SAGE
Premium Video

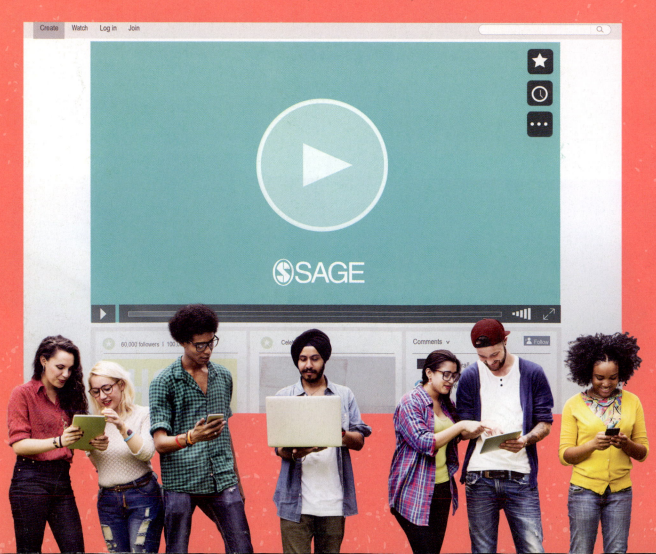

The Hallmark Features

A COMPLETE LEARNING PACKAGE

Packed with critical thinking opportunities, experiential exercises, and self-assessments, the new **Second Edition** provides students with a fun, hands-on introduction to the fascinating world of OB.

- **NEW EXPERIENTIAL EXERCISES AND NEW ONLINE EXERCISES** have been added to each chapter for easy use in face-to-face or online classes

- **YOU MAKE THE CALL VIDEOS** present students with realistic workplace dilemmas they must solve, giving students a chance to practice their critical thinking and decision making abilities

- **DID YOU KNOW? VIDEOS** expose students to counter-intuitive or little known OB facts, challenging student assumptions that OB is just common sense

EXERCISE 8.2: Decision-Making Process Role Play

Objective

The purpose of this exercise is to grasp the concept of the five-step decision-making process.

Instructions

This exercise looks at the five-step decision-making process and has volunteers from the class role-playing a simple decision making scenario.

Three students will join the instructor at the front of the class. With the help of the rest of the class, the volunteers will proceed through all five steps of the decision making process in an attempt to determine what will be had for lunch.

The five steps are:

1. Define the problem
2. Identify and weigh decision criteria
3. Generate multiple alternatives
4. Rate alternatives on the basis of decision criteria
5. Choose, implement, and evaluate the best alternative

As students tackle each step, the audience provides suggestions, questions, and input. In the final step, a selection is made, but it is up to the volunteers whether they want to report back in the following class the evaluation of the decision!

Hamdi Ulukaya

Organizational Behavior

Second Edition

Sara Miller McCune founded SAGE Publishing in 1965 to support the dissemination of usable knowledge and educate a global community. SAGE publishes more than 1000 journals and over 800 new books each year, spanning a wide range of subject areas. Our growing selection of library products includes archives, data, case studies and video. SAGE remains majority owned by our founder and after her lifetime will become owned by a charitable trust that secures the company's continued independence.

Los Angeles | London | New Delhi | Singapore | Washington DC | Melbourne

Organizational Behavior

A Skill-Building Approach

Second Edition

Christopher P. Neck
Arizona State University, Tempe

Jeffery D. Houghton
West Virginia University

Emma L. Murray

Los Angeles | London | New Delhi
Singapore | Washington DC | Melbourne

FOR INFORMATION:

SAGE Publications, Inc.
2455 Teller Road
Thousand Oaks, California 91320
E-mail: order@sagepub.com

SAGE Publications Ltd.
1 Oliver's Yard
55 City Road
London EC1Y 1SP
United Kingdom

SAGE Publications India Pvt. Ltd.
B 1/I 1 Mohan Cooperative Industrial Area
Mathura Road, New Delhi 110 044
India

SAGE Publications Asia-Pacific Pte. Ltd
18 Cross Street #10-10/11/12
China Square Central
Singapore 048423

Printed in the United States of America

ISBN 978-1-5443-1754-0

Acquisitions Editor: Maggie Stanley
Content Development Editor: Lauren Holmes
Editorial Assistant: Janeane Calderon
Production Editor: Andrew Olson
Copy Editor: Tammy Giesmann
Typesetter: C&M Digitals (P) Ltd.
Proofreader: Christine Dahlin
Indexer: May Hasso
Cover Designer: Anthony Paular
Marketing Manager: Sarah Panella

This book is printed on acid-free paper.

SUSTAINABLE FORESTRY INITIATIVE

Certified Sourcing
www.sfiprogram.org
SFI-01268

SFI label applies to text stock

18 19 20 21 22 10 9 8 7 6 5 4 3 2 1

BRIEF CONTENTS

DETAILED CONTENTS

©iStockphoto.com/g-stockstudio

Priyanka Parashar/Mint via Getty Images

PEOPLE

David Paul Morris/Getty Images

CHAPTER 3: PERCEPTION AND LEARNING 68

CHAPTER 4: EMOTIONS, ATTITUDES, AND STRESS 94

Getty Images via Vaughn Ridley

© Shutterstock.com/Keith Homan

YOSHIKAZU TSUNO/AFP/Getty Images

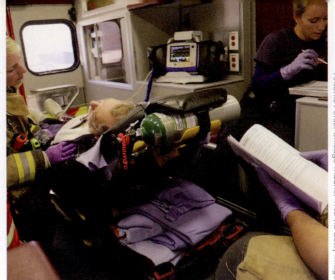

Antonio Perez/Chicago Tribune/TNS via Getty Images

Chris Coduto/Icon Sportswire/Corbis via Getty Images

Artur Widak/NurPhoto

Craig Ferguson/LightRocket via Getty Images

Rob Tringali/SportsChrome/Getty Images

Luke Sharrett/Bloomberg via Getty Images

Robert Nickelsberg/Getty Images

CHAPTER 13: INFLUENCE, POWER, AND POLITICS　372

Suzi Pratt/Getty Images for REI

©Shutterstock.com/Sundry Photography

PART V: ORGANIZATIONAL CONTEXT

PREFACE

Nikos Kazantzakis once wrote:

> Ideal teachers are those who use themselves as bridges over which they invite their students to cross; then having facilitated their crossing, joyfully collapse, encouraging them to create bridges of their own.

Our goal as an author team was to write an organizational behavior (OB) textbook that really engaged students—not one that involved memorizing its content for the sole purpose of passing exams and then quickly forgetting whatever they had learned. We wanted to write a textbook that students could use well after the semester was over to help them actively learn and think critically in order to understand how people behave as they pursue their career goals. In other words, we wanted to help students "build bridges" to their goals and dreams. We hope we have achieved our goal in *Organizational Behavior: A Skill-Building Approach* for students in organizational behavior classes across the world.

In our 21st-century business world, organizational behavior has taken on a new significance. In an environment in which competition is fiercer than ever, it is people who act as differentiators in the workplace. In every aspect of business, people are the cornerstone of success. This is why it is so important to understand human behavior.

The following quote from Curt Coffman and Gabriela Gonzalez-Molina in *Follow This Path: How the World's Greatest Organizations Drive Growth by Unleashing Human Potential* reinforces the importance of understanding human behavior in organizations:

> The success of your organization doesn't depend on your understanding of economics, or organizational development, or marketing. It depends, quite simply, on your understanding of human psychology: how each individual employee connects with your company and how each individual employee connects with your customers.

One of the earliest studies of organizational behavior was carried out at AT&T's Western Electric Hawthorne plant by Harvard's Elton Mayo in 1927. The principal findings of this study showed that when workers are given the opportunity to contribute their thinking and learning to workplace issues, their job performance improves. This finding is still relevant today. Studies in organizational behavior add to our understanding of the individuals working within all types of businesses, from corporate to entrepreneurial. *Organizational Behavior: A Skill-Building Approach* attempts to capture the body of knowledge that encompasses the organizational behavioral research into a book that is fun to read, captures the reader's attention, and imparts the organizational behavioral knowledge in a way that promotes critical thinking.

Our Vision

Organizational Behavior: A Skill-Building Approach is a textbook for college-level undergraduate students seeking insight into individual behavior, group behavior, organizational structure, and organizational processes through the lens of critical thinking.

Organizational behavior courses are defined by the following trends: larger course sizes, the need for continually changing content to stay relevant, and instructors working to make vast online resources meaningful to the student experience. The cumulative effect of these trends on instructors is a much more demanding environment for teaching and learning. In a quickly changing business environment, many books need a complete rewrite to be fully up-to-date. Even better, though, this is a new book—written from today's perspective, with an eye to the near future. Our goal in writing this book is to bring to the classroom a fresh view of human behavior in organizations.

What Makes Our Book Unique

Skill-building approach. Students are provided with opportunities to develop motivational, leadership, and teamwork skills that will help them to analyze behavioral patterns and take appropriate actions to help shape and influence those behaviors in positive ways. Supporting students in building and developing the skills and abilities that will allow them to make decisions and take actions that result in expected and desirable behaviors and related outcomes is the primary objective of our textbook.

Practical applications, self-assessments, experiential exercises, and additional pedagogical features make OB come to life and encourage students to engage with OB concepts in meaningful ways.

A Skill-Building Approach

We believe that in today's business world, organizational behavior is more important than ever. Companies are looking for employees and managers who have strong organizational behavior skills. Leadership, teamwork, motivational capabilities, decision making, communication, ethics, and creativity are valuable and essential people skills needed in organizations.

Our text provides a comprehensive overview of OB theories and processes with a strong emphasis on skill-building applications in order to equip students with the information and skills they need to thrive in organizations today.

Why Critical Thinking Matters in OB

Critical thinking is an essential skill; managers use critical thinking to understand, explain, predict, and influence behavior in the workplace. A critical thinker uses his or her intelligence, knowledge, and skills to question and carefully explore situations and to arrive at thoughtful conclusions based on evidence and reason. Someone thinking critically is able to get past biases and view situations from different perspectives to ultimately improve his or her understanding of the world.

Business leaders use critical thinking when making decisions, solving problems, gathering information, and asking questions. Time and again, research has shown the effectiveness of critical thinking in the workplace. In an article published in the journal *Current Directions in Psychological Science*, the authors report that cognitive ability tests, including critical-thinking tests, "are among the strongest and most consistent predictors of performance across academic and work settings."[1]

In *Organizational Behavior: A Skill-Building Approach,* we use the components and core skills of critical thinking to teach the many facets of organizational behavior to students. Adding critical thinking to these behaviors further enhances students' abilities to strategically think as well as analyze and solve problems. By seeking first to understand the dynamics of human behavior, then sharing the knowledge learned, they will be able to build more successful relationships within their personal and professional lives.

How Our Book Incorporates Critical Thinking

A lot of OB books claim to help students to develop their critical-thinking skills. What makes our book different? Our book incorporates critical thinking on every page. Instead of passively reading through each chapter, the student is asked to pause, reflect, and engage more critically with the content.

Chapter 1 explains the central role critical thinking plays in OB and introduces a five-step **critical-thinking framework** that students can apply to challenging scenarios, problems, decisions, and other issues.

> **Thinking Critically** questions don't necessarily have a right or wrong answer but rather are designed to challenge students to think critically and achieve higher levels of learning.

> **Examining the Evidence** boxes highlight a recent seminal OB study from high-quality OB journals and discuss its practical applications in the business world. Critical-thinking questions at the end of each box allow students to see how research in academe applies to real-life settings.

> **OB in the Real World** boxes feature real-world anecdotes, quotes, and examples from seasoned business professionals who share their knowledge and experience with students by describing how they used OB to positively influence outcomes and achieve organizational success. Critical-thinking questions help students see how OB concepts impact real people and organizations.

These critical-thinking elements are perfect for assignments or class discussions and lively debate.

Digital Resources

$SAGE edge™

SAGE edge for Instructors

A password-protected instructor resource site at **edge.sagepub.com/neckob2e** supports teaching with high-quality content to help in creating a rich learning environment for students. The SAGE edge site for this book includes the following instructor resources:

- **Test banks built on Bloom's Taxonomy** and **AACSB Standards** to provide a diverse range of test items, which allow you to save time and offer a pedagogically robust way to measure your students' understanding of the material
- **Sample course syllabi** with suggested models for structuring your course
- Editable, chapter-specific **PowerPoint® slides** that offer flexibility when creating multimedia lectures
- EXCLUSIVE access to full-text **SAGE journal articles** to expose students to important research and scholarship tied to chapter concepts
- **Video and multimedia content** that enhances student engagement and appeal to different learning styles
- **Lecture notes** that summarize key concepts on a chapter-by-chapter basis to help you with preparation for lectures and class discussions
- Sample **answers to in-text questions** that provide an essential reference

- Lively and stimulating **experiential exercises and activities** that can be used in class to reinforce active learning and the skill-building approach
- **Teaching notes for the cases** to guide analysis
- **Running case studies from the first edition** provide instructors with additional case study content to use for further analysis of chapter concepts
- Suggested film clips showing **OB in the movies** that include analysis and critical-thinking questions
- **Self-Assessments** pulled from the end of each chapter allow students to print and fill out assessments in or outside of the classroom

SAGE edge for students

The open-access companion website helps students accomplish their coursework goals in an easy-to-use learning environment, featuring:

- **Learning objectives** with summaries reinforce the most important material
- Mobile-friendly practice **quizzes** encourage self-guided assessment and practice
- Mobile-friendly **flashcards** strengthen understanding of key concepts
- Carefully selected **video and multimedia content** enhances exploration of key topics to reinforce concepts and provide further insights
- **Self-Assessments** pulled from the end of each chapter allow students to print and fill out assessments in or outside of the classroom
- EXCLUSIVE access to full-text **SAGE journal articles** to expose students to important research and scholarship tied to chapter concepts

SAGE coursepacks

SAGE coursepacks makes it easy to import our quality instructor and student resource content into your school's learning management system (LMS) with minimal effort. Intuitive and simple to use, **SAGE coursepacks** gives you the control to focus on what really matters: customizing course content to meet your students' needs. The SAGE coursepacks, created specifically for this book, are customized and curated for use in Blackboard, Canvase, Desire2Learn (D2L), and Moodle.

In addition to the content available on the SAGE edge site, the coursepacks include:

- **Pedagogically robust assessment tools** that foster review, practice, and critical thinking, and offer a better, more complete way to measure student engagement, including:
  - **Diagnostic chapter pretests and posttests** that identify opportunities for student improvement, track student progress, and ensure mastery of key learning objectives
  - **Instructions** on how to use and integrate the comprehensive assessments and resources provided
  - **Assignable video tied to learning objectives, with corresponding multimedia assessment tools** bring concepts to life that increase student engagement and appeal to different learning styles. The **video assessment questions** feed to your gradebook.
  - **Integrated links to the eBook version** that make it easy to access the mobile-friendly version of the text, which can be read anywhere, anytime

Interactive eBook

Organizational Behavior 2e is also available as an **Interactive eBook** which can be packaged with the text for just $5 or purchased separately. The Interactive eBook offers hyperlinks to original SAGE videos, including **You Make the Call videos,** which place students in the role of a decision maker within an organization who is faced with a real-world challenge, and **Did You Know videos** that provide students with unassuming research findings from sources such as Gallup and the Harvard Business Review to challenge the assumption that OB is a common-sense course. The Interactive eBook also includes additional case studies, as well as carefully chosen journal articles that students can access with just one click. Users will also have immediate access to study tools such as highlighting, bookmarking, note-taking/sharing, and more!

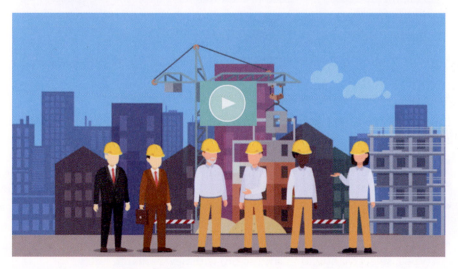

New to This Edition

In addition to updating 80 percent of the chapter references, we have added two new end-of-chapter exercises and one online exercise for use in online classes to each chapter. We have also moved the continuing case studies from the text to the instructor resource site and replaced them with chapter-opening cases on real-world companies, including Under Armour, Twitter, and Uber. We have updated all end-of-chapter cases and added new profiles for the OB in the Real World feature. Additionally, we have added a new chapter on ethics and social responsibility and added the topic of trust to Chapter 11 on conflict and negotiation. Please read the section below to see the chapter-specific changes that have been made.

Chapter-by-Chapter Changes

Chapter 1 (Why Organizational Behavior Matters)

- New opening case: Southwest Airlines
- New section explaining why OB is not just common sense
- New OB in the Real World (OBRW) featuring Tom Hatten, founder of Mountainside Fitness
- New OBRW featuring Dr. Karen Hardy, Director of Risk, US Department of Commerce
- More detailed explanation of the four functions of management and how they apply to OB
- Additional discussion on how human skills and communication skills directly relate to organizational behavior
- New case: CVS Health

Chapter 2 (Diversity and Individual Differences)

- New opening case: PepsiCo
- New OBRW featuring Kaia West, HR recruitment, KPMG
- Explores three diversity initiatives commonly used in the workplace (reducing bias, hiring tests, grievance procedures) and explains the reasons why they may not work
- Outlines positive ways for managers to promote diversity
- Describes cross-cultural diversity and how it can be managed within the organization
- Expands discussion of the Big Five model

Chapter 3 (Perception and Learning)

- New opening case: Twitter
- New OBRW, featuring Matt Nuyen, Head of Sales, Currency Capital
- Discusses perception in relation to fake news using current research and media examples
- Expands the discussion of common perceptual distortions (halo effect, stereotypes, selective attention, and so on) with new research

Chapter 4 (Emotions, Attitudes, and Stress)

- New opening case: Under Armour
- New OBRW featuring Clare Collins, founder of Silver Linings Bikinis
- Enhanced discussion of emotional contagion using real-world examples
- Updated information and real-world examples on employee engagement

- Greater coverage of stress in the workplace including the causes of stress, different ways to manage stress, and the impact of stress on job satisfaction
- More discussion on wellness illustrated by new research and real-world examples

Chapter 5 (Motivation: Concepts and Theoretical Perspectives)

- New opening case: AriZona Iced Tea
- Greater depth added to the definition of motivation and the process of motivation
- New OBRW featuring Mark Shoen, U-Haul
- New figure illustrating S.M.A.R.T goals
- Enhanced discussion, research, and examples on equity theory and expectancy theory

Chapter 6 (Motivation: Practices and Applications)

- New opening case: Disney
- Revised introduction to intrinsic motivation
- New "Examining the Evidence" feature discussing the possibility of family motivation as a replacement for intrinsic motivation
- New OBRW featuring Rob Kanjura, Savant Naturals
- New OBRW featuring Karen Sanders, manager, Virginia Tech
- Expanded discussion of performance-based pay
- New section, "Motivation over Time," examining research on the effects of rewards on employee motivation over time, illustrated by new figure
- New Examining the Evidence feature: "Family Motivation as a Substitute for Intrinsic Motivation?"
- New material focusing on differences in work values between the baby boomer, Generation X, and millennial generations
- Enhanced discussion of motivation through job design
- Explores the argument for and against flexible work options through research and real-world examples

Chapter 7 (Teams)

- New opening case: Pearson
- Enhanced explanation of the differences between groups and teams
- Updated research-based information on highly effective teams, highlighting the concept of psychological safety (illustrated with new figure)
- New OBRW featuring Derrick Hall, CEO, Arizona Diamondbacks
- Detailed discussion on virtual teams using current research, real-world examples, and a new figure
- Expanded focus on team formation using Tuckman's model
- Introduces Gersick's Time and Transition Model as a different perspective to the Tuckman model
- Provides new examples of team norms

- Updated Examining the Evidence feature: "Team Cohesion: Is Too Much More Than Enough?"
- New section on cyberloafing as a form of social loafing
- Enhanced discussion of groupthink with the inclusion of political groupthink
- New section on how to brainstorm

Chapter 8 (Decision Making, Creativity, and Innovation)

- New opening case: ASU
- Explains the difference between decision making and problem solving
- Clarifies the difference between creativity and innovation using real-world examples
- New OBRW featuring John Beck, CIO, ASU
- Enriched discussion on availability heuristics based on current research.
- New research and examples to illustrate the factors that inspire creativity.
- New case: McDonald's

Chapter 9 (Ethics and Social Responsibility in Organizations)

- New opening case: IBM
- New chapter on ethics
- Explains the importance of ethics in organizations
- Discusses ethical dilemmas and how to resolve them.
- New OBRW featuring Sam Heiler, plant manager, JMW Truss.
- New Examining the Evidence feature: "Ethical Leadership and Moral Judgments"
- Explains the different approaches to ethical decision making.
- Clarifies the differences between ethical leadership and ethical followership.
- Explores the approaches to social responsibility in organizations.
- Identifies the components of an ethical culture.
- New case: JetBlue

Chapter 10 (Effective Communication)

- New opening case: Uber
- Enhanced discussion of communication channels illustrated by real-world research
- New table describing some tips for email etiquette
- New OBRW featuring Destin Cook, Director of Finance, NextEra Energy
- Includes new research on the effect of modern technology on listening skills
- New Examining the Evidence feature: "Electronic Communication during Nonworking Hours"

Chapter 11 (Trust, Conflict, and Negotiation)

- New opening case: NFL
- New discussion on the concept of psychological contract
- New content on the topic of social networks

- New table outlining tips for building trust in organizations
- New OBRW featuring Ken Hill, CEO, Dorco
- New OBRW featuring Radha Abboy, 8020 Consulting
- New case: Disney

Chapter 12 (Leadership Perspectives)

- New opening case: Procter and Gamble
- Updated media examples and research
- New table highlighting the differences between charismatic, transformational, and transactional leaders
- New OBRW featuring Scott Whitfield, IBM
- New OBRW featuring Heather Clark, founder of Pomchies
- Real-world examples added to Empowering Leadership section
- New Examining the Evidence feature: "When Is Empowering Leadership Most Effective?"
- Expanded discussion on leadership and gender
- New section on LGBT employees in the workplace
- New case: Chobani Yogurt

Chapter 13 (Influence, Power, and Politics)

- New opening case: NextEra Energy
- Enhanced discussion of influencing tactics illustrated by real-world examples
- New figure illustrating inspirational leadership
- New Examining the Evidence feature: "Political Behavior: A Viable Coping Strategy for Organizational Politics?"
- New OBRW featuring Maurice S. Hebert, SVP, Tufts Health Plan
- New section added discussing four types of organizational politics

Chapter 14 (Organizations and Culture)

- New opening case: REI
- New OBRW, featuring senior account executive, Datavard
- New figure to illustrate the competing values framework
- New media examples to highlight strong and weak cultures

Chapter 15 (Organizational Change and Structure)

- New opening case: Google
- New introduction profiling sexual harassment using a real-world example
- New media examples illustrating the topic of external forces for change
- New OBRW featuring Cris Weekes, SVP, Central Garden and Pet
- New section on generational changes
- New section explaining the ten main reasons for resisting change
- New figure illustrating psychological reactions to change
- New section on Kotter's 8-Step change model featuring updated figure
- New case: General Electric

End-of-Chapter Features

In each chapter, we include traditional chapter review materials to help students check their comprehension and prepare for quizzes and exams.

In Review, organized by learning objective, summarizes key chapter information.

Up for Debate challenges students to think critically and develop and discuss their own viewpoints across a wide range of issues, including diversity, emotional well-being, and ethics.

Short exercises, experiential exercises, and online exercises are designed to help students build valuable experience and increase their skills through decision-oriented and hands-on exercises.

Self-assessments allow students to apply chapter content to their own lives and better understand their own behaviors, skills, and strengths.

Case studies profile real-world companies and people and illustrate how OB concepts function in the real world, providing students with engaging case examples and opportunities to apply OB concepts to the case studies.

Content and Organization

Each chapter is introduced by an OB model that provides students with a big-picture overview of how all the chapters and parts fit together.

Chapter 1, "Why Organizational Behavior Matters," explains how and why OB has become significant in today's organizations and describes how human skills and communication skills directly relate to organizational behavior.

Chapter 2, "Diversity and Individual Differences," explores different types of diversity, describes positive ways for managers to promote diversity, discusses how cross-cultural diversity can be managed within the organization, and explores personality theory in greater depth.

Chapter 3, "Perception and Learning," describes the ways in which we interpret our environment and discusses the effects of common perceptual distortions such as halo effect, stereotypes, and selective attention.

Chapter 4, "Emotion, Attitudes, and Stress," explores how emotions influence our behavior; common workplace attitudes; and the impact of stress in the workplace and how to manage it.

Chapter 5, "Motivation: Concepts and Theoretical Perspectives," discusses the process of motivation, and explores the theories of motivation and how they influence behavior in the workforce.

Chapter 6, "Motivation: Practices and Applications," outlines the practical ways and strategies used by organizations such as job design and flexible work options to encourage motivation and empower employees.

Chapter 7, "Teams," emphasizes the critical role of teams and teamwork, explores team norms, and explains the components that make up an effective team.

Chapter 8, "Decision Making, Creativity, and Innovation," addresses the main types of decision making in organizations, and highlights creativity and innovation processes and how they affect organizational behavior.

Chapter 9, "Ethics and Social Responsibility in Organizations," explains the importance of ethics in organizations, discusses ethical dilemmas, and explores different approaches to social responsibility.

Chapter 10, "Effective Communication," describes the different types of communication channels, explores the effect of modern technology on communication, and describes the key barriers to effective communication.

Chapter 11, "Trust, Conflict, and Negotiation," explains how managers can build trust in organizations, manage conflict, and learn to negotiate using a variety of different skills.

Chapter 12, "Leadership Perspectives," discusses different types of leaders and leadership theories, and explores gender issues in the workplace, such as those related to LGBT employees.

Chapter 13, "Influence, Power, and Politics," describes different types of influence tactics for influencing others, discusses the concept of power and its relationship to leadership, and explores different forms of organizational politics.

Chapter 14, "Organizations and Culture," explores the facets of organizational culture, how organizations can adapt their practices across cultures, and different ways in which culture is shaped in organizations.

Chapter 15, "Organizational Change and Structure," describes the forces for change in organizations, outlines resistance to change and how to reduce it, and discusses how organizational structure helps shape behavior in organizations.

Note

1. Kuncel, Nathan R., and Sarah A. Hezlett. "Fact and Fiction in Cognitive Ability Testing for Admissions and Hiring Decisions." *Current Directions in Psychological Science* 19, no. 6 (December 2010): 339-345.

ACKNOWLEDGMENTS

The authors thank all those people who have supported our efforts in writing this book. There are a plethora of people who contributed to making this text a reality. First, we thank all of the students who over the years have encouraged us to leave our teaching comfort zone to explore new and innovative ways of teaching. It was through these experiences that we obtained the courage to attempt to write such a book as the 2nd edition of *Organizational Behavior: A Critical-Thinking Approach*. We also thank our respective deans Amy Hillman at Arizona State (W. P. Carey School of Business) and Javier Reyes at West Virginia University's College of Business & Economics for their support for this project. We thank our department heads (Kevin Corley, Arizona State, and Abhishek Srivastava, West Virginia University) for their encouragement as well. Chris Neck thanks Duane Roen (Dean of the College of Integrative Sciences and Arts at Arizona State University) for his steadfast support and encouragement to excel in the classroom.

For their thoughtful and helpful comments and ideas on our manuscript, we sincerely thank the following reviewers. Our book is a better product because of their insightful suggestions.

Reviewer Acknowledgments

Tracy H. Porter, Cleveland State University

Samira B. Hussein, Johnson County Community College

Lisa M. Nieman, Indiana Wesleyan University

Tommy Nichols, Texas Wesleyan University

Steven D. Charlier, Georgia Southern University

Daniel S. Marrone, Farmingdale State College

Linda Hefferin, Columbia College of Missouri

Robert D. Gulbro, Florida Institute of Technology

Deborah S. Butler, Georgia State University

Christine R. Day, Eastern Michigan University

Janice S. Gates, Western Illinois University

Nathan Himelstein, Essex County College

Harriet L. Rojas, Indiana Wesleyan University

Andrea E. Smith-Hunter, Siena College

Maria D. Vitale, Brandman University, Chaffey College, and UCLA Extension

Audrey M. Parajon, Wilmington University

Frederick R. Brodzinski, The City College of New York

Michael J. Alleruzzo, Saint Joseph's University

Jacqueline Mayfield, Texas A&M International University

Milton Mayfield, Texas A&M International University

Bob Waris, University of Missouri-Kansas City

Ann Snell, Tulane University

Mike Shaner, Saint Louis University

Susan Knapp, Kaplan University

Jason Jackson, Kaplan University

Palaniappan Thiagarajan, Jackson State University

Maria Minor, Kaplan University

David J. Biemer, Texas State University

Marla Lowenthal, University of San Francisco

Avan Jassawalla, SUNY Geneseo

Warren Matthews, LeTourneau University

Eric B. Dent, Fayetteville State University

Dr. Patrick Coyle, Lycoming College

Dave Beaudry, Ph.D., Keene State College

Angela Balog, Saint Francis University

Vallari Chandna, University of Wisconsin, Green Bay

Jennifer Griffith, University of New Hampshire

Marjolijn van der Velde, Devenport University

Desiree Keever, State University of New York, Delhi

Kathleen Novak, University of Denver

Curt Beck, Concordia University

Chad Stevens, Keystone College

Kevin G. Love, Ph.D., Central Michigan University

Alex Chen, University of Central Arkansas

Jeffrey B. Paul, The University of Tulsa

Joseph Simon, Casper College

Kristin Holmberg-Wright, University of Wisconsin, Parkside

Annette B. Roter, Viterbo University

Laura Yu Hickerson, James Madison University

Stephanie A. Kodatt, Ph.D., Texas A&M University

Katrina Graham, Suffolk University

Keanon Alderson, California Baptists University

Min Carter, Southern Illinois University

Huaizhong Chen, West Virginia University

Yi-Yu Chen, New Jersey City University

Guorong Zhu, Salem State University

Todd A. Conkright, Creighton University

Michael L. Woodward, Shorter University

Adriana Machado Casali, Conestoga College

Alicia J. Revely, Miami University

Amanda L. Christensen, University of Cincinnati

Colleen A. McLaughlin, Liberty University

David Hofstetter, Clark University

Monica Law, Ph.D., Marywood University

Dr. Richard J. Vaughan, University of St. Francis

It takes a team to write a textbook, and we thank those behind-the-scenes individuals who assisted in the research, development, and/or editing of various parts of this second edition. Specifically, Chris Neck would like to thank George Heiler, Kevin Murphy, and Tristan Gaynor for their above and beyond help. This textbook was made better by their talents and contributions.

In addition, we thank the fine folks at SAGE for bringing this book to fruition. Our dream of creating an innovative OB textbook and ancillary package has become a reality because of our amazing, energetic, and encouraging acquisitions editor, Maggie Stanley. She has been a champion for this book and our ideas (and there were many!) every step of the way. We can't thank her enough for her dedication and support. Lauren Holmes, our talented developmental editor, pushed us to explore new ideas and kept us on track to write the best book possible. Andrew Olson, our production editor, made sure that everything that needed to happen did indeed happen and kept all of us on track. We appreciate all of their hard work, creativity, and attention to detail. We are also grateful to Ashlee Blunk and Mark Achenbach from SAGE, who planted the seeds for this book many years ago. We are grateful to Harriet Rojas (Indiana Wesleyan University), Milton R. Mayfield (Texas A&M International University), Jacqueline R. Mayfield (Texas A&M International University), and Steven Stovall (Southeast Missouri State University) for contributing valuable, hands-on experiential exercises. Designer Anthony Paular came up with an elegant and contemporary look for this book that visually brings to life our ideas more than we could have ever imagined. Alissa Nance took care of a myriad of tasks during the development of the manuscript with an energy and enthusiasm that was inspiring. Amy Lammers, our marketing manager, did a great job coordinating the promotion of our book, from organizing focus groups to overseeing all of the professor outreach efforts. And we thank our families for "living without us" as we worked diligently on completing this textbook.

ABOUT THE AUTHORS

Dr. Christopher P. Neck is currently an Associate Professor of Management at Arizona State University, where he held the title "University Master Teacher." From 1994 to 2009, he was part of the Pamplin College of Business faculty at Virginia Tech. He received his Ph.D. in Management from Arizona State University and his MBA from Louisiana State University. Neck is author of over 100 scholarly articles in seminal academic journals as well as a number of books. Some of his books include: *Self-Leadership: The Definitive Guide to Personal Excellence* (2017, SAGE); *Fit to Lead: The Proven 8-Week Solution for Shaping Up Your Body, Your Mind, and Your Career* (2004, St. Martin's Press; 2012, Carpenter's Sons Publishing); *Mastering Self-Leadership: Empowering Yourself for Personal Excellence, 6th edition* (2013, Pearson); *The Wisdom of Solomon at Work* (2001, Berrett-Koehler); *For Team Members Only: Making Your Workplace Team Productive and Hassle-Free* (1997, Amacom Books); and *Medicine for the Mind: Healing Words to Help You Soar, 4th Edition* (Wiley, 2012). Neck is also the coauthor of the principles of management textbook *Management: A Balanced Approach to the 21st Century* (Wiley 2013; 2017, 2nd Edition); the upcoming introductory to entrepreneurship textbook *Entrepreneurship* (SAGE, 2017); and the introductory to organizational behavior textbook *Organizational Behavior* (SAGE, 2017).

Dr. Neck's research specialties include employee/executive fitness, self-leadership, leadership, group decision-making processes, and self-managing teams. He has over 100 publications in the form of books, chapters, and articles in various journals. Some of the outlets in which Neck's work has appeared include *Organizational Behavior and Human Decision Processes, Journal of Organizational Behavior, Academy of Management Executive, Journal of Applied Behavioral Science, Journal of Managerial Psychology, Executive Excellence, Human Relations, Human Resource Development Quarterly, Journal of Leadership Studies, Educational Leadership,* and *Commercial Law Journal.*

Due to Neck's expertise in management, he has been cited in numerous national publications, including *The Washington Post, The Wall Street Journal, The Los Angeles Times, The Houston Chronicle,* and the *Chicago Tribune.* Additionally, each semester Neck teaches an introductory management course to a single class of anywhere from 500 to 1,000 students.

Dr. Neck was the recipient of the 2007 Business Week Favorite Professor Award. He is featured on www.businessweek.com as one of the approximately twenty professors from across the world receiving this award.

Neck currently teaches a mega section of Management Principles to approximately 500 students at Arizona State University. Neck received the Order of Omega Outstanding Teaching Award for 2012. This award is awarded to one professor at Arizona State by the Alpha Lambda Chapter of this leadership fraternity. His class sizes at Virginia Tech filled rooms up to 2,500 students. He received numerous teaching awards during his tenure at Virginia Tech, including the 2002 Wine Award for Teaching Excellence. Also, Neck was the ten-time winner (1996, 1998, 2000, 2002, 2004, 2005, 2006, 2007, 2008, and 2009) of the "Students' Choice Teacher of The Year Award" (voted by the students for the best teacher of the year within the entire university). Also, some of the organizations that have participated in Neck's management development training include GE/Toshiba, Busch Gardens, Clark Construction, the United States Army, Crestar, American Family Insurance, Sales and Marketing Executives International, American Airlines, American Electric Power, W. L. Gore & Associates, Dillard's Department Stores, and Prudential Life Insurance. Neck is also an avid runner. He has completed 12 marathons, including the Boston Marathon, the New York City Marathon, and the San Diego Marathon. In fact, his personal record for a single long-distance run is a 40-mile run.

Dr. Jeffery D. Houghton completed his Ph.D. in management at Virginia Polytechnic Institute and State University (Virginia Tech) and is currently an associate professor of management at West Virginia University (WVU). Dr. Houghton has taught college-level business courses at Virginia Tech, Abilene Christian University (Texas), Lipscomb University (Tennessee), the International University (Vienna, Austria), and for the US Justice Department-Federal Bureau of Prisons. Prior to pursuing a full-time career in academics, he worked in the banking industry as a loan officer and branch manager.

A member of the Honor Society of Phi Kappa Phi, Dr. Houghton's research specialties include human behavior, motivation, personality, leadership, and self-leadership. He has published more than 50 peer-reviewed journal articles, book chapters, and books, and his work has been cited more than 3,500 times in academic journals. He has coauthored three textbooks: *Self-Leadership: The Definitive Guide to Personal Excellence* (2017, SAGE), *Organizational Behavior* (2017, SAGE), and *Management: A Balanced Approach to the 21st Century* (Wiley 2013; 2017, 2nd Edition). He currently teaches undergraduate-, master's-, and doctoral-level courses in management, organizational behavior, and leadership. Dr. Houghton was named the 2013 Beta Gamma Sigma Professor of the Year for the WVU College of Business and Economics, awarded annually to one faculty member within the college as selected by a vote of the student members of Beta Gamma Sigma; and he received the 2008 Outstanding Teaching Award for the WVU College of Business and Economics, awarded annually to one faculty member for outstanding teaching.

In addition to his research and teaching activities, Dr. Houghton has consulted and conducted training seminars for companies including the Federal Bureau of Investigations, Pfizer Pharmaceuticals, and the Bruce Hardwood Floors Company. In his spare time, Dr. Houghton enjoys traveling, classic mystery novels, racquetball, and snow skiing. Finally, Dr. Houghton has trained for and completed two marathons, the Marine Corps Marathon in Washington, DC, and the Dallas White Rock Marathon in Dallas, Texas.

Emma L. Murray completed a Bachelor of Arts degree in English and Spanish at University College Dublin (UCD) in County Dublin, Ireland. This was followed by a Higher Diploma (Hdip) in business studies and information technology at the Michael Smurfit Graduate School of Business in County Dublin, Ireland. Following her studies, Emma spent nearly a decade in investment banking before becoming a full-time writer and author.

As a writer, Emma has worked on numerous texts, including business and economics, self-help, and psychology. Within the field of higher education, Emma worked with Dr. Christopher P. Neck and Dr. Jeffery D. Houghton on *Management* (Wiley 2013); and is the coauthor of the principles of management textbook *Management: A Balanced Approach to the 21st Century* (Wiley 2013, 2017–2nd Edition), the coauthor of *Organizational Behavior* (SAGE 2017), and the co-author of *Entrepreneurship: The Practice and Mindset* (SAGE 2018).

She is the author of *The Unauthorized Guide to Doing Business the Alan Sugar Way* (2010, Wiley-Capstone); and the lead author of *How to Succeed as a Freelancer in Publishing* (2010, How To Books). She lives in London.

PART I

Introduction

CHAPTER 1
Why Organizational Behavior Matters

Carolyn Van Houten/The *Washington Post* via Getty Images

1

Why Organizational Behavior Matters

The single biggest decision you make in your job—bigger than all the rest—is who you name manager. When you name the wrong person manager, nothing fixes that bad decision. Not compensation, not benefits—nothing.

—Gallup CEO Jim Clifton in the summary accompanying his organization's 2013 "State of the American Workplace" employee engagement study

Learning Objectives

By the end of this chapter, you will be able to:

OB

1.1   Explain the basic concept of organizational behavior (OB) and its value in organizations

1.2   Describe the key role of managing human capital in creating a sustainable competitive advantage for organizations

1.3   Identify the major behavioral science disciplines that contribute to OB

1.4   Demonstrate the value of critical thinking in the context of OB

1.5   Identify the major challenges and opportunities in the field of OB

1.6   Differentiate the three basic levels of analysis at which OB may be examined

1.7   Outline the benefits of positive OB and high-involvement management

CASE STUDY: SOUTHWEST AIRLINES' ORGANIZATIONAL CULTURE

The airline industry has been one of the most saturated and unprofitable businesses for at least the past three decades. It is a business where profit margins of 3 percent aren't uncommon and where customer satisfaction hovers around 60 percent. Seats are getting smaller, delays longer, and prices higher despite fuel prices being 30 percent lower.

The list of would-be competitors to Southwest Airlines and imitators is lengthy, all with plenty of money and plenty of brand recognition. What they all lacked was Southwest's intense focus on organizational culture. In an industry where profits are shrinking, Southwest Airlines stands as an example of a company that is finding opportunities where others are not with profit margins consistently around 10 percent. Southwest stands out in a well-saturated industry thanks to its organizational culture of putting employees before profits and before customers.

Southwest Airlines was founded in 1967 by Herb Kelleher and Rollin King, serving just three cities in Texas. By 1998 they had built Southwest Airlines to be the fifth largest US air carrier, serving over 50 million passengers a year. It only took until 1980 to be recognized as number one in customer service, a list that they consistently top to this day. Today Southwest has the mission of "dedication to the highest quality of customer service delivered with a sense of warmth, friendliness, individual pride, and company spirit."

What makes Southwest Airlines consistently stand out begins with the way that they look for employees and the manner in which they treat them. Southwest Airlines founder Herb Kelleher has long kept the recruitment motto at Southwest, "Hire for attitude and train for skill." When searching for employees, Southwest is not looking for the perfect résumé or the perfect work experience. Instead, Southwest is looking for someone whose devotion to the company and to its customers brings them to "a sense of mission, a sense that 'the cause comes before their own needs.'"

Southwest instills three main things into the hearts of its employees: a warrior spirit, a servant's heart, and a "fun-luving" (sic) attitude. These are far different directives than the typical "take the initiative" or "care about your customers" and that is why Southwest can bring in the kind of people that fits their mold for a trainable employee. In the past year, the company had openings for roughly 4,500 new employees and received more than 150,000 applications.

What motivates the employees at Southwest is something much greater than a paycheck; instead, they share a common purpose. The paycheck can get people to work on time consistently, but it takes something more inspirational to get employees to go the extra mile. Southwest CEO Gary Kelly says, "Southwest is a great place to work and brings the greatest joy because we have such meaningful purpose." The Southwest vision that guides its employees is "to connect people to what's important in their lives through friendly, reliable, and low-cost air travel." This vision guides Southwest's growth as well as the motivation of its employees to go the extra mile and serve the customers for a broader purpose than a paycheck.

To enforce this purpose to which all Southwest employees aspire to, Gary Kelly gives "shout outs" to employees who have gone above and beyond each month to show great customer service. The culture at Southwest Airlines is one that nurtures employees that go above and beyond and incentivizes them to show great customer service.

Despite Southwest's excellent reputation for customer service, like any large organization, it's experienced a few bumps in the road, largely related to technology problems. In July 2016, Southwest was forced to cancel thousands of flights following a technical failure, and in early 2017, a series of computer outages left hundreds of thousands of customers stranded.

President of Southwest Airlines, Tom Nealon, realizes the necessity of efficient technology for improving the customer experience, and for Southwest employees to adopt the technical skills needed to provide a higher level of service, but not at the sacrifice of the personal touch for which the airline is so well known.

"We need to be digital," he says. "We need to strengthen our customer experience. But our customer experience is always going to be centered with our people."

Indeed it is Southwest's "people" who went the extra mile and provided sleeping bags and pizzas to a girls' lacrosse team which had been stranded because of an outage. By going above and beyond the call of duty, Southwest's employees had saved the airline from a potential customer services disaster.

Another part of its technology program involves connecting with international customers. Since its 2010 purchase of AirTran Airways, trade on the international routes (gained by Southwest because of the acquisition) was not as good as it should be. Southwest is investing in technology to attract its international customers by building a new reservations system which includes foreign currency exchanges and point-of-sale programs.

Not only will the new system give Southwest better control over its flight fares, but it also provides the airline with the option to add ancillary charges, which is something that most of its competitors do. But despite the changes ahead, Nealon says that Southwest will still keep its policy to allow passengers to check in their first two bags for free.

"It's part of our brand," Nealon says. "It's part of our promise to our customers, and we're not going to change it."

However, a recent tragic event has forced Southwest to look beyond its technology inefficiencies to address a much more serious situation. In April 2018, a Southwest Airlines plane was forced to make an emergency landing due to an engine explosion which killed one passenger and injured seven more. The CEO of Southwest Airlines, Grace C. Kelly, has called for "enhanced inspection procedures" on its entire fleet of aircraft to ensure a terrible tragedy like this never happens again.

Resources:

Ahles, A. (2017). New Southwest Airlines president combines tech and people skills. *Star-Telegram*. Retrieved from http://www.star-telegram.com/news/business/aviation/sky-talk-blog/article146047379.html

Carbonara, P. (1996). Hire for attitude, train for skill. *Fast Company*. Retrieved from https://www.fastcompany.com/26996/hire-attitude-train-skill

Gallo, C. (2014). Southwest Airlines motivates its employees with a purpose bigger than a paycheck. *Forbes*. Retrieved from https://www.forbes.com/sites/carminegallo/2014/01/21/southwest-airlines-motivates-its-employees-with-a-purpose-bigger-than-a-paycheck/#de8246753769

Makovsky, K. (2013). Behind the Southwest Airlines culture. *Forbes*. Retrieved from https://www.forbes.com/sites/kenmakovsky/2013/11/21/behind-the-southwest-airlines-culture/#15e375a03798

Martin, E. (2015). A major airline says there's something it values more than its customers, and there's a good reason why. *Business Insider*. Retrieved from http://www.businessinsider.com/southwest-airlines-puts-employees-first-2015-7

Solomon, M. (2012, April 4). What you can learn from Southwest Airlines' culture. *The Washington Post*. Retrieved from https://www.washingtonpost.com/business/on-small-business/what-you-can-learn-from-southwest-airlines-culture/2012/04/03/gIQAzLVVtS_story.html?utm_term=.174c12262071

Case Questions:

1. Describe how Southwest Airlines builds their human capital.

2. What differentiates Southwest from any other airline?

3. What kinds of human skills is Southwest Airlines looking for in potential employees?

What Is Organizational Behavior and Why Is It Important?

>> LO 1.1   Explain the basic concept of organizational behavior (OB) and its value in organizations

Today's continually changing economic world needs managers who can understand, anticipate, and direct people in a fast-paced competitive market. In the past, organizations focused on numbers and how to achieve those numbers without paying too much attention to motivating and understanding their staff. However, fast-paced organizations like Southwest Airlines need the right people with the right skills to achieve success. This is why organizational behavior has taken on a new level of importance; people with organizational behavior skills are now regarded as a valuable and essential commodity. In an environment in which competition is fiercer than ever, people will differentiate your business from anyone else's. No matter what area of business you work in, people are the cornerstone of success.

We define **organizational behavior** (OB) as a field of study focused on understanding, explaining, and improving attitudes of individuals and groups in organizations.[1] An **organization** is a structured arrangement of people working together to accomplish specific goals. In short, OB focuses on figuring out how and why

SAGE edge™

Master the content
edge.sagepub.com/neckob2e

Organizational behavior: A field of study focused on understanding, explaining, and improving attitudes of individuals and groups in organizations

Organization: A structured arrangement of people working together to accomplish specific goals

individual employees and groups of employees behave the way they do within an organizational setting. Researchers carry out studies in OB, and managers or consultants establish whether this research can be applied in a real-world organization. Over the years this research has uncovered some surprising results. One study found that American employees would rather have a better boss than a pay raise.[2] This is certainly the case in Southwest Airlines where employees are more motivated by a good management with a clear vision, than they are by salary. Being treated well, respected, and rewarded for excellent service is more important to the Southwest Airlines employees than money. In another survey, people said they would rather have a better boss than a private office or free snacks![3] Management expert Victor Lipman believes that when people quit their jobs, they are quitting their managers, rather than the companies themselves.[4] The point is that managers who lack OB skills lose good employees. This is why it is important for you to learn OB skills in order to eventually become a manager who people will listen to and respect.

How will studying organizational behavior benefit you in the workplace?

Understanding the ways people act and interact within organizations provides three key advantages:

1. You can *explain* behavior. You can explain why your boss, coworkers, or subordinates are doing what they are doing.
2. You can *predict* behavior. You can anticipate what your boss, coworkers, or subordinates will do in certain circumstances and situations.
3. You can *influence* behavior. You can shape the actions of your subordinates, as well as your boss and coworkers in order to help them accomplish their goals and achieve organizational objectives.

Although explaining and predicting behavior are undoubtedly useful skills, *influencing* behavior is probably of the greatest interest to a practicing manager. Once you are equipped with knowledge about your employees' work behaviors, you can use it to optimize performance by providing effective direction and guidance. This explains why managing organizational behavior (i.e., focusing on the behavior and actions of employees and how they apply their knowledge and skills to achieve organizational objectives) is so important in today's organizations. There is a common belief among some people that OB is just common sense, but this is not the case. We cannot rely on just common sense to truly understand the behaviors of others. If that were the case we would be in danger of using inaccurate generalizations, incorrect suppositions, and common misconceptions to justify or define other people's behaviors. OB provides a systematic approach, based on scientific evidence, to further our understanding of behavior that goes far beyond common sense alone.

Put simply, OB is for everyone. It applies to everyday situations where you find yourself interacting with people, from the workplace, to home life, to the basketball court. Explaining and predicting behavior are of great interest to both formal managers in organizations and all employees given we all have the ability to influence coworkers. Throughout this book, we will show how OB concepts can relate to all employees at all levels of a company with a primary focus on formal managers. While the understanding of OB can benefit all employees and all levels in an organization, let's now focus on formal managers and what a manager actually does in the workplace.

Let's remind ourselves what a manager actually does in the workplace. Typically, managers carry out four main functions: planning, organizing, leading, and controlling.[5] (See Figure 1.1.)

In *planning,* a manager evaluates an organization's current position and where it wants to be in the future, and sets goals, designs strategies, and identifies actions and resources needed to achieve success. *Organizing* means arranging resources such as people and functions to implement the strategy made during the planning stage. Managers ensure goals are achieved by *leading* teams and individuals effectively, which means motivating and communicating with people to achieve goals. The *controlling* function allows managers to monitor employee performance, ensure milestones are being reached, and take corrective or preventative action where necessary.

OB is an integral part of these four functions as each function involves people "behaving" in certain ways to achieve specific tasks and duties. Successful planning, organizing, leading, and controlling would not be possible without managers following some fundamental OB principles.

Organizational members need to be equipped with specific skills to carry out their roles effectively.[6] First, they must have technical skills. A **technical skill** is an aptitude for performing and applying specialized tasks.[7] Today's members need to be proficient in using the latest technologies, including databases, spreadsheets, email, and social networking tools. Tom Nealon, president of Southwest Airlines, believes in combining people skills with technical skills in order to provide the best customer service to the airline's passengers.

Although technical skills are important, they can be learned on the job; to be really effective, managers need to possess **human skills** or the ability to relate to other people.[8] People with effective human skills take the feelings of others into account and are adept at dealing with conflict. These skills are essential for managing relationships not only with peers and employees but also with competitors, partners, suppliers, and stakeholders. Managers with human skills also realize the importance of communicating and sharing information across the organization in order to achieve goals. Southwest Airlines CEO Gary Kelly is a good example of someone who uses human skills to give "shout-outs" to the employees who have excelled in customer service. Kelly understands being acknowledged for hard work makes people feel good.

A key facet of human skills is **emotional intelligence** (EI), which is an awareness of how your actions and emotions affect those around you and the ability to understand and empathize with the feelings of others.[9]

Managers need to be technically proficient and know how to get along with people, but what about dealing with the complexities of the organization itself? Managers also need **conceptual skills** in order to see the organization as a whole, visualize how it fits into its overall environment, and understand how each part relates to the others.[10] Conceptual skills help managers solve problems, identify opportunities and challenges, and think creatively when making decisions.

Managers who embrace organizational behavior principles understand that the success of an organization lies with its people, and without people, there would be no companies, businesses, or industries. You may have a business that produces the highest-quality, most competitively priced product in the market or that prides itself on excellent customer service. However, if you don't have the right people in place to manufacture, market, and sell your product and take care of your customers, the business will suffer. Similarly, if some of your coworkers lose motivation and provide lower levels of customer service, the company will lose business, and perhaps even its reputation. Either of these problems can bring about a decrease in profits, reduced employee wages and bonuses, staff layoffs, and in extreme cases, bankruptcy.

FIGURE 1.1

The Four Functions of Managers

PLANNING   ORGANIZING

CONTROLLING   LEADING

Source: Carpenter, M., Bauer, T., Erdogan, B. (2012). "Chapter 15: The Essentials of Control." *Management Principles.* https://2012books .lardbucket.org/books/management-principles-v1.1/s19-the-essentials-of-control.html

Technical skill: The aptitude to perform and apply specialized tasks

Human skills: The ability to relate to other people

Emotional intelligence: The ability to understand emotions in oneself and others in order to effectively manage one's own behaviors and relationships with others

Conceptual skill: The capacity to see the organization as a whole and understand how each part relates to each other and how it fits into its overall environment

Studying organizational behavior can help you to understand how and why individuals and groups interact.

How do managers achieve the best outcomes for their organizations? A **strategic OB approach** is based on the idea that people are the key to productivity, competitive edge, and financial success. This means that managers must place a high value on **human capital**, which is the sum of people's skills, knowledge, experience, and general attributes.[11] Let's take a closer look at where human capital fits into organizations, and how it is managed.

Strategic OB approach: The idea that people are the key to productivity, competitive edge, and financial success

Human capital: People's skills, knowledge, experience, and general attributes

THINKING CRITICALLY

1. OB helps managers explain, predict, and influence behavior in the workplace. Identify the types of behavior you are most interested in explaining, understanding, and predicting in the workplace.

2. Of the four main functions managers fulfill (planning, organizing, leading, and controlling), which do you think is most likely to be enhanced by an understanding of organizational behavior? Why?

3. Managers need technical, human, and conceptual skills in order to succeed. Which of these skills are least likely to be learned on the job? Explain your position.

4. Compare the book's argument that the success of an organization lies with its people with the argument that every employee is replaceable and expendable. Which argument do you consider more compelling? Why?

THE BIG PICTURE:
How OB Topics Fit Together

Individual Processes
- Individual Differences
- Emotions and Attitudes
- Perceptions and Learning
- Motivation

Team Processes
- Ethics
- Decision Making
- Creativity and Innovation
- Conflict and Negotiation

Organizational Processes
- Culture
- Strategy
- Change and Development
- Structure and Technology

Influence Processes
- Leadership
- Power and Politics
- Communication

Organizational Outcomes
- Individual Performance
- Job Satisfaction
- Team Performance
- Organizational Goals

Managing Human Capital

>> **LO 1.2** Describe the key role of managing human capital in creating a sustainable competitive advantage for organizations

Organizations have two kinds of resources: tangible and intangible. Physical assets such as equipment, property, and inventory are examples of *tangible* resources. *Intangible* resources include an organization's reputation and culture, its relationships with customers, and the trust between managers and coworkers. Although it is difficult to measure intangible resources because of their subtle nature, they remain crucial for organizations competing in a global economy.

Human capital falls into the category of critical intangible resources. Today's managers focus on enriching their human capital by nurturing and enhancing their employees' knowledge and skills. The possibilities of building on human capital are endless—empowered, satisfied, knowledgeable employees can achieve so much for the organization and its customers. Human capital is essential for gaining **competitive advantage**, the edge that gives organizations a more beneficial position than their competitors and allows them to generate more profits and retain more customers.[12] (See Figure 1.2.) Southwest Airlines stands out among its competitors because of its commitment to nurturing its human capital. Three main aspects of human capital enhance true competitive advantage: value, rareness, and inimitability.[13]

FIGURE 1.2

How Human Capital Enhances Competitive Advantage

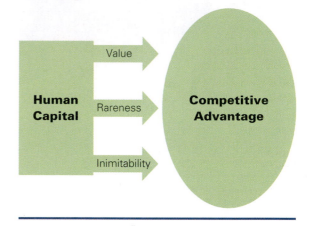

Value

Employees can add value in many different ways, but there is a difference between merely fulfilling the requirements of your job and working with an eye on company strategy. **Human capital value** accumulates when employees work toward the strategic goals of an organization to achieve competitive advantage. Although it is essential that employees have the skills and the abilities to execute a company strategy, they must also have a genuine willingness to contribute to the performance and success of an organization. Therefore, it is critical that managers make every effort to continuously nurture their high-performing employees, because regardless of labor market conditions, outstanding employees are always in short supply.

Rareness

Not everyone has the right skillset to further the progress of an organization. **Human capital rareness** is the level of exceptional skills and talents employees possess in an industry. For example, you may be an excellent computer programmer with an outstanding eye for detail, or you could have a gift for dealing with customer complaints and creating resolutions to resolve dilemmas. These are rare skills that employees may bring with them into an organization, but they can also be learned given the right training and encouragement. In our OB in the Real World feature, Dr. Karen Hardy, Director of the Risk Management Division and Deputy Chief Risk Officer at the US Department of Commerce, describes how managers can select the best talent.

Competitive advantage: The edge that gives organizations a more beneficial position than their competitors and allows them to generate more profits and retain more customers

Human capital value: The way employees work toward the strategic goals of an organization to achieve competitive advantage

Human capital rareness: The skills and talents of an organization's people that are unique in the industry

OB IN THE REAL WORLD

Dr. Karen Hardy, Director of the Risk Management Division and Deputy Chief Risk Officer at the US Department of Commerce

Dr. Karen Hardy is currently the Director of the Risk Management Division and Deputy Chief Risk Officer at the US Department of Commerce. Her specialty is in Enterprise Risk Management where she is a recognized industry pioneer and influencer, and with three decades of experience on her hands, is nationally recognized for excellence in many facets of her work. Dr. Hardy has worked for both the private and public sectors. She served as senior advisor on risk management to the Controller of the United States while on assignment to the White House Office of Management and Budget, where she was credited with influencing federal policy for instituting risk management in government. Dr. Hardy is an accomplished national and international speaker, and award-winning and best-selling author, achieving high accolades in anything she sets her mind to.

Due to her time in both the public and private sectors, and with a long tenure at the Department of Commerce, Dr. Hardy has a keen sense of the difference between both sectors, as well as what their future holds. Dr. Hardy vowed to never go into the public sector early on in her career, but after spending time in consumer banking, she found that she was missing a mission in her day-to-day life and decided to try something new.

One recurring theme in her description of public versus private sector management work is that goals in the private sector are driven by the bottom line while public sector work is mission driven. While a business worries about what investments are immediately paying off quarter to quarter, Dr. Hardy can think about the long-term impacts of programs and services designed to improve the quality of life for constituents. It takes longer to see the impact of her work because it is done on such a large scale. The public sector is a very complex environment, with systems inside of systems, and from time to time it is easy to feel like a cog in a machine, but Dr. Hardy says that this isn't unique to federal work. She states that the difference between the two industries is that in the public sector, at the end of the day, while you may be a small piece in a large machine, there is a purpose in the work you do to accomplish a mission. While this isn't necessarily in contrast to all private companies today, bottom lines can often get in the way of accomplishing missions for good.

The stereotype of public sector work has always been a comparison to bureaucratic red tape and this may have discouraged many prospective candidates from seeking federal work. Dr. Hardy says that while this is something they are always trying to improve, this isn't unique to government work. She states, "Bureaucracy is the result for any massive organization, both private and public, but it is becoming less and less tolerated." While in banking, she saw firsthand the amount of bureaucracy involved within a large for-profit institution and she stressed that this is how many large institutions order themselves.

So how can you, as a manager, ensure that you are attracting the best talent when the private sector will, in some cases, be able to pay more and offer benefit and bonus packages beyond what the public sector can provide? Dr. Hardy says that it may be getting easier as the next generation of leaders will seek out companies that have well-defined missions and purpose. Dr. Hardy says that while the public sector may be limited by salary thresholds, they can offer millennials what they are searching for—and that is purpose. Due to the profit-driven versus mission-driven dynamic, the next batch of employable students is more interested than ever. Increasingly millennials are caring more about what they are doing and how they are serving. They want a mission to accomplish and they may be willing to take a little less to do it, given the other trade-offs, such as telecommuting and a balanced work life. For this reason, Dr. Hardy says that they have always attracted a certain type of high-achieving applicant, but the outlook is even better now more than ever. Dr. Hardy believes that the new generation of public sector leaders are accustomed to functioning in sharing and transparent communities and that this adaptability is perfect for the management of key programs and services that benefit the American public. Dr. Hardy says "they will bring that behavior with them," and that "if we can make sure we continue to promote the service-oriented work found in government, I can't think of a better way to find a purpose-driven job than to serve in the federal sector."

As a manager, it is her duty to direct her workforce toward the identified mission of the Department of Commerce, and she sees it as her role to lead on principled strategy above all else. Dr. Karen Hardy looks fondly toward the next generation of federal workers and believes it will be a more capable workforce than ever. She finishes by saying that when she took her job she took an oath, one of the same oaths taken by Congress to serve the people of the United States and to serve with that oath in mind. She is forever loyal to that oath and sees it taken very seriously throughout her branch of government.

Critical-Thinking Questions

1. What differences are there between the public and the private sector regarding objectives?

2. What does the future hold for government employee recruitment according to Dr. Karen Hardy? ●

Source: Interview with Dr. Karen Hardy conducted on February 23, 2018.

Inimitability

Employees may be able to add real value and possess rare and important skills, but these attributes must be inimitable (i.e., unique and difficult to copy or replicate) for an organization to achieve success. **Human capital inimitability** is the degree to which the skills and talents of employees can be emulated by other organizations. The higher the level of inimitability, the more competitive an organization will be. For example, what's to prevent an excellent computer programmer from going to a competitor that offers the same services and opportunities? Successful organizations ensure that their talented employees possess skills and talents that are difficult to imitate. This means employees have a degree of *tacit knowledge:* they have a feel or an instinct for a method or a process but can't easily articulate it; they just know it is right. An organization's culture or values are also difficult to imitate and often determine why employees choose to work for one company over another that offers similar products and services. Usually, this comes down to the organization's shared values, attitudes, and type of culture.

Human capital inimitability: The degree to which the skills and talents of employees can be emulated by other organizations

Take a look at how Mountainside Fitness founder Tom Hatten managed human capital at his 13 fitness centers across the Phoenix Valley in the OB in the Real World feature.

THINKING CRITICALLY

1. Compare the relative importance of tangible and intangible resources. Can an organization succeed without adequate resourcing in both areas? Why or why not?

2. Explain in your own words how value, rareness, and inimitability in human capital contribute to an organization's competitive advantage.

Behavioral Science Disciplines That Contribute to OB

>> **LO 1.3 Identify the major behavioral science disciplines that contribute to OB**

In the early days of management theory, studies focused on how workers could perform manual labor more efficiently (on a factory assembly line, for example), and how physical working conditions could be improved for better employee performance. There was little focus on the human element (i.e., how individual characteristics,

OB IN THE REAL WORLD

Tom Hatten, Founder and CEO of Mountainside Fitness

In 1991, Tom Hatten opened a single fitness club in Arizona and built it into what is today Mountainside Fitness, a fitness chain with thirteen gym locations valued at 70 million dollars, employing over 1,200 people, and serving over 70,000 customers.

Tom started Mountainside Fitness after spending less than a semester at Arizona State University and with only $2,000 to his name. He renovated the original Mountainside Fitness himself and he and his friends and family built much of the equipment on their own. He even washed the sweat towels when he was trying to get the business off the ground.

Tom believes that his OB skills played a huge part in his business success, especially when he was starting out.

"You can't be great at anything until you absolutely master the fundamentals [of OB]. Once you treat people well and foster a positive culture, then you can be a great manager."

And it seemed that Tom's positive attitude was contagious—not only was he able to enlist friends and family to help out, but customers too. In fact, in the early days of Mountainside Fitness, many of the new members willingly helped Tom with cleaning the towels and wiping down machines despite paying a membership fee every month. Tom had created the sort of environment which inspired them to help because they felt invested in Mountainside's success.

Tom firmly believes that a clear mission statement and vision go a long way to keep him and his employees on the right path to organizational success. When he first had the idea, Tom knew how he wanted the business to be—the friendliest gym in town—and he was determined to make this vision a reality.

"No matter how many directions you might be pulled in when you're running a business, you have to stay true to the business fundamentals reflected in your vision and mission statement. Without this, the business will not last because employees need more than just a paycheck to go the extra mile."

Tom also has a different attitude toward recruitment. His hiring strategy is based on finding people who are willing to learn.

"I want to hire someone that is outgoing and fun. I don't care what they look like on the outside or their experience in the industry because I need someone I can teach."

For that reason, Mountainside Fitness has one of the lowest employee turnovers in the entire industry, for the simple reason that people love working there. In fact, Tom credits over 40 percent of his employees for some of the more innovative ideas that have been implemented in many of his fitness centers. Also, Tom typically hires the managers of his fitness centers from within. Almost all of his current center managers started at lower levels within the company.

Despite turning $2,000 into a $70 million business, Tom doesn't see himself as some sort of business guru, but rather as an air-traffic controller, listening to and directing his employees. He does not perceive himself as the absolute source of ideas and output and that's how he likes it. Because of his management ethos, people believe in Tom, and buy into his mission to make Mountainside Fitness "the friendliest gym in town."

Critical-Thinking Questions

1. What types of human capital do Tom and his team value most?

2. Why do you think Tom and his team hire from within? ●

Source: Interview with Tom Hatten conducted on March 21st, 2017.

communication, and interpersonal relationships affect organizations). Over the past one hundred years, however, researchers have carried out a host of studies on the practice and application of OB, taking full advantage of its strong links to five main behavioral science disciplines: psychology, sociology, social psychology, political science, and anthropology (see Figure 1.3).

Psychology

Psychology is the scientific study of the human mind that seeks to measure and explain behavioral characteristics. Early organizational psychological research and theory focused on the factors affecting work performance and efficiency, such as lethargy and boredom. More recently, psychologists have focused on the mental health and well-being of employees in relationship to their work performance and created methods to help employees deal with challenges such as job stress. Psychologists have also helped design performance appraisals, decision-making processes, recruitment techniques, and training programs.

Sociology

While psychology focuses on the individual, **sociology** looks at the way groups behave and how they communicate and exchange information in a social setting. Sociologists have made valuable contributions to OB within areas such as group dynamics, communication, power, organizational culture, and conflict.

Social Psychology

Social psychology mixes concepts from sociology and psychology and focuses on the way people influence each other in a social setting. Social psychologists look at behaviors, feelings, actions, beliefs, and intentions and how they are constructed and influenced by others. They have made significant contributions to reducing the level of prejudice, discrimination, and stereotyping by designing processes to change attitudes, build communication, and improve the way groups work together.

Political Science

Political science studies the behavior of individuals and groups within a political environment. Political scientists focus particularly on how conflict is managed and structured, how power is distributed, and how power is abused or manipulated for the purposes of self-interest. Their studies have helped improve our understanding of how different interests, motivations, and preferences can lead to conflict and power struggles between individuals and groups.

Anthropology

Anthropology is the study of people and their activities in relation to societal, environmental, and cultural influences. In a global organizational environment, anthropological research has become even more significant because it increases our understanding of other cultures and the types of values and attitudes held by others from other countries and organizations.

FIGURE 1.3

**Disciplines Contributing to the F...
Organizational Behavior**

Psychology: The scientific study of the human mind that seeks to measure and explain behavioral characteristics

Sociology: The study of the behavior of groups and how they relate to each other in a social setting

Social psychology: The social science that blends concepts from sociology and psychology and focuses on how people influence each other in a social setting

Political science: The study of the behavior of individuals and groups within a political environment

Anthropology: The study of people and their activities in relation to societal, environmental, and cultural influences

1. What factors are likely to have played a role in early management theory's emphasis on physical tasks and working conditions?

2. Of the five behavioral science disciplines listed, which one do you consider to be the most relevant to the field of management today? Explain your answer.

A Critical-Thinking Approach to OB

>> **LO 1.4** Demonstrate the value of critical thinking in the context of OB

Critical thinking: The ability to use intelligence, knowledge, and skills to question and carefully explore situations and arrive at thoughtful conclusions based on evidence and reason

In the section "What Is Organizational Behavior and Why Is It Important?" we outlined the four main functions of management (planning, organizing, leading, and controlling) and the skills (technical, human, and conceptual) managers need to be effective in an organization. However, another skill is becoming increasingly important for managers in the workplace: critical thinking. **Critical thinking** is the use of your intelligence, knowledge, and skills to question and carefully explore situations and arrive at thoughtful conclusions based on evidence and reason.[14] Increasingly used in business as a problem-solving tool, the critical-thinking approach is a powerful analytical method that helps managers consider intended and unintended consequences of individual behaviors on their teams and within their organizations and communities. Organizations need managers who think independently without judgment and bias, predict patterns of behaviors and processes, and ask the right questions—"How?" and "Why?" and not just "What?"—in order to make effective and thoughtful decisions.

At the moment, there is a skilled labor shortage in the United States, yet unemployment is still on the rise.[15] How can this be? Surely, if there are enough people available for work, then companies should be able to fill their vacancies. However, as the business environment changes, so do the types of skills expected from employees. New and recent graduates may find that their educational backgrounds do not fulfill the requirements of organizations and may be forced to change, adapt, or learn new skillsets to secure a job. Furthermore, many organizations are becoming more selective; for some positions, a degree is not enough.

Your ability to think critically will differentiate you from other job applicants. In an interview situation, critical thinkers take the time to think carefully about the questions they are asked, base their responses on facts or experience rather than emotion or bias, consider different viewpoints or perspectives equally, and compare their responses with similar examples that have occurred in the past. Once hired, critical thinkers are more likely to succeed. After all, most companies do not employ graduates to simply go through the motions or to be a mere cog in the wheel. They expect their employees to play a pivotal role in helping the company achieve its organizational goals. And when a company does well, everyone benefits. You don't need to be an expert in critical thinking to get a job. Many of these skills can be learned in the workplace. However, employers look for candidates who have a questioning mind, a willingness to embrace change, and a keen desire to learn.

Indeed, as research shows, businesses are desperate to attract employees with critical- thinking skills.[16] Why? Because organizations are undergoing such rapid change that they need their employees to consistently introduce new, fresh ideas to stay ahead of the competition. Consider the following:

1. When more than four hundred senior HR professionals were asked in a survey to name the most important skill their employees will need in the next five years, critical thinking ranked the highest—beating out innovation and information technology (see Figure 1.4).[17]

2. Senior executive development professionals report that future leaders are lacking chiefly in strategic thinking skills—which are closely related to critical-thinking skills.[18]

3. A 2009 study by Ones and Dilchert found that the most successful senior executives scored higher on critical-thinking skills than did the less successful ones.[19]

4. *Forbes* recently analyzed data from online databases of occupations and necessary skills in order to identify the skills most in-demand in 2013. Then the magazine went further and analyzed the key skills necessary for success in those roles. The number one skill should be no surprise at all: it was critical thinking.[20]

5. A 2014 survey involving 16,000 corporate employers conducted by the Penn State Office of Career Services found critical-thinking skills to be the most important attribute in employees.[21]

Business leaders use critical thinking when making decisions, solving problems, gathering information, and asking questions. Time and again, research has shown the effectiveness of critical thinking in the workplace.

These tables from an even more recent 2016 SHRM/Mercer survey show that critical thinking is important (93 percent) yet lacking in job applicants (see Figure 1.4).

Entrepreneur Daniel Ek, founder of Spotify, is a good example of a critical thinker.[22] Launched in 2008, Spotify is a digital music service that allows people legal paid access to millions of songs streamed directly from major and independent record labels. As a child, Daniel was fascinated by computers and computer games: "When he asked his mother what to do when one of his computer games broke, she told him, 'I don't know, why don't you figure it out?' So he did. 'And that was basically my life story,' says Mr. Ek." By using critical thinking and asking "How?" and "Why?" Ek has managed to build a cutting-edge company valued at $8 billion with more than 50 million paying users.[23]

Daniel Ek, founder of Spotify, shows critical thinking by asking "How?" and "Why?" and seeking out the answers.

Noam Galai/Getty Images

The process of critical thinking provides you with the tools to make better decisions as a manager and help you to predict the effects and consequences of those decisions. Most important, you will be better able to manage the complexities of human behavior and initiate behavioral changes by following the critical-thinking process. There are five steps to applying critical thinking in order to manage and change behavior (Figure 1.5): *observe* (recognize the behavior), *interpret* (understand the cause and effects of behavior), *analyze* (investigate the causes and effects of behavior), *evaluate* (assess the consequences of changing behavior), and *explain* (justify a change to behavior).

Let's use an example to illustrate the five steps of critical-thinking methodology. Suppose you are the manager of a restaurant owned by a local businesswoman. Samir, one of your wait staff, has failed to show up for several shifts without giving any

FIGURE 1.4

Importance of Skills for Entry-Level Positions

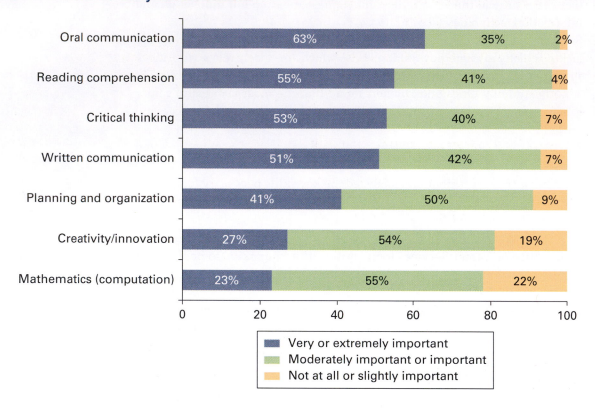

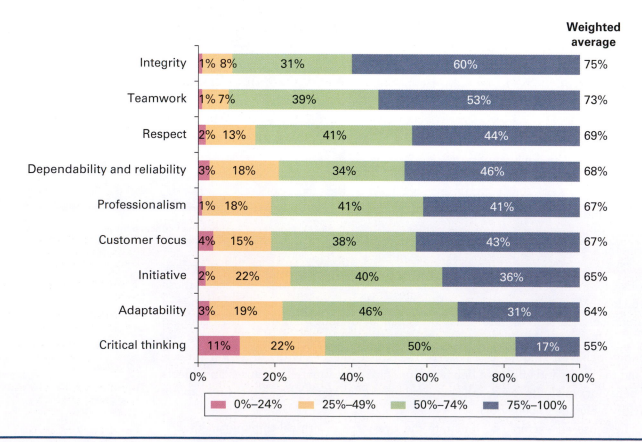

meaningful reason. Since Samir is usually reliable, you are puzzled by his absenteeism. Because you don't have all the facts, you decide to use critical-thinking skills to investigate the real source of the problem.

The next time Samir comes to work, you *observe* the situation objectively, suspending all bias and judgment. You notice that he is abrupt with customers, doesn't attempt to communicate with his fellow colleagues, and walks across the restaurant with a heavy gait. This helps you to *interpret* the situation better, giving you enough evidence to deduce that your employee is not happy. You might *analyze* these effects and think of a way to deal with the behavior. What should you do? You decide to *evaluate* the situation and assess the consequences of trying to change his behavior. Based on his performance, your boss, Jessica, the restaurant owner, tells you to fire Samir but you *explain* to your boss why you believe an attempt to change his behavior might be justified and she agrees to give Samir another chance.

You set up a meeting with Samir to discover the reasons behind his unexplained absences and unmotivated behavior at work. Samir apologizes and tells you he has become dissatisfied with his job and would much rather work on the front desk of the restaurant, greeting customers and taking reservations. He says he has been afraid to tell you because he has been worried he would be letting you down by switching roles. You explain that his absences have already disappointed you but that you are willing to give him a second chance. Following a trial period at the front desk, Samir immediately becomes more motivated, and his attendance is impeccable.

Of course, there could be many ways to handle this dilemma, but it is clear that critical thinking can help to find the best solution for each situation when dealing with the complexities of real-life challenges.

In the next section, we explore how managers use OB research findings to enhance their critical-thinking skills.

Research in OB

Researchers use the scientific method to conduct research that managers can use to understand their employees and enhance critical thinking in OB. Researchers often begin with a **theory**, a set of principles intended to explain behavioral phenomena in organizations.[24] OB researchers may also use **models**, simplified snapshots of reality, to summarize and illustrate the reasons behind certain behaviors such as absenteeism or employee turnover. Connecting the elements of these models are **independent variables,** which are factors that remain unchanged, and **dependent variables**, factors affected by independent variables. Researchers then write a prediction called a **hypothesis,** a statement that specifies the relationships between the two variables. For example, much OB research has been carried out on the **correlation,** or the reciprocal relationship between two or more factors, between job satisfaction (independent variable) and absenteeism (dependent variable).

Researchers discovered that employees who were more satisfied in their jobs had higher attendance at work than those who had lower levels of job satisfaction. At first glance, this seems pretty reasonable—you may feel more inclined to call in sick when

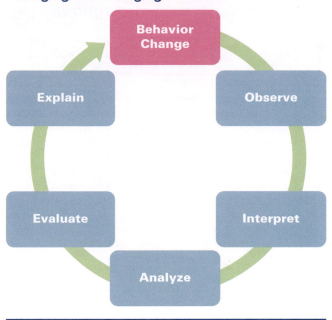

FIGURE 1.5

Five-Step Critical-Thinking Framework for Managing and Changing Behavior

Behavior Change

Observe

Interpret

Analyze

Evaluate

Explain

Source: Neck, C., et al., *Management* (Hoboken, NJ: Wiley, 2014): 5.

Theory: A set of principles intended to explain behavioral phenomena in organizations

Model: A simplified snapshot of reality

Independent variables: Factors that remain unchanged

Dependent variable: Factor affected by independent variables

Hypothesis: A statement that specifies the relationships between the two variables

Correlation: A reciprocal relationship between two or more factors

EXAMINING THE EVIDENCE

Evidence-Based Management

One of the strongest proponents of applying research evidence to management practice, Denise M. Rousseau, H. J. Heinz II University Professor of Organizational Behavior at Carnegie Mellon University, defines evidence-based management (EBMgt) as "the systematic, evidence-informed practice of management, incorporating scientific knowledge in the content and processes of making decisions."* EBMgt employs valid scientific findings in the context of critical thinking, decision making, and judgment to help managers obtain and use the best and most reliable information available to increase managerial and organizational effectiveness.*

But why is it important for managers to think critically about and incorporate current research findings into their management practices and decision making? A good parallel comes from the field of medicine. You may naturally assume that medical doctors and health care practitioners use the latest and best research evidence available in the field of medicine to make their decisions. Yet despite the thousands of studies conducted and published in the field of medicine each year, studies suggest that only about 15 percent of doctors make evidence-based decisions.^ Instead, they rely on obsolete information they learned in school, unproven traditions, personal experiences, and information provided by vendors selling medical products and services.^ During the past two decades, however, evidence-based medicine has begun to revolutionize the way medical practitioners make decisions and prescribe treatments.

Stanford Professors Jeffrey Pfeffer and Robert I. Sutton argue that managers should take a similar evidence-based approach in making decisions, taking actions, and prescribing cures for organizational ills: "Managers are actually much more ignorant than doctors about which prescriptions are reliable—and they're less eager to find out. If doctors practiced medicine like many companies practice management, there would be more unnecessarily sick or dead patients and many more doctors in jail or suffering other penalties for malpractice."^

Professor Rousseau suggests that EBMgt consists of four basic activities:* (1) obtaining the best scientific information available, (2) systematically assessing organizational facts, (3) using critical thinking and reflective judgment to apply the research evidence, and (4) considering key ethical issues. Throughout the remainder of the text, you will be presented with current research evidence from the field of OB and asked to think critically about how you might apply these findings in your current or future career as a management practitioner.

Critical-Thinking Questions

1. What are some of the primary advantages of evidence-based management practices?

2. What makes it difficult for managers to be evidence-based in their actions and decision making? ●

Sources:

*Rousseau, Denise M. "Envisioning Evidence-Based Management." In *The Oxford Handbook Of Evidence-Based Management*, 3–24 (New York: Oxford University Press, 2012).

^Pfeffer, Jeffrey, and Robert I. Sutton "Evidence-Based Management." *Harvard Business Review* 84, no. 1 (January 2006): 62–74.

you dislike your job. But it doesn't end there. OB researchers used critical thinking to examine the theory further in order to provide a solution to this work dilemma. What are the factors affecting job satisfaction? What makes employees happy or miserable in their jobs? How can organizations improve conditions to increase job satisfaction and decrease levels of absenteeism? By drilling down deeply into proposed theories, researchers have created practical resolutions to address these problems. OB researchers apply critical thinking to facets of an organization by questioning and exploring the reasons behind issues such as work stress, unethical behavior, lack of team cohesion, poor relationships between individuals and groups, and many more.

Similarly, we could apply the same critical-thinking method to the issue of work/life balance (independent variable) and its relationship to stress (dependent variable), which is one of the main issues facing today's organizations. Employees who sacrifice their personal lives for too many hours in the office may be subject to higher levels of stress. Conversely, workers who achieve a balance between their personal and working lives may have lower levels of stress. We may conclude from this that an acceptable work/life balance leads to higher levels of job satisfaction. Using critical thinking, managers explore how they can help their employees achieve a balance between work and play.

Yet, for all the research that exists on OB and the debates it continues to inspire, it is still universally agreed that there is no one best way of managing people. In fact, there is a theory for that too. It's called **contingency thinking,** and it states that our actions must be dependent on the nature of the situation. In other words, one size does not fit all. Every single circumstance brings about a whole new set of questions and solutions—this is where critical thinking comes into play. By asking the right questions to fit each scenario, managers have a better chance of resolving problems. Related to contingency thinking is **evidence-based management,** which relies on research-based facts to make decisions.[25] Successful OB managers use this wealth of research findings as a basis for understanding different situations.

Contingency thinking: The approach that describes actions as dependent on the nature of the situation; one size does not fit all

Evidence-based management: The practice of using research-based facts to make decisions

Open Systems Theory

A key OB research finding that has had a significant impact on the use of critical thinking by managers is called **open systems theory**. According to this theory, organizations are systems that interact with (are *open* to) their environments and use their environments to obtain resources, or inputs, and transform those inputs into outputs that are returned to the environment for consumption.[26] Open systems theory maintains that all organizations are unique and subject to internal and external environmental influences that can affect their efficiency. To ensure the smooth running of an organization, a defined structure should be in place that can

Open systems theory: The assumption that organizations are systems that interact with their environments to obtain resources or inputs and transform them into outputs returned to the environment for consumption

---

FIGURE 1.6

Open Systems Theory: Inputs and Outputs

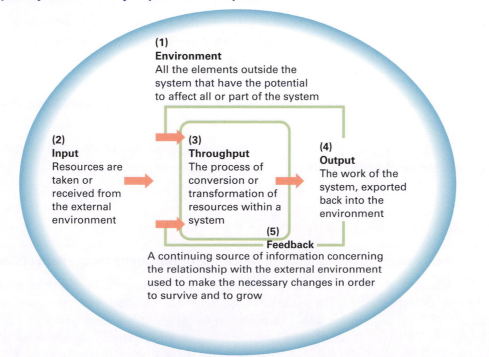

(1) Environment
All the elements outside the system that have the potential to affect all or part of the system

(2) Input
Resources are taken or received from the external environment

(3) Throughput
The process of conversion or transformation of resources within a system

(4) Output
The work of the system, exported back into the environment

(5) Feedback
A continuing source of information concerning the relationship with the external environment used to make the necessary changes in order to survive and to grow

Source: Basic Open System Model. CSAP Institute for Partnership Development. US Department of Health and Human Services. n.d. Public domain. https://commons.wikimedia.org/wiki/File:Basic_Open_System_Model.gif.

accommodate problems and opportunities as they arise. Let's take a look at how a car manufacturing company might operate, according to this theory (see Figure 1.6).

In this example, a car manufacturing company takes inputs from suppliers of certain goods or materials and then uses these resources to manufacture cars within the organization itself ("throughput" in the figure), before exporting them back into the environment as outputs. Put into a general context, this means organizations use input from their resources, such as technology, people, money, raw materials, information, and processes, and transform them into the finished product or output, which they sell.

Value chain: The sequence of activities carried out by organizations to create valued goods and services to consumers

When open systems work well, they create a **value chain**, the sequence of activities carried out by organizations to create valued goods and services to consumers.[27] In the car example, if every link in the chain is working efficiently, suppliers are satisfied with the way they have been treated by the car company and continue to meet its specifications, employees are productive and manufacture the car in good time and within budget, and consumers are gratified with their new purchase. However, a poorly managed value chain can have disastrous consequences. Suppliers that go out of business, high employee turnover, and a dissatisfied consumer base can all lead to the decline of an organization.

Open systems strive to find a balance between themselves and their environment and to remain harmonious, especially in the face of environmental changes. A strong open system can be crucial to organizational survival, especially in today's organizations that are continually adjusting to meet the demands of global challenges and opportunities.

THINKING CRITICALLY

1. Explain in your own words how critical thinking can be used as a problem-solving tool in the workplace.

2. Create a list of behaviors and skills that contribute to a manager's ability to think critically.

3. Imagine that you manage two employees who dislike each other and have engaged in heated arguments in front of customers. What specific steps could you take, following the 5-step critical-thinking model (observe, interpret, analyze, evaluate, and explain), to resolve the situation?

4. Identify the inputs, throughput, and outputs of a fast food chain according to Open Systems Theory.

5. Explain the meaning of "value chain" and provide an example of one way that a value chain may be enhanced and one way a value chain may be harmed.

OB Challenges and Opportunities

>> **LO 1.5**   Identify the major challenges and opportunities in the field of OB

Organizations are in a continual state of flux and transformation. In addition, within the past decade, the financial world has been in turmoil because of a lingering recession and high unemployment. The resulting uncertainty has immeasurably influenced the behavior of people and organizations. So what can you expect when you enter the workforce? Next we discuss some of the main challenges and opportunities facing organizations today (see Figure 1.7).

Globalization

Globalization is a process by which the world has become increasingly interconnected through trade, culture, technology, and politics. It has had a huge influence on OB. Many organizations now have offices all over the world, and it's not uncommon for employees to move between them. For example, you may be placed on a foreign assignment where you are expected to learn a different language and work with people from different cultures and backgrounds. Even at home, you are very likely to be working with people from abroad or from backgrounds different from yours. It is essential to be able to work well with others regardless of their location or cultural background. Communicating effectively across time zones and via the latest technological methods is equally important.

Economic Factors

Economic events have had a significant effect on the workplace. Recessions and financial crises have led to layoffs, reduced wages, unemployment, bankruptcy, and labor shortages. Organizations are continuously strategizing to overcome economic stumbling blocks by seeking out talent and focusing on the skill set of their workforce to find innovative ways to differentiate themselves from the competition. To flourish in a work environment that is continually in flux, you will need to be agile, adaptable, and open to learning new skills when required.

Workforce Diversity

The demographic profile of the United States is changing, and the resulting diversity in the workforce is encouraging organizations to foster inclusive working environments that do not discriminate against employees regardless of gender, race, ethnicity, age, sexual orientation, or disability.[28] In most large organizations, employees are educated about diversity and taught the importance of respecting individual differences. Forming and building good working relationships is central to achieving professional success. You will need to respect others and accept people without prejudice if you want to get ahead in the workplace.

FIGURE 1.7

Challenges and Opportunities Facing Today's Organizations

In an increasingly global economy with more companies expanding internationally, having a strong grasp of organizational behavior can help individuals to relate to and respect their colleagues.

© iStockphoto.com/Morsa Images

Customer Service

Organizations are creating customer-responsive cultures to meet the increasing needs and changing demands of their customer bases. Companies are striving to understand the customers' needs first and then tailor the product to customer requirements. In most businesses, you will carry out some level of customer service, whether you are dealing with external clients (customers) or internal ones (coworkers). In doing so, you will need to develop a customer-focused attitude and think creatively about how to satisfy customers' needs.

People Skills

Managers and employees must have excellent people skills, such as the ability to communicate and interact with others, in order to work harmoniously with their colleagues. Being able to relate to other people has just as much impact on success as your technical skills, especially when you are leading and managing teams.

Innovation and Change

Organizations need to simulate innovation and change by becoming faster and more agile than the competition. Tangible resources such as physical equipment are no longer the mainstay of an organization. The organization's most important assets are its people and their ability to continuously create, strategize, innovate, and convert their ideas into quality products and processes. Critical thinking is imperative in innovation; you will need to question, analyze, and create to come up with new, original ideas that will appeal to your customers to secure a competitive advantage.

Sustainability

Many organizations are striving to build a more sustainable and responsible global marketplace by taking environmental factors into consideration during decision making and goal setting. Whatever role you play, you will need to take into account the effects your decisions and the decisions of others may have on the environment, your community, and the organization itself.

Throughout this book, we explore these and other factors that influence OB, including leadership, and the effects of a new generation of workers on the workplace. In the next section, we analyze one of the most important elements of global OB: ethical behavior in organizations.

THINKING CRITICALLY

1. Of the seven challenges discussed in this section, which do you consider the most difficult to address? Which do you consider the easiest to address? Why?

2. Based on your own work or volunteer experience, have you ever experienced any of these seven challenges? Describe your experience and brainstorm ways for overcoming these challenges.

3. Select a company and research online to learn more about their sustainable business practices. Do they have a sustainability plan? What are some recommendations you might make that would benefit the organization as well as the environment and society?

Three Levels of Analysis in OB

>> **LO 1.6**   Differentiate the three basic levels of analysis at which OB may be examined

There are three main levels of analysis within the OB model: individuals, teams, and organizations.[29] (See Figure 1.8.) Each level builds on the previous one. For example, individuals working well together lay the foundation for effective teams, which in turn work together to achieve organizational goals.

Individuals

Individuals are the foundation of organizations, and the way they work and behave makes or breaks a business. The role of managers is to integrate individuals into the organization, nurture their skills and attributes, and balance their needs and expectations accordingly. When managers do this successfully, individuals will achieve high levels of job satisfaction, motivating them to work toward attaining organizational goals. For instance, Tom Hatten, founder of Mountainside Fitness featured in OB in the Real World, engages his employees by listening to their ideas and encouraging them to think for themselves.

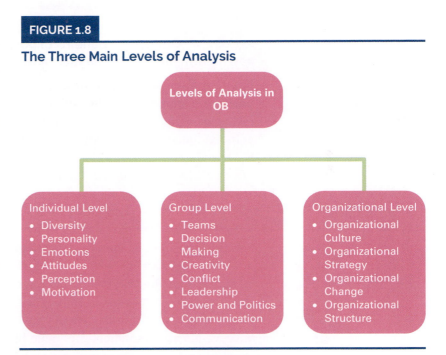

FIGURE 1.8

The Three Main Levels of Analysis

Levels of Analysis in OB

Individual Level
- Diversity
- Personality
- Emotions
- Attitudes
- Perception
- Motivation

Group Level
- Teams
- Decision Making
- Creativity
- Conflict
- Leadership
- Power and Politics
- Communication

Organizational Level
- Organizational Culture
- Organizational Strategy
- Organizational Change
- Organizational Structure

Teams

Teams or groups exist in all organizations, large or small, and their effective functioning is essential to the success of any organization. Teams are complex because they consist of many different personalities and attitudes. Managers who understand the dynamics of a team and the way it is structured also better understand the underlying behaviors of individuals within the group. A good example is the British football team Manchester United, whose players continually cooperate with each other in pursuit of a common goal, in spite of well-documented personality differences and the occasional feud.[30]

Organizations

Organizations provide individuals and groups with the tools and systems to achieve objectives and goals. The attitudes and behavior of employees are influenced by the way organizations are structured. For instance, Google's organizational structure is centered around employees from all disciplines working together to meet goals and generate innovative ideas. Google employees derive job satisfaction from a flexible working structure that provides them the freedom to set their own goals and standards.[31]

With organizations continually juggling market changes and customer demands, the success of a business depends on its workforce as never before. But how do managers get the best from individuals, teams, and the organization itself?

THINKING CRITICALLY

1. Discuss the relationship among the three levels of analysis in OB. How might individuals influence organizations? How might organizations influence individuals?

2. Teams play a critical role in OB. What are some of the benefits of working in teams? What are some of the challenges?

Positive OB and High-Involvement Management

>> LO 1.7   Outline the benefits of positive OB and high-involvement management

Positive organizational behavior: The strengths, virtues, vitality, and resilience of individuals and organizations

Drawing from a range of organizational research and theories, scholarship on **positive organizational behavior** focuses on the strengths, virtues, vitality, and resilience of individuals and organizations.[32] The idea is that nurturing the strengths of individuals rather than attempting to "fix" their weaknesses is far more beneficial to achieving organizational goals. Employees will gain more self-confidence and feel more positive about their skills and abilities, leading to better performance. Managers who practice positive OB value human capital as their most important resource.

Say you are the manager of a sales and marketing department. You need your sales team to reach a specific sales target by the end of each month. However, one of your new hires, a recent business graduate, is regularly failing to meet objectives, bringing down the department's sales total. When you arrange a one-to-one meeting with him, he admits he is finding the role tougher than he thought it would be. He knows the products and services inside out but finds it difficult to persuade people to meet with him to discuss a potential sale. As his manager, you arrange additional training to improve his sales technique and build his confidence in selling. Following extensive training, he succeeds in securing a couple of meetings with prospects but fails to sell anything. When you hired him, you felt he had potential. Do you fire him for not bringing in the business, or do you consider another position for him in the organization?

Managers who practice positive OB will choose the second option. This employee may not be a good fit for sales, but what else can he do that would benefit the organization? Perhaps he loves to write and feels more comfortable communicating through media rather than over the phone. As a Web content assistant, writing articles for the company website and working with project teams, designers, and developers to ensure information is presented in the best way, he can thrive.

This is just one example of how managers get the best from (and for) their employees using positive behavior. Most people are hired for a reason, but it is entirely possible that some may not be the best fit in the role for which they were hired. In such a case, managers who value their human capital should make every effort to match employees' skill sets with a more appropriate position. Otherwise, organizations could face the dilemmas of low job satisfaction and reduced productivity, leading to an increase in absenteeism and high turnover.

© iStockphoto.com/pixelfit

Managers who practice positive OB will communicate with their employees and learn their strengths to discover the position that is best suited to their skills.

Positive OB places the highest priority on the well-being of employees. This style of management is closely linked with **high-involvement management**, a strategy in which managers empower employees to make decisions, provide them with extensive training and opportunities to increase their knowledge base, share important information, and provide incentive compensation.[33] Increasing employee involvement in this way is a very democratic approach to management, giving all employees, including those who carry out basic duties, a say in how the work is conducted. They are then more likely to work hard, and more willing to adapt to new processes and learn new tasks. Empowered, satisfied employees strive to achieve organizational goals.

Again, this type of approach works only when the right employees are selected to work in an organization. They must be the right cultural fit and believe in the values and mission of the company. Equally, managers must treat employees with respect, listen carefully to their ideas, and be willing to admit to themselves and their employees that they don't have all the answers. When high-involvement management is effective, it helps to build strong relationships between employees and managers, fosters trust, and increases job satisfaction and productivity.

High-involvement managers have different ways of empowering their employees. Take Brandon Steiner, for instance. Steiner is the founder and CEO of Steiner Sports and a professional sports marketer, speaker, and author. He believes the well-being of his employees begins with the food they eat, and that there is a strong correlation between a healthy diet and work performance.[34] When new hires join Steiner Sports, he tells them, "I don't care about a lot of the things other managers do, but one thing you cannot do here is eat unhealthily."[35] How does Steiner encourage his employees to be healthy? The company pays for gym membership, ensures a continuous supply of fresh fruit is available in the break room, and makes personal side bets with heavily overweight employees to see who can lose the most weight in the healthiest way within a specified period of time. One of Steiner's mottos is, "If you don't feel your best, you can't do your best work."[36] Would you like to work for a company like Steiner Sports that strongly promotes employee health and well-being? Do you think you would fit in and buy into the ethos of this type of organization? If you are not the type of person who places as high a value on healthy living as Steiner, then perhaps this might not be the right work culture for you. Remember, high-involvement management works best when employees are a good fit for the organization.

Throughout this text, we present a number of real-world case studies which demonstrate a critical-thinking perspective in relation to OB. We have structured this book to explore the challenges and opportunities facing OB on an individual, group, and organizational level. We explore the complexities of human behavior, including individual behaviors, emotions, and attitudes. We also examine OB in the context of leadership, motivation, teamwork, and culture.

At the heart of every job, regardless of the industry, lies the need to get along with people and to fit in with the values and culture of the organization.

High-involvement management: The way managers empower employees to make decisions, provide them with extensive training and the opportunities to increase their knowledge base, share important information, and provide incentive compensation

Brandon Steiner of Steiner Sports is an example of a high-involvement manager.

AP Photo/Kathy Willens

However, in today's organizations, fitting in does not mean agreeing with everything to maintain the status quo, nor does it mean laughing at your boss's jokes (especially when you don't think they are very funny!). Instead, applying critical thinking by asking questions, suspending bias, and providing creative solutions, all of which you'll experience in this book, form the new norm. Understanding and gaining knowledge about OB is a lifelong learning process. Your career success depends on your ability to learn from your everyday experiences and on the way you conduct your relationships with others, behave, and communicate.

In a world where the only constant is change, it is more important than ever to manage our own behavior and understand the feelings, attitudes, and behaviors of others around us in order to work harmoniously and productively and succeed in a complex working environment.

THINKING CRITICALLY

1. Identify your top five strengths. Describe how each of these strengths might benefit an organization.

2. Could there be a downside or unintended consequences for managers who focus primarily on the findings of positive organizational behavior research? Explain your answer.

3. List three concrete ways a high-involvement manager could empower employees. ●

Visit **edge.sagepub.com/neckob2e** to help you accomplish your coursework goals in an easy-to-use learning environment.

- Mobile-friendly eFlashcards and practice quizzes
- Video and multimedia content
- Chapter summaries with learning objectives
- EXCLUSIVE! Access to full-text SAGE journal articles

IN REVIEW

1.1 Explain the basic concept of organizational behavior and its value in organizations

Organizational behavior studies how and why individual employees and groups of employees behave the way they do within an organizational setting. The three main reasons for studying organizational behavior in your organization are to be able to *explain* it, *predict* it, and *influence* it.

1.2 Describe the key role of managing human capital in creating a sustainable competitive advantage for organizations

Human capital is essential for gaining **competitive advantage**, the edge that gives organizations a more beneficial position than their competitors and allows them to generate more profits and retain more customers. Three main aspects of human capital enhance true competitive advantage: **value, rareness,** and **inimitability.**

1.3 Identify the major behavioral science disciplines that contribute to OB

Psychology is the scientific study of the human mind that seeks to measure and explain behavioral characteristics. **Sociology** is the study of the behavior of groups and how they relate to each other in a social setting. **Social psychology** blends concepts from sociology and psychology and focuses on how people influence each other in a social setting. **Political science** studies the behavior of individuals and groups within a political environment. **Anthropology** is the study of people and their activities in relation to societal, environmental, and cultural influences.

1.4 Demonstrate the value of critical thinking in the context of OB

Critical thinking is the ability to use intelligence, knowledge, and skills to question and carefully explore situations and arrive at thoughtful conclusions based on evidence and reason. The critical-thinking approach is a powerful analytical method that helps managers consider intended and unintended consequences of behaviors on their teams, organizations, and communities.

1.5 Identify the major challenges and opportunities in the field of OB

The process of *globalization* has had a huge influence on OB. The *economy* has had a significant effect on OB. Organizations are continually strategizing to overcome economic stumbling blocks by hiring talent and focusing on the skill sets of their workforce to find new, innovative ways to differentiate themselves from the competition. *Workforce diversity* develops when organizations foster working environments that do not discriminate against others regardless of gender, race, ethnicity, age, sexual orientation, and disability. Organizations are creating *customer-responsive cultures* to meet the increasing needs and changing demands of their customer base. Managers and employees must have excellent people skills to use on the job to work harmoniously with their fellow colleagues. Organizations need to simulate *innovation* and *change* by becoming faster and more agile than the competition. There is a growing commitment to fostering an *ethical culture* and improving ethical behavior in the workplace. Many organizations are striving to build a more *sustainable* and responsible global marketplace by taking environmental factors into consideration during decision-making and goal-setting practices.

1.6 Differentiate the three basic levels of analysis at which OB may be examined

There are three main levels of analysis within the OB model: individuals, teams, and organizations. Individuals are the foundation of organizations: the way they work and behave either makes or breaks a business. The role of managers is to integrate individuals into the organization, nurture their skills and attributes, and balance their needs and expectations accordingly. Teams or groups exist in all organizations, large or small, and have a significant influence on the behavior of individual team members. Managers who understand the dynamics of a team and how it is structured gain more knowledge about the underlying behaviors of individuals within the group. Individuals and groups work within the formal structure of organizations. Organizations provide employees with the tools and systems to achieve objectives and goals. The attitudes and behavior of employees are influenced by the way organizations are structured.

1.7 Outline the benefits of positive OB and high-involvement management

Positive organizational behavior focuses on the strengths, virtues, vitality, and resilience of individuals and organizations. **High-involvement management** occurs when managers empower employees to make decisions, provide them with extensive training and the opportunities to increase their knowledge base, share important information, and provide incentive compensation. This type of approach works only when the right employees are selected to work in an organization. When high-involvement management is effective it helps to build strong relationships between individuals and teams, fosters trust, and increases job satisfaction and productivity.

KEY TERMS

Anthropology 13
Competitive advantage 9
Conceptual skill 7
Contingency thinking 19
Correlation 17
Critical thinking 14
Dependent variable 17
Emotional intelligence 7
Evidence-based management 19
High-involvement management 25
Human capital 8
Human capital inimitability 11
Human capital rareness 9
Human capital value 9
Human skills 7

Hypothesis 17
Independent variables 17
Model 17
Open systems theory 19
Organization 5
Organizational behavior 5
Political science 13
Positive organizational behavior 24
Psychology 13
Social psychology 13
Sociology 13
Strategic OB approach 8
Technical skill 7
Theory 17
Value chain 20

UP FOR DEBATE: Hiring Qualified Candidates

When hiring employees, it is imperative that organizations hire the most qualified candidates for the position and refuse to settle for less. Agree or disagree? Explain your answer:

EXERCISE 1.1: Organizational Behavior in an International Firm

Objective

The purpose of this exercise is to gain a greater understanding of organizational behavior as it applies to globalization.

Instructions

Globalization is a major consideration for large, diversified companies and their understanding of organizational behavior. Suppose you work for an American organization that has been operating in this country for over one hundred years. The company manufactures a variety of light bulbs, but in the last ten years, has specialized in LED bulbs. As the business has grown, the leaders of the organization see opportunities to expand internationally for the first time in the firm's history. The CEO wants to begin international operations next year with a manufacturing plant in a country outside the United States.

In teams of three to six, first choose a country to open a new division of your company. Select one you are either familiar with or can readily find information about. Next, determine what you would need to know about the country and its culture for the new facility to be successful. For example, does the country and culture you selected value individualism or teams more? Is the country one where loud, expressive communication is commonplace, or does interpersonal communication tend to be more quiet and subdued? Assume that 95 percent of the employees will be hired from the country you selected, and only 5 percent will be expatriates from the United States.

Reflection Questions

1. How important is it for managers to understand both organizational behavior *and* globalization when operating an international organization?

2. Taking a look at your list of considerations, what could managers do to ensure that the employees hired have a firm understanding of the accepted standards of behavior in the company?

3. How about the 5 percent of the employees who will be relocating from the United States? What challenges will they have adjusting to this new country and culture? How can the company assist them in acclimating more quickly and easily to this new working environment?

Exercise contributed by Steven Stovall, Southeast Missouri State University.

EXERCISE 1.2: Discussion about Who Can Be CEO

Objective

The purpose of this exercise is to grasp the concept of human capital and its value to organizations.

Instructions

Human capital is described as the sum of people's skills, knowledge, experience, and general attributes. To be the president or chief executive officer (CEO) of a firm, one must be strong in all of these factors. The top leaders of organizations change over time due to the death or retirement of the CEO, the CEO moves on to a different organization voluntarily, or if the board of directors asks the CEO to step down because of poor performance.

When the board of directors at a major corporation has an opening for a CEO and they want to promote someone from within the organization, they examine all the qualifications of various candidates—the human capital of those vying for the position.

The question for the class to discuss is this: Can anyone be a CEO? Does every single employee in a company have the same skill set, knowledge about the firm and the industry, experience in the field, and other general attributes to step into the role of CEO? Why or why not?

Reflection Questions

1. If you feel that anyone can be CEO, what do you base this on? And if you feel otherwise—that only certain individuals can be CEO—what would prevent others from filling that role? What is it that they're missing?

2. How do companies identify human capital in their organization? What ways could a board of directors evaluate who is most qualified to be CEO?

What training and development could a company offer to prepare more candidates to be the top manager of an organization? Are all of the qualifications that a CEO should have ones that *can be* learned, or are they innate skills these individuals are born with?

Exercise contributed by Steven Stovall, Southeast Missouri State University.

EXERCISE 1.3: Your Experience with OB

Objective

This exercise will help you to better *understand* organizational behavior, its concepts, and its uses by helping you to *explain* and *discuss* your organizational experiences in terms of Chapter 1 concepts.

Instructions

Step 1 (10 minutes): Think about an organization that you are or have been a member of. This organization can be any type of organization as discussed in the first chapter of this text (i.e., a social, religious, charitable, or other type of organization). After selecting your organization, think about some problem that the organization has had. Write down a brief (no more than one-half of a page) narrative describing this problem. Be sure to explain the problem using the concept terms from Chapter 1. Also, try to identify the level at which this problem existed: individual, group, organizational, or across multiple levels.

Step 2 (10 minutes): Find a partner and read each other the problem you each wrote about. Select the most interesting of the two write-ups. Together rewrite the description so that it clarifies any points that are unclear and is more concrete in its use and application of chapter concepts.

Step 3 (10 minutes): Each pair should find another pair to form a quad. Each pair should read the situation write-up selected in step 2 to the other pair. Again, select the situation that is the most interesting, and work together as a group to improve the situation description. Clarify any misuse of terms and be sure that as much of the situation as possible is described using chapter concepts.

Step 4 (10 to 30 minutes): Select one person from the quad to read the write-up chosen by the entire quad as the most interesting to the entire class. The person who reads the situation should be someone other than the person who initially wrote about the situation, but everyone should be prepared to help clarify any points about the write-up using chapter concepts.

Reflection Questions

Think about the process of identifying organizational problems in terms of the organizational behavior concepts you are learning.

1. How did identifying the problem in this way change the way you thought about the problem?

2. How did linking the problem to the concepts help you think about methods for dealing with the problem?

3. How did thinking about the level of the problem shape the way you thought about the problem?

4. When listening to other groups, note how their descriptions used chapter concepts. Were there any usages that surprised you or you were uncertain about?

Exercise contributed by Milton R. Mayfield, Professor of Business, Texas A&M International University, and Jacqueline R. Mayfield, Professor of Business, Texas A&M International University.

EXERCISE 1.4: Testing a Hypothesis

Objective

The purpose of this exercise is to gain an understanding of organizational behavior research.

Instructions

Organizational behavior research seeks to help managers understand their employees and enhance critical thinking. In this exercise, you're going to test a hypothesis.

Select three volunteers from the class to be the organizational behavior researchers. These three should meet privately to discuss a simple hypothesis regarding the behaviors of students in the class. The volunteers will craft a hypothesis based upon something simple such as "the majority of students read the textbook prior to coming to class," or "half of all students eat breakfast in the morning," or "25 percent of students will go directly to graduate school after receiving their undergraduate degree," or something similar. Again, develop a hypothesis that can be easily tested among the students.

Once the hypothesis has been established, think about how you could determine if your hypothesis is correct. What questions would you need to ask the class to validate your hypothesis? Once you have a "script" for a simple survey, ask the class to respond and evaluate those responses.

Reflection Questions

1. Why is hypothesis testing important in organizational behavior research?

2. How can researchers use hypothesis testing to improve working conditions for employees?

3. If you were not one of the three volunteers, how reliable do you think the questions that were asked would prove the stated hypothesis? What additional questions would you have asked?

Exercise contributed by Steven Stovall, Southeast Missouri State University.

ONLINE EXERCISE 1.1: Understanding Skills

Objective

The purpose of this exercise is to gain an appreciation for technical, human, and conceptual skills.

Instructions

Technical, human, and conceptual skills are used in varying degrees by managers at all levels of an organization. For example, a forklift driver will have more technical skills, while the vice president of sales will have more conceptual skills.

Have each person on the discussion board post a job title that is familiar to that individual. If it is a job title that is peculiar to a particular industry or one that many will not readily know what it is, offer a brief description of the essence of the job. Once the job title is posted, discuss whether that job title should have more conceptual, human, or technical skills. Discuss why you think one job title would have more of one skill than another job title that has been posted.

Reflection Questions

1. What kinds of jobs have more conceptual skills? More human skills? More technical skills?

2. Are human skills important for every job title? Why or why not?

3. How effective would the president of a company be if she had strong technical skills, but weak conceptual skills? What about a janitor who has excellent conceptual skills, but poor technical skills?

4. In your current job, or jobs you have had in the past, which skill is most important: technical, human, or conceptual? Explain.

Exercise contributed by Steven Stovall, Southeast Missouri State University.

CASE STUDY 1.1: CVS Health

Time and time again, job satisfaction has been proven to have large effects on the bottom line; employee happiness and productiveness go hand in hand. As mentioned in the chapter, human capital, which is the sum of people's skills, knowledge, experience, and general attributes, is a key element of competitive advantage. One way to influence people and employees is from a sociological perspective, which involves managers and corporations committing to a bigger picture. The text speaks on the ways in which feelings, actions, and beliefs can influence the behavior of employees and consumers, and CVS Health has spent considerable time and resources forming a fulfilling mission.

Making Difficult Decisions to Inspire

In September of 2014, CVS Corporation made a landmark decision: they decided to cease all tobacco sales in their nearly 10,000 locations. The CVS bottom line took a $2 billion annual reduction, which is a risky move for a Fortune 500 company, but the CVS mission became clear to all employees and consumers. They have branded themselves as a leading provider of health services, and they could no longer square their cigarette sales with their genuine pursuits in healthcare. The people at CVS and the upper management team decided that a value chain must be valuable in the marketplace, but it must also reside within their corporation's bigger mission. While there may be short-term financial losses embedded in decisions like these, they give employees a reason to find more fulfillment in their work and have financially lucrative sociological side effects. For example, being that CVS was the first drugstore to eliminate tobacco, many prominent figures came out in support of the effort, ranging from Bill Gates, founder of Microsoft, to then-president Barack Obama. These larger societal implications can make short-term difficulties pay off in the long run, and studies have shown that this CVS decision led to a reduction of total cigarette purchases, from any seller, of 95 million packs in eight months.

The Value Chain

On first glance, it can be difficult to understand how a decline in sales could improve a company's value chain, described in the text as the sequence of activities carried out by organizations to create valued goods and services to consumers. But, according to executive Eileen Howard Boone, "For now, we focused on helping our customers lead tobacco-free lives. We believe passionately that is a powerful preventive health measure that will have a positive impact on their health and quality of life. I'm so proud that we are the first national pharmacy chain to stop the sale of tobacco products. While it produced $2B in annual sales, we wanted to take a bold step in support of the health and well-being of our patients and customers and I truly hope will continue to fuel the public health discussion." CVS and their employees are committed to creating healthy lives, and they believe they can now provide that valuable service better than ever, and they now maintain a more fulfilling, long-term outlook on their value chain.

Aside from making waves in their industry with their decision to nix tobacco sales, the leadership members at CVS have sought to define their business on their own terms. The text describes the value of having a purpose, from an individual employee level to a corporate level, and CVS describes theirs as such: "We're reinventing pharmacy to have a more active, supportive role in each person's unique health experience and in the greater health care environment." A consistent purpose like this one can play a key role in keeping a company on track in spite of financial gains and losses and the ebbs and flows of the market as a whole. CVS (NYSE: CVS) stock has seen some large fluctuations, but they have grown steadily on a long-term basis, and have risen all the way to #7 on the Fortune 500 list.

Ethics

It's no stretch to consider the ethical implications of the CVS tobacco-free decision: they believe it is worth short-term pains to benefit the health of their communities. Ethics are morals that guide behavior—but they never make answers black and white, and often create ethical dilemmas. While all their best practices do not fit into a case study, CVS takes a number of notable measures to ensure they promote ethical behavior. CVS ensures all their suppliers, of which they have thousands, go through application and compliance processes to guarantee ethical sourcing. They also offer a website for customers and employees to report any ethical dilemmas and offenses they notice, as the pharmaceutical and health industries present many difficult decisions and temptations.

Conclusion

In sum, many large corporations have issues, but many also have valuable best practices, from which all managers and business owners can learn. CVS has taken meaningful strides to improve their corporate culture, management style, and society as a whole, all the while investing in the growth and improvement of their value chain.

Case Questions

1. Describe the big decision that CVS Health made. How does it relate to the text?

2. How does the text describe ethics, and how do they play a role at CVS Health?

Sources

Clough, R., & Kochkodin, B. (2018, February 24). Markets: GE cuts $2.4 billion from biggest pension deficit on S&P 500. *Bloomberg*. Retrieved from https://www.bloomberg.com/news/articles/2018-02-23/general-electric-cuts-2-4-billion-off-s-p-worst-pension-deficit

Encyclopaedia Britannica. (Eds.). (2018, September 5). General Electric (American corporation). *Encyclopaedia Britannica,* Inc. Retrieved from https://www.britannica.com/topic/General-Electric

Forbes. (2011, May 26). The 10 oldest Dow components. Retrieved from https://www.forbes.com/2011/05/26/dow-at-115-longest-tenured-stocks_slide/#234d73084e14

Immelt, J. R. (2017). *How I remade GE*. Retrieved from https://hbr.org/2017/09/inside-ges-transformation

Yahoo Finance. (n.d.). General Electric Company (GE). Retrieved from https://finance.yahoo.com/quote/ge/

Follow the flow chart below to see what kind of a leader you are!

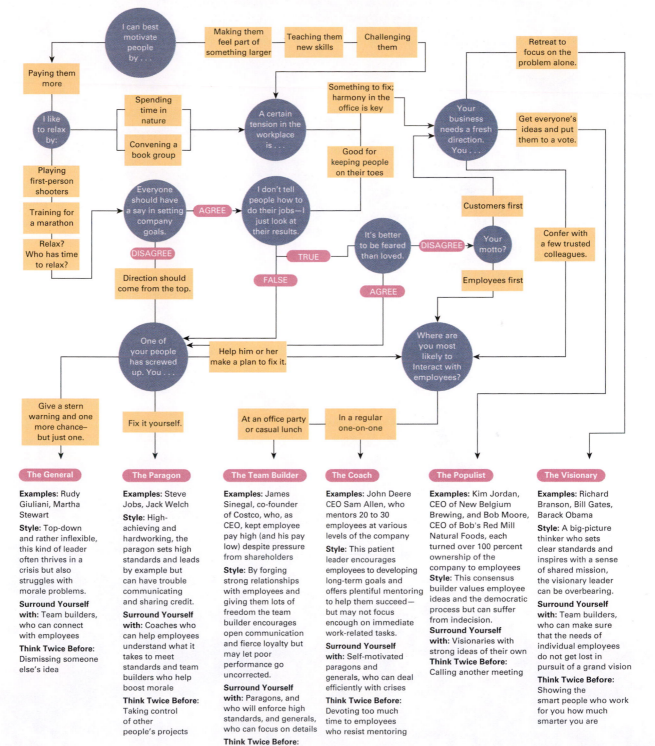

The General

Examples: Rudy Giuliani, Martha Stewart

Style: Top-down and rather inflexible, this kind of leader often thrives in a crisis but also struggles with morale problems.

Surround Yourself with: Team builders, who can connect with employees

Think Twice Before: Dismissing someone else's idea

The Paragon

Examples: Steve Jobs, Jack Welch

Style: High-achieving and hardworking, the paragon sets high standards and leads by example but can have trouble communicating and sharing credit.

Surround Yourself with: Coaches who can help employees understand what it takes to meet standards and team builders who help boost morale

Think Twice Before: Taking control of other people's projects

The Team Builder

Examples: James Sinegal, co-founder of Costco, who, as CEO, kept employee pay high (and his pay low) despite pressure from shareholders

Style: By forging strong relationships with employees and giving them lots of freedom the team builder encourages open communication and fierce loyalty but may let poor performance go uncorrected.

Surround Yourself with: Paragons, and who will enforce high standards, and generals, who can focus on details

Think Twice Before: Giving unqualified praise

The Coach

Examples: John Deere CEO Sam Allen, who mentors 20 to 30 employees at various levels of the company

Style: This patient leader encourages employees to developing long-term goals and offers plentiful mentoring to help them succeed—but may not focus enough on immediate work-related tasks.

Surround Yourself with: Self-motivated paragons and generals, who can deal efficiently with crises

Think Twice Before: Devoting too much time to employees who resist mentoring

The Populist

Examples: Kim Jordan, CEO of New Belgium Brewing, and Bob Moore, CEO of Bob's Red Mill Natural Foods, each turned over 100 percent ownership of the company to employees

Style: This consensus builder values employee ideas and the democratic process but can suffer from indecision.

Surround Yourself with: Visionaries with strong ideas of their own

Think Twice Before: Calling another meeting

The Visionary

Examples: Richard Branson, Bill Gates, Barack Obama

Style: A big-picture thinker who sets clear standards and inspires with a sense of shared mission, the visionary leader can be overbearing.

Surround Yourself with: Team builders, who can make sure that the needs of individual employees do not get lost in pursuit of a grand vision

Think Twice Before: Showing the smart people who work for you how much smarter you are

Source: www.inc.com/magazine/201310/adam-bluestein/what-kind-of-leader-are-you.html.

PART II

Individual Processes

2

Diversity and Individual Differences

We all should know that diversity makes for a rich tapestry, and we must understand that all the threads are equal in value no matter what their color.

—*Maya Angelou, American author*

Learning Objectives

By the end of this chapter, you will be able to:

2.1 Explain the importance of diversity in OB

2.2 Discuss why individual differences are important

2.3 Contrast the nature and nurture explanations of personality development

2.4 Describe the Myers-Briggs Type Indicator types

2.5 Identify the five personality factors of the Big Five model

2.6 Differentiate among the most common personality attributes

CASE STUDY: PEPSICO'S DIVERSITY

Growing up in the historically far-right-wing city of Madras, India, Indra Nooyi and her sister didn't have much to look forward to other than motherhood and managing a household—at least that is what societal norms told them. However, these girls did not succumb to these expectations and they grew up determined to become exactly who and what they wanted to be. A seemingly trivial activity ended up playing a huge role in empowering Nooyi to become the woman she is today. Nooyi recalls, "Every night at the dinner table, my mother would ask us to write a speech about what we would do if we were president, chief minister, or prime minister—every day would be a different world leader she'd ask us to play. At the end of dinner, we had to give the speech, and she had to decide who she was going to vote for. She gave us the confidence to be whatever we wanted to be." After many years climbing the corporate ladder in Indian companies and receiving an MBA from Yale, Indra became the CFO of PepsiCo in 2001. In 2006, Indra was promoted to CEO, becoming the fifth ever PepsiCo CEO. She is currently considered to be one of the most powerful women in business today.

This success has not come without obstacles. Nooyi claims that early in her career, she was constantly ignored in meetings and male managers wouldn't even make eye contact with her. Also, the data she often displayed during corporate meetings was constantly cross-checked by other male employees to make sure it was accurate. Instead of shriveling under the pressure, Nooyi voiced her concerns regarding her treatment and openly challenged her male counterparts. Her demands for respect and equal treatment sent shockwaves through her colleagues and they eventually came to realize that her abilities were just as good, if not better, than their own.

Under Indra's tenure as CEO, PepsiCo has become a world leader in inclusion, empowerment, and corporate diversity while still growing in profitability. In fact, net annual profits have risen from $2.7 billion to $6.5 billion since 2001. PepsiCo's success is attributed to its attitude toward diversity. Nowadays, stakeholders (customers, shareholders, etc.) are increasingly concerned about the behind-the-scenes work of the corporations that make the products they purchase. According to Nooyi, "PepsiCo needs to create a company that reflects the diversity of its customers. And that starts with creating a workplace where everyone feels welcome. Creating a culture of respect and trust is a part of PepsiCo's values and it is the source of our strength in the marketplace."

Including people for their talents, regardless of racial, gender and sexual orientation in the hiring process is a crucial step that PepsiCo implements to cultivate an environment like the one described by Nooyi. PepsiCo's commitment to involving minorities in the hiring process presents more people with opportunities they may not otherwise have access to. There is no quota or a specified amount of minorities that need to be interviewed for every position; rather, PepsiCo requires its recruiters to engage in a conscious effort to find more diverse applicants. In fact, PepsiCo has fired recruiters in the past for not making this conscious effort. Recently, a recruiter was required to find ten applicants for a senior-level position within the company. The recruiter submitted all ten applications, but only one of them was from a woman. When asked why there weren't more female applicants, the recruiter responded, "I can't find them." This is a problem that many recruiters claim to face. However, PepsiCo does not take that as an excuse, and it is constantly increasing its efforts to give diverse applicants equal opportunities.

Through many diversity-training programs, PepsiCo helps employees overcome their unconscious biases and realize that a diversity of talent will naturally lead to a diversity of thought. This is essential for competitive companies like PepsiCo because it allows for an innovative and creative workplace environment. This atmosphere, combined with much higher employee satisfaction built on mutual respect and trust for one another, drives productivity and gives PepsiCo the competitive advantage in the corporate world.

However, even the most culturally sensitive and prodiversity organizations can make mistakes. In 2017, Pepsi was heavily criticized for using the Black Lives Matter movement to promote its product. People protested that the ad trivialized the very serious issue of police brutality against black people. Pepsi pulled the ad and admitted it had "missed the mark":

> "Pepsi was trying to project a global message of unity, peace and understanding. Clearly, we missed the mark and apologize," the company said in a statement on Wednesday. "We did not intend to make light of any serious issue. We are pulling the content and halting any further rollout."[1]

Critical-Thinking Questions

1. How can a diverse workplace add to a company's competitive advantage in the marketplace?

2. How did the obstacles Nooyi faced early in her career impact her?

3. PepsiCo attacks this problem with a wide array of methods. What are some other ways a corporation can start to implement a sense of diversity?

Resources:

Feloni, R. (2015). Pepsi CEO Indra Nooyi explains how an unusual daily ritual her mom made her practice as a child changed her life. *Business Insider.* Retrieved from http://www.businessinsider.com/pepsico-indra-nooyi-life-changing-habit-2015-9

Forbes. (n.d.). *Power Women 2017, #11 Indra Nooyi.* Retrieved from https://www.forbes.com/profile/indra-nooyi/#5fe83ed05d6f.

PepsiCo. (n.d.). *Diversity and engagement.* Retrieved from http://www.pepsico.com/company/Diversity-and-Engagement

Pratap, R. (n.d.). Diversity at the workplace is a win-win, says Corporate India. *The Hindu Business Line.* Retrieved from http://www.thehindubusinessline.com/specials/diversity-at-the-workplace-is-a-winwin-says-corporate-india/article9574293.ece

Sherwood, I.-H. (2017). Why the president of PepsiCo's global beverage group fired a recruiter. *Campaign US.* Retrieved from http://www.campaignlive.com/article/why-president-pepsicos-global-beverage-group-fired-recruiter/1425787

Diversity in OB

>> **LO 2.1**   **Explain the importance of diversity in OB**

Diversity is a hot topic in organizations around the world. Banking heavyweights Morgan Stanley, and Bank of America Merrill Lynch have paid millions settling sex discrimination and race discrimination claims. Widely publicized cases like these have encouraged organizations to care more about diversity and realize the importance of respecting individual differences in order to form and build successful professional relationships. In broader terms, **workplace diversity** refers to the degree to which an organization includes people from different cultures and backgrounds; it involves recognizing, respecting, and valuing both individual and group differences by treating people as individuals in an effort to promote an inclusive culture.[2]

As our case study shows, PepsiCo is a great example of a company that implements recruitment strategies targeted specifically at minorities. PepsiCo has an excellent reputation for fairness because of its commitment to diversity. The issue of diversity has also been raised in popular culture. In 2016, celebrities such as actor Jada Pinkett Smith and director Spike Lee boycotted the Oscars due to the lack of diversity among the list of nominees.[3]

One of the most effective ways organizations can encourage acceptance of differences and create a harmonious workforce is through the management of diversity. Today's workplace welcomes more people from different backgrounds and different experiences than ever before. Combined, these individuals create a powerful force—studies have shown diverse groups working well together perform better and are more innovative, creative, and productive: factors essential for organizations when gaining competitive advantage in the workplace.[4] Similarly, a diverse workforce can increase market share by helping the organization more effectively communicate with customers from different backgrounds and cultures.

However, there are also challenges to managing a diverse workforce—diversity does not simply mean recognizing the differences between us. For diversity to succeed, managers must promote inclusiveness, tackle discrimination, and respect and value the differences between people.

In a recent survey of the Top 50 Companies for Diversity run by DiversityInc, healthcare provider Kaiser Permanente took the number one spot; medical technology company Medtronic came last on the list.[5] Organizations that do not currently foster a diverse workforce need to harness all the talent available and commit to these changing demographics or risk being left behind.[6]

Surface-Level and Deep-Level Diversity

There are two main types of diversity: surface-level diversity and deep-level diversity.[7] (See Figure 2.1.) **Surface-level diversity** describes the easily perceived differences between us, such as age and generation, race and ethnicity, gender and sexual orientation, and physical and/or mental ability. This type of diversity can lead to discrimination when managers or recruiters judge or stereotype others on the basis of superficial differences. For example, if they believe performance declines with age, they will choose a younger candidate over an older candidate.

In contrast, **deep-level diversity** describes verbal and nonverbal behaviors that are not as easily perceived because they lie below the surface. Deep-level diversity may include attitudes, values, beliefs, and personality traits. People first identify surface-level differences in others, and then become aware of deep-level differences as

**Master the content
edge.sagepub.com/
neckob2e**

Workplace diversity: The degree to which an organization represents different cultures

Surface-level diversity: Easily perceived differences between people, such as age/generation, race/ethnicity, gender, and ability

Deep-level diversity: Differences in verbal and nonverbal behaviors that are not as easily perceived because they lie below the surface, such as differences in attitudes, values, beliefs, and personality

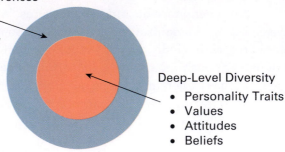

FIGURE 2.1

Surface-Level and Deep-Level Diversity

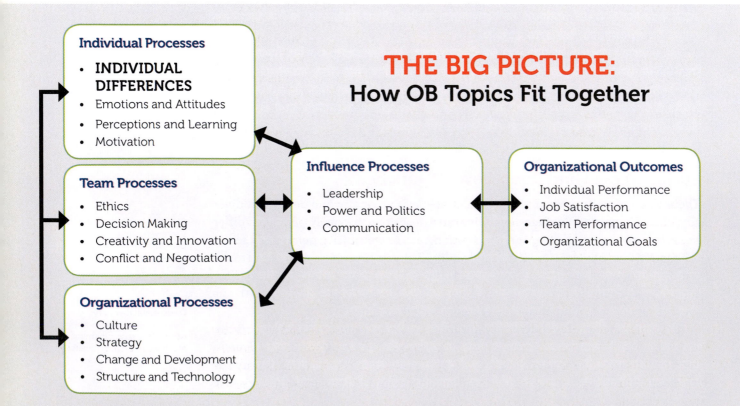

Surface-Level Diversity
- Age and Generational Differences
- Race and Ethnicity
- Gender and Sexuality
- Physical and Mental Ability

Deep-Level Diversity
- Personality Traits
- Values
- Attitudes
- Beliefs

Sources: Huszczo, G., and Megan Endres. "Joint Effects of Gender and Personality on Choice of Happiness Strategies." *Europe's Journal of Psychology* 9, no 1 (February 2013).

they get to know someone. For example, initially Myra and Jorge might treat one another with caution because of dissimilarities between their cultural background or native languages. As their relationship deepens and they learn about each other's underlying attitudes, values, and beliefs, however, their surface-level perceptions of difference may subside. Myra and Jorge may begin to find common ground and recognize the similarities they share with one other.

Age/Generation Diversity

Age diversity: People of all different ages included within the workplace

With workforce demographics shifting and the number of mature people in the workplace rising, many organizations are finding ways to leverage **age diversity,**

Individual Processes
- **INDIVIDUAL DIFFERENCES**
- Emotions and Attitudes
- Perceptions and Learning
- Motivation

Team Processes
- Ethics
- Decision Making
- Creativity and Innovation
- Conflict and Negotiation

Organizational Processes
- Culture
- Strategy
- Change and Development
- Structure and Technology

THE BIG PICTURE:
How OB Topics Fit Together

Influence Processes
- Leadership
- Power and Politics
- Communication

Organizational Outcomes
- Individual Performance
- Job Satisfaction
- Team Performance
- Organizational Goals

Media giant Oprah Winfrey is a notable member of the baby boomer generation.

Laura Alber, CEO of retailer Williams Sonoma, belongs to Generation X.

Facebook founder Mark Zuckerberg belongs to the generation deemed millennials.

which is including people of all different ages within the workplace.[8] This is no easy task given that today's workforce spans four generations: traditionalists (born before 1946); baby boomers (born 1946–1964); Generation Xers (born 1965–1981); millennials (born 1982–2000); and Generation Z (born 1998–2016). Managers need to treat age-diverse workforces thoughtfully, without falling prey to stereotypes often portrayed by the popular media. For example, traditionalists and baby boomers are often described as "old school," conservative, and not up to date with the latest technology, while younger employees such as Gen Xers and millennials are thought to be technology savvy yet lazy and with a tendency to flit from one job to the next. Generation Z is on the cusp of entering the workforce and have yet to make an impact but are regarded by some as being heavily influenced by millennials. However, a recent study carried out by research firm 747 insights shows some very important differences between Generation Z and other generations.[9] For instance, they are less patriotic, more inclined to have friends of different races (48 percent of Generation Z is non-Caucasian making it more racially diverse than any other generation), and more supportive of marrying people of different races.

Applying these stereotypes to individuals could lead to bias and conflict among differently aged workers in an organization. Organizations dealing with a multigenerational workforce need to focus on the strengths and weaknesses of their individual employees and should be able to foster the transfer of knowledge across age groups while bridging differences and building on commonalities in order to create a cohesive, dynamic workforce.

Race and Ethnicity

Today's workplace is made up of people from different racial groups and ethnicities, yet racial and ethnic prejudice still persist. Sometimes the terms *race* and *ethnicity* are used interchangeably, but **race** is related to factors of physical appearance such as skin, hair, or eye color, whereas **ethnicity** is associated with sociological factors such as nationality, culture, language, and ancestry.[10]

Race: Identifying biological factors such as skin, hair, or eye color

Ethnicity: Sociological factors such as nationality, culture, language, and ancestry

No one should ever feel uncomfortable because of their race or ethnicity. Racial and ethnic prejudice often stems from ignorance and stereotypes that individuals may not even be aware influence them. Racial and ethnic discrimination has played a prominent role in US history and it is only in the last few decades that significant strides have been made to overcome such discrimination. Making an effort to develop a deeper sense of racial and cultural awareness by becoming familiar with the history of racial and ethnic discrimination in the United States and learning about different languages and cultural traditions goes a long way toward building group harmony in the workplace. And, as with all workplace relationships, treating every person with whom you work as an individual rather than a collection of predetermined labels goes a long way toward establishing trust and understanding.

Gender Diversity and Sexual Orientation

Gender diversity: The way different genders are treated in the workplace

Gender diversity is the equal representation of both men and women in the workplace.[11] As with racial and ethnic minorities in the United States, the treatment of women in the workplace has come a long way during the past fifty years. In the past, wealthier women were often expected to take care of their children and their home rather than having a career, while poorer women often did double-duty caring for their own households as well as working to supplement their family's income. The jobs available to women were limited, paid less than similar jobs available to men, and most employers considered women to be physically, emotionally, and mentally inferior to men in their ability to contribute to the workplace.

Glass ceiling: An invisible barrier that limits one's ability to progress to more senior positions

Sexual orientation: A person's sexual identity and the gender(s) to which she or he is attracted

Today, women occupy positions and roles in every industry, and laws and regulations have been put in place to counteract discrimination against them. However, though women have made great strides in achieving equality, differences in salary and hiring practices remain. For example, many women are still hampered by a **glass ceiling,** an invisible barrier that limits their ability to progress to more senior positions.[12] In addition, in 2017, women are still paid less than men for comparable jobs and remain under-represented in more senior roles.[13] Like race, ethnicity, and gender, the organizational approach to **sexual orientation,** which refers to a person's sexual identity and the gender(s) to which she or he is attracted, in the United States has come a long way during the past few decades, yet achieving equal rights and protections in the workplace regardless of sexual orientation have only partially occurred. While there have been great strides made for workplace equality in the United States and around the world, in twenty-eight states employees can legally be fired by their employers for being lesbian, gay, bisexual, or transgender (LGBT), despite marriage being legal in all fifty states[14] (See Figure 2.2.)

Diversity of Abilities

Ability diversity: The representation of people with different levels of mental and physical abilities within an organization

Ability diversity is the representation of people with different levels of mental and physical abilities within an organization. More than 50 million people in the United States have a disability and more than 50 percent of those people are unemployed.[15]

Although people with physical and mental impairments may not be able to carry out certain tasks, there is still a huge range of tasks at which they can excel. Skills can be taught, and people can be trained to improve their skills; jobs may or may not require particular physical abilities, like the ability to walk unaided. Managing ability diversity begins with selecting employees with abilities that best fit the role. This, in turn, leads to increased productivity and job satisfaction.

FIGURE 2.2

Where Are LGBT Employees Most Vulnerable?

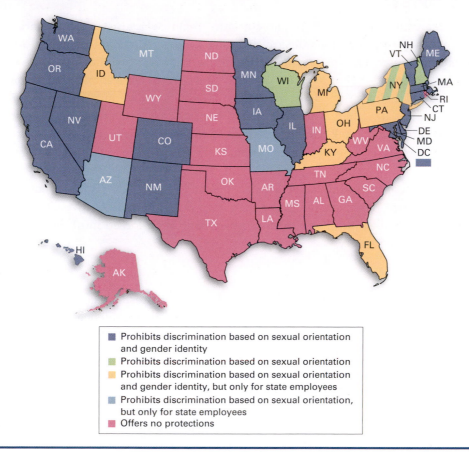

- ■ (dark blue) Prohibits discrimination based on sexual orientation and gender identity
- ■ (green) Prohibits discrimination based on sexual orientation
- ■ (yellow) Prohibits discrimination based on sexual orientation and gender identity, but only for state employees
- ■ (light blue) Prohibits discrimination based on sexual orientation, but only for state employees
- ■ (pink) Offers no protections

Sources: Vocativ. Used with permission; https://www.fastcompany.com/3057357/heres-everywhere-in-america-you-can-still-get-fired-for-being-lgbt.

Diversity Training

Diversity training can help reduce bias and break down prejudices or psychological barriers among those who struggle to accept coworkers they perceive as different. Many organizations institute mandatory diversity training programs with an emphasis on inclusion, in which each employee is asked whether he or she feels valued, respected, and welcomed in the organization. This provides a safe forum for employees to openly discuss diversity issues and consider the actions they would take when presented with different scenarios.

Although most organizations would agree that all employees should be treated fairly and equally, the rising number of lawsuits citing discrimination and bias has led some experts to question whether diversity training programs are as effective as organizations would like to believe. For example, a 2007 study of more than eight hundred companies over the course of thirty-one years showed that despite millions spent on diversity training, no positive impact was made on the workplace. In fact, in organizations with lawsuits made against them, diversity training had a negative influence.[16] Furthermore, statistics show that in US companies with more than one hundred employees, there has only been a very slight increase in black men in management despite diversity training.[17] In Silicon Valley, most tech jobs are dominated by white men.

Why is this? Why isn't equality improving in most organizations in the United States despite the investment in diversity training programs? In the following section, we explore three diversity initiatives commonly implemented by most companies—and why they may not be effective.

Reducing Bias

Bias refers to the tendency to show unfair prejudice against another person or group. Many organizations design diversity programs around reducing bias by giving managers a list of dos and don'ts in the hope that by following these rules, they will suspend their biases. Over a thousand studies have shown that people do not suspend their bias so easily. In fact, people who take diversity training soon forget the rules altogether. A number of studies have also found that these programs can also provoke a backlash, for example, managers who resent being ordered to give up their time to be lectured or being told what to do tend to harbor more bias as a result.

How do companies reduce bias? In some studies, voluntary training has helped to reduce bias. When people make their own decision to take diversity training (rather than perceiving it as something they have been forced into) they are more likely to be prodiversity.

Hiring Tests

Approximately 40 percent of US companies use hiring tests designed to fight bias to test candidates applying for front-line roles. Yet there is evidence to suggest that some managers use these test selectively. For example, one HR director at a West Coast food company discovered that during the hiring process, white managers would only make minorities or strangers take the test, but would hire people they already knew without making them take the test.

But even companies who do use the test can be guilty of ignoring the results. For example, Kellogg professor Lauren Rivera sat in on some hiring meetings at a firm which asked its candidates during the interviews to solve a series of math and scenario-based problems on the spot, as part of its hiring test. She found that when some of the candidates struggled with the problems, the hiring teams paid more attention to women and black candidates but little attention to white men when they made the same mistakes. Rivera concluded that the hiring test actually highlighted bias among the team rather than reduced it.

Grievance Procedures

The grievance system is supposed to give employees who feel discriminated a safe platform to air their grievances (such as pay, promotion, termination) against managers who are perceived to be biased. A successful grievance procedure outcome would involve the manager adjusting his or her behavior or address the level of discrimination among other employees. However, according to the Equal Employment Opportunity Commission, almost half of the ninety thousand discrimination complaints included a charge of retaliation. This means that people who have made the complaint have been retaliated against (possibly in the form of demotion or ridicule).

When employees witness the failure of a grievance procedure, it makes them less likely to report discrimination. The fewer complaints they receive, the more companies are likely to believe there are no problems to be addressed.

Positive Ways to Promote Diversity

Despite the evidence questioning the effectiveness of diversity training programs, it is still vital that organizations create environments that embrace every employee, regardless of background, age, culture, ethnicity, or other difference. Here are some positive ways managers can promote diversity:

- Implementing college recruitment programs specifically targeted at women and minorities. When managers get actively involved in the hiring process they become more focused on the goal itself, rather than their own biases. As our case study shows, PepsiCo's targeted recruitment strategies have succeeded in creating a workplace of equality.

- Mentoring encourages managers to get involved with people from different races, ethnicities, and genders, by coaching and sponsoring them for key projects and assignments, which again helps to reduce whatever biases they may hold. For example, Coca-Cola's mentoring initiative working specifically with minorities resulted in at least 80 percent of those mentees reaching some level of management over a period of five years.

- Increasing contact between diverse groups of people in the workplace also cultivates relationships and allows people to work together as equals. Studies show that companies who use self-managed teams or rotate employee roles through cross-training typically have a higher proportion of white women, and black men and women, as well as Asian-American men and women, in management positions.

- Encouraging social accountability is important as it targets our innate need to look good in front of others. For example, in 1992, Deloitte CEO Mike Cook implemented a task force to investigate the reasons behind the high turnover of women at the company. Once word spread that the task force was watching, women started to receive key assignments and mentoring. Over eight years, turnover started to drop and the percentage of female partners started to rise. In 2015, Cathy Engelbert was appointed CEO of Deloitte LLP—the first woman to head up a leading consultancy.

Cross-Cultural Diversity

Due to globalization, it has become more important for people working in a global economy to develop a global mind-set in order to fully understand cultural differences. According to a 2016 survey carried out by Culture Wizard—a New York–based cultural training company, corporate teams are almost entirely virtual, with just over 40 percent never meeting in person.[18] Furthermore, the survey showed that almost 50 percent of respondents revealed that more than half of their teams include members from different countries—up from 33 percent in 2012. Given these figures, it is clear that team members, virtual or otherwise, need to be able to rise to the challenge of working with culturally diverse colleagues.

Employees from different cultures with different languages provide companies with a greater reach into global markets because of their ability to communicate with people from similar backgrounds. A wide range of diverse employees with different perspectives and knowledge also offer a variety of solutions that help boost creativity and productivity, and increasingly, organizations like KPMG featured in OB in the Real World with diverse workforces have become desirable places to work because they are perceived as being fair and nondiscriminatory.

Managing Cross-Cultural Diversity[19]

Managing cross-cultural diversity isn't easy. It involves cultivating a deep appreciation and respect of other people's cultural differences and the willingness

OB IN THE REAL WORLD

Kaia West, Manager of University Recruiting at KPMG

KPMG is a multinational audit, advisory, and tax services firm and a world leader in workplace diversity. Many of the lessons outlined in this chapter are applied in the real world by Kaia West, Manager of University Recruiting at KPMG. A diverse workplace creates an environment of heightened creativity and productivity. This stems from a strong sense of belonging. When employees feel this sense of belonging, they have the confidence to bring forward their best contributions to the firm. According to Kaia, "having a myriad of perspectives allows us to do our jobs more effectively. Also, being able to rely on a multitude of ideas allows us to meet the needs of our clients, and function as a team in a more enlightened way." This is exactly why KPMG places such a huge emphasis on diversity. Kaia's responsibility of recruiting the future talent of the corporation while also ensuring that the talent has representation from diverse groups is not an easy task. Recruiting is an extremely interpersonal line of work and it requires someone with both strong communication

skills and the ability to communicate with people of different backgrounds. Additionally, it requires someone like Kaia to communicate its importance to the everyday employee of the firm. It is by no means a one-man job so success is contingent on a recruiter's ability to get the whole firm to buy into recruitment efforts. Once this is done, the process is run much more smoothly. Kaia is able to effectively leverage these skills and then she is able to use the various programs in place to help her get the job done.

"KPMG has a number of programs that allow me as a recruiting manager to target my efforts regarding Diversity and Inclusion. We have affinity networks that allow us to get connected to other minorities around the firm. We also have recruiting initiatives that allow us to create inroads for underrepresented minority candidates. Our Future Diversity Leaders program is a great example. The FDL program is one that allows younger minority candidates to get access to firm leaders and training as early as freshman year. This program goes hand in hand with our CMI internship program which allows students an opportunity to do an internship earlier than majority race/white candidates. This helps to provide a stepping-stone into the culture of KPMG while providing the proper resources necessary to accomplish our end goal, which is a diverse workplace. This is very effective!" With these tools at her disposal, Kaia is able to effectively contribute to the diverse environment that KPMG values and strives for.

Critical-Thinking Questions

1. In the end, who benefits the most from a diverse workplace?

2. Kaia can do her job well but what does she need to do to be totally successful in cultivating a diverse environment? ●

Source: Interview with Kaia West, March 31, 2017.

to change our behavior and perspectives in order to interact and communicate with other employees, teams, and even whole organizations. Research shows that people who are culturally competent tend to share certain characteristics. (See Table 2.1.) Organizations that fail to implement successful cross-cultural diversity are often guilty of bias, lack of effort when it comes to recruiting and retaining diverse talent, and promoting a "we" versus "they" mentality. This why it is so important that managers implement a healthy cross-cultural diverse workforce.

TABLE 2.1

Characteristics of Culturally Competent People

Openness to cultural diversity
Flexibility and adaptability
Emotional resilience
Curiosity
Tolerance and respect for differences
Patience
A nonjudgmental attitude
Global identity
Cultural intelligence
Global leadership behaviors
Multicultural experiences, such as being multilingual and having lived in more than one country

The first step to implementing a healthy diverse workforce is to understand how people experience cultural difference. Dr. Milton Bennett's Developmental Model of Intercultural Sensitivity (DMIS), comprising six world views, helps managers to assess the level of cultural awareness and sensitivity within different teams. The six stages start from least developed to most developed.

- Denial: when people don't really believe there are differences between people and aren't particularly interested in cultural differences.

- Defense/reversal: when people recognize cultural differences exist but feel threatened by these differences (defense). In contrast, reversal takes place when people denigrate their own culture in favor of another culture; for example, people who have immersed themselves in a different culture may prefer the new culture over their own.

- Minimization: when people are aware of cultural differences but focus on the human element rather than differences between people. They have a sort of "live and let live" mentality.

- Acceptance: when people have a deep understanding of their own and others' cultural identities and appreciate the value of different cultural perspectives.

- Adaptation: when people have the ability to view a certain situation from a different cultural perspective, and adapt their behavior in order to be more effective in managing that situation.

- Integration: when people have a deep understanding of one or more cultures and successfully integrate them into their own identity.

Once managers have a sense of the level of cultural awareness and sensitivity within their teams, they can begin to create some training initiatives to increase the level of cultural intelligence. At the core of cultural intelligence is **cultural metacognition** which refers to the level of conscious cultural awareness we possess during cross-cultural interactions. Research has shown that people who interact with others

Cultural metacognition: The level of conscious cultural awareness we possess during cross-cultural interactions

across different cultures (intercultural) have higher levels of cultural metacognition than those who communicate with those in the same culture. This may be because people who are communicating with different cultures take into account cultural backgrounds and differences which influence their responses to certain situations. This is called "cultural perspective taking"—a process whereby we tend to imagine the world from someone else's perspective. The ability to put ourselves in the shoes of another means that we are more likely to see ourselves as similar to another person, which tends to reduce bias and stereotyping. Developing these metacognitive skills together with cross-cultural training could benefit managers who work from their native country as well as those who work internationally.

Cultural intelligence training goes further than honoring different customs, but involves a full commitment to learning about different cultures. Spending time in a different culture, reading publications from other cultures, getting involved in global projects, learning a different language, socializing with an ex pat, or visiting an ethnic restaurant are all ways in which people can become more culturally intelligent.

Managers also need to be culturally aware in order to build relationships with foreign professionals. Managers need to be particularly conscious of pronouncing employees' names correctly and ensuring others do the same, learning cultural differences, assigning a new foreign professional a mentor to help navigate the organization and cultivate relationships, and engaging role-play in order to experience how the foreign professional might feel moving to a different country and working for a new organization.

The biggest challenge to successful cross-cultural diversity is communication. The following guidelines help to improve communications between multicultural teams:

- Be concise: words may be translated into several different languages so keep your message short and to the point.

- Avoid jargon/slang: people outside the United States may have no idea what "hitting a home run" or "making a slam dunk" means. Use language that you are confident everybody understands well.

- Listen better: many people struggle with different accents, but listening well and having more patience will help you to further your understanding.

- Be respectful of cultural and religious differences: people from different cultures celebrate different holidays and different religions. Any signs of religious bias will not be well received.

- Understand different communication styles: people in the United States tend to favor a more informal style of direct communication whereas people from the Middle East and Asia tend to prefer formal, indirect communication.

As they continue to expand, more organizations are offering formal global training programs for their employees. For example, Boston-based investment firm Loomis, Sayles & Co. spent a whole year training its workforce in global awareness before it opened new offices abroad. Global training programs may include role-play, training simulations (with feedback from managers, team members, etc.), global site visits (which give employees opportunities to communicate with each other in person), and open discussion around cultural differences and how they influence behavior. More important, it is essential to our own personal and professional relationships to be tolerant of our individual differences.

Let's see why.

THINKING CRITICALLY

1. Explain why a diverse work group might score higher on innovation, creativity, and productivity than a group made up of similar individuals.

2. Identify and list at least three surface-level and three deep-level aspects of diversity that describe you. Then list three surface-level and three deep-level aspects of diversity that describe one of your good friends. How do the similarities and differences between you and your friend affect your friendship?

3. Imagine that you work in an organization with a variety of people who differ from you in terms of age, race, ethnicity, gender, sexual orientation, and physical or mental ability. Which diversity category would you find it most difficult to understand and bridge? Which diversity category would you find it easiest to understand and bridge? Explain your answer.

4. What criteria would you use to determine the effectiveness of a workplace diversity training program? List at least three separate measurable variables that you could evaluate if you were conducting research in this area.

The Importance of Individual Differences

>> **LO 2.2** Discuss why individual differences are important

Diversity is not the only thing that makes us feel different from each other. Have you ever been teamed up with someone for a school or work project who just seemed so different from you? What made that person unique? Maybe he or she had opinions or beliefs different from your own, liked music you hated, or had hobbies you considered strange. How did you handle working together? Did you just focus on getting the job done, or did you make an effort to find some common ground?

In class and at work you are surrounded by a multitude of individual personalities and behaviors and are expected to work well with others regardless of how different they seem to you. As we mentioned in Chapter 1, people are the key to ensuring competitive advantage and organizational success, and today's managers keep a close eye on team dynamics and the relationships among team members. Hostility or tension between workers is simply not tolerated. Working in a harmonious organizational environment is the ultimate goal, but to realize this goal we need to understand more about the differences and similarities between us and the way they guide our behavior.

Being different from each other makes us each unique. We define **individual differences** as the behavioral and cognitive similarities and differences among people.[20] In short, we need to understand not only people who are like us (which is relatively easy), but also people who are not like us and who think, behave, and make decisions differently than we do. When you can analyze the differences and similarities among your coworkers, you will have a better idea why people act the way they do. To understand individual differences, we must also have a high degree of **self-awareness**, or awareness of our own feelings, behaviors, personalities, likes, and dislikes.[21] We must also possess an **awareness of others,** a consciousness of other people's feelings, behaviors, personalities, likes, and dislikes.[22] But how easy is it to define ourselves?

Individual differences: The degree to which people exhibit behavioral similarities and differences

Self-awareness: Being aware of our own feelings, behaviors, personalities, likes, and dislikes

Awareness of others: The way we are aware (or unaware) of the feelings, behaviors, personalities, likes, and dislikes in other people

Actress and model Emma Watson demonstrates self-esteem and self-efficacy through serving as the UN Women Goodwill Ambassador.

Self-concept: The beliefs we have about who we are and how we feel about ourselves

Self-esteem: The beliefs we have about our own worth following the self-evaluation process

Self-efficacy: The belief we have in our ability to succeed in a specific task or situation

We generally have a perception of ourselves as distinct human beings. This is called our **self-concept,** the belief we have about who we are and how we feel about ourselves.[23] Social and academic influences and the culture in which we are raised play a significant role in our belief system. For example, we might be influenced by the beliefs held by our parents, friends, teachers, or coworkers.

Our self-concept can be divided into two key components: self-esteem and self-efficacy. **Self-esteem** is the belief we have about our own worth.[24] People with high self-esteem perceive themselves to be confident, have a high sense of self-worth, and be capable of taking on challenges. In contrast, people with low self-esteem are full of self-doubt, have a rather low opinion of themselves, and tend to shy away from challenges.

The other part of self-concept is **self-efficacy**, our belief in our ability to succeed in a specific task or situation.[25] However, just because you have high self-esteem doesn't mean you have a strong sense of self-efficacy. For example, you may be confident about completing coursework but have a low sense of self-efficacy when taking the exams.

THINKING CRITICALLY

1. Identify at least three types of individual differences related to each of the following categories: behavior, thought, and decision making.

2. To illustrate your level of self-awareness and your awareness of others, imagine a scenario in which you are working under a tight deadline and a new coworker stops by your office and asks for help understanding a key report she needs to submit to her manager. How are you likely to respond given your stress level and overall personality? How would your response affect a new employee who didn't know you well?

3. Briefly discuss your levels of self-esteem and self-efficacy. What sort of an impact do these factors have on your ability to meet school and job expectations?

Nature versus Nurture

>> LO 2.3   **Contrast the nature and nurture explanations of personality development**

We often regard people as having "good personalities" or "bad personalities," but what does that really mean? Is someone's personality "good" because we have something in common with that person and get along with him or her? Or is someone's personality "bad" because he or she ignores or offends us? What is personality after all?

We define **personality** as a stable and unique pattern of traits, characteristics, and resulting behaviors that gives an individual his or her identity.[26] When we understand different personalities, we can better understand the behaviors and motivations of others rather than making snap judgments that are often inaccurate. Researchers have spent decades carrying out different studies of **personality traits**, the characteristics that describe our thoughts, feelings, and behaviors.[27] But we are such complex creatures that no one theory has yet established a clear definition of personality.

Where does personality come from? Research has proven that we inherit some physical characteristics from our parents; you may have your father's blue eyes or your mother's curly hair, for example. However, the origins of our personality traits have yet to be fully determined, and the nature versus nurture debate still rages. Is personality inherited (nature) or is it influenced by our environment and upbringing (nurture)? In an effort to differentiate the impacts of nature and nurture on personality, researchers have studied identical twins adopted by different sets of parents at birth. They discovered that though 40 percent of personality traits can be attributed to inheritance, the 60 percent that remain suggest that personality is more likely to be shaped by environmental and situational factors such as culture, religion, and family life. In the next section, we explore how many organizations use assessment tools to get a better understanding of their employees' personality traits.

Personality: A stable and unique pattern of traits, characteristics, and resulting behaviors that gives an individual his or her identity

Personality traits: Characteristics that describe our thoughts, feelings, and behaviors

THINKING CRITICALLY

1. Describe your personality by listing seven to ten adjectives that illustrate your behavior and approach to life. Now imagine your opposite personality type by listing seven to ten adjectives that are diametrically opposed to those you listed for yourself.

2. If you were a researcher who believed that individual differences were primarily determined by nature (i.e., inherited and hard-wired) what common-sense arguments could you use to support your belief?

3. If you were a researcher who believed that individual differences were primarily determined by nurture (i.e., shaped by one's upbringing and environment) what common-sense arguments could you use to support your belief?

4. Argue for a middle ground to the nature vs. nurture debate. How would you support the belief that BOTH genetics and environment influence personality and differences?

Myers-Briggs Type Indicator

>> **LO 2.4** Describe the Myers-Briggs Type Indicator Types

The Myers-Briggs Type Indicator (MBTI) is a psychometric questionnaire used to evaluate four psychological preferences that combine to describe sixteen personality types.[28] It was originally created by Katharine Cook Briggs and her daughter Isabel Briggs Myers during World War II to test a theory of psychological types advanced by the noted psychologist Carl Jung.[29] Initially drafted as a questionnaire, the test was developed into the official MBTI in 1962. It is the most widely used personality assessment instrument in the world.[30]

FIGURE 2.3

Myers-Briggs Preferences

Extraversion		Introversion
	Energy	
⬅ ➡		

Sensing		Intuiting
	Information	
⬅ ➡		

Thinking		Feeling
	Decisions	
⬅ ➡		

Judging		Perceiving
	Lifestyle	
⬅ ➡		

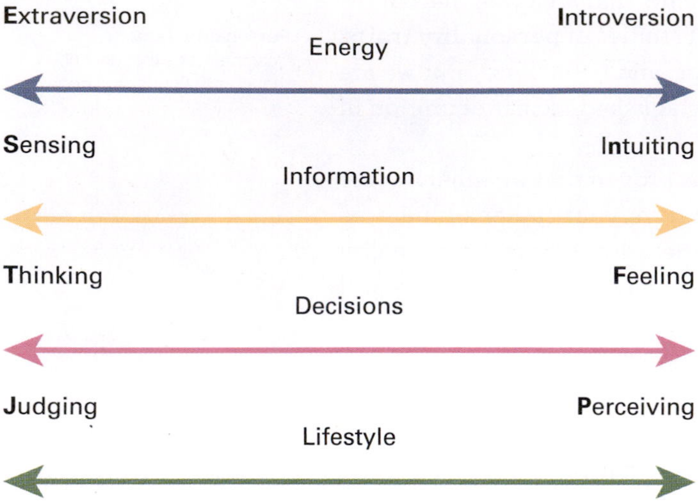

Although countless organizations all over the world still use the MBTI, it has been criticized by academics for providing a simplified, limited view of personality. It can be a valuable tool for increasing self-awareness and understanding others, but it is limiting in that it tends to box individual personalities into two main categories: introverts or extraverts. Whatever results you get after completing the questionnaire, remember they are not a definitive description of your personality type—they are merely suggestions based on psychological preferences, and are open to interpretation.

Myers-Briggs Preferences

Each MBTI profile is made up of four psychological preferences, each of which is one of a pair (see Figure 2.3). According to the theory, we have a tendency to lean toward one of the characteristics within each pair, which determines our preference in each case.

The four pairs of preferences are as follows:

- Extraversion (E) versus Introversion (I): Extraverts tend to be outgoing, talkative, and expressive; introverts tend to be reserved and like to work by themselves.

- Sensing (S) versus Intuitive (N): Sensing people prefer tangible, concrete, real-life information based on known facts; intuitive people tend to be imaginative, creative, and insightful.

- Thinking (T) versus Feeling (F): Thinking people use reason and logic to make decisions; feeling people draw from their own values when making decisions.

- Judging (J) versus Perceiving (P): Judging people prefer order, structure, plans, and rules; perceiving people are flexible and adaptable and like to keep their options open.

The Sixteen Myers-Briggs Types

To identify personality type, the four psychological preferences have been developed into a Preference Clarity Index (PCI) made up of 16 different typologies (Table 2.2).[31]

For example, if you think you are an introvert rather than an extravert, a sensing person rather than an intuitive one, a thinking person rather than a feeling person, and a judging person rather than a perceiving person, then you would be known as an ISTJ. Each type is associated with a list of personal characteristics. For instance, ISTJ people tend to be thorough, practical, determined, and calm in a crisis. However, they can be impatient and sometimes make impulsive decisions.

The MBTI can be beneficial in understanding yourself and increasing your self-awareness. It is also useful for identifying individual differences between us that can be a source of conflict and misunderstanding. The MBTI theory holds that by

TABLE 2.2

Sixteen Myers-Briggs Types

ISTJ 11–14%	ISFJ 9–14%	INFJ 1–3%	INTJ 2–4%
ISTP 4–6%	ISFP 5–9%	INFP 4–5%	INTP 3–5%
ESTP 4–5%	ESFP 4–9%	ENFP 6–8%	ENTP 2–5%
ESTJ 8–12%	ESFJ 9–13%	ENFJ 2–5%	ENTJ 2–5%
Estimated percentages of the 16 types in the US population			

Source: "Estimated Frequences of the Types in the United States Population." *Center for Applications of Psychological Type.* https://www.capt.org/mbti-assessment/estimated-frequencies.htm?bhcp=1.

broadening our perspectives of others, knowing what motivates them, and why they behave and communicate in the way they do, we will build better relationships.

THINKING CRITICALLY

1. How might knowing a coworker's Myers-Briggs type help you to more effectively work with her or him? How might knowing a coworker's Myers-Briggs type might hinder your ability to work together?

2. What other preference categories in addition to energy, information, decisions, and lifestyle that you think could be helpful in typing personality? List at least two.

The Big Five Model

>> **LO 2.5** **Identify the five personality factors of the Big Five model**

One important area of personality is **emotional stability,** the extent to which we can remain calm and composed. At the opposite end of the spectrum for this trait is **neuroticism,** a tendency to be tense, moody, irritable, and temperamental. The more emotionally stable you are, the lower your level of neuroticism. The MBTI tells us very little about these traits. Although MBTI is the most widely used approach to personality in the world, you may be surprised to learn that it doesn't get much respect from academics. Instead, academics tend to use other approaches more grounded in research. The dominant approach is the Big Five. The Big Five is based on the "lexical hypothesis" which is the idea that if there is a meaningful difference in personality, it is encoded in language—we have a word for it. One hundred years ago, researchers started compiling lists of adjectives from dictionaries: twenty thousand words, thirty thousand words. Then they reduced these words down to the fewest categories possible using a statistical technique called factor analysis. Over decades of research, five primary factors continued to emerge. In other words, you can't reduce the words to fewer categories and thus these five categories represent the five basic dimensions of human personality.

This model is widely accepted in academia and used more frequently in academic research. The **Big Five model,** outlined in Table 2.3, describes five basic dimensions of personality, including Extraversion, Agreeableness, Conscientiousness, Neuroticism (or Emotional Stability), and Openness to Experience and is frequently used to evaluate and assess people in the workplace.[32]

Emotional stability: The extent to which we can remain calm and composed

Neuroticism: A personality trait that involves being tense, moody, irritable, and temperamental

Big Five model: Five basic dimensions of personality to include neuroticism and frequently used to evaluate and assess people in the workplace

TABLE 2.3

The Big Five Model

Openness to Experience	The dimension of being curious, creative, and receptive to new ideas
Conscientiousness	The dimension of being thoughtful, organized, responsible, and achievement oriented
Neuroticism	The dimension of being tense, moody, irritable, and temperamental
Extraversion	The dimension of being outgoing, sociable, assertive, and talkative
Agreeableness	The dimension of being trusting, good natured, tolerant, forgiving, and cooperative

Source: Based on Barrick, Murray R., and Michael K. Mount. "The Big Five Personality Dimensions and Job Performance: A Meta-Analysis." *Personnel Psychology* 44, no. 1 (Spring 1991): 1–26; John, Oliver P., and Sanjay Srivastava. "The Big Five Trait Taxonomy: History, Measurement, and Theoretical Perspectives." In *Handbook of Personality: Theory and Research* (2nd ed.), 102–138 (New York: Guilford, 1999).

The Big Five personality test scores these personality dimensions from low to high, and a combination of these traits gives us an idea of what type of personality the individual possesses. For example, a person may score high in extraversion (very sociable), but low on conscientiousness (not very responsible). This analysis gives employers a better idea of the worker's profile and how he or she might fit into a certain role, and it is a useful way of assessing and predicting job performance. It also provides a more complete view of personality traits than earlier theories that saw traits as contradictory rather than as different in degree, because it allows for the many complexities of the human temperament.

The Big Five model has become the dominant trait theory of personality guiding research today. While the model has been subject to a certain amount of criticism,[33] the weight of evidence suggests that the five-factor structure remains remarkably stable over time, generalizes across cultures and languages, and shows substantial agreement across self and other rating sources.[34] This growing body of validating evidence further solidifies the Big Five model's status as the most widely accepted and influential modern trait theory of personality.

Researchers have proposed the concept of core self-evaluation (CSE), which refers to the appraisals that people make of their own abilities, self-worth, control, and capabilities.[35] For example, people who have a high core self-evaluation think of themselves in a positive way and have a high degree of confidence in their own skills and abilities whereas people with low core self-evaluation tend to lack confidence and think negatively of themselves. CSE involves four main personality dimensions: locus of control, emotional stability, self-efficacy and self-esteem. Research links these four traits with job satisfaction and work performance.

Earlier in the chapter, we described three of these dimensions: emotional stability, self-efficacy, and self-esteem. **Locus of control** is the extent to which people believe they have influence over events.[36] There are two types: **internal locus of control,** which allows people to believe they are responsible for influencing events; and **external locus of control,** which allows people to believe outside influences are responsible for their fate.

Yet the search for the most accurate personality test continues. The consultancy firm Deloitte teamed up with scientists from the fields of neuro-anthropology and genetics to create a 70-question personality test called "Business Chemistry." Devised with CFOs in mind, Business Chemistry helps people identify their own

Locus of control: The extent to which people feel they have influence over events

Internal locus of control: The degree to which people believe they control the events and consequences which affect their lives

External locus of control: The extent to which people believe their performance is the product of circumstances which are beyond their immediate control

EXAMINING THE EVIDENCE

The HEXACO Model of Personality

Although the Big Five model of personality has become a standard framework for personality in the field of OB, in recent years a competing model of personality has emerged that adds a sixth personality dimension to the basic five factors. The HEXACO model of personality consists of the six dimensions of Honesty-Humility (H), Emotionality (E), Extraversion (X), Agreeableness (A), Conscientiousness (C), and Openness to Experience (O).* Although aspects of all five factors are interpreted somewhat differently in the HEXACO model, the addition of the Honesty-Humility dimension represents the biggest departure from the classic framework.

The Honesty-Humility factor includes trait descriptors such as honesty, sincerity, fairness, and modesty, as opposed to greediness, conceitedness, deceitfulness, and pretentiousness—concepts that were traditionally elements of Agreeableness in the Big Five model.* Focusing on honesty-humility as a separate personality dimension may have important implications for managerial practice. For example, the results of a recent study by Professors Jocelyn Wiltshire and Kibeom Lee of the University of Calgary and Joshua S. Bourdage of Western University suggests that employees rating low on the honesty–humility dimension may be more likely to engage in

counterproductive work behaviors and impression management behaviors and to experience greater job stress and decreased job satisfaction when working in a highly political work environment,^ while another recent study found that low levels of honesty-humility were related to the intention to commit premeditated and calculated vengeful acts.

Critical-Thinking Questions

1. Why might it be important to consider the honesty-humility personality dimension in addition to the traditional Big Five dimensions?

2. What are some possible implications of the research findings outlined above for managerial practice? ●

Sources:

*Ashton, Michael C., Kibeom Lee, and Reinout E. de Vries. "The HEXACO Honesty-Humility, Agreeableness, and Emotionality Factors: A Review of Research and Theory." *Personality and Social Psychology Review* 18, no. 2 (May 2014): 139–152.

^Wiltshire, Jocelyn, Joshua S. Bourdage, and Kibeom Lee. "Honesty-Humility and Perceptions of Organizational Politics in Predicting Workplace Outcomes." *Journal of Business and Psychology* 29, no. 2 (June 2014): 235–251.

#Lee, Kibeom, and Michael C. Ashton. "Getting Mad and Getting Even: Agreeableness and Honesty–Humility as Predictors of Revenge Intentions." *Personality and Individual Differences* 52, no. 5 (April 2012): 596–600.

personality traits and recognize qualities in their colleagues. Deloitte believe this new personality test helps CFOs engage with stakeholders, manage the strengths and weaknesses of their teams, and use their capabilities to handle multiple tasks.[37]

As we have since learned, the diversity of a group is not the only thing that can cause challenges to working relationships—personality also plays a huge part.

THINKING CRITICALLY

1. Rank each of the Big Five dimensions of personality (Openness to Experience, Conscientiousness, Neuroticism, Extraversion, and Agreeableness) in order of importance to workplace performance. Then rank them in order of importance to getting along well with others. Provide an explanation and defense for the two sets of rankings and discuss the similarities and differences between the two.

2. Pick one of the Big Five dimensions of personality and describe a possible work scenario where an employee who rates high on the dimension you have chosen would be more effective at solving a conflict or problem than an employee who rates low on the dimension. Next, describe a different scenario where an employee rating low on the dimension would be more effective in solving a problem or conflict than an employee rating high on the dimension.

FIGURE 2.4

FIGURE 2.4

Dimensions of Personality

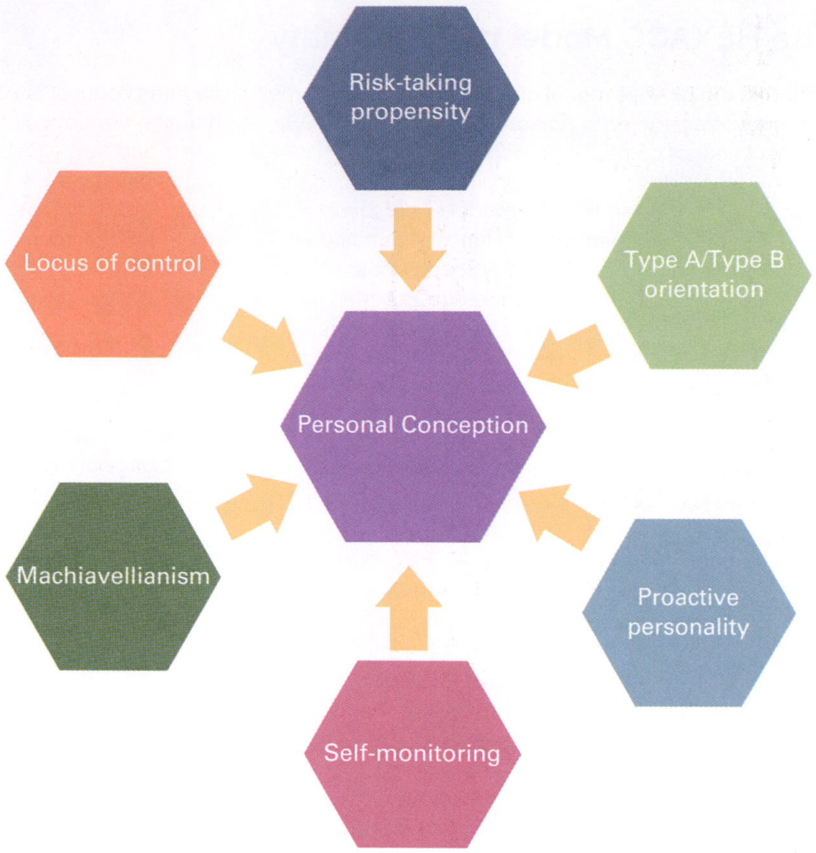

Other Personality Attributes

>> LO 2.6   **Differentiate among the most common personality attributes**

Personal conception is the degree to which individuals relate to and think about their social and physical environments and their personal beliefs regarding a range of issues. A person's conception of himself or herself is dependent on the following personality dimensions shown in Figure 2.4.

Machiavellianism

Some psychologists and sociologists use the term **Machiavellianism** to describe the behavior of people who manipulate others and use unethical practices for personal gain.[38] The term owes its origins to the 16th-century author Niccolo Machiavelli, whose book *The Prince* describes the true nature of power and its acquisition through cunning and ruthless means. People with high levels of Machiavellianism tend be pragmatic, may be prone to lying to achieve goals, are good at influencing others, and have the ability to distance themselves from conventional morality. Conversely, people with low levels of Machiavellianism are more likely to maintain moral standards and use ethical practices to achieve objectives. Russian president, Vladimir Putin, has been compared to Machiavelli owing to his manipulation of Russian public opinion through propaganda and using extreme measures and unethical practices in the guise of "protecting Russia" from its so-called "enemies" in the West.[39]

Personal conception: The degree to which individuals relate to and think about their social and physical environment and their personal beliefs regarding a range of issues

Machiavellianism: A philosophy that describes people who manipulate others and use unethical practices for personal gain

Self-Monitoring

Self-monitoring is the degree to which people adjust their behavior to accommodate different situations.[40] High self-monitors might hold back on expressing their true feelings and behaviors if they think the situation does not call for it, or that others might not approve. In short, they match their behavior to the requirements of the situation. In contrast, low self-monitors do not disguise their behaviors, have little regard for how others perceive them, and refuse to change any aspect of themselves to accommodate any given situation. Their attitude is "What you see is what you get." Google's CEO Sundar Pichai is thought to be a high self-monitor as he tends to adjust his behavior to cater for certain situations.[41]

> **Self-monitoring:** Adjusting our behavior to accommodate different situations

Proactive Personality

Proactive personality is the extent to which individuals take the initiative to change their circumstances.[42] Those who are high in proactive personality look for opportunities to change events and take action to ensure the desired change takes place. People who are low in proactive personality are generally more accepting of the status quo and take very little action to change the circumstances surrounding them. Today's organizations actively seek out proactive people because they are more likely to react positively to and adapt to an ever-changing work environment. Research has also shown that people with proactive personalities tend to be more successful when it comes to starting and running their own businesses.[43]

> **Proactive personality:** The tendency for individuals to take the initiative to change their circumstances

Type A/Type B Orientation

The way employees react to stressful situations is of particular interest to OB managers. For example, some people thrive under pressure and perceive tight deadlines as a challenge, whereas others may struggle and react negatively. Researchers have defined two main personality types to gauge how workers cope under pressure: Type A and Type B orientation.[44] People with a **Type A orientation** are characterized as competitive, impatient, aggressive, and achievement oriented. Conversely, those with a **Type B orientation** are characterized as relaxed, easygoing, more patient, and less competitive.

> **Type A orientation:** The way people are characterized as competitive, impatient, aggressive, and achievement oriented

> **Type B orientation:** The way people are characterized as relaxed, easygoing, patient, and noncompetitive

Risk-Taking Propensity

Risk-taking propensity is the tendency to engage in behaviors that might have positive or negative outcomes.[45] High risk takers make faster decisions based on less information, but they risk making mistakes if they don't adequately assess the consequences of their decisions. For example, excessive risk taking was one of the main causes of the housing market crisis between 2007 and 2008, because lenders granted high-risk mortgages loans to subprime (poorly qualified) borrowers who could not afford to pay back the loans. When the housing market bubble burst, prices dropped, resulting in high volumes of defaults, leaving the banks with foreclosed houses that were worth less than the amount of the original loan. This had a devastating effect on the lenders, banks, and investment institutions that were involved in selling or trading mortgage loans, many of which collapsed.[46]

> **Risk-taking propensity:** The tendency to engage in behaviors that might have positive or negative outcomes

Low risk takers tend to take more time with their decision making and require more information to assess the potential level of risk, yet they may become paralyzed by indecision if they spend too much time gathering information. Similarly, people can become paralyzed by having too much choice. Researcher Barry Schwartz of Swarthmore College conducted a study that showed that shoppers at a grocery store who were given a choice of six types of jam to purchase were more likely to make

John M. Heller / Stringer

Richard Branson, owner of Virgin Group, is a notorious risk taker.

a purchase decision and actually buy some jam than shoppers who were given a choice of twenty-four different types.[47] Schwartz labeled this phenomenon "The Paradox of Choice" and noted that our cherished freedom of choice may actually lead to decision-making uncertainty and dissatisfaction with decision outcomes. In other words, having too many choices may cause people to be unhappy with their decisions or to have difficulties in making any decision at all. Decision making can be especially difficult for "maximizers"—those individuals determined to make only the best choices.

As we have seen, despite the amount of research and theories carried out, the human personality still remains something of a mystery. However, by applying some of the research toward understanding our own differences and the differences of others, we have a better chance of building productive relationships inside and outside the workplace.

THINKING CRITICALLY

1. Imagine your ideal coworker based on where you fall on each of the dimensions of personality. Identify the dimensions where similarity would be most beneficial to an effective working relationship. Identify the dimensions where difference would likely benefit the relationship. Defend your answers.

2. What sorts of industries or types of businesses would most value workers rating high on each of the six dimensions of personality? What sorts of industries or types of businesses would most value employees rating low on the six dimensions of personality? Are there any dimensions where a particularly low or particularly high rating would be an obstacle to satisfactory work performance regardless of the type of industry or business? ●

 **SAGE edge™**

Visit **edge.sagepub.com/neckob2e** to help you accomplish your coursework goals in an easy-to-use learning environment.

- Mobile-friendly eFlashcards and practice quizzes
- Video and multimedia content
- Chapter summaries with learning objectives
- EXCLUSIVE! Access to full-text SAGE journal articles

IN REVIEW

2.1 Explain the importance of diversity in OB

Workplace diversity can be defined as the degree to which an organization includes people from different cultures and backgrounds, and recognizes, respects, and values both individual and group differences by treating people as individuals in an effort to promote an inclusive culture. One of the most effective ways organizations can encourage acceptance of differences and create a harmonious workforce is through the management of diversity. **Surface-level diversity** describes the easily perceived differences between us, such as **age/generation, race/ethnicity, gender, sexual orientation,** and **ability. Deep-level diversity** describes verbal and nonverbal behaviors that are not as easily perceived as they lie below the surface, such as differences in attitudes, values, beliefs, and personality.

2.2 Discuss why individual differences are important

Individual differences are defined as the effort to find behavioral similarities and differences. We don't need to just understand people who are different from us, but also those who are similar to us in the way they think, make decisions, and behave. When you figure out the differences and similarities of your coworkers, it will give you a better idea of why people act the way they do.

2.3 Contrast the nature and nurture explanations of personality development

Personality is defined as a stable and unique pattern of traits, characteristics, and resulting behaviors that gives an individual his or her identity. The origins of our personality traits have yet to be fully determined, and the nature versus nurture debate still abounds. The nature side of the debate argues that personality is inherited while the nurture side argues that personality is influenced by the environment.

2.4 Describe the Myers-Briggs Type Indicator Types

The **Myers-Briggs Type Indicator (MBTI)** is a psychometric questionnaire used to evaluate four psychological preferences, and developed into sixteen personality types. The four psychological preferences are as follows:

- Extraversion (E) versus Introversion (I): How the flow of energy is directed
- Sensing (S) versus Intuitive (N): How information is understood and interpreted
- Thinking (T) versus Feeling (F): How decisions are made
- Judging (J) versus Perceiving (P): How we cope with our surroundings

2.5 Identify the five personality factors of the Big Five model

The Big Five model describes five basic dimensions of personality to include neuroticism and is frequently used to evaluate and assess people in the workplace. The five traits are as follows:

1. *Openness to experience*: The dimension of being curious, creative, and receptive to new ideas
2. *Conscientiousness*: The dimension of being thoughtful, organized, responsible, and achievement oriented
3. *Neuroticism*: The dimension of being tense, moody, irritable, and temperamental
4. *Extraversion*: The dimension of being outgoing, sociable, assertive, and talkative
5. *Agreeableness*: The dimension of being trusting, good-natured, tolerant, forgiving, and cooperative

The Big Five personality test scores these personality dimensions from low to high; a combination of these traits gives us an idea of what type of personality the individual possesses.

2.6 Differentiate among the most common personality attributes

Personal conception is the degree to which individuals relate to and think about their social and physical environment, and their personal beliefs regarding a range of issues. A person's conception of himself or herself is dependent on the following personality dimensions:

- **Locus of control:** The extent to which people feel they have influence over events
- **Machiavellianism:** A philosophy that describes people who manipulate others and use unethical practices for personal gain
- **Self-monitoring**: Adjusting our behavior to accommodate different situations
- **Proactive personality:** The tendency for individuals to take the initiative to change their circumstances
- **Type A/Type B orientation:** The way people are characterized as possessing certain personality attributes
- **Risk-taking propensity:** The tendency to engage in behaviors that may have positive or negative outcomes

KEY TERMS

Ability diversity 42
Age diversity 40
Awareness of others 49
Big Five model 53
Cultural metacognition 47
Deep-level diversity 39
Emotional stability 53
Ethnicity 41
External locus of control 54
Gender diversity 42
Glass ceiling 42
Individual differences 49
Internal locus of control 54
Locus of control 54
Machiavellianism 56
Neuroticism 53

Personal conception 56
Personality 51
Personality traits 51
Proactive personality 57
Race 41
Risk-taking propensity 57
Self-awareness 49
Self-concept 50
Self-efficacy 50
Self-esteem 50
Self-monitoring 57
Sexual orientation 42
Surface-level diversity 39
Type A orientation 57
Type B orientation 57
Workplace diversity 39

UP FOR DEBATE: Diverse Business Environments Create Diverse Company Cultures

Firms around the world, especially in the United States, are placing a huge emphasis on acquiring talent from diverse ethnic, educational, and socioeconomic backgrounds. The claim is that building a diverse business environment directly translates into a culture of diverse and creative thinking, ultimately giving the firm a competitive advantage. Agree or disagree? Explain your answer.

EXERCISE 2.1: Personality: Core Self-Evaluations

Objective

The purpose of the exercise is to help you reflect upon and improve your own Core Self-Evaluation (CSE).

Instructions

Before starting this exercise, complete Self-Assessment 2.2 below. Did you score above or below average in CSE? Either way, the following exercise can help you increase your level of CSE.

- Write three statements about your self-worth. "I am … (valuable, important, worthless)."

   1. _____
   2. _____
   3. _____

- Write three statements about your capabilities. "I am … (competent, capable, mediocre, inept)."

   1. _____
   2. _____
   3. _____

- Write three statements about your performance at school or work. "I am … (successful, above average, a failure)."

   1. _____
   2. _____
   3. _____

Reflection Questions

1. What evidence do you have for these statements?
2. How could you reshape your view of your self-worth in more positive ways?

EXERCISE 2.2: Dimensions of Diversity

Objective

Differentiate between surface-level diversity and deep-level diversity.

Instructions

You have one minute to write down on a 3x5 card as many words as possible that come to mind when you hear the term "diversity." As a class or in small groups, compared your responses and note the number of times each word is used. Categorize the words into two categories: surface-level diversity and deep-level diversity.

Reflection Questions

1. How many of the words were surface-level? What aspects of surface-level diversity were mentioned the most?
2. How many of the words were deep-level? What aspects of deep-level diversity were mentioned the most?
3. Did your group list more surface-level or deep-level dimensions of diversity? Why do you think that was the case?

Exercise contributed by Harriet Rojas, Professor of Business, Indiana Wesleyan University.

EXERCISE 2.3: My Experience with Individual Differences

Objectives

In this exercise you will explore and *describe* the concept of diversity and its importance—including its benefits. In addition you will *develop* an understanding of the significance of individual differences.

Instructions

This exercise consists of four steps.

Step 1. Individually think about then write about an experience where you were unfairly treated for being different in an organizational group. The group can have been in any type of organization (i.e., work, school, social, religious, volunteer, etc.). Be as specific as possible about the following aspects of this experience and answer the following questions (10 minutes):

- In what way were you different from the group?
- How were you treated unfairly?
- What were the consequences of the unfair treatment? Describe the effectives in terms of how you were affected as an individual as well as how the group and organization were affected.
- What could the group have gained if that person had been treated fairly?

Step 2. Choose a partner, preferably someone who you do not know very well, and compare your situation and responses. Identify what your experiences share in common and how they differ. (10 minutes)

Step 3. Partners should now join groups of five to seven people. Repeat the comparison process among all team members. Be sure to focus on each of the four preceding specific questions. As a group, identify commonalities and divergence in member experiences. Finally, select one member's experience to be presented to the entire class. Choose a team spokesperson (the spokesperson should not be the author of the selected experience) to describe the situation and the answers to the four specific questions. (10 to 20 minutes)

Step 4. Each team spokesperson should be prepared to present the team's findings to the entire class. Again, the class should identify through discussion common points and differences in the various group's interpretations of unfair treatment based on differences from a group. (10 to 20 minutes)

Reflection Questions

1. How does your new understanding of chapter concepts better help you to grasp the negative consequences of excluding people based on non-performance-related differences?

2. Did you identify any structural or cultural issues in the exclusion process?

3. What similarities did you notice between different team presentations?

4. What concrete, specific behaviors and mind-sets could help ensure that such unfair treatment does not happen?

5. How can individuals, groups, and organizations themselves benefit from helping all members maximize their potential contributions?

Exercise contributed by Milton R. Mayfield, Professor of Business, Texas A&M International University, and Jacqueline R. Mayfield, Professor of Business, Texas A&M International University.

EXERCISE 2.4: Your Generation

Objective

The purpose of this exercise is to gain a greater understanding of age diversity.

Instructions

Your generation has been portrayed in movies, TV shows, and online as having certain peculiarities, which may or may not be accurate. It is obviously important not to stereotype any demographic group, but your generation especially has been the subject of numerous studies as to work ethic, understanding of technology, entitlement, and so on.

In groups of three to six, brainstorm a list of the characteristics of your generation—good and bad. As you capture these characteristics on a sheet of paper, discuss why these particular ones are peculiar to your age group. Try to make a list of ten positive characteristics and ten characteristics that might be perceived as negative.

Reflection Questions

1. How difficult was it to generate this list? Was it easier to come up with traits that are positive or ones that are negative? Why do you think that is?

2. Suppose a different generation, such as a baby boomer or Generation X member, were also asked to develop a list of characteristics of your generation. What differences would there be in the lists?

3. From where did you and your team draw the inferences for your list? In other words, did you base the items on your list from your own experiences or what you *think* other generations think of those your age?

4. Do you think your list is a fair assessment of individuals in your generation? How can you encourage other generations to recognize your positive traits and ignore or change their views on the negative characteristics you listed?

5. How can managers effectively manage the youngest workers entering the job market? What strategies work and which ones will turn off most people your age?

Exercise contributed by Steven Stovall, Southeast Missouri State University.

EXERCISE 2.5: Nature versus Nurture

Objective

The purpose of this exercise is to grasp the concept of nature versus nurture.

Instructions

The debate regarding nature versus nurture centers on where we acquire our personality. Researchers try to determine if our personality is a result of genetics (nature) or if environmental influences influence our personality (nurture). Certainly, some physical attributes you have such as eye or hair color are based upon genetics, but are mood swings dependent upon the DNA we receive from our parents or is that something that we develop over time on our own?

Talk to one or two people sitting next to you and determine which among you have siblings (if none of you have siblings, consider parents or cousins for this exercise). Find out as much as you can about your neighbors' brothers and sisters. Ask about education, sports, hobbies, and interests. But also ask about moods, emotions, and how they interact with others. As you discuss, ask questions that find out how different or alike your neighbor is compared to the siblings.

Reflection Questions

1. Based on your discussions, are the differences and similarities you learned about your neighbor and his or her siblings as well as perhaps you and your own siblings founded upon genetic predisposition or are they developed within individuals as they grow older?

2. Which side of the debate do you subscribe to? Are you one who believes our personality comes directly from our parents or is it something we develop on our own?

3. Given your response in question 2, why do you feel that way? What evidence can you cite that points in the direction which you believe?

Exercise contributed by Steven Stovall, Southeast Missouri State University.

ONLINE EXERCISE 2.1: Understanding the Big Five Model

Objective

The purpose of this exercise is to gain an appreciation for the Big Five model.

Instructions

This exercise requires the use of a discussion board and delves into the Big Five model. The Big Five model describes five basic dimensions of personality (each are summarized below). Your particular combination of these dimensions represents your overall personality. Some people are higher in some dimensions and lower in others. It is this high-low assessment that describes your personality type.

To begin the discussion, post which one of the five dimensions you think you are the highest in. Then, explain why you chose this particular dimension. Allow others to post their highest dimension as well. When you encounter another person who has posted the same dimension as you as the highest, engage in a dialogue about how you each might be similar when it comes to that dimension. After some discussion, then post the dimension you think is your second highest one. Once again, compare personality traits with those who share that dimension. Finally, post your third highest dimension.

The five dimensions are:

- **Openness to experience**—curious, creative, and receptive to new ideas
- **Conscientiousness**—thoughtful, organized, responsible, and achievement oriented
- **Neuroticism**—tense, moody, irritable, and temperamental
- **Extraversion**—outgoing, sociable, assertive, and talkative
- **Agreeableness**—trusting, good natured, tolerant, forgiving, and cooperative

Reflection Questions

1. How did you decide which of the Big Five dimensions was your highest? Second highest? And so on.

2. Given your highest dimension selected, how do you think you would get along in the workplace with someone with the same highest dimension? What about someone who does not share your highest dimension?

3. How accurate do you think your own assessment is? Do you think if you completed a full assessment of your personality, conducted by a trained researcher, the dimensions would still be in the same order that you have selected here? Why or why not?

Exercise contributed by Steven Stovall, Southeast Missouri State University.

CASE STUDY 2.1: W.L. Gore and Associates

He was ready for anything—or so he thought. Dressed in his finest and armed with an MBA degree fresh off the press, Jack Dougherty walked in for his first day of work at Newark, Delaware–based W. L. Gore and Associates, the global fluoropolymer technology and manufacturing giant that is best known as the maker of Gore-Tex.

But it turned out he wasn't ready for this: "Why don't you look around and find something you'd like to do," founder and CEO Bill Gore said to him after a quick introduction. Although many things have changed over the course of W. L. Gore and Associates' more than sixty years in business, the late Gore stuck to his principles regarding organizational structure (or lack thereof), a legacy he passed down to subsequent generations of management. Gore wasn't fond of thick layers of formal management, which he believed smothered individual creativity. According to Gore, "A lattice (flat) organization is one that involves direct transactions, self-commitment, natural leadership, and lacks assigned or assumed authority."

In the 1930s, Gore received a bachelor's degree in chemical engineering and a master's degree in physical chemistry. During his career, he worked on a team to develop applications for polytetrafluoroethylene (PTFE), commonly known as Teflon. Through this experience, Gore discovered a sense of excited commitment, personal fulfillment, and self-direction, which he yearned to share with others. Spending nights tinkering in his own workshop, he did what he had previously thought to be impossible: he created a PTFE-coated ribbon cable. It occurred to Gore that he might be able to start his own business producing his invention, so he left his stable career of seventeen years, borrowed money, and drained his savings. Though his friends advised him against taking such a risk, W. L. Gore and Associates was born in January 1958. The basement of the Gore home was the company's first facility.

Although no longer operating from a family basement (Gore boasts more than $3.5 billion in annual sales and ten thousand employees in more than fifty facilities worldwide), the sense of informality has stuck. "It absolutely is less efficient upfront," said Terri Kelly, chief executive of W. L. Gore. (Her title is one of the few at the company.) "[But] once you have the organization behind it . . . the buy-in and the execution happens quickly," she added.

Structure and Management of Unstructure and Unmanagement

Even as Gore started to grow, the company continued to resist titles and hierarchy. It had no mission statement, no ethics statement, and no conventional structures typical of companies of the same size. The only formal titles were "chief executive" and "secretary-treasurer"—those required by law for corporations. There were also no rules that business units within the company couldn't create such structures, and so some of them did create their own mission statements and such. Many called Gore's management style "unmanagement." What had started as twelve employees working in the Gore basement eventually evolved into a thriving company by the 1960s, with multiple plants.

There were two hundred employees working at a plant in Newark, Delaware. One day, Gore was walking around the plant, and it occurred to him that he didn't know all the employees there. Based on this realization, Gore established a policy that said no plant was to be larger than one hundred fifty to two hundred workers per plant, to keep things more intimate and interpersonal. He wanted to "get big while staying small."

Understanding and Leveraging Differences

With a global recession on the horizon in 2007, the company prepared for tough times by hunkering down, self-assessing, and embarking on a journey of self-improvement. A diversity leadership program was developed that focused on Gore's most important asset: people. The Gore team sought to understand "when, why, if, and how differences affect relationships, because the quality of relationships [among employees] has a lot to do with how well our business performs," adding that improving relationships [could] "decrease reactivity; increase professional capacity; and [help associates] learn about self while helping to make a more cohesive, diverse, and cross-discipline system." Intense analysis and discussion led to bold change:

Workshops, lunch and learn sessions, and other programs help promote a more inclusive environment and encourage associates to listen to and learn from each other on a regular basis.... [We created] space for self-exploration, learning from differences dialogues; meeting with enterprise diversity affinity groups; monthly 15 engagement survey; building space in global business meetings to talk about individual belief systems and the connection to enterprise belief systems; proactively ensuring that learning from difference dialogues are built into global and local business meetings; and once a year, teams form to create and raffle off diversity baskets, filled with items that celebrate their culture, ethnicity, religion, etc. In addition, these teams speak at plant meetings about the items and traditions represented in their baskets.

As the objectives were set into motion, monthly and annual employee survey results began to reflect increased satisfaction.

People Helping People

As the company grew, Gore also realized that there had to be some kind of system in place to assist new people on the job and to track progress. Instead of a formal management program, Gore implemented a "sponsor" program. When people applied for jobs with the company, they were screened and then interviewed by associates. An associate who took a personal interest in the new associate's contributions, problems, and goals would agree to act as a mentor, or sponsor. The new hire's sponsor would coach and advocate for him, tracking progress, encouraging the person, and dealing with weaknesses while focusing on strengths. Sponsors were also responsible for ensuring that their associates were fairly paid. The result of all this focus on mentoring and the right-sized teams has cultivated a feeling of intimacy and appreciation that attracts and retains a strong workforce.

"You feel like you're part of a family," said Steve Shuster, part of Gore's enterprise communication team. "I have been working at Gore for twenty-seven years, and I still get excited coming to work each day."

Case Questions

1. How did Bill Gore structure management within his company and why is this relevant to personality and individual differences?
2. Explain why the diversity leadership program developed by W. L. Gore and Associates is a positive way to better understand and foster individual differences.
3. Describe how the sponsor program developed higher levels of employee satisfaction as well as maintained the "unmanagement" culture.

Sources

"About Us." www.gore.com/en_xx/aboutus/culture/index.html.

Mayhew, Ruth. "Cons of a Lattice Organizational Structure." *Houston Chronicle*, http://smallbusiness.chron.com/cons-lattice-organizational- structure-3836.html.

Sacconey Townsend, Gail, and William Aubrey Saunders. "Cross-Functional Teaming through the Lenses of Differences: W. L. Gore & Associates, Inc., Case Study." October 8, 2013. http://c.ymcdn.com/sites/www.odnetwork.org/resource/resmgr/2013_education/gailt_aubreys_handout_whitep.pdf.

Shipper, Frank, and Charles C. Manz. "Classic 6: W. L. Gore & Associates." www.academia.edu/964711/Classic_Case_6_WL_Gore_and_ Associates_Inc; n.d.

"Workplace Democracy at W.L. Gore & Associates." *workplacedemocracy.com.* July 14, 2009; http://workplacedemocracy.com/2009/07/14/work- place-democracy-at-w-l-goreassociates.

How Accurately Can You Describe Yourself?*

Describe yourself as you generally are now, not as you wish to be in the future. Describe yourself as you honestly see yourself in relation to other people you know of the same sex as you are, and roughly your same age.

For each statement, check the circle that best describes you based on the following scale:

	NOT AT ALL ACCURATE	SOMEWHAT ACCURATE	A LITTLE ACCURATE	MOSTLY ACCURATE	COMPLETELY ACCURATE
1. Am the life of the party	O	O	O	O	O
2. Am interested in people	O	O	O	O	O
3. Am always prepared	O	O	O	O	O
4. Am relaxed most of the time	O	O	O	O	O
5. Have a rich vocabulary	O	O	O	O	O
6. Feel comfortable around people	O	O	O	O	O
7. Sympathize with others' feelings	O	O	O	O	O
8. Pay attention to details	O	O	O	O	O
9. Don't get stressed out easily	O	O	O	O	O
10. Have excellent ideas	O	O	O	O	O
11. Talk to a lot of different people at parties	O	O	O	O	O
12. Have a soft heart	O	O	O	O	O
13. Get chores done right away	O	O	O	O	O
14. Seldom feel blue	O	O	O	O	O
15. Have a vivid imagination	O	O	O	O	O
16. Start conversations	O	O	O	O	O
17. Take time out for others	O	O	O	O	O
18. Like order	O	O	O	O	O
19. Don't get upset easily	O	O	O	O	O
20. Am full of ideas	O	O	O	O	O

Scoring

Extraversion (add items 1, 6, 11, 16 and write your score in the blank) _____

The extent to which you are outgoing, sociable, talkative, and able to get on well with others

Agreeableness (add items 2, 7, 12, 17 and write your score in the blank) _____

The extent to which you are able to relate to others by being trusting, forgiving, kind, affectionate, and cooperative

Conscientiousness (add items 3, 8, 13, 18 and write your score in the blank) _____

The extent to which you exhibit thoughtfulness, organization, and responsibility

Emotional Stability (Neuroticism reverse scaled) (add items 4, 9, 14, 19 and write your score in the blank) _____

The extent to which you are calm, relaxed, and not tense, moody, irritable, or anxious

Openness to Experience/Imagination (add items 5, 10, 15, 20 and write score in the blank) _____

The extent to which you are able to have fun, experience elation and delight, foster a diverse sharing of ideas, and learn from contradictory points of view.

What was your strongest decision-making style? What are the advantages and disadvantages of this style?

What was your weakest decision-making style? What are the advantages and disadvantages of this style?

*These five scales were developed to measure the Big Five factor markers reported in Goldberg, L. R. "The Development of Markers for the Big-Five Factor Structure." *Psychological Assessment* 4 (1992): 26–42.

The Core Self-Evaluations Scale (CSES)*

Instructions: Below are several statements about you with which you may agree or disagree. Using the response scale below, indicate your agreement or disagreement with each item by placing the appropriate number on the line preceding that item.

1	2	3	4	5
Strongly Disagree	Disagree	Neutral	Agree	Strongly Agree

1. _____ I am confident I get the success I deserve in life.

2. _____ I rarely feel depressed.

3. _____ When I try, I generally succeed.

4. _____ When I fail, I rarely feel worthless.

5. _____ I complete tasks successfully.

6. _____ I usually feel in control of my work.

7. _____ Overall, I am satisfied with myself.

8. _____ I rarely experience doubts about my competence.

9. _____ I determine what will happen in my life.

10. _____ I feel in control of my success in my career.

11. _____ I am capable of coping with most of my problems.

12. _____ There are rarely times when things seem bleak and hopeless to me.

Scoring:

Sum the numbers above and divide the sum by 12 to produce an average CSES score

Total _____

÷12 _____ (Average Score)

Comparison Data

(Compared to psychology students, business students, practicing managers)

Mean score: 3.88

Top quartile: 4.41 or above

Third quartile: 3.88 and 4.40

Second quartile: 3.35 and 3.87

Bottom quartile: 3.34 or below

*Adapted from Judge, T. A., Erez, A., Bono, J. E., & Thoresen, C. J. (2003). The core self-evaluations scale: Development of a measure. *Personnel Psychology*, 56: 303–331.

David Paul Morris/Getty Images

3 Perception and Learning

Studies have shown that 90% of error in thinking is due to error in perception. If you can change your perception, you can change your emotion and this can lead to new ideas.

—*Edward de Bono, author and psychologist*

Learning Objectives

By the end of this chapter, you will be able to:

3.1 Describe the basic concept of perception

3.2 Explain the different types of perceptual distortions

3.3 Apply attribution theory to more effectively interpret behavior

3.4 Use reinforcement theory to understand learning and modify behavior

3.5 Apply social cognitive theory to social learning and cognitive processes

CASE STUDY: TWITTER'S ADAPTABILITY

A Tech Giant

The seemingly indestructible tech giant that we know as "Twitter" consistently finds itself at the front of the pack alongside the other tech giants of our day. Twitter generates over $600 million in revenues, employs over 3500 people all over the world, and reports over 300 million daily users. What started as a tiny podcast start-up in Silicon Valley is now a 21st-century cultural phenomenon. World leaders, professional athletes, students use Twitter as a means of making their voices heard.

Twitter is an incredibly powerful tool that is at the fingertips of everyone with access to the internet. In response to the ever-changing sphere of technology and global trends, Twitter's functions are constantly changing. Through regular updates and improvements to its user interface, Twitter is always one step ahead of its competitors. If Twitter was unable to adapt early on, it would have surely failed. Ever since Twitter's start under the name of "Odeo" back in 2005, it has proved to be a great example of the success that comes when a company masters the ability to adapt to changing market conditions.

Humble Beginnings

In 2005, Evan Williams and some friends moved to Silicon Valley and created the start-up Odeo. It was a podcasting platform which, at the time, was all the rage. With fourteen full-time employees finally rolling out their product in summer 2005, it looked as though Odeo could not fail. However, another company called Apple had just rolled out its free podcasting service, rendering Odeo's product irrelevant. CEO Evan Williams needed to pivot—and fast. Williams asked his employees to collectively come up with any potential solution. After long days and nights of throwing around new business ideas, the Odeo team decided to completely shift gears from a podcasting platform to a status-updating micro-blogging platform. The idea was originally conceived by Jack Dorsey, one of Odeo's web designers.

A Slow, Volatile Start

It took about six months for things to really kick off for Twitter. After the slow start, Evan Williams wrote a letter to investors urging them to pull out their money. He is quoted as saying, "By the way, Twitter, which you may have read about, is one of the pieces of value that I see in Odeo, but it's much too early to tell what's there. Almost two months after launch, Twitter has less than five thousand registered users. I will continue to invest in Twitter, but it's hard to say it justifies the venture investment Odeo certainly holds—especially since that investment was for a different market altogether."

The everyday tech consumer wasn't ready for the service that Twitter offered. This new service came with new challenges for Twitter's employees. Employees would stay long hours researching new marketing techniques, computer engineering designs, and new ways to grow Twitter's brand. The key to the ultimate success of Twitter was the team's ability to learn on the job and then quickly apply what they learned. At a conference in Austin, Twitter was introduced as a way for attendees to share their thoughts and experiences with other attendees via a "status." The platform was hugely popular at the conference and the number of users skyrocketed. After a few short months, Twitter became one of the world's most widely visited websites with over 1 million subscribers.

Management in Action

The theme of Twitter's success is, simply, adaptability. A business is most able to adapt to new trends and technology only when it has a workforce of employees who have the ability to learn on the fly. Managers play a huge role in empowering their employees to do this. Hence, the corporate culture of Twitter that originated when Evan Williams turned to his employees to come up with new ideas. Ever since, Twitter has maintained a corporate culture that emphasizes employee contributions, learning, and advancement. Twitter's corporate culture was ranked #1 in the United States. According to one employee, "Great people, great food, great compensation, great learning opportunities, great opportunities. You get to do what matters to the world. Great work/life balance as well." Twitter's managers do many different things to maintain this perception of their corporate culture. Twitter's culture of learning and development shapes employees' perceptions in a positive way that encourages them to buy into the overarching mission. There are programs in place at Twitter to help enhance employees' various skills whether they are learning to code, aiming to get an MBA, or planning to start a business venture of their own. Twitter's empowering environment then enables employees to put what they have learned into practice. Another employee said, "The amount of power entrusted to employees is huge. You are empowered to go explore and find data, build things, and generally choose the course of action you think will have the most impact." This has a powerful impact on employee self-efficacy, which is the belief one has in one's own ability to succeed in a specific task or situation. When employees believe in themselves, they will not be afraid to take risks, just like Jack Dorsey did by pushing for his idea of Twitter.

Additionally, by giving employees the power to contribute to the direction of the organization, managers also consequently give employees the choice whether to learn more or not. Naturally, employees who don't strive to learn will perform poorly and eventually lose their job. On the other hand, the employees who go out of their way to learn more naturally empower themselves to do more. They can do this by first setting goals through self-regulation, then finding learning methods that best work for them. Vicarious learning, or learning by emulating the behavior of managers, is just one of the very reliable methods that team members can employ to develop their skills in the workplace. Twitter managers are willing to help any employee seeking to grow by providing constructive criticism and giving employees an opportunity to take part in more advanced projects. Their performance is then evaluated and along with constructive criticism, various types of reinforcement are served as well. With a good balance, this makes for an ideal learning environment that pushes employees to grow while also empowering them to seek out guidance and growth on their own.

Critical-Thinking Questions

1. What was valuable about Evan Williams's decision to task his employees with mustering up a new business idea?

2. How are employee empowerment, adaptability, and on-the-job training related?

Sources:

Carlson, N. (2011). The real history of Twitter. *Business Insider*. Retrieved from http://www.businessinsider.com/how-twitter-was-founded-2011-4

Koetsier, J. (2012, November 18). The legendary pivot: How Twitter flipped from failure to success [video]. *VentureBeat*. Retrieved from https://venturebeat.com/2012/11/18/the-pivot-how-twitter-switch-from-failure-to-success-video/

MacArthur, A. (2018, August 27). The real history of Twitter, in brief: How the micro-messaging wars were won. *Lifewire*. Retrieved from https://www.lifewire.com/history-of-twitter-3288854

Nazar, J. (2013, October 8). 14 famous business pivots. *Forbes*. Retrieved from https://www.forbes.com/sites/jasonnazar/2013/10/08/14-famous-business-pivots/#2a8e17415797

Nisen, M. (2014). How Facebook and Twitter built the best employee training programs in Silicon Valley. *Quartz*. Retrieved from https://qz.com/185585/how-facebook-and-twitter-built-the-best-employee-training-programs-in-silicon-valley/

Perception: Interpreting Our Environment

>> LO 3.1   **Describe the basic concept of perception**

A number of years ago, the *Washington Post* carried out an experiment in perception by placing world-famous violinist Joshua Bell, disguised as a street musician, in a Washington Metro station.[1] Wearing a baseball cap, T-shirt, and jeans, Bell performed a 43-minute set of six classical pieces for unsuspecting commuters. Of the 1,097 who passed by, only seven stopped for just over a minute to listen to his virtuoso performance before continuing their journey. By the end of his performance, the virtuoso Bell had made a grand total of $30 and a few cents—hardly enough to buy a ticket to one of his own sell-out concerts.

So what does this experiment tell us about perception? Was it because Bell was dressed as a street musician that the commuters didn't stop to listen? Or was it because of the setting—after all, how likely is it that a world-famous musician would perform for free in a Metro station? Whatever the reason, we can conclude that most people perceived Bell to be someone other than who he was, which affected their ability to recognize and appreciate his talent as a musician.

We define **perception** as the process by which we receive and interpret information from our environment.[2] Managing perceptions in the workplace is important for nurturing a healthy organizational culture, especially when people hold different perceptions about their colleagues, how tasks are carried out, and even the organization itself.

As our case study shows, Twitter intentionally shapes employees' perceptions in a positive way by nurturing an empowering environment of learning and development that encourages them to buy into Twitter's overarching mission.

**Master the content
edge.sagepub.com/
neckob2e**

Perception: The process by which we receive and interpret information from our environment

FIGURE 3.1

Optical Illusion

Source: http://www.goillusions.com/2015/05/three-or-four-perspective-matters.html.

But there are times when information from our environment negatively affects our perception. In recent times, concerns have been raised by the level of fake news and its dangerous influence on the wider public. Most of the more notorious fake news headlines from 2016 involve politics and politicians.[3] They include Pope Francis's supposed endorsement of Donald Trump for presidency, and Hillary Clinton's sale of weapons to Islamic State terrorists (ISIS). Both stories were completely fabricated of course, but it didn't stop them being shared over social media. In the final three months leading up to the US presidential election, these stories attracted more engagement than legitimate stories reported by reputable news outlets *New York Times, Washington Post, Huffington Post,* and *NBC News.*[4]

According to a survey by Pew Research Center, over 60 percent of the 1,002 US adults surveyed believe that made-up news stories are causing confusion about the basic facts of current issues and events.[5] And the news only spreads faster when it is shared online.

When respondents were asked how fake news could be prevented, many felt that social networking providers and search engines, politicians, and the public itself should do its share to stop the level of fake news.

Although the respondents felt the negative impact of fake news, over one in four were confident in their ability to spot a fabricated news story, believing that their perception was not colored by the content of these reports.

Take a look at Figure 3.1. What do you see?

You might say you see three bars while someone else sees four. In this trick drawing neither answer is the "right" one. The cartoon illustrates the fact that we often perceive things differently from one another.

Components of the Perception Process

A number of factors may influence and distort perception, including the perceiver, the environment, and the focal object.

The Perceiver

Perceptions are shaped by past experiences, culture, attitude, values, upbringing, and more. This means the nature of the perceiver has a strong influence on the perceptual process. For example, say you were raised in an environment where working hard and being on time were considered very important. You might have a negative attitude toward a coworker who comes to work late or takes long work breaks. Once you have formed this perception, it might be difficult for you to change your mind about your coworker even if he performs well.

The Environment

The context or the setting also affects the perception process. For example, you may not notice a person dressed in athletic attire running on the street, but if she turned up at a high-level work meeting in the same clothes, she would definitely look out of place. People flocked to see Joshua Bell perform in a concert hall but failed to recognize him in the Metro station. The person remained the same, but the situation or context had changed, which in turn influenced the perception of him.

The Focal Object

The person, thing, or event being interpreted also affects our perception. Many businesspeople choose to drive expensive cars because they feel it makes a good impression on others, who they hope will perceive them as wealthy, successful, and

Michael Williamson/The Washington Post / Getty Images

Violinist Joshua Bell posed as a street performer in a Washington Metro station as part of an experiment by the *Washington Post*. At the end of the day, he had made just over $30 for performing six classical pieces.

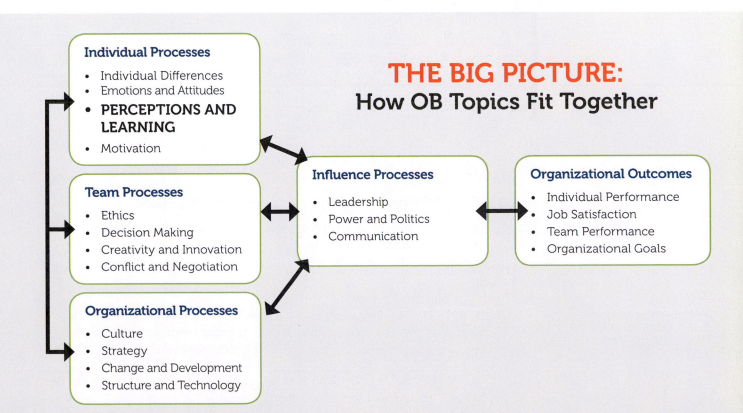

THE BIG PICTURE:
How OB Topics Fit Together

Individual Processes
- Individual Differences
- Emotions and Attitudes
- **PERCEPTIONS AND LEARNING**
- Motivation

Team Processes
- Ethics
- Decision Making
- Creativity and Innovation
- Conflict and Negotiation

Organizational Processes
- Culture
- Strategy
- Change and Development
- Structure and Technology

Influence Processes
- Leadership
- Power and Politics
- Communication

Organizational Outcomes
- Individual Performance
- Job Satisfaction
- Team Performance
- Organizational Goals

professional. However, in today's social context, do people really perceive owners of expensive cars in this way, or do they resent them for flaunting their success?[6] We tend to perceive objects in terms of contrast. For example, we might interpret the driver of the expensive car in a different way to someone else depending on their situation. Similarly, we perceive people who stand out differently from others—a work colleague who is vocal in meetings might be perceived differently from one who says very little.

Why Is Perception Important?

In 1936, psychologist Kurt Lewin observed that people act not upon the basis of reality, but upon their *perceptions* of reality.[7] In other words, we tend to interpret events differently from what actually happens in our environment. Therefore, understanding perception is a critical part of understanding behavior. In the workplace, the way we are perceived and the way in which we perceive others are crucial for career progress and for building our relationships. For example, a salesperson's success or failure depends on how he is perceived by prospective customers. He could have all the knowledge in the world about a product, but if he is perceived as overeager or too talkative, he is unlikely to make the sale. This is why many people in sales roles use self-critiquing techniques such as videoing themselves or seeking feedback from others in order to perceive themselves as others do. Salespeople who actively listen, communicate sincerely, and show a genuine interest in the person to whom they are selling tend to excel and to have more successful customer relationships.[8]

Uncritically allowing our perceptions to take control can create distorted versions of reality that can be very harmful to working relationships.

THINKING CRITICALLY

1. Consider the text's point that we often perceive things differently from others and that no one perception is necessarily right. What, from an OB perspective, are the benefits of differences of perception when a team of people is working on a project? What are the potential drawbacks of perceptual differences when a team is working together on a project?

Common Perceptual Distortions

>> LO 3.2   **Explain the different types of perceptual distortions**

Each and every day we take in and process a huge amount of complex information. Our attempts to organize and sift this information can lead to inaccuracies and clouds our perceptions of different people, situations, and events. Let's explore some common perceptual distortions:

Stereotypes: An individual's fixed beliefs about the characteristics of a particular group

- **Stereotypes** are an individual's fixed beliefs about the characteristics of a particular group.[9] When we have a particular feeling or attitude (often negative) toward members of a specific group, we call this *prejudice*. In a study of how people interact with avatars during an online game conducted by Penn State, researchers discovered that stereotypes in the real world relating to women and appearance were also reflected in the virtual world.[10]

For instance, women avatars tended to receive less help from players than male avatars, especially when male players operated an unattractive female avatar.

- **Selective attention** is the tendency to selectively focus on aspects of situations that are most aligned with our own interests, values, and attitudes.[11] Two classic experiments show the power of selective attention. In the first, participants are asked to watch a short video of six people playing basketball.[12] The challenge is to count the number of passes made by the three players wearing white T-shirts. During the game, a gorilla walks into the middle of the players, thumps his chest, and leaves. Over half of the participants in the experiment missed the gorilla because their attention was focused on counting the passes. The second experiment called "the Door Study" shows a man asking another man for directions.[13] At one point, people carrying a door passes between them, allowing the man who is asking directions to quickly swap places with another person. The person giving directions doesn't notice he is interacting with an entirely different person. Both these experiments reveal the extent of how much we miss around us without having any idea of what we are missing.

  > **Selective attention:** The tendency to selectively focus on aspects of situations that are most aligned with our own interests, values, and attitudes

- **Halo effect** is a perception problem in which our impression of someone is influenced by how we think or feel about their character.[14] Studies have found that we tend to ascribe positive personality traits to attractive people.[15] So if we perceive a person as good-looking, successful, and likable, then we also believe them to be intelligent, kind, and humorous. However this sort of perception can be dangerous—one study found that when the Halo effect is in force, jurors are less likely to give a guilty verdict to an attractive criminal.

  > **Halo effect:** A perception problem through which we form a positive or negative bias of an individual based on our overall impressions of that person

- **Primacy effect** is a perception problem in which an individual assesses a person quickly on the basis of the first information encountered.[16] Research conducted by *Harvard Business Review* based on recordings of over 160 candidates shows that small talk does have an influence on how interviewers perceive the candidates and vice versa.[17] By engaging in competent, friendly, informal talk before the formal interview, both parties will have a better chance of building a rapport and making a good impression, thus minimizing the primacy effect.

  > **Primacy effect:** A perception problem through which an individual assesses a person quickly on the basis of the first information encountered

- **Recency effect** is a perception problem in which we use the most recent information available to assess a person.[18] For example, if you test drive or buy a certain car, suddenly you see all kinds of these cars—same exact make and color—on the road that you never saw before.

  > **Recency effect:** A perception problem through which we use the most recent information available to assess a person

- **Contrast effect** takes place when people rank something higher or lower than they should as a result of exposure to recent events or situations.[19] Contrast effect occurs particularly among recruiters who tend to compare large volumes of résumés in a row, judging each résumé on the one that came before it, or when interviewing, forming an opinion on candidates based on the candidate before them.[20] This is problematic as recruiters should only be basing their opinions on how candidates' skills and attributes fit the job, rather than making comparisons with others.

  > **Contrast effect:** An effect that takes place when people rank something higher or lower than they should as a result of exposure to recent events or situations

- **Projecting** is a process in which people transfer their own thoughts, motivations, feelings, and desires to others.[21] For example, a person who takes a dislike to someone else may project their own feelings onto that person and convince themselves that the other person doesn't like them either.[22]

  > **Projecting:** A process through which people ascribe their own personal attributes onto others

Self-fulfilling prophecy: The way a person behaves based on pre-existing expectations about another person or situation so as to create an outcome that is aligned with those expectations

Impression management: The process by which we attempt to influence the perceptions others may have of us

Ingratiation: A strategy of winning favor and putting oneself in the good graces of others before making a request

- **Self-fulfilling prophecy** occurs when a person bases behavior on preexisting expectations about another person or situation in order to create an outcome aligned with those expectations.[23] One growing type of self-fulfilling prophecy is the "school-to-prison pipeline."[24] Sociologists believe that children who are labeled by others as delinquents or criminals has the effect of producing that same behavior.

- **Impression management** (IM) is the process by which we attempt to influence the perceptions others may have of us.[25] For example, we tend to engage in IM on social media sites such as Facebook and Instagram to make a certain impression on our friends and family but may engage in a different sort of IM when it comes to posting on professional sites, such as LinkedIn.[26] A facet of impression management is **ingratiation,** in which an individual attempts to influence others by becoming more attractive or likable. A recent HBR study found that the business executives who behave in the most ingratiating manner toward their CEOs are also the ones most likely to speak about those CEOs negatively or criticize them to the press.[27]

Forming accurate perceptions of others is a complex process. Awareness of these common perceptual distortions may help you to avoid making them about others and may also allow you to combat inaccurate perceptions others may form about you. In addition to perceptual distortion, it's also important to understand attribution theory.

THINKING CRITICALLY

1. Choose one of the perceptual distortions discussed (stereotypes, selective attention, halo effect, primary effect, recency effect, contrast effect, project, self-fulfilling prophecy, and impression management) and briefly describe a situation where your perception of another person was impacted by that distortion.

2. What do you think are the top three perceptual distortions that managers are most likely to be affected by when forming perceptions of their direct reports? Explain your answer.

3. What do you think are the top three perceptual distortions that employees are most likely to be affected by when forming perceptions of a new manager? Defend your answer.

Common Attribution Errors

>> LO 3.3   **Apply attribution theory to more effectively interpret behavior**

When we see someone behave in a certain way, we tend to try and make sense of it or at least attach some meaning to it. **Attribution theory** holds that people look for two causes to explain the behavior of others: *internal attributions,* which are personal characteristics of others, and *external attributions,* which are situational factors.[28]

Attribution theory: A theory that holds that people look for two causes to explain the behavior of others: internal attributions, which are personal characteristics of others, and external attributions, which are situational factors

For example, say you worked with a colleague called Tom who has a problem with absenteeism. How would you make sense of his behavior? Do you think he is lazy and indifferent? Or do you think he is so overloaded with responsibilities that he finds the prospect of coming to work overwhelming? If you choose the first option, you would ascribe Tom's behavior to internal causes: you believe Tom's absenteeism is a result of laziness and apathy. However, if you choose the latter option, you are attributing Tom's behavior to external causes: you blame overwhelming amounts of work for his poor attendance record.

Three factors influence our internal and external attributions: consistency, distinctiveness, and consensus, as outlined in Figure 3.2.[29]

Consistency is the extent to which a person responds in the same way over a period of time. For example, if Tom is late arriving at work every morning (high consistency in the same situation), we tend to ascribe his tardiness to internal causes and assume he is just not a punctual person. If, however, he is only late to work on Fridays (low consistency in the same situation), then we might assume an external cause, such as his wife must be at work early on Fridays and he must drop his children off at school.

Distinctiveness is the extent to which a person behaves consistently in similar situations. For example, if Tom tends to be frequently late to work, late returning from lunch, and late to mid-morning staff meetings (low distinctiveness across situations), we might ascribe his behavior to internal factors such as being lazy and indifferent. Conversely, if Tom is punctual in most situations but is sometimes late returning from lunch (high distinctiveness across situations), we might ascribe his tardiness in that particular situation to the fact that he sometimes visits his aging grandmother during lunch to see if she needs any heavy chores done around her house.

Consensus looks at how everyone else responds in the same situation. For example, if several people in the office are absent or late on the same day (high consensus with other people in the same situation), we might ascribe this behavior to an external attribution such as a dust storm that has slowed the morning commute for everyone or a virus or flu that has spread through the office. Conversely, if everyone else but Tom has arrived on time and is not absent on a given day (low consensus with other people in the same situation), we are more likely to attribute Tom's tardiness or absence to internal factors.

It is important to try and make sense of the behaviors of others in order to form the most meaningful conclusion. However, as the following section shows, it is also easy for us to make wrong judgments.

When perceiving others, we sometimes make erroneous judgments when assessing their behaviors. Take Nike employee Amanda, for instance. She traveled a lot but she still wanted to stay connected to her team, so whenever she was back in the office, she instituted an open-door policy. When she received her performance review, she was shocked to read that some people didn't feel they were being listened to. When she investigated further, she found that what she perceived as multitasking (such as replying to emails, etc.) during the meetings, they perceived as rudeness. So Amanda changed around her office and made sure she gave her full attention to the person she was talking to and kept her computer out of sight. In making these changes, she was able to change people's erroneous judgment about her behavior.[30]

FIGURE 3.2

Determinants of Attribution

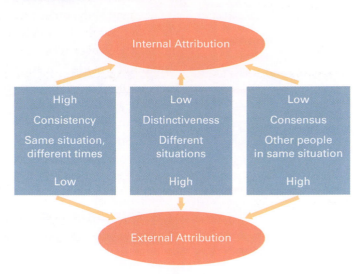

Source: Based on Mehlman, Rick C., and C. R. Snyder. "Excuse Theory: A Test of the Self-Protective Role of Attributions." *Journal of Personality and Social Psychology* 49, no. 4 (October 1985): 994–1001.

Fundamental attribution error:
The tendency to underestimate the influence of external factors and overestimate the impact of internal factors when making judgments about the behavior of others

Self-serving bias: The tendency for individuals to attribute their own successes to internal factors and put the blame for failures on external factors

There are two common attribution errors: fundamental attribution error, and self-serving bias. **Fundamental attribution error** is the inclination to attribute internal factors to the behavior of others more than external factors.[31] For example, if we are working with someone we perceive to be difficult or who keeps making mistakes, we might put the blame on some facet of their personality such as laziness or disorganized. However, when we make a mistake, we usually attribute the error to our own situation ("I made a mistake because I'm tired, stressed, working too hard…") rather than blaming our own personality.[32]

Self-serving bias is the tendency for individuals to attribute external factors more than internal factors for one's own failures.[33] For example, say you got top marks in an exam; you might attribute your success to studying hard (internal factors). But what if you failed? Instead of accepting your lack of study as the reason you failed, you might blame external factors such as the room being too warm, or being tired.[34]

THINKING CRITICALLY

1. Imagine that you are waiting in line to purchase groceries. You notice that your line is moving very slowly because the high school aged student who is bagging groceries is flirting with the cashier rather than working quickly and paying attention to customers. What internal and external attributions might you apply to this behavior? Try to generate at least 3 options for each type of attribution.

2. Briefly describe distinctiveness, consistency, and consensus. Apply these three concepts to a recent situation in your life at work, home, or school. Explain how these concepts attributed to your perception of the situation. Support your answer.

3. Describe what you could do in a difficult work situation to protect yourself from falling prey to fundamental attribution error.

4. Based on the chapter's discussion of self-serving bias, devise a list of questions you could ask yourself in order to determine whether you are attributing all positive outcomes to your own internal attributes and all negative outcomes to external attributes.

Learning Processes: Behavioral Theory

Learning: An ongoing process through which individuals adjust their behavior based on experience

>> LO 3.4   Use reinforcement theory to understand learning and modify behavior

Perception is shaped by **learning,** an ongoing process through which individuals adjust their behavior based on experience.[35] Understanding the way we learn is essential to OB because it has a direct influence on our work performance, our ability to relate to others, and our career progression. We all learn in different ways, and it is never too late to learn new skills. In fact, recent studies have shown that contrary to common thought, it is not just children who can easily absorb new languages; adults are just as capable of learning new linguistic skills with the same ease. Indeed, studies demonstrate that we are capable of learning any new skill, or even a few at a time, as long as we change our mind-set and focus on the task at hand.[36]

Learning opens up so many opportunities for us in every aspect of our daily existence. In the OB in the Real World feature, we see how Matt Nuyen of Currency Capital implements various techniques and strategies such as on-the-job training to help cultivate a culture that values learning.

To better understand learning behaviors, it is useful to evaluate the behavioral interpretations provided by different theorists over the past century. The behavioral view holds that behavior is shaped and learned as a result of external environmental stimuli. There are three important contributions within the behavioral perspective: classical conditioning, operant conditioning, and reinforcement theory.

Classical Conditioning

The concept of **classical conditioning** was developed by Russian physiologist Ivan Pavlov. Classical conditioning suggests that learning can be accomplished through the use of stimuli.[37] Pavlov's most famous experiment used different stimuli to elicit a behavioral response in dogs. Pavlov found that dogs began to salivate in response to the ringing of a bell—a *neutral stimulus*—before they were given food—an *unconditioned stimulus*. Eventually, the bell became a *conditioned stimulus* that caused the dogs to salivate *(conditioned response)* without the food being present. The steps are outlined in Figure 3.3.

We find evidence of classical conditioning in the workplace during fire drills. Most companies carry out fire drills to instill safety procedures in their employees in the event of a fire. When we hear the fire alarm (conditioned stimulus), we respond by leaving the building (conditioned response). However, if we saw a fire (unconditioned response) in the office without the fire alarm going off, many of us would react with the conditioned response of running away from the perceived danger. Although classical conditioning explains a great deal about why we react to certain stimuli, researchers have developed more sophisticated theories to explain why we behave the way we do.

Operant Conditioning Theory

Operant conditioning is the process of forming associations between learning and behavior that occurs when the consequences of behavior are being controlled.[38] At the root of operant conditioning is the law of effect theory devised by US psychologist E. L. Thorndike, which states that behavior followed by pleasant results is more likely to be repeated, whereas behavior followed by unpleasant results is not.[39] For example, if your boss reprimands you for being late to work, you are less likely to repeat the behavior. Theorists have since refined operant conditioning into the more comprehensive reinforcement theory.

Reinforcement Theory

Pioneered by psychologist B. F. Skinner and his colleagues, reinforcement theory is

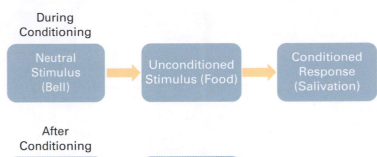

FIGURE 3.3

Classical Conditioning

During Conditioning

| Neutral Stimulus (Bell) | → | Unconditioned Stimulus (Food) | → | Conditioned Response (Salivation) |

After Conditioning

| Neutral Stimulus (Bell) | → | Conditioned Response (Salivation) |

Classical conditioning: A conditioning concept developed by Russian physiologist Ivan Pavlov that suggests that learning can be accomplished through the use of stimuli

Operant conditioning: The process of forming associations between learning and behavior by controlling its consequences

Operant conditioning follows the idea that a behavior followed by positive results is likely to be repeated. Rewarding employees for a job well done can encourage further positive performance.

FIGURE 3.4

Reinforcement Theory

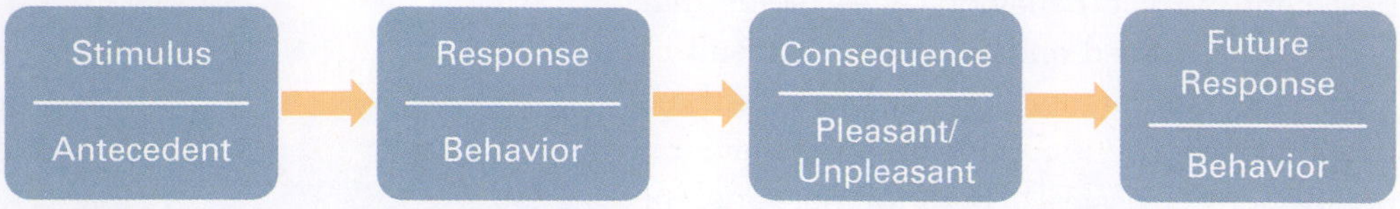

| Stimulus ——— Antecedent | → | Response ——— Behavior | → | Consequence ——— Pleasant/ Unpleasant | → | Future Response ——— Behavior |

the most fully developed theory of operant conditioning to date.[40] We define **reinforcement** as the application of consequences for the purpose of establishing patterns of behavior. Within **reinforcement theory,** behavior is a function of its consequences and is determined exclusively by environmental factors such as external stimuli and other reinforcers. The steps in the reinforcement process, sometimes referred to as the ABCs of behavior, are outlined in Figure 3.4.

For example, a curious child sees a hot stove (stimulus); the child touches the stove (response); the child gets burned and cries out in pain (consequence); the child avoids touching hot stoves in the future (future responses).

The practical application of reinforcement in the workplace is called **organizational behavior modification,** which is the use of behavioral techniques to reinforce positive work behavior and discourage unhelpful work behavior.[41] Research has shown that when employees are permitted to design their own roles in accordance with their skills, passion, and values—in organizations like Google, for example—it leads to a more positive work performance.[42] There are four main types of behavioral reinforcement techniques: positive reinforcement, negative reinforcement, punishment, and extinction.

Positive and Negative Reinforcement

Many managers use **positive reinforcement,** in which positive consequences are used to reinforce positive behaviors to make the employee more likely to behave in similar ways in the same or similar situations.[43] Disney applies positive reinforcement through recognition programs, and by showing sincere appreciation for its employees by writing personal thank you notes.[44]

Conversely, **negative reinforcement** is the removal of a particular item or stimulus following the demonstration of a certain behavior in order to increase that behavior. For example, say you hate when your mom nags you to wash the dishes. You might start doing the dishes immediately after the meal is finished in order to avoid your mom's nagging.[45]

In another example of positive and negative reinforcement, a group of university psychology students carried out a behavioral experiment on their professor. The professor had a habit of pacing back and forth and up and down the classroom during lectures, which the students found distracting and frustrating. To encourage him to remain in the center of the room where all the students could see and hear him, whenever he wandered there, the students applied the positive reinforcement of behaving as if they were fully engaged and focused on what he was saying. However, when the professor wandered to another point in the room, the students behaved as if they weren't listening until he returned to the center of the room, at which time they

Reinforcement: The application of consequences to establish patterns of behavior

Reinforcement theory: A theory that states that behavior is a function of its consequences and is determined exclusively by environmental factors such as external stimuli and other reinforcers

Organizational behavior modification: The use of behavioral techniques to reinforce positive work behavior and discourage unhelpful work behavior.

Positive reinforcement: A reinforcement contingency through which behaviors followed by positive consequences, are more likely to occur again in the same or similar situations

Negative reinforcement: A reinforcement contingency through which behaviors are followed by the removal of previously experienced negative consequences, resulting in the likelihood that the behavior will occur again in the same or similar situations

refocused their attention, thereby providing negative reinforcement. A quarter of the way through the semester, the students noticed a change in the professor's lecturing habit: he remained in the center of the classroom from then on.[46]

Punishment

Punishment is the administration of unpleasant consequences or removal of positive ones for the purpose of discouraging undesirable behavior.[47] There are two types of punishment: positive punishment—the administering of unpleasant consequences—and negative punishment—the removal of pleasant consequences.[48] For example, say your manager reprimands you for interrupting him during a meeting—this is positive punishment because your manager has administered unpleasant consequences that decrease the likelihood of your interrupting him again. Conversely, suppose that after the interruption your manager stops addressing comments to you and asking for your input; this is negative punishment because your manager has removed positively reinforcing consequences in an effort to eliminate your unappreciated behavior.

Punishment: A reinforcement contingency that discourages undesirable behavior by administering unpleasant consequences

Extinction

Using punishment techniques in the workplace can be risky and demotivating, which is why many managers often choose **extinction,** the absence of any consequences, which reduces the likelihood that the behavior will be repeated in the same or similar situations.[49] In one example, an employee continually makes jokes during important meetings, resulting in disapproving frowns from some of his teammates and laughter from others. In this situation, the employee may be seeking attention, which both the positive and negative reactions are rewarding. The manager instructs the rest of the team to pay no attention to this person during meetings. As a result, he no longer makes jokes because the reinforcing consequences of that behavior have been removed.

Extinction: A reinforcement contingency in which a behavior is followed by the absence of any consequence, thereby reducing the likelihood that the behavior will be repeated in the same or similar situations

Schedules of Reinforcement

Schedules of reinforcement determine how often specific instances of behaviors will be reinforced. In the real world, it is unrealistic to think that every single behavior will be reinforced every time it occurs, but some organizations select a reinforcement schedule when they are trying to reinforce specific desired behaviors. There are two main types of schedules: continuous reinforcement and intermittent reinforcement.

Continuous reinforcement is a reinforcement schedule in which behavior is rewarded every time it takes place.[50] For example, some companies reward their sales teams with commissions every time they make a sale.

In **intermittent reinforcement,** behavior is not rewarded every time it occurs.[51] There are four types of intermittent schedules:

Continuous reinforcement: A reinforcement schedule in which a reward occurs after each instance of a behavior or set of behaviors

Intermittent reinforcement: Reinforcement schedule in which a reward does not occur after each instance of a behavior or set of behaviors

- Many companies use a *fixed interval schedule*, a reward provided only after a certain period of time has elapsed, as the most common form of reinforcement schedule.[52] For example, employees receive a monthly or annual paycheck for working during a fixed period of time or interval.

- A *fixed ratio schedule* is followed when desired behaviors are rewarded after they have been exhibited a fixed number of times.[53] For example, production line workers may be rewarded with a cash incentive every time they produce a certain number of items.

- A *variable interval schedule* is designed to reinforce behavior at varying times.[54] For example, an employee may be rewarded with high praise following desirable behavior during periods of different length. However, employers need to ensure that too much time does not pass between reinforcements, because this might reduce the schedule's effectiveness.

- Finally, a *variable ratio schedule* rewards people after the desired behavior has occurred after a varying number of times.[55] For example, in a call center, the more calls workers make, the higher the chance of closing a sale, leading to greater financial compensation.

Behavioral theory provides a greater understanding of workplace behavior that occurs in response to external environmental stimuli. However, cognitive theorists believe the behavioral view is too limited, arguing that behavioral theorists do not take into account the mental processes behind the behavior. In the next section, we explore the cognitive view and the role it plays in shaping human behavior.

THINKING CRITICALLY

1. Re-read the fire alarm example in the classical conditioning section. Develop a different example of a type of classical conditioning response.

2. Praise can be a type of positive reinforcement used by managers. List at least three additional positive reinforcements that are used in the workplace. Of the reinforcements you list, which do you find most personally motivating and why?

3. You are the CTO of an educational startup focused on building a learning management system that out-performs Blackboard. You're concerned that your programmers are sticking to the same tried and true methods to improve your platform. What negative reinforcements might you apply in order to foster more creative and novel solutions? What positive reinforcements might you apply? Which of the two types of reinforcement do you believe would be most successful in fostering a spirit of innovation among your programmers?

4. You are an African American woman who has been hired to lead an all-white, all-male team of programmers. They don't have difficulty accepting your authority, but they do seem to have a hard time getting over the novelty of reporting to a woman and minority in an industry in which most workers are white and male. You're getting tired of their jokes and quips. How could you use the concept of extinction to reduce and eventually put a stop to this behavior? How could you use negative punishment to reduce the behavior? Do you believe one approach or the other would be more effective in diminishing the behavior? Why or why not?

5. Compare continuous reinforcement strategies to intermittent reinforcement strategies. What benefits would a company receive from implementing intermittent reinforcement strategies rather than continuous reinforcement strategies to achieve sales goals? What potential problems might arise as a result of this decision?

Learning Processes: The Cognitive View

>> LO 3.5   Apply social cognitive theory to social learning and cognitive processes

In **social cognitive theory,** psychologist Albert Bandura proposed that we learn by observing, imitating, and modeling the behavior of others within our social context.[56] The theory holds that our cognitive processes, which include awareness, perception, reasoning, and judgment, play important roles in how we learn new knowledge and skills.

This type of learning is particularly significant in the workplace, where employees tend to model the behavior of their managers. For example, a manager who demonstrates commitment, works late when needed, and completes projects on time is likely to lead a team with a similar work ethic. Conversely, if a manager arrives to work late, leaves early, and takes long lunch breaks, then employees are likely to imitate this behavior, leading to a decrease in work productivity and performance. Another example involves our OB in the Real World manager, Matt Nuyen, and his focus on mentorship. A mentor is a guide who advises less experienced employees to support them with their career direction help to develop new skills and abilities.

There are several important aspects of social cognitive theory. The first is **self-efficacy,** which describes our personal belief in our ability to perform certain tasks or behaviors.[57] For example, Twitter's policy of entrusting its employees to put their learning into practice gives them a high degree of self-efficacy.

The second component of social cognitive theory is **vicarious learning,** a process of learning by watching the actions or behaviors of another person. Twitter encourages its employees to learn by emulating the behavior of their managers. Similarly, Currency Capital fosters vicarious learning through its mentorship program where new hires learn from seasoned high-performing employees.

Vicarious learning is particularly important in organizations as it encourages the sharing of knowledge among employees. Studies have shown that Fortune 500 companies lose over $30 billion per year because of insufficient vicarious learning.[59] Google promotes vicarious learning by creating dedicated spaces (small kitchen spaces) where people can interact and hold learning conversations.[60]

This type of learning is also important in the sports world. For example, an amateur tennis player may find that her ground strokes are better after watching TV coverage of the Championships, Wimbledon tennis tournament, and seeing professionals hitting the ball so effectively.

Vicarious learning also influences our degree of self-efficacy.[61] For example, if you see a colleague on a similar career path successfully giving the weekly presentation during a meeting, you might be more inclined to volunteer to do the next one, because you have observed this event as a positive experience, thereby increasing your self-efficacy for doing presentations. However, if you observe the same colleague stumble nervously through the presentation, it might give you second thoughts about doing one yourself, resulting in low self-efficacy for giving presentations.

Social cognitive theory: A theory that proposes that learning takes place through the observation, imitation, and the modeling of others within a social context

Self-efficacy: The belief we have in our ability to succeed in a specific task or situation

Vicarious learning: A process of learning by watching the actions or behaviors of another person

Companies like Google promote vicarious learning by creating small kitchen spaces to encourage communication and learning opportunities.

OB IN THE REAL WORLD

Matt Nuyen, Head of Sales at Currency Capital

After the market crashed in 2008, small businesses found it increasingly difficult to get the financing they needed to expand their operations. Banks were lending less and when they were, the application process took way too long. In response to this, a team of financial gurus created a system that streamlined the lending process and made it easier for businesses to get the loans they needed. Initial approvals of loans and funding to a business's bank accounts can now happen overnight with Currency Capital's methods of gaining a more complete financial picture of a business at the beginning of the process. Currency's more than one hundred fifty employees are spread out between its headquarters in Los Angeles and satellite offices in Orange County, San Francisco, and Scottsdale. W Capital's operations reach much further than the West Coast as it funds businesses in every corner of the country.

Matt Nuyen, head of sales in the Scottsdale, AZ office, has been with the company since its beginning and has been a huge contributor to its current corporate culture. Matt's job is highly multi-faceted as he is responsible for revenue growth, human resources, business strategy, the sustainable growth of the Scottsdale office, and employee training. Matt has implemented various techniques and strategies to help cultivate a culture that values self-sufficiency, collaboration, and most importantly, learning.

Matt knows that his people are his greatest, most valuable assets so he invests in them. On-the-job training, especially in sales, is vital to the growth of any employee. Before even getting to work on the sales floor a new employee has two days of classroom training. After that, they are assigned a mentor and thrown onto the sales

floor. Mentorship is a very important tactic that Matt uses in training new hires. The mentors are typically seasoned, high-performing employees who receive compensatory benefits that are tied to the performance of their mentee. Their primary job is to help the new hires learn from their failures and gain confidence in their work.

According to Matt, "Confidence starts day 1. We want to build a culture of transparency where we encourage learning from failure. We want a very gritty group of individuals who accept challenges and embrace failures as learning opportunities."

This starts with the interview process. When Matt and his other hiring managers go to interview a potential new hire, they are constantly analyzing the candidate's "coachability." This job requires people who are coachable and who are hungry to learn and develop. Currency's employees are taught never to take short cuts and to embrace learning the skills their jobs require.

As Matt puts it, "rather than giving someone fish, we want to teach them how to fish."

Teaching the employees how to "fish for themselves" goes a long way in maintaining an extremely productive work environment and helps to develop future leaders of the business.

While reaching the point of self-sufficiency is valued, collaboration and learning from one's peers is what makes Currency's work environment so special. Employees know that they are encouraged to ask questions and seek advice from their colleagues and superiors. If you were to go and walk the sales floor at the Scottsdale office, you would see employees asking each other questions, constructively criticizing each other's work, and strategizing with one another for certain situations. You would also see Matt walking the floor, engaging with his employees, answering questions, and running an occasional spot check on an employee. Matt is a hybrid leader who has qualities of a directive leader but also knows how to empower his employees to take initiative, make recommendations, and get the job done the way they see fit (only if it is effective, of course).

1. Why might mentorship be a good strategy to develop new hires?

2. Explain Matt's mantra, "instead of giving people fish, we want to teach them how to fish," and how it relates to management.

3. How does social cognitive theory apply to Matt's approach to managing his employees? ●

Source: Interview with Matt Nuyen on May 1, 2017

EXAMINING THE EVIDENCE

Snakes, Self-Efficacy, and Task Performance: Too Much of a Good Thing?

Some very interesting early classic studies examining the concept of self-efficacy focused on people with a fear of snakes.* Albert Bandura and his colleagues set up an experiment using both an experimental group and a control group, with a pre-test indicating that both groups had strong fear of snakes and low self-efficacy for approaching and handling them. The researchers then carried out an intervention with the experimental group. They explained that the snakes were not poisonous and would not bite, and they described how the snakes would react when the subjects handled them. They also informed the group that the snakes were not cold and slimy, but actually dry and scaly. The researchers then measured the fear and self-efficacy levels in both groups again. Both groups still had a high fear of snakes, but the experimental group had a much higher level of self-efficacy for approaching and handling the snakes. Consequently, when members of both groups were asked to approach and handle the snakes, those from the experimental group whose level of self-efficacy had increased were able to do so at a much higher rate than those with low self-efficacy.

Although hundreds of studies have shown similar positive effects for self-efficacy on task performance, some recent studies have called this relationship into question.# These studies suggest that high levels of self-efficacy within an individual could cause that person to become overconfident and to allocate fewer resources and less effort to the task at hand, thereby resulting in lower levels of task performance. For example, one study of students playing an analytical game showed a negative relationship between self-efficacy and performance.[58] Self-efficacy resulted in overconfidence and the increased likelihood of making a logical error in the game.

Critical-Thinking Questions

1. Given the conflicting research evidence, how can self-efficacy affect individual task performance in the workplace?

2. What can managers do to try to enhance the positive effects of self-efficacy in their employees? ●

Sources:

*Bandura, Albert, and Nancy E. Adams. "Analysis of Self-Efficacy Theory of Behavioral Change." *Cognitive Therapy and Research* 1, no. 4 (December 1977): 287–310; Bandura, Albert, Linda Reese, and Nancy E. Adams. "Microanalysis of Action and Fear Arousal as a Function of Differential Levels of Perceived Self-Efficacy." *Journal of Personality and Social Psychology* 43, no. 1 (July 1982): 5–21.

#Vancouver, Jeffrey B., Charles M. Thompson, E. Casey Tischner, and Dan J. Putka. "Two Studies Examining the Negative Effect of Self-Efficacy on Performance." *Journal of Applied Psychology* 87, no. 3 (June 2002): 506–516.

The third factor of social cognitive theory is **self-regulation,** the process in which we set goals that create a discrepancy between a desired state and a current state.[62] This discrepancy creates tension, which drives us to increase effort to reduce tension and reach the goal. For example, your manager sets a goal for you to complete a complex project within two weeks; you might feel uncomfortable or nervous about your ability to achieve the goal within the allotted time frame, so you work harder in order to reduce your feelings of discomfort and to successfully complete the assignment on time.

Self-regulation: A process whereby people set goals, creating a discrepancy between the desired state and the current state

Triadic Reciprocal Model of Behavior

Bandura also believed human functioning is shaped by three factors that are reciprocally related: reinforcement, cognitive processes, and behavior.[63] The relationship is shown graphically in the **triadic reciprocal model of behavior** (Figure 3.5).

Figure 3.5 shows how cognitive processes mediate the effects of reinforcers on behavior and how behavior influences both reinforcers and cognitive processes. Consider two quarterbacks in a football game. The first throws an interception. This causes him to think that he is not an effective passer and lowers his self-efficacy for completing passes. Lower self-efficacy causes him to become tentative,

Triadic reciprocal model of behavior: A model that shows human functioning shaped by three factors that are reciprocally related: reinforcement, cognitive processes, and behavior

FIGURE 3.5

Triadic Reciprocal Model of Behavior

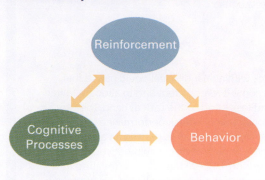

make more mistakes, and throw more incompletions and interceptions. His poor play encourages the defensive players to try even harder, which creates more negative reinforcers in the form of pressure.

In contrast, the second quarterback also throws an interception. However, unlike the first, he acknowledges his mistake and is determined to try harder; his self-efficacy remains constant. He increases his efforts, which leads to a touchdown pass. This success increases his self-efficacy even further. The defensive players become tentative because of his good play, which leads to even more success for the quarterback.

In this chapter, we have focused on the nature of perception and the differing ways in which we perceive each other and ourselves. We have also explored learning and its importance to our working, personal, and professional lives. In the next chapter, we look at how motivation, attitudes, and stress impact our behavior.

THINKING CRITICALLY

1. You join a company where managers regularly reprimand their direct reports in front of others, play favorites, and encourage coworkers to report one another for making small mistakes. Based on Bandura's social cognitive theory, what sort of company culture is likely to spring from these practices? How would a new employee seek to "get ahead" at such a company and to what extent would efforts to succeed in this culture directly benefit the company's shareholders?

2. Of the three key aspects of social cognitive theory (self-efficacy, vicarious learning, and self-regulation), which do you think is most important in adjusting to a new and particularly challenging job? Defend your response.

3. Apply the triadic reciprocal model of behavior to a recent situation in your life at work, home, or school. How does the model help to explain your behavior in this situation? ●

$SAGE edge™

Visit **edge.sagepub.com/neckob2e** to help you accomplish your coursework goals in an easy-to-use learning environment.

- Mobile-friendly eFlashcards and practice quizzes
- Video and multimedia content
- Chapter summaries with learning objectives
- EXCLUSIVE! Access to full-text SAGE journal articles

IN REVIEW

3.1 Describe the basic concept of perception

Perception is the process by which we receive and interpret information from our environment. A number of factors influence and perhaps distort perception, including the perceiver, the environment, and the focal object. Perceptions are shaped by past experiences, culture, attitude, values, upbringing, and so on. This means that the nature of the *perceiver* has a strong influence on the perceptual process. The context or the setting also affects the perception process. The person, thing, or event being interpreted also affects our perception.

3.2 Explain the different types of perceptual distortions

People process a huge amount of complex information, and their attempts to organize and sift this information can lead to inaccuracies. There are a number of common perceptual distortions. **Stereotypes** are an individual's fixed beliefs about the characteristics of a particular group. **Selective attention** is the tendency to selectively focus on aspects of situations that are most aligned with our own interests, values, and attitudes. **Halo effect** is a perception problem through which we form a positive or negative view of one aspect of an individual based on our overall impressions of that person. **Primacy effect** is a perception problem through which an individual assesses a person quickly on the basis of the first information encountered. **Recency effect** is a perception problem through which we use the most recent information available to assess a person. **Contrast effect** takes place when people rank something higher or lower than they should as a result of exposure to recent events or situations. **Projecting** is a process through which people transfer their own thoughts, motivations, feelings, and desires to others. **Self-fulfilling prophecy** occurs when a person bases behavior on pre-existing expectations about another person or situation in order to create an outcome aligned with those expectations. **Impression management** is the process by which we attempt to influence the perceptions others may have of us. A facet of impression management is **ingratiation,** by which an individual attempts to influence others by becoming more attractive or likeable.

3.3 Apply attribution theory to more effectively interpret behavior

Attribution theory holds that people look for two causes to explain the behavior of others: *internal attributions,* which are personal characteristics of others, and *external attributions*, which are situational factors. The theory holds that people tend to use two types of causal attributions to look for ways to explain the behavior of others: internal attributions, which are personal characteristics; and external attributions, which are situational factors.

There are three types of determinants of attribution that influence our internal and external attributions: distinctiveness, consensus, and consistency. *Distinctiveness* is the extent to which a person behaves consistently in similar situations. *Consensus* involves looking at how everyone else responds in the same situation. *Consistency* is the extent to which a person responds in the same way over a period of time.

3.4 Use reinforcement theory to understand learning and modify behavior

Learning is an ongoing process through which individuals adjust their behavior based on experience. **Reinforcement** is defined as the application of consequences to establish patterns of behavior. Within reinforcement theory, behavior is determined exclusively by environmental factors such as external stimuli and other reinforcers.

The practical application of reinforcement process in the workplace is called **organizational behavior modification,** which is the use of behavioral techniques to reinforce positive work behavior and discourage unhelpful work behavior.

3.5 Apply social cognitive theory to social learning and cognitive processes

The **social learning theory** proposes that learning takes place through the observation, imitation, and the modeling of others within a social context. There are several important components to social learning theory. The first is **self-efficacy,** which describes our personal conviction in our ability to perform certain tasks or behaviors. The second component to social learning is **vicarious learning,** a process of learning that involves watching the actions or behaviors of another person. Vicarious learning influences our degree of self-efficacy. The third factor of social learning is **self-regulation,** in which people set goals that create a discrepancy between the desired state and the current state.

KEY TERMS

Attribution theory   76
Classical conditioning   79
Continuous reinforcement   81
Contrast effect   75
Extinction   81
Fundamental attribution error   78
Halo effect   75
Impression management   76
Ingratiation   76
Intermittent reinforcement   81
Learning   78
Negative reinforcement   80
Operant conditioning   79
Organizational behavior modification   80
Perception   71
Positive reinforcement   80

Primacy effect   75
Projecting   75
Punishment   81
Recency effect   75
Reinforcement   80
Reinforcement theory   80
Selective attention   75
Self-efficacy   83
Self-fulfilling prophecy   76
Self-regulation   85
Self-serving bias   78
Social cognitive theory   83
Stereotypes   74
Triadic reciprocal model of behavior   85
Vicarious learning   83

UP FOR DEBATE: Setting High Expectations for New Hires

Large, world-class firms are known for setting very high expectations for new hires. In the financial services industry, for example, analysts often describe an "eat or be eaten" culture. They claim this stems from the expectation that analysts adjust and adapt the teaching style of the firm. Amidst all the criticism, these firms still tend to produce reliable, flexible, and hardworking employees that could bring tremendous value to virtually any industry. This goes to show that there is tremendous value in a rigid learning environment that drives out underperformers early on. Agree or disagree? Explain your answer.

EXERCISE 3.1: The Power of Perception

Objective

The purpose of this exercise is to gain a greater of perceptions.

Instructions

Perception is the process by which we receive and interpret information from our environment. Given that definition, think about your perceptions of this very course. In this exercise, you'll pair up with another student and discuss your initial perceptions of this course. Discuss what you initially thought based upon the professor, the syllabus, assignments, other students, and so on.

Recall the first day of the class and your very first thoughts. Whether the course is a traditional classroom style class, online, or a hybrid course, try and remember how you initially felt about the class.

Reflection Questions

1. What did you glean from the classroom environment on that first day that affected your perception of the course? What factors had the greatest influence? Do you still have these same perceptions about the course? Why or why not?

2. Did your partner have similar perceptions about the course? How were your and your partner's perceptions the same? Different?

3. What were your initial perceptions when you started your most recent job? How were those perceptions formed? Have your perceptions about the job changed? Why or why not?

EXERCISE 3.2: How Are Stereotypes Formed?

Objective

The purpose of this exercise is to grasp the concept of stereotypes.

Instructions

All kinds of stereotypes exist in business. As a class, brainstorm common business stereotypes you have heard of or you may even believe to be true. Your professor will capture the list on the board. Think in terms of every demographic—race, age, gender, social class, etc.

Once the list is complete, discuss why these stereotypes exist. Why do some continue while others are not so common? Are any of the stereotypes true? How does this affect our interactions with one another in the workplace?

Reflection Questions

1. How are stereotypes formed? Can our ideas about stereotypes change? Why or why not?

2. What stereotypes have you personally experienced in the workplace—as the one being stereotyped or where you stereotyped another person? How do you feel now about this experience?

3. How difficult was the process of identifying stereotypes in this exercise? Did any of the stereotypes make you feel uncomfortable? If so, why?

EXERCISE 3.3: Using OB to Improve Your Life

Objectives

After completing this exercise you will be able to better *understand* reinforcement theory concepts, and be able to *apply* reinforcement theory and social cognitive theory concepts to your personal and professional life.

Instructions

Step 1: Think about some behavior in your life you would like to improve and that you feel comfortable discussing with members of your class. Write down this behavior, and classify (i.e., does it relate to your school, personal, or work life?). Then decide if it is a behavior that you would like to increase the frequency of (such as exercising), or reduce the frequency of or eliminate (such as smoking). Note the key reasons you would like to change this behavior. Be sure to include what benefits the change would bring to you, friends, family, and colleagues. Then, using the reinforcement concepts you have learned in the chapter, set up a self-reinforcement plan for changing your behavior. Clearly define the behavior you want to change, set intermediate goals for your behavioral change (e.g., initially work out once a week, then advance to three times a week, and then reach five times a week). Next, set self-rewards for achieving and sustaining these behavioral changes. Be sure to specify the reward schedule and specific rewards that you will apply, and give the rationale behind your chosen schedule. Are there any natural rewards (related to changing the behavior) that might help? For example, would working out to your favorite music be more motivational? If possible, include ways that you can recruit friends, family, and other people to help you in your change plan. (10 minutes)

Step 2: Form into six groups based on behavioral change goal similarity. The groups are as follows:

- Behavior Frequency Increase—Work
- Behavior Frequency Increase—Social
- Behavior Frequency Increase—School
- Behavior Frequency Decrease—Work
- Behavior Frequency Decrease—Social
- Behavior Frequency Decrease—School

Once everyone has joined the appropriate group, each person should read their goal(s) and plan. In turn, the others should provide feedback on ways to improve the plan. (20 to 30 minutes)

Step 3: Be prepared to present your plan to the class, including any improvement suggestions from your group members. In your presentation, use chapter terms to describe your plan, and explain why you expect the plan to be effective using chapter concepts. (10 to 15 minutes)

Reflection Questions

This exercise is a good opportunity for you to think about and apply chapter concepts to personal, work, and educational goals and behaviors.

1. For your selected behavior, have you tried to change these behaviors before? How effective were you in making these changes?

2. Based on chapter concepts, if you implement your behavioral change plan, do you expect to see a different outcome?

3. Did the social cognitive aspect (discussing your plan with other people with similar behavioral plans) help you in the process?

4. As a manager, how might you apply similar methods to help workers reach their full potential at work?

Exercise contributed by Milton R. Mayfield, Professor of Business, Texas A&M International University, and Jacqueline R. Mayfield, Professor of Business, Texas A&M International University.

EXERCISE 3.4: The Maze Rat and Positive Reinforcement and Punishment

Objective

The purpose of this exercise is to grasp the concepts of positive reinforcement and punishment.

Instructions

This exercise requires several volunteers from the class and involves creating an obstacle course that a student will complete while blindfolded. First, a volunteer is chosen to be the "maze rat." Once this person is selected, he or she leaves the room for a moment. Then, three more volunteers come down to the front of the room and create a very simple obstacle course, consisting of tables and chairs. Again, nothing too complex—just something that keeps the "maze rat" from getting from point A to point B in a straight line. Finally, a volunteer is chosen to provide positive reinforcement.

Once the obstacle course is created, the "maze rat" is blindfolded (a scarf or jacket over his or her head should suffice) and brought by hand back into the classroom. The "maze rat" is placed at point A and told that he or she must get to point B in the obstacle course without removing the blindfold.

The "maze rat" is released and must slowly and carefully make his or her way to point B. If the "maze rat" goes in the wrong direction, the entire class should yell their disapproval. When the "maze rat" takes a step in the right direction, the person who volunteered to provide positive reinforcement will hand the "maze rat" a piece of candy.

The "maze rat" continues through the obstacle course—receiving positive reinforcement in the form of candy when the right path is chosen and punishment in the form of yelling from the audience when the wrong path is charted.

This continues until the "maze rat" completes the obstacle course and arrives at point B.

Reflection Questions

1. How effective was the punishment and positive reinforcement in helping the "maze rat" get from point A to point B?

2. What if no punishment or positive reinforcement occurred during this exercise? Would it have taken the "maze rat" longer to arrive at point B? Why or why not?

3. In the workplace, what forms of punishment and positive reinforcement are utilized? How effective are these?

Exercise contributed by Steven Stovall, Southeast Missouri State University.

ONLINE EXERCISE 3.1: Understanding Perceptions about Workplace Norms

Objective

The purpose of this exercise is to gain an appreciation for perceptions about workplace norms.

Instructions

On a discussion board, post a common normally accepted practice at your most recent job. For example, some companies highly value being on time for every meeting. Others, ensuring that PowerPoint presentations follow a particular format. Still, others have everyone using the same workplace jargon or wearing similar style clothes even though no uniform is required. Try and recall a particular norm from your job and explain it on your initial post.

Comment on others' posts asking, "How did that norm emerge?" or "Why is that important at your company?" and similar questions. Engage in a dialogue with one another as to why and how these norms occur and are perpetuated. Most importantly, also ask about perceptions of these norms. Do people seem to like the norm or do they resent it, or do they simply accept it without any real thought? Have their perceptions changed since they first encountered a particular workplace norm?

Reflection Questions

1. In the workplace, who do you think usually establishes a particular norm—the top leaders of the organization or the front line workers?

2. How has your own perceptions changed since the first day of the job you posted about? Do you still think of the norms associated with your organization as odd or have you accepted them as quite normal at this point? Why?

3. Were you surprised by anyone else's post? Did someone post a norm to which you had an instant negative reaction? What was it and what is your perception of this? If you worked at that particular company, do you think your perception would change about that norm that the other student posted? Why or why not?

Exercise contributed by Steven Stovall, Southeast Missouri State University.

CASE STUDY 3.1: Kempinski Hotels

Kempinski Hotels, headquartered in Switzerland, is Europe's oldest luxury hotel group, specializing in five-star properties that include the Emirates Palace in Abu Dhabi, the Hotel Taschenbergpalais Kempinski in Dresden, and the Çiragan Palace Kempinski in Istanbul. Founded in 1897, the Kempinski brand has an intriguing story to tell. "Our employees have been a part of creating history around the world," the website reads. "From historic buildings to the most avant-garde of modern architecture, our properties are the setting for some of life's greatest moments. We've witnessed historic meetings between world leaders, celebrities taking sanctuary in the world of calm we create for them, and created incredible memories for guests on a 'once-in-a-lifetime' journey."

In 2008, Kempinski was ready for a journey of its own: its portfolio of hotels was set to double by 2015, and its workforce was expected to grow from 7,500 to 37,500. How could Kempinski expand so dramatically without losing the soul that made it so unique?

Mia Norcao, vice president of corporate communication, realized that it was time to do some serious company soul-searching. Did employees understand the Kempinski brand? Were they armed with the knowledge and loyalty they needed to be true ambassadors to guests and to the world?

Norcao was part of a team that devised and implemented an elaborate plan to give every Kempinski employee a solid, intuitive understanding of what Kempinski was all about. The challenges were monumental. First and foremost, what *was* Kempinski all about? Despite its long, rich history, corporate values had never been consistently articulated—not in the Geneva-based boardroom, and certainly not at the front desk of any of its hundreds of hotels. Once those values had been identified, how could Norcao and her team communicate them to employees throughout the organization, given their widely varying levels of responsibility and education and the dozens of different languages they spoke?

Norcao knew she needed resources and buy-in from every level of the organization, starting with the top. "This last task was especially crucial—top management [the management board and regional presidents] had to commit their time and assign company resources to this program if we were to be successful with senior management on a group wide basis. They had to understand the link between delivering a consistent brand promise and guest experience, and actively managing our corporate culture," Norcao said. Explaining the benefits in dollars and sense was important. "We were able to demonstrate in business terms that when employee engagement is higher than 60 percent, total shareholder return can almost double, and conversely that if engagement drops below 25 percent, total shareholder return can be negatively impacted." Norcao's team showed that the organization already had 29 percent engagement—compared to the industry standard of 21—a solid start but with much room for improvement.

Once the top brass was on board, Norcao and her team conducted intensive interviews across the organization. Listening to the staff who lived the Kempinski experience every day helped shape what would eventually become five core values: "Being people oriented, being straightforward, encouraging entrepreneurial performance amongst staff, having the freedom to create traditions and being passionate about European luxury." The DNA of Kempinski's corporate culture had been identified. Now came the hard part: implementation.

How to reach every member of the organization in a meaningful way? How to make an impression on the concierge in Cairo and the maid in Munich? Clearly, an all-saturating, trickle-down approach was needed. But what was the model? "Our aim throughout was to create a corporate culture, which would empower staff to know instinctively what would be an appropriate way at Kempinski to solve a challenge, work with colleagues or serve our guests—not to limit them with strict rules," said Norcao.

Her team eventually opted for storytelling. "All cultures in the world have some form of story-telling tradition," Norcao said. Stories were collected from employees about emotional or memorable happenings at the hotel that represented one or more of the five core values. Campaigns were designed around the best of them, with "artwork and colors [that] were associated with each value, so that all collateral could have a consistent visual language—important again in helping illiterate staff identify values or stories."

Norcao started a storybook as her team built a wealth of tools to support managers: presentations, games, activities, session plans, Q&As, plus posters and brochures. A storytelling mini-site, "myStory", was constructed to collect touching, personal stories from employees all over the world. "The myStory space is among the most visited areas online and we've collected nearly 300 stories," Norcao commented. "This is very positive in an industry where most staff don't have time to regularly access a computer. Anecdotal evidence from sessions shows that staff often believe some or all of the original stories are about their hotel, which exhibits their pride, and belief in and ownership of these stories."

Today, Kempinski's growth plan is well underway, with more than seventy-five hotels worldwide in more than thirty countries and counting. "When I look back at the road we've traveled," Norcao continued, "I'm amazed to see how much we've accomplished with a relatively small budget but using a powerful storytelling approach to propagate our core values. . . . As part of my role, I spend time with senior managers when they first arrive at the company and often ask for their initial impressions of Kempinski (before mentioning our values) and am reassured that we haven't lost our soul—they always remark on how friendly, welcoming and practical everyone is. Some have even already heard of our values and can tell me their own stories."

Case Questions

1. Why did Norcao think that employee engagement was important? Can you explain the importance of perception in this case?

2. Describe how Kempinski used social cognitive theory to establish their corporate culture and core values.

3. What reinforcement activities were chosen to support the growth plan at Kempinski Hotels?

Sources

"About Us." *Kempinski.com.* www.kempinski.com/en/hotels/information/about-us/.

MacDiarmid, Ann. "Encouraging Employee Engagement." *CMA Management* (June/July 2004).

Mitchell, Colin. "Selling the Brand Inside." *Harvard Business Review.* http://hbr.org/2002/01/selling-the-brand-inside/ar/1.

Norcao, Mia. "Using Storytelling to Engage a Diverse Workforce at Kempinski Hotels," Melcrum, n.d.; www.melcrum.com/research/employee-engagement/using-storytelling-engage-diverse-workforce-kempinski-hotels#sthash.k23PPOU8.dpuf.

Rydberg, Isabella, and Lyttinen, J. P. "Internal Marketing in Hotel Chains" (Luleå University of Technology, 2005); http://epubl.ltu.se/1404-5508/2005/183/LTU-SHU-EX-05183-SE.pdf.

SELF-ASSESSMENT 3.1

General Self-Efficacy

Although Bandura originally conceptualized self-efficacy as a person's belief that he or she is capable of performing a *specific* task, many researchers have subsequently found it useful to expand it to describe general self-efficacy, our perceived ability to cope with daily hassles and adapt after experiencing stressful events.

For each statement, circle the number that best describes you based on the following scale:

	NOT AT ALL TRUE	HARDLY TRUE	MODERATELY TRUE	EXACTLY TRUE
1. I can always manage to solve difficult problems if I try hard enough.	1	2	3	4
2. If someone opposes me, I can find the means and ways to get what I want.	1	2	3	4
3. It is easy for me to stick to my aims and accomplish my goals.	1	2	3	4
4. I am confident that I could deal efficiently with unexpected events.	1	2	3	4
5. Thanks to my resourcefulness, I know how to handle unforeseen situations.	1	2	3	4
6. I can solve most problems if I invest the necessary effort.	1	2	3	4
7. I can remain calm when facing difficulties because I can rely on my coping abilities.	1	2	3	4
8. When I am confronted with a problem, I can usually find several solutions.	1	2	3	4
9. If I am in trouble, I can usually think of a solution.	1	2	3	4
10. I can usually handle whatever comes my way.	1	2	3	4

Scoring

Add the numbers you circled and write your score in the blank: _____

Interpretation

30 and above = You have very strong general self-efficacy. You are likely to be quite effective in coping with daily challenges and adapting to stressful events.

20 – 29 = You have a moderate level of general self-efficacy. Your confidence in your ability to perform difficult tasks and cope with adversity, though generally steady, may falter in certain situations.

19 and below = You have a low level of general self-efficacy. As a result, you may be more susceptible to the effects of stress, anxiety, burnout, and depression. You could benefit from the self-leadership strategies discussed in Chapter 13. Research has linked self-leadership with higher self-efficacy perceptions.

Source: Adapted from Schwarzer, R., & Jerusalem, M. (1995). "Generalized Self-Efficacy Scale." In J. Weinman, S. Wright, & M. Johnston (Eds.), *Measures in Health Psychology: A User's Portfolio. Causal and Control Beliefs* (pp. 35–37). Windsor, UK: NFER-NELSON.

4

Emotions, Attitudes, and Stress

If your emotional abilities aren't in hand, if you don't have self-awareness, if you are not able to manage your distressing emotions, if you can't have empathy and have effective relationships, then no matter how smart you are, you are not going to get very far.

—*Dr. Daniel Goleman, psychologist, scientist, and author*

Learning Objectives

By the end of this chapter, you will be able to:

4.1 Describe the basic concept of emotions in the context of organizational behavior

4.2 Discuss the various roles of emotions in the workplace

4.3 Explain the ways in which attitudes influence behavior in organizations

4.4 Identify some common workplace attitudes and related outcomes

4.5 Illustrate the ways in which stress can affect behavior in the workplace

4.6 Discuss different outcomes of stress and the benefits of wellness programs

CASE STUDY: KEVIN PLANK, FOUNDER OF UNDER ARMOUR

Stressful Beginnings

As a collegiate football player, Kevin Plank had a constant irritation: his undershirt always became too sweaty, to the point of annoyance. Like many other founders, Kevin began a new business called Under Armour in an effort to solve this problem. His solution? A new type of clothing, one that would stay dry and light in extreme heat—a type of revolutionized sportswear.

His idea has since grown into many products which made $4.3 billion of revenue in 2016.

But the path to success hasn't been easy. Throughout the process of beginning Under Armour, Plank had to deal with varying stressful roadblocks which challenged his positive outlook. For example, in 1996, Kevin invested $20,000 of his own savings and took on $40,000 of credit debt to begin producing and selling his product. However, his sales that year only amounted to $17,000. Making so little struck a real blow to Plank's hopes of getting his business off the ground. Yet Plank was determined not to let emotion cloud his judgment.

"You need to put your hands around the throat of your business, and you need to run it. There's no other way."

From the beginning, Plank has been determined to lead by facing his difficulties rather than letting these difficulties negatively affect the business.

Operational Pressure and Emotions

Today Under Armour still faces difficult situations at the organization's most important levels, and they require calm and effective solutions. Through a critical thinking approach consisting of many innovative tactics, Under Armour employees constantly receive treatment that limits the potential for unhealthy levels of stress, called distress, into healthy levels of stress, or eustress. A few things induce stress at Under Armour, but one primary example is its market share. Under Armour began trading as a public company in 2005, and since then its stock has seen times of extreme growth and times of extreme decline. This volatility paired with Under Armour's large sales creates constant expectations for positive financial reports, and the commentary on substandard reports can be scathing.

Constant pressure from the markets is felt in all public companies, especially those with varied years of great growth like Under Armour's. Furthermore, political turbulence and public opinion always play a role in valuing public companies like Under Armour, and in 2016, this was a significant issue to tackle. In the midst of a highly contested presidential race, CEO Plank made comments endorsing Donald Trump and his pro-business economics. This public statement saw backlash from some of Under Armour's lead athletes, and the company's stock price dipped. Limiting stress related to this issue to a healthy level, but also to a level where employees still constantly seek to manage the company in shareholders' best interests, involves managing the office behavioral environment accordingly.

Through a couple decades of massive growth and stressful market conditions, Under Armour maintains a relaxed atmosphere in its corporate setting. This is no accident; Under Armour strives to accommodate all levels of employees as well as possible, and, as mentioned above, they must innovate in order to do so. For example, to start the day, UA workers at one office in Baltimore take a water taxi to the building. According to primary interviews, many enjoy the ride and use it as a time to relax and refocus; there is even a company-sponsored yoga class offered after work. Under Armour encourages employees to dress in a laid-back manner, and offers them a 50 percent discount on UA products. According to employees at UA, an office space where members of the organization consistently wear its product and receive little things designed to relieve the emotional stress of a demanding business has been an important part of managing Under Armour's organizational behavior and success. Furthermore, formal suit-and-tie dress is one less thing for employees to stress about, and this assists in preventing employee anxiety from surpassing the healthy state of eustress.

Additional Management Methods

The CEO, Kevin Plank, has done more than just offer relaxing options for employees at corporate offices. Many employees have shared their experiences; for example, Under Armour often treats members of the organization to big sporting events—not just to see their brand in action, but to get in on the action. Plank advises his team to "stay humble," and reminds them that no one person, including himself, is bigger than the Under Armour brand. Another area in the business where effective team management can be seen is in the UA "performance center." As mentioned before, employees receive generous discounts on products, like those of many organizations, but at the performance center they work out using the gear. Over a hundred Under Armour workers can be seen exercising at the same company gym on a given day.

In another instance, employees recount stories about interactions with some of the greatest UA athletes, such as basketball player Stephen Curry. One even received an autographed shoe. This company involvement is a unique and simple way to engage employees: Let them partake in the outcome of their hard work. Not only does this build affinity within the brand, but a demanding workload becomes much more mentally and physically bearable when there are tangible benefits besides a paycheck.

It's important, in Kevin Plank's case, to make sure that his employees are comfortable, happy, and ready to succeed before putting them to work. Under Armour prides itself on having entrepreneurial team members, and this starts with their situation in the workplace. Scott Salkeld, the head of innovation at UA, describes his favorite perk as "limitless opportunities." He believes endless opportunities coupled with a healthy work environment, is the key to overcoming difficult tasks.

From beginning in a basement to becoming part of the soul of Baltimore, Under Armour has seen countless challenges and successes and has grown to be a useful study in organizational behavior. Today Under Armour constantly attempts to maintain four pillars of greatness, which they define as "Make a great product, tell a great story, provide great service, and build a great team." Although UA's primary concern is developing innovative sporting wear, a key piece of its successful business is building a great Under Armour team: innovative, passionate people working toward the same goal.

Successfully making that happen is a challenge for all organizations, large or small, and takes constant efforts to reduce stress and resolve conflicts. Each and every day organizations must find ways to solve these problems; there is a danger that emotions will get in the way of hard work and success.

Critical-Thinking Questions

1. How can personal stress affect the process of beginning and managing an organization, and how can you confront this?

2. What types of things can management do to relieve a demanding atmosphere, and why is this important?

3. Does managing one's own stress and attitude play a role in managing those of others? Explain.

Resources:

CEO.Com. (n.d.). *16 founder stories behind famous companies*. Retrieved from http://www.ceo.com/leadership_and_management/16-founder-stories-behind-famous-companies/

Fundable. (n.d.). *Under Armour startup story*. Retrieved from https://www.fundable.com/learn/startup-stories/under-armour

Schneider-Levy, B. (2016, May 11). Under Armour employees share Kevin Plank's best advice & company perks. *Footwear News*. Retrieved from http://footwearnews.com/2016/focus/uncategorized/under-armour-employees-share-kevin-planks-best-advice-220213/

Under Armour. (n.d.). *Welcome to the home of the best. Bring your A-game here*. Retrieved from http://www.underarmour.jobs/why-choose-us/our-history/

Under Armour. (n.d.). *Investor relations*. Retrieved from http://www.uabiz.com/results.cfm

Unger, M. (2013, August). A look inside Under Armour. *Baltimore*. Retrieved from http://www.baltimoremagazine.net/2013/8/1/a-look-inside-under-armour

Emotions in Organizational Behavior

>> **LO 4.1**   Describe the basic concept of emotions in the context of organizational behavior

Our Under Armour case study describes the rollercoaster of stress and emotions involved in running a business. The founder of Under Armour, Kevin Plank, believes the only way to battle these feelings and overcome difficulties is to persist. But what about the types of feelings and emotions you might feel on a daily basis? How do you deal with those? Say, one morning your professor hands you an important, complex assignment and tells you it has to be completed by the end of the day. How do you feel? Are you excited at the thought of a new challenge? Or fearful because the task is so complex? Do you feel angry with your professor because you have been given such a tight deadline?

People or events elicit a variety of feelings that cause us to respond in different ways. These feelings are called **affects**, a broad term covering a wide range of feelings, including emotions and moods.[1] We may react to certain situations with sadness, anger, or elation. These responses are **emotions**, which are defined as intense feelings directed at a specific object or person.[2] Emotions are numerous and intense, but they are usually also short-lived. For example, in the scenario described, it's likely that your intense feeling of anger toward your professor will dissipate as soon as you begin to focus on the task.

SAGE edge™

Master the content
edge.sagepub.com/neckob2e

Affects: The range of feelings in form of emotions and moods that people experience

Emotions: Intense feelings directed at a specific object or person

Moods: Generalized positive or negative feelings of mind

Positive affect: A mood dimension that consists of emotions such as excitement, self-assurance, and cheerfulness at the high end and boredom, sluggishness, and tiredness at the low end

Negative affect: A mood dimension that consists of emotions such as boredom, lethargy, and depression

But what if your professor has caught you on a day when you feel like you can't be bothered with working at all? In fact, now that you think about it, you've felt a bit down for the past few days and feel like a short deadline is the last thing you need since you're feeling so unmotivated. In this case, you are probably experiencing a negative **mood**, which consists of less intense and more generalized feelings not directed at a specific object or person.[3] Moods last longer than emotions. Of course, moods can also be positive, and we often categorize ourselves and others as being in a "good mood" or a "bad mood."

OB researchers have identified two basic types of mood dimensions: positive affect and negative affect. **Positive affect** includes emotions such as excitement, cheerfulness, and self-assurance, while **negative affect** includes emotions such as boredom, lethargy, and depression.[4] The sources of moods and emotions are complex. Factors such as lack of sleep and exercise, the weather, and the amount of stress we are under might play a part, but there are no concrete answers to explain the underlying reasons for our feelings and moods.

Although there are clear differences between emotions and moods, they do influence each other. Emotions can turn into moods when you lose focus on what caused the feeling in the first place, and good or bad moods can trigger a stronger, more intense emotional response. For example, your feelings of anger toward your professor for giving you a complex assignment on short notice may put you in a bad mood, which distracts you from focusing on the task. Conversely, if you were already in a bad mood before you were handed the project, your angry feelings may intensify even more after you receive the last-minute assignment. While your negative feelings are justified from your perspective, what about your classmates, friends, and others around you? How does your mood affect them?

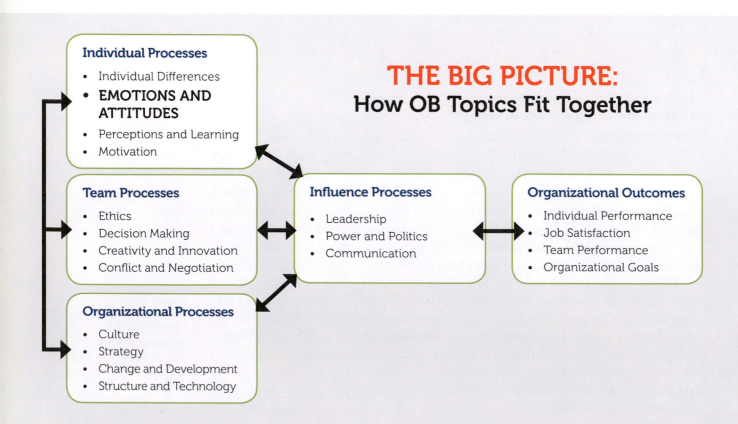

THE BIG PICTURE:
How OB Topics Fit Together

Individual Processes
- Individual Differences
- **EMOTIONS AND ATTITUDES**
- Perceptions and Learning
- Motivation

Team Processes
- Ethics
- Decision Making
- Creativity and Innovation
- Conflict and Negotiation

Organizational Processes
- Culture
- Strategy
- Change and Development
- Structure and Technology

Influence Processes
- Leadership
- Power and Politics
- Communication

Organizational Outcomes
- Individual Performance
- Job Satisfaction
- Team Performance
- Organizational Goals

THINKING CRITICALLY

1. Identify and list five separate emotions and five separate moods.

2. Imagine and describe a work situation where positive affect would be more effective in accomplishing key tasks. Imagine and describe a work situation where negative affect would be more effective in accomplishing key tasks.

3. In general, which type of affect (positive or negative) do you think would be more effective overall in a situation where you need to collaborate with a large team? Defend your response.

Emotions in the Workplace

>> LO 4.2   Discuss the various roles of emotions in the workplace

Awareness of our emotional state is paramount when making important career decisions. For example, people who are in heightened emotional states and are unhappy with their current roles or financially desperate sometimes jump into new positions without fully assessing the realities of what the new job has to offer. In this situation, job seekers need to consult someone else such as a friend, mentor, or coach who can view the situation objectively and help work through options without applying the same level of emotion.[5] Seeking the help of others helps you think more calmly and rationally and see the bigger picture.

Most of us experience heightened emotional states at least once in a while. When we are feeling frustrated, angry, or disappointed, we may choose to shout, storm out of a room, or curl up in a quiet place to calm down for a while. However, in the workplace, emotional outbursts could seriously damage your professional reputation and affect your work performance. For example, Uber CEO Travis Kalanick was recently caught on camera arguing with an Uber driver about falling fares. As the discussion became more heated, Kalanick lost his cool and delivered some personal insults to the driver. Following the release of the footage, Kalanick apologized in an email to his Uber staff for losing his temper and admitted he needed to "grow up."[6] As this example shows, a lack of self-control over your emotions not only affects you, but your negative responses can spread to others around you and disrupt the function of work groups.[7]

Emotional contagion: A phenomenon in which emotions which are experienced by few people of a work group are spread to the others

Emotional Contagion

Moods and emotions are contagious and have a strong influence on group behavior. **Emotional contagion** is a phenomenon in which emotions experienced by one or more individuals in a work group spread to the others.[8] Researchers have found that negative emotions tend to spread more quickly than positive emotions, which can affect morale, productivity, and motivation. Emotional contagion is the same kind of effect that occurred

Supporters reach for signatures and handshakes as Donald Trump greets the crowd after speaking at a campaign rally in Las Vegas, Nevada.

Jabin Botsford/The Washington Post via Getty Images

Waiters are expected to be friendly and approachable even when they are tired or dealing with difficult situations. This can create a burden of emotional labor for the employee.

at the Trump rallies where Trump's audience, fired up by his campaign rhetoric and by the powerful energy of the crowd, often had angry altercations with protesters.[9] Positive emotional contagion creates an environment in which people work better together, experience less conflict, and experience higher levels of work performance. Managers and leaders who have positive attitudes generally have the ability to inspire their employees to work well together. In our OB in the Real World feature below, Clare Collins describes how she inspired positive emotional contagion by correcting an error that could have dangerously affected morale.

Emotional Labor

Emotional labor: The process of managing one's feelings to present positive emotions even when they are contrary to one's actual feelings

The concept of **emotional labor** refers to the process of managing our feelings so that we present positive emotions even when they are contrary to our actual feelings.[10] Hotel employees, salespeople, flight attendants, wait staff, and tour operators are all examples of the types of service workers who are expected to smile and be pleasant even in the most demanding circumstances. Today's organizations are increasingly customer oriented, and many managers expect their employees to present a positive face when interacting with their external customers as well as with their internal clients and coworkers.

Display Rules

Display rules: Basic norms that govern which emotions should be displayed and which should be suppressed

Many organizations teach their employees **display rules**, the basic norms that govern which emotions should be displayed and which should be suppressed.[11] Different organizations have different rules that accord with their company culture. For example, call center workers may be given a script to read to customers and be instructed to be enthusiastic and conceal their frustration. Rules for retail or wait staff may require them to greet customers with a smile and treat them as if they are always right.

Emotional Dissonance

Emotional dissonance: A discrepancy between the emotions a person displays and the emotions he or she actually feels

It is challenging to put on a happy face all the time, especially if you are experiencing emotional upheaval at home or dealing with work stress. When you feel this way, sometimes the last thing you want to do is to be cheerful and helpful to difficult customers. Under these circumstances, you might experience **emotional dissonance**, a discrepancy between the emotions a person displays and the emotions he or she actually feels.[12] For example, you may feel angry with a particularly demanding and rude customer, but you are compelled to be polite regardless of your true feelings.

Surface Acting versus Deep Acting

Surface acting: A person suppresses their true feelings while displaying the organizationally desirable ones

When you engage in emotional labor, you are expected to regulate your true feelings in order to achieve organizational goals. People tend to use two emotional labor techniques to control their real emotions: surface acting, and deep acting.[13] **Surface acting**

FIGURE 4.1

Social Interaction Model

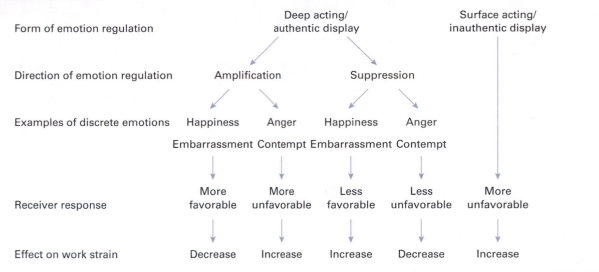

Source: Republished with permission of Academy of Management, from Côté, Stéphane. "A Social Interaction Model of the Effects of Emotion Regulation on Work Strain." *Academy of Management Review* 30, no. 3 (July 2005): 509–530; permission conveyed through Copyright Clearance Center, Inc. .

occurs when a person suppresses his or her true feelings while displaying the organizationally desirable ones. For example, you may fake a smile or use a soft tone of voice when dealing with a difficult customer even when, underneath, you are offended. In **deep acting** you try to change your emotions to better match the emotions your employer requires in the situation. For example, rather than feeling irritated by the demanding customer, you attempt to empathize by putting yourself in the customer's position and trying to feel his or her frustration.

> **Deep acting:** Efforts to change your actual emotions to better match the required emotions of the situation

Both surface acting and deep acting through social interaction can affect the level of work strain felt by individual employees (see Figure 4.1). As shown in the figure, people who amplify positive emotions like happiness or even embarrassment through deep acting will generate a favorable response from others which decreases work strain. Those who display high levels of anger or contempt will receive a negative response, thus increasing work strain. Similarly, those who put on a fake display of surface acting will also receive an unfavorable response from others, which again increases work strain.

Emotional Regulation

Every day we are exposed to situations that can trigger a range of strong emotions. Most of us try and control our feelings through **emotional regulation**, a set of processes through which people influence their own emotions and the ways in which they experience and express them.[14] The two main kinds of regulation strategies are antecedent focused and response focused.

> **Emotional regulation:** A set of processes through which people influence their own emotions and the ways in which they experience and express them

Antecedent-Focused Strategies

Antecedent-focused strategies[15] come into play before the emotional response has been fully triggered. They include the following:

- *Situation selection* lets you choose or avoid situations that have the potential to generate certain emotional responses. For example, if you dislike a coworker, you might avoid going by his desk so you don't have to engage with him.

- *Situation modification* involves altering a situation to change its emotional impact. For example, you might move physically closer to a person if you want to positively engage him or her in a serious discussion.

- *Attention deployment* consists of refocusing your attention to an area of a situation that results in a more positive emotional outcome. For example, if you are anxious about a looming deadline, you might distract yourself by taking a short break to recharge your energy levels and refresh your focus.

- *Cognitive change* lets you reassess an event or situation to see the bigger picture and bring about a more positive emotional reaction. For example, instead of being frustrated with your boss for being late for your meeting, you could use the extra time to do additional preparation or even take a moment to relax.

Antecedent-focused strategies help us to prevent strong emotional responses when we are confronted with certain situations. In the next section, we take a look at the second type of regulation strategies: response-focused strategies.

Response-Focused Strategies

We use response-focused strategies[16] after an emotional response has been fully triggered. There are two types:

- *Reappraisal* involves reevaluating a potentially emotional situation in a more objective way. For example, you are about to give a speech and you feel very nervous. Rather than allowing nerves to overcome you, you might take a few deep breaths or think about how interested your audience will be in what you have to say.

- *Suppression* occurs when we consciously mask inward emotional reactions with more positive or neutral behavioral responses. For example, you may feel inclined to laugh when a colleague mispronounces someone else's name, but you keep your emotions in check so as not to appear insensitive.

Response-focused strategies help us to prevent any outwardly perceivable expression of emotion in order to support us in coping with certain situations.

Emotional Intelligence

Imagine you are working on a complex project and one of your teammates is having such difficulty carrying out his role that he slows down the rest of the team and jeopardizes the deadline. Do you complain to your boss that this employee is letting the team down? Or do you try and manage the situation by supporting your teammate and helping him learn the right skills? If you chose the latter option, you probably have high levels of emotional intelligence (EI), the ability to understand emotions in ourselves and others in order to effectively manage our own behaviors and our interpersonal relationships.[17] Organizations are beginning to base hiring and promoting decisions on EI, and it is considered as important to professional success as other abilities such as technical skills.[18] In fact, according to the World Economic Forum's Future of Jobs Report, emotional intelligence is on track to become one of the top ten most desired job skills in 2020.[19] For example, American insurance company Aflac recruits people who can provide specific examples to illustrate their ability to stay calm in stressful situations.[20]

It is equally important to consider cultural variations in emotional expression. For example, in the United States it is acceptable to show enthusiasm in work when the situation is appropriate, and to debate points with passion in a meeting. However, in Japan and China, this sort of emotional expression is not tolerated and may be perceived as showing off. Similarly, people in the United Kingdom can be quite reserved and understated and tend to play down their emotions in a business setting. When dealing with different cultures, it is extremely important to learn the language of emotion in order to gain a greater understanding of emotional expression. Just because a person from a different culture may not seem enthusiastic doesn't mean they are not excited; they might just be showing their emotions in a different way.[21]

Related to EI is the use of "soft skills," or competencies that rely on personality traits such as empathy, listening abilities, and good communication to build work relationships. Job candidates with soft skills are in demand because they are generally better at conducting self-assessment, managing their emotions, and accepting feedback.[22] There are four dimensions[23] of EI (see Figure 4.2):

The Aflac booth at a job fair in Southern Florida. When recruiting new employees, Aflac looks for people who display high levels of emotional intelligence in addition to technical skills.

Joe Raedle/Getty Images

FIGURE 4.2

The Four Dimensions of EI

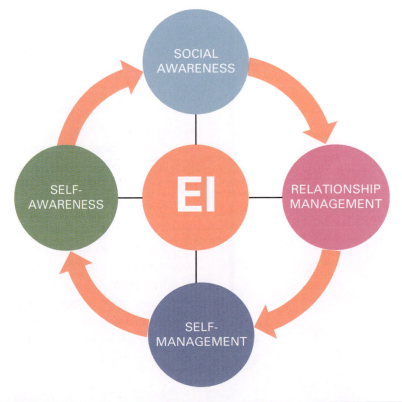

1. *Self-Awareness*: A good understanding of your own emotions
2. *Self-Management*: The ability to control and regulate emotions and impulses
3. *Social Awareness*: Skills in perceiving, empathizing with, and reacting appropriately to the emotions of others

4. *Relationship Management*: The ability to manage the emotions of others to build strong and healthy relationships with them

Despite its popularity during the past decade, some theorists question the validity of the EI concept, citing lack of evidence and criticizing the ways in which EI is tested and measured and the resulting conclusions.[24] Despite these criticisms, EI is becoming more popular in the workplace and more valued as a desired skill among employees. For example, a study conducted by Leadership IQ, investigating the reasons why new hires fail within the first eighteen months, shows low EI to be the second most common reason why new hires fail (the first being "coachability").[25]

THINKING CRITICALLY

1. Crowds at large sporting events, concerts, or in a movie theater typically experience emotional contagion in one form or another. Assume that your favorite professional sports team is in a close game and unexpectedly wins. What positive aspects of emotional contagion would you be likely to experience? If your team unexpectedly lost, perhaps to a bad call, what negative aspects of social contagion might you experience?

2. Take a close look at Figure 4.1. Describe an experience you have had with a friend, classmate, or coworker who displayed surface acting. What was your response to his or her display? How did your response affect her or his likelihood of displaying surface acting in the future?

3. You are the manager of a publishing group of twenty employees. Your parent company is closing your organization and you must inform your employees that they are being laid off. While you will receive a bonus for staying on an additional two weeks, you will also be losing your job. Discuss the antecedent-focused strategies (situation selection, situation modification, attention deployment, cognitive change) and/or response-focused strategies (reappraisal, suppression) you would use to regulate your emotions and behavior in this situation. Which strategy or strategies do you believe would be most effective? Least effective?

4. While emotional intelligence is considered an important and desirable quality in employees, discuss the ways in which emotional intelligence may be used in unscrupulous or unethical ways. For example, imagine you are running a Ponzi scheme similar to the one Bernie Madoff created and ran. How would social awareness, relationship management, self-awareness, and self-management benefit your efforts to swindle people and foundations? Rank the usefulness of each of the four dimensions of IE in this context and explain your rationale.

Attitudes and Behavior

>> LO 4.3   **Explain the ways in which attitudes influence behavior in organizations**

In the OB in the Real World feature, founder of Silver Lining Bikinis, Clare Collins, stresses the importance of possessing a good attitude. But what is attitude and why is it so important in the workplace? We define **attitude** as a learned tendency to consistently respond positively or negatively to people or events.[26] Attitudes determine our likes and dislikes and help us to make judgments about other people or

Attitude: A learned tendency to consistently respond positively or negatively to people or events

events. Our beliefs provide us with the necessary information to shape our attitudes, which in turn shape our behaviors.

How Attitudes Are Created

To truly understand attitudes, we need to understand how they are created (Figure 4.3). Three main elements form our attitudes.[27]

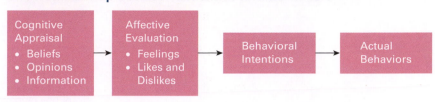

FIGURE 4.3

The Relationship between Attitudes and Behaviors

Source: Adapted from Fishbein, M., and I. Ajzen. *Belief, Attitude, Intention, and Behavior: An Introduction to Theory and Research* (Reading, MA: Addison-Wesley, 1975).

1. *Cognitive appraisal* reflects the sum total of a person's underlying beliefs, opinions, information, and knowledge about a specific object, person, or event. For example, my professor is overbearing; my girlfriend is smart and beautiful; the Steelers are the best team in the NFL.
2. *Affective evaluation* reflects a person's positive and negative feelings toward a specific object, person, or event. For example, I don't like my professor; I love my girlfriend; I like the Steelers.
3. *Behavioral intention* is the perceived likelihood that someone will behave in a particular way toward a specific object, person, or event. For example, I will not take another course with my professor; I will kiss my girlfriend; I will root for the Steelers.

While behavioral intention is the strongest predictor of actual behavior, it does not *necessarily* predict our behavior. Social norms and other behavioral controls may intervene, stopping us from carrying out our intended or most desired action. For example, perhaps Neda's boss has belittled her in front of her coworkers. While her behavioral intention may be to defend herself by telling her boss that his behavior is unprofessional and destructive, social norms suggest that telling off your boss will be considered professionally inappropriate. Meanwhile, in this example an especially relevant behavioral control is the knowledge that Neda might be fired if she responds to her boss in the way that her behavioral intention demands!

Cognitive Dissonance

Originally coined by psychologist Leon Festinger, **cognitive dissonance** is the stress and discomfort individuals experience when they face an inconsistency among her or his beliefs, attitudes, values, and behaviors.[28] Festinger observed that people prefer consistency and thus tend to alter their attitudes, beliefs, or behaviors in order to restore harmony.

For example, despite the evidence that smoking is detrimental to health, Matt likes to smoke and has a positive attitude toward smoking. However, it also makes Matt uneasy that he may be carrying out a behavior that has a negative effect on his health. To alleviate the psychological discomfort associated with his cognitive dissonance in relation to smoking, Matt has a number of choices:

- Change the behavior (Matt will stop smoking)
- Change the belief or attitude (Matt says he doesn't believe the evidence that suggests smoking is dangerous to his health)

Cognitive dissonance: The inconsistency between a person's beliefs, attitudes, or behaviors

OB IN THE REAL WORLD

Clare Collins, Founder of Silver Lining Bikinis

Clare Collins, a USC graduate, is a busy commercial real estate broker out of Southern California with a sporadic schedule; her little sister, Annie, is completing an undergraduate degree at USC on the path to becoming a doctor, all the while managing important aspects of her sorority, Delta Gamma. Their occupations didn't stop the two sisters from turning their longtime hobby of sewing clothing into a successful business: Silver Lining Bikinis officially began in Los Angeles in 2015. Since high school, Clare and Annie have been producing bikinis and other wear for friends and families, and their journey and current operation serve as great teaching points on effectively managing stress, heavy workloads, positive attitudes, and close relationships.

While still in undergraduate study at the University of Southern California, in an entrepreneurship course, Clare realized that her younger sister's unique ability to design and create bikinis could be turned into a business. Clare remembers thinking, "I am about to go graduate college, and I can either go work at a corporate desk or start my own business." Fueled by her ambition, she started by asking people she knew to help. "Friends and fellow sorority members began trying on Silver Lining's product, buying it and spreading the word."

Although Silver Lining Bikinis has been growing consistently and they have moved production away from their own hands and needles, Clare and Annie still operate the business alone. This means maintaining a healthy, stress-free relationship. They agree that they are sisters first and business partners second—this attitude has helped them share the workload when it becomes too cumbersome for one or the other. Speaking frankly while showing care for one another has been invaluable to their success.

Clare finds that Silver Lining Bikinis' organizational structure opens the door to some distressing possibilities, which she must manage accordingly. She has moments of weakness, because her business shares her own personal strengths and weaknesses. In Clare's words, always in the back of her mind is, "I could always do more: I could march into every bikini shop in California and ask them to buy bikinis," but she consistently replaces that unattainable goal with critical, relevant plans. She drives herself and her sister with high expectations.

When things go wrong it challenges their successful emotional management, and on one specific occasion, Clare and Annie actively avoided a dangerous emotional contagion. Clare had completed the backend work correctly with their bikini producer for a large shipment to a retailer, but the packages were sent with individual online purchases included. Annie was, at first, emotionally distressed about the error, but Clare made sure to reassure her. Instead of pointing fingers and exacerbating the mistake, Silver Lining Bikinis began fulfilling the misplaced orders immediately.

In a way that uniquely represents some of the important points in this chapter, Silver Lining Bikinis says this about their swimsuits: "All of the Silver Lining bikinis, made with love in Los Angeles, are lined with silver fabric to remind you to find the silver lining in everything!"

Clare and Annie fully believe that when it comes to running a business, seeing the silver lining is the key to success.

Critical-Thinking Questions

1. How can personal interest in a coworker's emotional state enhance the effectiveness of a team?

2. What is the relationship between critical thinking and maintaining a healthy stress level? ●

Source: Interview with Clare Collins conducted on March 14th, 2017

- Rationalize the inconsistency in his knowledge that smoking is unhealthy and his behavioral choice to keep smoking (Matt believes smoking is dangerous for most people, but not for him)

As this example illustrates, although we strive to quell the discomfort we feel when attitudes and behaviors contradict each other, the manner in which we try to reconcile dissonant beliefs, values, or attitudes may not be very rational.

THINKING CRITICALLY

1. Discuss the cognitive appraisal, affective evaluation, and behavioral intention that might contribute to your decision not to dress down on casual Friday in your workplace.

2. You work long hours at a start-up, routinely working weekends and while on vacation. Although you miss spending time with your family and friends, you believe that by working hard and exhibiting company loyalty you will be promoted as the company grows. When you are passed over for the promotion, you experience cognitive dissonance. List two to three options per category (changing your behavior, changing your belief or attitudes, or rationalizing away inconsistencies) that you could pursue in order to reduce the cognitive dissonance you feel.

Common Workplace Attitudes

>> LO 4.4   Identify some common workplace attitudes and related outcomes

As we have learned, attitudes play a big part in influencing our behavior at work. The attitudes we bring to the workplace are critical for three main areas: job satisfaction, organizational commitment, and employee engagement. **Job satisfaction** is the degree to which an individual feels positive or negative about a job.[29] In 2016, Facebook topped the list of best places to work with 97 percent of its employees reporting high job satisfaction.[30]

Table 4.1 lists common characteristics of job satisfaction in the United States. As Table 4.1 illustrates, factors such as relations with coworkers, job security, and the amount of on-the-job stress are correlated with job satisfaction. **Employee engagement** is a connection with the organization and passion for the job.[31] Job satisfaction and job performance are significantly related. Software firm Full Contact encourages employee engagement by offering their employees a paid vacation (worth $7,500).[32] The idea is that employees who take a proper break from the office (they are forbidden to do any work or take calls) will return from vacation with renewed energy and enthusiasm and perform better on the job. In addition, the realization that the business can still run smoothly without them encourages an enhanced sense of trust in their coworkers.

Southwest Airlines builds employee engagement by empowering their employees to achieve certain tasks, such as designing their own uniforms to putting innovative ideas into practice.[33] For example, in 2014, a fun video of one flight attendant rapping the safety information went viral which gave employees and customers a great experience and boosted the company image. Southwest employees also receive regular recognition for their work through public praise or "shout outs" or through a mention in Southwest's monthly magazine. Making sure employees know they are valued by a company is an important part of

Job satisfaction: The degree to which an individual feels positive or negative about a job

Employee engagement: A connection with the organization and passion for one's job

TABLE 4.1

Characteristics of Job Satisfaction

U.S. EMPLOYEES' SATISFACTION WITH 13 JOB ASPECTS—RECENT TREND % COMPLETELY SATISFIED, RANKED BY 2016			
	2015 %	2016 %	CHANGE OVER PAST YEAR (PCT. PTS.)
The physical safety conditions of your workplace	70	76	+6
Your relations with coworkers	72	71	−1
The flexibility of your hours	58	67	+9
Your job security	57	65	+8
Your boss or immediate supervisor	54	61	+7
The amount of work that is required of you	53	58	+5
The amount of vacation time you receive	57	56	−1
The recognition you receive at work for your work accomplishments	45	55	+10
The retirement plan your employer offers	35	44	+9
Your chances for promotion	35	43	+8
The amount of money you earn	33	41	+8
The health insurance benefits your employer offers	40	37	−3
The amount of on-the-job stress in your job	28	34	+6
Based on adults employed full or part time			

Source: Adapted from Newport, Frank and Jim Harter "U.S. Workers' Satisfaction with Job Dimensions Increases." *Gallup.* August 29, 2016. https://news.gallup.com/poll/195143/workers-satisfied-job-dimensions.aspx

employee engagement as it encourages commitment and the motivation to go the extra mile.

As Herb Kelleher, Southwest Airlines' founder, says, "They can buy all the physical things. The things you can't buy are dedication, devotion, loyalty—the feeling that you are participating in a crusade."

Organizational Citizenship

Organizational citizenship behavior: Discretionary and voluntary behavior that is not a part of the employee's specific role requirements and is not formally rewarded

Counterproductive work behaviors: Voluntary behaviors that purposefully disrupt or harm the organization

Organizational citizenship behavior (OCB) is discretionary and voluntary behavior that is not a part of the employee's specific role requirements and is not formally rewarded.[34] For example, kindergarten teacher Sonya Romero, based in Albuquerque, New Mexico, displays OCB by making sure her students (most of whom live in poverty) feel safe and comfortable by using her money to buy supplies (snacks, clothes, toothbrushes) to provide them to the children.[35]

Counterproductive work behaviors (CWBs) are voluntary behaviors that purposefully disrupt or harm the organization.[36] CWBs include avoiding work or taking shortcuts, creating conflict, harassing coworkers, being physically or verbally aggressive, and stealing or sabotaging work efforts. For example, long-standing cable news host Bill O'Reilly was recently forced out of Fox News as a result of multiple allegations of sexual harassment—a type of CWB.[37]

THINKING CRITICALLY

1. To what extent can organizational commitment and employee engagement contribute to a successful organization? Do situations exist where organizational commitment and employee engagement are counterproductive to organizational success? Explain.

2. List at least five specific behaviors that illustrate organizational citizenship behavior (OCB). How are coworkers likely to view and collaborate with those who display high levels of OCBs? Defend your answer.

3. List at least five specific behaviors that illustrate counterproductive work behaviors (CWBs). How are coworkers likely to view and collaborate with those who display high levels of CWBs? Defend your answer.

Stress in the Workplace

>> LO 4.5   Illustrate the ways in which stress can affect behavior in the workplace

Most of us know what it feels like to be stressed. We may feel under pressure about making a deadline, taking an exam, or giving a presentation in front of a large audience. Stress is a response that occurs when a person perceives a situation as threatening to his or her well-being when his or her resources have been taxed or exceeded.[38] In the United States, job stress is the leading source of stress for adults.[39] Stress in the workplace can affect the behavior of people working in an organization, leading to poor health and absenteeism. One million workers miss work every day due to stress.

High levels of workplace stress can lead to loss of productivity and even illness.

Statistics show that 60 percent of illnesses are caused by stress, which costs the United States $300 billion every year on medical bills and loss of productivity.[40]

As Figure 4.4 illustrates, the leading causes of stress include fear of job loss, difficult relationships with coworkers, the struggle to balance home and work life, and heavy workload. The resulting symptoms of stress in the workplace include back pain, fatigue, headaches, and complaining about being stressed. Additional symptoms may include anxiety, irritability, depression, apathy, poor concentration, stomach problems, and insomnia.

In a survey carried out by the RAND Corporation, one in four people blamed the cause of their stress on tight deadlines and lack of sufficient time to do their jobs properly, each resulting in working during their free time.[41] Others reported different reasons for stress including verbal abuse, bullying, threatening behavior, and sexual harassment.

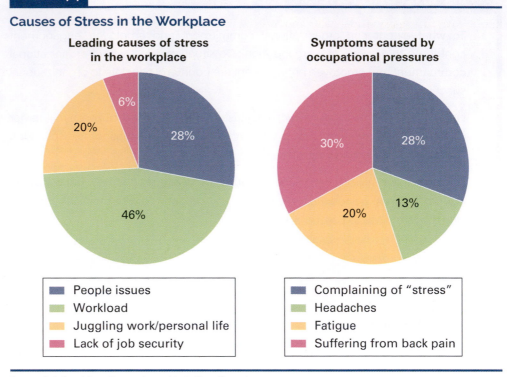

FIGURE 4.4

Causes of Stress in the Workplace

Leading causes of stress in the workplace

- People issues
- Workload
- Juggling work/personal life
- Lack of job security

Symptoms caused by occupational pressures

- Complaining of "stress"
- Headaches
- Fatigue
- Suffering from back pain

Source: Data from https://www.cdc.gov/niosh/docs/87-111/

Stressors

Stressors: Environmental stimuli that place demands on individuals

There are many sources of stress in the workplace. **Stressors** are environmental stimuli that place demands on individuals. There are two main types:[42]

- *Challenge stressors* are associated with workload, job demands, job complexity, and deadlines and are positively related to motivation and performance. Studies have shown that while challenge stressors can have a positive effect on employees' learning at work, the act of coping with challenge stressors can also increase pressure on employees, leading to a more stressful working environment.[43]

- *Hindrance stressors* inhibit progress toward objectives; examples are role ambiguity or conflict, hassles, red tape, and highly political environments. Research shows that while challenge stressors can improve job performance, hindrance stressors are negatively related to motivation and performance.[44]

Stress-Strain-Outcomes Model[45]

Strain: The physiological and psychological reactions to stress

Over time, hindrance stressors can lead to strains. **Strain** reactions include both physiological responses, such as adrenaline rush or increased heart rate and blood pressure, and psychological reactions, such as fatigue and irritability (for example, you may argue with a coworker). While strain reactions may disappear when the cause of the stress is removed, they can persist over a long time, which may result in damage to physical health (heart problems) or psychological health (burnout).

Research shows that people who can mentally detach themselves from work (psychological detachment) during their leisure time experience high life satisfaction and fewer psychological strains at work, without losing their sense of engagement.[46] In contrast, people who remain highly involved in work and do not mentally detach themselves tend to experience high strain levels such as low life satisfaction and burnout.

Figure 4.5 shows that unless organizations find ways to reduce stress, stressors can cause strains which can lead to poor performance and low motivation.

However, stress doesn't have to always be negative, nor is it a permanent condition. In the next section we explore different aspects of stress and ways of managing it.

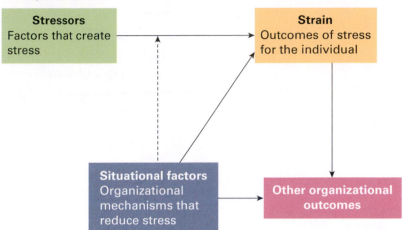

FIGURE 4.5

Workplace Stressors and Outcomes

THINKING CRITICALLY

1. Assume you are the manager of a team of employees and your team is experiencing a lot of stress due to the demands of the job. Do you feel that changing your management style would be an optimal solution to helping your team cope with the stress and ultimately perform better?

2. List possible challenge stressors and the hindrance stressors that could be affecting your team members. Is it possible for the same stressor to be a challenge stressor to one person and a hindrance stressor to another? Explain your answer.

Stress-Related Outcomes and Wellness

>> LO 4.6 Discuss different outcomes of stress and the benefits of wellness programs

Although high degrees of stress can be destructive to our behaviors and harmful to our health, stress isn't always negative. **Eustress** comprises a moderate level of stressors that have constructive and positive effects on effort and performance.[47] In other words, it is a "good" type of stress which can be attained by working out, achieving deadlines, or competing in a sports event. In contrast, bad stress, also known as **distress**, comprises high levels of stressors that have destructive and negative effects on effort and performance.[48] We tend to experience this sort of stress when we're having difficulty at work or struggling with personal problems such as divorce or a death in the family. Under Armour strives to transform distress to eustress by encouraging employees to dress informally which helps employees to feel more relaxed in a corporate setting.

There are three elements to distress:[49]

- The *physiological element* is manifested as negative physical health effects such as insomnia or exhaustion. According to research by wellness company Apollo Life, one in four CEOs admit to suffering from insomnia.[50]

Eustress: Moderate levels of stressors that have constructive and positive effects on effort and performance

Distress: High levels of stressors that have destructive and negative effects on effort and performance

- The *psychological element* appears as negative attitudes and emotions that can lower job satisfaction, among other results. Some experts attribute negative attitudes for the downfall of retail giant Sears, automotive company General Motors, and technology company Kodak among others.[51]

- *Job burnout* consists of emotional exhaustion, cynicism, and loss of interest in the job that can result from ongoing exposure to high levels of stressors. According to a national survey as part of its Employee Engagement Series conducted by workforce solutions company Kronos, almost 50 percent of HR leaders say that employee burnout is responsible for almost half of annual employee turnover.[52] This means that burnout also has a massive impact on job retention.

Managing Stress

Coping: The effort to manage, reduce, or minimize stressors

Problem-focused coping: A type of coping that aims at reducing or eliminating stressors by attempting to understand the problem and seeking practical ways in which to resolve it

Emotion-focused coping: An effort to try to change a person's emotional reaction to a stressor by using positive language and distracting techniques

Yet the good thing about stress is that it can be managed.

Coping is the effort to manage, reduce, or minimize stressors.[53] There are two types of coping:[54] **problem-focused coping**, which aims at reducing or eliminating stressors by attempting to understand the problem and seeking practical ways in which to resolve it; and **emotion-focused coping**, which is an effort to try to change a person's emotional reaction to a stressor by using positive language and distracting techniques (see Figure 4.6). Research conducted by TalentSmart shows a direct connection between coping skills and performance. Out of the one million people surveyed, 90 percent of the top performers are skilled in coping with their emotions in stressful situations.[55]

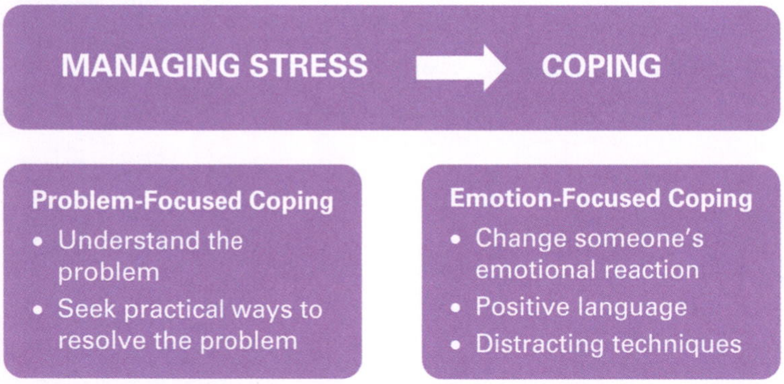

5 Ways to Manage Stress[56]

1. Meditate

Just a few minutes of meditating per day can help relieve stress. Find a quiet place and sit up straight, placing both feet on the floor. Close your eyes and repeat a positive mantra such as "I feel at peace" either out loud or silently. Focus on your breathing and allow your mind to clear.

FIGURE 4.6

Managing Stress

MANAGING STRESS → COPING

Problem-Focused Coping
- Understand the problem
- Seek practical ways to resolve the problem

Emotion-Focused Coping
- Change someone's emotional reaction
- Positive language
- Distracting techniques

2. Breathe Deeply

If you're feeling stressed or anxious, take five minutes to focus on your breathing. Deep breathing can help to slow down your heart rate and lower your blood pressure.

3. Be Present

Try and live in the moment and focus on what's around you. If you're going for a walk, deliberately note how the air feels on your face, or if you're eating, focus on how the food tastes. Being in the present can help relieve stressful symptoms.

EXAMINING THE EVIDENCE

Emotion-Focused Coping Strategies and Emotional Intelligence

When faced with stressors in the workplace, employees often choose problem-focused coping, tackling the problems head-on in an effort to eliminate or reduce stressors. However, recent research suggests that emotion-focused coping strategies may be very useful in helping employees to maintain their immediate task-performance levels. Researchers Janaki Gooty and Jane S. Thomas of the University of North Carolina at Charlotte, Mark B. Gavin of West Virginia University, and Neal M. Ashkanasy of the University of Queensland suggest that emotion-focused coping strategies such as denial, mental and behavioral disengagement, and venting could be effective short-term responses for dealing with discrete emotions such as anger, guilt, or joy. Their findings not only showed a significant positive relationship between emotion-focused coping strategies and task performance; they also indicated that people with high levels of emotional intelligence were more likely to choose emotion-focused strategies in response to their anger, guilt, and joy than were people with low levels of emotional intelligence.

Critical-Thinking Questions

1. What are the primary implications of this research regarding employee coping strategies?

2. What specifically can managers do to ensure that employees are using the most appropriate coping strategies to deal with their emotions in the workplace? ●

Source: Gooty, Janaki, Mark B. Gavin, Neal M. Ashkanasy; and Jane S. Thomas. "The Wisdom of Letting Go and Performance: The Moderating Role of Emotional Intelligence and Discrete Emotions." *Journal of Occupational and Organizational Psychology* 87, no. 2 (June 2014): 392–413.

4. Reach Out

Remember that you don't have to cope with your stressful feelings on your own. Reach out to your friends, relatives, or trusted colleagues. Talking to others and sharing the problem is a useful way to get some perspective on the issue.

5. Get Some Exercise

You don't have to be a professional athlete to get rid of stress. Many forms of exercise, including yoga, Pilates, and walking, can make you feel good. When you're feeling stressed, go for a quick walk around the block, or do some stretching exercises like head rolls and shoulder shrugs.

Wellness

We've seen that there are different degrees and types of stress and various ways of managing it. In recognition of the implications of stress, some organizations offer wellness programs as a way of helping their employees manage stress and otherwise protect and improve their health. A **wellness program** is a personal or organizational effort to promote health and well-being[57] through providing access to services like medical screenings, weight management, health advice, and exercise programs. The main aim of the wellness program is to cultivate a healthier and more productive workforce that are more satisfied with their jobs.

Another major benefit of wellness programs is that they save organizations money by reducing absenteeism and lower the cost of providing medical insurance,

Wellness program: A personal or organizational effort to promote health and well-being through providing access to services like medical screenings, weight management, health advice, and exercise programs

Fortune 500 companies often participate in Fitbit wellness programs to help increase morale, reduce employee turnover, and cultivate a healthier, more productive workforce.

both of which are major motivators for companies. According to a study carried out by Duke University, employees with health issues such as obesity can cost US companies over $73 billion per year in terms of medical costs and lost productivity.[58] This is one of the major reasons why more and more organizations are investing in wellness programs for their employees.

San Francisco–based consumer electronics company Fitbit provides activity tracking devices which measure data such as number of steps walked or climbed, quality of sleep, heart rate, etc. Thirty of the Fortune 500 companies participate in Fitbit wellness programs, including BP, Time Warner, Bank of America, and IBM. For example, BP runs a one million step challenge which rewards successful employees with a more deductible health plan.[59]

Fitbit runs its own internal programs such as "Workout Wednesdays," where employees can participate in different types of workouts throughout the day, and also encourages employees to use its own products for other fitness challenges.

Online shoe retailer Zappos operates "Wellness Adventures" where employees are taken on field trips to trampoline parks, laser tag venues, and local parks to play sports. Zappos' unique approach to wellness encourages team-building and engagement.[60]

Studies have also shown that effective wellness programs increase morale and reduce employee turnover while a recent study by research think tank Rand showed that properly executed wellness programs can save companies over $130 per wellness program member as well as a 30 percent reduction in hospital admissions.[61]

However, to be effective, wellness programs should be carefully planned. The most successful programs engage employees by inviting feedback and getting their buy-in through meetings, suggestion boxes, or staff surveys, and by tracking the level of employee participation and its impact on absenteeism, turnover, insurance costs, morale, and overall employee well-being. Managers are essential to a program's success, because they can communicate the many benefits to employees and lead by example by showing real commitment to the wellness program. The program's activities should also be attractive to employees and be designed to promote healthy eating and raise awareness of and knowledge about health. Companies are also expanding their wellness programs to include flexible working environments, teleworking (working from home), and stress management classes and education.[62] Studies have found that organizations that have instituted innovative measures to address the impact of stress on employees had a lower rate of turnover, less reports of chronic stress, and higher job satisfaction.[63]

More important, wellness programs should be fun! Walking and cycling clubs, golf, onsite fitness classes such as yoga, Pilates, Zumba, Piloxing (a blend of Pilates, boxing, and dance), and corporate challenge events such as half-marathons are popular activities run by organizations.

In this chapter we have explored the impact of emotions, attitudes, and stress on individuals and organizations. As you have seen, reducing stress and resolving conflicts requires the ability to communicate with people with different attitudes, behaviors, and personalities.

THINKING CRITICALLY

1. Consider what factors contribute to your own level of stress. Under what circumstances are you most likely to experience eustress? Under what circumstances are you most likely to experience distress? Do individual personalities play a role in how people experience stress? Support your answer.

2. Vikram, the father of a good friend, has been coaching Little League for over a decade. You attend a game and notice that Vikram is unusually harsh with his team, is making cynical remarks about their performance to other coaches, and seems lacking in energy or enthusiasm. Clearly he is suffering from job burnout. Discuss what physiological and psychological elements could be contributing to Vikram's burnout.

3. Based on your answer to Question 2 above, devise a list of at least five steps you and your friend could take to help Vikram manage his stress and job burnout. What problem-focused and emotion-focused coping strategies would you use? Do you believe that one type of strategy would be better than another in this situation? Why or why not?

4. Imagine that you are the human resources manager for a large nonprofit food bank that distributes groceries to hungry families and also offers cooking lessons, nutritional advice, and strategies for making scarce financial resources stretch further at the grocery store. Demand for your services is high and employees and volunteers are showing increased signs of stress as they struggle to meet the needs of hungry children and families. A wealthy patron offers to provide funding for wellness program that benefits food bank employees and volunteers and becomes self-sustaining after one year. What will the wellness program you create look like? ●

Visit **edge.sagepub.com/neckob2e** to help you accomplish your coursework goals in an easy-to-use learning environment.

- Mobile-friendly eFlashcards and practice quizzes
- Video and multimedia content
- Chapter summaries with learning objectives
- EXCLUSIVE! Access to full-text SAGE journal articles

IN REVIEW

4.1 Describe the basic concept of emotions in the context of organizational behavior

Emotions are intense feelings directed at a specific object or person. They are numerous and intense but they are usually fleeting and short-lived. **Moods** are less intense and more generalized feelings not directed at a specific object or person; they last longer than emotions.

Emotions can turn into moods when we lose focus of what caused the feeling in the first place; both good and bad moods can trigger stronger, more intense emotional responses.

4.2 Discuss the various roles of emotions in the workplace

In the workplace, emotional outbursts could seriously damage your professional reputation as well as your work performance. **Emotional contagion** is a phenomenon in which emotions experienced by a few people of a work group are spread to the others. **Emotional labor** takes place when, in the course of the job, service industry employees must display emotions different from those they are actually feeling. **Emotional regulation** is a set of processes through which people influence their own emotions and the ways in which they experience and express them. **Emotional intelligence (EI)** is the ability to understand emotions in ourselves and others in order to effectively manage our own behaviors and relationships with others.

4.3 Explain the ways in which attitudes influence behavior in organizations

An **attitude** is a learned tendency to consistently respond positively or negatively to people or events. *Cognitive appraisal* reflects the sum total of a person's underlying beliefs, opinions, information, and knowledge about a specific object, person, or event. These appraisals lead to *affective evaluation*, which reflects a person's attitudes and his or her positive and negative feelings toward a specific object, person, or event. This then leads to the individual's *behavioral intention,* the intention to behave in a particular way toward a specific object, person, or event. Attitudes do not necessarily predict behavior; social norms and other behavioral controls may intervene.

4.4 Identify some common workplace attitudes and related outcomes

Our workplace attitudes are critical in three main areas: job satisfaction, organizational commitment, and employee engagement. **Job satisfaction** is the degree to which an individual feels positive or negative about a job. **Organizational commitment** is the loyalty of an individual to the organization. **Employee engagement** is a connection with the organization and passion for one's job. There is a strong relationship between job satisfaction and job performance. **Organizational citizenship behaviors (OCBs)** are discretionary and voluntary behaviors that are not a part of the employee's specific role requirements and are not formally rewarded.

4.5 Illustrate the ways in which stress can affect behavior in the workplace

Stress is a response that occurs when a situation is perceived as threatening to a person's well-being when the person's resources are taxed or exceeded. **Stressors** are environmental stimuli that place demands on individuals. The outcomes of stress can be either positive or negative.

4.6 Discuss different outcomes of stress and the benefits of wellness programs

Eustress is a moderate level of stressors that have constructive and positive effects on effort and performance. In contrast, **distress** is characterized by high levels of stressors that have destructive and negative effects on effort and performance. **Coping** is the effort to manage, reduce, or minimize stressors. **Problem-focused coping** aims at reducing or eliminating stressors by attempting to understand the problem, and seeking practical ways in which to resolve it; **emotion-focused coping** is an effort to try to change our emotional reaction to a stressor by using positive language and distracting techniques. Many organizations offer wellness programs as a way of helping their employees manage stress. A **wellness program** is a personal or organizational effort to promote health and well-being.

KEY TERMS

Affects 97

Attitude 104

Cognitive dissonance 105

Coping 112

Counterproductive work behaviors 108

Deep acting 101

Display rules 100

Distress 111

UP FOR DEBATE: Employee Emotional Well-Being

The workplace demands hard work and consistent job performance, and employees and managers often don't have time to worry about much else. A member of a company is not responsible in any way for his or her fellow employee's emotional well-being, as this harms a professional environment. Agree or disagree? Explain your answer.

EXERCISE 4.1: Coping with Stress

Objective

The purpose of this exercise is to gain a greater understanding of how others cope with stress.

Instructions

Stress is unavoidable in our lives. You have stress associated with classes, but also in your social life, the activities you're involved with, and so on. Some have additional stress due to their health or home life. Given that there is always going to be some stress in our lives, being able to cope with it is important.

In groups of three to five, discuss the things that cause you the most stress. Is it tight deadlines or worrying about where you will work after graduation? Is it an upcoming assignment that you haven't started yet or is it an important conversation you need to have with a friend? Identify a stressor in your life and ask the others in the group to offer suggestions for how to cope with the stress. Take turns, permitting each person to provide their major stressor and others to offer methods for coping.

Reflection Questions

1. Were the suggestions you received helpful in alleviating your stress? Why or why not?

2. Sometimes just talking about something stressful is helpful. Did the process of revealing your stressor to the group in itself help you cope? Why or why not?

3. What coping suggestions did you receive that will help you in the workplace? Are the same coping mechanisms applicable for a work situation versus a personal stressor? Why or why not?

Exercise contributed by Steven Stovall, Southeast Missouri State University.

EXERCISE 4.2: Recognizing Emotions Role-Play

Objective

The purpose of this exercise is to grasp the concept of emotions and how to recognize them in others.

Instructions

Emotions are an integral part of our lives. We exhibit some blatantly and others we try to stifle. In this exercise, a series of role-plays will give you an opportunity to see if you can readily recognize emotions in others.

The professor will ask for volunteers or choose people at random for this role-play exercise. In teams of two, each pair of students will come up with a quick skit that demonstrates a particular emotion. Once the teams are formed, they take a few moments privately to determine what the skit will consist of—it might be verbal and/or nonverbal. Remember, emotions can be either positive or negative. One team might demonstrate *anger*, while another, *happiness*. One team may show the emotion of *betrayal*, while another, *pride*. After pairs are formed, determine which emotion you're going to demonstrate and act it out in front of the audience. The audience attempts to identify which emotion is being demonstrated. There should be between eight and ten different emotions exhibited among the pairings of students.

Reflection Questions

1. How easy was it to recognize each emotion? What elements—verbal or nonverbal—caused you to realize which emotion was being demonstrated?

2. In a workplace setting, how common are the emotions demonstrated in your class? Which emotions do we tend to see most often at work?

3. If you were one of those participating in the role-play, how did you decide what words or actions you would use to convey the emotion? If you were in the audience, what would you have done differently to convey that same emotion?

Exercise contributed by Steven Stovall, Southeast Missouri State University.

EXERCISE 4.3: Mourning at the Deco Chocolate Company

Objective

In this exercise, you will develop your ability to *describe* emotions in an organizational context, *discuss* the roles these emotions play in the workplace, and *develop examples* of the effects of workplace stress.

Instructions

You are a manager at the Deco Chocolate Company. Deco Chocolate is a small, boutique chocolate company that specializes in high-end, custom-designed, hand-crafted chocolates for special events such as large weddings and corporate banquets. The company has been highly profitable, but due to the nature of its service, it has remained relatively small with only 118 employees.

The company is very close knit, with all current employees having been personally selected by one of the founders, the former president (Mary Washington) or vice president of HR (her husband, Hank Washington). The founders would regularly invite workers at all levels to their home for dinners or parties. Reciprocally, there was rarely a wedding, birth, bar mitzvah, or other major life event that the founders were not invited to as well. In brief, Mary and Hank had developed the company into a true family.

This made the car crash and subsequent death of Mary and Hank last week a truly devastating loss to everyone in the company. A strong succession plan created by Mary Washington has ensured a smooth operational transition for the company, but the emotional fallout is quite different. There have been noticeable signs of grief, depression, and a general drop in worker morale and performance. In addition, more withdrawal behaviors such as absenteeism, lateness, and even looking for external employment have occurred.

While the company has provided grief counseling for the workers, the acting president realizes that the managers need to take an active role in helping the workers process their feelings and continue to sustain the company. To facilitate this process, the acting president has called a meeting of all company managers to discuss the situation, and how to best proceed.

Instructions: For the exercise, form into small groups (five to seven people). One person should take the role of the acting company president. This person's task will mainly be to make sure that everyone in the group has a chance to contribute to the discussion and to encourage exploration of ideas. Everyone else will assume the role of a company manager. In the group, discuss the expected emotional issues that company workers—and yourselves—are experiencing.

Discuss the role of how the company's family atmosphere both aids and hinders workers in processing the situation. You may want to have a special discussion about the extra emotional labor that workers (especially those who have to interact with the public as part of their jobs and the managers who have to maintain smooth business processes) are encountering. Also, discuss the role of stress in the situation. Finally, be sure to ground your discussion in concrete steps that can be taken to improve affected workplace outcomes such as performance, turnover, absenteeism, loyalty, and job satisfaction.

At the end of the discussion, have one person prepared to present an overview of the group's discussion and recommended steps to the class.

Reflection Questions

1. How did using chapter terms and concepts help shape how you understood and what you thought about the situation?

2. Did use of these concepts provide you with better insights into dealing with the situation? Also, look for differences between your group's presentation and other groups' presentations.

3. Were there any insights brought up that your group did not see?

4. Finally, while this exercise dealt with a negative situation, there are also many positive situations and attendant emotions at work. How could you use chapter concepts to recognize and promote such positive emotions?

Exercise contributed by Milton R. Mayfield, Professor of Business, Texas A&M International University, and Jacqueline R. Mayfield, Professor of Business, Texas A&M International University.

ONLINE EXERCISE 4.1: Understanding Attitudes and Job Satisfaction

Objective

The purpose of this exercise is to gain an appreciation for our attitudes and job satisfaction.

Instructions

An attitude is a learned tendency to consistently respond positively or negatively to people or events. Attitudes help shape our behaviors and whether or not we are satisfied with our jobs.

The website Glassdoor.com is an online platform that shows how satisfied employees (and former employees) are with a particular firm. Go to the website and look up companies in your town or city. Find three companies that are highly rated—above 4.0 stars. What comments tell you that this is an enjoyable place to work? Prepare a short report on all three companies, detailing why they are rated so highly. Submit this to your professor.

Reflection Questions

1. What conclusions can you draw about these three companies? Would you want to work for any of the three? Why or why not?

2. How reliable do you think the ratings and comments are for each company? How do those ratings and comments influence your opinion about the organizations? What do you think some of the attitudes are of those who posted comments on the website?

3. Why are some firms so highly rated and others have very poor ratings? What factors enable one company to have a high degree of job satisfaction, while another has a low degree of job satisfaction?

Exercise contributed by Steven Stovall, Southeast Missouri State University.

CASE STUDY 4.1: The Starbucks Experience

According to *CNN Money*, *barista* carries the dubious dual distinction of being one of the nation's most stressful jobs and among those with the lowest pay. Baristas face many challenges: not only do they have to deal with the physical demands of making and serving coffee, they also have the emotional stress of coping with early morning lines of impatient customers in a hurry. In a recent poll surveying coffee workers, 55 percent of respondents reported upper-body repetitive stress injuries, 37 percent complained of persistent sore muscles, 29 percent said they suffered from anxiety attacks, and 44 percent lamented high stress levels. Considering that the median pay of baristas is $21,895, is the stress worth it? How might their employers help baristas cope?

Howard Schultz is CEO of Starbucks Coffee, which is worth about $70.71 billion at the time of this writing and is projected to grow. There are more than 28,000 stores in 65 countries with 240,000+ employees, the bulk of whom are serving up your morning joe. After slashing jobs and closing stores in 2009 and 2018, Schultz and Starbucks are brewing up new business again. The company's China/Asia Pacific business grew revenue at 54 percent year over year as reported at the close of 2018.

When Starbucks was conceived by three friends on the Seattle waterfront in 1971, the number one principle of its mission statement was bold: "To provide a great work environment and treat each other with respect and dignity." Forty-five plus years later, Starbucks continues to provide an exception to *CNN Money*'s suggestion that the barista job is generally awful. The company frequently tops *Fortune*'s "100 Best Companies to Work For" list and has legions of fierce brand loyalists, many of them employees past and present. You can read employee testimonials on Glassdoor.com ("When I first started [with Starbucks] I had no intention of making a career out of Starbucks. Now, I have no intention of having a career without Starbucks"), plus numerous glowing blogs and the 2007 bestseller, *How Starbucks Saved My Life: A Son of Privilege Learns to Live Like Everyone Else*, by Michael Gates Gill.

Managers know that happy, healthy employees make for a better workforce, and a better workforce means a better experience for customers. To keep the money rolling in—while remaining true to its founding principles—Starbucks has had to be proactive about battling the barista blues. In the late 1990s, after conducting its own internal studies, Starbucks enlisted the help of La Marzocco, the Italian maker of espresso machines. La Marzocco in turn reached out to an osteopath and a physical therapist for insight into the company's concerns about the repetitive actions performed by the baristas. They found that lifting milk jugs and steaming milk, tamping, inserting and removing portafilters, and simply standing for long periods had serious health implications. The demands also placed a dampener on staff "happiness and effectiveness." To combat the effects, Starbucks worked with La Marzocco to develop a number of new employee-friendly technologies, including the auto-dosing and tamping Swift grinder. Throughout the decades, Starbucks has continued to innovate and automate processes with its employees' health and safety in mind.

In Peter Ubel's article in *Forbes*, "Do Starbucks' Employees Have More Emotional Intelligence Than Your Physician?" the author suggests that doctors have a lot to learn from Starbucks' baristas in terms of managing stress and communicating with constituents. He points out that, unlike physicians, Starbucks' employees are trained to be emotionally sensitive and intuitive and to act accordingly. In the "Latte Method," they undergo rigorous training on how to recognize and respond to customer needs. When a customer is unhappy, the Latte Method suggests, "We *Listen* to the customer, *Acknowledge* their complaint, *Take* action by solving the problem, *Thank* them, and then *Explain* why the problem occurred."

With a framework in place to manage customer anxiety, Starbucks also succeeds in soothing employees' nerves by providing the employee a basis for managing customers that reduces the fear of the unknown. The framework also empowers the employee (gives them tools) to handle stressful customer situations.

There are other ways in which Starbucks helps ameliorate employee stress—physical, emotional, and financial, too. Part-time employees who work at least 20 hours a week receive health care benefits. Salaries are higher than average for store managers and plans are in the works to raise wages for employees across the board; Starbucks' CEO, in fact, has been a vocal proponent of raising the minimum wage for workers in the service industry. The company recently revised its practices to give employees more consistent hours, which helps with financial planning, not to mention the demands of family life. What's more, Starbucks employees are eligible for bonuses, 401(k) matching, and tuition reimbursement, and most recently, a free online college education cosponsored by Arizona State University, one of the largest universities in the United States. Employees (called "partners") are also encouraged to move up the ladder. All these benefits help relieve the typical stress associated with service jobs. An employee who feels valued and who is encouraged to grow will be more invested in his or her job.

Schultz and Starbucks are clearly doing something right. Restaurant industry insider Eric Levine writes, "I'm fascinated how each and every Starbucks, while all corporately owned and part of a billion-dollar company, makes you feel that the owner and his wife are there, and that's why they care." Curious about what made Starbucks employees so happy, he decided to launch an informal poll. "I would have thought that the No. 1 reasons would have been benefits and stock options or growth and opportunity. To my surprise, the No. 1 answer—from eight out of ten employees—was that they love the product, people and culture."

The service industry is a notoriously stressful one, which Levine knows well. "I have seen servers yell at customers, 'I have five tables just seated. I'm doing the best I can.' This energy becomes anxiety and frustration, stressing customers, and costing both the company and the server money.... Starbucks employees deal with lines and stress like all the employees in our industry, but their stress is channeled into motion and productivity, not resentment and aggression."

Case Questions

1. Starbucks' core agenda is to provide an excellent work environment and for employees to treat each other with respect and dignity. How were they able to make this happen?

2. Describe the "Latte Method." How did it help grow Starbucks?

3. Employees say that they love Starbucks' company culture, and Starbucks regularly tops *Fortune*'s "100 Best Companies to Work For." How does Starbucks promote organizational commitment and job satisfaction?

SELF-ASSESSMENT 4.1

Emotional Intelligence Self-Assessment

Emotional intelligence is the ability to understand emotions in oneself and others in order to effectively manage one's own behaviors and relationships with others. More and more organizations are basing their hiring and promoting decisions on EI, and it is as important to professional success as other abilities such as technical skills. This assessment will help identify your EI strengths and areas for development.

Rank each statement as follows:

	NEVER 0	RARELY 1	SOMETIMES 2	OFTEN 3	ALWAYS 4
Self-Awareness					
I have a good understanding of my feelings.	0	1	2	3	4
I am aware of my individual strengths and weaknesses.	0	1	2	3	4
I usually know how I feel and understand why I feel that way.	0	1	2	3	4
I think about my own emotional reactions to the things that happen to me.	0	1	2	3	4
I analyze how my emotions may influence my behaviors.	0	1	2	3	4
Total: _____					
Self-Management					
I am able to effectively control negative feelings and impulses.	0	1	2	3	4
I am a person that other people can depend upon and trust.	0	1	2	3	4
I tend to be flexible when I encounter changing situations or difficult obstacles.	0	1	2	3	4
I always try to see the positive or the good in the things that happen to me.	0	1	2	3	4
I try to take advantage of opportunities when they are presented to me.	0	1	2	3	4

(Continued)

(Continued)

	NEVER 0	RARELY 1	SOMETIMES 2	OFTEN 3	ALWAYS 4
Total: _____					
Social Awareness					
I try to understand other people's emotions.	0	1	2	3	4
I am effective in reading and understanding the actions and decisions of others	0	1	2	3	4
I recognize and respond to the needs of other people.	0	1	2	3	4
I try to see things from other people's perspectives.	0	1	2	3	4
I show an interest in the concerns of other people.	0	1	2	3	4
Total: _____					
Relationship Management					
I can effectively guide and motivate other people.	0	1	2	3	4
I provide feedback and guidance to help others develop their abilities.	0	1	2	3	4
I am good at leading people in new directions.	0	1	2	3	4
I can effectively develop and maintain relationships with other people.	0	1	2	3	4
I enjoy cooperating with others in a team setting.	0	1	2	3	4
Total: _____					
You can assess your effectiveness on each EI dimension using the following scale:					
0–12 *Needs Improvement*: These dimensions should be targeted for additional consideration and refinement.					
13–17 *Adequate Functioning*: These dimensions are acceptable but could use additional strengthening.					
18–20 *Advanced Strengths*: These dimensions are key areas of strength that may be used to help develop lacking skills in other areas.					

5

Motivation: Concepts and Theoretical Perspectives

Motivation is the art of getting people to do what you want them to do because they want to do it.

—Dwight D. Eisenhower, 34th President of the United States

Learning Objectives

By the end of this chapter, you will be able to:

5.1   Explain the basic motivation process

5.2   Compare the various needs theories of motivation

5.3   Apply goal-setting theory in organizational contexts

5.4   Examine equity theory in the context of organizational justice and distinguish among the predictable outcomes of perceived inequity

5.5   Describe the expectancy theory of motivation and its practical implications

CASE STUDY: ARIZONA ICED TEA: ORGANIZATIONAL MOTIVATION

In one of the most competitive industries in the world, with competitors spending more on advertising than the GDPs of entire countries, AriZona Iced Tea stands out as an innovator. In a market for drinks without alcohol, Coca-Cola and Pepsi are the obvious leaders, but they do so with billions of dollars in advertising and with over a century each of growth. AriZona Iced Tea and its managers compete in the same space as these other beverage behemoths with a limited staff all motivated toward the goal of cost cutting. With companies like Pepsi and Coca-Cola devoting small armies toward marketing, a brand like AriZona needs an edge. Their advantage is a workforce that is fully motivated toward lowering costs and creating interest for their product without ever needing to do their own marketing.

AriZona Iced Tea broke into the market in 1992 after founders John Ferolito and Don Vultaggio saw the success of Snapple, founded in 1970. In a market for premixed tea drinks where Snapple was king, AriZona quickly shot to dominance with their larger size and lower price point of less than a dollar. Since 1992, AriZona Iced Tea has dominated their portion of the beverage market while growing their brand and keeping their price point the same.

So how does a beverage company produce a drink priced cheaper than water for twenty-five years? Founder Don Vultaggio says, "It comes down to incorporating new technology into our entire process." To a beverage company like AriZona, it comes down to a team of motivated employees continuously increasing efficiency without alienating the customer by raising the price of their product. Vultaggio understood his employees and his customer from the start and AriZona Iced Tea has built their brand around pleasing their loyal fan base.

Since 1992, AriZona has found a number of areas where they can increase efficiency and lower their own costs. The first of which is aluminum usage. AriZona currently uses 40 percent less aluminum per can than it used in the '90s. The AriZona team identified the easiest way to increase efficiency and avoid raw materials price volatility was to use less aluminum. The current price per can is between five and ten cents; in 1992, it was about half that, and in 2008 it was nearly double that. Because AriZona uses a larger can with thinner walls, their prices aren't affected by the volatile market for aluminum cans.

Another way that the AriZona team keeps prices down through efficient technology lies in their packaging methods. AriZona Iced Tea beverages are now packaged twice as fast as they were in 1992. This means that supply will always be at or above the level of demand, allowing them to sell more cans to more people and further hold down costs.

Most beverage companies have relatively centralized packaging operations that require all of their product to be distributed over long distances using a somewhat complicated supply chain. AriZona, on the other hand, has at least forty canning centers located across the United States that allow for shorter transport distances and lower fuel costs. This, paired with the policy that AriZona beverages are only transported at night to avoid traffic, greatly reduce transportation costs for their product.

All of these efficient uses of resources have allowed AriZona to keep their cost per can at ninety-nine cents, but the greatest advantage AriZona has in price leadership is their team's advertising strategy. Founder Don Vultaggio decided early on in AriZona's history that the best way to have a cheap product in the beverage industry is to not advertise anywhere but on the can.

Vultaggio says, "We feel like it's more important to spend money on something that our customer really cares about, instead of buying billboards or putting our cans in the hands of some celebrity for a few minutes."

AriZona and its employees decided at their inception that they needed to be different from other beverage companies in their advertising practices or they would get pushed out of the market. They decided that their team motivations needed to be a little different from those of the current top dogs in their market. AriZona needed to make it their motivation to cut costs anywhere they could and market their beverage by making it the best and cheapest product that they could. This is ultimately what made AriZona the brand they are today because without the huge advertising costs they were able to undercut larger beverage companies and create a following of loyal customers.

Customers are loyal to AriZona for the quirkiness of the brand and the taste and consistency of the product. One thing that is inseparable from the brand loyalty is the always low price of ninety-nine cents. It has been one of AriZona's most challenging goals so far to keep it at that price point for over twenty-five years but it has quite possibly been the main aspect of their product that has kept them relevant. The goal of ninety-nine cents has been the rallying point for the AriZona team and has motivated employees toward something.

As a result, AriZona has always kept the suggested retail price right on the can to keep merchants from marking it up and muddling their brand for the sake of higher profits. Vultaggio thinks that it is fair to think of this suggested retail price as an agreement that the merchant accepts when he chooses to sell their product. If AriZona is going to be motivated to that ninety-nine cent price point, the outcome cannot be higher profits on the merchant's end.

Vultaggio says, "We definitely try to protect that suggested retail price because, again, the price is part of us. That being said, it's hard to police that, nationwide."

Their price is intertwined with their brand as a whole, so he acknowledges that to change it is to tweak the ethos of the entire company.

A team that is motivated toward keeping their price low has kept a loyalty to the brand, which has in turn allowed AriZona to maintain itself as a staple of convenience stores across the nation. Of course, there is a reason that many merchants don't mind raising the price of the can above the recommended retail price. Due to AriZona being the least expensive beverage in convenience stores, the margin that these stores make off of AriZona cans is smaller than most other products. On the whole, if convenience stores had a choice, they would carry a product with higher profit margins in the place of AriZona Iced Tea. However, AriZona has gained a fair amount of market power due to the demand and consistency of its customer following. AriZona Iced Tea always sells, and if a convenience store doesn't sell it, many customers will go somewhere else to get it. This leaves merchants little choice but to carry a product that makes less per square foot than many other products.

The AriZona Iced Tea team has established itself as an effective cost leader in its segment of the beverage industry since its founding in 1992. Through innovation, lean thinking on the part of employees, and a creative advertising strategy, it has been able to keep its prices the same since 1992. In return for the low price, AriZona Iced Tea had a loyal fan base which will keep the beverage in stores for years to come.

Critical-Thinking Questions

1. What was the beverage market like in 1992 when AriZona entered?

2. How did AriZona Iced Tea differentiate itself from competitors and maintain dominance in their segment?

3. Why have merchants kept AriZona products in their stores despite low margins per can?

Sources:

Arizona Beverage Company. (n.d.). Retrieved from https://en.wikipedia.org/wiki/Arizona_Beverage_Company

Backman, M. (2015, July 1). Arizona Iced Tea is having a really hard time keeping its dollar cans at a dollar. *Quartz*. Retrieved from https://qz.com/427393/can-arizonas-dollar-cans-of-iced-tea-fend-off-a-bevy-of-snooty-competitors/

BevNET.com Staff. (2009). A brief history of Arizona. *Bevnet*. Retrieved from https://www.bevnet.com/magazine/issue/2009/a_brief_history_of_arizona

Fulton, W. (2016). Why Arizona Iced Tea is cheaper than water. *Thrillist*. Retrieved from https://www.thrillist.com/drink/nation/arizona-iced-tea-price-don-vultaggio-interview

Investopedia. (n.d.). *A look at Coca-Cola's advertising expenses (KO, PEP)*. Retrieved from http://www.investopedia.com/articles/markets/081315/look-cocacolas-advertising-expenses.asp

Rossen, J. (2016, November 16). Why is AriZona Iced Tea cheaper than water? *Mental Floss*. Retrieved from http://mentalfloss.com/article/88735/why-arizona-iced-tea-cheaper-water

Rovell, D. (2011). AriZona's Arnold Palmer brand aiming to top Snapple. *CNBC*. Retrieved from http://www.cnbc.com/id/45614646

The Motivation Process

>> **LO 5.1** **Explain the basic motivation process**

Have you ever successfully completed a goal such as passing an exam or getting a job and wondered how you did it? Think about the behaviors you exhibited to achieve your objectives. To pass the exam, you probably studied hard for long periods of time, and to get the job you likely prepared for the interview by researching the company and practicing responses to potential interview questions. Whatever your intended goal, you would not have achieved it without motivation. Take the AriZona Iced Tea employees featured in our case study. The individual goal for each employee was to boost efficiency and keep costs down, which has allowed the company to meet the organizational goal to sell its product

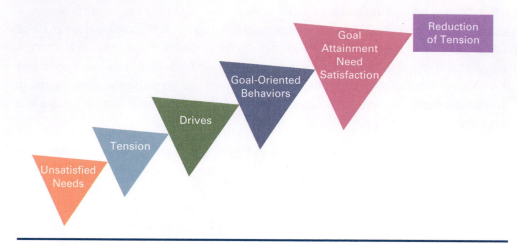

FIGURE 5.1

The Motivation Process

Motivation: Forces from within individuals that stimulate and drive them to achieve goals

at ninety-nine cents for the last twenty-five years without any investment in marketing. We define **motivation** as forces from within individuals that stimulate and drive them to achieve goals.[1] These forces help us to persist with our efforts to achieve specific objectives at work or in our daily life.

But how does motivation affect the way we behave? Motivation is a process by which behavior is *energized*, meaning we have the strength to keep going even when things aren't going our way; *directed*, meaning the efforts we invest in our work which also benefits the employer; and *maintained*, meaning our intention to work for some period of time to achieve objectives.[2] Take a look at how U-Haul motivates its employees in the OB in the Real World feature.

The motivation process is shaped by unsatisfied needs and the resulting tension, as shown in detail in Figure 5.1. For example, you may have an unsatisfied goal to achieve a high grade in an exam, which creates tension. The demand to satisfy this need and relieve the discomfort drives you to study hard, which helps you to attain your goal, thus reducing tension. Similarly, the AriZona Iced Tea team has a motivational goal to keep the price on the can at ninety-nine cents. Any change to this would lead to customer dissatisfaction. It is this discomfort that motivates employees to reduce costs to ensure the price point stays the same. The motivation process is best understood through several motivation theories, most of which we discuss in the next section.

THINKING CRITICALLY

1. List at least ten forces that have motivated you to attain simple and complex goals in your life. These forces may include those that affect your daily behavior such as preparing a meal or walking your dog or forces that affect work behavior such as meeting deadlines or arriving on time.

2. Apply the six-step motivation process shown in Figure 5.1 to a need in your own life (e.g., need to secure a job, need to improve your grades).

THE BIG PICTURE:
How OB Topics Fit Together

Individual Processes
- Individual Differences
- Emotions and Attitudes
- Perceptions and Learning
- **MOTIVATION**

Team Processes
- Ethics
- Decision Making
- Creativity and Innovation
- Conflict and Negotiation

Organizational Processes
- Culture
- Strategy
- Change and Development
- Structure and Technology

Influence Processes
- Leadership
- Power and Politics
- Communication

Organizational Outcomes
- Individual Performance
- Job Satisfaction
- Team Performance
- Organizational Goals

OB IN THE REAL WORLD

Joe Shoen, CEO of AMERCO, the Holding Company of U-Haul

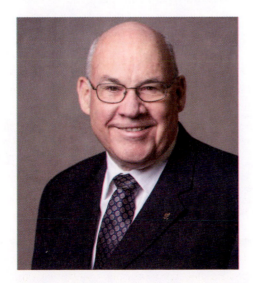

U-Haul has become an American staple since its founding over seventy years ago in Ridgefield, Washington, with an original investment of $5,000. Founded in 1945 by Leonard Shoen with his wife at the age of 29, the idea behind U-Haul was simple: to provide do-it-yourself moving resources to a returning generation of mobile young veterans and young families. The idea turned out to be exactly what people wanted and by 1955 there were over ten thousand U-Haul trailers on the road. Since that time U-Haul has expanded in all directions, with current revenues in the billions and with over sixteen thousand active dealers in the United States.

Joe Shoen, son of U-Haul founder Leonard Shoen, presides over a much different company than his father could ever have predicted back in 1945. With over eighteen thousand employees, Joe believes in using

(Continued)

(Continued)

a management style called "subsidiarity." Subsidiarity is the principle that a central authority should have a subsidiary function, performing only those tasks which cannot be performed at a more local level. Not unique to U-Haul, it happens to also be a general principle of European Union Law. As much as he can, he believes in letting the managers of each U-Haul dealer motivate employees in the ways that they see fit. This way, each dealer can be evaluated individually based on performance and what works and what doesn't work. Then, the things learned at each local dealer can be shared with other dealers to create best practices within the organization. It also gives dealers a fair amount of equity in the success/failure of operations. As long as each individual U-Haul dealer keeps to U-Haul guidelines they are free to make their own decisions. This method of leadership allows U-Haul to fulfill its mission of providing its service as cheaply as possible.

Not to be too disconnected from how his organization is being run, Joe, a manager of a company worth over $7 billion, has chosen to keep his number publicly posted. While he recognizes that this opens him up to some late night calls, he says that he consistently receives valuable critiques of how his business is being run that lead to continual improvement. He'll receive calls from people who feel they have been mistreated, from customers recommending employees for promotion, and even from customers with new ideas for U-Haul to pursue. He believes that this open-door policy keeps his business accountable and gives him insight into tasks that take place at a lower level than his. It allows for a certain amount of procedural justice so that if policies aren't being implemented, customers can easily access someone who can make immediate changes. Having his phone number public gives the idea of subsidiarity used by U-Haul more backbone in a corporate setting because if a customer can't get a problem solved through the usual ladder of command, Joe Shoen certainly can.

The primary motivation of U-Haul has been the same one since 1960. U-Haul's service objective is "To provide a better and better product or service to more and more people at a lower and lower cost." Its motivations and goals are what has kept U-Haul a major player in their industry for so long. They are at the heart of what they strive for at U-Haul and something that they repeat at the beginning of executive meetings. Joe points out that their goals and specifically their service objective has lined up with what has generally occurred for the American consumer over the past one hundred fifty years and he hopes it will continue to be this way for the consumer.

Most of U-Haul's motivations do not allow for applying the "next hot idea out of the marketing department" which he admits are not infrequent. The customer doesn't care about the next hot idea: they want a product or service at the lowest cost and at the highest quality. U-Haul has found over their lifetime that the best way to compete in a busy and competitive marketplace is to place the customer and their needs above all else. Joe says that the phrase that his father told him when he was young and the phrase that motivates his employees today is, "Don't worry about the competition, take care of the customer and let them sort out the competition." Generally, the businesses that function this way survive and prosper and those that don't tend to fall by the wayside.

In the end, Joe Shoen says there is one piece of advice that has stuck with him from the time he was in college that has motivated his career more than anything. Joe says above all else, "Don't learn any tricks. Try to do things for substantive reasons." He says that this is what all of U-Haul's other goals and motivations boil down to: they operate off of a basic set of principles that when consulted give them the tools to make major decisions. With these principles, the U-Haul organization has been able to keep an impeccable image while also becoming one of the most successful brands in their industry.

Critical-Thinking Questions

1. What method does U-Haul employ to manage their employees and their dealerships?

2. How does U-Haul grow their business? ●

Source: Interview with Joe Shoen on May 2nd, 2017.

Sources:

https://en.wikipedia.org/wiki/Subsidiarity

http://www.azfamily.com/story/35141990/u-haul-ceo-joe-shoen-named-w-p-carey-school-of-business-2017-executive-of-the-year

https://www.alumni.hbs.edu/stories/Pages/story-bulletin.aspx?num=5188

http://www.encyclopedia.com/social-sciences-and-law/economics-business-and-labor/businesses-and-occupations/amerco

http://www.bloomberg.com/research/stocks/people/person.asp?personId=345590&privcapId=345588

Needs Theories

>> **LO 5.2** **Compare the various needs theories of motivation**

There are many theories about motivation, but most focus on the idea that motivation is based on different needs and the behavioral outcomes of those needs.

Researchers have spent decades attempting to identify the underlying factors that motivate people. Needs motivation theories are generally divided into two categories: content theories and process theories.[3] **Content theories** explain why people have different needs at different times and how these needs motivate behavior. In other words, what are the types of factors that motivate people? There are four main content theories: Maslow's hierarchy of needs, Alderfer's ERG theory, McClelland's need theory, and Herzberg's two-factor theory. While content theories focus on what motivates us, **process theories** describe the cognitive processes through which needs are translated into behavior. Simply put, process theories look at how our needs drive, influence, and sustain our behavior. The process theories we investigate in this chapter are equity theory, goal-setting theory, and expectancy theory.

In this section we'll explore several needs theories of motivation: Maslow's hierarchy of needs, Herzberg's two-factor theory, McClelland's acquired needs theory, and money as a motivator.

Maslow's Hierarchy of Needs

Psychologist Abraham Maslow developed one of the most popular needs theories, referred to as the **hierarchy of needs theory**,[4] which is visually depicted as a pyramid of five levels of individual needs with physiological needs at the bottom and self-actualization needs at the top (Figure 5.2). Maslow's theory teaches that each need must be satisfied before we can move up the pyramid to satisfy the need above it. For example, at the base of the pyramid, we need to satisfy the physiological need to eat food and drink water in order to survive before we can satisfy our safety needs such as looking after our families or getting a job. Maslow's hierarchy is based on the belief that successfully accomplishing the lower-level needs leads to the achievement of higher-level needs such as gaining confidence, self-esteem, and finally self-actualization.

Content theories: Theories that explain why people have different needs at different times and how these needs motivate behavior, such as Maslow's hierarchy of needs, Alderfer's ERG theory, McClelland's need theory, and Herzberg's two-factor theory

Process theories: Theories that describe the cognitive processes through which needs are translated into behavior, such as equity theory, expectancy theory, and goal-setting theory

Hierarchy of needs theory: Maslow's theory that suggests people are motivated by their desire to satisfy specific needs, and that needs are arranged in a hierarchy with physiological needs at the bottom and self-actualization needs at the top.

FIGURE 5.2

Maslow's Hierarchy of Needs

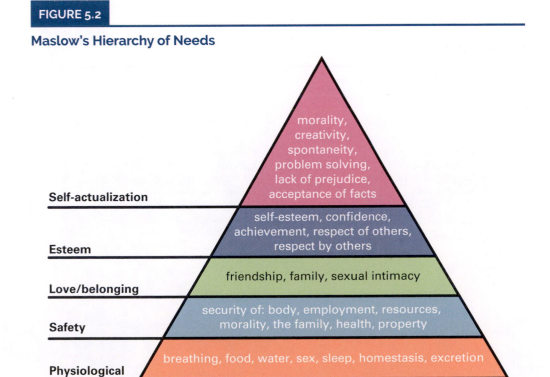

Source: Factoryjoe (Mazlow's Hierarchy of Needs.svg) [CC BY-SA 3.0 (http://creativecommons.org/licenses/by-sa/3.0)], via Wikimedia Commons.

Though Maslow's theory is useful for identifying categories of needs, there has been much debate about its implication that each need loses its importance as soon as it has been satisfied.[5] For example, according to the hierarchy, people who reach self-actualization won't be as concerned with gaining the respect of others. Researchers have also argued against the step-by-step sequence of Maslow's hierarchy, proposing that people may be motivated to satisfy these needs in a number of different ways or even simultaneously.[6]

ERG Theory

ERG theory: Theory that suggests that people are motivated by three categories of needs arranged in the form of a hierarchy

Developed by psychologist Clayton Alderfer, **ERG theory** also suggests that people are motivated by categories of needs arranged in the form of a hierarchy.[7] Instead of Maslow's five need categories, however, Alderfer includes only three: existence needs (E), relatedness needs (R), and growth needs (G). *Existence needs* are similar to Maslow's physiological and safety needs, *relatedness needs* are comparable to Maslow's love/belonging needs, and *growth needs* bear similarities to Maslow's esteem needs and self-actualization needs. Alderfer proposed that instead of satisfying needs one step at a time, we can satisfy different levels in any order or even at the same time depending on the circumstances. ERG theory has received more support from researchers than Maslow's hierarchy of needs, but further research needs to be carried out to fully test the validity of Alderfer's model.

Herzberg's Two-Factor Theory

Two-factor theory (*motivation-hygiene theory* or *dual theory*): The impact of motivational influences on job satisfaction

Hygiene factors: Sources of job satisfaction such as salary, status, and security

A third theory of motivation, developed by psychologist Frederick Herzberg, is called **two-factor theory** (or *motivation-hygiene theory* or *dual theory*). It explores the impact of motivational influences on job satisfaction.[8] Herzberg conducted interviews with hundreds of workers before identifying two main factors influencing employee behavior: hygiene factors and motivators (Figure 5.3). **Hygiene factors** are sources of job satisfaction such as salary, status, and security. Herzberg found that the first step to

---

FIGURE 5.3

Herzberg's Two-Factor Theory

Hygiene Factors	Motivator Factors
• Salaries, Wages, and Other Benefits • Company Policy and Administration • Good Inter-personal Relationships • Quality of Supervision • Job Security • Working Conditions • Work/Life Balance	• Sense of Personal Achievement • Status • Recognition • Challenging/Stimulating Work • Responsibility • Opportunity for Advancement • Promotion • Growth
When in place, these factors result in . . .	**When in place, these factors result in . . .**
✓ General Satisfaction ✓ Prevention of Dissatisfaction	✓ High Motivation ✓ High Satisfaction ✓ Strong Commitment

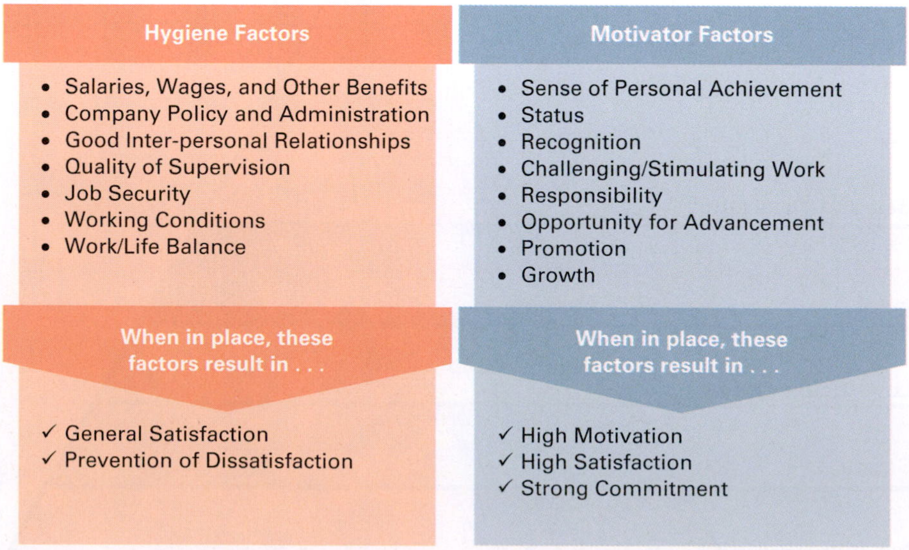

Source: Based on Herzberg, F., B. Mausner, and B. Snyderman. *The Motivation to Work* (2nd ed.) (Oxford: Wiley, 1959); Herzberg, Frederick, "One More Time: How Do You Motivate Employees?" *Harvard Business Review* 81, no. 1 (January 2003): 87–96.

employee satisfaction was to eliminate poor hygiene factors. For example, if employees don't feel they are being paid enough in comparison to industry standards, employers can remedy the situation by introducing fair and competitive wages. While eliminating poor hygiene factors will reduce job dissatisfaction, two-factor theory states that taking such steps will not increase job satisfaction.[9] To correct this, managers need to use **motivators** such as achievement, recognition, and responsibility to build job satisfaction.

According to Herzberg, effective motivators lead to a highly stimulated, motivated workforce, whereas in the absence of motivators, employees can become ambivalent or apathetic toward their roles. Over the years, Herzberg's two-factor theory has received a number of criticisms for being too narrow in scope. Some theorists have questioned Herzberg's assumption that satisfied employees are more productive. Others have argued that what motivates one person might not necessarily motivate another. The theory has also been criticized for not accounting for individual differences, meaning that some individuals may respond differently to hygiene or motivator factors.[10]

Despite these criticisms, Herzberg's two-factor theory has been an important influence on the motivational techniques employed by managers with their workforce in the areas of job security, job enrichment, and job satisfaction.[11]

Motivators: Sources of job satisfaction such as achievement, recognition, and responsibility

McClelland's Acquired Needs Theory

Developed by psychological theorist David McClelland, **acquired needs theory** holds that our needs are shaped over time and formed by our experiences and cultural background. McClelland classified needs into three main categories: need for achievement, need for affiliation, and need for power.[12] Although McClelland believed that in each of us one of these needs is the dominant motivator, he also believed that all three, in particular the need for achievement, can be learned through training.

Acquired needs theory: Theory that suggests three main categories of needs: need for achievement, need for affiliation, and need for power

- **Need for achievement** is the desire to excel. People who are achievement oriented are generally positive in nature, tend to set their own goals, thrive on feedback, and take ownership of their work. High achievers do well in challenging environments but may lose motivation in routine roles. Creator of shapewear product Spanx, and self-made billionaire, Sara Blakely is a good example of a person with a desire to excel.[13] When Blakely cut up a pair of pantyhose in an effort to find an undergarment to wear under her white trousers, she realized she had a viable product on her hands. She worked on the product for two years before showcasing it—in person—to department stores. When the product appeared on Oprah's "favorite things" list, it really took off, developing a celebrity following. Over the years, Spanx has added new products such as panties, bras, and jeans.

Need for achievement: Need to perform well against a standard of excellence

Need for affiliation: Need to be liked and to stay on good terms with most other people

Need for power: Desire to influence people and events

- **Need for affiliation** is the desire to belong to a group and to be liked. Generally, people who possess this need as a dominant motivator like to maintain the status quo; they tend not to make good managers because they don't like to make unpopular decisions or give orders for fear of falling out of favor with their colleagues. Without daily contact with others, people with strong affiliation needs might lose motivation, which may lead to job dissatisfaction.

- **Need for power** is the desire to control and influence the behavior of others. There are two types of power. *Institutional power* is the power an individual exerts for the good of the organization

Sara Blakely, creator of Spanx.

Sipa USA via AP

FIGURE 5.4

Comparison of the Four Content Theories of Motivation

Maslow's Need Hierarchy	Alderfer's ERG Theory	Herzberg's Theory	McClelland's Acquired Needs
Self-Actualization	Growth	Motivators	Need for Achievement
Esteem			Need for Power
Belongingness	Relatedness	Hygienes	Need for Affiliation
Safety	Existence		
Physiological			

Fidel Castro's need for personal power drove him to control his followers and become one of the most notorious dictators in the world.

and its employees, and *personal power* is power focused on controlling and manipulating others for personal gain. Dictators Kim Jong-un, Fidel Castro, and Adolf Hitler are examples of leaders who used their power to coerce and control their followers.

Each of the content theorists—Maslow, Alderfer, Herzberg, and McClelland—focused on our human needs and what motivate us to satisfy those needs (Figure 5.4). Yet, in many organizations, money is used as a prime motivator for employees.

Money as a Motivator

Money is one of the primary mechanisms managers use for motivating people in the workplace. This was the approach used by CEO Dan Price of Seattle-based credit card processing company Gravity Payments.[14] In 2015, Price not only announced he was cutting his own million-dollar annual salary to $70,000, but also made it the minimum salary for all his employees. Two years on, Price has no regrets about using money as a motivator, believing that it boosts employee engagement and makes an organization more competitive. He says, "If an organization focuses on paying everybody a living wage, it will have a competitive advantage." While Price may believe in the benefits of money as an incentive, how does this idea fit in with the content theories? Generally, money sits with lower-level needs: safety and physiological for Maslow's hierarchy of needs, existence for Alderfer's ERG theory, and hygiene factors for Herzberg's two-factor theory. Money provides us with food, housing, clothing, and all the necessities of life. If money is so important, why did the theorists not consider it a high-level need?

Most people who live in modern societies and work in contemporary organizations receive a paycheck that affords them a certain standard of living. This means their lower-level needs are already being satisfied. Instead, people focus on higher-level needs such as belongingness, esteem, self-actualization according to Maslow, relatedness and growth for Alderfer, and Herzberg's motivator factors. Money is not as important here according to these theorists. As the Beatles said, "I don't care too much for money, 'cause money can't buy me love."

Money can sometimes become a status symbol or an indication of success, and some people are paid far more than others. For example, CEO of WalMart US E-Commerce Marc Lore earned over $230 million in 2016, making him the highest-paid CEO in the United States. However, appealing as it might be to earn millions, money generally does not relate directly to the needs that people are trying to satisfy in the workplace. This is not to say that money is unimportant, but rather that it may not be the most important or most effec-

Marc Lore of Wal-Mart E-Commerce was the highest paid CEO in the US in 2016, but this does not mean that he was the most effective or successful.

tive motivator. For example, promising an employee a ten cent per hour raise or a $300 year-end bonus may not necessarily increase motivation. Instead, these theories suggest, people are motivated by their affiliation with others and the opportunity to achieve, grow, and be recognized for their accomplishments.

Drew Greenblatt, president of Marlin Steel, a US-based builder of steel wire baskets and sheet metal material-handling containers, uses a combination of lower-level and higher-level needs to motivate his workforce. An advocate of cross-training, Greenblatt ensures his employees undergo rigorous training courses in order to learn the skills necessary to carry out a variety of tasks and operate multiple machines. Each employee is rewarded with a bonus for every additional skill he or she acquires. Greenblatt believes his employees are motivated not only by the cash incentive but also by the opportunity

EXAMINING THE EVIDENCE

Money as a Motivator

Few behavioral researchers would argue that money has no motivational effect on employees. Indeed, a number of studies suggest that financial incentives can increase certain types of work performance.[*] However, a group of researchers conducted a series of experiments in which subjects completed basic tasks under different financial reward conditions ranging from relatively small to moderate to very large and across different types of tasks involving motor skills, creativity, and memory respectively. The researchers concluded, "One cannot assume that introducing or raising incentives will always improve performance." In short, these findings suggest that financial incentives—especially very large ones— could increase task motivation to a higher than optimal level, leading to "choking" under pressure and reduced performance. In contrast, small-to-moderate financial inducements may work best, especially when used to motivate the performance of noncognitive tasks that don't require employees to learn or develop specialized

skills or work collaboratively with others. These researchers conclude, "Perhaps there is good reason why so many workers continue to be paid on a straight salary basis."

Critical-Thinking Questions

1. Many companies offer large financial incentives for tasks that require creativity, problem solving, and memory. Based on the research findings described here, what is a possible limitation to this approach?

2. How can managers most effectively use nonfinancial incentives to increase employee performance? ●

[*]Rynes, Sara L., Barry Gerhart, and Laura Parks. "Personnel Psychology: Performance Evaluation and Pay for Performance." *Annual Review of Psychology* 56, no. 1 (February 2005): 571–600.

[^]Ariely, Dan, Uri Gneezy, George Loewenstein, and Nina Mazar. "Large Stakes and Big Mistakes." *Review of Economic Studies* 76, no. 2 (April 2009): 451–469.

to acquire new skills that increase their productivity and commitment.[15] Marlin Steel invests five per cent of its labor budget every year in cross-training. Greenblatt believes that training has "become a critical part of our business—it makes us more adaptable and more nimble, and helps us to weather turbulence in the economy. And it ensures that one person with all the skills is not a bottleneck."[16]

Marlin Steel is a large company, but what about smaller companies that cannot afford to pay cash bonuses or give monetary rewards, especially in difficult economic times? How do they motivate their employees? A San Francisco–based office catering company offers employees $500 each to pay for cooking classes every year.[17] Employees working at English-speaking start up Voxy, based in New York, have the opportunity to learn a new language courtesy of their employer (think Mandarin Mondays!). Universal Information Services, a news-media analysis company in Nebraska, offers "Free Beer Fridays" as a way of rewarding their employees for their hard work during the week; they also offer free sodas. These small companies have managed to create a committed and loyal workforce through their application of innovative motivators in lieu of high salaries and cash bonuses. Yet, regardless of the amount of cash incentives or creative perks, work will never get done without the existence of clear work-related goals.

THINKING CRITICALLY

1. Write a brief biography that assumes your development over time is following Maslow's hierarchy of needs precisely. To what extent does this version of your life story seem accurate? What problems and distortions do you perceive from this biography?

2. Revise your biography according to Alderfer's ERG theory so that it reflects the assumptions and categories (existence needs, relatedness needs, growth needs) of that theory instead. To what extent is this version of your life story more or less accurate than the version based on Maslow's hierarchy of needs? What aspects of your life are difficult to address when the main means of shaping/describing your life is based on your motivation to have particular needs met?

3. Based on your understanding of Herzberg's two-factor theory of job satisfaction, what types of incentives or employee programs are most likely to reduce job dissatisfaction? What types of incentives or employee programs are most likely to increase job satisfaction?

4. Compare McClelland's acquired needs theory and its emphasis on needs being shaped by experience and cultural background over time to Maslow's hierarchy of needs and ERG theory. Of these three theories, which do you think provides the most useful and realistic explanation for human development and motivation? Why?

5. Assume that you are the CEO of a midsize company that needs to increase employee retention and productivity. Based on the theories in this section and the text's discussion of money as a motivator, what sorts of payment/bonus strategies and benefits would you focus on providing or improving? Why?

Goal-Setting Theory

>> **LO 5.3**   **Apply goal-setting theory in organizational contexts**

What motivates us to go to work or even bother having a job at all? The answer is goals. Having goals to work toward gives us a sense of purpose and is the prime reason we get out of bed and go to work. One of the most important theories in practice

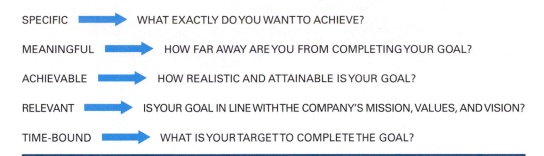

FIGURE 5.5

S.M.A.R.T. Goals

S.M.A.R.T. GOALS

SPECIFIC ➡ WHAT EXACTLY DO YOU WANT TO ACHIEVE?

MEANINGFUL ➡ HOW FAR AWAY ARE YOU FROM COMPLETING YOUR GOAL?

ACHIEVABLE ➡ HOW REALISTIC AND ATTAINABLE IS YOUR GOAL?

RELEVANT ➡ IS YOUR GOAL IN LINE WITH THE COMPANY'S MISSION, VALUES, AND VISION?

TIME-BOUND ➡ WHAT IS YOUR TARGET TO COMPLETE THE GOAL?

in organizations today is goal-setting theory. **Goal-setting theory** was developed by Edwin Locke and Gary Latham in the 1960s, and suggests that human performance is directed by conscious goals and intentions.[18] Studies of the effects of goal setting in the workplace showed that employees are motivated by clear goals accompanied by appropriate feedback.[19] In other words, employees benefit from goals as they provide direction and the amount of effort required to meet those goals.

Goals can have both direct and indirect effects. *Direct effects* motivate and energize us, helping to achieve objectives, and *indirect* effects encourage us to use cognitive skills such as planning and strategizing to attain goals. For example, the direct effect of buying a house involves the ownership of the house, but it also has the indirect effect of working out how to pay the mortgage.

Goal-setting theory: Theory that suggests that human performance is directed by conscious goals and intentions

Specific Goals

Research has shown that people respond more to clear, well-defined goals and produce better results than vague, or "Do Your Best," goals.[20] Managers can set specific goals by making them clear and easy to understand, ensure they are challenging but attainable, make them measurable, and set them within a distinct time frame. For example, a sales team might be set a goal to each acquire ten new customers or sell two hundred products a month. Because of the specificity of the goal, each team member knows exactly what to do to meet the challenge. Many organizations use the acronym S.M.A.R.T to guide their goal setting (see Figure 5.5).

Difficult Goals

Similarly, researchers found that goals set at a high but not unreasonable level of difficulty produce better results than less challenging or easier goals.[21] Vip Sandhir, CEO and founder of HighGround, an employee engagement software provider, believes that employees who set goals outside of their comfort zone and align them with the company goals are the most successful.[22]

Goal Acceptance and Commitment

In general, employees who accept and commit to goals set by or developed in participation with their managers have higher levels of performance and are more motivated to achieve the objectives.[23] The employees featured in the AriZona Iced Tea case study unite to meet the company's over-riding goal: to work efficiently as possible to maintain the beverage's long-standing price point. Companies with committed employees tend to have low turnover. For example, Nu Star Energy, based in San Antonio, rewards its employees for meeting goals with gifts, parties, and bonuses.

The company also builds trust and commitment with its "no layoff" policy which encourages employee retention.[24]

The Goldilocks Rule[25]

Have you ever wondered why you may achieve some goals but not others? Or why you start out so determined to reach a goal one week only to give up the next? This may be because your goal is either too hard, or too easy. The Goldilocks theory states that goals should fall somewhere in the middle in terms of difficulty (just right) in order to be achievable. For example, say you're playing tennis with a friend. If you're pretty good at tennis and your friend is just a beginner, you will mostly likely win easily, but you may also lose motivation because the game isn't challenging enough.

In contrast, say you're playing against a professional tennis player—the game is far more challenging but you might still lose motivation because the game is too tough and you're not good enough to win, let alone score many points. However, if you play against someone who is pretty equal to you in terms of skill, then the game becomes more engaging. Sure, you might lose a few points, but you will also win a few. You will be more motivated to finish the game because victory is possible. The point is that the most achievable goals are the ones that are "just of manageable levels of difficulty"—ones that are within our reach if we persevere enough.

How do you stay motivated to achieve your desired goals? Remember the Goldilocks Rule and work toward goals that fall within the margins of difficulty rather than extremes. Next, make sure to measure your progress and ask for feedback wherever possible so you know how far away you are from achieving your goal.

Feedback

Goals that are accompanied by regular feedback are more likely to motivate employees.[26] Microsoft cofounder Bill Gates is a big believer in feedback, saying, "We all need people who will give us feedback. That's how we improve."[27]

Goals are often arranged in hierarchies in order to assess which ones take priority.[28] For example, **behavioral goals,** which are short-term goals that provide employees with frequent feedback about their performance, are positioned further up the hierarchy than **performance goals,** which are long-term goals set into the future. Setting goals too far into the future can be demotivating for employees. But out-of-range goals are not the only catalyst for demotivated employees. Motivation can also be determined by our perception of fairness in relation to our own roles in an organization.

Behavioral goals (proximal goals): Short-term goals

Performance goals (distal): Long-term goals set into the future

THINKING CRITICALLY

1. Research suggests that having specific goals is more conducive to performance outcomes than nonspecific "fuzzy" goals. With this in mind, do you think writing your goals down (or typing them) can help you achieve your goals? Why or why not?

2. You are a manager and one of your staff members has expressed her long-term goal of getting an MBA but she is not making progress toward it. Based on the discussion of goals in this section what advice could you give her make progress toward this long term goal?

3. Assume you are a manager of an auto dealership and all your sales people employees are achieving the goals they have set for themselves in terms of weekly car sales. On the surface, this would seem to be a good thing. However, what could be the problem with this?

Equity Theory

>> LO 5.4 Examine equity theory in the context of organizational justice and distinguish among the predictable outcomes of perceived inequity

The concept of **equity theory**, introduced by psychologist J. Stacey Adams, holds that motivation is based on our perception of how fairly we are being treated in comparison with others.[29] In other words, people may be more motivated when they perceive their treatment as being fair, but demotivated if they consider their treatment to be unfair. According to this theory, our perception of what is fair depends on the ratio O/I where O equals outcomes like the recognition, pay, and status we enjoy and I equals inputs like our effort, experience, and ability (Figure 5.6).

People tend to compare their own perceived O/I ratio to their perceptions of the O/I ratio of *referent others*, or people whose situation is comparable to their own. As long as the ratios are similar there is no problem, but someone who perceives the other person's ratio as greater than his or her own will feel an inequity. For example, if you discover that a coworker's salary is higher than your own, you may experience a sense of unfairness. People adopt several behaviors in the face of such **perceived inequity**.

Equity theory: Theory that holds that motivation is based on our perception of fairness in comparison with others

Perceived inequity: The sense of feeling under-rewarded or over-rewarded in comparison with others

Change Inputs

Suppose you find out a coworker who does exactly the same job as you and has the same level of experience gets paid $2.00 per hour more than you. You respond to this by slacking off, investing less effort thereby lowering your inputs. Of the four components of the O/I self < O/I other equation, your own "I" is the one you have direct control over. When you are in a position of management and you come across an employee who appears unmotivated or seems to intentionally not do their job, it is very likely that their behavior is the result of a perceived unfairness or inequity. It is your job as a manager to try to find out what they think is unfair and restore a perception of fairness. While you might not think it is actually unfair, people will act based on their perceptions of fairness, not on the actual equity of the situation. Sometimes all that is necessary is to help them to see their misperception.

Attempt to Change Outcomes

Alternatively, if you find out you are underpaid, you could try to increase your "O" by approaching your manager and saying, "Hey I found out that Jamal, who does the same job as me, makes $2.00 per hour more than me! I deserve a raise!" (This incidentally, is one reason why discussing salaries is so taboo in many cultures. Companies and managers don't want to have this potential problem, so discussing salaries is viewed as inappropriate behavior. Do people still do it? Of course!)

Carry Out Cognitive Reevaluation

Suppose you find out that unbeknownst to you, your coworker went to night school and earned an MBA degree or perhaps they had ten years more experience than you while working at another company. Either of those could cause you to change how you perceive their Inputs. You realize, oh, they really do bring more compensable factors to the job than I do. Because equity theory is based on one's perceptions, any of the four components of the equation can be adjusted cognitively. For example, one study showed

FIGURE 5.6

Equity Theory

Equity theory says we perceive the fairness of rewards as a ratio of input to outcome and compare our ratio to other people's.

Person		Referent Other
$\dfrac{\text{Outcomes}}{\text{Inputs}}$	=	$\dfrac{\text{Outcomes}}{\text{Inputs}}$

that after a pay cut, employees increased their cognitive appraisal of nonmonetary job outcomes such as status, office furnishings, etc., in order to put the equation back in balance (I may be getting paid less, but I sure do have a nice office!).[30]

Attempts to Change Inputs or Outcomes

It's not easy to change the I or O of the referent other. You could ask your manager to cut their pay to match yours, but that would probably be met with icy indifference (at best). Even more ludicrously, you could ask your coworker to increase their inputs: "I found out recently that you make $2.00 per hour more than me and I was wondering if you could just do a little extra work off the clock at night or on the weekends—that would make me feel much better about things!" But they probably wouldn't be impressed.

Pick Another "Other"

Employees might compare themselves to different coworkers to perceive a more equitable situation. Suppose you find out that your coworker does have an MBA degree, but instead of doing a cognitive reevaluation, you might decide this person isn't an appropriate comparison for you anyway. This might lead you to choose another coworker who has more a more similar educational or experience level with whom to compare yourself.

Leave the Field

Finally, if the inequity (in this case underpayment) is severe enough and the employee can find no other means to restore equity (such as getting the manager to give them a pay raise or doing some type of cognitive reevaluation), they will often quit. Most people have quit a job or left an organization because they felt they were being treated unfairly. It's interesting to note that the term "leave the field" is based on some of the earliest equity theory studies in which researchers had some boys playing a game in a field involving inequitable outcomes for certain boys.[31] They noted the boys responding in all of the ways outlined above, but if the injustice were felt strongly enough, the boys would literally "leave the field"—they would "take their balls and go home" so to speak! Also of note, one weakness of equity theory is that it does not specify which of these predictable outcomes a person will engage. Will an employee simply slack off or will they quit their jobs? This is not predicted by the theory.

Organizational Justice

Organizational justice:
The perception of fairness in workplace practices

Equity theory includes the concept of **organizational justice,** which focuses on what people perceive as fairness in workplace practices.[32] In other words, the way an organization's behaviors, decisions, and actions as perceived by its employees influence their own attitudes and behaviors in the workplace. Organizational justice involves all matters of organizational behavior including pay, access to training, and gender equality. Employees who perceive themselves as being treated unfairly may call in sick more often, or become more unproductive and disengaged. It is essential that companies, big and small, promote a positive sense of organizational justice by building trust and encouraging communication among employees. Campbell Soup put "Inspiring Trust" as the top of its list over a ten-year period in order to engage its employees. The company has not only reached the top tier of the global food industry but has one of the highest levels of employee engagement in the Fortune 500.[33]

There are four main kinds of organizational justice: distributive, procedural, interpersonal, and informational.

Distributive justice is the degree to which people perceive outcomes to be fairly allocated. For example, employees doing the same job as others expect to be compensated equally. The concept of distributive justice is based on equity theory. When equal work does not produce equal outcomes, or when one employee is paid more or less than another for doing the same job, then there is a lack of distributive justice. Although the gender pay gap is narrowing, it is still present. Research shows that women in 2017 earned about 82 percent of what men earned during a study of full-time and part-time workers.[34] Another global study found that 65 percent of respondents quit their jobs because they weren't making as much as their similarly or less qualified male counterparts.[35] Organizations can provide equal distributive justice by taking the right steps to closing the gender pay gap.

Distributive justice: The degree to which people think outcomes are fair

Procedural justice is the degree to which people perceive the implementation of company policies and procedures to be fair. For example, if the organization has strict policies around dress code and tardiness, it can be frustrating for conscientious employees for a manager to turn a blind eye to an employee who has ignored the dress code or leaves work an hour earlier than the rest of the team.[36]

Procedural justice: The degree to which people perceive the implementation of company policies and procedures to be fair

If such a policy applies to all staff at every level, then employees will be more likely to accept it as fair. If some workers are exempt, then employees are unlikely to believe they are being treated equally. CEO of U-Haul, Joe Shoen, featured in our case study, implements procedural justice by ensuring he is accessible to both his employees and his customer base. This feedback allows him to find out the policies that aren't being implemented by his staff and sets him on the right path to resolving these issues.

Interpersonal justice refers to the level of dignity, politeness, and respect employees receive by supervisors during change implementation.

Informational justice refers to the degree of access people are given to information and the explanations provided to convey that information regarding why certain decisions are being made.

A classic research study was conducted in a company that was implementing 15 percent across-the-board pay cuts in two plants.[37] In plant A, the company president held a ninety-minute meeting in which the president showed concern for the workers and provided detailed information about why the pay cuts were necessary, particularly so that the company would not have to lay off any employees. In plant B, a vice president spent only fifteen minutes informing workers that the president had decided that 15 percent pay cuts were necessary. No additional information was provided except that the cuts were necessary because contracts had been lost. No apology or remorse was provided and detailed information regarding the rationale for the cuts was not offered. Subsequently, employee theft (an interesting way that employees try to restore equity by increasing outcomes in their O/I ratio!) increased in both plants, but to a much greater magnitude in plant B (1.5 percent increase in plant A and 5 percent increase in plant B). Also, turnover increased substantially in plant B, while in plant A it was unchanged. This was one of the first studies that helped us to begin to understand interpersonal and informational justice. The distributive justice was the same in both plants (15 percent pay cut) and the procedures to determine the pay cuts were the same in both plants (across the board for all employees). However, in plant A the company president took time with the employees, showing concern and compassion (interpersonal justice) and providing detailed information regarding the reasons for the cuts (informational justice). In contrast, in plant B the employees received an inadequate and impersonal explanation with much less of both types of justice, resulting in much different outcomes.

People who believe they are being treated poorly by an organization will become demotivated over time. However, organizations that meet or exceed employee expectations, reward good work, and treat people with respect have a greater chance of maintaining a more satisfied, productive workforce. This is where expectancy theory comes in.

THINKING CRITICALLY

1. What is organizational justice? Compare and contrast distributive and procedural justice.

2. Think of examples in your life when you faced or witnessed distributive and/or procedural justice. How did it impact your motivation at work?

3. To what extent are perceptions of procedural justice versus distributive justice a matter of perception? How could managers reduce inaccurate perceptions of workplace inequities?

Expectancy Theory

>> LO 5.5   Describe the expectancy theory of motivation and its practical implications

Expectancy theory: Theory that holds that people will choose certain behaviors over others with the expectation of a certain outcome

Vroom's **expectancy theory** holds that people will choose certain behaviors over others with the expectation of a certain outcome.[38] It was originally proposed by Yale School of Management professor Victor Vroom in 1964. Vroom's theory explores the motivation of individuals to maximize satisfaction and minimize dissatisfaction. In this context, motivation is a function of an individual's beliefs concerning effort-to-performance relationships (expectancy), work-outcome relationships (instrumentality), and the desirability of various work outcomes (valence).

Expectancy: The probability that the amount of work effort invested by an individual will result in a high level of performance

Expectancy is the probability that the amount of work effort invested by an individual will result in a high level of performance. In other words, it could be phrased as "What's the probability that, if I work very hard, I'll be able to do a good job?" It is measured in a range from zero to +1. If someone believes strong effort will not result in a higher performance level, his or her expectancy is zero; however, if the person believes a good effort *will* lead to high performance, expectancy is +1. For example, if you work hard on a project you will expect to reach the required deadline. **Instrumentality** is the probability that good performance will lead to various work outcomes. Another way of saying this is "What's the probability that, if I do a good job, that there will be some kind of outcome in it for me?" It can range from –1 to +1. An instrumentality of +1 would apply to people who believe that their performance would make an outcome likely, whereas people who think their performance will not result in outcomes would have an instrumentality of –1. For example, if you consistently reach your goals and perform well all year, then you might expect a bonus or a promotion (outcomes) as a reward for your efforts.

Instrumentality: The probability that good performance will lead to various work outcomes.

FIGURE 5.7

Expectancy Theory

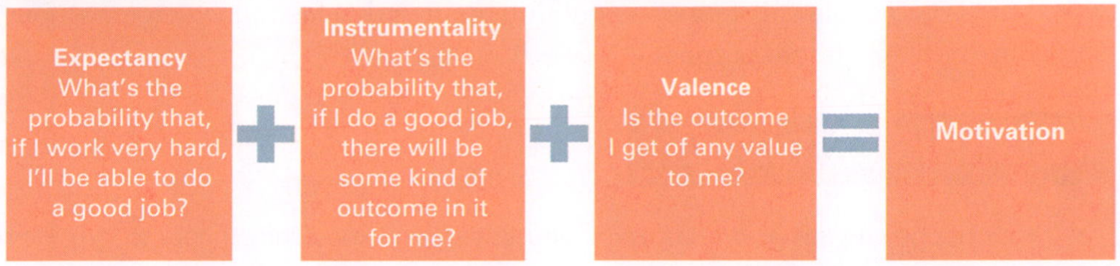

Valence is the value individuals place on work outcomes. Phrased a different way, "Is the outcome I get of any value to me?" Valences range from –1 to +1 and are positive or negative depending on the nature of the outcome. For example, if you expected a cash bonus as a reward but instead receive additional time off, you may see this as a negative outcome.

In addition, an article exploring the foundations of faking behavior reports that people may be motivated to engage in faking behavior as a means of successfully completing a test when (a) they believe that faking is essential for getting high scores on the test, thereby leading to positive work outcomes (instrumentality), (b) when people believe there is a high probability of faking behavior resulting in increased test scores (expectancy)."[39]

Expectancy theory can be summarized as follows. Say you work for a bank. The bank has a cross-sales incentive program. Cross-sales occur when someone comes in to buy one product and you sell them another. The classic example is, "Do you want fries and a drink with your burger?" So the bank has a cross-sales incentive program that works as follows: The top cross-sales person at each branch will be entered into a drawing (so as to give a chance to employees at small-volume branches) to win an all-expenses paid trip for two to Hawaii. Is this motivational? Well, that depends on the person. You see, expectancy theory is based on subjective assessments of each individual. For a married new accounts representative who sees 30 customers per day, the program might be very motivational: They think that because of their large number of customers and ease of cross-selling related products (e.g., a savings account with a checking account), that if they try, they have a good chance of being the top seller at their branch (expectancy), they often win prizes in drawings (instrumentality), and they would love to take their spouse on a trip (valence). In contrast, perhaps a young unmarried loan representative who sees three to four customers per day may NOT find the program motivational: They think that because of their low volume of customers and difficulty in cross-selling other products at a loan closing that even if they try they will not be the top seller in their branch (expectancy), they never win anything in drawings (instrumentality), and they aren't especially interested in the trip for two because they don't currently have a significant other to take along on the trip (valence).

The theory is summarized in Figure 5.7.[40]

As this chapter shows, motivation affects the way we behave in and outside the workplace. Motivation gives us energy, determination, and a sense of purpose. Without these motivational forces directed by clear goals, nothing would ever be achieved. Needs and contents theories help us to understand the complex nature of motivation by analyzing the underlying factors that drive us to successfully accomplish our goals. Equity theory and justice teaches us about the importance of fair

Valence: The value individuals place on work outcomes

treatment in the workplace, and expectancy theory shows the role our own expectations play when it comes to achieving our goals. As the next chapter shows, a large part of motivation comes from within us—a drive that incentivizes us to accomplish great things out of a sense of personal fulfillment. It is this feeling which empowers us to contribute to a larger purpose.

THINKING CRITICALLY

1. Your nephew in 4th grade has asked you to explain expectancy theory to him. How would you explain this theory in a way that a 4th grader would understand?

2. Think of a time you were not motivated to do something (to not study, work out, search for a job, etc.). How would you explain this lack of motivation in terms of expectancy theory?

3. What could be a weakness of using expectancy theory to explain one's motivation? ●

Visit **edge.sagepub.com/neckob2e** to help you accomplish your coursework goals in an easy-to-use learning environment.

- Mobile-friendly eFlashcards and practice quizzes
- Video and multimedia content
- Chapter summaries with learning objectives
- EXCLUSIVE! Access to full-text SAGE journal articles

IN REVIEW

5.1 Explain the basic motivation process

Motivation is a process by which behavior is *energized*, meaning how hard we work; *directed*, meaning what we choose to work at; and *maintained*, meaning how long we intend to work for to achieve objectives. **Content theories** of motivation explain why people have different needs at different times and how these needs motivate behavior. Maslow's hierarchy of needs, Alderfer's ERG theory, McClelland's need theory, and Herzberg's two-factor theory are all examples of content theories. **Process theories** describe the cognitive processes through which needs are translated into behavior. Examples of process theories include equity theory, expectancy theory, and goal-setting theory.

5.2 Compare the various needs theories of motivation

Maslow's hierarchy of needs identifies five levels of individual needs, with physiological needs at the bottom of the hierarchy and self-actualization needs at the top. **ERG theory** suggests that people are motivated by three categories of needs—existence, relatedness, and growth needs—that can be satisfied in any order or at the same time depending on the circumstances. **Herzberg's two-factor theory** proposes that the first step to employee satisfaction is to eliminate poor *hygiene factors*. Managers then need to use *motivators* such as achievement, recognition, and responsibility to build job satisfaction. **McClelland's acquired needs theory** suggests three main categories of needs: need for achievement, need for affiliation, and need for power. We all have a dominant motivator, and each of the motivators, in particular achievement, can be learned.

5.3 Apply goal-setting theory in organizational contexts

Goal-setting theory suggests that human performance is directed by conscious goals and intentions. Effective goals are specific, difficult, accepted by employees, and accompanied by regular feedback.

5.4 **Examine equity theory in the context of organizational justice and distinguish among the predictable outcomes of perceived inequity**

The concept of **equity theory,** introduced by psychologist J. Stacey Adams, holds that motivation is based on our perception of how fairly we are being treated in comparison with others. According to this theory, our perception of what is fair depends on the ratio O/I where O = their outcomes like the recognition, pay, and status we enjoy and I = inputs like our effort, experience, and ability.

Organizational justice describes how people perceive fairness in workplace practices. **Distributive justice** is the degree to which people perceive outcomes to be fairly allocated. **Procedural justice** is the degree to which people perceive the implementation of company policies and procedures to be fair. **Interpersonal justice** refers to the level of dignity, politeness, and respect employees receive by supervisors during change implementation. **Informational justice** refers to the degree of access people are given to information and the explanations provided to convey that information regarding why certain decisions are being made.

5.5 **Describe the expectancy theory of motivation and its practical implications**

Vroom's **expectancy theory** holds that people will choose certain behaviors over others with the expectation of a certain outcome. The theory describes motivation as a function of an individual's beliefs concerning effort-to-performance relationships (expectancy), work-outcome relationships (instrumentality), and the desirability of various work outcomes (valence).

KEY TERMS

Acquired needs theory 133
Behavioral goals 138
Content theories 131
Distributive justice 141
Equity theory 139
ERG theory 132
Expectancy 142
Expectancy theory 142
Goal-setting theory 137
Hierarchy of needs theory 131
Hygiene factors 132
Instrumentality 142

Motivation 128
Motivators 133
Need for achievement 133
Need for affiliation 133
Need for power 133
Organizational justice 140
Perceived inequity 139
Performance goals 138
Procedural justice 141
Process theories 131
Two-factor theory 132
Valence 143

UP FOR DEBATE: Raising Incentives to Increase Productivity

The best way to raise productivity amongst a workforce is to raise incentives. What do you think? Agree or disagree? Explain your answer.

EXERCISE 5.1: Understanding Equity Theory

Objective

The purpose of this exercise is to gain a greater appreciation of equity theory of motivation.

Instructions

In groups of two or three, discuss the following scenario:

> You discover that a student in the class currently has an A in the course. This student has the highest grades on every exam and has As on every paper that has been submitted. In questioning the student, you find out that she attends every class, reads each chapter four times, creates flash cards of every definition and concept, and meets with the professor every two weeks to go over material from the book and from classes.

The equity theory of motivation would indicate that some students would see this particular student receiving an "easy A" without knowing all the work and dedication the student is putting into the course. However, after talking to her, you know that she is putting in a significant amount of time and effort into the course and it is not an "easy A" at all.

In your group, answer the following questions:

a. Would you put in as much effort and time as this student with the hopes of earning an A in the course? Why or why not?

b. Could an A still be earned in the course *without* taking all the steps she is taking? Explain.

c. Would anyone in the group simply not take those actions, instead hoping for the best grade they can get by doing what they typically do? In other words, are you content with your current efforts even if the result is a B or C in the course?

Reflection Questions

1. How important is equity theory in organizations? What experience do you have with it in a job you have held?

2. If you see something as unfair at work—such as someone getting a better schedule than you or more money than you—would you change your behaviors so that you could also have a more accommodating schedule or additional money? Why or why not?

3. In what circumstances at an organization can equity theory backfire for managers? What scenarios might occur in which employees do *not* change their behaviors, but instead "give up" or protest the unfairness?

Exercise contributed by Steven Stovall, Southeast Missouri State University.

EXERCISE 5.2: Is Money a Motivator?

Objective

The purpose of this exercise is to grasp the concept of money as a motivator.

Instructions

This exercise utilizes a debate format to discuss money as a potential motivator of employees. The instructor will ask the group who believes money is a motivator and who does not. Once everyone has raised their hand for either side of this issue, move to the section of the room that believes the same as you about money motivating employees.

Once you are with those who feel similarly as you, elect two spokespeople to represent your side. The group will offer suggestions, making the case that money is indeed a motivator or that it is not. After ten minutes of preparation, the four representatives—two from each side—come to the front of the classroom and begin the debate.

The format of the debate is as follows:

A coin is tossed to determine which side goes first.

The first side has three minutes to make an opening statement. Then, the other side has three minutes to make their opening statement.

After the opening statements, the representatives who made the first opening statement have two minutes to respond. Then, the other side has two minutes for rebuttal.

This continues—two minutes per side—for thirty minutes (or an appropriate amount of time given any time constraints associated with the class).

Finally, three-minute closing statements are made. The side that gave the first opening statement goes first and then the side that gave the second opening statement has the final word.

During opening and closing statements as well as responses and rebuttals, there can be no interruptions or distractions from the other side or the audience.

Those who remain in the audience can still participate. If they readily see an opportunity for the perfect response, they should write their idea down and hand it to one of their representatives.

Reflection Questions

1. Based upon what you saw and heard during the debate, where do you stand on this issue? Do you think money is a motivator? Why or why not?

2. What instances in an organization can you think of where money *might* be a motivator to some employees? In which instances instances would money absolutely *not* be a motivator?

3. Does the amount of money in consideration make a difference as to whether a person *might* be motivated ($5 versus $10,000)? Explain.

Exercise contributed by Steven Stovall, Southeast Missouri State University.

EXERCISE 5.3: Your Motivation for Selecting Your Major

Objective

This exercise will help you develop your ability to *explain* the basic motivation process, *compare* the different needs motivation theories, and *select* a needs motivation theory that is most useful in understanding situations.

Instructions

This exercise will help you to apply chapter concepts for analyzing your decisions, and give you a foundation to make choices that are more likely to fulfill your expectations. In this exercise, you will be applying decision-making models and concepts that you have learned in this chapter to better analyze the process of selecting a major.

Step 1. Select a partner for the exercise. Ideally this person should be someone who you do not know well or work with on a regular basis. The person who has had a birthday most recently will take the role of the *teller* and the other person will be the *analyzer*. Both partners will have a chance to play each role. Introduce yourselves to each other, and tell each other your majors. (5 minutes)

Step 2. The *teller* should tell the process by which he or she chose a major.
The *teller* should be as explicit as possible about this decision-making process.
It may be that the decision about a major was not a direct decision about a major—the person may have been following the advice of a parent or older sibling. If this is the case, then the decision to be analyzed is why the person chose to follow someone else's advice on major selection. (10 to 15 minutes)

The *analyzer* should restate the major selection in terms of chapter concepts. Specifically, select one of the chapter needs theories, and describe the *teller's* needs in terms of the theory. Once you and the *teller* agree on the needs, describe the selection process based on *the motivation process* model.

Step 3. Switch roles and repeat step 2. (10 to 15 minutes)

Step 4. Be prepared to report your analyses to the class. (10 to 20 minutes)

Reflection Questions

1. How conscious and rational was your major selection?

2. Does your major selection meet the needs identified in this exercise?

3. After examining your major selection choice using chapter concepts, do you see any way to improve future decision processes to better meet your needs?

4. How could you apply this process to selecting a career or new job?

Exercise contributed by Milton R. Mayfield, Professor of Business, Texas A&M International University, and Jacqueline R. Mayfield, Professor of Business, Texas A&M International University.

ONLINE EXERCISE 5.1: Which Theory for Your Favorite Characters?

Objective

The purpose of this exercise is to gain an appreciation for various theories of motivation.

Instructions

For this exercise, you will be utilizing a discussion board. Think about one of your favorite shows on TV or that streams on an online platform. On the discussion board, choose three of the main characters from that show and talk about which theory presented in this chapter might be most applicable for motivating that particular character if he or she worked in your organization.

For example, if you chose *Family Guy*, you might say that Stewie, one of the characters on that series, might be motivated by power from McClelland's acquired needs theory because he seeks to take over the world. However, for Peter, equity theory could be more applicable because he sometimes sees that someone is getting something that he is not and he considers that unfair. If Chris were your employee though, you may find that an understanding of Maslow's hierarchy of needs is more relevant as he attempts to satisfy his most fundamental needs first before moving on to the next need.

As others post their favorite shows and characters, if you are familiar with those characters, offer agreement or other theories you think would be more applicable.

Reflection Questions

1. Why is it important for managers to know various theories of motivation?

2. As you were learning about the theories of motivation, which one or ones did you readily grasp and see how you could apply that theory of motivation in the workplace? Explain.

3. Which theory or theories of motivation do you feel would be difficult to understand and implement in the workplace? Explain.

Exercise contributed by Steven Stovall, Southeast Missouri State University.

CASE STUDY 5.1: The Whole Culture of Whole Foods

There's a palpable delight in the atmosphere of a business whose employees are actually *happy* and there is a visible difference when that atmosphere changes. Smiles come naturally. Help is offered without reservation. Prices may be a little steeper, but customers are less likely to balk. They know they are getting more for their money—an experience with their product.

Whole Foods Market is a prime example of what can happen when you create a culture that keeps employees happy, empowered, and engaged. The organic grocery super-chain booked $178 billion in fiscal year 2017 and currently has four hundred eighty stores in the United States, Canada, and the United Kingdom with another 100 stores under development. By the end of 2018, the company wants to reach five hundred locations; the ultimate goal is said to be one thousand. Yet despite its mammoth size and the notoriously staffing-challenged industry it occupies, Whole Foods has a remarkably low turnover rate—about 26 percent annually compared to the 90 percent standard. It's been named one of *Fortune* magazine's "100 Best Companies to Work For" every year since the list began in 1998; the distinction is earned, in large part, by independent surveys of its employees.

How does Whole Foods keep its 91,000+ team members motivated? Founder and co-CEO John Mackey says it doesn't. You can't really motivate someone, he told a student audience in 2011; it's better to focus on selecting the right people from the start and create a "conscious culture" in which motivation perpetuates itself. If that sounds a bit philosophical, it is. Mackey studied philosophy during the 1970s is the author of *Conscious Capitalism*, a book whose title has since become a buzzword in business. "Conscious capitalism" refers to an "evolved" capitalism, shaped by humanistic and environmental principals. This approach is not just a reflection of Mackey's social leanings; he argues that it is smart business. Increasingly, consumers want to purchase from businesses they can feel good about. And Whole Foods, as well as their new owner

Amazon, have principles that are aligned with the desire of the millennial workforce to make a difference in the world; they help Whole Foods attract motivated, high-quality employees.

Mission (Not Profit) Driven

Whole Foods makes money, to be sure, but Mackey makes it clear that profit is not his or Amazon's primary motivation. It's telling that among Whole Foods' eight core values (Table 5.1), only one of them is tied to the quality and performance of the physical goods in consumers' grocery carts, and there is not a single mention of price or convenience (compare that to the focus of a traditional grocery chain, like Safeway). Although "We create wealth through profits and growth" gets the number four spot, the other core values focus on ethical pursuits: sustainable and ecological farming practices, fair trade, and helping the community. In this way, Whole Foods positions itself more as the leader of a food/product *movement* rather than simply a food/product provider. These were all reasons for Amazon to see Whole Foods as a great opportunity for them to further their own goals of "selling everything to everyone" in a new and efficient way.

Employees as Stakeholders

Investors are important, but Whole Foods stresses they are not the most important of stakeholders. For Whole Foods, *stakeholder* is defined broadly: it means anyone who has "an investment in what we do or sell," which includes customers, employees, suppliers, and the communities within which they operate. Decisions are made, ideally, with the interests of all these stakeholders in mind—not just those of the investors, as is the case in traditional capitalism.

And to keep its employee stakeholders happy, Whole Foods aims to empower them: employees at every level have input on decisions about policy, including benefit options, plus product offerings and more. Robust compensation doesn't hurt, and a stock option plan is available to workers at all levels, even the front-line staff manning cash registers or stocking shelves. A whopping 94 percent of the company's stock options are distributed to nonexecutives. At the same time, Whole Foods' open-book policy gives team members access to the firm's financial records, including compensation information for all associates, including the top management team and the CEO. Since 2007, Mackey himself earns a symbolic $1 per year, and executives may make no more than nineteen times that of the lowest-paid associate (the US average for top executive-to-worker pay ratio is 30:1). Together, these policies help to enforce a shared identity under which everyone feels equal and valued.

Other stakeholder-benefiting programs include the distribution of $10 million in grants to small food producers each year. Whole Foods holds seminars that teach small farmers and producers how to get their products onto its shelves. The company also donates 5 percent of its annual profits to a variety of nonprofit and community organizations. In the stores, employees are

---

TABLE 5.1

Whole Foods' Core Values

1. We sell the highest quality natural and organic products available.
2. We satisfy, delight, and nourish our customers.
3. We support team member excellence and happiness.
4. We create wealth through profits and growth.
5. We serve and support our local and global communities.
6. We practice and advance environmental stewardship.
7. We create ongoing, win-win relationships with our suppliers.
8. We promote the health of our stakeholders through healthy eating education.

Source: Whole Foods. "Our Core Values." www.wholefoodsmarket.com/mission-values/core-values.

encouraged to recycle and reuse (a nod to the community in which a store operates, another stakeholder). Whole Foods was also the first to build its stores to meet Leadership in Energy and Environmental Design (LEED) Green Building Rating System.

Cultivating Conscious Leadership

From empowering employees with fair pay, ample benefits, and decision-making powers, to grants that benefit small farmers, Whole Foods, especially with Amazon behind it, aims to be a corporation with a conscience. To that end, Mackey created the Academy for Conscious Leadership, located in Austin, Texas. With conscious capitalism as the guiding principle, the academy is another opportunity for Whole Foods to reinforce the culture it's worked so hard to build, through courses on sustainable agriculture, whole and organic foods, and fair trade. During four-day retreats and other special events, the academy "prepares leaders to lead from a place of service by guiding them through experiences that identify their higher purpose and create cultures of meaning."

Whole Foods' brand of conscious capitalism is no longer the relative novelty it was in 1997—it's hard to find a large company these days without some sort corporate social responsibility program or a philanthropic arm. Though skeptics may argue the shift is all about marketing or positioning, paying attention to a broad swatch of "stakeholders"—with a special focus on employees—can be a win-win. As Mackey's co-CEO Walter Robb told Snagajob in 2015: "[Whole Foods'] strong culture of empowerment is really the secret to the company's success. . . . Culture is the living, breathing heart of the company."

Case Questions

1. What role does personal motivation play in Whole Foods' success?
2. How does Whole Foods help employees fulfill the needs in Maslow's hierarchy?

Sources

"Academy for Conscious Leadership Mission Statement." http://academyforconsciousleadership.com/our-mission.

Egan, John. "Despite Falling Share Prices, Whole Foods Envisions Massive Expansion in U.S." *Austin Culture Map*. February 13, 2014. http://austin.culturemap.com/news/innovation/02-12-14-whole-foods-envisions-1200-stores-in-us-expansion-grocer/.

Farfan, Barbara. "Kroger Supermarkets Mission Statement—Being the Leader with Values." *Retail Industry*. n.d., http://retailindustry.about.com/od/retailbestpractices/ig/Company-Mission-Statements/Kroger-Mission-Statement.htm.

Katchen, Joe. "Whole Foods CEO: I Don't Think Obamacare Comment Will Hurt Sales." *NBCNews.com*, January 18, 2013, http://www.nbcnews.com/id/50508631/t/whole-foods-ceo-i-dont-think-obamacare-comment-will-hurt-sales/.

Layton, Joe. "Whole Foods CEO Lectures about Business Philosophy." *Daily Texan Online*. March 28, 2011. www.dailytexanonline.com/news/2011/03/28/whole-foods-ceo-lectures-about-business-philosophy.

"100 Best Companies to Work For." *CNNMoney.com*. http://money.cnn.com/magazines/fortune/best-companies/2013/snapshots/71.html.

"Opening Case Study: Whole Foods, Whole People." *Mysafaribooksonline.com*. http://my.safaribooksonline.com/book/hr-organizational-management/9780470528532/opening-case-study-whole-foods-whole-people/opening_case_study_colon_whole_foods_com.

"Our Core Values." *Wholefoods.com*. http://www.wholefoodsmarket.com/mission-values/core-values.

"Our Visions, Our Mission." *Safeway.com*. www.careersatsafeway.com/why-work-for-us/missionvision-statement.

Sriram, S. "Whole Foods' John Mackey among CEOs Drawing $1 Salary." *Citybizlist*. March 26, 2013. http://dallas.citybizlist.com/article/whole-foods%E2%80%99-john-mackey-among-ceosdrawing-1-salary.

"Whole Foods Market® Celebrates 17 Years on *Fortune*'s '100 Best Companies to Work For' List." *Businesswire.com*. January 14, 2014. www.bloomberg.com/article/2014-01-16/aufPXNX7AyfU.html.

"Whole Foods Market Q1 2014 Earnings Conference Call Summary," Thompson Reuters, February 12, 2014, www.alacrastore.com/thomson-streetevents-transcripts/Q1-2014-Whole-Foods-Market-Earnings-Conference-Call-B5273163.

SELF-ASSESSMENT 5.1

Leadership Motivation Assessment

For each statement, circle the number that best describes you based on the following scale:

	STRONGLY DISAGREE	SOMEWHAT DISAGREE	NEUTRAL	SOMEWHAT AGREE	STRONGLY AGREE
1. I take pride in my ability to influence others.	1	2	3	4	5
2. I am often the "creator" or "idea generator" in group or team projects.	1	2	3	4	5
3. I enjoy providing feedback and/or praise to my coworkers as we work toward achieving a goal or objective.	1	2	3	4	5
4. People look to me for ideas and direction.	1	2	3	4	5
5. When working in a team context, I tend to share my ideas and thoughts about how best to proceed.	1	2	3	4	5
6. I often challenge my team or coworkers when we are working on projects or tasks.	1	2	3	4	5
7. Seeing my team or those around me succeed is more important to me than my own personal gain.	1	2	3	4	5
8. I enjoy providing recognition and rewards for other people's achievements.	1	2	3	4	5
9. I enjoy serving as a mediator in resolving conflict among my coworkers.	1	2	3	4	5
10. When working in a team context, I often work to build team cohesion and shared norms.	1	2	3	4	5
11. When working in a team context, people often advance and refine ideas that I originated.	1	2	3	4	5
12. When working in a team context, I enjoy coaching and mentoring other members of the team.	1	2	3	4	5

Total Score: _____

Score Interpretation

12–23	This implies a low motivation to lead.
24–47	This implies some uncertainty over your motivation to lead.
48–60	This implies a strong motivation to lead.

YOSHIKAZU TSUNO/AFP/Getty Images

6

Motivation: Practices and Applications

What I have learned is that people become motivated when you guide them to the source of their own power and when you make heroes out of employees who personify what you want to see in the organization.

— Anita Roddick, founder of the Body Shop

Learning Objectives

By the end of this chapter, you will be able to:

6.1   Explain the concept of intrinsic motivation and its primary determinants

6.2   Differentiate among the various types of extrinsic rewards

6.3   Discuss the various facets of job design

6.4   Discuss psychological empowerment and its components

6.5   Evaluate various approaches to nontraditional work schedules

CASE STUDY: WALT DISNEY COMPANY'S MOTIVATION TECHNIQUES

The $170 billion Walt Disney Company of today has passed through over ninety years of formation and strategic management, and it has seen countless forms of organizational behavior. Today, the executive team at Disney describes their vision as "A commitment to excellence, creativity and innovation. Our executive team's vision and strategic direction deliver stories, characters and experiences that are welcomed into the hearts and homes of millions of families around the world." This lofty vision, which the Walt Disney Company constantly lives, plays an essential role in the organizational management and motivational techniques behind Disney's immense success.

Walt Disney himself began the company's long-standing tradition of motivating its employees in unique, convincing ways. Decades ago, according to Disney's former employee Mike Vance, Walt Disney had a team of seven people designed to help him solve a number of problems. First, Walt needed to get more money out of his Walt Disney World park in order to fund movie production. The team orchestrated a plan to open the park, which previously ran for half of the week, on Mondays and Tuesdays, and to incentivize customers to come by activating a discount-loyalty program. After the program's outstanding success, Walt Disney gave each of the seven team members 100 shares of Disney stock and $25,000 on Christmas day.

For these seven team members, a similar reward system occurred multiple times, and through each iteration the team made some of the most important changes in the history of the company. These serve as examples of extrinsic rewards, but they carry with them an intrinsic incentive to help Disney, because if Disney does well, then their ownership of the company in shares becomes more significant. In this particular case, employee stock ownership served to motivate Disney innovation effectively. Many large corporations have mandatory stock ownership plans for this reason, but Walt Disney found a unique method in order to drive the continued success of his team.

Now, Disney's parks are widely known for their charitable employees with huge smiles. They are consistently rated highly for customer service, and among the Fortune 100 list of businesses, Disney is the most desirable employer. It takes an active approach to motivate employees to the point where they serve customers well and love the work they do. In order to reach this point and maintain it, the Walt Disney Company employs a few tactics, a few of which have been defined in the preceding chapter.

The organization is just as innovative today about the way it motivates Disney employees at all levels to consistently fulfill the Walt Disney Company's vision. For example, the Disney Corporation uses clear goal setting as an effective measure to motivate employees. Specifically regarding the environment, Disney has annual goals to reduce their emissions as a corporation, divert their waste in an environmentally friendly way, and conserve water responsibly. They provide employees and the world with the raw data on their success in these pursuits, which allows workers to satisfy their need for competence. When there are accurate measures of success, all members of a company have the chance to stretch their effort to excel. These clearly defined short- and long-term goals can fire up employees who need more than just the daily hum of work to put in maximum effort.

As many employees of Disney are high-achieving workers with a desire for constant improvement, job enrichment through social responsibility has served as a practical motivational technique for decades. Each and every year becomes more important to employees, from ground-level workers to corporate executives, and they publicly report their conservation progress annually. Goals such as environmental conservation encourage teamwork and meaningfulness, which are both effective methods of motivation. When employees feel a sense of duty not only to their management but also to one another and to the world around them, they have important reasons to work hard.

On top of providing rewarding work, the Walt Disney Company always puts its employees first. In response to a story about a theme park staffer helping a little girl recover her doll, a senior member of the Disney Institute says this, "What motivates employees to go above and beyond the call of duty to provide this kind of a memorable customer experience? It's not magic, but method. The theme park team didn't consult a script or take instructions from their manager. They did what they did because Disney has created a culture where going the extra mile for customers comes naturally." He says that creating a culture of motivated employees requires that they have an emotional attachment to their work—it must be work that they truly enjoy. For that reason, the company places many resources into the process of finding the right frontline employees and then treating them well. Disney even gives a list of the steps they take in this process: First, always listen to the needs of employees. The company tries to find ways to respect and hear the needs of all employees, and to provide assistance in as many matters as possible. Next, they "hire for attitude, not aptitude." Management finds that investing in their employees' skill development is easier than forcing a great attitude. Lastly, for all levels of employment, the Walt Disney Company puts purpose ahead of strict guidelines. It is important to have protocol for as many things as possible, but in the world of customer service there is no way to chart out all interactions. For this reason, employees must provide a certain type of service, as opposed to a set of specific services.

To the ordinary vacationer, Disneyland, Walt Disney World, and Disney films provide entertaining stories, characters, and experiences. From the top down, the Walt Disney Company works to achieve this mission, and managers motivate Walt Disney employees the same way that Disney pleases its customers: by providing them with meaningful stories. The Walt Disney Company shows that giving employees the drive to complete their work effectively is instrumental to growth and success, and Walt Disney himself launched this campaign.

Critical-Thinking Questions

1. How does the Walt Disney Company use both intrinsic and extrinsic rewards to motivate simultaneously?

2. Explain the effects of ESOPs (Employee Stock Ownership Plans).

3. How does Disney's mission relate to corporate motivation?

Resources:

Bradt, G. (2015, May 20). Disney's best ever example of motivating employees. *Forbes.* Retrieved from https://www.forbes.com/sites/georgebradt/2015/05/20/disneys-best-ever-example-of-motivating-employees/2/#58b46a47182a

D23. Com. (n.d.). *Disney history.* Retrieved from https://d23.com/disney-history/

Disney Institute. (n.d.). *Disney institute blog.* Retrieved from https://disneyinstitute.com/blog/tag/motivating-employees/

Forbes. (n.d.). *#72 Walt Disney.* Retrieved from https://www.forbes.com/companies/walt-disney/

The Walt Disney Company. (n.d.). *Recent news.* Retrieved from https://thewaltdisneycompany.com/

Zillman, C. (2016). Disney is named the company Americans want to work for most. *Fortune.* Retrieved from http://fortune.com/2016/06/06/fortune-500-disney-most-desired-employer/

Master the content
**edge.sagepub.com/
neckob2e**

Intrinsic Motivation

>> LO 6.1 **Explain the concept of intrinsic motivation and its primary determinants**

Have you ever participated in a sport just for the excitement of playing, written a piece of music just for the pleasure of listening to it, or participated in a video game for the thrill of it? If so, you have been inspired by **intrinsic motivation** which is the performance of tasks for our own innate satisfaction. As our case study shows, Disney employees also engage in intrinsic motivation by being personally and professionally motivated by their work. Disney nurtures a culture where employees are taught that going the extra mile feels good.

Intrinsic motivation consists of two main mechanisms: need for competence, and need for self-determination.[1] **Need for competence** is the motivation we derive from stretching and exercising our capabilities. For example, Disney consistently challenges its employees by setting them goals especially in the areas of environmental conservation. Every time an environmental goal is met, the employees feel motivated to continue to achieve bigger and better results.

Need for self-determination describes the feeling of motivation and control we get from making efforts that do not rely on any external influences. For example, although Disney employees are not financially rewarded for meeting their environmental goals, the positive feeling derived from being socially responsible is enough to motivate them to keep going. In contrast to intrinsic rewards, **extrinsic rewards** are external awards to employees such as salary, bonuses, and paid vacations. If we apply the concept of extrinsic rewards to the opening examples in this chapter, it means that rather than simply playing a sport, writing music, or engaging in gaming for the "feel good factor," you might carry out these activities for other incentives such as money or recognition. Extrinsic rewards can either increase intrinsic motivation, if the rewards are high, or decrease it if they are low. On the one hand, extrinsic rewards act as a source of competency information. That is, financial rewards directly and concretely show the employee he or she is valued and thus increase employee feelings of competence and self-determination and increase intrinsic motivation. For example, the Disney employees involved in orchestrating the park to open on more days were rewarded with shares of Disney

Intrinsic motivation: The performance of tasks for our own innate satisfaction

Need for competence: The motivation derived from stretching and exercising our capabilities

Need for self-determination: The state of motivation and control gained through making efforts that are not reliant on any external influences

Extrinsic rewards: External awards to employees such as salary, bonuses, and paid vacations

Poor extrinsic rewards can demotivate employees by failing to show them their value to the organization.

stock and a large paycheck. This validated their feelings of competence and self-determination, encouraging them to work even harder for the company.

On the other hand, when people feel they are being under-rewarded, their feelings of self-determination decrease, as does their intrinsic motivation.[2]

How do real-world managers inspire intrinsic motivation in their employees? Take a look at how Rob Kanjura, at protein bar supplier Savant Naturals, motivates his employees by using effective intrinsic and extrinsic rewards in the OB in the Real World feature.

Types of Extrinsic Rewards

>> LO 6.2 Differentiate among the various types of extrinsic rewards

Rob Kanjura of Savant Naturals uses both intrinsic and extrinsic rewards to motivate his employees. Let's explore the different types of extrinsic rewards.

Seniority-Based Pay

Seniority-based pay:
Guaranteed wages and salary increases based on the amount of time the employee has spent with the organization

Guaranteed wages and salary increases based on the amount of time the employee has spent with the organization are called **seniority-based pay**.[3] These wages, which are paid at fixed intervals such as monthly or weekly, tend to encourage

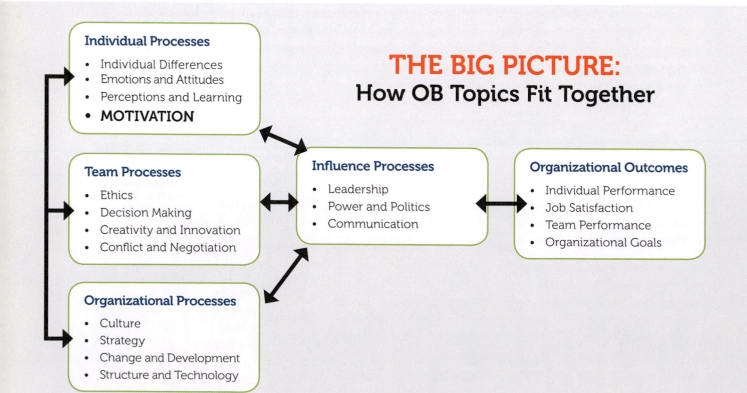

THE BIG PICTURE:
How OB Topics Fit Together

Individual Processes
- Individual Differences
- Emotions and Attitudes
- Perceptions and Learning
- **MOTIVATION**

Team Processes
- Ethics
- Decision Making
- Creativity and Innovation
- Conflict and Negotiation

Organizational Processes
- Culture
- Strategy
- Change and Development
- Structure and Technology

Influence Processes
- Leadership
- Power and Politics
- Communication

Organizational Outcomes
- Individual Performance
- Job Satisfaction
- Team Performance
- Organizational Goals

OB IN THE REAL WORLD

Rob Kanjura, Operations Director, Savant Naturals

Rob Kanjura went to college at Northern Illinois and for a large chunk of his career worked in construction. The housing and development industries took a huge hit when the economy fell in 2008, and Rob had grown weary of his day-in and day-out monotonous work life in construction. That's why Rob chose to work as operations director with Savant Naturals, a dessert protein bar supplier. He works in Scottsdale, Arizona, in an office with three other colleagues. Savant currently supplies three delicious, all-natural flavors to over four thousand RiteAid stores, as well as electronically via Amazon; they are currently growing rapidly into the retailer business, which is part of Rob's job.

It seems that an office run by only four people could lend itself to lulls, but Rob is always excited about his work for a few important reasons. First and foremost, the intrinsic rewards he receives keep Rob motivated; his own lifestyle is healthy and fit, and the idea behind the all-natural dessert protein bars he sells is that they provide a healthy and tasty solution. He says healthy food "is what I eat, so I wanted to be involved with it." Beyond this, Rob and his coworkers always find ways to stay busy. Testing their own limits and always challenging themselves to get the job done has been a practical motivational technique for the Savant Naturals team. Going hand in hand with their heavy workload, Savant Naturals employees have clearly defined roles and tasks—Rob says, "We all have our roles, so we all better get it done."

Rob actively makes sure to avoid boredom at work. Back when he did construction, Rob needed a change, and so he made a large career change. This was not an isolated experience—job rotation on a smaller scale takes place often in his life, as Rob and his coworkers often move around the departments of Savant Naturals and help out wherever they can.

Along with job rotation options, they receive performance and bonus-based pay. Savant Naturals employees, besides being intrinsically rewarded by their mission to sell healthy products, are externally motivated to earn extra pay by excelling with their work. The Savant Naturals team also exercises the right amount of freedom with their work schedules to serve as a motivator. Rob and the other members of the office believe it is valuable to be able to stay late and finish some work one evening in order to leave early the next day. Having some flexibility with office time is useful for self-motivation in Rob's work life.

Savant Naturals has a simple mission: "We're challenging the status quo. We believe taste matters and that natural and nutritional indulgence shouldn't hold you down." Rob's daily motivation is something like a challenge to status quos; he involves enough variety, hard work, and rewards in his professional life in order to keep it stimulating. Rob and all those who run Savant Naturals have developed an office life that interests them and gives them constant incentives to produce, and because of this Savant is currently growing at a steep pace. Managers of all companies can learn from some of the tactics Rob uses, both in their own personal motivation, as well as their employees' motivation.

Critical-Thinking Questions

1. Name and describe some of the concepts from this chapter which Rob uses in his own office.

2. Are there similarities between motivating oneself and motivating one's employers? ●

Source: Interview with Rob Kanjura conducted on April 14th, 2017

---

longevity and commitment, which reduces turnover. However, seniority-based pay can also be demotivating because employees know they will get paid regardless of how they perform, which also encourages poor performers to stay in an organization much longer. From the 1950s to the 1990s, Japanese companies rewarded the people who had been there the longest with the most money. In other words, the older you were the more you were rewarded. As employees tended to stay in a job for life, the system worked by rewarding people for their loyalty. However, when the economic bubble burst in Japan, many employees were made redundant, and graduates were reluctant to join the first company that offered them roles. Today, despite the efforts of big companies like Sony, Hitachi, and Fujitsu to steer away from seniority-based pay, it appears as though Japan has yet to find an alternative pay scheme to satisfy all its employees.[4]

EXAMINING THE EVIDENCE

Family Motivation as a Substitute for Intrinsic Motivation?

We've seen that intrinsic motivation occurs when the performance of tasks provides innate satisfaction by satisfying employees' needs for competency and needs for self-determination. But some jobs are simply not designed to provide intrinsic motivation. For example, many jobs in the manufacturing, service, and agricultural industries provide employees with little discretion in performing tasks, setting schedules, making decisions, and determining work methods. This leads to low levels of job autonomy, which is a primary predictor of feelings of self-determination and intrinsic motivation. When jobs are not intrinsically motivating, valued outcomes can often substitute as important motivating factors. A recent study* explored the possibility that the desire to support one's family may be one such motivating factor. The study found that family motivation, defined as the desire to expend effort to benefit one's family through work, may be an important source of motivation that enhances energy and job performance, especially for jobs lacking intrinsic motivation. The researchers conclude that although family motivation does not actually change employees' enjoyment of their work, it can help employees to view their jobs as more meaningful and motivating because of how their work contributes to their family lives. These findings suggest that organizations may be able to increase employee job performance by providing employees with more opportunities to experience family motivation through implementing family-friendly policies and events that make the family more salient for employees at work and by making structural changes to jobs and pay that enhance family-focused job outcomes.

Critical-Thinking Questions

1. What specific actions can managers take to help employees feel family motivation at work? Why would these actions be effective?

2. What factors could limit the effectiveness of interventions designed to increase family motivation? How could these limitations be overcome? ●

*Menges, Jochen I., Danielle V. Tussing, Andreas Wihler, and Adam M. Grant. 2017. "When Job Performance Is All Relative: How Family Motivation Energizes Effort and Compensates For Intrinsic Motivation." *Academy of Management Journal* 60, no. 2: 685–719.

Job Content-Based Pay

Job content-based pay: A salary paid based on the evaluation of a job's worth

Skill-based pay: A system of pay that rewards employees for the acquisition and the development of new skills that lead to enhanced work performance

Job content-based pay is based on an evaluation of a job's worth to the organization and its relationship to other jobs within the organization.[5] Many organizations use this compensation structure because it is thought to be one of the best ways to maintain pay equity. Employees also tend to be more motivated to compete for promotions and a higher rate of pay. At the same time, employees who are competing against each other may exaggerate their duties to their managers to try and impress, or they may hoard resources to get ahead. These activities can also create a psychological distance across teams and hierarchies. Technology company Cisco, clinical specialist Genentech, and law firm Perkins Coie are among the many organizations that follow this payment structure.[6]

Skill-Based Pay

Skill-based pay rewards employees for the acquisition of new skills that lead to enhanced work performance.[7] As we learned in Chapter 5, Marlin Steel uses this type of extrinsic reward by paying its employees bonuses every time they acquire a new skill. Skill-based pay can be a useful way to motivate employees while providing them with an

Andrew Harrer/Bloomberg via Getty Images

Employees of Marlin Steel are rewarded with bonus pay each time they learn a new skill.

opportunity to showcase their new skills and competencies. As a result, workers are more flexible and productive. However, there can be some disadvantages. There is the high cost of additional bonuses and training to consider, as well as the possibility that employees may max out their skill levels, which means they cannot receive any additional pay increases unless they change jobs. Journalist and digital consultant John Boitnott believes there is such a thing as being too good at your job and says he has changed jobs multiple times in order to progress professionally.[8]

Performance-Based Pay

Performance-based pay is a financial incentive awarded to employees for meeting specific goals or objectives.[9] Two levels of performance-based pay exist: individual level and team and organization level.

Performance-based pay: A financial incentive awarded to employees for meeting certain goals or objectives

Individual-Level Performance-Based Pay

Individual-level pay includes:

- **Piece rate** is a pay plan in which workers are paid a fixed sum for each unit of production completed. In other words, people are rewarded for the quantity of goods they produce regardless of how long it has taken them. While this used to be the type of play plan most common in the manufacturing and construction industries, it is less so now since the introduction of the minimum wage.

  Piece rate: A pay plan in which workers are paid a fixed sum for each unit of production completed

- **Merit pay** links pay increases directly to performance. In other words, it rewards performance by increasing the employee's salary on a long-term basis. However, a study conducted by Willis Towers Watson on the value of incentive plans based on feedback from senior managers from one hundred fifty large and midsized companies shows that merit plans are the least effective of all the pay plans with only 20 percent of managers believing they drive "higher levels of individual performance."[10]

  Merit pay: A pay plan consisting of a pay rise which is linked directly to performance

- **Bonus pay** rewards employees for good performance in addition to their base salary. While most top companies in the United States pay out bonuses as part of their compensation schemes, a report by Seattle-based online compensation company PayScale found that despite the bonus system, a high percentage of employees still felt that there wasn't enough open communication about pay, still didn't feel valued at work, and also didn't believe they were fairly compensated. PayScale president and CEO Mike Metzger believes it is time for companies to step away from traditional pay practices toward more innovative approaches. He says, "Our research shows there is significant benefit in abandoning traditional compensation practices in favor of more transparency around compensation and variable pay practices that recognize an individual's contribution to the business."[11]

  Bonus pay: A pay plan that rewards employees for recent performance rather than historical performance

Overall, research conducted by the University of East Anglia in the United Kingdom shows that performance-based pay can have negative effects on employee well-being. A study recently published in the *Human Resources Management Journal* based on a survey of almost fourteen thousand employees revealed that people who receive performance-based pay not only work harder, but also end up with higher stress levels and lower levels of job satisfaction.[12]

As head researcher Chidiebere Ogbonnaya says, "By tying employees' performance to financial incentives, employers send signals to employees about their intention to reward extra work effort with more pay. Employees in turn receive these signals and feel obliged to work harder in exchange for more pay."[13] The result? Overworked employees who end up feeling exploited by their employer.

Employers can try and decrease the negative effects of performance-based pay by providing a balance between the amount of work carried out by employees and the type of rewards on offer. Talking to employees about their compensation is a good way to gauge their thoughts and address any concerns they may have.

Team- and Organization-Level Performance-Based Pay

There are three types of team and organization performance-based plans:

Gain sharing: A system whereby managers agree to share the benefits of cost savings with staff in return for their contribution to the company's performance

Profit sharing: Sharing profits with employees of an organization by the owners

Employee stock ownership plans (ESOPs): Plans in which employees purchase company stock, often at below-market price, as part of their benefits.

- **Gain sharing** is a system whereby managers agree to share the benefits of cost savings with staff in return for their contribution to the company's performance.[14] United Steelworkers uses a gainsharing program to pay its employees bonuses up to 14 percent per month on their gross wages.[15]

- **Profit sharing** is a pay system in which the organization shares its profits with employees.[16] In February 2017, for the third year in a row, Delta Airlines awarded over $1 billion in profit-sharing bonuses to its employees, distributing the checks on Valentine's Day. The generous pay scheme is widely credited for Delta's positive corporate culture.[17]

- **Employee stock ownership plans (ESOPs)** allow employees to purchase company stock, often at below-market price, as one of their benefits.[18] Many small businesses use ESOPs because of their big tax benefits and because they allow the owner to keep control of the business until the time comes to hand over the reins to eligible employees. Seattle-based pet supplies retailer Mud Bay, wholesaler Charlie's Produce, Timberland Bank, and engineering firm Hart Crowser are just a few companies that offer ESOPs to their employees.[19] Gain sharing: A system whereby managers agree to share the benefits of cost savings with staff in return for their contribution to the company's performance.

Motivation over Time

Rewards can either be motivators or demotivators depending on the situation and the individual. But when it comes to those employees who respond well to rewards, does it mean that they stay motivated over time? Not necessarily. Research shows that as we get older our ability to reason, focus, and remember (fluid intelligence) declines, yet our capacity to absorb educational and experiential knowledge (crystallized intelligence) increases.

In other words, as we reach middle age and above, we may struggle more with roles that demand high levels of fluid intelligence, such as engineering for example, which could affect our performance, motivation, and self-esteem. In contrast, we may perform better in roles that require crystallized intelligence as it alleviates the pressure of the factors associated with fluid intelligence. So, how does performance change with age? Researchers propose that stronger rewards and incentives are necessary in order to motivate aging employees in jobs requiring crystallized intelligence in comparison with younger employees.

However, despite the decline in fluid intelligence over time, further research shows that it is entirely possible to make up for this decline with crystallized intelligence. For example, say you were a student training to be a pharmacist. Learning about pharmacy requires high levels of fluid intelligence in order to absorb the huge amounts of complex facts and procedures. However, after years of study, you will have gathered a huge body of information and knowledge (crystallized intelligence) which means you will have less to learn over time. As you get older, you will be able to use this expert knowledge to not only function in your role as a pharmacist but also to use your wisdom to advise others.

Yet, there are some jobs that require consistent levels of fluid intelligence more suited to younger workers. In a 2009 study of US air traffic controllers, researchers discovered that experienced controllers aged between 53 and 64 took around the same time to reroute two planes heading for a collision as the younger, more inexperienced controllers.[20] In contrast, the younger and experienced controllers took half the time. The study shows that in this particular role, where decisions have to be made quickly and problems need to be solved in uncertain situations, fluid intelligence is more valuable than crystallized intelligence. It also explains why the US Federal Aviation Authority requires that air traffic controllers retire by the age of 56.[21]

FIGURE 6.1

Fluid Intelligence and Crystallized Intelligence across the Lifespan

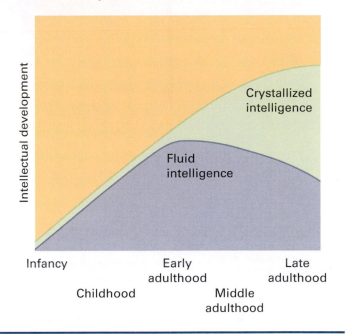

However, that's not the only difference between generations when it comes to motivation. In a study of US high school seniors in 1976, 1991, and 2006 to find out the differences in work values between the baby boomer, Generation X, and millennial generations showed a higher emphasis on leisure values than work values.[22] Specifically, extrinsic values (status, money) were highest among Generation X, followed by millennials, and then baby boomers. With regards to intrinsic work values, millennials placed less importance on these types of values than baby boomers. In other words, millennials are more likely to value leisure activities over the workplace.

These researchers also discovered that millennials are no better than previous generations when it comes to altruistic work values (e.g., helping others, contributing to society), social values (e.g., making friends), or intrinsic values (e.g., intellectual stimulation, interesting job).

It is important that employers take these findings into account when it comes to hiring people from different generations. For example, the knowledge that Generation X tends to value extrinsic rewards over millennials should prove to managers that millennials may need to be motivated by more than a paycheck and bonus.

Similarly, in order to recruit and retain millennials, companies need to focus on work-life balance and flexible schedules. Millennials who work under these conditions are more likely to stay with an organization and less likely to job hop.

While more recent generations may need more than a bonus to become motivated, most people in the workforce regardless of their generation have the same thing in common: to work in a job designed to challenge, stimulate, and enhance personal achievement.

THINKING CRITICALLY

1. Create a chart that lists the types of extrinsic rewards discussed in the section. Provide an example of a useful application and a detrimental application for each type of reward.

2. Imagine that you are the manager of a small clothing manufacturer. You wish to retain your more senior employees, who typically work faster in completing each item of clothing than newer employees. Nevertheless, because 80 percent of your current workforce is over 50 you need to incentivize new hires in order to be sure you have an adequate supply of skilled workers in ten years' time. Devise an extrinsic reward plan that rewards skilled workers as well as new workers who need to acquire skills.

Motivation through Job Design

>> **LO 6.3**   Discuss the various facets of job design

Job design: A method of setting duties and responsibilities of a job with the intention of improving productivity and performance

Scientific management: Early 20th-century theory introduced by Frederick Taylor and his colleagues that analyzes workflow through systematic observation or reasoning

Job design is a method of setting forth the duties and responsibilities of a job with the intention of improving productivity and performance.[23] Read how psychologist Karen Sanders, featured in OB in the Real World, uses the components of job design to motivate her employees. The concept of job design can be traced back to the theory of **scientific management**, introduced in the early 20th century by Frederick Taylor and his colleagues, who analyzed workflow through systematic observation of the tasks to be performed. Taylor designed experiments to calculate the motions and time required to complete workplace tasks in order to improve efficiencies. For example, he tested the various motions required for laying bricks to understand how workers could complete the task more quickly.

Through these "time and motion" studies Taylor not only discovered better and faster ways to complete tasks, he also found that certain people could work more efficiently than others. Therefore, he advocated selecting the right people for the job as another important part of workplace efficiency.

Also known as "Taylorism," scientific management focused on how to make people, assembly line workers in particular, more efficient at their jobs through training, monitoring, and detailed planning.

There are three main approaches to job design: job enlargement, job rotation, and job enrichment.

Job enlargement: An increase in the range of tasks and duties associated with a job

Job enlargement is a method of job design that increases the range of tasks and duties associated with a job.[24] For example, if you were a host at a restaurant, you might leave your station during quiet periods to collect glasses for the bar staff. In doing so, your job will have become expanded to include other duties.

Job rotation: A process of periodically moving staff employees from one job to another

Job rotation is a process of periodically moving employees from one job to another.[25] Companies are increasingly using job rotational programs for millennials in order to appeal to some common traits such as desire to learn, progress, and make an impact. Typically, rotational programs offer at least three different roles with a set amount of time assigned to each role. This way, millennials can try out each role and decide which one they like the best. Companies such as global confectionary giant Mars Inc. are noticing higher levels of employee retention and long-term commitment as a result.[26]

Laura Lawson, Chief People Officer at United Shore Financial Services, a financial and wholesale mortgage company, also believes in the value of rotational programs for millennials. She says, "I think millennials are attracted to rotational programs

FIGURE 6.2

Job Characteristics Model

Core Job Characteristics
- Skill variety
- Task identity
- Task significance
- Autonomy
- Feedback

Psychological States
- Meaningfulness
- Responsibility
- Knowledge of results

Outcomes
- Motivation
- Performance
- Satisfaction
- Low absenteeism
- Low turnover

Source: Hackman, J. R., and G. R. Oldham. *Work Redesign* (Reading, MA: Addison-Wesley, 1980).

like ours because of the continuous training," and "Millennials typically crave the ability to learn new skills and continuously improve and that's what our program is designed to provide."[27]

Job enrichment means increasing the scope of a job to make it more complex, stimulating, and satisfying for employees.[28] Job enrichment differs from job enlargement by the complexities of the tasks included in the role. In the example above, your tasks as a restaurant host may have been expanded to collecting glasses, but that duty in itself is unlikely to challenge you or allow for personal growth. However, if you were given more responsibility or empowered to work on your own ideas, and make decisions that would normally have been made by senior management, then you may experience the positive effects of job enrichment. IBM, AT&T, and Texas Instruments are just a few companies that offer job enrichment programs for their employees.[29]

Job enrichment can be further explained through the Hackman and Oldham **job characteristics model** (see Figure 6.2) which identifies five core dimensions of jobs: skill variety, task identity, task significance, autonomy, and feedback.[30] Hackman and Oldham created a scoring system based on these five characteristics. The higher the score for each of the characteristics, the more positive are employees' psychological states and outcomes.

Skill variety is the extent to which workers utilize a variety of skills. For example, Savant Naturals employees move around the different departments in order to learn and apply their skills.

Task identity is the extent to which an employee completes an entire piece of work from start to finish. A recent study shows that employees who are given autonomy and task identity to see a project through are generally more productive.[31]

Task significance is the extent to which employees see meaning in the impact of their roles on the organization. Several studies show that people who find meaning in their work feel a sense of purpose, are more loyal and committed to their employers, and are happier overall.[32]

Autonomy is the extent to which employees are given the freedom and independence to schedule and perform tasks.

Music, video, and podcast streaming company Spotify provides its two thousand employees with autonomy by dividing them into teams, called squads. Each squad is responsible for an aspect of a product which it owns from start to finish. Spotify's autonomous culture works because it allows for personal growth and development.[33]

Job enrichment: An increase in the scope of a job to make it more complex, interesting, stimulating, and satisfying for employees

Job characteristics model: Five core dimensions of jobs: skill variety, task identity, task significance, autonomy, and feedback

OB IN THE REAL WORLD

Karen Sanders, Associate Vice Provost for College Access, Virginia Polytechnic Institute and University

Karen Sanders is a first-generation college student born and raised in Virginia, but she did not stop with her undergraduate degree. After graduating from Virginia State University, an HBCU, she got her masters in clinical psychology and then a PhD in psychology. Her field of choice evolved throughout her educational career, ultimately settling on developmental education—a field dedicated to providing a collegiate education to low-income, first-generation, or otherwise underprepared students. Karen finds a deep passion in helping students from difficult circumstances make it to college so that those students can then, in turn, improve their communities.

Karen's passion leads her to be strongly intrinsically motivated. She says, "I believe that work should be so fulfilling that you would do it for free if you had the means," and her path has led her to an important managerial role at Virginia Tech, where she is the associate vice provost for college access. Karen is also the chief diversity officer at the Virginia Tech Carilion School of Medicine. Although Karen is intrinsically motivated and fulfilled by her work, she believes that there is a place for both intrinsic and extrinsic motivation in a healthy workplace. She knows that for many people, their work is their total source of income, and managers should reward their employees financially and with rewards like time off and professional networking for performing well. At the same time, Karen speaks of the importance of a holistic approach to employee motivation: "As a manager, I have to use various strategies to motivate employees, and I need to do more than just reward them financially. To create a work environment that is comfortable, I sit down with my team and ask them what their passion is and make it an important part of their workplace."

In running a productive workplace and managing a great team, Karen utilizes multiple tools mentioned in the text. For example, various elements of job design not only serve as effective motivational tools, they have also played significant roles in her own professional success and development. The first is job enlargement, the process by which a manager increases a position's scope of responsibilities to keep an employee motivated and provide new challenges. Job enlargement has played a huge role in Karen's professional life—starting as the director of one department, she expanded it and connected it to the institutional mission at Virginia Tech. She set benchmarks and data-driven outcomes to measure success and was promoted twice over the next seven years to run larger teams.

Another job design technique is job rotation, the process of moving an employee within the organization. Karen believes "it is important to constantly look at each employee individually and match their position with their strengths and abilities." An employee's strengths often change and improve over their time with a company, and job rotation is an effective method by which managers can keep the employee engaged and refreshed by his or her work, as well as use the employee to his or her full potential.

One reason Karen and her team find success is that they are open to new ideas and innovations. According to Karen, working in higher education has been fulfilling, and she does some things to mimic the efficiency of the private business sector. For example, Karen is very particular about her hiring process. In Karen's department, psychological empowerment, the extent to which employees feel personal fulfillment and intent while carrying out their work, "starts from the very beginning in the search and hiring process." The most valuable asset in her department is her people, and she works diligently to find the right ones. When asked how she does it, Karen says, "Look at the gaps in your organization and be selective when adding a member to fill a gap. If you are very deliberate for picking the right people for the job, you will succeed." Being that Karen specializes in diversity, she looks for employees with diverse perspectives and backgrounds, but, in one key way, Karen looks for employees that have a homogenous overarching goal for the organization. In this way, employees all become psychologically committed to a mission.

In conclusion, Karen has used the motivational tactics mentioned in this chapter throughout her whole career.

She leaves a final word on what it takes to achieve success in a higher-ed management role: "We have to connect the institutional mission to an individual's specific job. We make expectations clear and hold our people accountable for outcomes." Karen says she strives to educate her community, the people of Virginia, and the world, one student at a time.

Critical-Thinking Questions

1. Name and describe some motivational tools that have played a role in Karen's professional experience.

2. Is Karen evidence that multiple sources of motivation should exist, or is she evidence that you should only find motivation in one source? ●

Feedback is the extent to which employees are provided with timely information regarding their job performance. Yet some CEOs welcome it too. It is said that Google cofounder Larry Page invites feedback, regardless of how brutal it is in the quest to arrive at the best possible outcome.[34]

The Hackman and Oldham job characteristics model enables companies to design new jobs better and redesign existing ones in order to enhance employee motivation. According to the theory, an uninspiring, monotonous job tends to stifle motivation, while a more challenging, stimulating role increases it. Managers who ensure workers are exposed to a variety of skills, provide them with a sense of authority and ownership, impose an awareness of the significance of the task, and give regular feedback tend to have more motivated employees.

While it is important to design or redesign roles to motivate employees, this approach is unlikely to succeed without the benefit of psychological empowerment.

THINKING CRITICALLY

1. What positive outcomes could result from implementing job enlargement, job rotation, and job enrichment in an organization with which you are familiar? What objections or obstacles might be encountered?

2. Use Hackman and Oldham's job characteristics model to assess a job you have held in the past or one with which you are familiar. Consider each of the five core dimensions (skill variety, task identity, task significance, autonomy, and feedback) for the job. Based on your assessment, what positive changes could be made to enhance the job?

Psychological Empowerment

>> **LO 6.4** Discuss psychological empowerment and its components

Another facet of the job characteristics model is the concept of **psychological empowerment**, the extent to which employees feel a sense of personal fulfillment and intent when carrying out tasks, along with a belief that their work contributes to some larger purpose.[35] There are four main factors associated with psychological empowerment: *competence, self-determination, impact,* and *meaningfulness*.

Competence is the ability to perform work tasks successfully.[36] It stands to reason that employees who are regarded as the most competent are assigned more tasks and responsibilities than the less competent. However, recent research from Duke University, the University of Georgia, and the University of Colorado shows that competent people may feel resentful bearing the burden of more work, especially in situations where other coworkers receive the same rewards for doing less.[37]

Psychological empowerment: The extent to which employees feel a sense of personal fulfillment and intent when carrying out tasks, together with a belief that their work contributes to some larger purpose

Competence: The ability to perform work tasks successfully

When a problematic issue in the workplace is resolved, employees are motivated to work harder.

Self-determination: The understanding of skills, knowledge, and strengths that enable a person to make choices and initiate work tasks

Impact: The feeling of making a difference

Meaningfulness: The value of work tasks in line with a person's own self-concepts and ideals

Self-determination is the understanding of skills, knowledge, and strengths that enable a person to make choices and initiate work tasks.[38] Studies have found that employees who have a higher level of autonomy, the freedom to choose how to carry out their tasks and duties, and more control over decision making tend to display higher levels of performance than people who had less control.[39] This means that employees with self-determination tend to be more effective, motivated, and more satisfied with their jobs overall.

Impact is the degree to which an individual can influence work-related outcomes.[40] Kristen Hadeed, founder and CEO of all-student company Student Maid, is a good example of someone who has made a valuable impact on both customers and employees.[41] Employees are trained to respect their customers and build relationships with their "fellow maids" in order to create a positive environment. As a consequence, the student maids are motivated to do good, even going as far as cleaning for cancer patients for free.

Meaningfulness is the value of work tasks in line with a person's own self-concepts and ideals.[42] Disney employees find meaning in their work by working hard on environmental issues. In an effort to find out what makes work meaningful, researchers at MIT Sloan recently carried out a study of one hundred thirty-five people from ten different occupations (including retail, law, music, garbage collection, academia, and entrepreneurship), asking them about times where they found meaning in their jobs.[43] The study found that people find work meaningful when it transcends the workplace and becomes part of our personal life. For example, one garbage collector found his work meaningful when he was asked to distribute clean water to residents whose water supply had become contaminated. Doing good and helping people gave his work meaning.[44]

THINKING CRITICALLY

1. Think of a job that you have done in your life that you really enjoyed. Now also think of a job that you did that you hated going to work. Now with both the job you loved and the one you hated, what were the levels of competence, self-determination, impact, and meaningfulness that you felt in each job? Compare the two lists. What do you see?

2. Do certain types of jobs automatically lead to lower motivation over time? Why or why not?

Nontraditional Work Schedules

>> **LO 6.5**   Evaluate various approaches to nontraditional work schedules

Flexible work schedules are becoming more popular with today's workers and their employers. Rather than putting in the traditional forty-hour week, many employees are permitted to work from home, choose their own working hours, and even work remotely from different countries. Free agents and part-time workers are two types of workers who adhere to nontraditional work schedules. **Free agents** are independent workers who supply organizations with short-term talent for projects that need to be completed within a certain amount of time.[45] A freelancer is a type of free agent who can work for multiple employers, giving a limited amount of time to each. Similarly, **part-time workers** are independent workers who supply organizations with part-time talent for projects that need to be completed within a certain amount of time. Part-time workers work fewer hours than full-time workers but may supplement these hours by working for other employers.

Why are more companies implementing flexible working arrangements for their employees? According to recent studies, members of Generation Y, or the millennials, are driving the change.

According to a recent FlexJobs survey of almost three thousand people made up of Gen Xers and baby boomers, 82 percent of the millennials surveyed rated flexible work options as one the most important factors in a job, and over a third of those had actually quit a job due to lack of flexibility.[46] In fact, work flexibility is so important to some millennials that they reported that they would be more loyal to employers that offered flexible work arrangements and would even take a 10 to 20 percent cut in pay for the privilege.

Because 60 percent of these young employees switch employers every three years, companies seeking to avoid the high cost of turnover are looking for ways to keep their employees satisfied so they'll stay longer. These efforts seem to be working as recent research suggests that millennials aren't job hopping any faster than Gen Xers did.[47]

Yet, despite the recent surge of flexible work arrangements, not every organization is keen to implement them. Yahoo is one company that has bucked the trend by announcing an end to working from home, with former CEO Marissa Mayer stating that Yahoo employees need to be "physically together" in order for the organization to be at its most productive.[48] Almost a year after the work-from-home ban, Mayer still defended her decision claiming that employees were more collaborative and innovative when they were physically together.[49] Technology company IBM—one of the first pioneers of flexible work arrangements—has recently followed suit by bringing more people from its marketing department from digital workspaces into the office. Employees who work from home or different locations will need to relocate to one of six US cities, including Atlanta, Austin, Boston, New York, Raleigh, and San Francisco. Those who choose not to move have been told they will need to find another job. Why after all these years is IBM championing in-office work for its marketing department over its flexible work schedules? Michelle Peluso, IBM's chief marketing officer, believes that being physically together makes for a more productive workplace. "There is something about a team being more powerful, more impactful, more creative, and frankly hopefully having more fun when they are shoulder to shoulder," she said. "Bringing people together creates its own X Factor."[50]

These are the four main nontraditional work schedules commonly adopted by employers in today's workplace (see Figure 6.3).

Flextime means flexible working hours whereby an employee can customize his or her own work hours within limits established by management.[51] For example, an employee might work a 7:00 a.m. to 3:00 p.m. shift rather than the more traditional 9:00 a.m. to 5:00 p.m. workday.

Compressed workweeks give employees the benefit of an extra day off by allowing them to work their usual number of hours in fewer days per pay period.[52] For

Free agents: Independent workers that supply organizations with short-term talent for projects or time-bound objectives

Part-time workers (similar to *free agents*): Independent workers who supply organizations with part-time talent for projects or time-bound objectives

Flextime: Flexible working hours in which employees customize their own work hours within limits established by management

Compressed workweeks: A work arrangement that gives employees the benefit of an extra day off by allowing them to work their usual number of hours in fewer days per pay period

FIGURE 6.3

Examples of Nontraditional Work Schedules

WORK SCHEDULE	MONDAY	TUESDAY	WEDNESDAY	THURSDAY	FRIDAY
Flextime	7 a.m.–3 p.m.	8 a.m.–4 p.m.	10 a.m.–6 p.m.	8 a.m.–4 p.m.	9 a.m.–5 p.m.
Compressed Workweek	9 a.m.–7 p.m.	9 a.m.–7 p.m.	9 a.m.–7 p.m.	9 a.m.–7 p.m.	off
Job Sharing	Lucy 9 a.m.–2 p.m., Nathan 2 p.m.–6 p.m.	Lucy 9 a.m.–2 p.m., Nathan 2 p.m.–6 p.m.	Lucy 9 a.m.–2 p.m., Nathan 2 p.m.–6 p.m.	Lucy 9 a.m.–2 p.m., Nathan 2 p.m.–6 p.m.	Lucy 9 a.m.–2 p.m., Nathan 2 p.m.–6 p.m.
Telecommuting	9 a.m.–5 p.m.	9 a.m.–5 p.m.	9 a.m.–5 p.m.	Work from home	Work from home

example, the employee might work four ten-hour days each week and then enjoy a three-day weekend, or work eighty hours in nine days with an extra day off every other week.

Job sharing: An employment option in which one full-time job is divided among two or more people according to predetermined hours

Job sharing divides one full-time job among two or more people who work predetermined hours.[53] Job sharers can hand over their work to the next person when their part of the shift ends and the next begins. For example, you might work Monday to Wednesday and then hand over to your job share partner who then works from Wednesday to Friday, resulting in each of you working two and a half days per week. The US federal government is a big advocate of job sharing because it benefits those who need a more flexible lifestyle to either look after their families, pursue further education, or have other reasons for wanting to work part-time.[54]

Telecommuting: Working from home or from a remote location on a computer or other advanced telecommunications that are linked to the office

Telecommuting means working from home or from a remote location on a computer or other advanced telecommunications system linked to the main office.[55] This gives workers greater flexibility of working hours and location. Though more companies are using at least one of these alternative work schedules, other businesses are coming up with even more creative ways to meet the needs of their employees.

Take Oregon-based Urban Airship—a company that helps big brands engage with their mobile users. Employees are permitted to work from anywhere they like—from the home or the beach. The company also has an unlimited vacation policy—another great perk that appeals to its employees. An account manager, Urban Airship's Daniel Nguyen, says, "You can have a family, be healthy, and be ambitious and work hard. When you come to work here, you get that vibe right away."[56]

Like Urban Airship, many other companies are seeing the

The company Yahoo has stopped allowing employees to work from home since the former CEO, Marissa Mayer, feels the employees need to be physically together to be more collaborative and innovative.

FIGURE 6.4

Unlimited Vacation

IS UNLIMITED VACATION RIGHT FOR YOU?	
Probably Not If . . .	Probably Yes If ...
Employees are paid an hourly wage.	Employees have feast-or-famine workloads, such as in the tech and sales fields.
Productivity is not easily measured.	Productivity is easily measured.
Employees work in retail or other industries that need a set number of people on the job at any given time.	The culture is one of high trust between employees and managers.
The culture is intense and deadline-oriented, so people feel pressure to always be working.	Employees have the freedom to structure their own time.

Source: Reprinted from Milligan, Susan. (2015). "The Limits of Unlimited Vacation" with permission of the Society for Human Resource Management (SHRM).

benefits of providing unlimited vacation or "take what you need" as long as the job gets done. Mammoth HQ, LinkedIn, and Netflix are just a few of the larger companies that offer its employees as much vacation as they want or need. While this policy may sound easy to exploit, it does work in companies with a culture of respect and trust.

However, unlimited vacation may not be right for all companies as Figure 6.4 illustrates.

Yet even the most flexible working arrangements have their drawbacks. Some people who work remotely or telecommute may feel isolated or cut off from coworkers, while others may not be suited to working from home and the potential distractions of family life. Job sharing can be frustrating if the sharers don't work well together; and holding down a multitude of part-time or free agent jobs can lead to overwork and stress. This is why companies need to tailor their alternate work schedules to their employees with a view to retaining a productive, efficient, and committed workforce.

In this chapter, we have explored the application of motivation and its impact on employees, the difference between intrinsic and extrinsic motivation, the powerful effect of job design, and the motivational components of psychological empowerment and nontraditional work schedules. As we have seen, motivation is unsustainable without the support of teams and managers. In Chapter 7, we explore the nature of teams and the way people actively work together to achieve organizational goals.

THINKING CRITICALLY

1. List each of the work schedules discussed in the section and provide a list of the strengths and weaknesses of each approach.
2. Imagine you are considering starting a new job or leaving your old job for a new one. What aspects of a company's integration of work and life would you consider an important factor in your decision?
3. Imagine that you have replaced Marissa Mayer as CEO of Yahoo. Based on what you have learned in this chapter about intrinsic motivation, extrinsic rewards, and the job characteristics model would you continue or rescind the no telecommuting policy she implemented? Why or why not? ●

Visit **edge.sagepub.com/neckob2e** to help you accomplish your coursework goals in an easy-to-use learning environment.

- Mobile-friendly eFlashcards and practice quizzes
- Video and multimedia content
- Chapter summaries with learning objectives
- EXCLUSIVE! Access to full-text SAGE journal articles

IN REVIEW

6.1 Explain the concept of intrinsic motivation and its primary determinants

Intrinsic motivation moves us to perform tasks for our own innate satisfaction. The two main mechanisms of intrinsic motivation are *need for competence* and *need for self-determination*. The **need for competence** motivates us to gain satisfaction by stretching and exercising our capabilities. The **need for self-determination** motivates us to achieve the feeling of satisfaction and control gained through making efforts that are not reliant on any external influences.

6.2 Differentiate among the various types of extrinsic rewards

Extrinsic rewards are external contributions awarded to employees such as salary, bonuses, paid vacations, and so on. **Seniority-based pay** is guaranteed wages and salary increases based on the amount of time the employee spends with the organization. **Job content-based pay** is a salary paid based on the evaluation of a job's worth. **Skill-based pay** rewards employees for the acquisition and the development of new skills that lead to enhanced work performance. **Performance-based pay** is a financial incentive awarded to employees for meeting certain goals or objectives.

6.3 Discuss the various facets of job design

Job design is a method of setting duties and responsibilities of a job with the intention of improving productivity and performance. **Job enlargement** increases the range of tasks and duties associated with a job. **Job rotation** is a process of periodically moving staff employees from one job to another. **Job enrichment** entails increasing the scope of a job to make it more complex, interesting, stimulating, and satisfying for employees.

6.4 Discuss psychological empowerment and its components

Psychological empowerment is the extent to which employees feel a sense of personal fulfillment and intent when carrying out tasks, together with a belief that their work contributes to some larger purpose. There are four main beliefs associated with psychological empowerment. **Competence** is a belief in a person's ability to perform work tasks successfully. **Self-determination** is the understanding of skills, knowledge, and strengths that enable a person to make choices and initiate work tasks. **Impact** is the feeling of making a difference. **Meaningfulness** is the value of work tasks in line with a person's own self-concepts and ideals.

6.5 Evaluate various approaches to nontraditional work schedules

Free agents are independent workers that supply organizations with short-term talent for projects or time-bound objectives. **Part-time workers** (similar to free agents) are independent workers that supply organizations with part-time talent for projects or time-bound objectives.

There are four main nontraditional work schedules commonly adopted by employers. **Flextime** means flexible working hours where you customize your own work hours within limits established by management. **Compressed workweeks** give you the benefit of an extra day off by allowing you to work your usual number of hours in fewer days per pay period. **Job sharing** is when one full-time job is divided among two or more people according to predetermined hours. **Telecommuting** means working from home or from a remote location on a computer or other advanced telecommunications that are linked to the office.

Bonus pay   159
Competence   165
Compressed workweeks   167
Employee stock ownership plans
    (ESOPs)   160
Extrinsic rewards   155
Flextime   167
Free agents   167
Gain sharing   160
Impact   166
Intrinsic motivation   155
Job characteristics model   163
Job content-based pay   158
Job design   162
Job enlargement   162
Job enrichment   163

Job rotation   162
Job sharing   168
Merit pay   159
Meaningfulness   166
Need for competence   155
Need for self-determination   155
Part-time workers   167
Performance-based pay   159
Piece rate   159
Profit sharing   160
Psychological empowerment   165
Scientific management   162
Self-determination   166
Seniority-based pay   156
Skill-based pay   158
Telecommuting   168

UP FOR DEBATE: Using Pay Raises and Pay Cuts for Motivation

A firm's greatest tool for encouraging employees to work hard is through pay raises and cuts.
Agree or disagree? Explain your answer.

EXERCISE 6.1: Understanding Job Design

Objective

The purpose of this exercise is to gain a greater appreciation of job design.

Instructions

In groups of two to three, attempt to improve the overall job design of the following jobs. For
each job title, decide whether you would use job rotation, job enlargement, job enrichment, or
a combination of these. Explain how you would implement each form of job design.

- University president
- Cashier at a fast food restaurant
- Janitor
- President of a major corporation
- College professor

Reflection Questions

1. What challenges did you have in enhancing the overall job design of each job? How did you
   overcome those challenges?

2. Which was the most difficult job to enhance job design? Explain.

3. Which was the easiest job to enhance job design? Explain.

4. Choose a job you have held either in the past or currently. If your supervisor gave you
   permission to enhance the job design of that job in any way you wanted, how would you
   change the job through effective job design?

5. Why do managers attempt to improve job design in the workplace? What benefit do the
   managers receive from this?

Exercise contributed by Steven Stovall, Southeast Missouri State University.

EXERCISE 6.2: Extrinsic Rewards and Intrinsic Motivation

Objective

The purpose of this exercise is to grasp the concept of extrinsic rewards and intrinsic motivation.

Instructions

For this exercise, find a partner. Think about your pursuit of a college degree. Also, consider the motivation required to attain a college degree. With your classmate, brainstorm at least four extrinsic rewards and four elements of intrinsic motivation that you both have for the ultimate goal of graduating college.

Remember that extrinsic rewards are external awards such as salary. Intrinsic motivation is the performance of tasks for our own innate satisfaction.

After ten minutes of brainstorming, the instructor will ask for volunteers to share their results.

Reflection Questions

1. Did you and your partner readily agree on each extrinsic reward or intrinsic motivation? How were they alike? Different?

2. Was your list similar to other teams who volunteered their list? How alike or dissimilar were they?

3. Thinking about your current job, what are the extrinsic rewards and intrinsic motivation of this job?

Exercise contributed by Steven Stovall, Southeast Missouri State University.

EXERCISE 6.3: Charity Begins with Motivation

Objectives

In completing this exercise, you will have practiced your ability to *explain* intrinsic motivation and its determinants, *differentiate* between various types of extrinsic rewards, and *discuss* work duties in terms of a job design.

Background

You are part of a group that is in charge of recruiting and staffing a charity car wash to raise money for a university scholarship fund. The car wash is expected to last from 8:00 a.m. to 5:00 or 6:00 p.m. with lunch provided on a rotating basis for each volunteer. In addition to the free lunch, the university can provide a small fund for compensation (approximately $5 to $10 per volunteer) to be used in any reasonable way the committee decides is appropriate. In addition to this fund, the university is planning on posting the volunteers' names and pictures on the university website along with a brief story about the event.

From your OB class, you realize the importance of a good job design in motivating people: both in terms of quality work outcomes and in being able to better recruit people for tasks. Using this knowledge, you were able to convince everyone to hold a meeting just to develop a clear plan for maximizing the volunteers' motivation for this event. You are about to go into that meeting.

Instructions

Step 1. Form into groups (maximum of seven members), and create a motivation plan for the volunteers. This plan should include intrinsic and extrinsic motivations, as well as any job design aspects that are appropriate. Be creative in developing this plan, but also be sure to link your ideas back to chapter concepts, and use chapter terms in your descriptions. Then use this plan to make suggestions of how the job aspects can be used to promote the recruitment process. Also, provide information on how the job design and motivational aspects of the task are likely to affect volunteer outcomes. (20 minutes)

Step 2. Select a spokesperson to present your plan. (If possible, the spokesperson should be someone who has not had an opportunity to speak in front of the class before. If everyone has presented in front of class, select the person who has presented the least.) Before the person presents, give your group a unique name. (20 to 30 minutes)

Step 3. Vote on the plan that should be the most motivational. (You cannot vote for the team you were a member of.) In addition to writing the group's name on a sheet of paper, write down why you believe the plan will be the most motivational using chapter terms. (10 to 15 minutes)

Reflection Questions

1. What difficulties did you encounter in developing motivational methods with such constrained resources? How are these difficulties similar to what supervisors for entry level personnel face?

2. Which type of motivations do you expect to be stronger in this situation—intrinsic or extrinsic?

3. How might that motivational balance differ for supervisors of entry-level personnel?

4. How did using chapter terms and concepts better help you frame and understand this situation?

5. What other teams came up with creative ways to motivate the volunteers? Were there motivators that you found difficult to classify as intrinsic or extrinsic?

Exercise contributed by Milton R. Mayfield, Professor of Business, Texas A&M International University, and Jacqueline R. Mayfield, Professor of Business, Texas A&M International University.

EXERCISE 6.4: Role-Playing Job Design

Objective

The purpose of this exercise is to grasp the concept of job design through a role-play.

Instructions

There are three ways a manager could enhance the design of a job: job rotation, job enlargement, and job enrichment. Job rotation is periodically moving employees from one position to another. Job enlargement is increasing the range of tasks and duties associated with a job. And job enrichment is increasing the scope of a job to make it more complex, interesting, stimulating, and satisfying for employees.

For this role-play, a stack of blank paper will be needed and the instructor will ask for four volunteers from the class. These four are the employees. In addition, two more volunteers will be the managers.

The task is simple. The four employees will use an assembly line to construct paper airplanes. The first employee will make a fold or two, the second employee will make another fold or two, and so on until the paper airplane is finished by the fourth employee (the managers will provide training on how to properly construct the airplane).

The role-play consists of the following phases:

Phase 1: The managers determine one specific model of paper airplane and train the employees on how to make that particular model. The managers then divide the steps among the four employees.

Phase 2: The employees construct four identical paper airplanes to the one demonstrated during training.

Phase 3: The employees construct four more identical paper airplanes, but this time, job rotation is used where employees are assigned a different step along the production line than they originally had in Phase 1 (additional training from the managers may be necessary so that employees understand their new role).

Phase 4: Employees may remain in the same position or may move back to their original positions—this is entirely up to the managers. Four more planes will be constructed; however, for this phase job enlargement will be introduced (additional tasks will be given to each employee). Managers can decide what these additional tasks will be—decorating the plane in a certain prescribed way, cleaning up around the area, etc.

Phase 5: For this phase, four more paper planes will be constructed and the managers will introduce job enrichment (they will give the employees more decision-making authority as to how their tasks are done). Again, it is up to the managers as to how this should be implemented, but possible ideas are permitting them to construct a different airplane of their choice, choosing which tasks are to be completed by which employees to make the production process faster or more efficient, etc.

Reflection Questions

1. How well did the managers introduce each method of job design? What did they do right, and what would you have done differently?

2. Take each method of job design—job rotation, job enlargement, and job enrichment—and think about a job for each that would benefit from that particular type of job design. For example, in which type of job would employees be most motivated if job rotation was available? Job enlargement? Job enrichment? Why did you choose those particular jobs?

3. What difficulty would managers have in implementing each method of job design? How could the manager overcome these difficulties?

Exercise contributed by Steven Stovall, Southeast Missouri State University.

ONLINE EXERCISE 6.1: Finding Examples of Individual Performance-Based Pay

Objective

The purpose of this exercise is to gain an appreciation for various forms of individual performance-based pay.

Instructions

Go to a job-listing website and look through the listings of available job postings. Read through the posts and find one example of each of the following forms of individual performance-based pay:

- Piece rate
- Bonus pay
- Merit pay

Keep in mind, many companies do not readily reveal their pay practices in these posts so you may have to visit more than one career website to find an example of each. Once you have located one of each, copy the link or the post and submit that to your instructor, being sure to label it as an example of piece rate, bonus pay, or merit pay.

Reflection Questions

1. Which of these three forms of individual performance-based pay do you think is most common in the workplace? Explain.

2. Which form of individual performance-based pay would you like to receive/earn most? Why?

3. What are the advantages and disadvantages of each of these forms of pay?

4. Why are some companies secretive about their pay practices?

Exercise contributed by Steven Stovall, Southeast Missouri State University.

Netflix's new employee practices have grabbed attention, to put it mildly. In 2012, a simple internal PowerPoint explaining them went viral and was viewed more than 5 million times on the web. Sheryl Sandberg, chief operating officer of Facebook, said it "may well be the most important document ever to come out of [Silicon] Valley." Dozens of bloggers and journalists scrambled to analyze its contents. And Netflix is surely doing something right: In 2013, the company's stock value tripled; in 2017–2018 the same is true. It has reached over 200 million subscribers and won an Academy Award and thirty-seven Emmy Awards for its original shows like *House of Cards*.

What was revealed in that game-changing PowerPoint? It was simply a "commonsense" approach, according to Patty McCord, then Netflix's chief talent officer and one of the presentation's authors. Netflix treats the people it hires as grownups. It grants them a great deal of freedom, and it expects them to use it wisely.

Game Changers

Conventional human resources (HR) is full of structure and documentation. Directors spend hours drafting standard operating procedures about time off, performance appraisals, training, and more. Netflix has simplified the process by doing away with many of these policies and focusing on results rather than processes.

McCord realized that motivating employees to produce outstanding results had a lot to do with trusting them with greater independence. That didn't mean installing an arcade or skateboard park, as other tech companies have done. Instead, Netflix started doing away with formal procedures. Among the first to go was the leave procedure. Gone were the standard ten days of vacation, ten holidays, and handful of sick days. The new policy? Take what you need when you need it.

Giving employees the leeway to take as much vacation time as they'd like might strike many HR professionals as reckless. Wouldn't people abuse such a liberal leave plan? McCord, however, had shifted to a different philosophy. Written policies, she reasoned, were mainly designed to eliminate problems created by a very small percentage of employees. The vast majority of people, and particularly the type of person Netflix tries to recruit, could be counted on to use common sense in their decision making.

This approach was extended to other areas. Travel and expense accounts are generally kept under a watchful eye, policed by HR or accounting to ensure that money is being spent in an acceptable manner, with plenty of documentation and accountability. Netflix turned tradition on its head, creating what may be the shortest expense policy any company has ever set: "Act in Netflix's best interests." Employees are also allowed to book their own travel online rather than going through a designated travel agent, allowing them to choose the best price.

Netflix compensates its employees very well, but there's freedom there, too. People can choose what portion of their pay they would like to receive in direct compensation and what portion in stock options. This allows them to consider what sort of risk level they're comfortable with (the value of any company's stock will fluctuate over time) and what is best for them and their families. Netflix also eliminated performance-based bonuses, preferring to pay people fairly and trust them to do good work. There are no "golden handcuffs"—a form of retention plan that does not allow employees to receive stock options or other incentives until they've reached a certain number of years of service. Employees are also encouraged to research and interview with competitor companies and then have frank discussions with HR. This helps both the department *and* the employee know what is are good salaries for various positions.

The company also decided to forego conventional performance reviews. It eliminated the performance metrics typical of many companies' evaluations, like grading an employee on a five-point scale in a variety of different tasks and expectations. Instead, a "360-degree review" is performed, which is an open conversation between employees and their managers about feedback from people inside (and occasionally outside) the company who have any contact with the employee. The evaluation is largely centered on one question for the manager, known as the "keeper test": "Which of my people, if they told me they were leaving in two months for a similar job at a peer company, would I fight hard to keep at Netflix?" If someone's skills and abilities are no longer a match for the company, the person is given a generous severance package upon exit. As CEO Reed Hastings told the *Harvard Business Review*, paraphrasing a section of the now-famous PowerPoint: "'Adequate performance gets a generous severance package.' It's a pretty blunt statement of our hunger for excellence."

The document is "our version of *Letters to a Young Poet* for budding entrepreneurs," Reed continued. "It's what we wish we had understood when we started." He goes on to argue that a relatively new industry—online, on-demand entertainment—demands new paradigms. "As a society, we've had hundreds of years to work on managing industrial firms, so a lot of accepted HR practices are centered in that experience. We're just beginning to learn how to run creative firms, which is quite different. Industrial firms thrive on reducing variation (manufacturing errors); creative firms thrive on increasing variation (innovation)."

The Payoffs

Netflix's overhaul of its HR policies has yielded positive results. Despite the lack of carefully outlined procedures, the expectations are still clear: you have the freedom to make decisions, but keep in mind what is best for the company. The HR department at Netflix has realized that it isn't necessary to beat its people over the head with exactly *how* to make good decisions.

Freedom equals reduced stress, arguably. The level of flexibility and self-management that Netflix also offers creates more efficiency. Employees don't have to worry about whether they've racked up enough days off to take a trip or whether they've worked long enough hours to impress the boss. They aren't fretting over how the big annual review will go, or whether they'll get the score that will earn the bonus they've been counting on. Eliminating these typical workplace stressors motivates employees to stay focused on creating ideas and solutions for the business.

At Netflix, clear and honest communication thrives. Employees don't fear retribution for looking into openings with other companies; they can go to HR and openly discuss other possibilities. Managers no longer have to spend time "in the weeds" developing improvement plans and riding mediocre workers for results. Likewise, employees are less likely to have to pick up slack for colleagues who are not performing. While Netflix lets people go whose knowledge and skills are no longer relevant, it's candid about why. As McCord puts it, "People can handle anything as long as they're told the truth."

Being straightforward has costs, but having direct conversations with and offering a generous severance package to employees who are no longer a good fit has resulted in *zero* lawsuits over termination to date. HR is also empowered to find someone who fits the bill rather than continuing to invest in someone who cannot do what's needed while risking the morale and motivation of fellow coworkers.

By allowing its employees plenty of liberty to make decisions for themselves, Netflix has reaped great rewards in employee motivation, efficiency, and productivity. While the premise may have seemed risky, it proved to be a commonsense solution for issues most HR departments face. Considering the way it revolutionized and streamlined the movie rental process for changing times, it is hardly surprising that Netflix seems to have done the same for employee motivation.

Case Questions

1. How does Netflix use intrinsic motivation to support its HR practices?

2. Why would a creative firm choose to use intrinsic motivation where an industrial firm would probably choose to use extrinsic rewards?

3. Explain the appeal of nontraditional work schedules and how Netflix has chosen to implement them.

Sources

Baer, Drake. "Netflix's Major HR Innovation: Treating Humans Like People." *Fast Company*. March 13, 2014. www.fastcompany.com/3027124/lessons-learned/netflixs-major-hr-innovation-treating-humans-like-people.

Fenzi, Francesca. "3 Big Ideas to Steal from Netflix." *Inc.* February 5, 2013. www.inc.com/francesca-fenzi/management-ideas-to-steal-from-netflix.html.

Grossman, Robert J. "Tough Love at Netflix." *HR*. April 1, 2010. www.shrm.org/Publications/hrmagazine/EditorialContent/2010/0410/Pages/0410grossman3.aspx.

Kamensky, John. "Netflix's 5 Tenets of HR." *Government Executive*. February 14, 2014. www.govexec.com/excellence/promising-practices/2014/02/netflixs-5-tenets-hr/78827/.

McCord, Patty. "How Netflix Reinvented HR." *Harvard Business Review* (January–February 2014). http://hbr.org/2014/01/how-netflix-reinvented-hr.

Nisen, Max. "Legendary Ex-HR Director from Netflix Shares 6 Important Lessons." *Business Insider.* December 30, 2013. \www.businessinsider.com/netflix-corporate-culture-hr-policy-2013-12.

No Author. "Netflix Wins Three Emmys." *Huffington Post.* September 23, 2013. www.huffingtonpost .com/2013/09/22/netflix-emmys-house-of-cards-wins_n_3973794.html.

SELF-ASSESSMENT 6.1

Is Job Enrichment Motivational to Me?

For each statement, circle the number that best describes you based on the following scale:

	STRONGLY DISAGREE	SOMEWHAT DISAGREE	NEUTRAL	SOMEWHAT AGREE	STRONGLY AGREE
1. I prefer a job that requires me to use a number of complex and high-level skills.	1	2	3	4	5
2. I prefer a job in which the work is arranged so that I have the chance to complete an entire work process from beginning to end.	1	2	3	4	5
3. I prefer a job that provides many chances for me to figure out how well I am doing.	1	2	3	4	5
4. I do not prefer work that is quite simple and repetitive.	1	2	3	4	5
5. I prefer a job in which a lot of other people can be affected by how well the work gets done.	1	2	3	4	5
6. I prefer a job that provides me the opportunity to use my own personal initiative and judgment in carrying out the work.	1	2	3	4	5
7. I prefer to completely finish the work processes that I begin.	1	2	3	4	5
8. I enjoy work that provides information about how well I am performing.	1	2	3	4	5
9. I prefer considerable independence and freedom in how I do my work.	1	2	3	4	5
10. I am interested in work that is very significant or important in the broader scheme of things.	1	2	3	4	5
11. I prefer a job that allows me to decide on my own how to go about doing the work.	1	2	3	4	5
12. I prefer a job that provides me with information about my performance.	1	2	3	4	5

Scoring

Add the numbers circled above: _____

Interpretation

48 and above = You have a strong desire for complex, challenging work. You would find an enriched job to be very motivational.

25–47 = You have moderate desire for complex, challenging work. You would find an enriched job to be moderately motivational.

24 and below = You have a low desire for complex, challenging work. You would not find an enriched job to be motivational. You would prefer a job that is more simple, straightforward, and uncomplicated.

Source: Adapted from Hackman, J. R., and G. R. Oldham. *The Job Diagnostic Survey: An Instrument for the Diagnosis of Jobs and the Evaluation of Job Redesign Projects.* Technical Report No. 4 (New Haven, CT: Yale University, Department of Administrative Sciences, 1974).

YOSHIKAZU TSUNO/AFP/Getty Images

PART III

Teams and Teamwork

7

Teams

Alone we can do so little, together we can do so much.

—*Helen Keller*

Learning Objectives

By the end of this chapter, you will be able to:

7.1 Distinguish between teams and groups

7.2 Explain how team processes affect team outcomes

7.3 Compare the various types of teams in organizations today

7.4 Apply the model of team effectiveness to evaluate team performance

7.5 Identify the advantages and disadvantages of different team decision-making approaches

CASE STUDY: THE TEAM AT THOMAS JEFFERSON UNIVERSITY HOSPITAL EMERGENCY DEPARTMENT

Have you ever made a trip to the emergency room? If so, how long was your wait? Often times, patients will go to the emergency room with a legitimate emergency medical condition but wait up to an hour to be seen by a physician. Many people choose not to wait and simply walk out the door. Hospitals around the country have adopted a metric to keep track of patients who leave, called "left-without-being-seen" rates or LWBS. Naturally, high LWBS rates correspond directly to an overcrowded emergency room and a poorly functioning staff of nurses and physicians. When patients leave without being seen, they put themselves in a situation where their health can decline further by not being treated.

Additionally, the nursing teams at hospitals with high LWBS rates typically perform subpar due to the excessive sense of urgency they have when treating patients. Currently, it is not uncommon for the public to keep track of individual LWBS rates to avoid hospitals that have a history of long waits and poor service. In fact, Medicaid Services and the Centers for Medicare require hospitals to report the LWBS rates to the public on a quarterly basis. According to the quarterly reports for Thomas Jefferson University Hospital in the first quarter of 2015, it has a door-to-provider time of 43 minutes and an LWBS of 5.7 percent, among the worst in the country. However, those numbers are a significant improvement in comparison to the numbers that the hospital saw in 2008 to 2009 when the door-to-provider time was averaging around 122 minutes and the LWBS rate was between 6 percent and 8 percent.

Thomas Jefferson University Hospital Emergency Department is located in Philadelphia, Pennsylvania, and sees around 65,000 patients per year with its busiest time between 2 p.m. and 10 p.m. The emergency department is made up of a team of physicians and nurses who run the day-to-day operations. The team at Thomas Jefferson Hospital decided to make it a goal of theirs to bring down LWBS rates below the national average of 2 percent along with decreasing the door-to-provider times, and improving overall service. This led to the creation of the "Emergency Department 2.0" initiative at Thomas Jefferson.

Stephen McDonald, manager of the emergency department, said of the initiative, "We adopted it as our mantra and challenged ourselves to become a more patient—and family-centric emergency department. Jefferson wants to be the best in all areas. It is a privilege to care for 65,000 people in the Philadelphia area, and we don't take that lightly."

With a strong mission, the emergency department had the foundation it needed to make positive changes; however, without proper management, the team would likely fail. The nature of this change called for increased interdependence between team members within the department, meaning teams would need to rely on each other, work closely together on a piece of work, consult with each other, provide each other with advice, and exchange information, during the process of implementing the new process improvement strategies. The executive physicians stepped up to the plate and engaged deeply in the redesign and processes of the operations in the department alongside the nurses and technicians. McDonald acknowledges, "The support (from leadership) was the only way we could institute such radical change."

While the leadership played a huge role in the ultimate success of the project, it was the integration of the nurse's perspectives that were the key factor in determining the best strategy moving forward. When it comes down to it, the nurses in the emergency department know the operations better than anyone and have a much more useful perspective on how it can be improved than anyone else. The department leadership employed the Delphi Technique, which is a method of decision making in which information is gathered from a group of respondents within their area of expertise. Stephen McDonald recalls, "We wanted to leverage the amazing nursing staff and we really worked hard to engage them throughout the process. They were at the table and their voices were heard." This is by far one of the most important aspects of a successful team.

Management that opens the floor to the perspective of all the team members is much more likely to make better decisions when they have their hands on the perspectives of the people that make up the backbone of their team. Silencing and excluding team members from discussion will only cause harm to the team and the operation as a whole. By being inclusive to all team members, everyone has access to more knowledge and learning opportunities. Also, empowering team members to contribute in their own special ways is sure to help any team succeed in accomplishing its goals. Teamwork has benefits that are both morale boosting and psychological: team members will be happier, more motivated, and more likely to contribute ideas that can improve productivity when they feel empowered.

A cohesive team with a strong mission, like the team at Thomas Jefferson, is a force to be reckoned with. Susan Cissone, administrative supervisor of the department, describes the instant benefits that including the nurses in decision making had for the company as it pushed toward its goal. "Anyone looking to change their intake model needs to be bold; including our nursing staff in decisions led to our success." In the first week of ED 2.0's implementation, Thomas Jefferson's Emergency Department saw a 0.42 percent LWBS rate, a number that far exceeded original expectations. The team at Thomas Jefferson has been able to sustain their early success with an LWBS rate under 1 percent and an average door-to-provider time hovering around ten minutes which is among the best in the nation. Joseph Anton, VP of clinical support and services, explains, "We are extremely proud of what the team has accomplished. While ED 2.0 was a call to action to ensure we were putting the patients and their families at the center of all we do, it was also a tremendous example of the power of teamwork and staff engagement."

Critical-Thinking Questions

1. What types of problems might the hospital have encountered had it not included the nursing staff in decision making?

2. What was so valuable about seeing management engage in the new initiative alongside their subordinates?

Sources:

Goodman, P. (2018). 15 advantages of teamwork in the workplace. *Toughnickel*. Retrieved from https://toughnickel.com/business/15-Advantages-of-teamwork-in-the-workplace

HRH Global Resource Center. (n.d.). *Why is teamwork in health care important?* Retrieved from http://www.hrhresourcecenter.org/HRH_Info_Teamwork

Jefferson Health. (n.d.). *Quality & safety*. Retrieved from http://hospitals.jefferson.edu/quality-and-safety.html

Leonard, K. (2018). Elements of teamwork in the workplace. *Chron*. Retrieved from http://smallbusiness.chron.com/elements-teamwork-workplace-692.html

Love, D. B. (2016, May 2). *Thomas Jefferson University Hospital*. Retrieved from http://nursing.advanceweb.com/Features/Articles/Thomas-Jefferson-University-Hospital.aspx

Thomas Jefferson University Hospital. (n.d.). *Improving ED flow through the UMLN II*. Retrieved from http://www.hpoe.org/Case_Studies/ThomasJEffersonUniversityHospital_EDFlow_UMLNII.pdf

The Difference between Teams and Groups

>> **LO 7.1** Distinguish between teams and groups

Teams and teamwork play a critical role in the success of 21st-century organizations. In the Thomas Jefferson Hospital case study, the team was empowered to contribute to the initiative to reduce the amount of time patients spent waiting for practitioners, which led to the team successfully accomplishing its goals. The most successful organizations value and understand the nature of teams and create a productive environment in which teams flourish. A **team** is a collection of people brought together to apply their individual skills to a common project or goal.[1]

Regardless of the type of organization, most employees work in some form of a team in today's workplace. Compared to a few decades ago, teamwork has become commonplace in contemporary organizations. But what has caused this dramatic shift to team structures? Global competition means that organizations need to respond quickly to competitive pressures. Efficient, collaborative teams are one way for organizations to meet the growing demands of their customers and stay ahead of the competition. Some organizations take collaboration so seriously that they are changing the traditional office layout and replacing cubicles with low walls or no walls between desks. Many are creating small, informal areas designed to encourage spontaneous discussion and problem solving.[2]

Organizational restructuring and downsizing have brought leaner, more efficient, and more productive structures to many companies. Rather than viewing layoffs as a negative, some companies perceive a trimmer organization as an optimal way for employees to collaborate more intensely, to become more engaged in the decision-making processes, and to contribute their own ideas and initiatives. In addition, employees have become more empowered through **decentralization**, the distribution of power across all levels of the organization.[3] Employees are encouraged to be creative and innovative and given more freedom to make decisions.

Finally, many employees, especially in the United States and Europe, are working in high technology or knowledge information industries where close collaboration is viewed as a positive forum for innovation and creativity. However, collaboration in today's working world doesn't necessarily mean physically sitting

Team: A group of people brought together to use their individual skills on a common project or goal

Decentralization: The distribution of power across all levels of the organization

together in the same office. Thanks to increasing technology, people are more connected than ever before. Take global design company IDEO for instance. While employees often meet in person in order to conduct field research, there are times when teams agree to work remotely using agreed methods of communication (email, Slack, group messaging) to share information and ideas.[4]

Teams versus Groups

The terms *teams* and *groups* are often used interchangeably, but there are subtle differences between them.[5]

Group: Three or more people who work independently to attain organizational goals

A **group** usually consists of three or more people who work independently to attain organizational goals.[6] In other words, it focuses on achieving individual goals. For example, in a small business, there might be three people in the marketing department; one might be focused on sales, another on branding, and a third on the administration associated with those tasks. Each employee will work independently and produce individual projects but all group members will still work toward the organization's common goals. Outside work, friends who come together to watch a football game on television would be classified as a group.

In contrast, teams consist of a number of people, usually between three and seven, who use their complementary skills to collaborate in a joint effort. Teams engage in interdependent, collaborative, and cooperative work to achieve purposeful goals. For example, players playing on a game of football would be classified as a team.

Teams with fewer than three people tend not to derive the benefits of a collaborative team, and teams with more than seven tend to have communication and control issues. In this chapter we focus on teams.

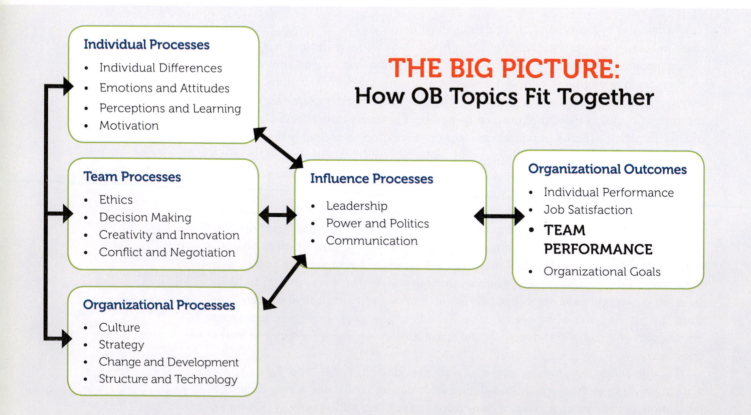

THE BIG PICTURE:
How OB Topics Fit Together

Individual Processes
- Individual Differences
- Emotions and Attitudes
- Perceptions and Learning
- Motivation

Team Processes
- Ethics
- Decision Making
- Creativity and Innovation
- Conflict and Negotiation

Organizational Processes
- Culture
- Strategy
- Change and Development
- Structure and Technology

Influence Processes
- Leadership
- Power and Politics
- Communication

Organizational Outcomes
- Individual Performance
- Job Satisfaction
- **TEAM PERFORMANCE**
- Organizational Goals

Are Teams Effective?

The effectiveness of work teams depends on how well they are managed and treated within the organization. A well-run team is usually productive, innovative, loyal, and adaptable. Organizations that consistently nurture teams tend to experience reduced turnover and absenteeism. Over a period of two years, researchers at technology giant Google carried out a study of over 180 teams at the company in an effort to discover the components of an effective team.[7] The results were surprising. It turned out that it didn't matter so much about who was on the team, but rather how team members interacted with each other, structured their work, and viewed their contributions.

The researchers found that most highly effective teams shared the same team dynamics. Teams were made up of dependable members who were clear about their roles and goals, attached personal meaning to their work, and understood the impact of their work. Interestingly, the findings showed that the most important component of an effective team was **psychological safety**, which is a shared belief held by team members whether it is safe enough to trust each other well enough to take risks.[8] When people feel psychologically safe in a working environment, they will feel more inclined toward open communication, voicing their concerns and actively seeking feedback.

A psychologically safe environment produces a number of positive outcomes on both the individual and team levels, such as better communication, knowledge sharing, greater reporting of errors, improved learning behaviors, and a higher ability to learn from failure. Research also shows a positive link between creativity and employees' perceptions of psychological safety, particularly in R&D teams where innovation performance is high.

While psychological safety may sound similar to trust, there is an important difference. Trust focuses on how one person might perceive another, but psychological safety is more focused on how team members perceive the behaviors of the team as a whole (see Figure 7.1).

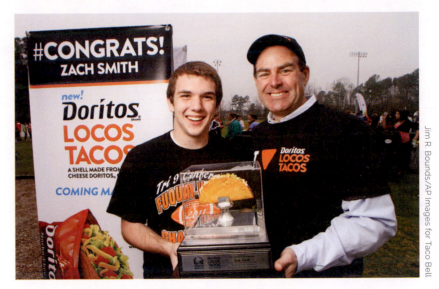

Taco Bell COO Rob Savage poses for a photo with the winner of a social media contest promoting Doritos Locos Tacos.

Jim R. Bounds/AP Images for Taco Bell

FIGURE 7.1

The Impact of Psychological Safety

1. **Psychological Safety**
Team members feel safe to take risks and be vulnerable in front of each other.

2. **Dependability**
Team members get things done on time and meet Google's high bar for excellence.

3. **Structure and Clarity**
Team members have clear roles, plans, and goals.

4. **Meaning**
Work is personally important to team members.

5. **Impact**
Team members think their work matters and creates change.

Source: Thomson, Stephanie. (2015). "Google's Surprising Discovery about Effective Teams." *World Economic Forum.* https://www.weforum.org/agenda/2015/12/googles-surprising-discovery-about-effective-teams/

Psychological safety: A shared belief held by team members that the team trusts each other enough to take risks

How to Build an Effective Team[9]

All teams have the potential to be high-performing when they have the right leader. Here are a few tips that help leaders get the most out of their teams:

1. Nurture relationships

It's not always easy to get along with everybody on the team, but investing in relationships builds trust and loyalty—both of which are key to a high-performing team.

2. Honest feedback

Some leaders tend to shy away from giving "bad news" or negative feedback. Learning how to give honest feedback is a skill, but one that must be adopted to cultivate a culture of openness.

3. Identify common goals

Effective leaders identify and prioritize common goals to solidify the team—the message being that the team will only succeed if everyone works together.

However, teams can fail if they are mismanaged; if they are not implemented properly, they can cause more harm than good. Explore the concept of teams further from the point of view of Derrick Hall, president and CEO of the Arizona Diamondbacks in the OB in the Real World feature.

THINKING CRITICALLY

1. What types of tasks are best suited to a group? What types of tasks are best suited to a team?

2. Which of the four aspects of a well-run team (productive, innovative, loyal, adaptable) do you think is the most important? Which do you think is least important? Explain your response.

A Model of Team Effectiveness: Processes and Outcomes

>> LO 7.2   **Explain how team processes affect team outcomes**

A high-performing team does not happen overnight. It takes time for team members to build rapport and trust. When teams first come together they go through a number of stages in the process of becoming a team. In his original model of group development in 1965, psychologist Bruce Tuckman named the stages "forming, norming, storming, and performing" (Figure 7.2).[10] Tuckman believed that these stages are essential for teams in order to grow together to confront challenges, solve complex problems, find solutions, make decisions, meet goals, and deliver results. Twelve years later, Tuckman created a fifth stage called "adjourning."

Forming.   In the first stage of group development the members meet for the first time, get to know each other, and try to understand where they fit within the team structure. They may discuss opportunities and challenges ahead, decide on goals, and assign tasks. They may work independently from each other until they feel

Forming: A process whereby team members meet for the first time, get to know each other, and try to understand where they fit in to the team structure

FIGURE 7.2

The Tuckman Model of Team Development

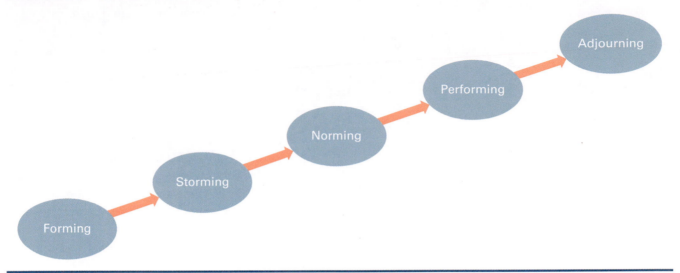

Source: Tuckman, Bruce. "Developmental Sequence in Small Groups." *Psychological Bulletin* 63 (1965): 384–399.

comfortable enough to raise difficult topics. During this period, team members focus on learning about each other, are polite to each other, and tend to avoid conflict.

Storming. After a period of time, tensions may arise between members and different personalities might clash, leading to conflict within the team. For instance, team members might question the actions of a team leader, perceive the leader as too weak or dominant, or feel annoyed with another team member for being frequently late or shirking responsibility. Tension and arguments may result when these opinions are voiced. However, if a team has any chance of being successful, the team members must find a way to manage these conflicts in order to resolve their differences and move past the issues. Some teams do not survive the storming stage, but the ones that do become all the stronger for it. By openly discussing and resolving issues, the team can put its differences aside and focus instead on the work at hand.

> **Storming:** A phase during which, after a period of time, tension may arise between members and different personalities might clash, leading to tension and conflict in the team

Norming. The team members resolve the conflict and begin to work well together and become more cohesive. Members become more tolerant and understanding of each other's differences and begin to appreciate different strengths. During this stage, team members may start to socialize together and make more of an effort to get to know each other. When rapport starts to build, team members feel more comfortable asking each other for help, or providing constructive feedback. Because the team is becoming more cohesive, reaching goals, hitting milestones, and achieving deadlines becomes more realistic. However, it is not all smooth sailing during the norming stage. It is very common for the team to revert to the storming stage especially when new tasks are assigned.

> **Norming:** The process by which team members resolve the conflict and begin to work well together and become more cohesive

Performing. The team becomes invested in achieving its goals and operates as a unit. At this stage, there is high loyalty and trust between members. Team members are motivated on achieving common goals and can make decisions without supervision. Any dissent that occurs is handled easily and members work in harmony in order to successfully complete common goals. Despite this congenial

> **Performing:** The way in which a team is invested toward achieving its goals and operates as a unit

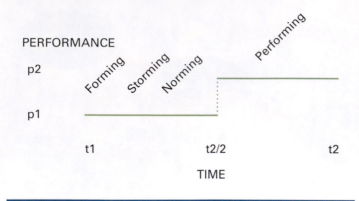

Source: Based on Gersick, Connie J.G. 1988. 'Time and Transition In Work Teams: Toward A New Model Of Group Development.' *Academy of Management Journal* 31. no. 1: 9-41

work environment, it is still possible for high performing teams to lapse back into the storming stage, particularly if there is a change in leadership which challenges the team dynamics.

Adjourning. The final stage takes place when individuals either leave the team or have no reason to be in further contact with their teammates—successfully completing a group project, for example. Even long-standing teams may be forced to disband in the event of an organizational restructure. Although adjourning is usually inevitable, this can be a difficult stage for some team members who have built relationships with fellow colleagues and grown used to the routine and norms of the team itself. When teams lose members which are then replaced by new members, the whole team development cycle is likely to start again.

Punctuated equilibrium. While Tuckman's model is a popular theory for team formation, the punctuated equilibrium model developed by Connie Gersick suggests that teams do not develop in this sequence (see Figure 7.3). **Punctuated equilibrium** is a method of understanding organizational change by illustrating where change is relatively stable and where it becomes more volatile.[11]

For instance, when teams first come together they tend to perform at a low level for a period of time that is more or less equal to half the time until the deadline or due date. At some point, the team transitions upward to a higher level of performance when the team task(s) are really accomplished. Within the context of the Tuckman model, this means that groups tend to start off by combining the forming and norming stages, before going through a period of low performance, followed by storming, a period of high performance, and then finally adjourning.

Tuckman's model is the most commonly used framework for team development today. It illustrates that team development is not always a linear process and provides a useful way for organizations to identify the reasons behind team behaviors in order to find ways to resolve issues in order to optimize team performance and productivity.

Team Norms and Cohesion

The effectiveness of many teams depends on it **norms**, or the informal rules of behavior that govern the team.[12] Team norms are ground rules that impact the functioning of the team, for example, how team members communicate, agree on email response times, how decisions are made, expected work hours, timekeeping, and so on. Teams that adhere to norms tend to perform better and are more cohesive. Here are some other examples of norms:[13]

- Treat each other with dignity and respect.
- Avoid hidden agendas.
- Be genuine with each other about ideas, challenges, and feelings.
- Have confidence that issues discussed will be kept in confidence.
- Listen to understand.

Adjourning: The stage when individuals either leave the team or have no reason to be in further contact with their teammates

Punctuated equilibrium: A method of understanding organizational change by illustrating where change is relatively stable and where it becomes more volatile

Norms: The informal rules of a team's behavior that govern the team

- Practice being open minded.

- Don't be defensive with your colleagues.

- Give your colleagues the benefit of the doubt.

- Support each other; don't throw each other under the bus.

- It's okay to not know the right answer and to admit it.

- Present problems in a way that promotes mutual discussion and resolution.

- Practice and experience humility.

- If you commit to doing something, do it.

- Respect the time and convenience of others.

A recent study called Project Aristotle carried out by Google showed that team norms were more important than team smarts when it came to successfully completing an assignment.[14] Researchers found that dysfunctional teams failed more often because of wrong norms in spite of how many smart people were on it; whereas teams with healthy norms tended to succeed on every assignment. In sum, the right norms can increase a team's intelligence whereas the wrong norms can hamper it.

As Tuckman's team development model shows, teams need to be cohesive in order to perform well. **Cohesion** is the degree to which team members connect with each other.[15] In most cases, cohesiveness is essential for team effectiveness because it encourages members to work together to reach the same goal. Social and emotional bonds between members help to maintain consistent work efforts, steering everyone toward the same objective. A cohesive team is more motivated, communicates better, and reports higher levels of satisfaction than less cohesive teams.

Cohesion: The degree to which team members connect with each other

However, there is such a thing as too much cohesion in a team, which can have negative consequences. For example, an overly cohesive team may be prone to inflexibility or resistance to change. It may also limit team members' ability to express their own personal thoughts and feelings for fear of upsetting the group dynamic. Too much cohesion can also lead to lack of accountability and decision making.

Team Charters

Another good way to ensure good team communication and positive work cohesion is to provide team charters for every project.[16] A charter is a type of document that outlines the purpose of the team, the benefits of the project, the required objectives, and expected timeframe. Ideally, team charters should be created in the early stages of team formation. Managers are responsible for ensuring that team members have been given clear direction and feel confident enough in their roles in order to achieve the goals of the project described in the charter efficiently and effectively.

Synergy: Process Gains and Losses

Team are more likely to perform well when they have good **synergy**, or the interaction that makes the total amount of work produced by a team greater than the amount of work produced by individual members working independently.[17] The Arizona Diamondbacks baseball team featured in OB in the Real World has good

Synergy: The concept that the total amount of work produced by a team is greater than the amount of work produced by individual members working independently

synergy, mostly because of its familial culture where every team member is given a voice. Positive synergy is achieved by good leadership as well as ensuring the right people are hired for the right roles. Teams with good synergy are more committed to goals, apply more diverse skills and abilities to tasks, and show greater willingness to share information and knowledge. Typically, teams that share common interests and values have a better chance of creating and maintaining positive synergy.

However, bad synergy within teams can lead to toxic negativity, especially when one or more team members exhibits negative behavior. Research has shown that it only takes one "bad apple" to impact a whole team.[18] These bad apples tend to work less than the other members, or attack and bully others. For example, in one study analyzing team dynamics in fifty manufacturing teams, researchers found that the teams with at least one irresponsible or negative team member were more likely to experience conflict, poor communication, and lack of cooperation.[19] Managers can address this issue by making an effort to try and change the negative behavior, but if this doesn't work, there may be little choice but to let the bad apple go.

Process gains: Factors that contribute to team effectiveness

Teams that achieve positive synergy will produce a number of **process gains**, which are the degree to which certain factors contribute to team effectiveness.[20] Process gains include a sense of shared purpose, plans, and goals; the confidence team members have in their own abilities to achieve objectives; a shared vision of the way the work should be carried out; and constructive task-focused conflict, which can help teams with their problem solving and decision making. In many cases, the level of process gains leads a team to exceed its performance.

Process losses: Factors that detract from team effectiveness

In contrast, a team without good synergy can lead to **process losses**, the factors that detract from team effectiveness.[21] Team members who are afraid to disagree with other team members inhibits decision making and problem solving. Process losses include personality clashes or unproductive conflict; and the inability to focus on certain tasks. It also includes **social loafing**, also known as "free riding," which is the reduced effort people exert in a team compared to the amount they supply when working independently. In fact, sometimes working in teams can achieve less than people working alone. For example, in a brainstorming session, people may make less effort to contribute because they know that other people will put forward ideas instead.[22] People are more likely to engage in social loafing when they work in large teams where they can slip below the radar, when clear goals are not given, or when they believe they lack the skills and abilities necessary to complete the tasks.

Social loafing: A phenomenon wherein people put forth less effort when they work in teams than when they work alone

Cyberloafing: A phenomenon whereby people access the internet for personal use while pretending to work

Another form of social loafing facing today's organizations is **cyberloafing** or accessing the internet for personal use while pretending to be working, such as checking Facebook or playing YouTube videos.[23] According to a University of Nevada study, cyberloafing is estimated to cost US businesses up to $85 billion per year.[24] Not only does it cost organizations money, but it also affects productivity, drains bandwidth, and makes systems vulnerable to computer viruses. In a different study conducted by Kansas State University, participants admitted to spending between 60 to 80 percent of their time cyberloafing at work.[25] So how can organizations tackle this problem? Blocking employees from browsing sites unrelated to work may sound like the obvious solution, but there are some sites such as LinkedIn or Facebook used by organizations for legitimate work reasons. How can managers tell if employees are using a site for work purposes or cyberloafing?

In an effort to find a solution to cyberloafing, Jeremy Glassman and his team of fellow researchers at Arizona State University created some software designed

EXAMINING THE EVIDENCE

Team Cohesion: Is Too Much More Than Enough?

Team cohesion is a necessary prerequisite for effective team performance, as indicated by the model of team development. But is it possible to have too much team cohesion? The answer is yes!

In 1951, Solomon Asch of Swarthmore College published the results of his now-famous conformity study. In the study, college students were asked to participate in a perceptual activity. Eight participants were shown a card with a single line, followed by another card with three lines (labeled A, B, and C as shown).

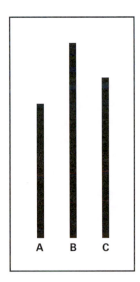

Participants were then asked to state which of the three lines matched the line on the first card in length. In the first couple of trials, all eight participants agreed it was C.

However, in the third trial, the first seven participants all gave the same obviously incorrect answer, because they were actually confederates working in collusion with the researchers. The only true participant was the eighth student, and the real focus of the study was on how this student would react to the confederates' behavior. Remarkably, one of every three true participants responded with an obviously incorrect answer in order to conform to the answers given by the seven confederates! If there is that much pressure to conform in an ad hoc group brought together temporarily for a research study, imagine how much pressure there might be to conform in a permanent and highly cohesive work group. It's certainly possible that too much cohesion could be a bad thing. A more recent study provides additional support for this idea. The study of 180 teams in a national travel agency found that social ties within the teams had a curvilinear effect on team performance over time, first increasing and then decreasing performance as the negative effects of cohesion such as groupthink began to take a negative toll on team performance.

Critical-Thinking Questions

1. How can managers recognize when there is too much cohesion on their teams?

2. What specific actions can managers take to reduce ineffective levels of team cohesiveness? ●

Sources: Asch, Solomon E. "Effects of Group Pressure upon the Modification and Distortion of Judgments." In *Groups, Leadership and Men: Research in Human Relations*, 177–190 (Oxford: Carnegie Press, 1951); Wise, Sean. "Can a Team Have Too Much Cohesion? The Dark Side to Network Density." *European Management Journal* 32, no. 5 (October 2014): 703–711.

---

to prevent cyberloafing.[26] This system permitted employees to use certain sites and used on-screen warnings to remind employees not to access sites that were not work-related. Sites that used up bandwidth (video sites) or could cause legal issues (pornography) were blocked. While employees were still allowed to access some leisure sites, they were limited to ten minutes at a time, with a maximum limit of ninety minutes per day. When the ninety minutes expired, employees were blocked from those sites and if they needed further access would have to explain to their managers the reason why.

When Glassman tested his system at a real agricultural company, the results showed a significant decrease in cyberloafing.

© iStockphoto.com / Izabela Habur

A group's effectiveness can be attributed to social facilitation, when individuals perform better in the presence of others.

FIGURE 7.4

A Model of Process Gains and Losses

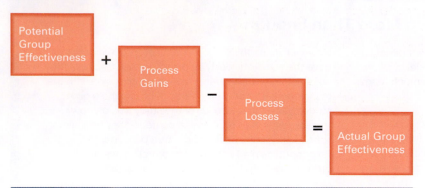

Sources: Based on Miner, Frederick C. "Group versus Individual Decision Making: An Investigation of Performance Measures, Decision Strategies, and Process Losses/Gains." *Organizational Behavior and Human Performance* 33, no. 1 (February 1984): 112–124; Steiner, Ivan D. "Models for Inferring Relationships Between Group Size and Potential Group Productivity." *Behavioral Science* 11, no. 4 (1966): 273–283.

Social facilitation: The tendency for individuals to perform tasks better when they are in the presence of others

"It provided them with a reminder of the acceptable uses for Internet resources while at work and what is expected of them," Glassman says. "With a greater amount of interaction with the system, the more likely they will be using the Internet resources for work-related purposes."[27]

While social and cyberloafing tend to negatively impact team dynamics, there are several factors that contribute to group effectiveness (see Figure 7.4). The first factor is **social facilitation,** which occurs when individuals perform tasks better in the presence of others.[28] However, social facilitation applies to simple rather than complex or novel tasks. For example, you may play soccer better when people are watching, but you might not be able to cook a meal as easily in front of an audience!

Another factor that contributes to group effectiveness is the number of favorable outcomes a team engineers. Effective teams usually produce high-quality goods and services, a satisfied customer base, a capacity to consistently work well together, and a high degree of team member satisfaction.

THINKING CRITICALLY

1. Recall a time you were part of a team at work or at school. Did your team experience all of the stages of Tuckman's model? Explain. Do you think a team can skip over one of the stages? Why or why not?

2. Discuss the ways in which team cohesion can contribute to overall team effectiveness. What questions would you ask to determine whether a team was suffering from too much team cohesiveness?

3. Once again, recall a time you were part of a team at school or work. Apply the model of process gains and losses to this scenario you recalled. What gains and losses did you identify? Based on this assessment, what could you have suggested to improve the team's performance?

Types of Teams

>> LO 7.3 Compare the various types of teams in organizations today

The technological revolution has turned the original concept of what a team means on its head. Many global companies now operate in virtual teams. A **virtual team** is a group of individuals who work together from different geographic locations and rely on communication technology, such as email, video conferencing, instant messaging, and other electronic media, to collaborate.[29] See Figure 7.5 for the types of tools virtual teams use to communicate with each other. Virtual team members have great flexibility because they are able to work anywhere, including their own homes. According to a 2016 survey carried out by

Virtual teams: Groups of individuals from different locations work together through email, video conferencing, instant messaging, and other electronic media

Global Workplace Analytics, the amount of people working regularly from home has increased by 103 percent since 2005, and 3.7 million Americans work from home at least half the time.[30]

Organizations value the virtual team model because it saves on travel costs by eliminating in-person meetings and allows for greater sharing of information between employees from different countries. San Francisco–based Buffer, a web-based platform that helps users share social media content, has a team of twenty-five employees working virtually from all over the world, with employees from Hong Kong, London, New York, and Cape Town. Buffer founder Joel Gascoigne strongly believes in the benefits of a totally virtual team.

Because working remotely can be a challenge to some people, Gascoigne makes sure new team members learn the art of self-motivation and productivity by monitoring them over a forty-five-day trial period. He also ensures Buffer team members take advantage of the flexibility of working remotely by encouraging them to share travel photos, go on adventures, or simply spend time with family.

Teams are also encouraged to use the latest tools to communicate regularly whether it's online chat, virtual conference rooms, or instant messaging. Furthermore, Buffer is a diverse group which helps members from different cultures and backgrounds learn new things from each other. To avoid the perils of faceless contact, Gascoigne ensures the whole team convene for retreats three times a year to encourage bonding and relationship-building.

Finally, Buffer maintains its high productivity because of its global virtual team—different time zones means that Buffer is always operational. Software provider in the education sector Fire Engine RED, app automation company Zapier, and professional job service provider Flexjobs are all examples of companies that successfully run their businesses using the virtual model.[31]

However, there are a few disadvantages to working in a virtual team. Time differences between countries can cause confusion, lack of face-to-face contact can result in miscommunication, and cultural differences can also compound misunderstandings related to distance. Recall that Yahoo famously put an end to virtual working to encourage more face-to-face collaboration and since then other big companies have followed suit, including healthcare provider Aetna, multinational conglomerate Honeywell, and more recently technology giant IBM. However, according to a recent survey, faceless interaction is not the only challenge of working in a virtual team.

In 2016, New York–based consulting firm RW3 CultureWizard conducted a survey of global virtual teams with 1,372 respondents from eighty countries.[32] The results showed how dominant virtual teams have become in the corporate world with the majority of corporate teams operating virtually. It also highlighted the fact almost half of those respondents had never met their virtual team members face to face. The report also showed that faceless interaction is also the cause of many cultural problems, especially when virtual workers include members from other nations. In fact, 68 percent of respondents stated that cultural challenges were the most difficult to overcome in working in a virtual team. Overall, the survey emphasizes the urgent need for increased intercultural training in order to improve relationships between teams from different cultures.

The survey shows that communication and cultural understanding are key to operating successful virtual teams (Figure 7.5).

In many instances, virtual teams work successfully. Take the author team of this book, for example. Chris Neck lives in Arizona; Jeff Houghton is in West Virginia; and Emma Murray lives in London, United Kingdom. Despite their locations, the

FIGURE 7.5

Virtual Communication

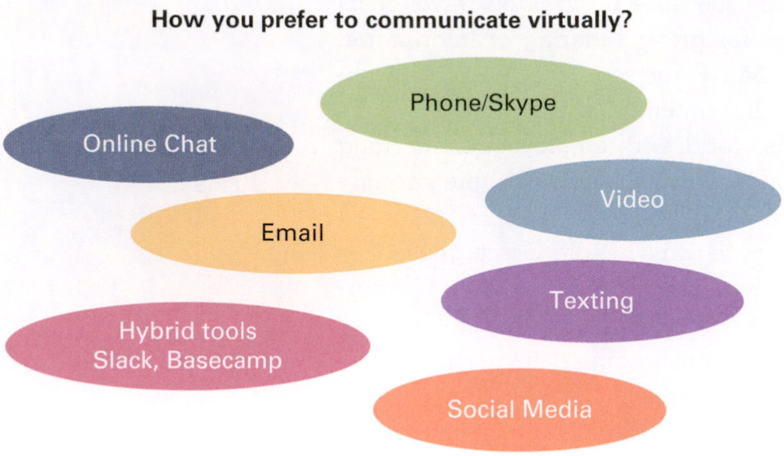

How you prefer to communicate virtually?

Online Chat

Phone/Skype

Email

Video

Hybrid tools
Slack, Basecamp

Texting

Social Media

Virtual teams can communicate with each other more easily with video conferencing software like Skype.

Self-managing team: A group of workers who manage their daily duties under little to no supervision

Problem-solving team: A group of workers coming together for a set amount of time to discuss specific issues

Cross-functional team: A group of workers from different units with various areas of expertise, assembled to address certain issues

team has managed to successfully work together over a number of years, thanks to email and Skype.

Other types of teams include self-managing teams, problem-solving teams, and cross-functional teams. A **self-managing team** is a group of workers who manage their own daily duties under little to no supervision.[33] Manufacturing company W. L. Gore, systems engineering and management company Semco, and technology solutions firm Barry Wehmiller are among many companies composed of highly effective self-managing teams, in which team members are expected to make decisions without consulting higher management.[34] The concept of self-managed teams is growing in popularity because of the benefits it brings to organizations. Numerous examples show that companies with self-managed teams tend to grow faster, are more productive and profitable, and have a lower turnover of employees.[35] However, self-managing teams are not without their downsides. Research suggests that self-managing teams often struggle with internal conflict, trust, and accountability issues.[36] A **problem-solving team** consists of a small group of workers who come together for a set amount of time to discuss and resolve specific issues.[37] While it has been generally thought that teams comprised of different ages, ethnicities, and gender are the more effective for finding solutions, recent research shows that cognitively diverse teams (how they think about and perceive new complex situations) are the best for fast problem solving.[38]

Finally, a **cross-functional team** is comprised of a group of workers from different units with various areas of expertise to work on certain projects.[39] The cross-functional model can be effective in both large and small companies and is growing in popularity. A recent survey conducted by Robert Half Management Resources and Robert Half Technology discovered that 51 percent of CFOs collaborate more frequently with their company's CIO, in comparison to three years ago.[40] Tim Hird, executive director for Robert Half Management Resources, believes cross-functional teams are vital to today's organizations.

"Before, these functions were run as silos," says Hird, "but business has become more complex and organizations continue to invest in technology to make strategic decisions. A few years ago it wasn't necessary to work together—now it's essential."[41]

OB IN THE REAL WORLD

Derrick Hall, President and CEO, Arizona Diamondbacks

The Arizona Diamondbacks (D-Backs) are a major league baseball (MLB) team located in Phoenix, Arizona. With a world championship, multiple division championships, and countless other non-baseball-related honors awarded to them since their inaugural season in 1998, the organization has proven to be an industry leader in fan experience, corporate performance, financial efficiency, community, and culture. The Diamondbacks organization is not one of the famed cash-cow MLB organizations that can seemingly throw money at any internal problem that arises and solve it right away. Rather than putting out fires with cold hard cash, the D-Backs have invested in its people to prevent problems from arising in the first place. The result is an organization that has been named one of the best places to work in baseball and has a work culture that is described as "familial" by the majority of its employees. Under the direction of President and CEO Derrick Hall, this middle market baseball organization is doing big things in the industry by constantly investing in its workplace culture.

Fostering this coveted familial culture starts with a work environment supported by successful teams. Teams are what drive the success of this organization and the D-Backs know that their people are the most crucial component of this. Derrick Hall provides a very interesting perspective on how to foster a successful workplace culture by investing in people.

"The customer doesn't come first, the fan doesn't come first, the employee comes first. If the employee feels respected, developed, invested in, and rewarded he/ she will treat the customers the way we want them to be treated. When the employee is valued the most it feels like a family. It feels like a team."

By focusing on the employee first, each employee feels a sense of responsibility toward the organization and buys into its mission. Once everyone is bought in, the organization's teams are ready to meet the customer's needs across the various different departments.

The team on the field playing baseball is only one of over thirty highly successful individual teams that work in the Diamondbacks organization. What lies at the core of each of these teams is a mutual commitment to excellence amongst members. This means that team members can openly disagree with each other and can challenge each other to bring their best individual work to the table. When this is done, the teams function at maximum production and efficiency.

Derrick Hall sits on top of the organization. However, he is a member of multiple smaller teams which have adopted this culture. For example, the members of Derrick Hall's executive team know that they have a voice in the executive meetings and that their opinions matter. Also, Derrick has made it clear that the only way the executive team will put forth its best work for the organization is if each member brings forth a different perspective. This is so crucial to the success of any team because it prevents missed opportunities, groupthink, and power imbalance.

Teams are the backbone of any organization and the backbone of every team is its people. By investing in his people, Derrick Hall lays the groundwork for an environment where individual teams can thrive. The culture within these teams, where each member has a voice and each member can openly challenge another's work in a healthy, productive way, is what has made the Diamondbacks such a successful organization.

Critical-Thinking Questions

1. Do you agree with the "employee is always first" philosophy? Why or why not?

2. Why might an investment in an organization's employees be more valuable than an investment elsewhere?

3. What kind of work would a team experiencing groupthink put forward?

4. Is there value in creating a culture where disagreements and healthy conflict is encouraged? Why or why not? ●

Source: Interview with Derrick Hall, April 22, 2017.

THINKING CRITICALLY

1. Imagine that you are assigned to work with a virtual team. What challenges and drawbacks might you encounter? What technological methods of communication would you use most often to communicate? Why?

2. What industries and types of businesses would be most likely to be open to the use of self-managing teams? What industries and types of businesses would be least open to the use of self-managing teams? Explain your answers.

3. What criteria would you as a manager use in determining whether a problem-solving team should also be a cross-functional team? In other words, what types of issues would a problem-solving team from the same functional area solve most efficiently and what types of issues would a problem-solving team that is also cross-functional solve most efficiently?

4. Given the nature of self-managing teams, what could be some potential problems facing such a team in the workplace? How would you overcome such problems?

A Model of Team Effectiveness: Context and Composition

>> LO 7.4   Apply the model of team effectiveness to evaluate team performance

Not all teams are effective. Effective teams in an organization are characterized by their ability to improve quality, reach goals, and change processes. One classic way of understanding teams and their effectiveness is to consider teams in terms of the contextual influences that affect their functioning, their composition, the processes they use, and the outcomes they achieve.[42] Figure 7.6 shows how these factors influence team effectiveness.

FIGURE 7.6

A Model of Team Effectiveness

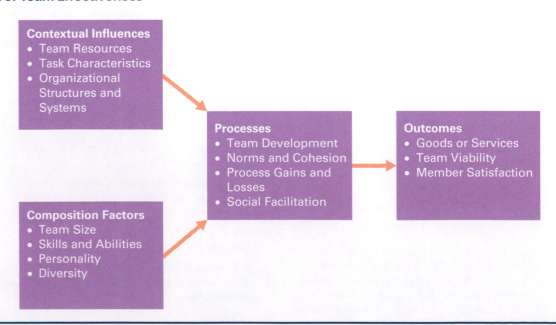

Source: Figure adapted from Hackman, J. R. "The Design of Work Teams." In *Handbook of Organizational Behavior*, edited by J. W. Lorsch, 315–342 (Englewood Cliffs, NJ: Prentice-Hall, 1987); McGrath, J. E. *Social Psychology: A Brief Introduction* (New York: Rinehart and Winston, 1964); Resick, C. J., M. W. Dickson, J. K. Mitchelson, L. K. Allison, and M. A. Clark. "Team Composition, Cognition, and Effectiveness: Examining Mental Model Similarity and Accuracy." *Group Dynamics: Theory, Research, and Practice* 14, no. 2 (June 2010): 174–191; Doolen, Toni L., Marla E. Hacker, and Eileen M. Van Aken. "The Impact of Organizational Context on Work Team Effectiveness: A Study of Production Team." *IEEE Transactions on Engineering Management* 50, no. 3 (August 2003): 285–296.

Team Contextual Influences

There are three main contextual influences: team resources, task characteristics, and organizational systems and structures.

Team resources are important for effective teams because they equip the team members with the tools to successfully perform their roles. Resources consist of the equipment, materials, training, information, staffing, and budgets the organization supplies to support the team's goals.

Tasks are the specific steps the team must perform to achieve its goals. They can be structured or unstructured, complex or simple, and characterized by more or less interdependence among team members. **Interdependence** is the extent to which team members rely on each other to complete their work tasks.[43] For example, in the Thomas Jefferson University Hospital case study, the new initiative to improve patient service required team members to work closely together and depend on each other to complete work tasks. There are three levels of interdependence (see Figure 7.7):

- **Pooled interdependence** occurs when each team member produces a piece of work independently of the others. Sandwich fast-food restaurant Subway and Bank of America branches are both examples of pooled interdependence. Though each restaurant unit is a part of the overall Subway organization, the units work independently of each other. Similarly, bank branches in different cities carry out the same duties but have no real need to interact with each other.[44]

- **Sequential interdependence** takes place when one team member completes a piece of work and passes it on to the next member for his or her input, as on an assembly line. Car manufacturer Toyota's production system is partly based on sequential interdependence.[45]

- **Reciprocal interdependence** happens when team members work closely together on a piece of work, consulting with each other, providing each other with advice, and exchanging information. For example, the teams at Southwest Airlines rely on reciprocal interdependence to manage the intense coordination of the different services provided to its customers in real time.[46]

Team Composition

Typically, a team is characterized by four qualities: its size as well as the skills and abilities, personalities, and diversity of its members.

The appropriate *size* of a team depends on the task the team needs to

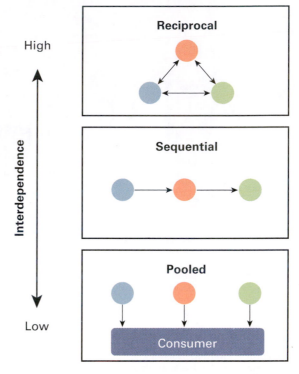

FIGURE 7.7

Levels of Task Interdependence

Interdependence

High

Reciprocal

Sequential

Low

Pooled

Consumer

Interdependence: The extent to which team members rely on each other to complete their work tasks

Pooled interdependence: An organizational model in which each team member produces a piece of work independently of the other members

Subway restaurants are an example of pooled interdependence. While all Subway restaurants are part of the larger organization, they operate independently of one another.

© iStockphoto.com/ MrNovel

While it may be tempting to congratulate or reward individual employees, this could create conflict or resentment among team members.

Sequential interdependence: An organizational model in which one team member completes a piece of work and passes it on to the next member for their input, similar to an assembly line

Reciprocal interdependence: An organizational model in which team members work closely together on a piece of work, consulting with each other, providing each other with advice, and exchanging information

FIGURE 7.8

Attraction-Selection-Attrition Model

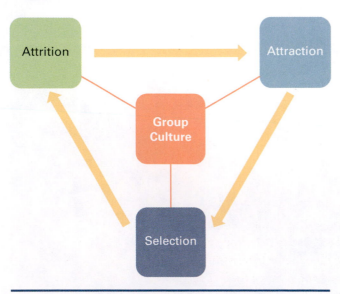

Source: Based on Schneider, Benjamin. "The People Make the Place." *Personnel Psychology* 40, no. 3 (September 1987): 437–453; Schneider, Benjamin, Harold W. Goldstein, and D. Brent Smith. "The ASA Framework: An Update." *Personnel Psychology* 48, no. 4 (Winter 1995): 747–773.

perform. In general, teams tend to consist of four to seven members. A recent study by management consulting firm Bain shows that decision-making effectiveness is reduced by 10 percent when more than seven people join a team.[47] If all that being a team player meant was having *skills* and *abilities*, professional baseball teams with the highest payrolls (like the New York Yankees) would win the World Series every year. Instead, however, it's the way talent interacts in the context of team processes that brings results. In terms of *personality*, teams typically need a balance between extraverts and introverts.[48] Having too many extraverts can mean too much talking and not enough listening, and having too many introverts can mean very little communication among the team members. Generally, people who are agreeable and conscientious are effective team members.[49]

Ensuring *diversity* on a team can be a challenge. Recall from Chapter 2 that diversity includes surface-level factors such as race and ethnicity, gender, sexuality, and age, as well as deep-level factors such as personality and beliefs. From a team composition perspective, managers are most concerned with the ways that deep-level diversity factors, like introversion and extraversion, affect team functioning. Typically, team members who share similarities in values, personalities, and interests tend to have positive social relationships with each other, which helps the team to be more effective.

Psychologist Benjamin Schneider's attraction-selection-attrition (ASA) model (see Figure 7.8) states that people are functions of three interrelated dynamic processes: attraction, selection, and attrition, all of which influence organizational culture.[50] For example, new employees are *attracted* to a team because of a perceived similarity in values, interests, and goals. New hires are *selected* based on how well they fit in to an organization. Over time, *attrition* occurs when employees feel they do not fit in, causing them to leave the organization.

This theory explains why team members who are perceived as sharing similarities are selected as a good "fit," while those who do not fit in tend to leave the team.[51] However, there must be a balance between diversity and similarity, because too many people behaving in a similar way can stunt growth and have a negative effect on insight and creativity due to the lack of unique viewpoints.

THINKING CRITICALLY

1. Based on this section and Figure 7.6, the model of team effectiveness, explain how problems in each one of the three contextual influences (team resources, task characteristics, and organizational structure and systems) could affect team success. Provide an example for each of the three influences.

2. Explain how problems in each one of the composition factors (team size, skills and abilities, personality, and diversity) could affect team success. Provide an example for each of the four composition factors.

3. Do you think there are any types of situations where either contextual influences or composition factors would have a bigger influence on successful team functioning? Explain.

4. Assume you work in a restaurant that specializes in a broad variety of Chinese-style dumplings and potstickers. Identify the likely level of task interdependence (pooled, sequential, or reciprocal) for each of the groups involved with the operation of the restaurant (dumpling makers, hosts, servers, runners, bartenders).

5. Consider diversity as it was discussed in Chapter 2 and its impact on and interplay with the ASA Model. How might a lack of surface-level diversity in a team affect the attraction and selection process discussed in the ASA Model? What are the potential weaknesses of teams that lack diversity in these areas?

Team Decision Making

>> LO 7.5 **Identify the advantages and disadvantages of different team decision-making approaches**

One approach to team decision-making is the concept of **brainstorming**, which is generating creative, spontaneous ideas from all members of a group without making any initial criticism or judgment of them.[52] While brainstorming is a popular method of idea generation among many organizations, decades of studies have shown that simply gathering a group to toss out as many ideas as possible within a certain amount of time does not work.[53] In fact, studies show that people who follow this type of brainstorming produce less ideas (and less good ideas) than if they had been on their own. This is because people in a group setting are more likely to be influenced by the ideas of others which causes them to think similarly, resulting in stagnation of creative and original thinking.

Brainstorming: The process of generating creative, spontaneous ideas from all members of a group without any criticism or judgment

However, while the evidence points to flaws in the brainstorming process, this does not mean that people should stop brainstorming altogether; it merely calls for a new approach.[54]

Brainstorm Alone—At First

Brainstorming alone is a useful way of coming up with new, creative ideas without being influenced by the group. Then when everyone has had a chance to brainstorm alone, they can get together as a group and build on those ideas. One brainstorming technique includes the 6-3-5 method. Six people write down three ideas each. These ideas are passed to the person on their right who builds on those ideas. The stack is passed around five times, ensuring that everyone in the group has a chance to develop each idea. When everyone is finished the group then gets together to discuss.

Slow Down the Creative Process

Some people don't like brainstorming. They would rather get the brainstorming process over and done with quickly in order to start implementing the solution. These people have a high level of the personality characteristic "need for closure." However, it is important that enough time is given to the brainstorming process so enough ideas are generated to find the right solution to the problem. The 6-3-5 method slows down the creative process by giving people individual turns to write down their ideas. This also helps people who have a need for closure as it teaches them that everyone needs to wait until ideas are generated and built upon.

Start Drawing

Studies show that a combination of drawing and writing is highly beneficial to idea generation and coming up with creative solutions to problems. Drawing is useful because it helps describe ideas that are difficult to explain in words, and also appeals to part of the brain dedicated to visual processing. It is also helpful to include words in sketches or diagrams to aid interpretation. Google employees use pictures during their brainstorming sessions, believing that "pictures are usually louder than words and harder to misinterpret."[55]

While using the right approach to brainstorming can be a useful way to make decisions, many organizations use other team decision-making techniques. The **nominal group technique** is a structured way for team members to generate ideas and identify solutions.[56] Each member is asked the same question in relation to a work issue and requested to write down as many solutions as possible. Answers are read aloud and recorded for discussion. Then the ideas are put to the vote. No criticism or judgment of any ideas is allowed. The nominal group technique is particularly useful in bigger groups where often only the loudest voices are heard. Using this technique allows each group member to put forward their ideas and solutions, thereby taking everyone's opinions into account.

The **Delphi technique** is a method of decision making in which information is gathered from a group of respondents within their area of expertise.[57] Questionnaires are sent to a select group of experts, whose responses are collated and reviewed, and then a summary is returned to the group with a follow-up questionnaire. Again, the experts provide their answers. The process continues until the group agrees on a common answer and a decision is reached. The Delphi technique was applied during the implementation of the new patient efficiency program at the Thomas Jefferson University Hospital, profiled in our case study. This method allowed the group of executive physicians to gain new insights into the hospital's operations by gauging the thoughts and perspectives of the nurses in the emergency department. In this chapter, we have focused on the different types of teams and how teams generate ideas and find solutions. In the next chapter, we will explore how managers make decisions and how organizations, teams, and individuals engage in creativity and innovation.

When it comes to decision making, teams play an important part. According to enterprise platform Cloverpop's business decision database, teams make better decisions 75 percent of the time, and are more effective in making decisions than managers and executives acting alone.[58] Going by these results, it stands to reason that decision making drives business performance which in turn positively impacts an organization's bottom line. However, there are both advantages and disadvantages to team decision making.

Nominal group technique: A structured way for team members to generate ideas and identify solutions in which each member is asked the same question in relation to a work issue and requested to write as many answers as possible. Answers are read aloud and voted upon

Delphi technique: A method of decision making in which information is gathered from a group of respondents within their area of expertise

Advantages and Disadvantages of Team Decision Making

Some of the key benefits include increased engagement of staff, consensus decisions that when implemented already have buy-in from the staff that do the work, and finally and most importantly: better decisions.

Team decision making has its advantages. It often gives those involved a broader perspective, provides more alternatives, clarifies ambiguities, and brings about team satisfaction and support. By involving each team member in the decision, it also increases engagement, gains buy-in from the people who will have to do the work, and overall results in better decisions being made.

However, team decision making also has its disadvantages. Meetings can be time consuming; too much attention can be paid to simple matters; nobody may take responsibility for the decision; and team members might end up agreeing on a compromise that satisfies nobody.

One important factor that can negatively affect team decision making is **groupthink**, a psychological phenomenon in which people in a cohesive group go along with the group consensus rather than offering their own opinions.[59] Groupthink is a major disadvantage to team decision making, because the team members are more concerned with preserving harmony in the group than with risking opinions that may cause conflict or offense. In doing so, people lose the ability to "think outside the box" or think creatively in their decisions. This leads to an environment where ideas and perspectives simply remain unchallenged, which over time can prevent an organization from innovating, progressing, and competing. Being in this kind of group confers an illusion of immunity, an "us against the world" view that the group members know better than outsiders, even given evidence to the contrary. The executive team at the Arizona Diamondbacks prevents groupthink by encouraging each member to bring forth different perspectives, and in doing so gives them a safe space to air their opinions without fear of reprisals.

The rise of social media has contributed to "political groupthink." For the first time in history, people are able to air their political views to a large audience without the help of television networks, radio, or other media reserved for the select few.

However, not only do we like to express our political opinions on social media, but according to Pew research, we are more willing to share our political views with a like-minded audience.[60] According to author Eli Pariser, this creates "filter bubbles" containing people with the same views, but, where those views go unchallenged, leading to polarization.[61] In fact, a study conducted by the University of Chicago discovered that "people held more-extreme positions after they spoke with like-minded others," which further cements groups together, limiting diversity of thought.[62] However, there is hope that social media will eventually become a tool that fosters wider political discussion rather than restricting it to the shared views of like-minded groups.

Organizations are far more likely to be successful when their employees work well together to meet required objectives. But as we have seen, it doesn't take more than one negative member to destroy team dynamics. This is why managers must work hard to nurture a positive team culture by giving clear direction, treating each member equally, and ensuring that teams are cohesive, communicative, and collaborative.

Groupthink: A psychological phenomenon in which people in a cohesive group go along with the group consensus rather than offering their own opinions

THINKING CRITICALLY

1. Define the team decision-making approaches of brainstorming and nominal group technique. In your opinion, is one of these techniques better than the other? Or does it depend on the situation? Why or why not?

2. Do you think the management style (e.g., more or less authoritative) of a group's manager can impact the group's performance?

3. What are the pros and cons of having a team leader for a particular team? What problems might the addition of a team leader create for a group?

Visit **edge.sagepub.com/neckob2e** to help you accomplish your coursework goals in an easy-to-use learning environment.

- Mobile-friendly eFlashcards and practice quizzes
- Video and multimedia content
- Chapter summaries with learning objectives
- EXCLUSIVE! Access to full-text SAGE journal articles

IN REVIEW

7.1   Distinguish between teams and groups

A **team** is a group of people brought together to use their individual skills on a common project or goal. Regardless of the type of organization, most employees work in some form of team in today's workplace. A **group** usually consists of three or more people who work independently to attain organizational goals.

7.2   Explain how team processes affect team outcomes

Process gains are factors that contribute to team effectiveness. They include a sense of shared purpose, plans, and goals; the confidence team members have in their own abilities to achieve objectives; a shared vision of how the work should be carried out; and constructive task-focused conflict that can help teams with their problem solving and decision making.

Process losses are factors that detract from team effectiveness. They include social loafing, wherein people in a group put in less effort than when working independently; personality clashes or conflict; and the inability to focus on certain tasks.

7.3   Compare the various types of teams in organizations today

Many global companies now operate in **virtual teams,** whose members are from different locations and work together through email, video conferencing, instant messaging, and other electronic media. A **self-managing team** is a group of workers who manage their own daily duties under little to no supervision. A **problem-solving team** is a group of workers coming together for a set amount of time to discuss and resolve specific issues. A **cross-functional team** is a group of workers from different units with various areas of expertise.

7.4   Apply the model of team effectiveness to evaluate team performance

Team contextual influences include team resources, task characteristics, and organizational structures and systems. Team resources are the level of support provided by the organization, such as equipment, materials, training, information, staffing, budgets, and such. Task characteristics can be structured or unstructured; complex or simple; and measured by a degree of interdependence. Performance management systems, compensation and reward systems, and organizational and leadership structures must be aligned with team structures to maintain smooth running of operations.

Typically, a team has four main elements: team size, skills and abilities, personality of team members, and team diversity. Teams tend to consist of four to seven members. The skills and abilities of the team members are very important, but the way this talent interacts in the context of team processes is also important. Typically, teams need a balance between extraverts and introverts. Team members who share common interests or certain similarities tend to have positive social relationships with each other that help the team to be more effective.

7.5 **Identify the advantages and disadvantages of different team decision-making approaches**

Groupthink is a psychological phenomenon in which people in a cohesive group go along with the group consensus to preserve harmony rather than offering their own opinions.

Brainstorming generates creative, spontaneous ideas from all members of a group without any criticism or judgment.

The **nominal group technique** is a structured way for team members to generate ideas and identify solutions. Each member is asked the same question in relation to a work issue and requested to write as many answers as possible. Answers are read aloud and recorded for discussion. Then the ideas are put to the vote. No criticism or judgment of any ideas is allowed. **The Delphi technique** is a method of decision making in which information is gathered from a group of respondents within their area of expertise.

KEY TERMS

Adjourning 190	Pooled interdependence 199
Brainstorming 201	Problem-solving team 196
Cohesion 191	Process gains 192
Cross-functional team 196	Process losses 192
Cyberloafing 192	Psychological safety 187
Decentralization 185	Punctuated equilibrium 190
Delphi technique 202	Reciprocal interdependence 200
Forming 188	Self-managing team 196
Group 186	Sequential interdependence 200
Groupthink 203	Social facilitation 194
Interdependence 199	Social loafing 192
Nominal group technique 202	Storming 189
Norming 189	Synergy 191
Norms 190	Team 185
Performing 189	Virtual teams 194

UP FOR DEBATE: Hiring Teams Instead of Individuals

Companies are beginning to entertain the idea that they could hire teams rather than individuals. For example, firms in Silicon Valley have claimed that hiring a team of three people who already know how to work with each other eliminates multiple steps in the team-building process. This allows the team to hit the ground running on their first day of work. Agree or disagree? Explain your answer.

EXERCISE 7.1: Practicing 6-3-5 Brainstorming

Objective

The purpose of this exercise is to gain a greater appreciation of brainstorming.

Instructions

Brainstorming is ubiquitous in the business world. Companies use brainstorming for developing new products, adding features to existing products, crafting new marketing campaigns, improving services provided by human resources, and many more uses. One technique that has gained a foothold in businesses in recent years is the process of 6-3-5 brainstorming. With this method, team members spend some time alone developing ideas before bringing those to the group as a whole. It works like this: first, teams of six members are formed; second, each of the six team members writes down five ideas without input from anyone else; and third, the pieces of paper with the ideas are passed to the right, where new ideas are added (and this is done a total of five times).

This exercise utilizes the 6-3-5 method of brainstorming. Form teams of six people (if there aren't enough people to make this work exactly, it's ok if some groups have five or seven team members). The scenario is as follows: your team works for a restaurant and the dessert menu has been exactly the same for the last five years. The owner wants some new, fresh ideas for desserts. Using the 6-3-5 method, brainstorm as many new ideas as possible. Then, once the papers have been passed around five times, narrow the list down to the top three desserts you can all agree on to ultimately submit to the restaurant owner.

Reflection Questions

1. Traditional brainstorming simply has a group of people all working together to develop as many ideas as possible. The 6-3-5 method is individual-based first and *then* the other team members get involved in adding ideas. What are the advantages and disadvantages of traditional brainstorming and the 6-3-5 method of brainstorming?

2. Which do you prefer as a brainstorming technique: traditional brainstorming or the 6-3-5 method? Explain.

3. What are ways you could utilize the 6-3-5 method of brainstorming at your current or most recent job?

Exercise contributed by Steven Stovall, Southeast Missouri State University.

EXERCISE 7.2: A Nominal Brainstorm about the Delphi Technique

Objectives

This exercise will help you to *identify* the advantages and disadvantages of different team decision-making approaches.

Instructions

Form into a group of six to eight members. Your task is to develop a set of recommendations on using the Delphi Technique and explain its appropriateness for generating management ideas. You will be developing these recommendations using the brainstorming and nominal group methods. To complete this task, complete the following steps:

Step1. Select a person to write down the ideas generated in this exercise and to tally votes in the later steps. (1 to 2 minutes)

Step 2. Use the brainstorming method to generate ideas about when using the Delphi technique would not be successful. These ideas can either be statements about the general characteristics of a situation or about a specific job situation. (5 minutes)

Step 3. Combine ideas where appropriate. Soliciting feedback from everyone in your group, determine whether an idea is relevant or not for your guidelines. In order to be considered relevant, an idea must be true (based on chapter concepts) and useful in a business setting. Write down the list of ideas that are voted as being relevant. (1 to 2 minutes)

Step 4. Use the nominal group technique to generate ideas about when the Delphi technique would be successful. These ideas can either be statements about the general characteristics of a situation or a specific job situation. (5 to 10 minutes).

Step 5. Repeat step 3. (1 to 2 minutes).

Reflection Questions

1. Which idea generation method did you prefer? Why?

2. Which idea method generation method generated the most ideas?

3. Which idea generated the most relevant ideas?

4. What new ways of employing the Delphi technique did you discover?

Exercise contributed by Milton R. Mayfield, Professor of Business, Texas A&M International University, and Jacqueline R. Mayfield, Professor of Business, Texas A&M International University.

EXERCISE 7.3: Consulting at Bella Nota

Objective

This exercise will help you to *distinguish* between teams and groups, *compare* different types of teams, and *apply* the team effectiveness model.

Background

You are in a consulting group who is working with Bella Nota—a company in Austin, Texas, that provides background and incidental music for commercials and industrial videos. The company has enough steady business to sustain ten musicians, two composers, two sound engineers, and one conductor as full-time employees. The musicians and conductor usually work together on a regular basis, rotating between the composers and engineers. When business picks up or there is a call for a larger set of musicians, the local talent pool provides an easy source for short-term hires. While many of the same people are hired frequently, none of these people work for Bella Nota on an ongoing basis.

The company president, Natalie Bell, realizes how critically important high-quality team processes is to her business. She has brought in your consulting group to help develop guidelines for developing effective teams. To develop these guidelines, you will need to provide information the following:

- Create a guideline that distinguishes between groups and teams. Include the differences between a team and a group, and when the use of teams would be more appropriate at Bella Nota.

- Develop a guideline for classifying different types of teams. While not all team types will be represented in the musical side of the company, there are other business activities and teams that will find these guidelines useful.

- Develop a guideline for evaluating the musical teams/groups on process. This guideline will be used for developing suggestions for future team/group improvements.

Instructions

Step 1. Form into teams to complete the three tasks outlined in the background section. (20 to 30 minutes)

Step 2. Present your guidelines to the class and be prepared to answer questions from the class and the instructor. (20 to 30 minutes)

Reflection Questions

1. How did using chapter terms and concepts help you to better structure your thinking about teams and team processes?

2. If you have been working in a team in this or another class, how can you use the guidelines in improving team outcomes?

3. How do processes differ in team work situations compared with individual work situations? How do team processes differ between different types of teams?

Exercise contributed by Milton R. Mayfield, Professor of Business, Texas A&M International University, and Jacqueline R. Mayfield, Professor of Business, Texas A&M International University.

ONLINE EXERCISE 7.1: Virtual Team Project

Objective

The purpose of this exercise is to gain an appreciation for virtual teams.

Instructions

Utilizing a discussion board, a virtual team will be created to complete a project. The scenario is as follows: you work for a very small company that had a very successful app for phones two years ago. The app was for runners who wanted to connect with other runners nearby for training or for just partnering with another runner to enjoy the company of a fellow runner. Though the app was free, income was garnered through ads on the app. However, the initial popularity of that app has faded and sales of ads have diminished greatly. The president of the company desperately wants to introduce a new app to the public and she does not care what that app is.

The president has asked all of you to develop a new app from start to finish. Using the discussion board, brainstorm a new cell phone app. Once you all agree on what the concept is, virtually partner with others on the discussion board and divide up the following roles among you:

- Sales (how the app will generate income)
- Images (what the graphics will look like)
- Text (what words and wording will be used)
- Functions (what the app will actually do)
- Marketing (how consumers will know that the app exists)

After these roles have been divided among the discussion board participants, develop the app. Obviously, those working on functions will have to work closely with the images and text personnel to ensure the app's interface is attractive to users—which is important for marketing. And, if sales personnel want to place ads within the app, the sales people will need to work closely with all the other groups to make the ads as seamless and unobtrusive as possible to the end users.

Reflection Questions

1. What difficulties did you have in building an effective team for this exercise? What successes did you have?

2. How did the team resolve conflict?

3. In what ways was this exercise similar to team-building projects you have had at your current or most recent job? How was it different?

4. What did you learn from this exercise that you can utilize in your current or most recent job? How will this help you as your career progresses?

Exercise contributed by Steven Stovall, Southeast Missouri State University.

CASE STUDY 7.1: International Game Technology (IGT)

You may not know the company by name, but if you've ever been to a casino, chances are you've had an IGT experience. The global powerhouse Nevada-based International Game Technology (IGT) specializes in computerized gaming machines and is the designer and manufacturer of well-known slot machines such as Red White & Blue, Double Diamond, and the ever-popular Wheel of Fortune games. Although IGT was acquired in 2015 by Italy-based GTECH—uniting the world's largest provider of lottery systems (GTECH) with the world's largest slot-machine maker—IGT's manufacturing hub remains stationed in its hometown of more than 45 years, Reno, Nevada. A formidable player in the $430 billion global gambling business, the combined company retains the iconic IGT name and boasts 13,000+ employees and thousands of gaming machines in casinos all over the world. As longtime GTECH executive and IGT CEO

Marco Sala told *Bloomberg Business* at the time of the acquisition, "This is a transaction that we firmly believe will transform the gaming industry. We will have a library of games that will surpass that of any other company in the industry."

But during the Great Recession, IGT had experienced significant cuts in revenue and profit and worrying drops in share price. Competitors like Bally Technologies were eager to step in and grab market share, and grab they did. Like many companies, IGT was struggling to regain its footing in 2009—and its approach to team management on several different fronts is among one of its key strategies for recovery.

Streamlining Teamwork in "The Shop"

IGT had been focusing on teams since the early 2000s to keep its market position and to stay on top. In 2004, the company invested in iMaint, which helps IGT's maintenance crew team manage work orders, scheduling, parts and inventory, and purchasing, as well as track costs and budget and project progress with easy-to-use graphs and charts—no small feat in a global company whose maintenance department alone is spread over a 1.2 million-square-foot facility. Although the system cuts out paperwork and streamlines streamlined processes, there is a very human element involved: its users. John Butterfield, facilities maintenance supervisor based in Reno, praised the system but insisted that training is the key. "Investing in training is money well spent for two reasons. First, it helps employees understand how important their data is and thus provides better data and better history. Second, it enhances the mechanics' overall knowledge in the maintenance field. Now they not only know how to turn wrenches, but also have an understanding of how all the maintenance processes are put together (scheduling, parts ordering, contractor work) which in turn increases the entire team's effectiveness." Butterfield dedicated every second Friday of the month to continued training. "At our once a month training the employees learn more and I learn more. It's a win-win."

iMaint gave IGT an additional advantage: what would otherwise be costly and potentially disruptive—the testing of new processes—could occur in the virtual environment first. When Butterfield's crew wants to implement something new—be it changes to parts ordering, inventory management, scheduling, or codes—they could test it in iMaint's training database first. Initiatives are either quashed or implemented, with the added benefit that those rolling it out have already developed a comfort level with the new process, and could anticipate possible challenges.

Virtual Teams

Enter virtual teams. In 2009, Chris Satchell was hired by as chief technology officer (CTO) to help battle IGT's financial woes. Satchell's job was to keep an eagle eye trained on the competitive marketplace, to make sure IGT-wannabes weren't out-innovating the gaming giant. One of Satchell's strategies was deploying virtual teams throughout the organization. He started small-scale efforts within his information technology (IT) department, perhaps the ideal testing ground, because its members were already accustomed to working on problems remotely and through machines.

Satchell found that the IT experiment proved his case: the benefits of virtual teams were tangible. Beyond the obvious benefits, like the ability to rely on top talent the world over without travel costs (because meetings could take place online), working remotely helped the company realize faster time to market. Satchell also noticed greater innovation, because the online environment, by its very nature, skirts bureaucratic interference, allowing employees a level of semi-autonomy.

Yet Satchell found that, as in the face-to-face workplace—and perhaps more so—building relationships among team members was vital. "We're always pushing employees to understand that people in other groups have different perspectives. They have something you need, and you have something they can use." And even as virtual teams move beyond the IT department, traveling for occasional "face time" is still necessary, although not as frequently, and not for the whole team. "It's a misconception to think that you can do away with your travel budget," Satchell noted.

Teamwork and Emergenetics

IGT has implemented technology to help with its human resources strategy as well. Emergenetics Solutions utilizes research in brain science, psychometric evaluation, and organizational development to help analyze the way people think and behave, providing actionable solutions and suggestions for better teamwork. Specifically, Emergenetics' ESP

System helps companies match candidate profiles against the job description, while the Emergenetics Profile offers companies (and individuals) a portrait of individual strengths and weaknesses, predicting how these might play out in different team arrangements.

Emergenetics helped IGT generate a "picture" of who they were as an organization—and, with deeper analysis, "extract performance themes, identify strengths and opportunities across the organization and formulate groups to better meet specific business needs." Although not a requirement, many IGT employees displayed their Emergenetics profiles in their workspaces, which IGT says helps create a feeling of openness, stimulate dialogue, and encourage collaboration.

IGT also used Emergenetics tools during the hiring on-boarding process, helping potential team members and leaders recognize strengths and potential pitfalls in the team the former may be joining. "Specific practices are then developed based on the team's overall Emergenetics make-up and the team's objectives," Emergenetics authors noted in a case study on their work with IGT. Goals and benchmarks can could be developed, and tracked, accordingly.

The IGT of today is far removed from its struggles of the mid- and late 2000s. IGT's official headquarters have shifted to London. Asked how the new IGT will compare to the "IGT as Reno knew it," CEO Marco Sala responded, "[It] will be a combination of the two companies. We're putting in teams of different experiences, and some guys will join Nevada. I think these combinations will bring new ideas for future innovation. That is what we intend to pursue."

Case Questions

1. What role did competition play in IGT's decision to implement stronger team management for recovery?

2. Describe the benefits as well as shortcomings that IGT saw after implementing virtual teams.

3. Explain how IGT used systems like iMaint and Emergenetics to increase team effectiveness.

Sources

"Case Study: IGT." *Emergentics.com*. www.emergenetics.com/wp-content/uploads/2010/12/Emergenetics-International-Case-Study-IGT.pdf.

"How to Deploy Collaborative Virtual Teams." *Economist*. www.economistinsights.com/technology-innovation/analysis/next-generation-cios/casestudies.

"Success Stories: International Game Technology," *DSPI.com*. www.dpsi.com/success-stories/international-game-technology/.

"What Is Emergentics?" *Emergentics.com*. www.emergenetics.com/whatis.

SELF-ASSESSMENT 7.1

Dealing with a Difficult Team Member

What do you do when a team member arrives late for or misses meetings, does not contribute a fair share toward the team's effort, is offensive or disruptive, or has some other problem? The following self-assessment will provide you with some feedback that may help you improve your ability to communicate with a difficult team member.

For each statement, circle the number that best describes how you would talk to a problem team member based on the following scale:

	NOT AT ALL ACCURATE	SOMEWHAT ACCURATE	A LITTLE ACCURATE	MOSTLY ACCURATE	COMPLETELY ACCURATE
1. I am specific rather than general, giving good, clear, and recent examples of the problem behavior.	1	2	3	4	5
2. I present the situation as a problem that disrupts the whole team not just one individual.	1	2	3	4	5

		NOT AT ALL ACCURATE	SOMEWHAT ACCURATE	A LITTLE ACCURATE	MOSTLY ACCURATE	COMPLETELY ACCURATE
3.	My comments focus on things that the team member has control over and can actually do something about.	1	2	3	4	5
4.	I try to provide constructive criticism at a time when the team member is prepared to receive it, rather when they are busy doing something else.	1	2	3	4	5
5.	I don't try to embarrass or put my team member on the spot, but remember that the purpose of my comments is to improve the team member's behavior.	1	2	3	4	5
6.	I try to keep feedback professional, avoiding labels such as *stupid* or *incompetent*.	1	2	3	4	5
7.	I make sure that my criticisms are concise and complete enough that the team member understands the problem.	1	2	3	4	5
8.	I talk to the team member as an equal, not as a controlling parent, supervisor, or boss.	1	2	3	4	5

Scoring

Add the numbers circled above and write your score in the blank _____

Interpretation

32 and above = You have very strong skills for communicating with a problem team member. You are likely to be naturally effective at constructively influencing the behaviors of your problem team member.

24–31 = You have a moderate level of skills for communicating with a problem team member. You may want to consider reshaping your approach to communicating with a difficult team member based on the previous statements.

23 and below = You have room to improve your team communication skills. You and your team will be more effective if you can successfully reshape your communication approaches based on the previous statements.

Source: Adapted from Manz, C. C., C. P. Neck, J. Mancuso, and K. P. Manz. *For Team Members Only: Making Your Workplace Team Productive and Hassle-Free* (New York: AMACOM, 1997).

Chris Coduto/Icon Sportswire/Corbis via Getty Images

Decision Making, Creativity, and Innovation

It's not hard to make decisions when you know what your values are.

—Roy E. Disney, former Disney executive and nephew to Walt Disney

Learning Objectives

By the end of this chapter, you will be able to:

8.1 Identify the primary types of decisions managers make to solve problems

8.2 Identify factors that influence the way we make decisions in the real world

8.3 Discuss the critical nature of creativity and innovation in today's organizations

8.4 Describe the three-component model of creativity

8.5 Identify the three types of support for creativity

8.6 Outline the steps in the innovation process

CASE STUDY: CREATIVITY AND INNOVATION, ARIZONA STATE UNIVERSITY

"Let's go to the number one party school in the U.S.!" Such an exclamation was typical of prospective Arizona State University students for many years through the 1990s and early 2000s. Including graduate and undergraduate enrollment, Arizona State University has more than 82,000 students, so it makes sense that ASU became primarily a symbol of social life. There are almost 15,000 employees on staff, and that combined with the student body adds up to the size of a bustling city. Arizona State University has become a behemoth of an organization, and it must answer to the taxpayers of an entire state; it is difficult for any person or group to run an organization with so many facets. Led by President Michael Crow and his handpicked team, ASU is now regarded as the number one university for innovation—a title they achieved by, not surprisingly, innovating.

Exploratory Innovation

In an attempt to pursue innovation and diversity, Arizona State University began adopting policies previously considered taboo in the world of higher education. Administrators decided to find ways to enroll as many capable students as possible; as President Crow often says, "We measure our success by the people we let in, not by the people we keep out." Since setting aside the traditional industry metric of the acceptance rate, the university has seen record numbers of enrollment, and it is a place of cultural, social, economic, and ideological diversity. It is currently ranked near the very top in universities for veterans, and it is ranked at the very top of places to study for international students.

The research funding at ASU has rapidly increased over fifteen years to its current $450 million+. In both 2015 and 2016, the widely trusted *U.S. News* report on higher education ranked ASU as the most innovative university in the country. The leadership at Arizona State University risked becoming a school known for its simple academic standards by bringing in so many students, but they delivered on bringing in a huge supply of idea creation. This bold and innovative move to search for creativity through diversity plays a fundamental role in maintaining the university's accommodative approach for vast numbers of students.

Organizational Structure and Innovative Change

Michael Crow is not hesitant to introduce new methods of organization and management at Arizona State University, a trait which assists managers in increasing their operations' success. In an interview, President Crow says, "The big thing that would be different in 2016 is all of this hesitancy about the integrated, aggregated tools—both software and hardware—that we now have available to us," and, "We need to get about the business of integrating technology-based learning platforms as enhancements of our faculty and enhancements of our instructional environment." Crow came to ASU in 2002, and even up until 2016 he was focused on harnessing and honing the latest technological opportunities for professors and students. Just like a business, ASU has budgets to meet, revenue to produce, and a service to render, and ASU has succeeded in becoming a reputable university by keeping up with the same industry innovations as corporations.

Arizona State University has many different vice presidents and directors, and they use this as a chance to bring about people innovation. There are fifteen vice presidents of the university, and twenty-four vice provosts and deans, so management at the university intentionally works in a large web in order to ensure diversity of ideas and creativity. Many organizations struggle with silos and a lack of delegation, whereas the dozens of departments at ASU all run differently, but all with the same mission: to educate as many people as possible. In that way, ASU has taken tips from retailers and production corporations with similar structures, whose goals are to sell product to as many people as possible, and applied them to the pursuit of education.

Competitive Innovation

Another reason Arizona State University sticks out as an innovative institution compared to its peers is that it competes with other universities, and it does so through innovative means. Colleges and universities in the United States of America have always jousted for position in rankings and reputation, but ASU put a new twist on competition when they began accepting and educating so many thousands of undergraduate students. Instead of the traditional path of marketing their university in an attempt to increase application numbers and push acceptance rates down, the managers of Arizona State University market the university as a feasible path for any person genuinely seeking a higher education. This mind-set is a form of innovation within the industry, as is the methodology propping it up.

ASU tracks the statistics and benchmarks of dozens of nearby universities and community colleges, but not necessarily to find weaknesses. In fact, this process is an attempt to find strengths: Arizona State University partners with a number of universities across the United States; as long as a new, innovative program or research opportunity exists, the management at ASU hunts it down. This competitive edge extends into the business world. Arizona State University has one of the largest corporate sponsorships in the university world. Starbucks and ASU are partnered to bring education to thousands of baristas, and the CEO, Howard Schultz, spoke at the 2017 commencement. In sum, Arizona State University exposes the cornucopia of opportunities for organizations led by innovative people and ideas, and its managers provide a useful exhibit of the constant search for improvement that goes hand in hand with innovation.

Innovation in Philanthropy

Universities such as ASU who strive to top the list of innovators often pride themselves on the work of their graduates. Recently, students out of Arizona State began a group called 33 Buckets, and they travel across South America installing affordable water filters and training local citizens on their maintenance. This was born out of a program called EPICS: Engineering in Community Service, where students and professors spend class time actively innovating, and then launch as many real-world projects as possible. This program serves as an example for organizations who seek creative potential in their team members, and it shows that organizations can engage in practiced creativity by creating a space for it.

Critical-Thinking Questions

1. What innovative decision boosted Arizona State University's enrollment?

2. How does ASU think about enrollment differently than competitors, and why do they do this?

3. How could the practices mentioned in this chapter and case report be integrated into your workplace?

Resources:

Arizona State University. (n.d.). *Guiding an innovative, transformative new American university.* Retrieved from http://www.asu.edu/admin/

Arizona State University. (2014). *ASU ranked among top schools for veterans.* Retrieved from https://asunow.asu.edu/content/asu-ranked-among-top-schools-veterans

Arizona State University. (2016, September 13). *ASU selected nation's most innovative school for second straight year.* Retrieved from https://asunow.asu.edu/20160912-asu-news-asu-selected-nations-most-innovative-school-second-straight-year

Arizona State University. (2016). *Global engagement: Addressing global water crisis with 33 Buckets.* Retrieved from https://asunow.asu.edu/20160721-solutions-addressing-global-water-crisis-33-buckets

Arizona State University. (2017). *Facts at a glance: Fall 2016 - Metropolitan campuses.* Retrieved from https://uoia.asu.edu/sites/default/files/asu_facts_at_a_glance_-_fall_2016_final_0.pdf

ASU Knowledge Enterprise Development. (n.d.). *Facts and figures.* Retrieved from https://research.asu.edu/about-us/facts-figures

O'Brien, J. (2016). *Innovative cooperation, at scale: An interview with Michael M. Crow.* Retrieved from https://president.asu.edu/node/2245

U.S. News. (n.d.). *Most innovative schools National universities.* Retrieved from https://www.usnews.com/best-colleges/rankings/national-universities/innovative

Decision Making and Problem Solving

>> LO 8.1 Identify the primary types of decisions managers make to solve problems

The ability to make decisions and solve problems is a key aspect of organizational behavior. We make decisions, big and small, every single day in our professional and personal lives. Living in the technology era means we are subject to a continuous flow of information that needs to be processed and absorbed. When we are deciding what to do with this abundance of information, our understanding of a rational decision-making process can guide us toward the right course of action. **Decision making** is the action or process of identifying a strategy to resolve problems.[1] There is a tendency to use decision making and problem solving interchangeably, but they are not the same thing. Problem solving is a method that requires analytical thinking and intuition to find a solution, whereas decision making is a process that takes place during problem solving and involves judgment to decide on the right course of action.

SAGE edge™

Master the content
edge.sagepub.com/neckob2e

Decision making: The action or process of identifying a strategy to resolve problems

Amazon has a reputation for having high-quality customer service.

Programmed decisions:
Automatic responses to routine and recurring situations

Nonprogrammed decisions:
New or nonroutine problems for which there are no proven answers

There are two main types of decisions: programmed decisions and nonprogrammed decisions.[2]

Programmed decisions are automatic responses to routine and recurring situations. Usually these situations have occurred in the past and are familiar to the people dealing with them. Decisions are generally made by following company policies and guidelines that have been put in place to deal with specific issues. For example, Costco, Amazon, Apple, and Salesforce are just a few companies that are market leaders in customer service because of their excellent policy for responding efficiently to customer queries and resolving customer complaints. Thanks in large part to meticulous programmed decision making, these companies have thrived over the last decade. Amazon uses programmed decision making in its customer service guidelines which state that customers who report a lost package must always be compensated with an immediate replacement.[3]

Nonprogrammed decisions respond to new or nonroutine problems for which there are no proven solutions. In these situations, employees will not find the answer they are looking for in the company handbook or policy guidelines. Very often, the problems are complex in nature with few past occurrences for employees to draw on.

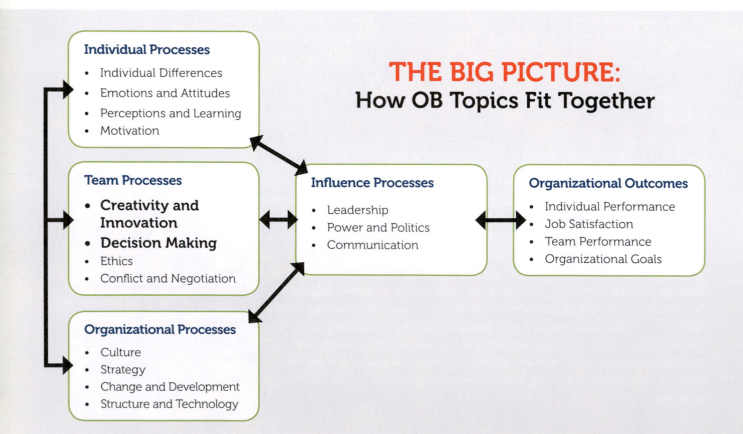

Individual Processes
- Individual Differences
- Emotions and Attitudes
- Perceptions and Learning
- Motivation

Team Processes
- **Creativity and Innovation**
- **Decision Making**
- Ethics
- Conflict and Negotiation

Organizational Processes
- Culture
- Strategy
- Change and Development
- Structure and Technology

THE BIG PICTURE:
How OB Topics Fit Together

Influence Processes
- Leadership
- Power and Politics
- Communication

Organizational Outcomes
- Individual Performance
- Job Satisfaction
- Team Performance
- Organizational Goals

For example, the rising number of cybersecurity threats and cybercrimes is an example of a complex problem that has not occurred so much in the past. Battling cybercrime will require serious decisions, given it is one of the biggest challenges facing organizations today, regardless of their size. Dotan Bar Noy, CEO and cofounder of ReSec technologies, believes that all companies are at risk. Noy says, "No one can say that they're not a target, no matter the size of the company. If you have a business and it generates money, then that means you have something of value for the attackers."[4]

We make dozens of decisions in our personal lives every day—from what we're going to wear, to who we're going to meet, to what we're going to eat for lunch. Some of these decisions are conscious while others are instinctive. However, in business, decisions need to be made with more care and analysis. The skill of decision making is one of the more important tools for managers and can make the difference between good and poor outcomes.

Managers often use the five-step decision-making process to help them make good decisions and resolve complex issues (Figure 8.1).

Define the Problem

The first step in the decision-making process is to define the problem. You need to fully understand the nature of the problem and be able to describe it in clear, concise terms in order to arrive at a solution. For example, say you are the manager of an assembly line in a manufacturing plant where work-related injuries have increased, leading to higher levels of absenteeism and falling profits due to reduced productivity. In this instance, the problem is the rise of work-related injuries and the goal would be to reduce the number of work-related injuries in the plant as soon as possible (Figure 8.2).

Identify and Weigh Decision Criteria

Now that the problem has been defined, you will need to identify and weigh the criteria in the decision. For example, the hazards and risks involved in the injuries, the degree to

FIGURE 8.1

A Five-Step Model of Decision Making

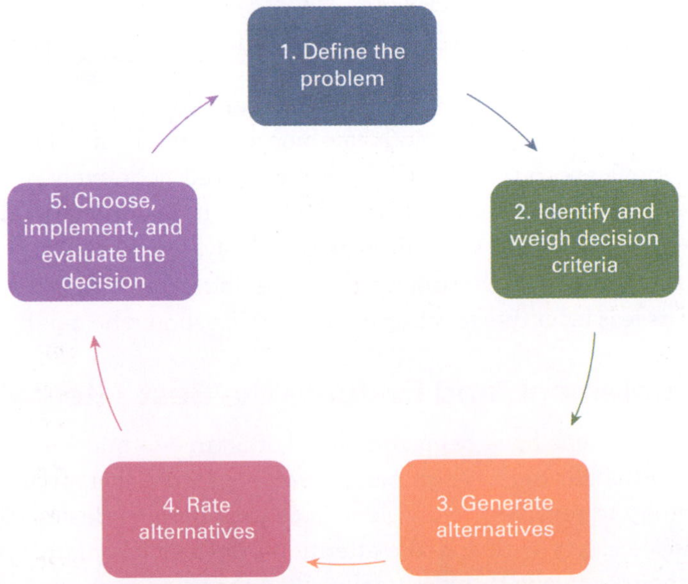

1. Define the problem
2. Identify and weigh decision criteria
3. Generate alternatives
4. Rate alternatives
5. Choose, implement, and evaluate the decision

FIGURE 8.2

Distribution of Selected Occupational Injuries for Selected Private Sector Occupations, 2013

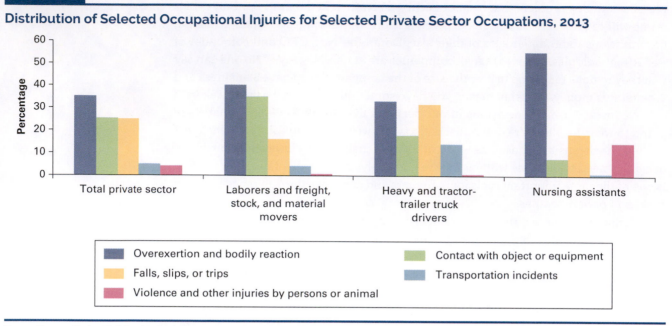

Source: Bureau of Labor Statistics. *Nonfatal Occupational Injuries and Illnesses Requiring Days Away From Work, 2013*, p. 2 (Washington, DC: US Department of Labor, 2014). www.bls.gov/news.release/pdf/osh2.pdf.

which employees follow safety procedures, and why injuries are becoming more common. One solution might be to increase employee focus on safety and encourage employees to care about safety procedures in a way that will not be viewed as a threat or a negative.

Generate Multiple Alternatives

Next, you may think of alternate solutions to the defined problem. Perhaps if you discover that employees are not adhering to safety guidelines, then stricter sanctions and punishments should be imposed for violations of safety standards. Alternatively, a reward system such as bonuses or vacation time for low injury rates would be a more beneficial way to highlight the safety initiative.

Rate Alternatives on the Basis of Decision Criteria

During this step, you might spend some time weighing the two possible solutions against each other and find they both rate poorly on the basis of the criteria. For example, sanctions and punishments could be viewed negatively and as a threat, and employees might fail to report injuries for fear of punishment. Similarly, though the reward system might be viewed more positively, there is also a concern that because rewards would be contingent on achieving a lower number of reported injuries, there is less incentive to report incidents that should be legally reported.

Choose, Implement, and Evaluate the Best Alternative

Once the first four steps have been completed, it is time to make a decision on the basis of the information you have gathered. In this example, you might use a critical-thinking strategy to resolve the problem. This may involve designing a program around employee safety with specific attention drawn to the plant's machinery. It could ask each employee to think critically about the work environment in terms of potential energy sources including the plant's machines, which produce pressure, mechanical, chemical, electrical, gravity, and heat/cold energy. This initiative might encourage all employees to do three things relative to these energy sources: identify-act-review. First identify the energy source, and then take mitigation actions to eliminate it, control it, or if necessary protect yourself from it. If that is not possible, for example, if the machine is malfunctioning, then the employee should stop, call, and wait for a supervisor to review the situation. By making this decision, you have introduced a way to reduce work-related injuries in a nonthreatening way, as well as encouraging employees to think more seriously about their safety around machinery at work.

THINKING CRITICALLY

1. Defend the perspective that the first step in the Five-Step Decision-Making Model is the most important.

2. Defend the perspective that generating and evaluating alternatives (steps 3 and 4) are the most important steps in the model.

3. Do you believe that any one step is more or less important than any other step in the model? Why or why not?

Decision Making in the Real World

>> **LO 8.2** **Identify factors that influence the way we make decisions in the real world**

We've seen that decision making requires taking multiple steps to arrive at a clear solution. But what other factors affect an individual's ability to make rational decisions?

Bounded Rationality

Bounded rationality is the idea that we are restricted by a variety of constraints when making decisions.[5] This concept is in contrast with **complete rationality**, which assumes we take into account every single criterion or possible alternative to make a decision.[6] (See Figure 8.3.) In reality, most of us don't have the time or mental processing capacity to deal with so much information; instead, we tend to narrow the options to a few key criteria. For example, when buying a new car, we are more likely to use bounded rationality. First, we identify a few main benchmarks, like mileage, options, and price, and then we choose the models that meet our benchmarks to test drive. However, if we were to adopt a completely rational approach, we would need to consider every single car in production as a viable option, which is not realistic.

Bounded rationality: The idea that we are restricted by a variety of constraints when making decisions

Complete rationality: The assumption that we take in to account every single criterion or possible alternative to make a decision

Satisficing Decisions

Satisficing decisions aim for acceptable results rather than for the best or optimal solutions.[7] Satisficing is useful for less important decisions. For example, when purchasing a pack of chewing gum, we tend to choose something that looks good. We don't spend time researching the merits of all the different chewing gum brands and flavors on the market. If it turns out that we made a bad decision in choosing that particular brand, it's not a big deal because gum isn't expensive. We simply make a

Satisficing decisions: Solutions that aim for acceptable results rather than for the best or optimal ones

FIGURE 8.3

Bounded versus Complete Rationality

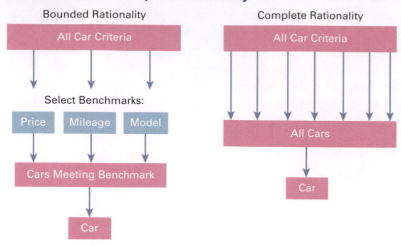

Apple's classic slogan, "Think Different," alludes to founder Steve Jobs's tendency to rely on his intuition to make creative decisions and innovations.

Intuition: An unconscious process of making decisions based on imagination and possibilities

Heuristics: Shortcuts or "rules of thumb" that allow us to make judgments and decisions quickly and efficiently

Availability heuristic: A rule of thumb for making judgments on examples and events that immediately spring to mind

Anchoring and adjustment heuristic: A process whereby people base their decisions on the first piece of information they are given without taking other probabilities into account

different decision the next time. However, satisficing is not appropriate for important decisions. For example, when diagnosing illness, doctors cannot afford to make an incorrect decision that causes harm; they need to consider a great deal of information to establish the right course of treatment for the patient.

Intuition

Intuition is the unconscious process of making decisions based on imagination and possibilities.[8] Relying on "a feeling" may not seem a totally reliable decision process. Some research suggests, however, that intuitive decisions often represent information we are already holding at an unconscious level, and thus it may lead to effective decisions.[9] Reed Hastings, CEO of tech company Netflix, relies on his intuition when it comes to making decisions about new products. Hastings says, "We start with the data," said Hastings. "But the final call is always gut. It's informed intuition."[10]

Heuristics

Another aspect of decision making is **heuristics**, shortcuts or "rules of thumb" that allow us to make judgments and decisions quickly and efficiently.[11] There are three types of heuristics: availability heuristic, anchoring and adjustment heuristic, and representativeness heuristic.

Availability heuristics allow us to make judgments based on examples and events that are available and immediately spring to mind.[12] Sometimes we can make incorrect judgments about certain issues because of our reliance on information that is more readily available to us. This is called *availability bias*. Extensive media coverage can also bias our opinion; for example, a plane crash that is widely reported could lead many people to believe flying is unsafe, whereas it's more likely that one would be killed in a car accident than in the air.[13] Psychologist Daniel Kahneman uses this example of availability bias in his book *Thinking Fast and Slow*: "Because of the coincidence of two planes crashing last month, she now prefers to take the train. That's silly. The risk hasn't really changed; it's an availability bias."[14]

Anchoring and adjustment heuristics lead us to base decisions on the first piece of information and then adjust it, leading to *anchoring bias*, which is the tendency to over-rely on initial information while overlooking other important criteria.[15]

For example, a shopper might "anchor" on the discount of 25 percent on a pair of jeans worth $150, rather than considering that even with the discount the jeans are still more money than the shopper intended to spend.

With **representativeness heuristic** we base a decision on our existing mental prototype and similar representative stereotypes.[16] For example, two candidates turn up for an interview; one is well groomed, neatly dressed in a shirt and trousers, and the other has untidy hair and dresses in jeans and an old T-shirt. Based on past experience, you might assume the better-groomed candidate to be the more serious and committed person.

Biases and Errors

Our decision making is often influenced by different types of bias. Recognizing and minimizing these biases is crucial for making accurate decisions.

Common-information bias is the inclination to overemphasize information held by the majority of group members while failing to consider other perspectives held by the minority.[17] For example, in a voting situation, people often go along with the common or majority view rather than take the time to learn about and discuss other views.

We use representative heuristics to make decisions, using our existing expectations or experiences to predict an outcome. For example, you may expect someone dressed in a suit when interviewing for an office job to be a better fit for the company than someone who shows up in a sleeveless shirt and jeans.

© iStockphoto.com/alvarez

Confirmation bias is the tendency to seek out information that fuels or confirms our preexisting views and to discount information that conflicts with them.[18] For example, say you want to move to a country in Europe for a couple of years. During your research, you only look at the aspects that support your own beliefs about that country (historic, scenic, cultural) and overlook information that presents alternate viewpoints (unpredictable weather conditions, cultural differences, cost of living).

Ease-of-recall bias is the propensity to over-rely on information recollected from memory when making a decision.[19] For example, an investor might provide inaccurate information about a stock by plucking figures from his memory instead of taking the time to locate the exact information.

Hindsight bias is the tendency to overestimate our ability to predict an outcome of an event.[20] For example, before a baseball game you "predict" that your favorite team is going to win. When your team does win, you might say, "I knew that was going to happen!," even though it is clearly impossible to predict these things.

Projection bias is the inclination to believe that other people think, feel, and act the same way we do (we project our thoughts and attitudes onto them).[21] For example, you might assume that all of your coworkers agree with your opinion of the company CEO, even though you've never asked them their opinion.

Escalation of commitment is the increased commitment we may make to a decision despite receiving negative information about the consequences.[22] For example, a manager may choose to invest in more and more training for an underperforming employee even though the evidence suggests that the employee's work is unlikely to improve. Figure 8.4 suggests a number of factors that can contribute to the escalation of commitment effect.

Sunk cost bias is the decision to continue an unwise investment based on past investments of time, effort, and/or money.[23] For example, you might be reluctant to sell

Representativeness heuristic: A shortcut that bases a decision on our existing mental prototype and similar stereotypes

Common-information bias: The inclination to overemphasize information held by the majority of group members while failing to consider other perspectives held by the minority

Confirmation bias: The tendency to seek out information that fuels our preexisting views and to discount information that conflicts with our worldview

Ease-of-recall bias: The propensity to over-rely on information recollected from memory when making a decision

Hindsight bias: The tendency to overestimate the ability to predict an outcome of an event

Projection bias: The inclination to believe other people think, feel, and act the same way we do

Escalation of commitment: The increased commitment to a decision despite negative information

Sunk cost bias: The decision to continue an investment based on past investments of time, effort, and/or money

FIGURE 8.4

Escalation of Commitment Effect

Source: Adapted from Staw, B. M. "The Escalation of Commitment to a Course of Action." *Academy of Management Review* 6 (1981): 577–587.

Framing error: The tendency to highlight certain aspects of a situation depending on whether they are positive or negative to solve a problem while ignoring other aspects

Lack of participation error: The inclination to exclude certain people from the decision-making process

Randomness error: The tendency for people to believe they can predict the outcome of chance events based on false information or superstition

your car for a reasonable price because you spent so much to fix it (your sunk cost) and you think it's worth more than it is.

Framing error is the tendency to highlight certain aspects of a situation, either positive or negative, to solve a problem while ignoring other aspects.[24] For example, suppose the company president tells her executive team that the company, which employs 2,000 workers, has an annual turnover of 2 percent. A positive frame views this percentage as low, requiring very little action, whereas a negative frame perceives the loss of 40 employees a year as unacceptable and is likely to spark discussions about how to resolve this perceived problem.

Lack of participation error is the inclination to exclude certain people from the decision-making process. For example, in hierarchical companies, most of the lower-level employees are not invited to partake in decision making even though their feedback may prove very useful.

Randomness error is the tendency for people to believe they can predict the outcome of chance events based on false information or superstition. For example, people believe it is possible to have a run of luck at the poker table, when in fact the probability of winning is the same every game.

THINKING CRITICALLY

1. In what types of work situations would satisficing be appropriate? List at least three occupations or industries where satisficing would not be an appropriate strategy for decision making?

2. Provide two examples of each of the three heuristics (availability, anchoring and adjustment, and representative) that are not discussed in the text.

3. Which of the biases and errors discussed do you think are most likely to lead to miscommunication issues with colleagues and friends? Devise a series of questions you could ask yourself in order to avoid falling prey to the biases and errors you identify.

4. Which of the biases and errors discussed are most likely to lead to budget and timeline problems in an organization? Defend your answer.

Creativity and Innovation in Individuals, Teams, and Organizations

>> **LO 8.3**   Discuss the critical nature of creativity and innovation in today's organizations

In the previous sections, we have discussed the art of decision making and its importance to today's organizations. Creativity and innovation can aid decision making by giving people a greater understanding of the company needs and its customers. Many of the world's leading organizations like Apple, Facebook, and Google have transformed the way we live and interact with others and encouraged us to want more. What do these organizations have in common, and why are they so wildly successful? The reason is that their business models are largely based on promoting **creativity**, which is the generation of meaningful ideas by individuals or teams,[25] and **innovation**, which is the creation and development of a new product or service.[26] But of course, it's not just the Silicon Valley companies that create and innovate. For example, IDEO maintains a creative culture during brainstorming sessions by applying seven rules to ensure that the discussion is as productive as possible.[27] These rules encourage open dialogue, provide people with the confidence to share their ideas, and give them a platform to be as creative as they desire.

Creativity: The generation of meaningful ideas by individuals or teams

Innovation: The creation and development of a new product or service

To further innovation, multinational services firm EY has set up some global labs, for instance, the Data Analytics Center of Excellence and the Software Robot Center, to enable employees to experiment with groundbreaking artificial intelligence (AI) technologies.[28]

Creativity and innovation affect organizational behavior in those organizations in which employees are expected to generate creative products, processes, and strategies. The contribution from a group of individuals with varying knowledge, skills, backgrounds, and experiences can be a powerful force in creating innovative ideas, making decisions, and generating solutions. It is not just technology companies that have embraced this business model. Most successful organizations, whether in media, fashion, architecture, medicine, or engineering, are emphasizing creativity and innovation in order to stay competitive. They recognize the need to redefine, reinvent, and repurpose brands and products to keep up with market demand.

In 2017, cloud-computing giant Amazon topped the list as the world's most innovative organization according to *Fast Company*'s World's Most Innovative Companies ranking. Since being founded in 1994 by Jeff Bezos, it has sold books, clothes, digital content (movies, music, apps), cloud-based services for businesses all over the world, and consumer electronics. In the future, Amazon aims to deliver packages under five pounds via its own fleet of drones through its Amazon Prime Air initiative.

Every business, large or small, needs to innovate in order to compete. Fortunately, with the right training and a willingness to learn, every one of us has the ability to be creative on an individual level. "Business as usual" is no longer an option.

THINKING CRITICALLY

1. Discuss the relationship between creativity and innovation. Is it possible to innovate without creativity? Is it possible to be creative without innovating? Defend your position.

2. List at least three key technological advances and how they have affected consumer behavior within the last decade. Then discuss the ways in which consumer behavior changes have put more pressure on businesses to be more innovative and creative.

A Three-Component Model of Creativity

>> LO 8.4 Describe the three-component model of creativity

When speech scientist Rupal Patel happened to overhear a conversation between a young girl and a man using assistive devices, each of which used a male voice, she knew something had to be done. Patel says, "We don't give people the same

OB IN THE REAL WORLD

John Beck, Chief Innovative Officer, Arizona State University

John Beck has a résumé that checks all the boxes in both industry and academia. John has worked at such consulting firms as Monitor, Accenture, and Jump and has taught at schools like Hult, Thunderbird, and is currently a Senior Research Fellow at USC. A Harvard graduate PhD, John has worked for some of the top consulting firms but has transitioned the second leg of his career toward academia. Always an academic at heart, he has written multiple books such as *The Attention Economy*, *Good vs. Good*, and *The Kids Are Alright*, but right now he wants to change education altogether.

All of these accolades lead up to his current title of chief innovation officer at Arizona State University, the *U.S. News* top-ranked university in the country for innovation. He is doing his best to reinvent the way we teach and the way that students learn at the largest university in the United States. His experience in the consulting industry has brought him to the conclusion that students are coming out of universities unprepared for professional life and he intends to help change that.

John has traveled around the world and interviewed ninety executives, most of them CEOs, along with a handful of recruiters to hear what they really want from college graduates. The result was a list of traits that these executives see as rarities amongst their incoming employees. He found that these executives want employees who will push the boundaries in their field.

They want employees for their companies who are willing to embrace change and innovation. John says that traits such as "creativity, critical thinking, comfort with ambiguity, and execution skills are really what employers want out of the next generation workforce". With his list and a general idea of what universities are lacking, John seeks to change the way that we think of higher level education. The only way to do this is through innovation and creativity, both of which he considers his specialty, thanks to a career of pushing boundaries.

John wants to create a university system that better prepares students for the reality of professional life by innovating from within. John explains that he has spent much of his career fighting to make changes in businesses as a consultant. He explains, "People don't like to do new things," and "People are extremely hesitant to any sort of change." This may seem obvious, but to many organizations this proneness to not change can be fatal. In the case of the American higher education system, this proneness toward tradition has left many universities worse off than they were a century ago.

He goes in depth on the importance of change on a biological level, "Synapses in our brain are taught to do certain things over and over." We are biologically prone to build a routine for ourselves and to stay in that routine and to leave it is difficult. This is especially true in large organizations where it is easiest to get into a routine and to prefer to stay in it. This explains why it is common for smaller firms to innovate faster while larger firms are prone to a stagnation of new ideas. It is easy to fall into a routine in an established organization while it is much harder to do so in a start-up.

College students are learning in almost the same manner as they always have been while businesses have been forced to evolve. This type of system has created incongruencies between what the university system has prepared students for and what businesses need in graduates. John seeks to reverse this skill gap by addressing the issue of an antiquated style of teaching head-on using innovation and creative thinking. One of his biggest barriers will be the people who are comfortable with the way of doing things that they know, a barrier he has been working against for the entirety of his career. With his goal in mind, John will seek to make change at Arizona State University and across all academia. He hopes that the entire university system could gain from his work at ASU and feels he has the resources and ambition to be more than equipped to achieve success.

Critical-Thinking Questions

1. What makes an organization fall behind their competitors according to John?

2. What traits should you cultivate in order to make yourself more valuable to a company according to John? ●

Source: Interview with John Beck conducted on March 31st, 2017

prosthetic limbs, and yet we're doing that with the prosthetic voice."[29] So in 2014, she founded VocaliD, a synthetic-voice start-up based in Belmont, Massachusetts, which creates unique voices for people who struggle with speech impairments, often caused by autism, diseases, or cerebral palsy. These unique voices allow the person to communicate more naturally in a way that represents their age, gender, and personality. Many of us would describe Rupal Patel as a creative person. She created an innovation that filled a gap in the market and succeeded admirably. But what makes someone creative?

Researchers have spent years trying to figure out what makes a person creative. Some theorists have focused on the personalities of history's most creative geniuses, such as Einstein, Plath, Edison, Plato, and Mozart, to try and find the common thread associated with creativity. Other theorists argue that the study of personality traits is not sufficient to explain the foundations of creativity. Creativity researcher Teresa Amabile believes that creativity is a process rather than a list of traits, and she proposes a **three-component model of creativity** to describe the factors necessary for an individual to be creative. The three components of Amabile's model are domain-relevant skills and expertise, creativity-relevant processes, and task motivation (Figure 8.5).[30]

Cirque du Soleil constantly reinvents and innovates what we traditionally think about the circus, drawing on more high-end concepts like opera and theatre, to attract a higher-paying customer base.

Three-component model of creativity: A model proposing that individual creativity relies on domain-relevant skills and expertise, creativity-relevant processes, and intrinsic task motivation

Domain-Relevant Skills and Expertise

Amabile argues that we must have what she calls *domain-relevant skills and expertise,* that is, knowledge about the subject and the skills and talent to provide the most creative and productive responses. An increase in knowledge leads to higher levels of creativity. For example, say you work in the graphics section of your firm and your boss asks you to come up with a new product logo. If you are a brand expert, you will draw on your knowledge and experience of certain brands to come up with creative responses that accurately represent the product. Even without any brand knowledge, you can still produce creative responses because such knowledge can be learned, but it usually takes longer to generate creative suggestions because it takes more time to acquire the relevant knowledge.[31]

Creativity-Relevant Processes

According to Amabile, *creativity-relevant processes,* work methods dependent on particular personality characteristics, methods of thinking, and knowledge of heuristics, are a second component needed for creativity. Personality traits such as self-discipline, perseverance, delayed gratification, and independence, for instance, appear to be associated with creative minds.[32] In addition, creative people tend to adopt a work style consisting of long periods of concentration and focus. They also have the ability to use **productive forgetting**, which allows them to abandon a solution that isn't working in favor of a new one.[33] People with creativity-relevant skills

Productive forgetting: The ability to abandon a solution that isn't working in favor of a new one

---

FIGURE 8.5

Three Components of Creativity

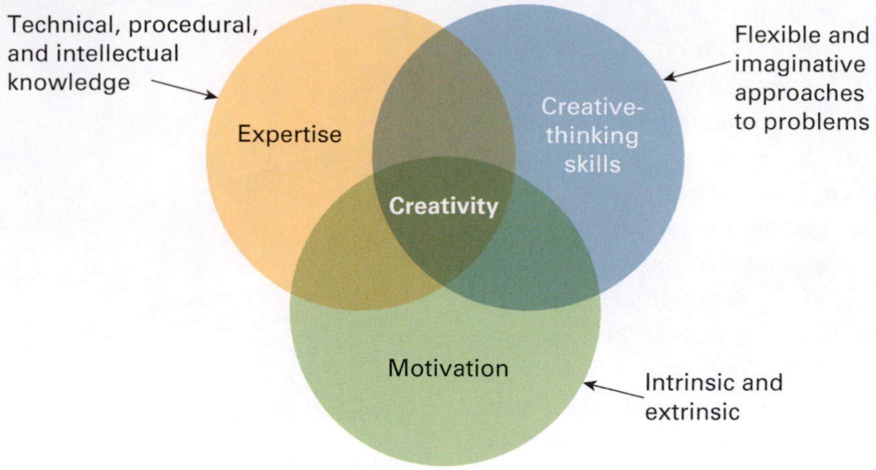

Technical, procedural, and intellectual knowledge →

Expertise

Creative-thinking skills

Flexible and imaginative approaches to problems

Creativity

Motivation

Intrinsic and extrinsic

Source: Adapted from Amabile, Teresa M. "How to Kill Creativity." *Harvard Business Review* 76, no. 5 (September 1998): 76–87.

can also suspend judgment, adopt viewpoints different from their own, persist in overcoming obstacles, and ignore social approval. Finally, they use mental shortcuts or heuristics rather than strict rules to find creative ways to resolve a problem. For example, if you spend most of your day manually inputting data into a computer system, you might try and find practical ways to make the process more efficient. Like domain knowledge, creativity-relevant skills and processes can be learned through training and on-the-job experience.

Intrinsic and Extrinsic Motivation

People who have an innate interest in a chosen task tend to be more motivated to produce creative ideas. It stands to reason that if we find a task interesting and stimulating, then we will be more inclined to engage with it. In contrast, a task that we perceive to be tedious and boring will not provoke the same degree of attention or inspiration.

In the past, it was believed that extrinsic or external factors that control the way a person deals with the task tend to inhibit creativity. For example, you might feel intimidated or overly cautious if your manager is looking over your shoulder while you answer emails. This level of control may indeed stifle your creativity and your willingness to take risks, while people who are given the freedom to explore creative options may feel less inhibited and more inclined to share their ideas. Similarly, extrinsic rewards such as bonuses or other monetary rewards may stunt employee creativity, because many people have a tendency to focus solely on the steps it takes to obtain the reward rather than thinking of creative ways to reach their work goal.

More recent research suggests that extrinsic motivation, when used in the right way, could support intrinsic or inner motivation, especially when the levels of intrinsic motivation are already high.[34] For example, you might be told that your team is going to participate in a brainstorming session during which each of you is expected to come up with at least five ideas to redefine a product. You are likely to find this task creatively stimulating, particularly if you have a real interest in the product already. In other words, people who are explicitly told exactly what they need to do to be creative tend to produce creative responses.

THINKING CRITICALLY

1. What types of issues could you tackle most creatively given the three components of Amabile's model (domain-relevant skills and expertise, creativity-relevant processes, and task motivation)?

2. To what extent can Amabile's model of creativity explain varying levels of creativity among individuals? Explain your answer.

Creative Potential versus Practiced Creativity

>> LO 8.5 **Identify the three types of support for creativity**

People with **creative potential** tend to possess the skills and capacity to generate ideas. As OB in the Real World shows, one of the most desired traits CEOs want from college graduates is the potential to be creative.

In contrast, **practiced creativity** is the ability to spot opportunities to apply these skills in the workplace.[35] Brian Scudamore, founder and CEO of O2E Brands and 1-800-GOT-JUNK, inspires practiced creativity by encouraging his staff to write their own business dreams on a wall.[36] Anybody can write their vision and goals on the wall under the words "Can You Imagine?" Scudmore believes that this creative method empowers employees to accomplish goals and boosts employee engagement.

Research shows that creative people are more likely to flourish in a work environment that supports creativity.[37] If companies get it right, a creative mind-set can lead to innovative thinking, better performance, increased job satisfaction, and a positive impact. Rachel Light, associated director of global employee engagement at California-based talent management solutions provider Cornerstone on Demand, believes that being creative has led to a much-improved workplace. She states, "Taking a creative approach to our employee engagement program has directly impacted our team's productivity and employee satisfaction."[38]

Those who perceive their work environment to lack support for creative expression may feel reluctant to express their ideas. This may create a gap between the person's creative potential and the application of their creative skills.[39]

Organizations that do not cultivate an environment open to creativity are at a disadvantage because they are neglecting resources that could help the company operate and compete more effectively. Organizations can narrow the creativity gap by fostering an environment that employees perceive as supportive to creative expression.[40]

Three Types of Support for Creativity

There are three main types of support for creativity in organizations: organizational support, supervisory support, and workgroup support, all of which have an influence on whether and how creativity flourishes in an organization.

Organizational Support for Creativity

Researchers have identified a range of environmental factors controlled by the organization that can either stimulate or stifle creativity.[41] Creativity flourishes when

Creative potential: The skills and capacity to generate ideas

Practiced creativity: The ability to seize opportunities to apply creative skills in the workplace

EXAMINING THE EVIDENCE

Organizational Support and Creativity

Research findings support the idea that employee perceptions of a supportive organization help to facilitate creativity.[*] But exactly how does organizational support translate into employee creativity? Researchers Chongxin Yu and Stephen J. Frenkel of the University of New South Wales examined this question in a study of 206 bank employees in China.[^] Their findings demonstrate that perceived organizational support, which is the extent to which employees perceive that they are valued and cared for by the organization, as delivered by middle managers, affected employee creativity by strengthening two factors: employees' identification with their work unit and their expectations of career success. These results suggest that factors that engage intrinsic motivation—as heightened work group identification and career success expectations do—will be more likely to result in creative behaviors than extrinsic motivational factors such as felt obligation to care about and to assist the organization in the process of achieving its goals. To facilitate more creativity in the workplace, then, managers should engage in supportive behaviors that encourage employees to feel connected to their peers and to anticipate the possibility of a successful career path in the organization.

Critical-Thinking Questions

1. In what ways can managers help employees feel more connected to their work group and to have expectations a successful career path?

2. What can managers do to try to avoid feelings of obligation among employees that could undermine creativity? ●

[*]Amabile, Teresa M., Regina Conti, Heather Coon, Jeffrey Lazenby, and Michael Herron. "Assessing the Work Environment for Creativity." *Academy of Management Journal* 39, no. 5 (October 1996): 1154–1184.

[^]Yu, Chongxin, and Stephen J. Frenkel. "Explaining Task Performance and Creativity from Perceived Organizational Support Theory: Which Mechanisms Are More Important?" *Journal of Organizational Behavior* 34, no. 8 (November 2013): 1165–1181.

employees are provided with the autonomy and resources they need to implement their concepts and when they are given license to take risks. In addition, organizations that provide appropriate rewards and feedback and that encourage a collaborative environment tend to possess a more creative culture.[42]

In contrast, organizations that impose too many constraints or controls over their employees, and that do not provide feedback, resources, or sufficient rewards, tend to create an environment that fails to encourage teamwork and collaboration. This type of organization stifles creativity.

Supervisory Support for Creativity

Employees who perceive their supervisor as supportive will feel more comfortable about speaking up and making suggestions. Supervisors who communicate, set clear goals, and are confident and protective of their teams tend to nurture a creative environment.[43] Michael Crow, president of Arizona State University, is an example of someone who is a good model as he supports creativity through diversity by providing education to thousands of students.

Work Group Support for Creativity

Group members can support creativity by establishing certain norms, such as welcoming different perspectives, actively listening, fostering collaboration, being open-minded, and clearly communicating their views and approaches. As former Yahoo! CEO Marissa Mayer says, "While we need [constraints] to spur passion and insight, we also need a sense of hopefulness to keep us engaged and unwavering in our search for the right idea. Innovation is born from the interaction between constraint and vision."

The Innovation Process and Types of Innovation

>> **LO 8.6** Outline the steps in the innovation process

Every innovation starts with an idea. Take new innovation Pouncer, for instance. Pouncer is an edible drone designed by company Windhorse Aerospace to deliver humanitarian aid to remote places with impassable roads.[44] The drone carries food, firewood, and materials for shelter. The company hopes that Pouncer will eventually revolutionize aid for people struggling in the wake of natural disasters.

A model of a drone that will be made of edible materials and is conceived for delivering food to disaster zones stands on display at the stand of UK startup Windhorse Aerospace at the CUBE Tech Fair for startups.

Sean Gallup/Getty Images

Idea Generation

The first step in the innovation process is the creation of the idea itself (Figure 8.6). Usually an idea is born out of the recognition of a need for a solution and generated from existing information, experience, and knowledge. Entrepreneur Didier Rappaport credits his focus on "painful issues" for his idea for Happn, a location-based dating app. Unlike conventional dating apps, Happn allows users to cross paths with each other in the real world and instantly connect if desired, making it less "virtual," and reducing the burden of fake profiles. Since 2013, Happn has gained 25 million users worldwide in 30 major cities, including Tokyo, New York, London, Brazil, and Copenhagen.[45]

Problem Solving

The second step of the innovation process is to identify any advantages and disadvantages associated with the innovation, explore costs and value, and set goals and priorities. For example, the Transit Elevated Bus which hovers over cars on the road was created by top engineers in China to tackle traffic jams, provide more road space, and decrease pollution.[46] Yet there are many problems (design and safety issues) to be solved before this prototype becomes a reality.

A Model of the Innovation Process

Idea Generation
- Recognition of a need or problem
- Synthesis of information to create ideas for development and testing

Problem Solving
- Setting goals and priorities
- Sharing and evaluating ideas using goals and priorities
- Determining the feasibility and practicality of ideas

Implementation and Diffusion
- Bringing the prototype solution or invention to its first use (process) or market introduction (product/service)

Source: Based on Utterback, James M. "The Process of Technological Innovation within the Firm." *Academy of Management Journal* 14, no. 1 (March 1971): 75–88.

Implementation and Diffusion

The final stage of the innovation process is producing and distributing the new product or idea. Without implementation, there is little chance of an idea becoming a reality. Apple implements its products through an efficient design process and distributes them through carefully staged events and conferences intended to create a buzz before the product is even officially launched.

Types of Innovation in Organizations

We often think of innovation as a process that produces a tangible product, but in fact there are six main types of innovations in organizations: product innovation, process innovation, organizational structure innovation, people innovation, exploitative innovation, and exploratory innovation (see Figure 8.7). Let's apply the six types of innovation to the tractor assembly plant case.

Product innovation is the development of new or improved goods or services that are sold to meet customer needs.[47] The Amazon Kindle would be an example of a new product innovation, while enhancing the digital camera resolution on the iPhone 7 would be an example of an improved product innovation.[48] **Process innovation** is the introduction of new or improved operational and work methods.[49] Footwear manufacturing company Nike is focusing on 3D printing as a way of revolutionizing its manufacturing process for mass scale production.[50] It also hopes to make 3D printing technology available in retail stores for customers who want customized footwear.

Product innovation: The development of new or improved goods or services that are sold to meet customer needs

Process innovation: The introduction of new or improved operational and work methods

Organizational structure innovation is the introduction or modification of work assignments, authority relationships, and communication and reward systems.[51] Tony Hsieh, founder and CEO of online shoe retailer Zappos, famously restructured the organization by making it a holacracy—a self-management system whereby employees do not have managers and are more involved in decision making.[52]

People innovation includes the changes in beliefs and behaviors of individuals working in an organization.[53] Organizations use a variety of training methods to foster positive behavioral change in their employees. For example, Virgin Atlantic airline pilots who had their fuel conservation performance assessed over an eight-month period during an experiment to reduce fuel usage, changed their behavior by cutting down on the amount of fuel they used during flights. Not only did the experiment reduce pollution but also saved the company almost four million dollars.[54]

Exploitative innovation focuses on the enhancement and reuse (exploitation) of existing products and processes.[55] Online hospitality service Airbnb successfully exploited the conventional hospitality industry (hotels, guesthouses) by offering innovative approaches to accommodation.

Exploratory innovation focuses on risk taking, radical thinking, and experimentation.[56] To work, exploratory innovation has to be supported by a management team that advocates the freedom of radical thinking. For example, Arizona State University enrolls as many capable students as possible rather than adhering to the traditional acceptance rate, successfully creating a thriving, diverse culture. Researchers believe organizations need to strike a balance between the contradictory natures of exploitative and exploratory innovation. Many organizations play it safe by focusing on the refinement of existing products rather than taking risks to explore new avenues.

This approach can lead to **organizational cultural lag**, an effect that occurs when organizations fail to keep up with emerging innovations and so risk missing lucrative opportunities to capitalize upon.[57] To avoid cultural lag, organizations need to continuously focus on their existing products and processes at the same time they are investigating new innovations. For example, when enhancements to the Web made it possible to deliver news online, some newspapers capitalized on this opportunity and sought to attract readers through creatively presenting the electronic news while maintaining their traditional paper editions.[58] As a result, those newspapers remained successful. In contrast, newspapers with managers who perceived the delivery of news online as a threat rather than an opportunity lost readers.

The Transit Elevated Bus in China is an example of how a problem can be solved through prototypes.

FIGURE 8.7

Types of Innovations in Organizations

Organization structural innovation: The introduction or modification of work assignments, authority relationships, and communication and reward systems within an organization

People innovation: Changes in the beliefs and behaviors of individuals working in an organization

Exploitative innovation: The enhancement and reuse of existing products and processes

Exploratory innovation: Risk taking, radical thinking, and experimentation

Organizational cultural lag: The deficit in organizations that fail to keep up with new emerging innovations

To achieve the desired combination of exploitation and exploration, senior managers need to achieve a balance; encourage their employees to think in terms of sustaining an existing product while developing innovation; provide a forum for creative discussion; assign roles and set goals to get the process in motion; and introduce a reward system to help motivate teams and reinforce the importance of the organization's strategy.

To be successful in today's workplace, organizations need to nurture an environment of creativity and innovation, and give people a platform to share their thoughts and ideas, as well as the confidence to make mistakes. Organizations also need good decision makers to process and make sense of the continuous stream of information coming through every day. A large part of a manager's role is to make good ethical choices, but as the next chapter illustrates, not all managers make the right ethical decisions.

THINKING CRITICALLY

1. Provide at least two real-world examples of each of the six types of innovation (product, process, organizational structure, people, exploitive, and exploratory). To what extent do you believe that innovation in organizational structure and people enhances the likelihood of other types of innovation in an organization?

2. Consider the newspaper illustration used to explain cultural lag in the section. Newspapers are heavily dependent on advertising revenue for their profitability. A complicating factor for the newspaper industry has been the move of advertising dollars from traditional print products to the Internet. Using this additional information about the newspaper industry, revise the text's illustration to provide a more complex explanation of the factors spurring newspaper innovation over the past decade.

3. While the section discusses the need to balance exploitive and exploratory innovation in a successful organization, do you believe it is possible for an organization to remain profitable by focusing solely on one of these two types of innovation? Why or why not? ●

 **Visit edge.sagepub.com/neckob2e** to help you accomplish your coursework goals in an easy-to-use learning environment.

- Mobile-friendly eFlashcards and practice quizzes
- Video and multimedia content
- Chapter summaries with learning objectives
- EXCLUSIVE! Access to full-text SAGE journal articles

8.1 Identify the primary types of decisions managers make to solve problems

The ability to make decisions and solve problems is a key aspect of organizational behavior. **Programmed decisions** are automatic responses to routine and recurring situations. **Nonprogrammed decisions** address new or nonroutine problems for which there are no proven answers.

The first step in the five-step decision-making model is to define the problem in clear and concise terms. Second, we identify and weigh decision criteria. Next, we generate multiple alternatives to solve the defined problem. The fourth step is to rate the alternatives on the basis of defined decision criteria. Finally, we choose, implement, and evaluate the decision.

8.2 Identify factors that influence the way we make decisions in the real world

Bounded rationality is the idea that we are restricted by a variety of constraints when making decisions. This is in contrast with **complete rationality,** which assumes that we take into account every single criterion or possible alternative to make a decision. **Satisficing decisions** aim for acceptable results rather than for the best or optimal solutions. **Intuition** is an unconscious process of making decisions based on imagination and possibilities.

Heuristics are shortcuts or "rules of thumb" that allow us to make judgments and decisions quickly and efficiently. **Availability heuristics** allow us to base judgments on examples and events that immediately spring to mind. The **anchoring and adjustment heuristic** is a process of basing decisions on the first piece of information we are given without taking other probabilities into account. **Representativeness heuristic** bases a decision on our existing mental prototype and similar stereotypes.

Confirmation bias is the tendency to seek out information that fuels our preexisting views and to discount information that conflicts with our worldview. **Ease-of-recall bias** is the propensity to over-rely on information recollected from memory when making a decision. **Hindsight bias** is the tendency to overestimate the ability to predict an outcome of an event. **Projection bias** is the inclination to believe that other people think, feel, and act the same way we do. **Escalation of commitment** is the increased commitment to a decision despite negative information. **Sunk cost bias** is the decision to continue an investment is based on past investments of time, effort, and/or money. **Framing error** is the tendency to highlight certain aspects of a situation depending on whether they are positive or negative to solve a problem while ignoring other aspects. **Lack of participation error** is the inclination to exclude certain people from the decision-making process. **Randomness error** is the tendency for people to believe they can predict the outcome of chance events based on false information or superstition.

8.3 Discuss the critical nature of creativity and innovation in today's organizations

Creativity is the generation of meaningful ideas by individuals or teams. Innovation is the creation and development of a new product or service. Organizations need to redefine, reinvent, and repurpose brands and products to keep up with market demand. Creativity and innovation are the lifeblood of successful organizations.

8.4 Describe the three-component model of creativity

The three-component model of creativity proposes that creativity depends on the presence of domain-relevant skills and expertise, creativity-relevant processes, and intrinsic task motivation. *Domain-relevant skills and expertise* provide knowledge about the relevant subject and the skills and talent to provide the most creative and productive responses. *Creativity-relevant processes* are work methods dependent on certain personality characteristics, methods of thinking, and knowledge of heuristics. Personality traits such as self-discipline, perseverance, delayed gratification, and independence appear to be associated with creative minds. *Intrinsic task motivation* ensures that people who have an innate interest in a chosen task will be more motivated in producing creative ideas.

People with creative potential tend to possess the skills and capacity to generate ideas. In contrast, practiced creativity allows people who perceive the appropriate opportunities to apply these skills in the workplace. Organizations that do not cultivate an environment for creativity are at a disadvantage because they are neglecting potential resources that could help them operate and compete more effectively.

The three types of support for creativity are organizational, supervisory, and work group. Organizations that provide support for creativity, appropriate rewards and feedback, and encourage a collaborative environment tend to possess a more creative culture. Supervisory support for creativity takes place when supervisors have the ability to communicate, set clear goals, and are confident and protective of their teams. Work group support for creativity takes place when the work group members communicate well, respect each other, are committed to their work, have diverse backgrounds and perspectives, and are willing to help each other out.

In the first step an idea is born out of recognition of a need for a solution and generated from existing information, experience, and knowledge. The second step is to identify any advantages and disadvantages associated with the innovation, explore costs and value, and set goals and priorities. The final stage is the production and distribution of the innovation. It is in this stage that the idea is brought to life.

8.5   Identify the three types of support for creativity

The three types of support for creativity includes **organizational,** which flourishes when employees are provided with autonomy to implement their concepts, **supervisory,** which is successful when employees perceive their supervisor as supportive, and **work group,** in which group members support creativity by establishing certain norms such as collaboration.

8.6   Outline the steps in the innovation process.

Every innovation starts with an idea. **Idea generation** is the first step in innovation, followed by **problem solving,** and then **implementation and diffusion**.

KEY TERMS

UP FOR DEBATE: Compromising Values for Profit

While it is important that a company stay true to its values, at the end of the day you are in business to make money. Compromising on your values may occasionally be necessary to remain in business. Agree or disagree? Explain your answer.

EXERCISE 8.1: Practicing Innovation

Objective

The purpose of this exercise is to gain a greater appreciation of innovation.

Instructions

Innovation is the creation and development of a new product or service. In this exercise, you will be in groups of two to four students. The goal of each group is to practice innovation by developing a new course for college students. This new course will present "life lessons" for students such as how to get a loan, what to look for when you need an attorney, how to pay taxes, how interest works, how to negotiate the price of a car, and so forth.

Your group should go through all three steps in the innovation process in developing this new course for your university:

1. Idea generation

2. Problem solving

3. Implementation and diffusion

For the final step, obviously you won't be able to actually *implement* the new course, but describe *how* you would do so. The instructor will then ask each group to report on what they developed and how.

Reflection Questions

1. How did your group go through each of the three steps in the innovation process? Describe in detail how you approached each step.

2. What challenges did you have in developing this new course? How did you overcome those challenges?

3. Describe one way you could use the innovation process at your current or most recent job.

4. Discuss ways in which the innovation process might be difficult to perform in the workplace? In what circumstances would it be an easy process?

Exercise contributed by Steven Stovall, Southeast Missouri State University.

EXERCISE 8.2: Decision-Making Process Role-Play

Objective

The purpose of this exercise is to grasp the concept of the five-step decision-making process.

Instructions

This exercise looks at the five-step decision-making process and has volunteers from the class role-playing a simple decision-making scenario.

Three students will join the instructor at the front of the class. With the help of the rest of the class, the volunteers will proceed through all five steps of the decision-making process in an attempt to determine what will be had for lunch.

The five steps are:

1. Define the problem

2. Identify and weigh decision criteria

3. Generate multiple alternatives

4. Rate alternatives on the basis of decision criteria

5. Choose, implement, and evaluate the best alternative

As students tackle each step, the audience provides suggestions, questions, and input. In the final step, a selection is made, but it is up to the volunteers whether they want to report back in the following class the evaluation of the decision!

Reflection Questions

1. Though this was a very simple scenario, what challenges presented themselves during the decision-making process? How did the student volunteers overcome those challenges?

2. Think about a scenario at your current or most recent job. Go through the five-step decision-making process about a decision you had to make. Evaluate that decision.

3. Provide three to five examples of when the decision-making process would be utilized in-depth for an important work-related decision. Why are these kinds of situations more involved in the decision-making process versus simple decisions (such as what to eat for lunch)?

Exercise contributed by Steven Stovall, Southeast Missouri State University.

EXERCISE 8.3: Watch Me Get Creative Here

Objective(s)

This exercise will help you to better *understand* the various creativity and innovation concepts presented in this chapter.

Instructions

Step 1. Find a partner and select a concept you want to present to the class.
(1 to 2 minutes)

Step 2. Develop a creative way to present this concept to the class. You will need to present the following elements of the concept:

- An overview of the concept.
- The importance of the concept to organizations.

The presentation needs to be brief (1 to 3 minutes), but it can take any creative form you want. Some examples include writing a short story about the concept, singing a song about the concept, writing a poem about the concept, or performing a short skit demonstrating the concept.

When selecting a concept, you may want to use the major chapter headings as a guideline.
(15 minutes)

Step 3. Present your concept in the selected creative way. (1 to 3 minutes)

Reflection Questions

1. How did the process of having to present a concept in a creative way aid your understanding of the creative process?

2. Which creative presentations of others were most memorable and why?

3. What barriers did you face in developing a creative presentation?

4. How did completing a creative activity increase your confidence about future creative activities?

5. How could organizations use similar exercises to increase overall creativity in the organization?

Exercise contributed by Milton R. Mayfield, Professor of Business, Texas A&M International University, and Jacqueline R. Mayfield, Professor of Business, Texas A&M International University.

ONLINE EXERCISE 8.1: Programmed and Nonprogrammed Decisions Discussion

Objective

The purpose of this exercise is to gain an appreciation for programmed and nonprogrammed decisions.

Instructions

There are two types of decisions: programmed and nonprogrammed decisions. A programmed decision is one that is an automatic response to routine and recurring situations. Nonprogrammed decisions, on the other hand, are for new or nonroutine problems for which there are no proven answers. An example of a programmed decision would be what to wear to work, while a nonprogrammed decision might be whether or not you should look for another job.

On a discussion board, provide five programmed decisions you have made in the last week. Comment on others' posts about how similar or common their programmed decisions have been. Then, post five nonprogrammed decisions you have made in your lifetime or will need to make in the coming years. Again, engage in a dialogue with other students about how their nonprogrammed decisions are like your own or how they are very different.

Reflection Questions

1. How easy was it to develop your list of programmed decisions versus nonprogrammed ones? Explain.

2. In your current or most recent job, what programmed decisions do you make? Nonprogrammed decisions?

3. What has been your most difficult nonprogrammed decision to make at this point in your life? Why was it so difficult? How did you ultimately make the decision?

CASE STUDY 8.1: McDonald's Decision Making and Innovation

McDonald's is home to far more than a good deal on a Big Mac, and the corporation engages in many effective practices, especially in the realm of decision making and innovation. Created as one location in 1940 and turned into a corporate chain in 1955, McDonald's has been through some significant change, while at the same time holding on to its core offerings. They are a unique company: There are about 37,000 locations worldwide, and only about 3,000 are owned by the corporation—the rest are franchised to others who pay a start-up cost and yearly franchise fees. The chapter speaks about programmed decisions and nonprogrammed ones; these are both common at a company that must somehow manage the practices of 34,000 locations that they don't physically own. To operate a consistent business, McDonald's must figure out how to program as many decisions as possible across the fleet, but at the same time each and every location presents its own financial, supply chain, hiring and sales challenges, and each location must have leaders who use nonprogrammed decisions to solve them and provide a desirable offering to local customers.

Managing 37,000 Businesses

Managing a business is difficult. You always have to meet your minimum sales numbers to keep your doors open, but to get to that point there are often dozens of problems that must be solved and decisions that must be made. For McDonald's, that applies to 37,000 storefronts. Corporate McDonald's has a solution for this, which they call their Operations Management unit. According to the Panmore Institute, "McDonald's Corporation's operations management (OM) supports the company's position as the largest fast food restaurant chain in the world. The ten decisions of operations management represent the various strategic areas of operations that must be coordinated for optimal productivity and performance."

The text explains the fundamental process behind decision making: Define the problem, look at decision criteria to create alternatives, and then select the best option available. McDonald's goes through this process in each of their ten primary Operations Management areas. For example, McDonald's describes the founder, Ray Kroc, and his vision: "Ray Kroc wanted to build a restaurant system that would be famous for providing food of consistently high quality and uniform methods of preparation. He wanted to serve burgers, fries and beverages that tasted just the same in Alaska as they did in Alabama. To achieve this, he chose a unique path: persuading both franchisees and suppliers to buy into his vision, working not *for* McDonald's but *for* themselves, together *with* McDonald's. He promoted the slogan, 'In business for yourself, but not by yourself.'" This is a nearly insurmountable goal, but retailers today have made it look easy. To approach this goal, with the problems defined, McDonald's made a firm decision on quality management: They would provide the best food they could, as long as it was reasonably priced and could be duplicated everywhere using the same production line at every location. After considering alternatives, like letting franchisors figure out production on their own or changing the nature of the business, the leadership at McDonald's picked their current strategy and committed to it. Implementing this decision has not been easy, and the team at corporate McDonald's and the leaders at all 37,000 locations have to continually work together to do so.

Quality

A common decision-making problem in the business world is that managers do not know precisely what they want. Either they become obsessed with too many goals and ideas at once and exhaust their resources, or they cannot commit to anything consistently. McDonald's and its founder Ray made sure to avoid this tendency from the very beginning. Kroc famously said this, "If I had a brick for every time I've repeated the phrase *Quality, Service, Cleanliness and Value*, I think I'd probably be able to bridge the Atlantic Ocean with them." It seems simple: Four goals, repeated so many times that they become an echo in the corporation. Saying them just once would never be enough—another franchise is always around the corner, or a longstanding location may hit a rough patch, and managers must find a way to implement the four goals time and time again.

By defining your mission, you can make the decisions necessary to support it. While it is not easy to keep track of the quality in 37,000 restaurants, managers from the top down at McDonald's all agree on their primary focus. The decisions that go into maintaining the chain will never be simple, and they will never be uniform, but they can always be directed toward the goal: *Quality, Service, Cleanliness,* and *Value*. With the end in mind, a manager can gather the right people, the right resources, and execute a plan. To the customer, McDonald's seems as basic as it gets—but it takes an immeasurable amount of hard work from the start and each coming day to make it seem that way. If the burger was different every day, the coffee cold one morning and hot the next, the booths messy one evening and clean the next, no customer would trust the brand. The person making the food and the person running the entire corporation must be on the same page, and they have to trust one another's decisions.

Next time you visit a McDonald's, ask yourself: How is the quality, service, cleanliness, and value for my dollar? If they are up to par, try to imagine the decade's worth of specialization and decision making—some good, some bad—that went into creating the restaurant in which you sit. If they are lacking in one of those four departments, try to figure out why. It could have been a mistaken decision that an employee made five minutes ago, or it could have been an organizational mistake that a regional manager made months ago. Regardless of which scenario you find, your experience will be dependent on the ability of McDonald's employees to think critically about problems and solve them adequately.

Critical-Thinking Questions

1. Why is McDonald's uniquely challenged when it comes to decision making?

2. What department at corporate McDonald's is in charge of making strategic decisions, and how many areas of focus does it have?

3. What are Ray Kroc's four original goals, and why are they still useful today?

What Is My Decision-Making Preference?

This assessment will help you to determine the extent to which you tend to be rational, satisficing, or intuitive in your decision-making processes.

For each statement, circle the number that best describes how you would approach a decision of average importance based on the following scale:

	NOT AT ALL ACCURATE	SOMEWHAT ACCURATE	A LITTLE ACCURATE	MOSTLY ACCURATE	COMPLETELY ACCURATE
1. I tend to establish specific criteria before I make a decision.	1	2	3	4	5
2. I tend to select the first option I find that meets my needs.	1	2	3	4	5
3. I tend to trust my instincts when making decisions.	1	2	3	4	5
4. I generally consider a significant number of possible alternatives before I decide on the best course of action.	1	2	3	4	5
5. I generally select a course of action that meets most of my needs, rather than searching for an "optimum" solution.	1	2	3	4	5
6. I am more likely to follow a given course of action if it "feels right" to me.	1	2	3	4	5
7. I always take the time to clearly identify the situation and/or problem I am facing before I decide how to handle it.	1	2	3	4	5
8. When working in a group, I tend to look toward a solution everyone can agree on even if it may not be the best.	1	2	3	4	5
9. If I were faced with a life and death situation, I would trust my immediate reactions on how to respond.	1	2	3	4	5

Scoring

Preference for Rational Decision Making

Total for items 1, 4, and 7 _____

Preference for Satisficing Decision Making

Total for items 2, 5, and 8 _____

Preference for Intuitive Decision Making

Total for items 3, 6, and 9 _____

What was your strongest decision-making preference?

What are some of the strengths and weaknesses to this approach?

Under what circumstances might if be beneficial for you to attempt to incorporate more of your weakest decision-making preference?

SELF-ASSESSMENT 8.2

Creative Potential versus Practiced Creativity

Creative potential refers to the creative capacity, skills, and abilities a person possesses. In contrast, practiced creativity is the ability to take opportunities to use creativity skills and abilities. The following assessment will help you to determine both your creative potential and the extent to which you have the opportunity to practice creativity in your work or school situation.

For each statement, circle the number that best describes how you would approach a decision of average importance based on the following scale:

	STRONGLY DISAGREE	DISAGREE	NEITHER AGREE NOR DISAGREE	AGREE	STRONGLY AGREE
1. I am good at generating novel and original ideas.	1	2	3	4	5
2. I have the ability to use my creativity to solve problems.	1	2	3	4	5
3. I have a talent for helping to further develop the creative ideas of others.	1	2	3	4	5
4. I am able to find creative ways to solve problems.	1	2	3	4	5
5. I have the talent and skills to do well in my work.	1	2	3	4	5
6. I feel comfortable trying out new ideas.	1	2	3	4	5
7. I have opportunities to use my creative skills and abilities at work or school.	1	2	3	4	5
8. I am invited to submit ideas for improvements in the workplace or in the classroom.	1	2	3	4	5
9. I have the opportunity to participate on team(s) at work or at school.	1	2	3	4	5
10. I have the freedom to decide how my job tasks or school work get done.	1	2	3	4	5
11. My creative abilities are used to my full potential at work or at school.	1	2	3	4	5
12. I have opportunities to put my creative ideas into practice at work or at school.	1	2	3	4	5

Scoring

Creative Potential

Total for items 1–6 _____

Practiced Creativity

Total for items 7–12 _____

Was your score higher for creative potential than for practiced creativity? If so, this gap could indicate that you are not able to fully tap into your creative potential at work or at school.

What are some ways in which you might be able to increase the opportunities to apply your creative potential at work or at school?

Source: Adapted from DiLiello, T. C., Houghton, J. D. "Creative Potential and Practiced Creativity: Identifying Untapped Creativity in Organizations." *Creativity and Innovation Management* 17 (2008): 37–46.

Chris Coduto/Icon Sportswire/Corbis via Getty Images

9

Ethics and Social Responsibility in Organizations

We have got to change our ethics and our financial system and our whole way of understanding the world. It has to be a world in which people live rather than die; a sustainable world. It could be great.

—Vivienne Westwood, British fashion designer

Learning Objectives

By the end of this chapter, you will be able to:

9.1 Defend the importance of ethics in organizations and effectively evaluate and resolve ethical dilemmas

9.2 Compare and contrast various approaches to ethical decision making

9.3 Differentiate between the challenges of ethical leadership and ethical followership

9.4 Describe the primary approaches to social responsibility in organizations

9.5 Identify the components of an ethical culture

CASE STUDY: IBM'S ETHICAL SUPPLY CHAINS

For a long time now, high-flying tech start-ups have offered the best employment perks in business. Encouraging employees to work more effectively and sustain a happier lifestyle while doing it. While it may seem like a concept that started at the dawn of the tech bubble in the nineties, this type of organizational culture was actually the brainchild of Thomas J. Watson Sr. of IBM from the early years of the 20th century. He is pegged as the source of extravagant organizational culture as we know them today, creating IBM's own symphony, giving employees country club memberships, and even creating a songbook for IBM employees. At the same time, high-benefits corporations like IBM have a duty to ensure that employees are rewarded fairly and incentives are healthy. The result of this strong organizational culture is a company that is devoted to continually showing themselves to be the gold standard of ethical business practices.

To really understand how this can be, it is necessary to investigate the beginning of IBM and the beginning of Thomas Watson. In 1914, a man was confronted with a company that had recently been formed after the merging of three smaller firms that were geographically separated from each other. He understood that it was his primary task to integrate the three small firms operationally and organizationally toward a common initiative. By many, he is credited as the first business leader to consciously create a common organizational culture for a company. This was Thomas Watson and the company he helped form was the Computing-Tabulating-Recording Company (CTR), which became what we know today as IBM. The culture that Watson hoped to create for a company that was split between Washington DC, New York, and Ohio was one that pressed innovation and outside-the-box thinking. He made the company motto "THINK" for a company that made devices that helped people work faster and more precisely. Watson knew the limitless potential of these types of machines and also knew the value of the people who could create and sell them. Encouraging each employee to be a thinker was what would knit his newly formed organization together. Over the years after this initiative, the newly renamed International Business Machines or "IBM" developed a set of guidelines that would be the basis for their organizational culture. IBM called these "Basic Beliefs" and they were "Respect for the individual, the best customer service in the world, and Excellence."

Today, IBM is one of thirty companies included in the Dow Jones Industrial Average, and it employs nearly 380,000 people worldwide, and it spends over $3 billion a year just supplying its production. IBM employees have been awarded five Nobel Prizes, Six Turing Awards, and ten National Medals of Technology. With yearly revenues of $80 billion in 2016, it is hard to believe that even Watson could have predicted where his "THINK" motto would get them. As all successful large companies do, IBM consistently finds ways to maintain an ethical work environment for employees, and ethical relationships with suppliers, partners, investors, and all other market participants. According to their own corporate reports, one of the most useful tools in this pursuit has been communication. It is important that employees are trustworthy, that they trust each other, and that all those involved with the company give and receive respect. In order to monitor these character traits, IBM is in full communication at all times with all members of their business. Employees, partners, and suppliers always have a contact point within the company, so that everyone can report problems and expectations can be clear.

IBM, for all its size and strength, however, has had its fair share of hills and valleys leading up to today. For much of the 20th century, IBM had a firm grasp on the business of corporate computing. This changed abruptly when the semiconductor ushered in a new era of personal computing and IBM lost market share to the likes of Microsoft and Apple. IBM didn't stay at the leading edge of technology and allowed themselves to just follow along with the market. They lost their purpose and stopped developing new technologies of great significance, leading to their decline as the new millennium arrived.

IBM stopped innovating and the technology giant lost market share in an industry it helped build. From the 1950s to the 1980s, under Thomas Watson, IBM produced everything from the original computer languages to ATMs and even supermarket checkouts. IBM was a dominant force and, in 1990, the company was the second most profitable enterprise in the world. By 1991, earnings had dropped to -$2.8 billion and dropped 60 percent for the next two years. By 1993, a newly appointed CEO decided that the company needed to reintegrate all of their systems together and become "One IBM" saying, "[We had to change] the view that IBM was a group of fiefdoms. We needed to have a sense that we were going to operate as a team, as a global entity." After over 80 years of doing business, the new CEO of IBM, Louis Gerstner, embarked on the same initiative that Thomas Watson had in 1914, to create an integrated company using corporate culture.

By the end of 1994, profits had risen to $5 billion and, by 2000, IBM Global Services had become the world's largest IT consulting and web services organization. IBM had clawed its way back to the top through the same practices that had put them there. IBM after 1994 was much leaner and much more devoted to its mission and to making itself a leader in its industry.

Since then IBM has become the gold standard of sustainable business practices with one of the most ethically focused supply chains of any business and a culture motivated toward focusing on making a difference in places that need it. Now that they are so firmly rooted as a technology giant, they have an additional duty to promote ethical markets in ways that only become apparent upon critical thinking. Specifically, IBM purchases billions of dollars of supplies annually, and has "more than 30,000 supplier locations spread out over more than 60 countries." This means that they have massive bargaining power in many companies and around the globe, including places where products can be sourced through unethical forms of labor. IBM puts out a report each year about its effort to ensure its suppliers are being socially responsible.

Current management says this about ethics, "Expectations and legislation are increasing, such as the growing concerns about conflict minerals, anti-slavery and human trafficking, and other important social responsibility issues." So ethical concerns in today's business world affect all companies, and they have a social and legal responsibility to make money in the right way. IBM has taken the various sections of their business and united them behind a common initiative to be the guiding light of ethical practices to other large cap technology giants. Due in part to this reintegration, IBM has climbed its way back to the top and prepared itself for another successful one hundred years.

Critical-Thinking Questions

1. What was Thomas Watson's initial dilemma in uniting the Computing-Tabulating-Recording Company?

2. Why did IBM stagnate in the early '90s?

3. What is one tool that IBM uses to monitor the ethical decisions across their company and supplies?

4. What makes IBM very influential in the market regarding ethical supply chains?

Resources:

Braswell, S. (2014). From IBM to Google, the birth of company culture. *USA Today.* Retrieved from https://www.usatoday.com/story/money/business/2014/11/22/ozy-ibm-google-company-culture/19345427/

IBM. (n.d.). *Corporate responsibility at IBM.* Retrieved from https://www.ibm.com/ibm/responsibility/supplychain.shtml

IBM. (n.d.). *Supply chain social responsibility.* Retrieved from http://www-03.ibm.com/procurement/proweb.nsf/contentdocsbytitle/United+States~Supply+chain+social+responsibility

IBM Archives (n.d.). *A culture of think.* Retrieved from http://www-03.ibm.com/ibm/history/ibm100/us/en/icons/think_culture/

King, R. (2011). IBM: Corporate culture stands in way of enterprise analytics adoption. *ZDNet.* Retrieved from http://www.zdnet.com/article/ibm-corporate-culture-stands-in-way-of-enterprise-analytics-adoption/

Sellers, P. (2011). IBM exec: Culture is your company's No. 1 asset. *Fortune.com.* Retrieved from http://fortune.com/2011/03/10/ibm-exec-culture-is-your-companys-no-1-asset/

Weller, C. (2017). IBM was a pioneer in the work-from-home revolution — now it's cracking down. *Business Insider.* Retrieved from http://www.businessinsider.com/ibm-slashes-work-from-home-policy-2017-5

Ethics in Organizations

>> LO 9.1 **Defend the importance of ethics in organizations and effectively evaluate and resolve ethical dilemmas**

IBM sets the gold standard for business practices through its firm commitment to ethics which is applied to the culture of its organization as well as to its external partners, such as suppliers, to ensure social responsibility. **Ethics** are moral principles of duty and virtue that prescribe how we should behave.[1] We often hear that businesspeople must be ruthless, willing to stab people in the back as they climb up the ladder of success. What place do ethics have in business decision making? Should we even study ethics in a business class? There are at least two good reasons to study ethics: firstly for reasons of virtue meaning it's the right thing to do. Most people have learned values and developed character that steer them toward making the right ethical decisions over the wrong ones.

SAGE edge™

Master the content
**edge.sagepub.com/
neckob2e**

Ethics: Moral principles that guide our behavior

Secondly, for reasons of prudence, meaning it's the smart thing to do. Even for people who don't care about doing the right thing, often making ethical decisions tends to be in their own self-interest. People who cheat, lie, cut corners, and break trust rarely end up as successful in the long run when they caught out by others. Overall, good things tend to happen to companies and individuals that consistently do the right thing, while bad things tend to happen to companies and individuals that even occasionally do the wrong thing.

More than a decade ago, the unethical behavior of some major US-based organizations hit the headlines worldwide. One of the most infamous cases brought about the fall of energy giant Enron. In 2001, it was discovered that Enron's CEO Kenneth Lay had used unethical accounting practices and led his team to commit one of the largest corporate frauds in US history.[2] One of the biggest corporate casualties of the Enron scandal was the company's auditors, the accounting and consultancy firm Arthur Anderson, which until then had enjoyed a sterling reputation. Because of the unethical choices made by a few members of the Enron team, such as the decision to destroy evidence of wrongdoing, the company was eventually dissolved.

More recently, Wells Fargo came under fire for creating fake bank accounts under the names of real customers, pharmaceutical giant Mylan created an ethical scandal by raising the price of its EpiPen (a life-saving medication used to treat very serious allergic reactions), and plant-based food startup Hampton Creek was accused of buying vast quantities of its own products from retailers in order to inflate its sales numbers.[3]

Company scandals have also made many people more aware and less tolerant of perceived unethical behavior. For example, footwear company Skechers was fined $40 million for falsely claiming that its Shape-Ups shoes would tone legs and help burn calories.[4]

As the Enron, Skechers, and other scandals prove, making unethical decisions can have huge consequences. Yet it is not only enormous organizations that deal with ethical problems. Breaches of ethics happen all over the world; in many countries corruption is

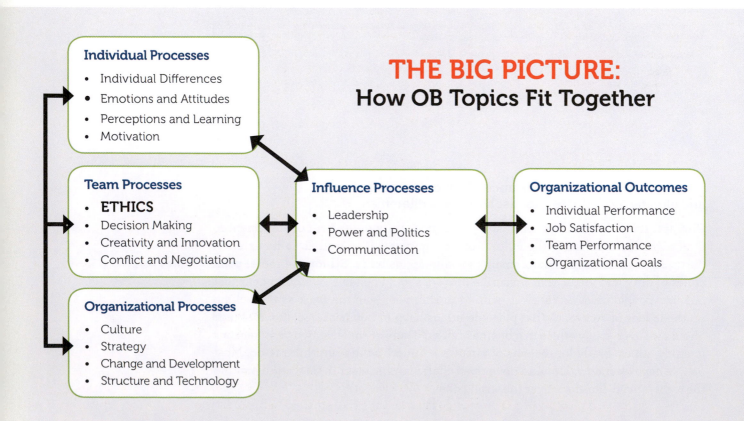

Individual Processes
- Individual Differences
- Emotions and Attitudes
- Perceptions and Learning
- Motivation

THE BIG PICTURE:
How OB Topics Fit Together

Team Processes
- **ETHICS**
- Decision Making
- Creativity and Innovation
- Conflict and Negotiation

Influence Processes
- Leadership
- Power and Politics
- Communication

Organizational Outcomes
- Individual Performance
- Job Satisfaction
- Team Performance
- Organizational Goals

Organizational Processes
- Culture
- Strategy
- Change and Development
- Structure and Technology

prevalent, and instances of bribery to win business are commonplace. Similarly, some organizations exploit labor by hiring children, paying very low wages, and forcing employees to work in poor conditions. An organization is unethical if it violates the basic rights of its employees and ignores health, safety, and environmental standards.

One of the more recent ethical debates springs from the rapid development of artificial intelligence (AI) technology. With enhanced speech recognition available, robot dogs in development, "killer robots," and solar-powered drones and self-driving cars on the horizon, the risks associated with AI have quickly come to the fore. Tesla Motors founder Elon Musk

Tim Sloan, president and CEO of Wells Fargo, speaks during a Bloomberg Interview about the company's fallout from the fake-accounts scandal that occurred in 2017.

and the noted physicist Stephen Hawking are among those who have expressed concern about the ethical consequences of advanced technology.[5] Still to be answered are questions about the danger of building robots for military use, the safety of self-driving cars, the possibility that jobs will be lost to drones and robots, and the general risk of creating software designed to help computers think like humans. Google, owner of several robotics companies, has set up an ethics board to ensure that AI technology is not exploited.

However, Google is not the only company conscious of ethical risks. In many organizations, employees attend training programs, workshops, and seminars that present ethical dilemmas and how to overcome them. In most workplaces, there is a growing intolerance for unethical behavior, and there is an expectation that employees will align their work practices with the organization's code of ethics.

Indeed, such is the demand for a better understanding of ethical organizational behavior that many business schools, including the Catholic University of America, have integrated ethics into their business and economics courses on a daily basis to teach students the importance of behaving ethically in the workplace.[6]

TOMS Shoes, founded by entrepreneur Blake Mycoskie in 2006, is a good example of a company that prides itself on its ethics. Thanks to its "give away one pair of shoes for every pair sold" scheme, over 60 million pairs of shoes have been given away over the last 10 years.[7]

Although ethics are useful in helping us make decisions and come to certain conclusions, they don't always give a clear answer to every moral question. For example, complex issues such as abortion and euthanasia have been the subject of strong debate over many years, yet people do not agree on a "right" or "wrong" moral answer to these issues. By following a code of ethics, however, we can make many decisions based on sound guiding principles.

Ethical Dilemmas

In Chapter 1, we introduced ethics and showed how it can be useful in helping us make decisions in cases where there may not be easy answers. We described bad ethical decisions in organizational settings may result in harm to employees as well as lost profits, bankruptcy, and litigation. Because of these instances, many of today's organizations have committed to fostering an ethical culture and improving ethical behavior in the workplace by providing employee training programs, workshops, and

Ethical dilemma: A conflict between two or more morally unpleasant alternatives

seminars on dealing with ethical dilemmas. Individuals and companies frequently face large and small **ethical dilemmas**, or conflicts between two or more morally unpleasant alternatives.[8] Ethical dilemmas represent difficult ethical decisions.

Scott Gerber, CEO of hospitality industry leader Gerber Group, faced an ethical dilemma when he discovered that an employee was clocking in his wife three hours before she turned up to work. Although Gerber immediately fired the employee, he ended up having a change of heart when the employee's father (a long-term Gerber loyal employee) approached Gerber to beg that he give his son another chance. Gerber made the decision to take the employee back based on that employee's father's loyalty to the company, but it wasn't an easy decision to make:

"[We] made the decision to [rehire] him," says Gerber. "The decision was extremely difficult because we caught him technically stealing from the company, and we generally have a zero-tolerance policy for such behavior. But because his father has worked for us for over 20 years, and vouched that his son would never do this again, we decided to give him another chance."[9]

Many decisions include some sort of ethical choice. For instance, what would you do if you saw a good friend in your class cheating on an exam? It's tough to know the right decisions to make in certain circumstances. This is where ethical decision making can be useful in guiding us to do the right thing.

The cheating example mentioned earlier represents an ethical dilemma. You could tell the professor you witnessed the student cheating, but then you might feel guilty for betraying a friend. However, you could keep quiet, but you might feel bad allowing the cheater to gain an unfair advantage over you and the rest of the students in the class. So how do you make the right choice?

The key to being an ethical person or organization is to *consistently* choose to do the right thing. Most people have strong values and the character to make morally correct decisions, and even people who are immoral can be sensible enough to know that cheating, lying, and breaking trust will not help them get very far in the workplace in the long term.

TOMS founder Blake Mycoskie and TOMS employees took off their shoes for TOMS' annual One Day Without Shoes event to raise awareness about children's health and education.

THINKING CRITICALLY

1. Analyze the relationship between ethics and technology. How might technology lead to unethical behavior? How might technology help businesses develop more ethical and transparent business practices?

2. Recall a recent news story related to unethical behavior by a company. What were the effects of the ethical breach in terms of their reputation and profitability?

3. Write a mission statement or list of rules that sums up what "consistently doing what's right" means to you.

Ethical Decision Making

>> **LO 9.2** **Compare and contrast various approaches to ethical decision making**

Organizations often face ethical dilemmas in which they have to choose a certain course of action. There are three classical ethical decision-making approaches: utilitarian approach, rights approach, and justice approach.

The **utilitarian approach** focuses on taking action that results in the greater good for the majority of people.[10] For example, an organization that is struggling financially may choose to outsource some of its operations more cheaply overseas in order to stay in business and retain its US workforce.

The **rights approach** fosters decisions made on moral principles that infringe as little as possible on the entitlements of others.[11] For example, a business owner might believe it is morally wrong to pay overseas workers low wages and decide to close down his US-based company rather than betray his principles.

The **justice approach** advocates basing decisions on fairness.[12] For example, a struggling organization might choose to turn down the best candidate for CEO if that person expected compensation that wasn't in line with the company's fairness-based compensation structure.

There are no easy answers to most ethical decisions. The organization that saves its domestic workforce by outsourcing some functions to inexpensive labor overseas may discover that the overseas workers don't receive a fair wage or work in unsafe conditions. Similarly, the business owner who refuses to hire inexpensive labor because of ethical concerns will nevertheless lose his company and leave his current employees jobless. A struggling organization may choose a less-qualified candidate who is willing to accept their compensation structure, but to what extent is justice served if they are failing to hire the best-qualified candidate who is more likely to save the business?

Utilitarian approach: Action that results in the greater good for the majority of people

Rights approach: A decision-making method based on using moral principles that least infringe on the entitlements of others

Justice approach: A way to base decisions on the basis of the fairness

Contemporary Views of Ethical Decision Making

Lynn Paine, ethics professor at Harvard, proposed a four-part "moral compass" to help managers make ethical decisions.[13] This involves factoring ethical considerations into every single part of organizational decisions. There are four types of lenses through which managers can explore the moral dimensions of their own decisions.

Lens 1: Is this action worthwhile?

This first lens explores the end results of the action. Does it serve a worthy purpose? Will it have an ethically successful outcome? To answer these questions, managers need to gather data and arm themselves with as much information as possible to reach the right conclusion.

Lens 2: Does this action comply with company principles?

Most companies have a set of ethical standards, code of conduct, business norms, and values and ideals. Each action must be in line with the company's ethical standards.

Lens 3: What impact does this action have on others?

This involves analyzing how other people, such as stakeholders, may be affected by the decision. Learning about their different perspectives, how they might feel about the action, and preparing compensation if necessary are all important ways to research the decision before it is made.

Lens 4: Had this action been approved by the right authority?

There is little point in exploring the first three lenses unless the action has been signed off by the relevant authority (such as a senior manager, or CEO). It is also essential to check that the organization itself has the right to take this action, as well as the necessary resources.

The consequences of organizations making immoral decisions can be devastating. For example, in 2017, credit reporting agency Equifax waited over three months before publicly divulging that hackers had gained access to personal information, such as driver's license and social security numbers, stored in 143 million customer accounts.[14] Equifax has been criticized for sitting on the information, with some believing that it should have announced the breach when it first happened, and focus on telling customers how to safeguard their data. Worse still, the website that was eventually set up to respond to customers' questions was beset by more vulnerabilities. As well as suffering a loss in credibility, Equifax may also face some serious legal consequences for failing to protect so many of its customers' private information.

The Foursquare Protocol is another contemporary ethical decision-making approach proposed by Catholic University law professor Stephen Goldman.[15] Like the moral compass, this approach focuses on reaching the right ethical conclusions.

Protocol Element 1: Gathering all the facts

Information is key to making the right ethical decisions. Goldman equates this first step to a doctor diagnosing a patient. In the same way a doctor will gather information about a patient's symptoms, managers must follow the same process in order to identify relevant facts.

Protocol Element 2: Reflecting on past experiences

Just as doctors use past experience to treat patients, managers should follow the same process. How did the organization react to a similar case in the past? What was the outcome? How did other managers deal with the situation? How certain situations were handled at the time will influence the ethical culture going forward. For example, if sexual harassment has been tolerated in the past, it is likely there will be more cases in the future.

Protocol Element 3: Identifying the differences between the present and the past

It is important for managers to compare the similarities and differences between different cases in the past in order to come to a fair conclusion in the present. Just because one case was handled in a particular way before doesn't mean the same approach automatically follows for a similar case.

Protocol Element 4: Analyzing the situation

Once all the information has been gathered, three factors must be taken into consideration in order to reach the most ethical decision. Firstly, do you have any self-interest that might compromise your judgment? For example, you may turn a blind eye to your top salesperson's tendency to accept corporate gifts (although this goes against company policies) because his sales contribute to your annual bonus. Secondly, consider how you would feel if you were on the receiving end of the decision being made. For example, if your decision involves layoffs, think about how you would feel if you were to be laid off. Third, listen to your own moral instincts, and ask yourself some honest questions. Is the right thing to do to overlook a high performer's missteps? Or lay off people who have been with the company the longest?

Once all the steps of the Foursquare Protocol have been completed, you will have a much better chance of making the right ethical decision.

FIGURE 9.1

Levels of Moral Reasoning

- Preconventional—moral reasoning is based on external rewards and punishments
- Conventional—laws and rules are upheld simply because they are laws and rules
- Postconventional—reasoning based on personal moral standards

How Individuals Make Ethical Decisions

Most of the decisions we make, we make as individuals. According to American psychologist Lawrence Kohlberg, we go through several stages of moral development which influence our decision-making—an adaptation of a theory originally introduced by Swiss psychologist Jean Piaget.[16] To illustrate these stages, Kohlberg carried out a famous experiment using a storytelling technique. One of the stories involved a man called Heinz whose wife was dying of cancer. Heinz found a local chemist who claimed he had a cure, but the chemist has priced the drug too far out of Heinz's reach. In desperation, Heinz borrowed enough money to pay half the price, promising the chemist he would pay the rest at a later date. The chemist refused. That night, Heinz broke into the chemist's and stole the drug.

Kohlberg used this story to monitor how moral reasoning changed from childhood to adulthood, interviewing a total of seventy-two boys from Chicago whose ages ranged between 10 and 16 years, fifty-eight of whom he followed up for the next twenty years.[17] The results of these interviews formed the basis of Kohlberg's theory.

There are three main stages of moral development: preconventional morality, conventional morality, and postconventional morality (see Figure 9.1).[18]

1. Preconventional morality

This stage applies to very young children whose morality tends to be based on obedience, self-protection, and self-interest. For instance, Heinz should never steal because stealing is wrong and against the rules.

2. Conventional morality

During the second stage (adolescence and early adulthood) moral decisions are based on standards set by adult role models and societal norms. Those people who abide by these conventions are more likely to be accepted by society than those who do not. For instance, Heinz was right to steal the medicine to save his wife, or he was wrong because he was breaking the law which is against societal norms.

3. Postconventional morality

In the final stage of moral development (mature adults), individual judgment is based on a chosen belief system, which shapes moral views. In the Heinz example, people may consider the human rights side of the issue such as the wife's right to the drug because there is a higher value on human life than money. Equally, it could be argued that Heinz had no right to steal the drug as his wife's life was no more precious than anyone else in the same position.

While Kohlberg's theory has given us a greater understanding of morality, the Heinz experiment in particular has been called into question. For instance, the story is clearly fictional, leading some experts to question if a group of boys aged between 10 and 16, who have never experienced marriage or indeed ever been in a similar position, should have been involved in this sort of process.

Secondly, Kohlberg's theory has been criticized for gender bias, given it is based on an all-male assessment, which neglects to take into account women's views of morality.

Finally, the Heinz dilemma is hypothetical and the boys' responses may not accurately reflect the decisions they would make if they were confronted with the same predicament in real life.

Despite the challenges of ethical decision making, having a clear ethical code that guides your actions will make it easier to choose the most appropriate path.

The Josephson Institute was founded in 1987 with a mission to change personal and organizational decision making and improve ethics and character development in society.[19] CHARACTER COUNTS! is a program established by the institute to promote and teach the Six Pillars of Character it believes define ethical behavior.[20] Today, this program is the most widely used approach to character education in the United States, reaching millions of young people through thousands of affiliated schools, agencies, and organizations.[21] Both Democratic and Republican presidential administrations have proclaimed the third week of October as CHARACTER COUNTS! Week, while a bipartisan group of US senators form the congressional CHARACTER COUNTS! Working Group.[22] In addition, dozens of mayors and governors have endorsed the CHARACTER COUNTS! framework and programming in their communities.[23]

The Six Pillars of Character are not based on political, religious, or cultural leanings in making ethical decisions. The Six Pillars are:[24]

> *Trustworthiness*. Be trustworthy and willing to build trust with others. Honesty, sincerity, and loyalty are core qualities necessary for ethical behavior.
>
> *Respect*. Treat others with courtesy, appreciation, and tolerance. Avoid judging others and using aggressive language.
>
> *Responsibility*. Work hard, and be conscious of the way you behave and communicate toward others. Practice self-awareness and always strive toward self-improvement.
>
> *Fairness*. Be impartial and make decisions based on sound knowledge. Follow the rules but question injustices when they arise.
>
> *Caring*. Exercise forgiveness, compassion, gratitude, and kindness in relationships with others.
>
> *Citizenship*. Be sure to vote and play your part in improving the lives of the people in your community. Be kind to the environment and make time to volunteer in social enterprises.

The Six Pillars of Character offer a framework of commonly held ethical values that may be useful in discussing ethical issues and making ethical decisions in the workplace. Josephson suggests the following process for making ethical decisions:[25] First, take into account the interest and well-being of all stakeholders. Next, put the core ethical values (the Six Pillars) above all other values. For example, a person may value money, success, or winning, but these values should not be put above core values such as integrity, courtesy, or kindness. Finally, this approach suggests that if you must violate one core value in order to honor another, do what you believe will provide the greatest amount of good in the long run (apply the utilitarian approach). Take a look at how Sam Heiler, plant manager of manufacturing company JMW Truss, applies some of the Six Pillars when setting ethical standards for his employees.

It is rare that the core values in the Six Pillars will conflict with one another, but it is possible, for example, that honesty might conflict with kindness and compassion; for example, if any employee asks for feedback from their boss on a new idea, the boss does not want to stifle the employee's creativity in the long run and may suggest to the employee that the idea is okay when in fact it is not.

THINKING CRITICALLY

1. Consider the strengths and weaknesses of each of the three ethical decision-making approaches (utilitarian, rights, and justice). Is one of the three more appealing to you than the other two? Why or why not?

2. Compare the moral compass and the Foursquare Protocol. How are they similar? How do they differ? Do you think one approach is better toward helping you make an ethical decision? Why or why not?

3. Fast rewind to an ethical dilemma you faced in the past. Pretend you had to make the decision over again and apply both the moral compass and Foursquare decision approaches to the situation. Did both approaches result in you making the same decision? Explain.

OB IN THE REAL WORLD

Sam Heiler, Plant Manager, JMW Truss

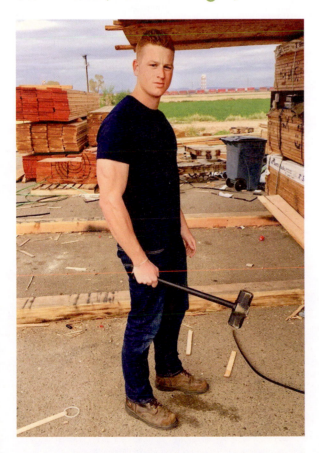

JMW Truss is a plant in sweltering, sunny Yuma, Arizona, where the summer temperatures exceed 110 degrees. Manufacturing mainly trusses and wall panels, JMW provides finished product for a large portion of the multifamily housing development market in Southern California. Southern California is the largest market in the world for this type of framing development, and JMW is the largest framing provider in this market. The work at the plant is laborious, and they have a constant demand to fill orders—this environment calls for constant creativity in production, employee management, and customer management. Perhaps more importantly, through growth and hard work, the company must maintain ethical standards.

The plant manager, Arizona State University graduate Sam Heiler, joined the team in May of 2016, then as an assistant plant manager coming out of school with a finance degree—not exactly a typical career route. He says the day he showed up, "I didn't have a clue what I was doing in Yuma. I didn't feel I was serving any real purpose." But that all began to change for him when he started thinking critically about how to improve the success of the plant, and thereby improve the success of the company. The first thing he noticed after becoming accustomed to the fast-paced and grueling work at the plant was that there seemed to be a shortage of well-trained employees. The high demand

(Continued)

(Continued)

often kept the plant running past normal work hours, so JMW Truss had to compensate with heavy overtime pay for many of the employees.

For a while, the crew rather enjoyed working 10-hour days plus Saturdays, as they were making plenty of money putting in all the extra work. But after a month of this, it became physically and mentally taxing for employees, many of whom travel long distances to get to work, to continue operating at this level. Sam felt that a work environment as difficult as this can be unethical to his workers, so he defined the problem by speaking with the employees and with the other managers about the current workload. Sam decided that he could use a utilitarian and rights approach to ethics, where he benefits as many members of the organization as possible while treating individuals as they deserve to be treated. In order to make things easier on the employees, the plant, and the financials, Sam proposed and implemented a second shift, with an entire new set of floor workers, with all but a few of them having no experience on how to manufacture their products. This new influx of workers allowed for an ethical work environment, where employees were working hours suited to their needs and Sam and his team could feel good about requiring hard work from themselves and their crew. This approach solidified an important pillar of character among members of the plant: responsibility. The plant now comes with responsibility to work hard.

The effects were immediate. Sam says, "JMW pays less overtime than they had to before, more employees benefit from having a steady and reliable job, and shifts with rested workers produce more finished product than ever." The idea is in full force now, as Sam manages over two hundred employees and a plant that runs twenty-four-hour days and puts out more than 100,000 board feet of finished goods per day. When he first arrived at the plant in 2016, there were fifty-five employees. On this rapid growth, Sam had this to say: "We had such a huge demand to meet, and the only way to do it was to quadruple in size. When you do that, there are all kinds of challenges that present themselves, and you have to be able to find solutions to them. If you don't, the results can be disastrous." But, he mentioned, "With rapid growth comes a duty to ensure ethical and fair treatment of employees, and a duty to ensure ethical behavior on the job."

Having to manage his personnel is often an ethical challenge for Sam. Many occasions which test his ethics arise when someone is not performing at a high level and he has to decide whether or not to keep that individual on staff. He says, "Look, in this type of work there are always going to be people who just can't

do it. It's manual labor, and it's well over 100 degrees sometimes. You have to find the people who can do it, and you have to weed out the people who cannot—you give them all the same chance, but you have to recognize that of five prospective employees, you are going to get one good one." This company serves as an example of how ethics should always be a concern, even with seemingly simple decisions. In this case, staffing the plant means giving all applicants a chance to show their willingness to help.

He also added that they have implemented as many comfort-increasing benefits around the plant as possible—most of the plant is underneath an 88,000-square-foot roof, there are fans and a misting system, and they provide unlimited ice, water, coolers, and Gatorade for the entire staff. Sam says they pride themselves on treating their employees as well as they can, and this has become less of an ethical dilemma and more of an obvious choice for him: "You want to provide them with as much comfort as you possibly can, and you want to reward them as much as you possibly can. They give you their hard work day in and day out, and without their hard work we couldn't do what we do." This treatment results in respect, caringness, and fairness among Sam's team, which are key elements of character involved with professional relationships.

Sam also said that such rapid institutional growth like the kind JMW has undergone also presents lots of opportunity, in the form of a cultural shift. "A benefit to adding so many new members to the team is that they don't have any of the bad habits you might see from those who have worked at the plant for fifteen years. You get to mold them exactly how you want to, and by doing that you actually affect change in all the veteran employees as well." Sam is talking about organizational behavior, and he says it is the lifeblood of this industry. He says a top-down dynamic of hard work and excellence permeates the plant, and it all starts with the leadership team they have created. They elevate their best workers into these leadership roles, and it motivates the entire crew. By managing this small crew of leaders, Sam can manage over two hundred people. By molding them, he can mold the entire operation.

Critical-Thinking Questions

1. Which of Sam's ethical dilemmas at JMW Truss are similar to those of all managers?

2. List and explain the Pillars of Character mentioned in Sam's article. ●

Source: Interview with Sam Heiler conducted on April 20th, 2017

Ethical Leadership and Followership

>> **LO 9.3** **Differentiate between the challenges of ethical leadership and ethical followership**

Business leaders have greater responsibility for decision-making and organizational outcomes. Usually, leaders have a number of followers who have less responsibility but play a key role in implementing plans set out by the leader. Ideally, leaders and followers collaborate and work together to achieve common goals. However, sometimes ethical challenges can upset the dynamics of a relationship.

Leaders and Power

With leadership comes greater influence and power. Some leaders misuse that power to exert their influence over their followers. This sort of abuse can come in the form of bullying, verbal or physical abuse, and sexual harassment. Recent surveys have reported that one in four women and 10 percent of men have experienced workplace sexual harassment in the United States.[26]

Studies carried out by social scientists show the dangerous effects of power on the behavior of ordinary people.[27] They found that when certain people are put in a powerful position, they tend to lack empathy, are less able to detect emotion, and fail to understand other perspectives. In one experiment, the people in power were able to take candy from children without feeling any sense of guilt or remorse. In relation to inappropriate sexual behavior in men, studies show that the most powerful tend to believe that women are more attracted to them than they really are, and are prone to looking for opportunities where they can engage in unacceptable sexual conduct.

Leaders and Privilege

The more power a leader possesses, the greater the privilege. Typically, top CEOs are paid enormous amounts which some use to fund lavish lifestyles. For example, Facebook CEO Mark Zuckerberg used some of his wealth to not only buy his own house in Palo Alto, California, but also the four houses surrounding it, in order to ensure personal privacy.[28] Yet these high salaries are in stark contrast to those paid to the average worker. According to a 2016 report from the Economic Policy Institute, CEOs from the three hundred fifty companies studied made two hundred seventy-one times more than the average employee.[29] In fact, some top CEOs made more over two days than the typical employee did in one year.

Chobani's CEO, Hamdi Ulukaya, is an example of a CEO who has taken action to reduce the pay gap between CEOs and their employees.

This growing gap between the wealthiest and the poorest raises some interesting ethical questions. While CEOs bear the risk, pressure, scrutiny, and responsibility of their roles, do they deserve to get paid over two hundred times more than the average employee? How can the pay gap be narrowed? Some CEOs are already recognizing this massive disparity and making an effort to put it right. For example, Hamdi Ulukaya, founder and CEO of Chobani—a yogurt-making company—has pledged to award two thousand employees with a 10 percent stake in the company.[30] Those employees could receive up to $1 million if the company is sold or goes public.

Leaders and Responsibility

While some CEOs enjoy considerable perks and wealthy lifestyles, they also have a huge amount of responsibility. In fact, due to the numerous instances of fraud and unethical conduct over the past few years, CEOs are being held to higher levels of accountability than ever before. Unethical behavior such as bribery, fraud, insider trading, environmental disasters, and sexual harassment no longer goes unnoticed or unpunished. The consequences for engaging in unethical behavior are serious, sometimes resulting in criminal indictments, dismissals, and huge financial penalties. Today's business leaders are very much under the spotlight from the public and the media and cannot afford to engage in corporate misconduct if they want their organizations to survive. According to the 2017 Edelman Trust Barometer, only 37 percent of people consider CEOs credible—the lowest it has ever been.[31]

If leaders want to be considered reputable, credible, and trustworthy, they need to be transparent with their followers about the tasks and duties they are undertaking; make an effort to actively prevent crimes and injustices; take immediate action to correct ethical problems; accept accountability for decisions and actions; and maintain the same standards as their followers.

Leaders and Information Management

By the very nature of their senior positions, leaders tend to have more access to information than followers, and are often the first to receive that information. The challenge for leaders is how to deal with that information. Do they share it immediately with followers or keep it to themselves? Consider the case of a senior manager who is told about upcoming layoffs. She has been instructed to withhold this information until an official announcement is made. Yet rumors have started flying around about the layoffs and her team is agitated. Does she tell them the truth about the layoffs or does she stay silent until the announcement is made?

Leaders who fail to meet the ethical challenges of information management often behave in the following ways: lying about what they know; using the information for their own gain; denying having the knowledge at all; and telling certain followers to withhold information when others have a right to know.

Hisao Tanaka, former president and CEO of electronics giant Toshiba, resigned over a scandal involving managers who withheld information regarding operating profits over a period of six years. Management had lied about the real profit numbers, resulting in Toshiba declaring over $1.2 billion in false profit.[32]

Leaders and Consistency

It's human nature to prefer some people over others, and in an ideal world, leaders and followers would treat each other equally and respectfully. However, this is often not the case. Some leaders may show favoritism to certain followers by paying them more attention, overlooking tardiness, or giving them more time off when they need it. Treating some followers more favorably than others has a tendency to breed resentment and lower morale and productivity. It also stunts creativity. As Karen Dillon, author of the *HBR Guide to Office Politics*, says, "We tend to want to be surrounded by people who see the world as we do and think like we do."[33] However studies show us that being around people who have different perspectives and ideas

EXAMINING THE EVIDENCE

Ethical Leadership and Moral Judgments

The corporate scandals of recent years have highlighted the importance of both ethical leadership and good ethical decision making by all members of an organization. Recent research by University of Memphis researchers Robert Steinbauer, Robert W. Renn, Robert R. Taylor, and Phil K. Njoroge explores the possible relationship between these two processes. Their research suggests that ethical leadership, which involves both demonstrating and promoting effective ethical conduct to organizational members, is likely to influence the moral judgments of organizational members. The effects of this type of leadership are likely enhanced by the extent to which organizational members perceive that they will be held accountable for their ethical actions and the degree to which they engage in ethics-focused self-leadership, which entails leading and motivating one's own behavior to achieve goal-oriented outcomes. The research further suggests that the effects of the ethics-focused self-leadership will be greater when coupled with conscious, active judgment processes rather than unconscious, reflexive, or intuitive approaches. This research suggests that organizations may be able to encourage better ethical decision making by providing ethical leadership and self-leadership training for their leaders and other organizational members.

Critical-Thinking Questions

1. In what ways can ethical leaders encourage ethics-focused self-leadership in their organizations?

2. How might organizations best hold their members accountable for their ethical decisions and actions? ●

Source: Steinbauer, R., Renn, R. W., Taylor, R. R., & Njoroge, P. K. (2014). Ethical Leadership and Followers' Moral Judgment: The Role of Followers' Perceived Accountability and Self-Leadership. *Journal of Business Ethics, 120,* 381–392.

inspires creative thinking as well as personal growth. Dillon says, "You are not going to grow if you only work with people like you."[34]

Leaders need to be consistent in their behavior toward their followers by learning how to cater for each individual's needs; how to choose an appropriate time to bend the rules; and how to treat those followers that may not be as competent as others. They must also offer equal opportunities when it comes to promotions and bonuses and treat everybody around them with respect.

Leaders and Loyalty

From their followers and shareholders, to investors, wider communities, and the environment, leaders have to juggle a range of loyalties. Ideally, all leaders would act in the best interests of their followers and prioritize the environment over financial gain, but as recent scandals have demonstrated, this is often not the case. For example, Matthias Mueller, CEO of German car manufacturer Volkswagen, was forced to issue an apology for betraying the trust of the company's shareholders following reports of emissions-cheating software being installed in over 11 million diesel engines worldwide.[35] In another example, Isaac Choi, CEO of job search start-up WrkRiot, betrayed his followers by cheating them out of their wages and misleading them about his own credentials. As a result, Choi has been indicted on five counts of fraud by the US Department of Justice.[36]

The Ethical Challenges of Followers

Like leaders, followers also face a number of ethical challenges in their working roles. As followers do not have the same power and status as their leaders, these challenges if not met can affect the dynamics of the leader-follower relationship. Here are some of the challenges that followers are confronted with.

Followers and Obligation

Good followers have a strong allegiance and commitment to their organizations, leaders, customers, and shareholders. For instance, Costco employees have an obligation to their organization to provide the best customer service possible, which is why the giant wholesaler is ranked as one of the best companies for customer service in the world.[37] However, followers also need to determine the extent of their obligation to a company. Should followers be expected to sacrifice their personal lives in favor of working long hours and weekends? Being overworked is a rising problem, particularly in Japan. According to a recent report issued by the Japanese government, employees in almost one in four companies work more than eighty unpaid extra hours per month.[38] Pushing workers too hard has led to a dramatic increase of fatal health conditions. Followers need to assess the degree of their own obligation to their companies and think about how much they want to give in order to strike the right work-life balance.

Followers and Obedience

In the business world, followers are expected to carry out orders and demands in order to further the mission of the organization. However, there is a difference between carrying out orders and blind obedience. This is particularly important given society's belief that people can no longer resist responsibility for their actions by claiming they were merely following orders (known as the Nuremberg Defense used by Nazi war criminals following World War II). However, a recent study shows that some people who have been coerced to do something they ordinarily wouldn't tend to experience a reduced sense of responsibility.[39] When faced with unethical situations, followers must ask themselves if obedience might lead to unethical behavior, dangerous consequences, or damage to the organization's mission.

Followers and Cynicism

In times of economic turbulence, rising lay offs, corporate scandals, and continued austerity measures, it is easy for employees to become cynical. Too much cynicism can lead to lack of trust, lower commitment levels, reduced job satisfaction, and decreased performance and productivity. Yet cynicism does have its place when it comes to questioning ethical decisions made by leaders. According to a University of Toronto researcher, Professor Kristin Scott, "People who are very cynical can ask the tough questions and examine decisions that their company is making with a critical lens. This kind of feedback may be beneficial for organizations if their own employees are holding them to account for their actions."[40]

In addition, Scott believes that too much cynicism can be alleviated when employees have the right support. A survey assessing workplace cynicism carried out in partnership with her colleague, Professor David Zweig, found cynical employees tend to become more positive about their workplace when they have a supportive manager on board.[41] Zweig says, "Treating employees with respect, offering support and helping them understand the necessity of change within an organization are all the hallmarks of a good supervisor, but it also has the benefit of mitigating the negative effects of cynicism."[42]

Followers and Dissent

For most followers, there will be a time when they become dissatisfied with the organization, in relation to areas such as organizational policies, pay, working conditions, promotions, bonuses, and so on. For organizations to be successful, employees need to be given the opportunity to express their dissent regarding organizational practices and to raise questions about unethical practices.[43] However, not all organizations encourage dissent and not all followers feel comfortable expressing it. Some people prefer to stay silent rather than share their views with their leaders for fear of being seen in a negative light. Others keep quiet out of mistrust—they don't believe their leaders will help solve the problem even if they share it. When followers decide to express their dissent, they need to choose the right person to help solve the problem; suggest solutions to the issue; think about what they might say if their opinions are dismissed; and plan the steps they may have to take if they still want to be heard (such as escalating the problem to higher management). If the situation does not improve then followers may threaten to resign. However, resignation should really only be a last resort and only warranted if raised concerns have been repeatedly ignored by leaders over a lengthy period of time.

Followers and Bad News

Very few of us like to be the bearer of bad news, especially when we are directly at fault. Confessing a mistake may incur the wrath of our leaders, damage our reputations, and negatively influence our bonuses and promotional opportunities. However, organizations that don't provide a forum for sharing bad news can suffer catastrophic consequences. For example, Wells Fargo employees feared termination if they spoke out against the fraudulent customer accounts that they were pressured to set up in order to meet sales quotas. In turn, when the news finally broke about the extent of the fraud and unethical practices, leadership at Wells Fargo also stayed silent, only owning up to the bad news to its customers and shareholders when CEO John Stumpf was called in front of the US Senate Committee.[44] As the Wells Fargo scandal shows, followers must be given the freedom to report bad news to their leaders so those leaders can take corrective steps to address the problem before it gets out of hand.

Delivering bad news takes courage and if possible is better communicated face-to-face to the most appropriate person, rather than over email or phone. But sharing unpleasant information doesn't always have to be a negative experience. When bad news is shared in a positive tone, respondents tend not to react as defensively as with a negative tone. Take animation studio Pixar, for instance.[45] Over the course of the film-making process, Pixar's creative teams undergo a series of critique sessions. Instead of focusing on what's wrong with the work, they give each other feedback on how things could be improved. As a result, creators are more likely to accept the feedback because it is not perceived as a personal attack.

THINKING CRITICALLY

1. Assume you found your dream job working for a company for which you have always wanted to work. Once you start, you find everyone works a lot of overtime and weekends. Do you think it is ethical for you to be expected to sacrifice your personal life in favor of working long hours and weekends? Why or why not?

2. Often employees are fearful of speaking up about poor behavior in a company. How can companies encourage employees to speak up when they see unethical behavior in the company? Explain.

3. Have you ever witnessed an unethical act by someone at your school or place of business? If so, did you speak up? If you did speak up, what gave you the courage to do so? If you did not, what prevented you from doing so?

Social Responsibility

>> **LO 9.4**   **Describe the primary approaches to social responsibility in organizations**

While ethical values need to be upheld by both leaders and followers, it is even more important that organizations as a whole set a good example by behaving ethically and responsibly. One way organizations can do this is through practicing **corporate social responsibility (CSR),** defined as a business approach that delivers economic, social, and environmental benefits to stakeholders in order to contribute to sustainable development.[46]

Good CSR is especially important to today's consumers who tend to buy from companies that have a beneficial impact on the environment. In a 2015 Nielson survey, almost two-thirds of consumers said that they would pay more for sustainable products.[47]

There are four main levels of CSR: economic responsibility, legal responsibility, ethical responsibility, and discretionary responsibility.[48]

1.   Economic Responsibility

Corporate social responsibility (CSR): A business approach that delivers economic, social, and environmental benefits to stakeholders in order to contribute to sustainable development

Economic responsibility means that organizations must be economically and financially sound to enable them to become socially responsible in the first place. This means that its services and products must be sold at a reasonable price, and the business run as efficiently as possible. If the company doesn't manage to become profitable, then employees lose their jobs. In other words, the company must first fulfill its responsibilities to employees before it can contribute to the greater social good.

Economic responsibility: Means that organizations must be economically and financially sound to enable them to become socially responsible in the first place

2.   Legal Responsibility

Legal responsibility means that organizations must make every effort to comply with legal requirements. Types of legal responsibility include labor law, tax regulations, environmental law, and criminal law. Alongside these laws is the expectation that organizations conduct their business affairs in a sound and fair manner. The penalties for breaking the law can be severe. In 2017, twenty-six companies in the United Kingdom were fined over $2 million for breaking environmental laws relating to pollution and lack of recycling.[49]

Legal responsibility: Means that organizations must make every effort is made to comply with legal requirements

3.   Ethical Responsibility

Ethical responsibility means being morally aware enough to do the right thing in relation to the environment, fair wages, or who the company does business with. Yet not everything unethical is illegal. Take the infamous case of Martin Shkreli, former CEO of Turing Pharmaceuticals.[50] Shkreli created a huge amount of controversy when he made the decision to raise the price of the drug Daraprim (used to treat the condition toxoplasmosis which can affect pregnant women, people with HIV, and others with weakened immune systems) from $13.50 to $750 per pill—an increase of 5,000 percent. While Shkreli's actions were not illegal, he received a massive backlash from the public who perceived his conduct to be immoral and unethical.

Ethical responsibility: Means being morally aware enough to do the right thing in relation to the environment, fair wages, or who the company does business with

On a much lesser scale, when Blake Mycoskie founded TOMS Shoes, he ran the company out of his apartment without permission from his landlady.[51] He made sure that he and his team hid all signs of the business from her whenever she visited because he felt she would not approve. Again, Mycoskie wasn't breaking the law, but his behavior could have been regarded as unethical.

4. Discretionary Responsibility

Discretionary responsibility involves going beyond the call of duty to benefit society. When an organization achieves its economic, legal, and ethical responsibilities, it can begin to focus on its discretionary or philanthropic responsibilities. These responsibilities involve going beyond the call of duty to benefit society. Examples are charitable donations, running initiatives that benefit the community, providing aid to people affected by natural disasters, or engaging in projects that have a positive impact on the environment. A 2015 survey of the top one hundred fifty most generous companies conducted by *Fortune* magazine counts retail giant Walmart, oil and gas company Exxon-Mobil, and food company General Mills among the top twenty most philanthropic organizations in the Fortune 500.[52]

Social Entrepreneurs and CSR

While corporates tend to cycle through the various levels of responsibilities before being considered socially responsible, social entrepreneurs entrench CSR into their start-up business model. While there are similarities between traditional entrepreneurs and social entrepreneurs, there are differences too. For instance, although both traditional and social entrepreneurs found organizations, identify new opportunities, and create innovative products and services, they may differ in their original goals and objectives. Traditional entrepreneurs tend to start off with making profit as a goal, whereas a social entrepreneur may start off with the intention of tackling social and environmental problems to bring about social change.

In 2016, the World Economic Forum announced their top twelve social entrepreneurs who are making a significant impact on a global scale.[53] One of these social entrepreneurs is Poonam Bir Kasturi, founder of India-based Daily Dump—a home-composting company that provides well-designed products like leaf composters and sorting bags. Since founding the company in 2006, almost thirty thousand Indians have used the products, saving over twenty-eight tons of organic waste per day. Other social entrepreneurs on the list include former Microsoft and Amazon executive David Risher, and a former marketing director of ESADE business school in Spain, Colin McElwee. In 2010, Risher and McElwee cofounded Worldreader, a nonprofit organization with the mission to improve literary rates by providing free access to digital books to people all over the world. It has a store of over thirty thousand book titles in forty-three languages and is available to people in sixty-nine countries.

While the social entrepreneurs described above operate nonprofit companies, there are many successful social entrepreneurs who run for-profit businesses. These types of organizations make a profit and benefit society at the same time. For example, Jack's Soap is a for-profit company based in Los Angeles set up by founder Bridget Hilton to help combat common ailments arising in children from not washing their hands properly.[54] The company donates one bar of luxury organic soap to a child in need for each bar sold and educates children on the importance of hygiene.

THINKING CRITICALLY

1. Can a company be legally responsible yet not be ethically responsible? Or vice versa? Please explain.

2. Is it ethical for a social entrepreneur to make profits from his socially responsible business? Please explain.

Building Ethical and Socially Responsible Organizations

>> LO 9.5   Identify the components of an ethical culture

Regardless of the different types of organizations, building an ethical culture requires a shared sense of meaning to help positively influence ethical behavior. Some components of ethical behavior include core values, mission statements, codes of ethics, structure, boards of directors, reward and performance evaluation systems, reporting and communication systems, and ethics officers.

Core values are deeply held beliefs or guiding principles shared by everyone working at a particular company. They are the essence of a company's identity and help to support a company's vision. Common core values include integrity, honesty, perseverance, and accountability. Troy Guard, chef and owner of Denver-based Tag Restaurant Group, is so invested in his company's core values (passion, harmony, humility to name just a few) that he showcases them on the walls of his restaurants in order to inspire and motivate his employees.[55]

Mission statements communicate the company's purpose as reflected by its members. It is essential that mission statements are continually reinforced to ensure every employee adheres to the message. Eyewear manufacturer Warby Parker, which operates a Buy a Pair, Give a Pair scheme, has a mission statement that represents its commitment to both social and business goals: "Warby Parker was founded with a rebellious spirit and a lofty objective: to offer designer eyewear at a revolutionary price, while leading the way for socially conscious businesses."[56]

Codes of ethics (sometimes called code of conduct) are a written set of guidelines that define acceptable and unacceptable behavior. The main purpose of a code of ethics is to help employees make the right choices when confronted with difficult situations. Most organizations have codes of ethics, with almost 90 percent of the Global Fortune 200 companies.[57] PepsiCo's code of ethics is written in a way that leaves no room for error. The code includes a special provision to guide employees on the ethics of receiving gifts, specified to the exact dollar amount. Other provisions in an ethics code may include expected conduct when dealing with the competition, suppliers, and government agencies; the ramifications of conspiring against the company, price-fixing, and insider trading; and strict rules around gender and racial discrimination, sexual harassment, violence, and drug use. The code of ethics may also include provisions relating to health and safety, use of company technology, and treatment of the environment.

For a code of ethics to be successful, it must be supported by senior management who should lead by example by behaving ethically at all times, and acknowledging or rewarding those employees who follow the same code. Equally, leaders must also reprimand employees who break the ethical code. For example, in 2017, Google CEO Sundar Pichai sent a memo to his employees admonishing an employee who had circulated a controversial memo claiming that women were less capable than men of succeeding in technology because of their biology. In his memo, Pichai said that the parts of the employee's memo "violate our Code of Conduct and cross the line by advancing harmful gender stereotypes in our workplace." Pichai went on to say that the employee's beliefs were "contrary to our basic values and our Code of Conduct, which expects 'each Googler to do their utmost to create a workplace culture that is free of harassment, intimidation, bias and unlawful discrimination.'"[58]

However some leaders believe that codes of conduct alone do not always help with ethical dilemmas. In a study carried out by the University of Pennsylvania, thirty leaders interviewed recalled almost ninety ethical dilemmas, and not all of them were covered under the ethical code.[59] Many of these dilemmas related to the challenges of dealing with different cultures as a result of global business expansion. Some examples included the cultural and ethical consequences of breaking a verbal promise in China or shutting down a sales office in Japan.

Researchers of the study recommend that leaders must ensure that ethical behavior is practiced throughout the organization by staying in tune with how employees feel about the company, making sure that employees are being paid fairly and given opportunities for promotion, and building a diverse network which could help to circumnavigate cultural issues. Finally, if leaders witness unethical behavior then they must speak up and remain true to their own personal values.

Warby Parker is committed to upholding a socially conscious mission statement while still offering affordable prices to consumers.

Pat Greenhouse/The Boston Globe via Getty Images

Organizational structure also influences ethical behavior. For example, a command and control structure where leaders have a high amount of power and followers are expected to obey sometimes inspires unethical behavior. Some experts believe that leaders at Wells Fargo operated a command and control structure which pressured employees to behave unethically by opening thousands of fraudulent bank accounts.[60]

Boards of directors sit at the head of the organizational structure and are responsible for overseeing top management and ensuring loyalty to shareholders. However, not all boards act in the best interests of the organization and some have even approved unethical practices. Enron, HealthSouth, Tyco, Arthur Andersen, Siemens, Barclays, BP, General Motors, Takata, Volkswagen, and Wells Fargo are just a few of the corporate scandals that have taken place over the last few years.[61] Because of these ethical failures, it has become even more important for board members to ensure that top management is practicing good ethical behavior.

Ethics hotlines allow employees to report unethical conduct anonymously without fear of retaliation. Many organizations use ethics hotlines to provide employees, who may not be comfortable reporting ethical incidents to management, with a safe place to share their concerns. According to the 2017 Navex Global Ethics & Compliance Hotline & Incident Management Benchmark Report, the number of reports has increased significantly over the last six years.[62] The results show that more employees are engaged enough with the company to report unethical practices.

Ethics officers are responsible for ensuring their organizations adhere to legal and ethical practices. Expanding organizations in particular can create challenges with respect to new employees and new regulations. Chief ethics officers need to continuously convey the company's ethical code and values to ensure all employees work to the same ethical standards. In 2016, Emmanuel Lulin, senior vice president and chief ethics officer of cosmetics giant L'Oréal, was awarded the Carol R. Marshall Award for Innovation in Corporate Ethics from the Ethics & Compliance Initiative (ECI). L'Oréal has been consistently voted as one of the top companies for global corporate ethics. Lulin is a firm believer in the importance of ethics for business success,

FIGURE 9.2

An Integrative Framework

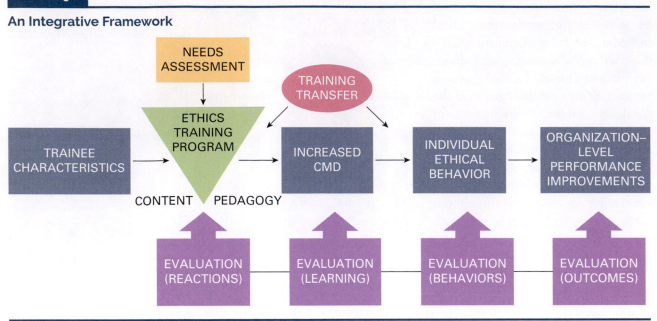

Source: Adapted from D. Wells and M. Schminke, "Ethical Development and Human Resources Training: An Integrative Framework," *Human Resource Management Review* 11 (2001): 135–158.

saying, "Good ethical practices are now strategic. Companies who want to be leaders in our 21st century must address them to win trust and keep their license to operate. Innovative thinking, and strong cooperation of the players, are required to address the deep ethical challenges of today and of tomorrow."[63]

Ethics Training

One important way to prevent unethical behavior from occurring in organizations is to ensure all employees receive ethics training. According to management research, there are four components of successful ethical training programs: (1) trainee characteristics, (2) needs assessment, (3) training transfer, and (4) evaluation (see Figure 9.2).[64]

1. Trainee Characteristics

Before designing an ethics training program, successful facilitators assess the characteristics of their trainees. This may involve documenting their moral profiles, their levels of integrity, their capabilities to be honest with themselves and others, and if there is any evidence of a predisposition toward unethical behavior. Other areas to assess would be the levels of assertiveness, intelligence, and general demographic (age, gender, ethnicity) of the audience. Another important factor to take into account is the degree to which the trainees have already been exposed to unethical behavior, as victims of such tend to be more engaged in these types of training programs.

2. Needs Assessment

Following an appraisal of the trainee characteristics, facilitators can carry out a needs assessment to establish the requirement for ethics training. Information gathered from employee surveys, advisory committees, exit interviews, and group discussions can be useful when planning an ethics training program. It is also important to plan a statement to give at the beginning of a session outlining the code of conduct, standards of excellence, behavioral expectations, and the overall goals of the program. The ethics program should also include topics on the fundamentals of ethics knowledge, assertiveness, productivity, and self-leadership. A good facilitator will ensure that senior management taking part are provided with access to training content which is relevant to their roles in the organization. Typically, an ethics training program will include discussions on dilemmas, personal growth, role-playing, scenario-based games, and interactive simulations.

3. Training Transfer

A successful ethics training program transfers the knowledge gained during the program to trainees so that they will remember to apply that behavior when they return to their working roles. To engage trainees from the outset, facilitators should provide them with a pretraining pack which introduces them to the topics being explored. In addition, trainees should be asked what they hope to achieve from the training session to ensure what is being discussed aligns itself with their own goals.

4. Evaluation

It is important that evaluation takes place after the training session in order to measure its effectiveness. As part of this evaluation, facilitators should note the reactions of the trainees and analyze the knowledge or skill tests completed by trainees. In the long term, facilitators need to continue their evaluation by documenting any positive change in workplace behavior and organizational performance results that may be attributed to the ethics training program.

THINKING CRITICALLY

1. In this section, we list various components of an ethical culture in organizations. In your mind, which of these components is the most important toward ensuring ethical behavior in organizations?

2. Think of a company that you worked for that had an unethical culture. What organizational characteristics created such a culture?

3. Think of a company that you worked for that had an ethical culture. Were any of the components in this chapter present in this company? What else besides these components lead to this ethical culture?

4. Do you believe someone can be trained to be more ethical? Why or why not? ●

Visit **edge.sagepub.com/neckob2e** to help you accomplish your coursework goals in an easy-to-use learning environment.

- Mobile-friendly eFlashcards and practice quizzes
- Video and multimedia content
- Chapter summaries with learning objectives
- EXCLUSIVE! Access to full-text SAGE journal articles

IN REVIEW

9.1　Defend the importance of ethics in organizations and effectively evaluate and resolve ethical dilemmas

Ethics are moral principles of duty and virtue that prescribe how we should behave. Individuals and companies frequently face large and small **ethical dilemmas**, or conflicts between two or more morally unpleasant alternatives. The key to being an ethical person or organization is to *consistently* choose to do the right thing.

9.2　Compare and contrast various approaches to ethical decision making

There are three classical ethical decision-making approaches: utilitarian approach, rights approach, and justice approach. Some contemporary approaches to help managers make ethical decisions include the four-part "moral compass" and the Foursquare Protocol.

9.3　Differentiate between the challenges of ethical leadership and ethical followership

Ideally, leaders and followers collaborate and work together to achieve common goals. However, sometimes ethical challenges in leadership such as misuse of power, privilege, and abuse of responsibility can upset the dynamics of a relationship. Like leaders, followers also face a number of ethical challenges in their working roles, such as blind obedience, cynicism, and obligation. As followers do not have the same power and status as their leaders, these challenges if not met can affect the dynamics of the leader-follower relationship.

9.4　Describe the primary approaches to social responsibility in organizations

Organizations as a whole set a good example by behaving ethically and responsibly. One way organizations can do this is through practicing **corporate social responsibility (CSR)** defined as a business approach that delivers economic, social, and environmental benefits to stakeholders in order to contribute to sustainable development. There are four main levels of CSR: economic responsibility, legal responsibility, ethical responsibility, and discretionary responsibility.

9.5　Identify the components of an ethical culture

Building an ethical culture requires a shared sense of meaning to help positively influence ethical behavior. Some components of ethical behavior include core values, mission statements, codes of ethics, structure, boards of directors, reward and performance evaluation systems, reporting and communication systems, and ethics officers.

KEY TERMS

Corporate social responsibility (CSR)　260
Discretionary responsibility　261
Economic responsibility　260
Ethical dilemmas　248
Ethics　245

Ethical responsibility　260
Justice approach　249
Legal responsibility　260
Rights approach　249
Utilitarian approach　249

UP FOR DEBATE: Reporting Ethical Violations

If you see your boss violate ethical codes of conduct and mishandle client information on multiple occasions, you know he or she should be disciplined for it. If you try to go over your boss's head and report an ethical violation to his or her boss, you could lose your job and it would make you look like a whistle blower who reports your own coworkers. Agree or disagree? Explain your answer.

EXERCISE 9.1: Ethical Situations

Objective

The purpose of this exercise is to gain a greater appreciation of ethics.

Instructions

We face ethical dilemmas everyday—some are broad in scope and some are relatively minor. These relatively minor ethical situations are just as important as the major ones. Below are several instances you may have found yourself in. In groups of three to five, discuss what you would do in each situation.

- You hand the cashier at a grocery store a $20 bill to pay for $16.50 worth of groceries. When she hands you back the change, instead of giving you $3.50, she inadvertently gives you $13.50, but does not realize her mistake.

- You borrow your grandmother's car for a few days. She has a "disabled driver" tag hanging from the rearview mirror. As you drive around town, you see several open parking spaces for cars with this disabled driver permit.

- At your favorite retail store, you put away the cart after placing your purchases in your car. As you do, you discover that someone left their purchases in a cart that was put away, including about $100 worth of merchandise.

- Your boss asks you to "pad" a report that you produce each week detailing the amount of overtime that employees work. Your boss has been getting in trouble from the president of the company because of this particular report. If you would just pad the report for one week—showing that there is actually less overtime—your boss feels that he'll have more time to take actions that will ultimately reduce overtime for the company.

- You work in a cubicle with twenty other employees. You have a fun, friendly work environment. However, you notice that the employee in the cubicle next to you is continually visiting pornographic websites. The manager is not aware that he is doing this on a regular basis.

Reflection Questions

1. How did you and your group members approach each of these ethical situations?

2. Was everyone in your group in agreement as to what should be done in each situation? Explain.

3. What similar examples of ethical dilemmas have you faced in your career? How did you handle those situations?

Exercise contributed by Steven Stovall, Southeast Missouri State University.

EXERCISE 9.2: Creating a Code of Ethics

Objective

The purpose of this exercise is to grasp the concept of a code of ethics.

Instructions

A code of ethics is a written set of guidelines that define acceptable and unacceptable behavior. It helps employees make the right choices when faced with difficult situations.

The instructor will invite two volunteers to come to the front of the class. One volunteer will write on the board, while the other will lead a brainstorming session with the students in the class. The purpose of the brainstorming is to develop a code of ethics for this course.

As participants in the brainstorming session, students will help craft a code of ethics that specifies what is acceptable conduct and behavior, how those who follow the code of ethics will be acknowledged or rewarded, and how those that break the ethical code will be reprimanded. As ideas are provided, the student volunteer at the board will capture each idea by writing it so that everyone can see it. Once there are enough ideas, the person leading the discussion will help the class craft a code of ethics specifically for this course.

Reflection Questions

1. Describe the process for developing this code of ethics.

2. Do you think codes of ethics are effective? Why or why not?

3. Does your current or most recent employer have a code of ethics? What is contained in the firm's code of ethics?

Exercise contributed by Steven Stovall, Southeast Missouri State University.

EXERCISE 9.3: What Is Fair?

Objectives

After successfully completing this exercise, you will be able to better *explain* different methods for resolving ethical dilemmas, and *contrast* different approaches to ethical decision making.

Instructions

You are the member of the board of directors for a medium-sized light aircraft parts manufacturing plant. The company has been in operations for over fifty years, and has been moderately successful throughout its history. However, due to changes in manufacturing processes, your current manufacturing methods are becoming obsolete and relatively costly compared to your competitors. You can upgrade your current manufacturing methods, but that will mean that 20 percent of your workforce will no longer be needed.

Your company has always prided itself on supporting the community through providing well-paying jobs, and strong employment guarantees to all of your workers. If you put the automation processes in place, you will not need to hire new workers for the foreseeable future. Additionally, all workers were promised (though not contractually guaranteed) lifetime employment as long as they did a good job.

If you do not implement the technological changes, your projections show a 20 percent chance of going bankrupt (and ceasing all operations) in the next five years due to increased competition.

Due to the nature of this decision, the company president has asked the company's board for advice on the ethical dimensions of this decision. You and the other board members have decided to meet to examine the situation using the utilitarian, rights, and justice approaches to the situation.

Step 1. Form into groups of five to seven members. Examine the decision from all three ethical approaches and make a recommendation on what steps to take from one selected approach. You can bring up alternative solutions to those currently being considered, but those alternatives must fall within the presented business constraints, and also be evaluated for ethical considerations. You will need to report your recommendation, and you will also need to report which approach you finally decided to use, why you chose it, the elements you used in making your decision, and if you would have made a different choice if you used another approach. (30 to 40 minutes)

Step 2. Choose a spokesperson to make your report to the entire class. However, all group members should be prepared to answer questions from the instructor and classmates. (5 minutes)

Reflection Questions

1. What difficulties did you have in making your recommendation?

2. Did using the different ethical approaches help you in making your decision?

3. What were the major ways in which your discussions differed using the different approaches?

Exercise contributed by Milton R. Mayfield, Professor of Business, Texas A&M International University, and Jacqueline R. Mayfield, Professor of Business, Texas A&M International University.

ONLINE EXERCISE 9.1: Good and Bad Examples of Social Responsibility

Objective

The purpose of this exercise is to gain an appreciation for positive and negative examples of social responsibility.

Instructions

Corporate social responsibility is a business approach that delivers economic, social, and environmental benefits to stakeholders in order to contribute to sustainable development. There are four main levels—economic responsibility, legal responsibility, ethical responsibility, and discretionary responsibility. Your text explores these in detail.

Search online for one example of an organization that exhibited social responsibility in a positive way and one example of another organization that demonstrated social responsibility in a negative way. For each, write one double-spaced page detailing what the organization did and how the issue was resolved—if it was resolved. Submit these two pages to your instructor.

Reflection Questions

1. Which is more difficult to find: a good example of social responsibility or a bad one? Why?

2. For both the good and bad examples you found, which level of responsibility is represented—economic, legal, ethical, or discretionary?

3. For your positive example, what costs do you think the organization had to endure to take the action it did?

4. For the negative example, will the organization ever fully recover from this incident? Explain.

Exercise contributed by Steven Stovall, Southeast Missouri State University.

CASE STUDY 9.1: JetBlue's Ethical Response to a Crisis

Crisis happens to even the best companies, and the larger a company becomes, the more prone to crisis it will be due to more reach and more to lose. A crisis will quickly test the mettle of any company and will expose the relationship between corporate values and organizational processes in a very public way. The best CEOs are the ones that are students of the game of crisis management and public relations (PR) fiascoes, studying cases of mismanagement like many study basketball. Especially in the modern era of social media, where even the actions of a small-time employee could affect an entire brand and the way it is perceived, it is fundamental to have corporate processes in sync with corporate values. Small things matter more than ever now and the companies that can consistently get out ahead of PR mishaps are the ones that will continue to build brands that people trust.

A good example of this lies within the airline industry. In an industry where power is consolidated and the main factor in deciding which brand to use is price, JetBlue has shined as a player that consistently goes above and beyond. JetBlue, founded in 1998 in one of the most competitive markets in the most competitive industry with the highest barriers to entry, has always sought to "bring the humanity back to air travel." In the early days this took better amenities, friendlier staff, and less emphasis on the bottom line. They modeled much of their philosophy off of Southwest Airlines, a company with a very similar backstory to entry. Commonly one of the highest rated airlines in the United States for consumer satisfaction, JetBlue was faced with a serious dilemma one winter.

In the middle of the winter of 2007, a major ice storm hit the East Coast where JetBlue has the majority of its flights. This meant that in the span of just five days, JetBlue had to cancel over a thousand flights. This left passengers caught all over the East Coast sleeping in airports with no way to get home. The entire industry was caught in what seemed like the worst case scenario during holiday season. While JetBlue wasn't alone in this crisis situation, they knew that they had to do something immediately or their brand would suffer. The founder and David Neeleman immediately came out to the media pleading his case that he was "humiliated and mortified" that something like this could happen at a scale like this. He also immediately launched a full-fledged investigation into what went wrong internally and what could have been managed differently. On top of these actions, he also made himself available in every media platform to answer questions and to walk customers through exactly how JetBlue would seek to make this right to them.

Where most airlines would see a situation like this as an unavoidable part of doing business, JetBlue took it as a sign that they weren't doing nearly enough for their customers and for what JetBlue stood for. The findings of the internal investigation found that JetBlue had failed to equip itself with enough infrastructure to handle a situation like this. David Neeleman quickly announced amidst the chaos that they had failed to provide themselves with reservation and employee communication systems large enough for a corporation their size. They had been using systems that were identical to the ones put together near the time of their founding. They stepped out in front of a crisis that could have been shaken off, instead using it as a way to strengthen their organizational communication systems and their brand in a single step.

Going forward, JetBlue changed everything they could to better themselves. Neeleman announced once the investigation was completed, "This is going to be a different company because of this. It's going to be expensive. But what's more important is to win back people's confidence." From then on JetBlue focused on building a system that is scalable and that customers can depend on in difficult situations like storms.

In conclusion, JetBlue stepped out in front of an unfortunate situation and managed to make it a teaching moment for them and for their industry. They could have blamed the weather or settled claims silently but instead they reformed themselves as a company focused on over-delivering in easy times and hard. Other companies have a lot to learn from crises like this one and the ones that can take lessons from situations like these are the ones that will continuously succeed.

Discussion Questions

1. Describe the options that JetBlue had when faced with the ice storm crisis.

2. What can any business learn from the mistakes that JetBlue made?

Sources

Bailey, J. (2007, February 19). JetBlue's C.E.O. is 'mortified' after fliers are stranded. Retrieved from https://www.nytimes.com/2007/02/19/business/19jetblue.html

Business Insider. (2007). *JetBlue's week-long operational breakdown*. Retrieved from http://www.businessinsider.com/pr-disasters-crisis-management-2011-5#jetblues-week-long-operational-breakdown-2007-6

Sachs, A. (2007, April 19). The new world of crisis management. *TIME*. Retrieved from http://content.time.com/time/magazine/article/0,9171,1612698,00.html

Smith, D. J. (2011, January 28). Jet Blue crisis management. *The Marketplace of Life*. Retrieved from http://themarketplaceoflife.blogspot.com/2011/01/jet-blue-crisis-management.html

SELF-ASSESSMENT 9.1

Corporate Social Responsibility

Corporate social responsibility (CSR) is defined as a business approach that delivers economic, social, and environmental benefits to stakeholders in order to contribute to sustainable development. People hold varying views on the level or extent to which organizations should be involved in CSR. The following brief assessment will help you to determine your views regarding the most appropriate level of CSR in organizations.

For each pair of statements below, choose the letter of the statement with which you agree the most.

1.

W – The primary responsibility for businesspeople should be to run an efficient and effective business.

X – Organizations should "play by the rules" doing whatever is most effective so long as they don't break any laws.

2.

W - Businesspeople are best equipped to run an effective business, not to solve the problems of society.

Y - The organization should hold itself to a higher standard than basic economic expediency or legal compliance.

3.

W - Solving social problems is a task best left to specialized nonprofit and government organizations.

Z – Organizations should go above and beyond the call of duty in taking actions for the public good.

4.

X – Organizations should comply with laws but should not be expected to go beyond legal requirements.

Y - Even if there's now a law against dumping waste in the river and it will be more expensive to dispose of the waste by other means, the organization should choose not to dump in the river if it appears it could do damage to the environment.

5.

X - An organization should be able to dump waste into the river if there is no law against it and it is in its own best interest. However, the organization should comply with any laws making such a practice illegal.

Z - The organization should take proactive actions in an effort to make the world a better place.

6.

Y – The organization should choose the action that represents the right thing to do.

Z – It is the responsibility of wealthy individuals and organizations to use their wealth for the betterment of society.

Scoring:

Add the number of times you chose W: _____

This score is an indicator of the strength of your preference for an *economic responsibility* level of CSR.

Add the number of times you chose X: _____

This score is an indicator of the strength of your preference for a *legal responsibility* level of CSR.

Add the number of times you chose Y: _____

This score is an indicator of the strength of your preference for an *ethical responsibility* level of CSR.

Add the number of times you chose Z: _____

This score is an indicator of the strength of your preference for a *discretionary responsibility* level of CSR.

10 Effective Communication

Intelligence, knowledge or experience are important and might get you a job, but strong communication skills are what will get you promoted.

—*Mireille Guiliano, French author*

Learning Objectives

By the end of this chapter, you will be able to:

10.1 Describe the basic model of communication

10.2 Compare the types of communication channels

10.3 Identify key barriers to effective communication

10.4 Describe types of communication networks within organizations

10.5 Discuss the elements of effective cross-cultural communication

CASE STUDY: UBER'S ORGANIZATIONAL COMMUNICATION

With more than $6.5 billion in annual revenues, around seven thousand full-time employees, operations in more than 570 cities worldwide, and an innovative service that has changed the way we look at business, Uber has been an example of excellence in the tech start-up community since its inception in March of 2009. In fact, the company's name has its roots in the German word *uber*, meaning super or topmost; a testament to the company's commitment to excellence. However, Uber has run into some trouble that has tainted this image, stemming from recent trends in the organization's communication.

As Mike Issac of the *New York Times* puts it, "The focus on pushing for the best result has also fueled what current and former Uber employees describe as a Hobbesian environment at the company, in which workers are sometimes pitted against one another and where a blind eye is turned to infractions from top performers." Historically, the verbal communication practices that flow through the formal and the informal networks at Uber have been very detrimental to the company's image and productivity over time.

In any organization, there are two networks through which communication flows: formal networks and the informal networks. The formal networks represent the transmission of messages established and approved by the organizational hierarchy. This type of communication is typically imposed by the chain of command through policies and procedures and can be observed through a manager's downward communication.

Downward communication is defined as messages sent from the upper levels of the organizational hierarchy to the lower levels. Simply put, the way managers communicate with their inferiors is crucial to their effectiveness as managers. Managers who communicate expectations through clear, concise, and respectful messages are much more likely to receive the highest quality of work from their employees than managers who communicate very vague expectations and use verbal abuse toward employees whom they deem incompetent. An employee is much more responsive when receiving messages that make them feel empowered and cared for. Accusations of verbal abuse at Uber, like the claim that an Uber manager threatened to beat an underperforming employee's head in with a baseball bat, are an indication of a culture rooted in verbal abuse. Managers have an ethical responsibility to provide verbal, nonthreatening constructive criticism to their inferiors. If nothing else, managers who communicate in this healthy way will, at the very least, see more improvement from their employees over time.

Additionally, there has been no room for employees to share their differing perceptions with one another. Differing perceptions are the way in which our interpretations of situations clash with the perceptions of others. What the management at Uber failed to realize is that the different perceptions of their employees is one of their most valuable assets. Some of the best ideas are brought to the tables by employees who see a situation a different way. By suppressing an employee's ability to do so, managers at Uber effectively put a halt to its internal creativity and hurt its own productivity. On one occasion, a director shouted a homophobic slur at a subordinate during a heated confrontation in a meeting. This verbal abuse toward a subordinate not only is another example of the presence of faulty downward communication at Uber but it also likely sent a message to other subordinates that differing perceptions had no place in the company.

Informal communication is defined as a casual form of sharing information between employees across company divisions. This is the everyday, free-ranging communication that employees partake in to build relationships and share opinions. Informal communication takes place through what is called the grapevine. It is simply an unofficial line of communication between individuals or groups. Informal communication through the grapevine will happen naturally in any organization and it can be a healthy contributor to the well-being of employees. However, if informal communication is let loose in a belligerent workplace it can have some seriously adverse effects to the organization as a whole. The grapevine in an organization with a culture like that of Uber has the potential to give rise to gossip chains. Gossip chains are a type of communication that occurs when one individual creates and spreads untrue or inaccurate information through the organization. At Uber, the excessively competitive culture has created an environment where stepping on the toes of fellow employees and damaging other's reputations is considered acceptable behavior. In Uber's case, "people wind up 'stepping on toes' in the wrong direction. Instead of challenging managers or superiors with bad ideas, they put down their peers." The formal and informal communication networks of Uber have been tainted by these past trends. Currently, Uber is taking steps to remedy the situation and start fresh.

The corrupt culture of Uber started to be brought to light to the public in 2016 and since then the company has taken steps toward fixing the problems they have caused for themselves. There has been pushback from upper management and high employee turnover rates have made it difficult to get new culture initiatives to find a foothold within the company. In June of 2017, Uber hired HR consultant Frances Frei to serve as its senior vice president of leadership and strategy. Prior to this engagement, Ms. Frei was a professor at Harvard University with a bio that said that she was "a personal advisor to senior executives embarking on cultural change and organizational transformations." This is exactly what Uber needs and the hiring of people like this is a true testament to Uber's commitment to changing its workplace culture by bringing in management who will actively challenge what used to be the status quo. Continued practices such as this are the key to any problems that originally stem from poor management. Many companies in the past, like Enron and WorldCom, have not been able to rebound from poor communication practices in management and this led to even larger problems like fraud and embezzlement. This is a huge step forward in the right direction for Uber, and the company should continue on this track as it strives to be a leader once again.

Critical-Thinking Questions

1. Why is important that differing perspectives are encouraged and praised as opposed to shut down and ridiculed like they were at Uber?

2. What network, formal or informal, is most important for a company to administer?

Sources:

Bradt, G. (2017). Why Uber needs a mu sigma culture to survive. *Forbes.* Retrieved from https://www.forbes.com/forbes/welcome/?toURL=https://www.forbes.com/sites/georgebradt/2017/06/10/why-uber-needs-a-mu-sigma-culture-to-survive/&refURL=https://www.google.com/&referrer=https://www.google.com/

Feldman, B. (2017, June 5). Uber hires business-school academic Frances Frei to reshape the company. *Intelligencer.* Retrieved from http://nymag.com/selectall/2017/06/uber-hires-frances-frei-to-reshape-the-company.html

Forbes. (n.d.). *#104 Travis Kalanick.* Retrieved from https://www.forbes.com/profile/travis-kalanick/#2a9656366199

Griswold, A. (2017). Uber is designed so that for one employee to get ahead, another must fail. *Quartz.* Retrieved from https://qz.com/918582/uber-is-designed-so-that-for-one-employee-to-succeed-another-must-fail/

Isaac, M. (2017, February 22). Inside Uber's aggressive, unrestrained workplace culture. *The New York Times.* Retrieved from https://www.nytimes.com/2017/02/22/technology/uber-workplace-culture.html?_r=1

Uber. (n.d.). *Move the way you want.* Retrieved from https://www.uber.com/

The Role of Effective Communication in Influencing Others

>> LO 10.1   Describe the basic model of communication

The Uber case demonstrates what can happen when communication breaks down in an organization. People hurling abuse at each other or making verbal threats brings down morale, and can turn a culture toxic. In an increasingly connected world, communication is more important than ever in the workplace. Today's organizations have no choice but to adapt quickly to the rise of new technologies and social networking tools in order to keep up with the competition and stay in touch with the needs of their customer bases. We define **communication** as the act of transmitting thoughts, processes, and ideas through a variety of channels.[1] Efficient communication leads to better functioning of organizations, which benefits both employees and customers.

Communication: The act of transmitting thoughts, processes, and ideas through a variety of channels

Inside the organization, effective communication must take place within and among peer groups and between different hierarchical levels. One of the most important roles of a manager is to encourage and nurture a collaborative working environment by effectively communicating with teams to ensure that tasks are accomplished and organizational goals achieved. Take a look at how renewable energy company NextEra Energy implements effective communication in the OB in the Real World feature.

In 1947, mathematician Claude E. Shannon created a communication model that was later developed further by Warren Weaver. The Shannon-Weaver model (see Figure 10.1) is the cornerstone of communication models and is still in use today.[2]

The Shannon-Weaver model assumes that communication relies on two main components: the *sender* of the message, also known

FIGURE 10.1

Shannon-Weaver Communications Model

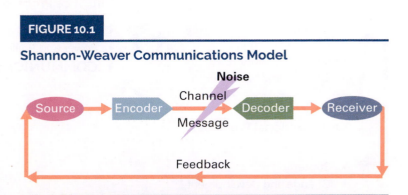

Source: Adapted from Shannon, C. E., & Weaver, W. *The Mathematical Theory of Communication* (Urbana: University of Illinois Press, 1949).

as the source, and the *receiver* of the message. When the sender transmits a message through a communication channel—the route the message travels along—the content of the message is encoded into its intended meaning through different formats such as written, oral, or electronic; the receiver then decodes or interprets the message into a perceived meaning. The receiver provides feedback or a response to the sender to confirm the message has been received and its meaning understood.

Although this sounds like a fairly simple process, disturbances known as *noise* often occur. Background noise such as people talking loudly, construction work, or telephones ringing can all interfere with our ability to communicate effectively. Noise in the context of the Shannon-Weaver Model does not necessarily refer to sound, however; noise refers to interference that can muddy a message between the sender and receiver. In this context, noise might refer to complex or difficult language or cultural differences that distort meaning. It is essential for sender and receiver to clear their communication channels of any noise that may disrupt the meaning of the message.

THINKING CRITICALLY

1. To what extent have technological advances (smartphones, laptops, tablet devices) made it easier to communicate effectively in organizations? To what extent have these advances made miscommunications more likely? Explain your answers.

2. Consider the Shannon-Weaver Communications Model. At what junctures in the model can miscommunications occur? To what extent is noise or some other factor to blame for miscommunication?

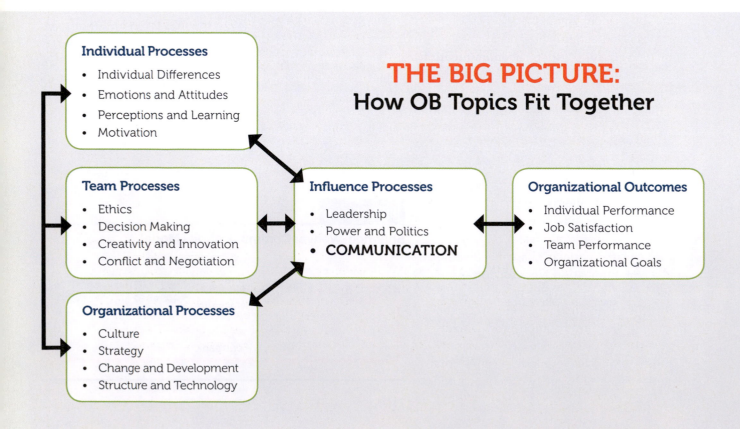

THE BIG PICTURE:
How OB Topics Fit Together

Individual Processes
- Individual Differences
- Emotions and Attitudes
- Perceptions and Learning
- Motivation

Team Processes
- Ethics
- Decision Making
- Creativity and Innovation
- Conflict and Negotiation

Organizational Processes
- Culture
- Strategy
- Change and Development
- Structure and Technology

Influence Processes
- Leadership
- Power and Politics
- **COMMUNICATION**

Organizational Outcomes
- Individual Performance
- Job Satisfaction
- Team Performance
- Organizational Goals

Types of Communication Channels

>> **LO 10.2** Compare the types of communication channels

As recently as 30 years ago, only a handful of communication channels were available to us. But thanks to the rapid rise of technology, we now have myriad ways to send and receive messages (Figure 10.2). Let's explore the different types of communication channels we use in daily life.

Oral communication is the exchange of information, ideas, and processes verbally, either one on one or as a group. In the workplace, we regularly communicate orally through telephone conversations, presentations, meetings, and conferences. For instance, Hillary Clinton's commencement speech at Wellesley College outside Boston in May 2017 is an example of oral communication.

Oral communication:
The ability to give and exchange information, ideas, and processes verbally, either one on one or as a group

OB IN THE REAL WORLD

Destin Cook, Director of Finance, NextEra Energy

Headquartered in Juno Beach, Florida, NextEra Energy is the largest renewable energy company in the United States and the world. Through its subsidiaries, NextEra boasts over $18 billion in revenues, generation of over 41,000 megawatts of energy, a $66 billion market cap, and active energy production in 24 states and Canada. Not to mention a workforce of over fifteen thousand employees, countless awards in customer service and workplace culture, and great relationships with some of the largest banks worldwide.

One statistic that is a real head turner is the fact that NextEra spends over $10 billion every year purely on capital expenditures. Only a handful of even the largest companies in the world can sustain this type of spending. In fact, NextEra is ranked in the top three companies worldwide for capital expenditures. So how does NextEra Energy spend all this money without killing itself? The hardworking men and women who are managers in the finance department are tasked with finding alternative ways to finance NextEra Energy's pricey operations.

Destin Cook, director of finance in NextEra's treasury department, oversees some portion of virtually every financing deal that NextEra engages in. Destin has been working in the treasury department at NextEra for ten years now. After climbing the corporate ladder and leveraging his critical thinking and quantitative skillsets, Destin has found himself leading as a direct liaison to the company's executive management, a direct point

of contact for many of NextEra's banking clients, and he even runs his own small team of analysts and interns. In order to consistently perform at a high level, Destin needs to leverage a wide array of skills when running all these different operations. The most important skill Destin needs to excel should be no surprise, communication.

Communication is defined as the act of transmitting thoughts, processes, and ideas through a variety of different channels. Communication plays a huge role in how effective a business functions and has great benefits to the company's employees and employers. One of Destin's most important tasks as a manager is to cultivate a collaborative working environment that pushes the department closer to reaching organizational goals. Communicating with peers on different hierarchical levels and countless different external parties is not an easy task for a manager. However, Destin has mastered the art of organizational communication which has led to not only his personal success as a manager but also to the success of the company as a whole.

There are many types of communication that take place in the office at NextEra: nonverbal, oral, written, and electronic. According to Destin, while he has learned to use all types of communication, he thinks that face-to-face oral communication is by far the most effective. Oral communication is considered to be the ability to give and exchange ideas and processes verbally, either one on one or as a group. Destin uses this type of communication while

(Continued)

(Continued)

working with superiors and working with his own team through upward communication and downward communication. Upward communication occurs when Destin speaks with his managers and is formally defined as messages sent from the lower levels of the organizational hierarchy to the higher levels. Downward communication occurs when messages are sent from the upper levels of the organizational hierarchy to the lower levels. According to Destin, he tries not to differentiate the way he communicates with people above or below him on the organizational chart. "We work in an organization where our management isn't afraid to roll up our sleeves and work alongside our employees as teammates rather than superiors."

This mind-set has translated into a very healthy communication environment for the members of Destin's team. The members of Destin's team enjoy open lines of communication where they are able to openly express alternative perspectives on issues. Destin values "being upfront and open to differing perspectives." As he puts it, "I am not an expert on

every subject by any means. Different perspectives and different backgrounds bring new ideas and solutions and I am happy to have my opinion swayed." It is important that, as a manager, Destin keeps an open mind and stays clear of letting his emotions control him. In business communications, emotions should only play a limited role and a delicate balance is needed; that is exactly how Destin operates. "There is a delicate balance. I think about my own emotions and other's emotions and I want myself and others to be passionate about what we do. Candidly, I want people who care a lot about their job. Passion is good but, just like anything, too much of a good thing can be a hindrance, off-putting the people you work with or are negotiating with."

Critical-Thinking Questions

1. In what ways can emotions hinder a manager's ability to lead?

2. What are the benefits of empowering employees to freely communicate with their superiors? ●

The State of the Union is one example of oral communication, when the President of the United States gives a speech to the country about the status of the country and its government.

Written communication:
Messages communicated through the written word, such as email, reports, memos, letters, and other channels

Electronic communication:
The ability to transmit messages through email, Skype, videoconferencing, blogs, fax, instant messaging, texting, and social networking

Advantages and disadvantages of oral communication. Talking to people in person or on the phone or in a video chat is an excellent way to network and build relationships. Another major advantage of oral communication is that messages are sent and received almost instantaneously, and feedback is given just as fast, so misunderstandings can be quickly cleared up. However, sometimes the informal nature of oral communication means that messages or parts of messages are forgotten or misunderstood later.

Written communication makes use of the written word in the form of reports, memos, and letters to communicate messages. Notice of acceptance to college or a formal job offer is usually delivered in a written letter.

Advantages and disadvantages of written communication. Senders can review written messages before sending and record and archive them if necessary. However, unless the receiver provides feedback, the sender will not always know whether the message has reached its destination or has been interpreted correctly.

Electronic communication is the transmission of messages through email, Skype, videoconferencing, blogs, fax, instant messaging, texting, and social networking (Twitter, Snapchat, Viber, LinkedIn, Facebook, YouTube, Pinterest, Instagram, and more). Many companies and social activist groups use "hashtag campaigns" to quickly and broadly disperse information and start conversations around certain topics, events, and products.

Advantages and disadvantages of electronic communication. There is no better way of instantly reaching a large audience across a global network than through forms of electronic communication. However, electronic communication can be hindered by technical problems, misinterpretation, and privacy breaches. Take the rise of hacker ransoms, for instance. Hackers use ransomware (malicious software) to make electronic devices unusable or threaten to publish data until a ransom is paid by the owner. In 2017, over 300,000 computers worldwide were affected by a ransomware attack, called "WannaCry," including some hospital systems in the United Kingdom which blocked doctors from accessing patient records.[3]

Written electronic communication can be an especially poor channel for delivering negative news because it does not provide an adequate means for expressing emotion. When delivering negative feedback, it is always best to do it over the phone or in person. Overall, it is easy to make mistakes over email, especially when dealing with a huge volume of correspondence. Table 10.1 provides some tips for email etiquette.

Nonverbal communication is the transmission of wordless cues between people. Examples of nonverbal cues include facial expression, eye gaze, gestures, tone of voice, the way we walk, stand, dress, and position ourselves.[4] From the way we shake hands to the color of the clothing we wear, nonverbal details show others who we are and influence the way we are perceived. The type of body language we use in the workplace is especially important when communicating with our colleagues.[5] For example, jiggling legs, hair twirling, or face touching may be perceived by others as boredom, nervousness, or some other insecurity. Similarly, failure to make eye contact might make the other person think that you're not interested in what they have to say. Being aware of our body language and what it means goes a long way toward building good working relationships. Figure 10.3 illustrates how different types of body language may be interpreted by others.

Nonverbal communication occurs in popular sitcoms like *Modern Family* as in many sitcoms, where the characters often engage in different facial expressions and gestures to convey thoughts and emotions.

Advantages and disadvantages of nonverbal communication. Nonverbal communication can be an important way of interacting with others because it allows for transmission of subtle messages through eye contact, vocal tone, and posture. However, because we are usually unaware of the nonverbal messages we are sending, we are at risk of unintentionally conveying the wrong message, which, in turn, may give the wrong impression. There can also be confusion and discrepancies between the nonverbal cues we convey and the words we are saying. For example, you might tell your

FIGURE 10.2

Communication Channels

Source: Neck, C. *Management* (Hoboken, NJ: Wiley, 2013): 379.

Nonverbal communication: The transmission of wordless cues between people

professor you are happy to stay after class and take on an extra assignment, but defensive body language such as folded arms, downcast eyes, and legs crossed away from your professor will suggest otherwise.

TABLE 10.1

Tips for Email Etiquette[6]

1. Write a clear subject line
Remember that people are more likely to click on an email that has a clear, relevant subject line. For example, if your email is about changing a date for a meeting, then simply use "Meeting date changed" as the subject line.
2. Use the company email address
It may sound obvious, but when you're working in a company, don't be tempted to use your personal email address for professional interactions. Even if you are self-employed, you're better off choosing a more professional email address rather than one like "beerlover@. . ."
3. Beware of "reply all"
It is a common irritation at work to receive emails from people that have nothing to do with you, and it's even worse when those people hit "reply all" sending dozens of messages into your mailbox. Unless there is a good reason why everyone on the mailing list needs to see your email, think twice about hitting the "reply all" button.
4. Use professional greetings
Regardless of how well you think you know the person (or people) you are emailing, do not be tempted to open an email with, "Yo," or "Hey you guys," or "Hi folks." Informal greetings sound amateurish and unprofessional. It is fine to use "Hi" or "Hello" instead. Furthermore, try to avoid shortening people's names unless you know for sure they are comfortable with it. For example, if you're sending an email to someone called David, don't address him as "Dave" unless you know that this is his preference.
5. Don't overuse exclamation points
Too many exclamation points in an email can come across as being overly emotional and immature. Only use exclamation points to convey excitement where relevant. For example, "We made the deadline. Well done team!"
6. Be careful with humor
Using humor in work emails is particularly risky as without the right tone or facial expression, the message often gets lost in translation. Besides, just because you think it's funny doesn't mean someone else will.
7. Understand cultural differences
It is common for miscommunication to occur because of cultural differences. Make sure you take cultural expectations into account when composing your emails. In general, Japanese, Arab, or Chinese cultures tend to be more personal in their emails, mainly because they like to get to know someone first before committing to a professional relationship. In contrast, people from German, American, or Scandinavian cultures tend to favor emails that get to the point quickly. We discuss cross-cultural communication later in the chapter.
8. Always proof your emails before sending them!
Spell-check can only take you so far. Make sure you read over your emails before pressing "send." Remember, your recipient is likely to spot your mistakes and will judge you for them.
9. Remember that every email leaves a trail
There is no such thing as a "forgotten" email. Impulsive, hotheaded emails could easily come back to haunt you. As a guideline, never write anything that could jeopardize your job, hurt others, or harm your reputation. If the recipient forwards it on, you never know who may end up reading it.
10. Try to avoid the emoji craze
Finally, avoid using smiley faces (emoticons) or other types of emojis in professional emails. According to a new study by researchers at Ben-Gurion University of the Negev in Israel, the use of smiley faces and emojis might undermine your overall competence. "Our findings provide first-time evidence that, contrary to actual smiles, smileys do not increase perceptions of warmth and actually decrease perceptions of competence," said researcher Dr Ella Gilkson.[7]

Most of the rules about emails also apply to texting but remember only to use text if you're working in a role that allows you to text business clients.[8] If not, it is best to put your phone away and avoid texting at work; otherwise it may appear as though your mind is not on the job. Some companies have strict rules about texting. For instance, investment banking giant Deutsche Bank has banned employees from using all texting apps, including Facebook Messenger, iMessage, and WhatsApp.[9]

Texting during meetings, business lunches, and other work-related activities can be perceived as lack of interest by your colleagues and clients. Even texting from the relative privacy of your desk can look unprofessional; it is always better to find a private space if you genuinely need to text. Finally, if you do really need to send or receive a text at your desk, make sure your phone is on silent—continuous beeping from text alerts is bound to frustrate and distract your colleagues from their own work.

Similarly, try to avoid making and answering personal calls on your smartphone at work, especially in front of your manager or during team meetings. If the call is urgent, briefly explain why and then find a place to talk quietly so as not to disturb your coworkers. Remember to keep the call as brief as possible so it doesn't affect your working day. If you get a missed call, try to avoid returning the call immediately especially if you know it is not urgent. Instead, wait until your designated break time to respond. Most importantly, be mindful of the people around you when answering your phone, and don't let your smartphone distract you from your work responsibilities.

FIGURE 10.3

Different Types of Body Language

Openness vs. Defensiveness   Expectancy vs. Frustration

Evaluation vs. Suspicion   Self-control vs. Nervousness

Readiness vs. Boredom   Confidence vs. Insecurity

Engaging Approachable Body Language

Source: Tutorials Point. "Cracking Interviews - Quick Guide." https://www.tutorialspoint.com/cracking_interviews/cracking_interviews_quick_guide.htm

Characters on ABC's *Modern Family* often convey their thoughts and emotions through nonverbal communication such as facial expressions and body language.

With so many communication channels to choose from, how do we choose the most appropriate one for certain situations? One way is to weigh **channel richness**, the degree to which a channel allows us to easily communicate and understand information sent between people and organizations (Figure 10.4). Face-to-face communication during meetings or videoconferencing is thought to be the richest form of communication. It allows for immediate feedback, the understanding of verbal and

Channel richness: The capacity to communicate and understand information between people and organizations

FIGURE 10.4

Channel Richness

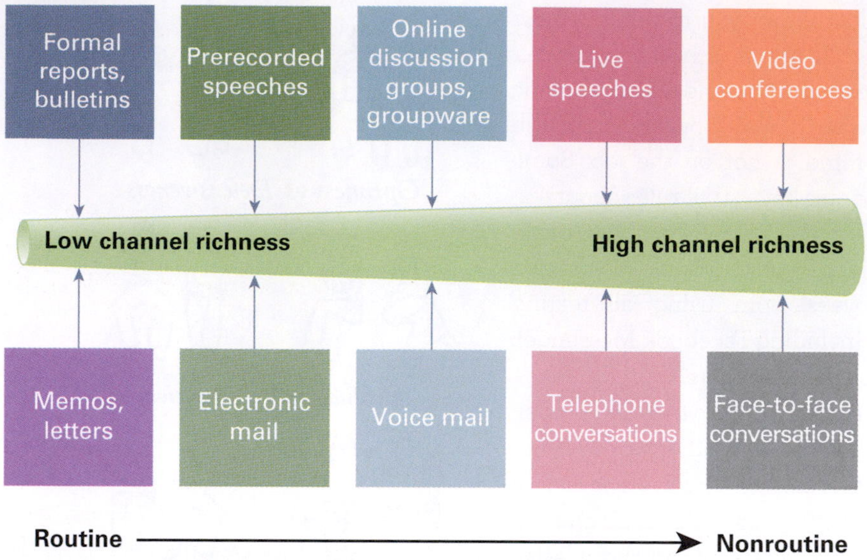

| Formal reports, bulletins | Prerecorded speeches | Online discussion groups, groupware | Live speeches | Video conferences |

Low channel richness ←→ **High channel richness**

| Memos, letters | Electronic mail | Voice mail | Telephone conversations | Face-to-face conversations |

Routine ————————————→ Nonroutine

nonverbal cues, and opportunities for building relationships. But like many other forms of electronic communication, videoconferencing still has its disadvantages: technical hitches, hacking, and time lags (which tend to interrupt the flow of the conversation) can sometimes make smooth communication difficult.

The second-richest channel is the phone. During phone conversations we are able to listen to verbal cues, detect levels of emotion, and pick up on nonverbal cues such as tone of voice. Despite their popularity, emails, text messages, blogs, memos, e-bulletins, and so on are considered to be at the lower end of channel richness, especially when the information becomes sensitive or complex. By far the most effective way of resolving a situation or dealing with a difficult issue is to call a face-to-face meeting or pick up the phone.

THINKING CRITICALLY

1. Make a list of all the channels of communication you use on a regular basis. Do you ever choose your communication channel based on the content of your message? Why or why not?

2. Discuss a misunderstanding you have had with a friend or work colleague and how you went about clearing up the misunderstanding. Did the channel of communication that you chose to convey the message contribute to the misunderstanding? Did you correct the misunderstanding using the same channel of communication you used or switch to a different channel to address the misunderstanding? Explain your answer.

3. Review the list of channels of communication that you use on a regular basis compiled for Question 1 and label them as low in channel richness or high in channel richness. Based on the text discussion, are you inclined to begin using channels higher in communication richness? Why or why not?

Barriers to Communication

>> **LO 10.3** **Identify key barriers to effective communication**

Because communication is central to our relationships with others, it is essential that we understand the barriers that can hamper our ability to communicate successfully and learn how to overcome them.[10] Here are some of the barriers most often encountered at work.

Filtering. When someone screens and then manipulates a message from a sender before passing it on to the intended receiver, that person has filtered the message. Research suggests that too much information (information overload) is one of the main reasons that we are five times more susceptible to marketing and political manipulation than we were thirty years ago.[11]

Emotions. Our emotions have an effect on the way we communicate. When we are happy and relaxed, we are more likely to accept constructive criticism in a positive way and convey our messages succinctly and accurately. However, when we are stressed or angry, we might snap at others or feel attacked or defensive when someone tries to offer advice. It is essential that we are aware of our emotions and keep them in check before they spiral out of control. For example, former Uber CEO Travis Kalanick suffered irreparable damage to his reputation when video footage (which went viral all over the world) showed Kalanick losing his temper when quizzed by Uber driver Fawzi Kamel about the falling of fare prices.[12]

Information overload. At times, we can become overwhelmed by the wealth of information surrounding us. This can lead us to make hasty decisions or lose our ability to prioritize. Studies have found that information overload reduces creativity, decreases productivity, impacts workflow, and can even cause headaches, stress, and insomnia.[13] Being able to prioritize our workload helps us to make better decisions and prevents us from getting overloaded by information.

Differing perceptions. Sometimes the way we interpret situations clashes with the perceptions of others, leading to confusion and misconception. For example, clashing perceptions between millennials and older generations have led to conflict in the workplace. In one survey, over 70 percent of Americans considered millennials to be selfish, while 65 percent thought them to be entitled.[14] We can overcome this communication barrier by challenging our own assumptions about other people and situations and by seeking advice from others to clarify our perceptions. Proper training for employees in organizations helps to align perceptions.

Filtering: The process of screening and then manipulating a message from a sender before passing it on to the intended receiver

Emotions: A state of feeling that affects the way we communicate

Information overload: Exposure to an overwhelming amount of information

Differing perceptions: The way in which our interpretations of situations clashes with the perceptions of others.

Active Listening

The Greek philosopher Epictetus once said, "We have two ears and one mouth so we should listen twice as much as we speak." This quote references one of the biggest obstacles to successful communication: poor listening. Within organizations, failure to listen properly can lead to misunderstandings that can damage personal and work relationships. Ineffective listening also comes at a high price—it is estimated that millions of dollars are wasted every year due to the time it takes to repeat information, correct misunderstandings, and make up for loss of productivity.[15]

A way to overcome poor listening is through **active listening,** which consists of concentrating on the true meaning of what others are saying.[16] It is an essential skill for employees in the workplace because it allows the receiver to hear and understand the message and reassures the speaker that the message has been heard in the same terms in which it is delivered. Good active listeners remove all distractions so they can concentrate on what is being said, show a real interest in the message the speaker is trying to deliver, and provide appropriate responses to the speaker at suitable times. More and more business leaders are realizing the value of active listening; for example, Peter Hill, CEO of leading golf management company Billy Casper Golf, says, "When I am speaking, I'm not learning."[17]

Active listening: The act of concentrating on the true meaning of what others are saying

In addition, studies have shown that our increasing tendency to communicate through modern technology has negatively impacted our listening skills. According to estimates by consultants Ed Keller and Brad Fay, 90 percent of our most productive conversations take place offline, while only 8 percent occur online. Keller and Fay explain, "Social media is big and growing, but it is still dwarfed by the analog world in which people live and interact."[18] In other words, they believe that interpersonal communication is more powerful and human than conversing through the medium of technology. One of the main reasons for this is the inability to interpret body language and tone of voice. However, people who learn to be active listeners can overcome these problems by paying close attention to the people with whom they are communicating, whether in-person or online.

FIGURE 10.5

The Active Listening Process

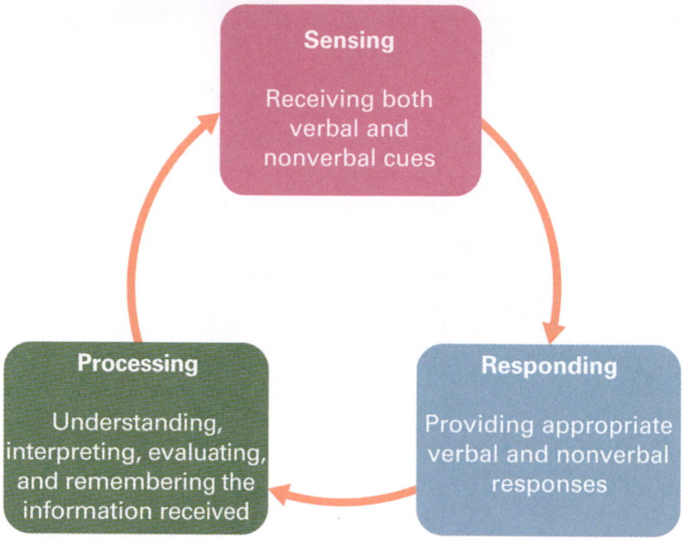

Source: Based on Comer, Lucette B., and Tanya Drollinger. "Active Empathetic Listening and Selling Success: A Conceptual Framework." *Journal of Personal Selling and Sales Management* 19, no. 1 (Winter 1999): 15–29.

There are three main components to active listening: processing, sensing, and responding (see Figure 10.5).[19]

Processing involves actively understanding and remembering what is being said as well as making an effort to empathize with the speaker's feelings and thoughts and the situation at hand. Active listening also requires looking for nonverbal cues such eye contact or lack thereof, poor posture (slouching, sitting upright, and tense), and tone of voice (sarcastic, angry, confident) to really understand the entire message.

Sensing involves paying attention to the signals sent from the speaker. The listener avoids forming an opinion or interrupting the speaker until he or she has finished and consciously remains attentive to what the speaker is saying.

Finally, **responding** is the way active listeners provide feedback to the speaker ("I see what you mean") and clarify the message by repeating some of the key points at appropriate breaks ("So, you're saying that . . .").

As we have illustrated, communication between individuals can be complex and is often the cause of conflicts and misunderstandings. In the next section, we explore how the different directions of communication affect the functioning of organizations.

Processing: The act of understanding and remembering what is being said as well as making an effort to empathize with the speaker's feelings and thoughts and the situation at hand.

Sensing: The way listeners pay attention to the signals sent from the speaker

Responding: The way active listeners provide feedback to the speaker

EXAMINING THE EVIDENCE

Electronic Communication during Nonworking Hours

Increases in electronic communication technologies such as smartphones, tablets, laptops, and wireless Internet have made it easier than ever for organizations to communicate with their employees outside of working hours. But what are the effects of these after-hour communications on employee well-being? In a recent study, researchers Marcus M. Butts of the University of Texas at Arlington, William J. Becker of Texas Christian University, and Wendy R. Boswell of Texas A & M University explored this question. They found that the emotional reaction and amount of work-nonwork role conflict experienced by employees receiving after-hours communications depended on the affective content and time demands of the messages. Messages with a positive affective tone involving encouragement, support, and recognition and that demanded less communication time resulted in more employee happiness and ultimately less work-nonwork conflict. In contrast, messages with a negative affective tone involving uncivil, degrading, or hostile content and those that demanded more communication time resulted in greater employee anger and more work-nonwork conflict. These findings suggest that communications sent outside of regular working hours should focus on positive feedback and accomplishments and not focus on problems, criticisms, and deficiencies. Organizations may be well advised to provide employees with training and guidelines on the appropriate use of electronic communications outside normal working hours.

Critical-Thinking Questions

1. Would it be advisable for organizations to implement policies prohibiting electronic communication after normal working hours? Why or why not?

2. Specifically, what types of messages would be best delivered electronically outside of working hours? Provide some examples of effective after-hour communications. ●

Source: Butts, Marcus M., William J. Becker, and Wendy R. Boswell. 2015. "Hot Buttons and Time Sinks: The Effects of Electronic Communication during Nonwork Time On Emotions and Work-Nonwork Conflict." *Academy Of Management Journal* 58, no. 3: 763–788.

THINKING CRITICALLY

1. Review the barriers to communication (filtering, emotions, information overload, differing perceptions). Provide at least one strategy for counteracting or overcoming each one of these barriers.

2. Active listening is described as the best solution for poor listening skills. In what, if any, situations can you imagine being an adept active listener? Defend your answer.

3. Review the three active listening steps (processing, sensing, responding). Given the text description of these steps, what obstacles to active listening will channels of communication low in information richness present? Explain your answer.

Communicating in Organizations

>> **LO 10.4** Describe types of communication networks within organizations

The flow of communication in an organization can move in three main directions depending on how an organization is structured.[20] (See Figure 10.6.)

Downward communication sends messages from the upper levels of the organizational hierarchy to the lower levels. For example, in hierarchical organizations like the military, there is a tendency to use downward communication. One of the major

Downward communication: Messages sent from the upper levels of the organizational hierarchy to the lower levels

FIGURE 10.6

Three Directions of Communication in Organizations

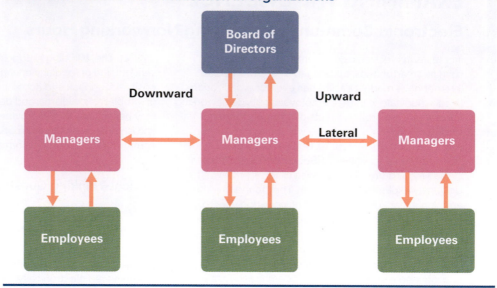

Source: Based on Lunenburg, Fred C. "Formal Communication Channels: Upward, Downward, Horizontal, and External." *Focus on Colleges, Universities, and Schools* 4, no. 1 (2010). www.nationalforum.com/Electronic%20Journal%20Volumes/Lunenburg,%20Fred%20C,%20Formal%20Comm%20Channels%20FOCUS%20V4%20N1%202010.pdf.

functions of downward communication is to maintain discipline and employee compliance through positive influence. When downward communication is successful, it is totally transparent. This means that lower-level employees consistently receive clear messages and feedback from their superiors regarding organizational performance, strategies, developments, and goals. Sharing information down the levels provides employees with a sense of involvement and minimizes doubt and insecurity about how the company is performing. However, when downward communication goes wrong and messages fail to be transmitted effectively down the chain of command, it can cause confusion, distrust, and anxiety among the rest of the workforce.

Upward communication sends messages from the lower levels of the organizational hierarchy to the higher levels. Some organizations value feedback, suggestions, and advice from lower-level employees who are "on the ground" and may be closer to knowing the needs of the customer. For example, Virgin founder Richard Branson makes a point of talking to his staff and getting feedback. Branson believes his staff on the front line are key to running a successful organization. He says, "And the people out on the front line, they know when things are not going right and they know when things need to be improved. And if you listen to them you can soon improve all those niggly things which turns an average company into an exceptional company."[21]

These employees are also encouraged to share any problems or thoughts they have about the organization and their roles and provide recommendations for improvement. If lower-level employees do not effectively communicate with their superiors and instead withhold or filter information, this can leave those at the higher levels ignorant of what is really going on in the organization.

Lateral communication sends messages between and among similar hierarchical levels across organizations. Lateral communication can be an effective way for people from different departments to communicate the information they need quickly and accurately. Organizations that foster a collaborative environment encourage lateral communication between their employees. For example,

Upward communication: Messages sent from the lower levels of the organizational hierarchy to the higher levels

Lateral communication: Messages sent between and among the same hierarchical levels across organizations collaborative organizations like IDEO use lateral communication to gather ideas from employees across several disciplines in order to generate creative solutions.[22] Although lateral communication supports teamwork and helps build morale, it requires managerial control to minimize potential interpersonal conflict that may arise as a result of many participants collaborating at once.

Let's take a look at the communication network operated by Trader Joe's.

Thriving US food retailer Trader Joe's owes much of its success to its communication process. When employees join Trader Joe's they participate in a training program that teaches them management, leadership, and communication skills. The retailer operates a hierarchy in which employees work in a collaborative environment and multitask regardless of their job descriptions. For example, store managers sweep the floor or operate the checkout register when the need arises. Every employee, from vice president to store clerk, is encouraged to contribute ideas about how the store is run, which inspires loyalty and a genuine interest in the business and its customers. Frequent feedback and communication from managers and supervisors means that employees are kept informed about their tasks and duties and how they fit into the goals of the organization. Employees use a novel way to communicate with each other during the working day; as Trader Joe's has no PA system, employees use nautical golden bells to signal when action needs to be taken. For example, one ring of the bell means that another register needs to be opened; two rings means a question from the cashier or the customer at checkout; and three rings requires managerial assistance.[23]

Companies like IDEO utilize lateral communication to increase collaboration across departments and to promote creativity.

By fostering a strong upward and downward communication chain, Trader Joe's has succeeded in building a successful enterprise equipped with a high-performing, loyal, and committed workforce.[24]

Regardless of the direction of the flow of communication within organizations, most messages are sent through two main communication networks: formal and informal.[25] **Formal networks** transmit the messages established and approved by the organizational hierarchy. Usually, formal networks are imposed by the chain of command, which sends official messages such as policies and procedures to the rest of the staff. For example, when a CEO needs to tell employees about a new company policy, management sends the information in the form of an email. In contrast, **informal networks** handle the unofficial sharing of information between employees and across company divisions. Informal networks can help employees communicate freely with one another, build relationships, exchange opinions, and share grievances. For instance, informal networks allow minimum wage workers to share their grievances about low pay, teachers to share classroom management strategies, and students to rate their professors and study for a major exam.

One of the main forms of informal networks is the **grapevine,** the unofficial line of communication between individuals or groups.[26] Grapevines are a useful method of

Formal networks: The transmission of messages established and approved by the organizational hierarchy

Informal networks: A casual form of sharing information between employees across company divisions

Grapevine: An unofficial line of communication between individuals or groups

© iStockphoto.com/Peopleimages

Trader Joe's employees at all levels are encouraged to contribute thoughts and ideas about how the store is run.

Teachers share stories and tips with each other as part of an informal network of communication.

Gossip chains: A type of communication that occurs when one individual creates and spreads untrue or inaccurate information through the organization

Cluster chain: A type of communication that occurs when a group of people broadcast information within a larger group

communicating messages quickly and efficiently in person, more than emails, blogs, or through other technological tools. They can bring about a sense of unity among the employees who meet and share information. However, they are more common where management keeps employees in the dark about what is going on in the organization. Indeed, much of what is said on the grapevine can be inaccurate and is usually based on rumor. As some employees have discovered, missteps on modern-day grapevines like blogs or tweets can lead to termination. For example, disgruntled barista Matt Watson was fired for criticizing his boss (and his job) in a blog which he wrote during working hours, and Carly McKinney, a tenth-grade math teacher, was fired for tweeting inappropriate messages about her students and her dubious personal habits.[27]

Grapevines also give rise to **gossip chains,** communication networks in which one individual creates and spreads untrue or inaccurate information to others through the organization.[28] Each person who hears the gossip has the choice to keep it confidential or to pass it on. For example, one employee might spread gossip to others to discredit an unpopular supervisor. In contrast, a **cluster chain** consists of a group of people who broadcast information only within their group.[29] In both gossip chains and cluster chains, the information moves very quickly and can be damaging to an organization regardless of management's confirming or denying the rumors. Successful organizations actively control rumors and gossip through effective, honest, and consistent communication.[30]

THINKING CRITICALLY

1. Would you prefer to work in an organization that depends on downward communication, upward communication, lateral communication, or some combination of the three? Explain your reasoning.

2. Are informal networks necessary in a healthy organization? Why or why not?

3. Office grapevine and gossip are prevalent in today's workplace and can often lead to ineffective communication. As a manager, what are some steps you could take to combat the office grapevine and gossip?

Cross-Cultural Communication

>> **LO 10.5**   **Discuss the elements of effective cross-cultural communication**

The success of global organizations depends on the quality of cross-cultural communication, and without the necessary preparation, it can be a minefield. Cultural misunderstandings are all too common. When is kissing a business associate appropriate? Or bowing to a colleague? When is it of the utmost importance to arrive on time for a business meeting? And what sort of behavior is expected during a meal? Figure 10.7 illustrates the types of dining etiquette in different countries. When it comes to advertising, it is imperative that the message not get lost in translation through cultural error. For example, KFC's "Finger-Lickin' Good" was interpreted as "Eat your fingers off" in China; Swedish vacuum maker's ad campaign for Electrolux centered on the slogan "Nothing sucks like an Electrolux," which understandably failed to appeal to many US consumers; and Braniff Airlines advertised its leather seats with the slogan "Fly in leather," which was translated in Mexico as "Fly naked"—not what the airline intended to convey.

FIGURE 10.7

Dining Etiquette in Different Countries

FIGURE 10.8

"Southside Up" Global Map

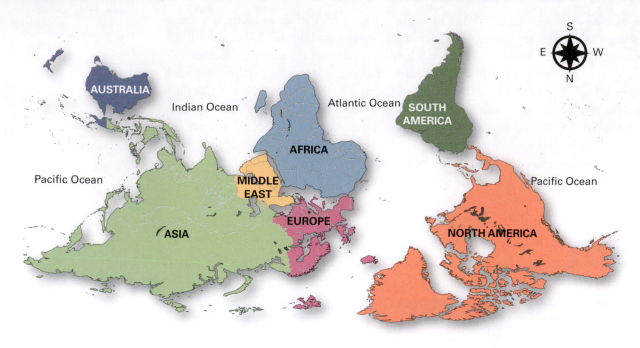

Source: Anna Versluis/SAGE

To avoid these costly blunders, many organizations encourage their employees to learn a second language and carry out extensive research to increase their understanding of other cultures. In answer to the questions mentioned, by the way, it is appropriate in France to greet business associates with a kiss on the cheek; bowing is a traditional form of greeting in East Asia; and punctuality is essential when attending meetings in the United Kingdom, Germany, and Switzerland, among others.

Ethnocentrism: The tendency to believe that your culture or ethnicity is superior to everyone else's

One of the major barriers to cross-cultural communication is **ethnocentrism,** the tendency to believe your culture or ethnicity is superior to everyone else's.[31] For example, members of Western cultures might judge negatively people from other cultures in which it is customary to use the hands to eat rather than use utensils, or they might belittle other cultures for their passive or formal nature. Figure 10.8 shows a map of the world.

Why does this map appear "wrong" to many people? Because it is shown from a different perspective than what one normally sees on a map. The famed Uruguayan artist Joaquin Torres-Garcia painted South America in this way in his painting *América invertida* to contrast the South with the North, where an ethnocentric perspective lead many in the so-called dominant northern hemisphere to look down on their southern neighbors. For those in the South, however, including Torres-Garcia, that view is simply upside-down.[32]

Low-Context versus High-Context Cultures

The role of language has a major influence on culture and vice versa. In the United States, it is common to use sports references in a business environment. "He's a team player," "You're way off base," and "She threw me a curve" are all popular phrases that are familiar in the United States but might be confusing to people from other cultures. Anthropologist Edward T. Hall studied the variety of ways different cultures use language and divided cultures into two main groups on that basis: low-context and high-context.[33]

Low-context cultures depend more on explicit messages conveyed through the spoken or written word. Most English-speaking and Germanic countries have a fast, direct, logical, efficient, "What you say is what you mean" communication style. In business environments in these countries there is less emphasis on interpersonal relationships and more on the individual.

In contrast, in **high-context cultures,** most messages are conveyed through body language, nonverbal cues, and the circumstances in which the communication is taking place. According to Hall, many Middle Eastern and Asian cultures fall into this category. The Japanese, for example, have an indirect, intuitive, unemotional, contemplative, and passive style of negotiation. In short, what you say is not necessarily what you mean. High-context cultures value silence as a way of absorbing information and getting a sense of the people they are communicating with.

Over the years, there have been many well-documented clashes between low-context and high-context cultures. In 2017, President Trump used inflammatory language directed at North Korea's leader Kim Jong-Un when speaking about the nuclear crisis. Some commentators believe this approach temporarily escalated tensions between the two countries.[34]

Social Context

Communication also depends on the social setting. We tend to use different vocabulary depending on the situation or the person we are talking to, and our response to these social contexts differs by culture. For example, you are unlikely to greet your professor the same way you would your baseball teammate or fellow student.

The way people from different cultures use language can provide a richer understanding of their society. For example, the Japanese base their linguistic styles on status and choose from three different styles to express the appropriate level of social respect: basic speech, average speech, or elegant speech. Novice speakers of Japanese might inadvertently offend someone to whom they are speaking if they mistakenly choose the incorrect linguistic style.[35]

Gender differences can be reflected in language and can, in turn, affect communication. In some areas of the West Indies, for example, women and men use different words to refer to the same thing.

Other Complicating Factors

Several other factors can further complicate our communication with members of other cultures.[36]

Slang and Idioms

Slang is informal language applied in a particular context or group. Although it is not usually appropriate in business communication, slang is often used in daily life. For example, in the United Kingdom and Ireland, "knackered" means "exhausted," while in the United States the slang phrase "in a New York minute" means to do something very fast.

An *idiom* is a word or group of words used to convey a meaning other than its literal one. For example, US businesspeople sometimes use expressions such as "dead in the water" for a project or action that has stalled. Even native English-speakers communicating with people from other English-speaking countries may encounter difficulties with idioms. For example, in a business setting, the US expression, "Table

Low-context cultures:
Cultures that depend on explicit messages conveyed through the spoken or written word

High-context cultures:
Cultures in which meaning is conveyed through body language, nonverbal cues, and the circumstances in which the communication is taking place

it" means not to discuss a matter further, whereas in the United Kingdom, it means to bring the matter to the table for discussion.

Euphemisms

Most languages include *euphemisms*, vague or general words used in place of those considered to be too blunt or harsh. Popular business euphemisms include "giving (someone) his or her marching orders" instead of firing the person; "under the table" to describe an illegal or concealed transaction; and "pushing the envelope," which means going beyond the limits of performance. Without understanding euphemisms and the social context in which to use them, businesspeople have difficulty appreciating and successfully integrating into different cultures.

Proverbs

Proverbs or wise sayings are common to many different cultures. Common proverbs used in a US business environment include: "A fool and his money are soon parted," "Too many cooks spoil the broth," and "Better late than never." Once again, it is essential to understand the way different societies use proverbs and how they are applied to behavior.

Verbal Dueling

Certain cultural subgroups engage in *verbal dueling*, a form of competitive communication in which the participants exchange insults until one "wins." Although verbal dueling is generally associated with male adolescents (African American adolescents in the United States verbally duel in a game called "The Dozens," and Turkish adolescents play a similar game), verbal battles also take place among political leaders and in a number of societies where exchanging insults is regarded as a better way of diffusing conflict than using weapons.[37] When you are interacting with other cultures, it is useful to become aware of different forms of verbal dueling to truly understand the nature of cross-cultural communication.

Actor and comedian Will Ferrell utilized humor when giving a memorable commencement speech at University of Southern California in 2017.

Humor

Most cultures value humor, but what is perceived to be funny in one culture can easily fall flat in another because some jokes are inappropriate for the audience or get lost in translation. While it is common for a British or US businessperson to begin a speech or a presentation with some light humor or an anecdote, that is not the case in Asia where humor is less pervasive in formal business settings. When presenting to people from different cultures, it is essential to know the audience and avoid jokes that could be perceived as inappropriate—or not to joke at all if that is the better course. Actor and comedian Will Ferrell was praised for his humorous commencement speech to students at University of Southern California.[38]

Conversational Taboos

Regardless of the participants' cultural background, a degree of small talk usually takes place before the beginning of a meeting, especially when people are meeting for the first time. US businesspeople tend to talk about the weather or sports and avoid taboo or contentious subjects such as religion, politics, and personal matters. Members of other cultures are accustomed to openly discussing religion and politics or asking personal questions in a business setting. What qualifies as taboo varies from culture to culture, so it is vital to know what to expect before the initial meeting.

Overcoming Difficulties in Cross-Cultural Communication

With so many potential obstacles to avoid, communicating with different cultures can seem a daunting prospect. The more knowledge and understanding we have, the smoother and more successful the communication will be. With this in mind, what can we do to reduce misunderstandings and misinterpretations?

- Do your homework and make sure you are familiar with the language and customs of different cultures.

- Never make assumptions; it is better to believe there are differences until similarities have been established.

- Be an active listener and summarize points to confirm you understand what the other party has said.

- Make an effort to be supportive, encouraging, and empathic, particularly toward those interacting in an English-speaking nation for whom English is a second language.

- Avoid slang, jargon, and euphemisms; they often cause confusion.

The most successful cross-cultural teams work in an environment which cultivates openness, trust, and respect. However, in many organizations, communication does not go so smoothly. Researchers have identified three work situations where communication most commonly breaks down. They are eliciting ideas, surfacing disagreement, and giving feedback.[39]

Eliciting Ideas

The level of participation in discussions which involve the sharing of ideas varies across different cultures. For example, people from low-context cultures like the United States and Australia are used to openly expressing their thoughts and opinions, while those from high-context cultures like Japan tend to wait until the more senior colleagues voice their thoughts before speaking up. Similarly, Finnish people are more hesitant in contributing, for fear of looking foolish, and prefer to think before they speak. In contrast, Americans are more confident in "shooting from the hip."

One way to ensure that all participants are contributing is to go around the table at least once, so everyone is given a chance to speak. Another solution is to rein in our own thoughts at first in favor of hearing what the others have to say, and asking plenty of open-ended questions to further explore their ideas. Research based on teams of Americans and East Asians showed these tactics significantly increased the contributions from both sides.

"Instead of taking five times as many opportunities to speak and using nearly ten times as many words as their Chinese, Japanese, Korean, or Taiwanese colleagues, Americans took just 50 percent more turns and spoke just 4 percent more words when an inclusive team leadership approached was used."

Surfacing Disagreement

When conflict arises during business discussions, some cultures are more comfortable with it than others. For example, people from Latin and Middle Eastern countries may be used to engaging in fiery exchanges and making loud arguments, whereas people from Asia or Scandinavia may employ the power of silence and rigid body language to convey their opposition.

To motivate participants to engage in healthy debate, it is a good idea to designate a devil's advocate—someone who is responsible for encouraging each party to discuss the different challenges associated with each of the proposals. Another tactic would be to ask each participant to share their pros and cons to enable both parties to freely argue both sides.

Giving Feedback

Providing feedback is essential for personal development, collaboration, and productivity, but it can also be a cultural minefield. In the United States, feedback is generally received as an opportunity to develop, and well received in front of a group. In contrast, people from other cultures may prefer meeting one-on-one in order to save face in front of their colleagues. Cultures also differ in the language they use to deliver feedback. In low-context cultures like the Netherlands or the United States, managers tend to use direct language, while in high-context cultures, such as India, managers use more subtle language.

When delivering feedback across different cultures, it is important to find a middle ground. This might involve using positive language to soften the critical aspects or, where appropriate, delivering feedback to the whole team rather than one particular individual.

In this chapter, we have explored communication in organizations and its importance across different cultures. In the next chapter, we explore how communication plays a significant role in building trust, dealing with conflict, and preparing for negotiation.

THINKING CRITICALLY

1. List at least three strategies or steps advertisers introducing a product in a new country should take to ensure that their marketing message isn't culturally misconstrued.

2. What difficulties are businesspeople from low-context cultures likely to encounter when doing business in high-context cultures?

3. Assume that you are a product manager based in North America and will be collaborating with a team of software engineers based in India. Describe the steps you would take to prepare to work effectively with your new colleagues. ●

Visit **edge.sagepub.com/neckob2e** to help you accomplish your coursework goals in an easy-to-use learning environment.

- Mobile-friendly eFlashcards and practice quizzes
- Video and multimedia content
- Chapter summaries with learning objectives
- EXCLUSIVE! Access to full-text SAGE journal articles

10.1 Describe the basic model of communication

Communication is the act of transmitting thoughts, processes, and ideas through a variety of channels. The Shannon-Weaver Model of communication is based on two components: the sender of the message, known as the *source*, and the receiver of the message. The sender encodes and then transmits a message through a communication channel where it is decoded by the receiver. The receiver must then provide feedback or a response to the sender to confirm that the message has been received and its meaning understood. Disturbances in the communications process are called *noise*.

10.2 Compare the types of communication channels

Oral communication is the verbal exchange of information, ideas, and processes one on one or as a group. **Written communication** makes use of the written word through reports, memos, letters, and other channels. **Electronic communication** transmits messages through email, Skype, videoconferencing, blogs, fax, instant messaging, texting, and social networking. **Nonverbal communication** is the transmission of wordless cues through posture, facial expression, gestures, tone of voice, and so on.

10.3 Identify key barriers to effective communication

Filtering is screening and manipulating a message from a sender before passing it on to the receiver. Our *emotions* have an effect on the way we communicate. The wealth of information surrounding us can lead us to make hasty decisions or prioritize poorly because of *information overload*. Because of *differing perceptions,* the ways we interpret situations can clash with the perceptions of others, leading to confusion and misconception. We can overcome this communication barrier by challenging our own assumptions about other people and situations for accuracy and by seeking advice from others to clarify our perceptions.

10.4 Describe types of communication networks within organizations

Downward communication sends messages from the upper levels of the organizational hierarchy to the lower levels, and **upward communication** sends messages from the lower levels of the organizational hierarchy to the higher levels. **Lateral communication** flows between and among similar hierarchical levels across organizations. **Formal networks** transmit messages established and approved by the organizational hierarchy. In contrast, **informal networks** are a means of unofficially sharing of information between employees across company divisions.

10.5 Discuss the elements of effective cross-cultural communication

Strategies for effective cross-cultural communication include doing your homework and making sure you know the language and customs of different cultures, never making assumptions, believing there are cultural differences until otherwise established, being an active listener, and summarizing points to confirm you understand what the other party has said, being supportive and empathic toward those for whom English is a second language, and avoiding slang, jargon, and euphemisms.

KEY TERMS

UP FOR DEBATE: Lines of Communication

Regular meetings designed to keep a team on track are absolutely essential. The team gets together and delegates work for the upcoming week. But what happens after these teams break? Do all lines of communication cease? They shouldn't. Managers must be proactive and engage the members of their teams to ensure that the members know what to do, that they are being productive, and that they can ask for help if they need it. Agree or disagree? Explain your answer.

EXERCISE 10.1: Overcoming Barriers to Effective Communication

Objective

The purpose of this exercise is to gain a greater appreciation of the barriers to communication.

Instructions

The text discusses four different barriers to effective communication. They are:

- **Filtering**—the process of screening and then manipulating a message from a sender before passing it on to the intended receiver

- **Emotions**—a state of feeling that affects the way we communicate

- **Information overload**—exposure to an overwhelming amount of information

- **Differing perceptions**—the way in which our interpretations of situations clashes with the perceptions of others

In groups of three to five students, discuss each of these barriers in the context of the workplace. For each barrier, provide an example where this barrier has occurred and ways it could have been avoided or ameliorated altogether. Approach each example from the standpoint of the sender of the message as well as the receiver.

Reflection Questions

1. How similar were your experiences to those of the others in the group? Discuss.

2. If you were the manager and you discovered that employees were not receiving a message from you accurately due to information overload, what steps would you personally take to correct the situation?

3. Describe a situation at work or in the classroom where you engaged in filtering.

Exercise contributed by Steven Stovall, Southeast Missouri State University.

EXERCISE 10.2: There's an App for That

Objectives

Identify key barriers to effective communication.

Discuss the elements of effective cross-cultural communication.

Instructions

Step 1. Write down as many barriers to intercultural communication as you can think of. (1 to 3 minutes)

Step 2. Find a partner and combine lists. Then, for as many barriers as possible, write down one communication or information technology that can help overcome each barrier. (5 to 10 minutes)

Step 3. Each pair should find another pair and form a quad. These quads should combine lists and reconcile any differences. Then they should examine the combined list and look for areas where information or communication technology *cannot* help to overcome intercultural communication barriers. (5 to 10 minutes)

Step 4. Choose a spokesperson for your quad and be prepared to discuss your list when called upon by your instructor. (3 to 5 minutes)

Reflection Questions

1. In what ways do you think using information or communication technologies could actually hurt intercultural communications?

2. What was the most interesting technology use you heard?

3. Were there any overall trends in technology use that you heard from the exercise?

4. Are there any ways that you have personally used information or communication technologies to overcome intercultural communication barriers? If so, which were most effective?

Exercise contributed by Milton R. Mayfield, Professor of Business, Texas A&M International University, and Jacqueline R. Mayfield, Professor of Business, Texas A&M International University.

EXERCISE 10.3: The Telephone Game

Objective

The purpose of this exercise is to grasp the concept of how a message can be easily altered as it travels through a communication channel.

Instructions

This is a very old exercise known as the "telephone game," as it refers to a message that is told to one person over the phone, who then calls someone else to relay the message, who in turn, calls someone else, and so on.

Starting at one corner of the back of the room, have that person secretly think of a sentence to whisper to the student sitting next to him or her. Sentences should be somewhat complex, such as, "Carl collected coins, coincidentally, Sarah sought stamps," or "Three foxes brought five loaves of bread to eight little pigs," and similar statements.

The rules are simple. As the message is whispered to the next person, it is spoken only once. The goal is to try and be as accurate as possible—intentionally garbling the message is not as fun. The message continues to work its way to the front of the room. When the last student hears the message, that student stands up and announces the sentence as it was heard. The student who originated the message then stands up and repeats the message as it was intended initially.

Reflection Questions

1. How different was the final sentence from the original sentence? Why does this happen?

2. What examples have you experienced at work where an intended message gets mixed up or completely altered during the communication process?

3. Discuss ways a situation like the one that played out during the telephone game could be avoided in the workplace.

Exercise contributed by Steven Stovall, Southeast Missouri State University.

ONLINE EXERCISE 10.1: Examples of Poor Communication

Objective

The purpose of this exercise is to gain an appreciation for examples of poor communication in the workplace.

Instruction

Conduct an online search, seeking an example of when a company communicated poorly with customers or employees. It might be a sale that was incorrect, or a new policy that went into effect, or even where employees were terminated from their positions via a text message or email.

Once you discover an example of poor communication in an organization, draft a report to your instructor. Assume that you work for the organization in question and your instructor is the CEO of the company. In the report, describe the situation that occurred and what steps you will be taking to ensure that this does not happen again. The report should be approximately two to three double-spaced pages.

Reflection Questions

1. Why does poor communication happen in the workplace? With some companies employing tens of thousands of employees, how could poor communication still occur with customers? With employees?

2. What examples of poor communication have you experienced so far in your career? Describe at least two.

3. Discuss a time when you did not utilize effective communication at work. What lessons did you learn from the experience?

Exercise contributed by Steven Stovall, Southeast Missouri State University.

CASE STUDY 10.1: Open Communication at 3M

With more than $30 billion in annual sales, 88,000 employees, and more than 55,000 products from adhesives to medical device parts to car care products, 3M has been a leader in innovation for over a century. Innovation is, after all, its slogan. How does the company sustain its pioneering attitude? The answer lies in great communication. As it has done with its evolving products, 3M continues to think of new ways to communicate with its employees.

In 2006, 3M executives felt that innovation and efficiency were slowing down, and they needed to do something about it. George W. Buckley had recently become CEO. He and the executive team outlined a strategy to engage employees that they believed would lead to positive effects in creativity and efficiency and, in turn, allow management to set more ambitious market-share goals.

Several areas that needed attention were identified by talent VP Sandra Tokach. Communication needed to be improved throughout; this included fostering collaboration and teaching leaders how to both supervise and develop people. Improved communication also entailed ensuring that employees found meaning in their work, that the work supported the market-focused mission, and that people understood their pay and benefits.

The team realized that implementing a lot of change at once is difficult and can unsettle employees. To combat this, they built upon existing approaches meant to foster innovation and communicated while changes were taking place. Two main initiatives that went hand in hand. First, leaders and employees needed to be educated about work factors that mattered to them, from company mission to pay. Next, open communication, a cornerstone of the company, was to remain front and center to preserve trust as a part of all interactions and relationships within the business.

Education of supervisors was implemented that aimed to give them the necessary skills to "Develop, Teach and Engage Others." A series of short videos, each about ten minutes in length, was created to demonstrate the relevant aspects of these proficiencies and to teach supervisors how to bring more authenticity to their communication methods and use a coaching perspective to develop their employees. The training focused on defining employee engagement as the leader's responsibility.

An emerging leaders program encouraged leaders to teach other employees by serving as a mentor, sponsor, and champion. As leaders help their employees achieve, those same employees develop leadership skills and help the next generation of workers. The emerging leaders program encouraged collaboration and candid conversation, behaviors that made their way back into the company culture.

Training emphasized the need for a leader to be open, honest, and available. Leaders were given guides on how to ask the right questions and listen to their employees when discussing their work. This inspired more understanding among colleagues as leaders began to understand each employee's different needs and wants.

Engagement extended to raising awareness of the role of everyone in society, not just at 3M. The company's three components of commitment are taking care of the environment, taking care of others, and taking care of yourself. Methods were put into place to communicate the importance of each of these aspects and train employees about how to articulate them to others.

All supervisors were trained to explain how pay is determined. 3M realized that the combination of rank-and-file layoffs and bloated executive bonuses at other companies sent a bad message to employees. Instead of treating pay as secret, the company made discussing it part of its open communication system, knowing that more understanding leads to more trust and stronger perceptions of fairness.

Many new systems for opening channels of communication were put into place. Several relied on modern technology, such as the online brainstorming tool InnovationLive. Blogs, wikis, and an internal social networking site have also been introduced. Other new methods didn't rely on technology at all. "Random lunches" are voluntary monthly meetings in which people sign up and get randomly assigned to have lunch with three other people. This helps employees get to know people across different divisions and work areas and has proved very popular within the company. All these techniques improved both communication and innovation.

3M has never been satisfied with the status quo. By continually examining and improving internal communication, the company provides work environments conducive to pursuing opportunities. This is what creates the innovative mind-set 3M is famous for.

Case Questions

1. Explain why 3M attributes so much of its success to open communication.
2. Describe how 3M has utilized electronic communication.
3. Identify the direction of communication in 3M.

Sources

Govindarajan, Vijay, and Srikanth Srinivas. "The Innovation Mindset in Action: 3M Corporation," *Harvard Business Review*. August 6, 2013. http://blogs.hbr.org/2013/08/the-innovation-mindset-in-acti-3.

McCauley, Cynthia D., and Morgan W. McCall Jr. *Using Experience to Develop Leadership Talent: How Organizations Leverage On-the-Job Development* (San Francisco: Jossey-Bass, 2014).

Oakes, Kevin, and Pat Galagan. *The Executive Guide to Integrated Talent Management* (Alexandria, VA: American Society for Training and Development; 2011).

SHRM Staff. "3M: In the Company We Trust." *Society of Human Resource Management*. August 8, 2011. www.weknownext.com/workforce/3m-in-the-company-we-trust.

SELF-ASSESSMENT 10.1

Listening Skills Self-Assessment

For each statement, circle the number that best describes you based on the following scale:

	NOT AT ALL ACCURATE	SOMEWHAT ACCURATE	A LITTLE ACCURATE	MOSTLY ACCURATE	COMPLETELY ACCURATE
1. I give people my full attention and maintain eye contact when they are speaking.	1	2	3	4	5
2. I maintain an attentive posture and respond with nonverbal cues to show that I am listening.	1	2	3	4	5
3. I appreciate hearing other people's perspectives.	1	2	3	4	5
4. I try to keep an open mind when I am listening.	1	2	3	4	5
5. I can effectively identify other people's emotions when speaking with them.	1	2	3	4	5
6. I can tell when someone is withholding information or not telling me the truth.	1	2	3	4	5
7. I have good comprehension and recall of what is communicated to me.	1	2	3	4	5
8. I ask for more information or ask follow-up questions as needed.	1	2	3	4	5
9. I try to be patient and understanding when listening to people who are upset.	1	2	3	4	5
10. I make others comfortable in sharing their feelings with me.	1	2	3	4	5
11. I carefully evaluate the information that is shared with me.	1	2	3	4	5
12. I let people know what I think of their message, even if I disagree with them.	1	2	3	4	5

Scoring

Add the numbers circled: _____

Interpretation

48 and above = You have outstanding listening skills that help you overcome communication barriers to be an effective communicator.

25–47 = You have moderate listening skills. You could improve some key aspects of your listening capabilities to become a more effective communicator.

24 and below = You need to make some substantial improvements in your listening skills in order to effectively communicate with others.

Source: Adapted from Zabava Ford, Wendy S., Andrew D. Wolvin, and Sungeun Chung. "Students' Self-Perceived Listening Competencies in the Basic Speech Communication Course." *International Journal of Listening* 14 (May 2000): 1.

11

Trust, Conflict, and Negotiation

If you want to bring an end to long-standing conflict, you have to be prepared to compromise.

—Aung San Suu Kyi, Burmese politician

Learning Objectives

By the end of this chapter, you will be able to:

11.1 Outline the bases of trust and predictable outcomes of trust in organizations

11.2 Describe the conflict process and the various types of conflict

11.3 Identify the five basic conflict management strategies

11.4 Describe the negotiation process

11.5 Compare distributive and integrative bargaining approaches

CASE STUDY: DISTRUST IN THE NATIONAL FOOTBALL LEAGUE (NFL)

The National Football League (NFL) is the most profitable professional sports association in the United States and arguably the most profitable in the world. The sport of American football was invented over the course of about twenty years between 1869 into the 1880s. As the sport grew in popularity throughout America's universities, graduates started to form their own clubs. These individual clubs were the beginnings of what would later become the first professional teams.

To look at the history of the National Football league, one must go to Canton, Ohio, where, in August of 1920, representatives from the largest professional football clubs met to form the American Professional Football Conference. According to the *Canton Evening Repository*, the purpose of the meeting was to "raise the standard of professional football in every possible way, to eliminate bidding for players between rival clubs and to secure cooperation in the formation of schedules." The organization allowed for the franchising of each team, which meant that each team operates under its own corporate model and is responsible for its own operations; however, a portion of its profits are paid back to the league which handles regulations, officiating, scheduling, and countless other logistical measures that lift a burden of the individual team owners. In 1922, the American Professional Football Conference changed its name to the National Football League.

The competition for the best talent and the best schedules often resulted in conflicts between two different clubs. There are times where conflict can be healthy and improve the functionality of an organization or group; however, in the case of the unorganized world of professional football, the conflict was very dysfunctional meaning it had negative effects on individuals and teams. The creation of an organized league improved the working relationships between the teams, which by late 1920 grew in number to fourteen. Only two of the original fourteen teams remain today: the Decatur Staleys (now the Chicago Bears) and the Chicago Cardinals (now the Arizona Cardinals).

As the professional sport started to increase in popularity, the league began to grow with more clubs vying for a spot in the mix. Yet, the NFL faced an unusual dilemma. Between the 1930s and the 1950s, many rival leagues began to sprout up. There was the American Football League (AFL), the All-America Football Conference, and various regional leagues. In 1966, the NFL and the AFL merged (keeping the NFL name) to create what is now a 32-team league that hosts the largest sporting event in the nation, the Super Bowl.

Today, the NFL boasts annual revenues averaging well over $10 billion a year which, again, ranks #1 in the world for professional sports. The sport seemingly has the United States wrapped around its finger, with over 200 million unique viewers tuning in every Sunday to watch the NFL's games on television. With such high popularity and revenues, the NFL has enabled its individual teams to pay some of the world's largest salaries to their players. Becoming an NFL player is no small feat. These men (and potentially women in the near future) have mastered the art of physical and mental toughness in addition to pinpoint accuracy in various athletic skillsets. Because of the sport's popularity, NFL players have become cultural icons, hometown heroes, spokespersons for social justice, famous actors, and expensive but effective marketing tools. In 2017, the highest paid NFL player is expected to receive $27.5 million. While the top percent of the players earn over $10 million a year, the average earnings of an NFL player ranks last in comparison to the other major American professional sports leagues behind the NBA, MLB, and the NHL. This statistic and others that essentially put a greater burden on the NFL players and increase the profits for the various team owners became antecedents to conflict. Essentially, these are factors that set the scene for potential conflict and in the end they resulted in the 2011 NFL Player Lockout.

In 2011, a meeting between the NFL Players Association and the owners resulted in a disagreement on a new collective bargaining agreement which is the process of negotiation between employers and employees on salary regulation, benefits, working conditions, etc. Because a consensus was not reached, the NFL owners "locked out" all the NFL players from all practices, facilities, and coaching. In the case of the NFL lockout, negotiations took eighteen weeks and four days before a consensus was reached. It required time in court, player testimonies, and millions of dollars to pay for the services of arbitrators, conciliators, and mediators.

On July 30th, 2011, the lockout officially ended and the NFL along with its players resumed operations. The end result of the lockout was that both parties, the players and the owners, achieved maximum value from the negotiations. The players received better benefits from increased minimum salaries, access to healthcare for life, newly allocated retirement benefits, improved player safety procedures, and increased roster size. The owners received more equitable revenue sharing between teams, avoidance of fines if they pay over the salary cap, franchise tags, increased share of revenue from regular season games, and increased credit for stadium upgrades. Essentially, rather than both parties trying to claim a "fixed pie" of resources, the negotiations were administered so that the pie was enlarged to ensure everyone got a piece.

Many people claim that this lockout stemmed from the general lack of trust that the NFL players had toward the league. The distrust seems to have been well placed given the unfair conditions that the players found themselves in. The NFL has learned its lesson and today works toward better relationships with its players. However, the lack of trust still lingers throughout the league and the NFL is constantly trying to repair it. They should continue to try to gain back the players' trust because trust has great benefits to an organization. Rather than focusing on commotion surrounding the league and spiraling negativity, when trust is high people tend to work better together and are better focused on the task at hand. Trust plays a huge role in preventing conflicts like the 2011 lockout from ever arising in the first place.

Critical-Thinking Questions

1. What role did trust play in the NFL Lockout of 2011?

2. Why was organizing a league in 1920 a better option than allowing independent clubs to take up much of the professional football market?

Resources:

Barrabi, T. (2017, February 28). NFL highest-paid players 2017: Where Antonio Brown's contract ranks. *Fox Business*. Retrieved from http://www.foxbusiness.com/features/2017/02/28/nfl-highest-paid-players-2017-where-antonio-browns-contract-ranks.html

Goodell, R. (n.d.). *History of the NFL commissioner*. Retrieved from https://en.wikipedia.org/wiki/National_Football_League#Corporate_structure

Kutz, S. (2016). NFL took in $13 billion in revenue last season — see how it stacks up against other pro sports leagues. *MarketWatch*. Retrieved from http://www.marketwatch.com/story/the-nfl-made-13-billion-last-season-see-how-it-stacks-up-against-other-leagues-2016-07-01

McGinnis, H. (2011, February 12). NFL lockout for dummies: Explaining the NFL labor dispute in Layman's terms. *NFL Lockout for Dummies*. Retrieved from https://bleacherreport.com/articles/606091-nfl-lockout-for-dummies-explaining-the-nfl-labor-dispute-in-laymans-terms

Pro Football Hall of Fame. (n.d.). *Birth of pro football*. Retrieved from http://www.profootballhof.com/football-history/birth-of-pro-football/

American studies professor Maya Angelou was rated highly on a *Reader's Digest* poll of most trustworthy celebrities

The founder of Silicon Valley-based venture capitalist firm 500 Startups, David McClure, lost credibility with his employees after he admitted to sexual harassment claims by several women.

Trust in Organizations

>> LO 11.1 Outline the bases of trust and predictable outcomes of trust in organizations

Trust is a critical factor for organizational performance. For people to successfully work together and build relationships, they need to have a high degree of trust in one another. We define **trust** as dependence on the integrity, ability, honesty, and reliability of someone or something else.[1] In US celebrity culture, Tom Hanks ranks as the most trustworthy celebrity, according to a 2016 poll conducted by *Reader's Digest*.[2] Actor Denzel Washington and American studies professor Maya Angelou also ranked high on the list. In contrast, other public figures have lost our trust, such as Silicon Valley 500 start-ups founder David McClure, who admitted to sexually harassing his female employees, and professional tennis player and endorser Maria Sharapova who was initially banned from playing for two years (since reduced to fifteen months) after testing positive for taking a banned drug.[3]

Trust: The dependence on the integrity, ability, honesty, and reliability of someone or something else

Types of Trust

How do we know when to trust someone? Say a new team leader has been appointed to your work team. You have never met this person before, yet you are expected to work with him or her every day for the foreseeable future. How do you make up your mind that your team leader is someone you can trust?

Three Types of Trust

Disposition-based trust	• Derived from possessing personality traits that include a general propensity to trust others
Cognition-based trust	• Derived from relying on factual information as a basis for trust
Affect-based trust	• Derived from putting faith in others based on feelings and emotions

Sources: Based on Mayer, Roger C., James H. Davis, and F. David Schoorman. "An Integrative Model of Organizational Trust." *Academy of Management Review* 20, no. 3 (July 1995): 709–734; McAllister, Daniel J. "Affect- and Cognition-Based Trust as Foundations for Interpersonal Cooperation in Organizations." *Academy of Management Journal* 38, no. 1 (February 1995): 24–59.

Generally, we can form three types of trust: disposition-based trust, cognition-based trust, and affect-based trust (see Figure 11.1).[4]

Disposition-based trust exists when people possess personality traits that encourage them to put their faith in others. For instance, you might be the kind of person who will trust the new team leader unless you are given a reason not to.

In contrast, in *cognition-based trust,* people rely on factual information such as someone's past experience and track record as a basis for trust. You might be wary of a new team leader until you recognize that he or she demonstrates the character, integrity, abilities, and benevolence to lead the team.

Finally, *affect-based trust* occurs when people put their faith in others based on feelings and emotions. For example, you are more likely to trust a new team leader if you feel you have made an emotional connection with him or her, such as by finding out you grew up in the same town.

Outcomes of Trust

When trust is high in the workplace, people tend to work better together and are more focused on their duties. Recent research found that people working in a high-trust environment tend to take more risks, such as initiating new ideas or admitting mistakes, display citizenship behaviors like going the "extra mile" on a work task or project, and exhibit fewer ineffectual or counterproductive behaviors like absenteeism or social loafing.[5] Trust is key when it comes to building and maintaining relationships, increasing morale and productivity, and effectively preventing unhealthy conflict. In contrast, employees working in a low-trust organizational environment are more likely to be distracted from their duties, lack engagement in their tasks, exhibit defensive behaviors, display apathy toward organizational goals, and have higher levels of absenteeism (see Figure 11.2).[6] Lack of trust between the NFL players and the league was considered to be at the heart of the disagreement that led to the 2011 Lockout. Although that event occurred several years ago, lack of trust still exists between the two parties and the damage has been difficult to repair.

Let's explore the issue of trust and how it affects organizational behavior.

Just as trust is important in how we interact with others in our personal lives, we also have expectations about how we are treated within an organization. This type of unwritten expectation between employees and organizations is called a **psychological contract**.[7] Essentially, this contract determines the degree to which employees trust their organizations to value their efforts, and how well employees meet the expectations of the organization in terms of their work contributions. For instance, if employees do not feel that they are being treated fairly, then this might affect their work performance, commitment, and overall job satisfaction. Similarly, if the organization does not feel that employees are fulfilling their side of the contract, then they are likely to be reprimanded or let go.

Trust also plays an important part in how we relate to others in work through our social networks. In this context, **social networks** describes the recurrent patterns of interaction with others that take place when carrying out work activities (for example,

TABLE 11.1

Tips for Building Trust in Organizations

1.	Always tell the truth even if it does not portray you in the best light.
2.	Never make promises you know you can't keep.
3.	Stay true to your values, especially when it comes to respecting the rights of others.
4.	Build a reputation of someone who has integrity and always does what's right.
5.	Don't let your personal ambition get in the way of being fair and honest.
6.	Take a moment to remind yourself that being selfish will not serve you well.

FIGURE 11.2

A Model of Trust within Organizations

exchanging information or working on projects).[8] People who demonstrate their *competence* (the skills and abilities to successfully support the completion of a task), *character* (the ability to keep confidence, respect others, and stand up for what's right), and *goodwill* (the ability to listen, offer positive remarks, and provide gentle encouragement) in their interactions with others tend to be perceived as being trustworthy.[9] However, those who fail to portray these characteristics can come across as untrustworthy, regardless how skilled they are at their roles. For example, in 2016, Matt Harrigan, CEO of cybersecurity firm PacketSled, was forced to resign after posting a threatening message to President Trump on Facebook while intoxicated. Harrigan has apologized profusely for his actions, but his rash behavior has cost him his credibility and lost him trust among his employees and peers.[10]

Trust is essential for building relationships as well as our own reputations. Lack of trust can

Some employees use cognition-based trust, or evidence of someone's qualifications, when deciding to entrust new leaders.

lead to serious conflicts between teams and organizations. The next section describes the conflict process and different types of conflict.

Conflict in Teams and Organizations

>> **LO 11.2**   **Describe the conflict process and the various types of conflict**

Conflict: A clash between individuals or groups in relation to different opinions, thought processes, and perceptions

Teams and organizations of all types face many challenges and it is inevitable that conflicts will naturally arise, especially when there is a significant lack of trust. We define **conflict** as a clash between individuals or groups because of different opinions, thought processes, and perceptions.[11] Many types of clashes can occur within organizations and between them and their constituents. For instance, the NFL (featured in our case study) has experienced its fair share of conflict over the years, particularly in relation to salary and benefits which eventually culminated in a lockout until an agreement between the owners and players was reached. As another example, in 2016, Muslim employees working for Cargill Meat Solutions came into conflict with senior managers when they were told their religious breaks (typically once or twice per shift lasting ten minutes) were to be shortened owing to staff limitation. As a result, dozens of employees walked out in protest, and 150 were fired for leaving their roles unattended. Despite Cargill working hard to try and resolve the religious dispute, only ten of the fired employees have since returned to the organization.[12] As a member of an organization you will have opinions that differ at times from those of other teams or individuals. Disagreements and clashes generally cause stress and discomfort, but does this mean all conflict is bad? Not necessarily. There are times when conflict helps teams and organizations be more creative and innovative. One of the most widely publicized business conflicts occurred between the late Steve Jobs, founder of Apple and Apple's board of directors. Jobs came into conflict with the board because of his dual roles as VP and chair of the board. Although he left on bitter terms, he returned to Apple several years later with a clear creative vision of what the company needed, and in doing so steered the organization to the success it is today.[13]

Depending on how it is handled, conflict can have either positive or negative effects on an organization. As the American psychologist and author Kenneth Kaye once said, "Conflict is neither good nor bad. Properly managed, it is absolutely vital."[14] Consultant Radha Abboy describes her approach to conflict in our OB in the Real World.

Functional and Dysfunctional Conflict

Functional conflict: A constructive and healthy dispute between individuals or groups

When conflict is constructive it can help improve work performance, redefine company goals, and encourage people to communicate better. Such **functional conflict** consists of productive and healthy disputes between individuals or groups.[15] For functional conflict to be successful, individuals from opposing sides need to be genuinely interested in finding a resolution to the problem and willing to listen to each other. Providing individuals with a forum to express their opinions often gives rise to critical thinking and helps to generate new ideas and solutions.

OB IN THE REAL WORLD

Radha Abboy, 8020 Consulting

With experience in three years in public accounting, nine years in the entertainment industry, and now the past two and a half years in consulting, Radha Abboy brings an insightful and well-rounded style to leadership. Her approach is very people-centric and trust based. This stems from an understanding that a manager must be very flexible in their ability to work with different types of people, especially in situations of conflict.

In her various positions working with large and small teams alike, Radha has observed that not all conflicts are necessarily things to avoid. Rather, oftentimes conflict can be very constructive. For example, conflicts surrounding technicalities and processes are often beneficial to a team because they force the team members to really think about the *why* with regards to their strategies. As a manager overseeing this type of conflict, Radha stresses the importance of guiding the team though the activity. "Healthy conflicts are constructive. Managers must take advantage of these situations because they are excellent teaching tools. They must guide each employee as they work through the process to find the best solution." It definitely isn't easy to do, as these situations tend to be very tense. **With the right care, however, managers are more than able to leverage the situation in such a way that will actually improve the functionality of the team**.

On the flip side, unhealthy conflicts create a toxic environment and have a drastic effect on any team's efficiency and effectiveness. For example, many industries like finance and accounting function around hard deadlines and the ability to meet these deadlines is often put at risk by any unhealthy festering.

Conflicts are a part of everyday life. The people we find ourselves working with essentially become a second family. Conflicts don't have to be unhealthy. Oftentimes, they can serve as great teaching tools and will make a team better off than before. At all times, however, **managers must ensure that they are taking preventative measures to ensure that unhealthy conflict is kept to a minimum**. According to Radha, that starts with managers building strong relationships with their employees. "Always invite staff to give feedback, me to them and them back to me. A manager is a direct reflection of their staff and vice versa. If, as a manager, you are uninformed, you can't solve anything. You have to be open to voice a concern but you also need to be able to listen and invest long hours, just like any relationship you may have."

There is much debate regarding where unhealthy conflicts arise but Radha's analysis seems to point that it typically stems from the top. Managers have a strong influence on how subordinates perform and behave. Managers should definitely not be enablers of poor behavior but they should also not lead through fear. They must find a happy medium and uphold the values of their team while exploring new ways for their employees to develop and grow.

In the event that an unhealthy conflict does arise, Radha stresses the importance of acting quickly. Unhealthy conflicts can quickly get out of hand and **there isn't a cut and dried method of solving them**. Being objective, keeping emotions out of the picture, and taking time to assess the root of the issue at hand will likely start a manager on the right path to a solution.

Critical-Thinking Questions

1. What are some preventative measures that managers should make to mitigate unhealthy conflicts?

2. Explain how managers can enable unhealthy conflict in the workplace. ●

Source: Personal interview with Radha Abboy, April 3, 2018.

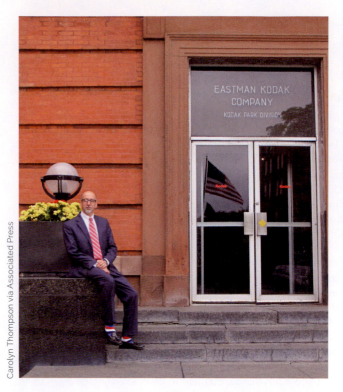

A business park owner sits outside the former New York offices of Kodak after the company paid millions in fines for violating state environmental laws.

Dysfunctional conflict:
A dispute or disagreement that has negative effects on individuals or teams

In contrast, **dysfunctional conflict** consists of disputes and disagreements that negatively affect individuals and/or teams.[16] This type of conflict often arises from an unwillingness to listen to each other or a reluctance to agree on a resolution or goal. High levels of dysfunctional conflict can lead to absenteeism, turnover, and a substantial drop in work performance, all of which can have a devastating effect on organizational goals and objectives.

Types of Conflict

The three main types of conflict in organizations are task conflict, relationship conflict, and process conflict.[17]

Task conflict refers to a clash between individuals about the direction, content, or goals of a work assignment. High task conflict can lead to disagreements that may raise negative emotions such as resentment, anger, and aggression. In contrast, low levels of task conflict are believed to have the most positive effect on organizations by stimulating creativity, healthy competition, and critical thinking among the individuals discussing the various ways to approach a task. Another benefit of low-level task conflict is that, if handled appropriately, it allows every viewpoint to be heard and discussed, giving the individuals a sense of recognition and job satisfaction.

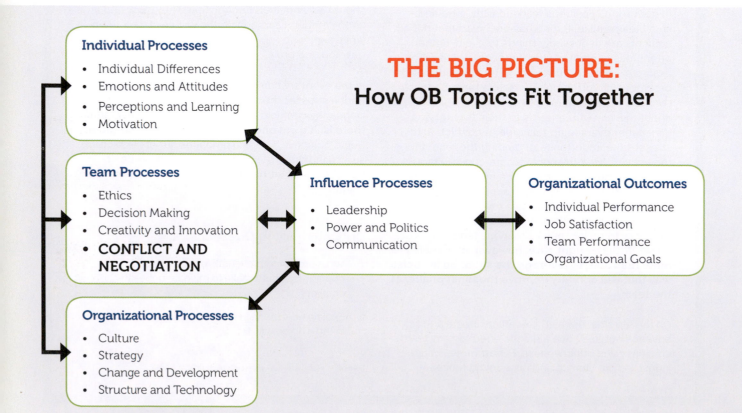

THE BIG PICTURE:
How OB Topics Fit Together

Individual Processes
- Individual Differences
- Emotions and Attitudes
- Perceptions and Learning
- Motivation

Team Processes
- Ethics
- Decision Making
- Creativity and Innovation
- **CONFLICT AND NEGOTIATION**

Organizational Processes
- Culture
- Strategy
- Change and Development
- Structure and Technology

Influence Processes
- Leadership
- Power and Politics
- Communication

Organizational Outcomes
- Individual Performance
- Job Satisfaction
- Team Performance
- Organizational Goals

Relationship conflict refers to personality conflicts between two or more individuals in the workplace. This type of conflict can be useful in resolving disputes if the parties are willing to communicate in a constructive and effective way. However, overall, it is considered the most destructive and harmful to organizations because it can give rise to hostility, mistrust, fear, and negativity. Managing relationship conflicts can also be time consuming and take resources away from other goals and priorities. A challenge for organizations today is that workforce diversity brings together a greater number of people from different backgrounds with different personalities, attitudes, and viewpoints, and managers must be vigilant to ensure that workplace relationships remain as harmonious as possible.

Process conflict refers to the clash in viewpoints about how to carry out work. Like task conflict, process conflict can be beneficial to organizations as long as it operates at a low level. When individuals and groups are given the chance to express their thoughts and opinions, they are more likely to generate new ideas regarding the best way to approach and define the process. However, high levels of debate about process can lead to resentment, apathy, and job dissatisfaction.

The Conflict Process

As we have learned, conflicts can have positive or negative outcomes depending on how the situation is managed. The following example illustrates the four different stages of the conflict process: *antecedents of conflict, perceived/felt conflict, manifest conflict,* and *outcomes of conflict.*[18]

Recently you arrive at work at 9:00 a.m. even though company policy states that employees should start work at 8:30 a.m. You haven't communicated the reason for your tardiness to the rest of your team. When you arrive at your desk, you take off your coat, grab a cup of coffee from the kitchen, and turn on your computer. By the time you actually start working it is 9:30 a.m. Without your realizing it, your tendency to arrive later than everyone else is an **antecedent of conflict**. You have set the scene for potential disputes. Antecedents of conflict include lack of communication, incompatible personalities, and collisions in value systems. In this case, your tendency to arrive late is clashing with the rest of the team's value of timeliness.

At 9:35, shortly after you have settled into your workday, one of your coworkers says, "Glad you could join us," which prompts a chuckle from the rest of the team. You perceive that the team has a problem with your tardiness and you feel their disapproval directed toward you. This is the **perceived/felt conflict stage**, during which emotional differences are sensed and felt.

Now you have a choice. Do you address the conflict head on or do you ignore it? In the **manifest conflict stage** people engage in behaviors that provoke a response. You can either try to resolve the conflict by bringing the matter out into the open, or you can suppress it, which may temporarily solve the problem but may also leave the situation open to future conflict and escalation.

The final stage is the **outcomes of conflict stage**, which encompasses the consequences of the dispute. Depending on how you and the rest of the team handle the manifest conflict stage, there will be either functional or dysfunctional outcomes. For example, if you choose to address the team in a professional manner and open up the lines of communication by explaining your lateness and pointing out that you stay an hour later than they do on most days to make up for your later arrival at work, then you are more likely to bring about a positive outcome. In contrast, if you decide to angrily retort to the sarcastic comment that when you arrive and leave is none of their business so long as the work gets done, you may make the situation even worse, which will lead to a dysfunctional outcome.

Task conflict: The clash between individuals in relation to the direction, content, or goal of a certain assignment

Relationship conflict: The clash in personalities between two or more individuals

Process conflict: The clash in viewpoints in relation to how to carry out work

Antecedents of conflict: Factors that set the scene for potential dispute

Perceived/felt conflict stage: The stage at which emotional differences are sensed and felt

Manifest conflict stage: The stage at which people engage in behaviors that provoke a response

Outcomes of conflict stage: The stage that describes the consequences of the dispute

While conflict can be difficult to deal with, there are ways in which it can be resolved. The next section focuses on some useful strategies managers can adopt when challenged with conflict in the workplace.

THINKING CRITICALLY

1. Based on the discussion of the differences between functional and dysfunctional conflict, write a series of ground rules that you believe could help individuals and teams resolve conflicts in a functional manner.

2. Why do relationship conflicts (as opposed to task or process conflicts) potentially lead to the most dysfunctional and harmful outcomes? Explain your answer.

3. Consider a disagreement you have recently had with a friend, family member, or colleague. Briefly describe the conflict by breaking it into the four stages of the conflict process (antecedent of conflict stage, perceived/felt conflict stage, manifest conflict stage, outcomes of conflict stage). What might you have done during the manifest conflict stage to lead to a more functional outcome to the conflict?

Conflict Management Strategies

>> **LO 11.3**   **Identify the five basic conflict management strategies**

Conflict is inevitable in the workplace. But we often focus more on how the other person responds rather than how we respond. Given that statistics show that workplace violence is on the rise (almost 2 million US workers report some level of violence in the workplace every year) it is more important than ever for organizations to set strategies in place to help manage conflict.[19] By analyzing and understanding the five basic conflict-management strategies, employees will be able to choose how to respond to others and manage conflicts so they are productive and don't escalate out of control.

The five strategies (see Figure 11.3) are *avoidance, accommodation, competition, compromise,* and *collaboration.*[20]

Avoidance

Avoidance is an attempt to suppress a conflict and pretend it doesn't exist. People who avoid conflict often hope that the problem will go away by itself or that someone else will take responsibility and confront the issue instead. Avoidance is a lose/lose situation. If you don't address the conflict then the people around you will have no idea how you're really feeling, or think that you don't care enough to get involved, and most likely, the problem will continue to go unresolved. The longer the issue is left unaddressed, the unhappier and frustrated you may feel, which may ultimately lead to an angry or negative outburst. However, there are certain situations in which avoidance makes sense. For example, rather than rushing into making a decision, you may benefit from taking some time to think more about it; or if you've had a difficult conversation with a coworker, giving that person space to calm down may be more sensible than trying to resolve the issue there and then.

Accommodation

Accommodation is an attempt to adjust our views to play down differences between parties. People who accommodate others tend to neglect or hide their own

FIGURE 11.3

Conflict Management Strategies

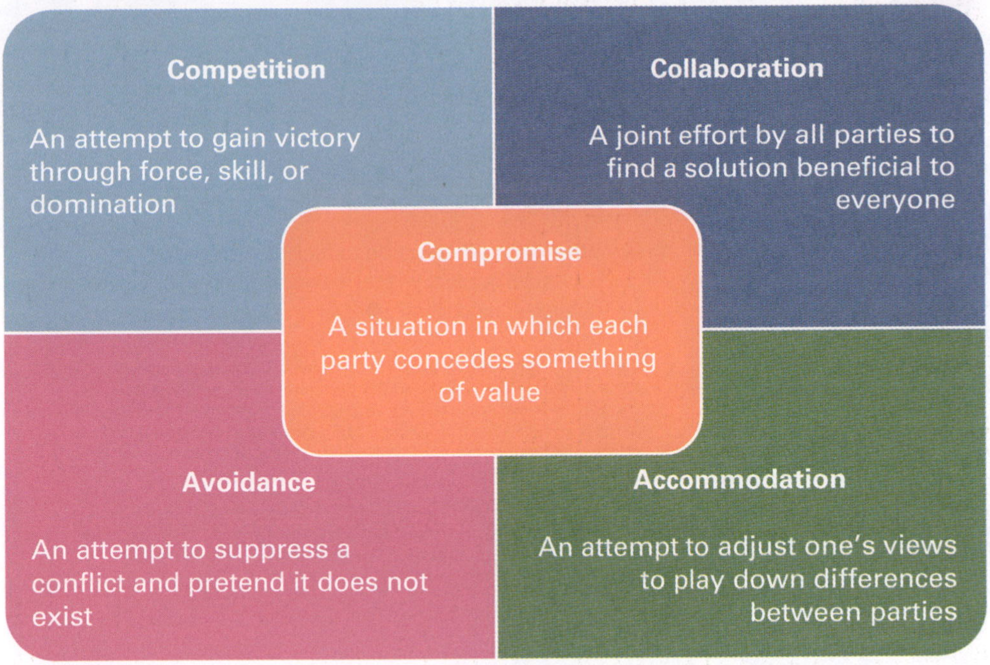

Competition

An attempt to gain victory through force, skill, or domination

Collaboration

A joint effort by all parties to find a solution beneficial to everyone

Compromise

A situation in which each party concedes something of value

Avoidance

An attempt to suppress a conflict and pretend it does not exist

Accommodation

An attempt to adjust one's views to play down differences between parties

true feelings or opinions about a certain issue in order to keep the peace or avoid rocking the boat. In sum, accommodating means giving people what they want. For example, say your boss gives you a 5 percent raise rather than the 10 percent you were expecting. Instead of voicing your disappointment and telling your boss that your needs aren't being met, you accept the raise without argument, thereby giving your boss what he or she wants, rather than what you want. In doing so, you are sacrificing your own personal needs to please your boss. This will give rise to resentment and anger over time. However, accommodation can be useful in certain situations, particularly when it comes to areas you're fairly relaxed about. For instance, if some people on the team feel strongly about the venue for an upcoming team-bonding day and you don't, then it's appropriate to accommodate those people by agreeing to their choice.

Competition

Competition is an attempt to gain victory through force, skill, or domination. When people compete against each other, it is at the other person's expense: one side wins and the other loses. In the workplace, a competing style of managing conflict is a way to gain power and pressure others into falling into line with certain methods and beliefs. People who use a competitive style tend to communicate aggressively, try to control discussions, and have little regard for preserving future relationships.

However, competing has its place in certain situations, for example, when it comes to important issues such as standing up for rights in the workplace or implementing a controversial decision regarding layoffs. However, both these scenarios regardless of their importance are likely to lead to divisions and resentment.

EXAMINING THE EVIDENCE

Task and Relationship Conflict

Researchers and practitioners have long asserted that task-related conflict can be beneficial by stimulating creativity and critical thinking in group decision making. However, two recent meta-analyses examining the effects of task-related conflict across multiple studies failed to find support for an overall positive relationship between task conflict and group performance.[*] These findings led researchers Frank R. C. de Wit and Daan Scheepers of Leiden University and Karen A. Jehn of the Melbourne Business School to delve a little deeper into the relationships between task conflict, relationship conflict, and decision making.[^] They found that when relationship conflict was present during task conflict, group members were more likely to rigidly hold onto less than optimal starting positions during group interactions, leading to poor decision outcomes. The findings suggest that task conflict is neither universally good nor universally bad. Instead, its potential benefits in group decision making may depend on whether relationship conflict is also present.

Critical-Thinking Questions

1. Why is relationship conflict so detrimental to group decision making? Why can task conflict be potentially beneficial?

2. What can managers do to facilitate potentially beneficial conflict while minimizing potentially detrimental conflict? ●

[*]De Dreu, Carsten K.W., and Laurie R. Weingart. "Task versus Relationship Conflict, Team Performance, and Team Member Satisfaction: A Meta-analysis." *Journal of Applied Psychology* 88, no. 4 (August 2003): 741–749; de Wit, Frank R. C., Lindred L. Greer, and Karen A. Jehn. "The Paradox of Intragroup Conflict: A Meta-analysis." *Journal of Applied Psychology* 97, no. 2 (March 2012): 360–390.

[^]De Wit, Frank R. C., Karen A. Jehn, and Daan Scheepers. "Task Conflict, Information Processing, and Decision-Making: The Damaging Effect of Relationship Conflict." *Organizational Behavior and Human Decision Processes* 122, no. 2 (November 2013): 177–189.

Compromise

Compromise is a situation in which each party concedes something of value. The main objective of compromising is to find a solution that satisfies both parties. For example, say you and a coworker have been assigned a project analyzing customer feedback. Both of you want to present the results of the analysis to your boss. In this situation, you might agree to split the presentation—your coworker presenting the first half and you presenting the rest. While compromising involves an element of sacrifice, it can be a useful way to settle differences, maintain relationships, and agree on middle-ground solutions.

However, sometimes compromising can lead to resentment on both sides, especially when neither party gets exactly what it wants. Using the example above, while you may have reached an agreement with your coworker, you may not feel totally happy to split the presenting responsibilities especially if you think you are the better presenter. Furthermore, compromising often and too easily can also stunt creativity when it comes to finding deeper solutions to the issue.

Collaboration

Collaboration is a joint effort by all parties to find a solution beneficial to everyone. Parties that engage in collaboration take the time to truly understand each other's underlying needs, wants, and goals. Collaborations between two people might involve analyzing the source of a disagreement in order to generate new insights or working together on creative solutions to a shared problem. Successful collaboration involves good communication and cooperation resulting in a better solution than either party could have achieved alone. It also helps to maintain and build long-term relationships.

However, collaboration takes a lot of time and commitment and may not be appropriate in all situations, for example, when it comes to minor issues or relationships that you don't regard to be beneficial or important.

While each of the five strategies can be applied to different situations, some people are more comfortable using certain approaches over others. However, when it comes to handling conflict, take a moment to ask yourself whether you are using the best conflict strategy to resolve the problem. If not, you may need to go in a different direction.

Overall, relationships that are based on trust and respect tend to have less conflict. When conflict arises, it is often resolved quickly and effectively thanks to negotiation skills.

THINKING CRITICALLY

1. Think of a personal conflict. Describe how you could have approached the conflict using each of the five conflict management strategies (avoidance, accommodation, competition, compromise, and collaboration) and how each strategy would have affected the outcome of your conflict.

2. Of the five conflict management strategies, which do you believe are most likely to occur in a conflict between two unequal parties (a manager and employee, a board of directors and its CEO, or a large company and a small supplier)? Which do you believe are most likely to occur in a conflict between two equal parties (similarly sized companies, team members, or department heads)? Explain your reasoning.

3. Consider a time that you managed conflict through avoidance. What did you actually avoid by putting off and waiting to deal with the conflict? Did avoidance make the conflict situation better? Why or why not? What types of conflict situations are best addressed through avoidance? Explain your answer.

4. Which type of trust (disposition-based, cognition-based, or affect-based) best describes the way you form relationships with new coworkers? Does a different type of trust best describe how you form new friendships and intimate relationships? If so, explain why this may be the case.

5. Discuss a situation which reflects the outcomes of a low-trust environment. What steps could you take to reestablish trust?

Negotiation and Dispute Resolution

>> LO 11.4 Describe the negotiation process

We may not realize it, but most of us negotiate on a daily basis in every aspect of our lives, with family members, friends, classmates, roommates, and partners, as well as with our coworkers, team leaders, and bosses. We define **negotiation** as the process of reaching an agreement that both parties find acceptable.[21] Since disagreements are common in a range of OB issues, including task allocation, work schedules,

Negotiation: The process of reaching an agreement that both parties find acceptable

OB IN THE REAL WORLD

James Kenyon Hill, President and CEO, Pace Shave and Dorco USA

Dorco was founded in 1955 in Seoul, South Korea, and has become a worldwide leader in disposable men's and women's shaving products. Now headquartered in the United States, Dorco's products are sold in over ninety countries worldwide. Ken Hill, the president and CEO of Pace Shave and Dorco USA, heads the operations in the United States. With around 350 full-time employees and well over 100 suppliers worldwide, Ken has his hands full with very unique managerial duties.

Because Dorco is a multinational corporation, Ken must ensure that conflicts originating from cultural differences are mitigated on top of the typical, everyday conflicts that managers must deal with. The primary conflicts that Ken faces arise from "terms and conditions failures." Miscommunication with suppliers, a lack of mutual understanding of timing, payment structure disagreements, and quality issues all play a role in these types of cross-border conflicts. It is important to remember that a manager's job isn't supposed to be to put out fires; rather, a manager should focus a lot of effort on the prevention of conflicts. Ken swears that honesty and transparency are the most effective methods of mitigating these types of conflicts when dealing with international partners. "If you come across as genuine, not playing games, and transparent in the information you give to those you are dealing with, you build trust." Trust is the key here. To prevent conflict from arising internally or externally, whether a manager is dealing with his or her shareholders, employees, or suppliers, one must build trust. Trust increases the morale of a workplace, it encourages employees to take risks and work harder, and it gives external business partners motivation to keep coming back. In order to build trust and effectively prevent unproductive conflict, an environment founded on trust must be fostered by the manager.

Ken is always working toward building an environment founded on trust: where making a mistake doesn't mean instant termination. Employees will feel comfortable taking risks by trying new things and voicing their opinions by making recommendations. This is something that is highly valued in the American business culture. If a manager can maintain the respect for the individual, innovation and increased productivity are sure to follow. It takes a lot of time to build a work environment like this and the cultural differences Dorco faces doesn't make it easy. Yet, after six years of booming business, thoughtful negotiations, and the persistent building of trust, it's safe to say that Ken has helped Dorco establish a workplace free of unhealthy conflict.

Dorco's relations with its external suppliers and business partners are just as important as its relations internally. Trust externally, especially across international borders, might actually be even more difficult to build than internal trust. When dealing with international suppliers, for example, Ken stresses the importance of humility. As a successful corporation, it is hard to not come across as arrogant and demanding so being respectful and kind in deliberations with suppliers and other international partners is key to building trust. Oftentimes, that trust is breached when a supplier feels that they are getting ripped off or if the terms agreed upon in the contract are broken, either intentionally or accidentally. In these situations Ken stresses, "Just be honest and apologize. It is not about pride or anything like that it is about getting the business done so both parties benefit from it. If we made a mistake, we own up to it." That goes both way as suppliers are expected to do the same from Ken and his team. Trust can only be built when both parties demonstrate their abilities to be humble and respectful toward each other.

A manager of a multinational corporation faces an entirely unique host of problems from cultural differences clashing within the organization to cultural differences when dealing with corporate suppliers and partners across borders. Whether the problems are internal or external, Ken has identified that trust is the key to remedying present problems and preventing problems from arising in the future.

Critical-Thinking Questions

1. What are some of the dilemmas that an international corporation might face that a domestic one will not?

2. Describe the benefits that come along with a strong sense of trust within a corporation. ●

and salaries, the art of negotiation is a necessity in life as well as in the workplace. Table 11.2 illustrates ten useful tips for negotiation.

Let's explore the negotiation process.[22]

TABLE 11.2

10 Tips for Negotiation[25]

Do your homework. Make sure you carry out some research on what is to be discussed and spend some time thinking through various outcomes before the meeting.
Consider different points of view. Think about the situation from the other person's perspective, not just your own. Try and understand their needs and concerns.
Clarify your goals. Make sure you define your main objectives before the discussion and have a clear BATNA in mind.
Choose the time for discussion carefully. Make sure there is enough time for the discussion to take place and during a period where both parties are relaxed.
Try to control your emotions. Remain calm and avoid getting emotional. Remember—high emotions can confuse our thinking which hampers the negotiation process.
Listen! Make sure you actively listen to the other parties, and do not interrupt until it is your turn to talk.
Explain your needs. Tell the other side what you would prefer the outcome to be, and why. Explain your needs calmly and concisely.
Avoid laying blame. Even if you have some misgivings toward the other party, do not air them during the negotiation process. Focus on the facts, and never make your comments personal.
Collaborate to find a creative solution. Try to not think of negotiation as one party winning and the other losing. The best negotiations end with each party walking away satisfied. Working together to find creative ways to meet everyone's needs is also a good way to build and sustain long-term relationships.
Remember that tomorrow is another day. If emotions start to run high and tempers flare, then it's reasonable to table the discussion for another day. The space gives the parties involved some time to calm down and think through the issues more rationally.

Getting Ready to Negotiate

Before any negotiation, it is critical for each party to outline the goals and objectives they would like to achieve. It is also essential for each party to do its homework on its opponent—to consider the other party's position and decision-making power, the length of time it has been in business, and whether it has any other negotiating history. Professor Jared Curhan of MIT Management Sloan School also advises preparing for an alternative outcome or BATNA (Best Alternative to Negotiated Agreement) should the deal not work out as planned. Curhan suggests the following question should be asked during the preparation stage: "Before any negotiation, ask yourself, 'What am I going to do if I don't reach a deal?'"[23]

Shaping Expectations

Defining the ground rules of negotiation before talks begin is key to shaping expectations. It is essential that each party understands the rules and agrees to adhere to them during the negotiation process. Opening with something like "Let's agree on some ground rules for our negotiation before we get started" is a good way to set expectations. These rules might include an agreement that the parties involved must only talk one at a time, listen to each other, treat one another with respect, and share a mutual intolerance of derogatory language or any other kind of verbal attacks. The rules may also include conditions for termination and an agreement that either party can halt the discussion at any time. With the ground rules set, the parties can begin their negotiation. Often, the ground rules can take longer than the negotiation itself, but establishing the rules before the conversation starts encourages cooperation, prevents misunderstandings, and overall makes for a smoother negotiation.

Providing Supporting Evidence

Providing supporting evidence is key to a successful negotiation. Parties entering a negotiation must show supporting evidence as proof to back up their arguments. Each party should describe the evidence and explain the facts clearly and concisely using jargon-free language. This is a good opportunity for each party to educate each other about their position.

Negotiating the Deal

Once each party has a chance to explain their positions, it is time to negotiate the deal. The goal during this stage is for the parties to convince each other of the validity of their demands, and to persuade the other side to concede to those demands. Each argument must be presented logically and clearly. It is possible for the discussion to become heated as each party strives to win the best deal, but too much emotion may negatively impact the negotiation. In fact, recognizing our own emotional triggers is a good way to defuse negative emotions in the heat of the moment. A study led by author and Nobel Laureate Daniel Kahneman showed that Americans experience the most distress when they are speaking to their bosses or commuting.[24] Being aware of these negative emotions and their potential to impact your ability to negotiate goes a long way to minimizing emotional behavior during the crucial stages.

When engaging in negotiations, both parties should outline their goals for the discussion and understand the other party's position.

TABLE 11.3

Third-Party Dispute Resolution Approaches

MEDIATOR	ARBITRATOR	CONCILIATOR
Reinstates communication between two parties	Issues judgment based on statements from both parties	Persuades opponents to communicate
Offers no opinions or judgment	Judgment is binding for all parties	Offers nonbinding opinion

Agreement and Implementation

With the bargaining process complete, the parties move on to the final stage of negotiation—formalizing an agreement and implementing the deal. They spend time clarifying the deal and ensuring that everyone understands the outcome of the negotiations and the specifications of the final agreement. Pending due diligence, the agreement will be formalized in writing and signed by each party by an agreed-upon date. Following the process, it is important that each party keeps its promises and adheres to the terms of the agreement.

Third-Party Dispute Resolution Approaches

What if the parties had reached a stalemate in their negotiations or failed to find a mutually beneficial solution to the price war that was harming both their companies? In these instances, it is useful to introduce a neutral third party to help settle disputes. There are three types of third party roles: mediator, arbitrator, and conciliator (see Table 11.3).[26]

A **mediator** is a neutral third party who attempts to assist parties in a negotiation to find a resolution or come to an agreement using rational arguments and persuasion. The chief role of mediators is to get the opposing parties to communicate rather than provide a solution or a decision. A mediator has no right to impose his or her views on the parties.

An **arbitrator** is a neutral third party officially assigned to settle a dispute who listens to both sides of the argument as stated by the parties. Unlike a mediator, an arbitrator has the power to issue a judgment, which is final and binding for all parties.

Finally, a **conciliator** is a neutral third party who is informally assigned to persuade opponents to communicate. The conciliator is allowed to offer an opinion, but unlike that of an arbitrator, this judgment does not carry any legal weight.

Many businesses in conflict choose one or more of these third-party dispute resolution approaches because they can be a useful way to resolve differences and can prevent an issue from escalating.

For example, Major League Baseball teams and players often engage in arbitration to determine a player's salary. The process begins with both the team and the player's agent submitting their "last best"

Mediator: A neutral third party who attempts to assist parties in a negotiation to find a resolution or come to an agreement using rational arguments and persuasion

Arbitrator: A neutral third party officially assigned to settle a dispute

Conciliator: A neutral third party who is informally assigned to persuade opponents to communicate

Major League Baseball players' salary arbitrations are complicated processes where a player's market salary is compared against offers from the player and the team.

George Nikitin via Associated Press

salary offer. Each side then presents their case and a rebuttal to the opposing side's case in a salary hearing to a panel of three arbitrators chosen from a slate of sixteen arbitrators determined jointly by major league baseball and the players association. The panel considers the evidence presented in order to reach a decision on what they consider to be the correct "market salary" for that player. This figure is compared to the two "best final offers," and whichever figure is closest is likely to be selected. For example, suppose that a player's agent submits a best final offer of $20 million, and the team submits a best final offer of $15 million. Theoretically, the panel of arbitrators would need to determine whether the player's market value is more or less than $17.5 million, the midpoint figure. If the arbitrators find the correct price to be higher than the midpoint, they will choose the $20 million figure requested by the player; if they determine that the player's market value is lower than the midpoint, then they will select the team's offer.[27]

THINKING CRITICALLY

1. Explain how the three steps prior to negotiating the deal (getting ready to negotiate, shaping expectations, and providing supporting evidence) can contribute to a successful negotiation.

2. Review earlier sections in the chapter regarding conflict. What factors could contribute to a dysfunctional negotiation process and an unsuccessful outcome?

3. Consider the three types of third-party dispute resolution. What types of situations would lend themselves most easily to mediation, to arbitration, or to conciliation? In what circumstances would businesses likely prefer mediation or conciliation over arbitration?

Bargaining Approaches

>> LO 11.5   **Compare distributive and integrative bargaining approaches**

Bargaining and negotiating are often thought to be one and the same, but there are important differences. Although a subset of negotiation, bargaining focuses more on price, where one party may agree to give the other a lower price than initially suggested. In contrast, negotiation goes further than just the price; it is a process of give and take, where each side engages in thoughtful discussion to reach an agreement to satisfy both parties.

The ultimate goal of a negotiation should be to provide an agreement that satisfies everyone and leaves all the parties on good terms. But in reality the process is not always straightforward. The reason is that the way people negotiate has an influence on its outcomes. In general, people use two main bargaining strategies: distributive bargaining and integrative bargaining (see Figure 11.4).

Distributive bargaining:
A strategy that involves two parties trying to claim a "fixed pie" of resources

Distributive bargaining occurs when two parties both try to claim a "fixed pie" of resources.[28] For example, say you are trying to buy a used car. You know you will need a certain amount of money to fix the car up the way you want it, and for that reason you want a reduction in the price. However, the car salesperson wants the maximum price he can get for the car and tells you to take it or leave it. This is known as a win/lose situation, in which one party only gains and the other one only loses.

Another approach to distributive bargaining is to compromise just for the sake of ending the negotiation. For example, say you and the car salesperson have been haggling for a long time and each of you is getting frustrated. The rep agrees to let you have a small percentage off the price, but you do not feel it is enough. Eventually you both give up something in order to agree on a price, but neither of you is satisfied with the outcome.

In many instances, distributive bargaining can be time consuming and inefficient. It can lead to a contest of wills, especially when egos get in the way. It is better suited to short-term bargaining with people you are unlikely to deal with again than to the building of long-term relationships, which require a degree of give and take.

Integrative bargaining occurs when both parties negotiate a win-win solution.[29] It is about enlarging the pie so everyone gets a piece. This type of bargaining applies to businesses that want to build long-term relationships with each other. For example, a clothing manufacturer is looking to negotiate with its fabric supplier to reach a mutually beneficial agreement. The manufacturer wants the supplier to consistently provide it with high-quality fabrics at a fair price within the allotted time frames. The fabric supplier agrees and a formal contract is arranged. In the end, both parties win: the clothing manufacturer has negotiated a long-term contract with the fabric supplier at a fair price, and the fabric supplier is guaranteed a stream of business from the clothing manufacturer. Both parties have achieved the maximum value from the negotiation.

Integrative Bargaining Strategies

There are four basic strategies for integrative bargaining.[30] The best choice will vary depending on the situation. For example, let's say you are preparing to negotiate a salary raise at work and are looking for the best ways to approach the situation.

- Separate the people from the problem

You may not be crazy about your boss, but this shouldn't influence your approach to negotiating a higher salary. In this instance, the focus needs to be on the facts; emotion should never influence your strategy. This is about sitting down with your boss and putting your feelings aside to find a solution that satisfies you both.

- Focus on interests, not positions

When preparing for a negotiation each party must understand its own interests as well as the interests of the other party. Why do you want a raise? And why should your boss give it to you? You may need more money for a mortgage or to pay off your college loans, but frankly this is not of any interest to your boss. From your boss's perspective, a raise is deserved only when the employee promises to deliver more in the future. You need to list all the ways you can benefit the company in the long term.

- Generate a variety of possibilities

It is a mistake to go into a negotiation with only one possible outcome. What if your boss simply says she can't give you a raise? Before the negotiation, consider some other possibilities. What about an increase in benefits, more vacation days, or

FIGURE 11.4

Bargaining Approaches

Distributive Bargaining

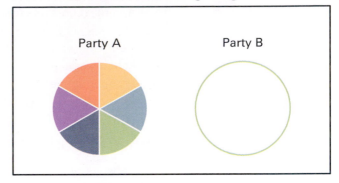

Integrative Bargaining

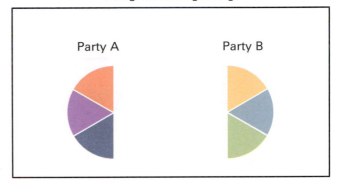

Integrative bargaining: A strategy that involves both parties negotiating a win-win solution

flexible work options such as a day or two of working from home? When you compile a list of acceptable possibilities, you will probably have a better chance of gaining something out of the negotiation, even if it's not the salary raise that you wanted.[31]

- Insist on some fair standard

Referring your boss to some fair standard other than your opinion, such as a published wage and salary survey, could be helpful. If you succeed in obtaining the salary raise, then ensure that the agreement is formalized. This will give clarity to the negotiations and prevent any misunderstandings further down the line.

Other Negotiating Strategies

It is always wise to have a best possible alternative to a negotiable agreement (**BATNA**), which is the best outcome you could achieve if the negotiation fails and you must follow another course of action.[32] For example, say you want a salary raise of $5,000 per year, but you will accept $3,000 if it is offered. What will you do if you are unable to get the $3,000 raise? Will you settle for your current salary? Will you quit your job and try to find a higher-paying job in another organization? Once you have identified your BATNA, you will be in a better position to figure out your zone of possible agreement (**ZOPA**) (see Figure 11.5), which is the area where two sides in a negotiation may find common ground.[33] For example, say you request your $5,000 salary raise and your boss tells you that the best offer will be $3,500. Since this figure lies within the zone that both parties find acceptable, then it is likely an agreement will be reached.

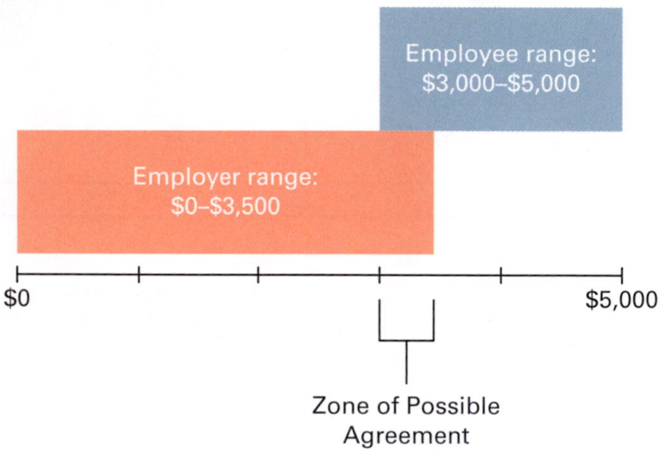

In this chapter, we have explored the complexities of conflict and negotiation and examined the different types of negotiation strategies that can help resolve conflict. In the next chapter, we explore the concept of leadership.

BATNA: The best possible alternative to a negotiable agreement

ZOPA: The zone of possible agreement, the area where two sides in a negotiation may find common ground

FIGURE 11.5

Zone of Possible Agreement

Employee range: $3,000–$5,000

Employer range: $0–$3,500

$0 $5,000

Zone of Possible Agreement

THINKING CRITICALLY

1. Discuss the integrative bargaining strategies used in the case negotiation discussed in the previous section. Which of the four strategies (separate the people from the problem; focus on interests, not positions; generate a variety of possibilities; insist on some fair standard) were used?

2. What is the primary strategic benefit of entering a negotiation with a clearly defined BATNA (best possible alternative to a negotiable agreement)? What are some possible emotional benefits of having a BATNA in place?

3. In what situations might it be useful to let the other party know your BATNA at the beginning of a negotiation? In what situations would it be best to keep that information to yourself? Explain your answer.

Visit **edge.sagepub.com/neckob2e** to help you accomplish your coursework goals in an easy-to-use learning environment.

- Mobile-friendly eFlashcards and practice quizzes
- Video and multimedia content
- Chapter summaries with learning objectives
- EXCLUSIVE! Access to full-text SAGE journal articles

IN REVIEW

11.1 Outline the bases of trust and predictable outcomes of trust in organizations

We define **trust** as the dependence on the integrity, ability, honesty, and reliability of someone or something else. Generally, there are three types. People with *disposition-based trust* tend to possess personality traits that encourage them to put their faith in others. In contrast, people with *cognition-based trust* base their faith in others on factual information such as the person's past experience and proven track record. Finally, *affect-based trust* occurs when people put their faith in others based on feelings and emotions.

When trust is high in the workplace, people tend to work better together and are more focused on their duties. They tend to take more risks, display citizenship behaviors, and exhibit fewer ineffectual or counterproductive behaviors.

11.2 Describe the conflict process and the various types of conflict

We define **conflict** as a clash between individuals or groups in relation to different opinions, thought processes, and perceptions. **Functional conflict** consists of constructive and healthy disputes between individuals or groups. In contrast, **dysfunctional conflict** consists of disputes and disagreements that have negative effects on individuals or teams. It often arises from an unwillingness to listen to each other or a reluctance to agree on a resolution or goal.

Task conflict refers to the clash between individuals in relation to the direction, content, or goal of a certain assignment. **Relationship conflict** refers to the clash in personality between two or more individuals. This type of conflict is considered to be the most destructive and harmful to organizations because it can give rise to hostility, mistrust, fear, and negativity. **Process conflict** refers to the clash in viewpoints about how to carry out work. It can be beneficial to organizations as long as it operates at a low level.

The four different stages of the conflict process are antecedents of conflict, perceived/felt conflict, manifest conflict, and outcomes of conflict. **Antecedents of conflict** are the factors that set the scene for potential disputes: lack of communication, incompatible personalities, and collisions in value systems. In the **perceived/felt conflict stage**, emotional differences are sensed and felt. The **manifest conflict** stage consists of behaviors that provoke a response. The final stage is the **outcomes of conflict stage,** which describes the consequences of the dispute.

11.3 Identify the five basic conflict management strategies

Avoidance is the attempt to suppress a conflict and pretend it does not really exist. **Accommodation** is one party's attempt to adjust his or her views to play down the differences between the parties. **Competition** is the attempt to gain victory through force, skill, or domination. **Compromise** is a situation in which each party concedes something of value. **Collaborating** occurs when all parties work together to find a solution beneficial to everyone.

11.4 Describe the negotiation process

We define **negotiation** as the process of reaching an agreement that both parties find acceptable. Before any negotiation, it is critical that each party get ready to negotiate by outlining the goals and objectives they would like to achieve. The second step is to shape the expectations for the negotiation. Next, both parties take turns in bolstering their demands with supportive evidence. Then the parties bargain back and forth until they both agree upon a deal. This leads to the final stage of the process, known as the agreement and implementation stage. During this stage, the agreement will be formalized in writing.

There are three types of neutral third-party roles in the event of a stalemate. A **mediator** attempts to assist parties to find a resolution using rational arguments and persuasion. A mediator has no right to impose his or her views on the parties. An **arbitrator** listens to both sides before issuing a judgment considered final and binding for all parties. Finally, a **conciliator** is informally assigned to persuade opponents to communicate. The conciliator is allowed to offer an opinion but it does not carry any legal weight.

11.5   **Compare distributive and integrative bargaining approaches**

Distributive bargaining occurs when two parties try to claim a "fixed pie" of resources. It is more suitable for short-term bargaining with people you are unlikely to deal with again than for long-term relationships, which require give and take. **Integrative bargaining** occurs when both parties negotiate a win-win solution by enlarging the pie so everyone gets a piece.

KEY TERMS

Antecedents of conflict   311
Arbitrator   319
BATNA   322
Conflict   308
Conciliator   319
Distributive bargaining   320
Dysfunctional conflict   310
Functional conflict   308
Integrative bargaining   321
Manifest conflict stage   311

Mediator   319
Negotiation   315
Outcomes of conflict stage   311
Perceived/felt conflict stage   311
Process conflict   311
Relationship conflict   311
Task conflict   311
Trust   305
ZOPA   322

UP FOR DEBATE: Global Standardization of Negotiations

In a world where globalization increases daily, interactions between firms from different countries are much more common. Many manufacturers have a network of thousands upon thousands of suppliers around the world. Firms engage in long and expensive negotiations to ensure that conflicts are avoided. This waste of time and resources shows that there is a growing need for firms around the world to standardize the way business is practiced to minimize conflict and streamline negotiations. Agree or disagree? Explain your answer.

EXERCISE 11.1: Which Is More Important? Handling Conflict

Objective

The purpose of this exercise is to gain a greater appreciation of conflict and how to work through it.

Instructions

In groups of three to five, rank the following items in order of their importance to society. Clearly, there will be conflict among group members. Your group should probably first determine what the word *importance* means—affecting the most people, impacting in a negative way, impacting in a positive way, etc. Also, you should define *society*—the local or regional society, American society, the world, etc. Remember to utilize concepts regarding conflict from this chapter as your group ranks the following from the most important to the least important:

- Abortion rights
- Diversity in the workplace
- Terrorism preparedness
- Equal pay for equal work
- Sexual harassment
- Welfare
- Labor unions
- Cure for cancer
- Unemployment
- Compensation of CEOs

Reflection Questions

1. How did your group determine a strategy for ranking these? Describe.

2. What challenges did you have in accomplishing the task? How did you overcome those challenges?

3. Did you use negotiation at any point during the process? Explain.

4. Describe an example of conflict at your current or most recent job. How has that conflict been resolved?

5. Discuss instances in which conflict resolution might be difficult to accomplish in the workplace.

Exercise contributed by Steven Stovall, Southeast Missouri State University.

EXERCISE 11.2: Tension, Conflict, Resolution

Objectives

This exercise will help you to be able to better *describe* the conflict process, *describe* the various types of conflict, and *identify* the five basic conflict management strategies.

Instructions

Step 1. Think of a conflict you are currently in (one that you are willing to share with the class), or, if you are not currently in any conflict, one that you have recently been in but were not able to resolve satisfactorily. Write this conflict down in as much detail as possible. (Note, you can give other parties in this description pseudonyms if you want to.) (5 minutes)

Step 2. Find a partner and give each other a brief overview of your conflicts. Choose the conflict that you both agree is the most interesting, and closely related to chapter topics on conflict management. (If one person has chosen an ongoing conflict, and the other person has chosen a past conflict, choose the ongoing conflict.) Both partners should then analyze the conflict for the following elements:

- Determine if the conflict is functional or dysfunctional.
- Determine the type of conflict (task, relationship, or process).
- Describe the conflict development using the four stages of conflict (antecedents of conflict, perceived/felt conflict, manifest conflict, and outcomes of conflict).
- Identify which of the five conflict management strategies were used in the conflict. (10 to 15 minutes)

Step 3. Be prepared to present your analysis to the class or provide details on specific aspects of the analysis when asked by your instructor. (5 minutes)

Reflection Questions

1. How did analyzing your conflict help you to better understand the reasons for your conflict?

2. How did working through the conflict with someone else help you to understand the conflict more clearly?

3. What new insights did you gain about avoiding dysfunctional conflicts, or better resolving functional conflicts?

4. How could you use this process in future conflicts?

5. As a manager, how could you use this or similar methods to help workers in dealing with a conflict?

6. In what ways would it be beneficial to have all parties in a conflict work through a similar process?

Exercise contributed by Milton R. Mayfield, Professor of Business, Texas A&M International University, and Jacqueline R. Mayfield, Professor of Business, Texas A&M International University.

EXERCISE 11.3: Win as Much as You Can

Objective

The purpose of this exercise is to grasp the concept of trust in group settings.

Instructions

This exercise is based on the "prisoner's dilemma" activity and involves trust of others as well as negotiation. The class will be divided into four groups. Each group should elect two representatives. Those four pairs of representatives will come to the front of the room. If the size of the class is small enough, the students should sit near their elected representatives (if this is not possible, the representatives will be seated by themselves). The four pairs of representatives should be seated far enough away from one another to ensure that conversations cannot be heard.

Each pair of representatives will receive from the instructor a single card that has a large "A" on one side and a large "B" on the other. The instructions are as follows:

- Both pairs of representatives will be reminded that the name of this exercise is "win as much as you can".

- There will be ten rounds and each pair of representatives will determine for each round whether they will hold up the "A" side or the "B" side of their card (if it is a smaller class, the other students will help confer with the representatives; in larger classes, the representatives will simply confer with each other).

- Each pair of representatives must agree on whether they will hold up an "A" or a "B."

- Scoring is as follows:

  o 4 Bs = each team loses 1 point

  o 3 Bs = each team wins 1 point

  o 1 A = that team loses 3 points

  o 2 As = each team wins 2 points

  o 2 Bs = each team loses 2 points

  o 1 B = that team wins 3 points

  o 3 As = each team loses 1 point

  o 4 As = each team wins 1 point

Here is the format for the ten rounds:

Round:

1. Pairs of representatives discuss only with one another which card they will show (for each round, if the class is small, the other students associated with the representatives may also provide input). There can be no communication—verbal or nonverbal between the pairs of representatives. After conferring, each pair of representatives holds up the card showing either an "A" or a "B" to the other pairs. This must be done at the exact same time to avoid cheating (the instructor will say something along the lines of "Ok, on the count of three, hold up your card...one, two, three!").

2. Again, representatives confer with one another and after about a minute of conferring, hold up the cards at the same time.

3. Same as round 2.

4. Here, the pairs of representatives may discuss with other pairs. They can negotiate, agree to hold up a certain card, meet with one pair separately from the other pairs, and so forth. After a few minutes of discussion and negotiations, the pairs of representatives return to their seats. They then confer with one another and determine whether they will do what was agreed or hold up a different letter. However, keep in mind, that in this round, the points are *doubled*.

5. Same as round 2.

6. Same as round 2.

7. Same as round 4. However, the points are 4 times the amount.

8. Same as round 2.

9. Same as round 2.

10. Same as round 4. However, the points are 8 times the amount.

At the conclusion of round 10, the instructor will total the points to see who won the most points. Discussion will then ensue as to the process, negotiations, and how trust played a role.

Reflection Questions

1. What did you learn from this game about trust and negotiations?

2. How important is trust in the workplace? When it comes to negotiations, what role does trust play?

3. The name of this exercise is "win as much as you can." You probably noticed that at least one team could not be trusted despite agreeing to hold up a particular card—they had the approach that they wanted to *win as much as they could*. Does this happen in the workplace? Explain.

4. What can we do as employees to earn trust and maintain trust among those with whom we work?

Exercise contributed by Steven Stovall, Southeast Missouri State University.

ONLINE EXERCISE 11.1: What Conflict Management Strategy Do You Use?

Objective

The purpose of this exercise is to gain an appreciation for different conflict management strategies.

Instructions

Take a look at the following five conflict management strategies:

- **Avoidance**—an attempt to suppress a conflict and pretend it doesn't exist
- **Accommodation**—an attempt to adjust our views to play down differences between parties
- **Competition**—an attempt to gain victory through force, skill, or domination
- **Compromise**—a situation in which each party concedes something of value
- **Collaboration**—a joint effort by all parties to find a solution beneficial to everyone

Be sure to read the chapter, as the text delves into each of these in more detail. After studying these five types of conflict management strategies, which one or ones do you tend to use when faced with conflict? On a discussion board, post which strategy or strategies you utilize most often and give an example. After each participant has had a chance to post something, comment on others' posts. For those who use the same strategy as you, discuss why you tend to find that strategy helpful. For those who use a different strategy than you, ask how and why their strategy is useful.

Reflection Questions

1. Do you utilize a different conflict management strategy in your personal life versus at work? Explain.

2. Which conflict management strategy would you never use in the workplace? Why?

3. Think of a current or recent manager you have had. Which conflict management strategy did he or she use? How effective was that manager in resolving conflicts?

Exercise contributed by Steven Stovall, Southeast Missouri State University.

CASE STUDY 11.1: Conflict and Negotiation at Disney

The great dreamer Walt Disney himself couldn't have dreamt of the corporate fairy tale that his company has become in the past forty years. The Walt Disney Company or just "Disney" is a company worthy of multiple books to discuss the amount of continued excellence that it has taken to get them to where they are today. The factor of Disney that is most worthy of study in this modern era of media is its ability to consolidate and merge with other companies to become the largest media company in the world. Today, as mass media consolidates further and further into three to five major conglomerates, Disney's strong culture and affinity for acquisitions has put them at the top of their industry.

Disney's competitors could not have seen the wave of movie power that Disney would be able to churn out due to a handful of what were at the time pricey purchase. When Disney purchased Marvel for $4 million and Lucasfilm for $4 billion, their competition could never have known that the fruits of these acquisitions would be so sweet. With movies from each of these purchases making well over $100 million within the first few weeks of release, Disney could not have imagined such great returns.

Year after year Disney movies dominate the box office and networks owned by Disney dominate the small screens. With huge growth in their theme park business and both Marvel and Lucasfilm in their stable, Disney looks to remain a powerhouse for the long haul. The thing that has gotten them here is their ability to use their unique future-oriented culture to absorb outside cultures as they acquire their competition. While they have gotten bigger and bigger so too has their competition with NBC Universal and Warner Media both owned by Comcast and AT&T respectively. And even with the rise of Netflix and other streaming platforms, Disney has consistently bought companies that could soon give them an edge in the streaming space where they plan to release a platform hosting all of their content companywide. Their ability to think ahead and buy into the future is going to remain a vital component to their success as we see further consolidation in the mass-media sector.

One of the most substantial acquisitions of the Disney story was Pixar in 2006, a move by both companies that has been seen as the gold standard in acquisition synergy. At the time Pixar was a big player in the animation realm with mega-hits like *Toy Story* and *Finding Nemo*. However, their vision for the entertainment industry always coincided with their intent to remain a fiscally solvent business due to their high operating costs, long turnover time, and limited release schedule. This meant that while they were making fantastic movies, they were having trouble balancing art with business and innovation. For this reason, Disney as a company with many streams of income and a very similar industry vision was the perfect fit to acquire Pixar.

While Pixar was one of Disney's easiest acquisitions, they have been able to make dozens more like this that keep them competing in every corner of media. With organizations like 21st Century Fox, Marvel, Fox Family Worldwide, and ABC all under the arm of the Walt Disney Company, they have consistently managed to facilitate a culture that consistently cohabitates and assimilates other organizations into their own. Even now, as smaller companies are being bought up by the largest players, Disney is willing to pay top dollar for a company with solid structure that is compatible to its goals and values.

Disney, one of the most recognizable brands in the world, has managed to maintain the same association with the brand that they have had since the visionary founder was still in charge. They have maintained the magical side of their brand while incorporating dozens of other companies into their everyday operations. There have been very few hiccups along the way, with a workforce more loyal to their brand name than any in the industry. This culture also permeates into the way that they handle their business regarding acquisitions. They have never made themselves the cutthroat negotiators often seen in the business from top studio heads but instead tend to pay more than what an asset is worth as long as it is an asset trending upward.

When they purchased the rights to make Marvel movies, they were entering a space that had never been successful, meaning that many said that they overpaid at $4 million. The same is also true for the rights to Star Wars, both thought to be extravagant purchases despite being so far apart. Disney knew what they were getting into and had no fear paying more than what they could have gotten each entity for and the results speak for themselves. Disney's ability to absorb companies into their own culture has allowed them to build themselves from a small-scale cartoon movie studio into the purveyor of high-quality media content that they are today. Due to their "all in" negotiation strategy of investing in the best content, they have made themselves the first choice of any studio looking for partners.

Discussion Questions

1. Discuss how Disney's negotiation tactics differ from most in their industry.

2. Discuss briefly the characteristic that has led Disney to its current size.

Resources

Hagey, K., & Schwartzel, E. (2018). 21st century fox agrees to higher offer from Disney. *The Wall Street Journal*. Retrieved from https://www.wsj.com/articles/fox-disney-announce-new-deal-1529496937

PBS. org. (n.d.). Walt Disney Co. *FRONTLINE*. Retrieved from https://www.pbs.org/wgbh/pages/frontline/shows/cool/giants/disney.html

Ruesink, M. (2015). Top corporate mergers: The good, the bad & the ugly. *Rasmussen College*. Retrieved from https://www.rasmussen.edu/degrees/business/blog/best-and-worst-corporate-mergers/

Samson, R. (2017). The conglomerate structure of The Walt Disney Company. *Profolus*. Retrieved from https://www.profolus.com/topics/conglomerate-structure-walt-disney-company/

SELF-ASSESSMENT 11.1

What Is My Preferred Conflict Management Strategy?

This assessment will help you to determine the extent to which you tend to use the avoiding, accommodating, competing, compromising, or collaborating conflict management styles.

For each statement, circle the number that best describes how you would respond when you have a conflict with another person:

	NOT AT ALL ACCURATE	SOMEWHAT ACCURATE	A LITTLE ACCURATE	MOSTLY ACCURATE	COMPLETELY ACCURATE
1. I usually give in to the other person.	1	2	3	4	5
2. I attempt to identify a middle-of-the-road resolution.	1	2	3	4	5
3. I force my own perspective.	1	2	3	4	5
4. I explore the situation in an effort to find an outcome that satisfies my interests as well as those of the other person.	1	2	3	4	5
5. I generally avoid confronting the other person about our disagreement.	1	2	3	4	5
6. I tend to simply agree with the other person.	1	2	3	4	5
7. I stress that we should find a good compromise agreement.	1	2	3	4	5
8. I look for opportunities to gain an advantage.	1	2	3	4	5
9. I try to represent both my interests as well as those of the other person.	1	2	3	4	5
10. I try to avoid disagreements as much as I can.	1	2	3	4	5
11. I do my best to accommodate the other person's wishes if possible.	1	2	3	4	5
12. I suggest that we both budge from our positions in order to reach an agreement.	1	2	3	4	5
13. I strive to get the best possible solution for myself.	1	2	3	4	5
14. I work with the other person to examine both sides of the story in order to find the most mutually beneficial resolution available.	1	2	3	4	5
15. I do my best to make our disagreements seem less important.	1	2	3	4	5
16. I tend to adjust my thinking to the other person's point of view.	1	2	3	4	5
17. I try to facilitate a 50–50 compromise if possible.	1	2	3	4	5
18. I do my best to win at all costs.	1	2	3	4	5
19. I attempt to craft an outcome that meets the other person's interests as well as my own.	1	2	3	4	5
20. I will avoid confronting the other person if at all possible.	1	2	3	4	5

Scoring

Preference for Accommodating

Total for items 1, 6, 11, and 16 _____

Preference for Compromising

Total for items 2, 7, 12 and 17 _____

Preference for Competing

Total for items 3, 8, 13, and 18 _____

Preference for Collaborating

Total for items 4, 9, 14 and 19 _____

Preference for Avoiding

Total for items 5, 10, 15 and 20 _____

1. What was your strongest conflict management strategy (the one with the highest score)?
2. What are some of the strengths and weaknesses of this approach?
3. Under what circumstances might it be beneficial for you to attempt to incorporate more of one of your weaker conflict management strategies?

Source: Adapted from a scale employed by De Dreu, Carsten K. W., Arne Evers, Bianca Beersma, Esther S. Kluwer, and Aukje Nauta. "A Theory-Based Measure of Conflict Management Strategies in the Workplace." *Journal of Organizational Behavior* 22, no. 6 (September 2001): 645–668.

PART IV

Leadership and Influence Processes

12

Leadership Perspectives

As a leader, it's a major responsibility on your shoulders to practice the behavior you want others to follow.

—*Himanshu Bhatia, Rose International, Inc.*

Learning Objectives

By the end of this chapter, you will be able to:

12.1 Explain the basic concept of leadership

12.2 Distinguish between formal and informal leadership and between leadership and management

12.3 Contrast the four basic types of leadership

12.4 Describe the trait, behavioral, and contingency leadership perspectives

12.5 Compare the inspirational, relational, and follower-centered leadership perspectives

12.6 Discuss the power-distributing leadership perspectives of empowering, shared, and self-leadership

12.7 Describe the values-based leadership perspectives of authentic, spiritual, servant, and ethical leadership

12.8 Discuss leadership across cultures

12.9 Identify gender issues in the context of leadership

CASE STUDY: PROCTER AND GAMBLE'S LEADERSHIP TRAINING PROGRAM

Whether you realize it or not, there is a company that has quietly inserted itself into most aspects of your day-to-day routine. To some it may seem like a soap and shampoo company but those that know its past know that it has created the market that it now leads. It has ridden the wave of modern hygiene to what it is today and is responsible for many of the consumable products you use every day in your home. This company is Procter and Gamble. Originally founded by William Proctor and James Gamble in 1837 as a soap company, P&G's products really took off during the Civil War when it won contracts with the Union army to provide supplies to its soldiers. Back then, most consumer products were made using home remedies with recipes passed down for generations. P&G were the first to streamline the process and to make brands with consistent ingredients. It was through this effort, that they effectively invented branding as we know it.

With over $85 billion in sales and sixty-five brands in its portfolio, Procter and Gamble is the world's largest advertiser. They sell all types of consumer goods—from cleaning agents to razors. You may not know it, but Gillette, Febreze, Vicks, and Olay are all P&G brands.

Today, Procter and Gamble products sell around the world (apart from North Korea and Cuba) and P&G employs over 100,000 people. While it all started with soap, over the last 150 years P&G have created new products by using out-of-the-box thinking. Before 2014, its portfolio included foods, snacks, and beverages. However, since then, they decided to cut one hundred of their brands and kept the sixty-five brands that made 95 percent of their profits. With this streamlining, we have the modern-day Procter and Gamble.

As a leader in new and innovative products, P&G knew it would constantly need to reinvent itself in order to keep up with the competition and meet the needs of consumers. If it only sold soap, it would quickly have its business stolen away by another company making a newer kind of soap. According to former chairman Richard Deupree, "The Procter & Gamble Company never has gone in circles, never followed footsteps, but rather has continually broken new trails, entered new fields, set new records, even raised its own high standards."

P&G also adopted this mind-set in its approach to advertising. It knew that reinventing its product line along with how it was presented would be crucial. For that reason, P&G is regarded by many as the inventor of advertising as we now know it and seen as the first household name brand. Its desire to advertise neatly coincided with the age of the newspaper and the rise of print advertising.

Along with being at the forefront of product innovation and advertising, P&G has also been a leader in its field for product testing and the proper vetting of all its products. It set a standard for the importance of safety, and even in the early days of mainstream advertising it made the safety of its product a huge priority. Thanks to the early groundwork laid by P&G, consumers rarely have to worry about the safety of cleaning products.

P&G has been the proud recipient of many awards, including being #1 on Fortune's Global Top Companies for Leaders or #15 for World's Most Admired Brands. It is consistently ranked a top company for its organizational culture, brand recognition, and leadership development programs. It has one of the most efficient employee training programs of any major companies and prides itself on mentorship and leadership skills even at entry level. As a result, P&G has become a very sought-after place to work. Its leadership in the industry applies to everything it does, from how it treats its workforce to how it manages its brand and its success shows no sign of slowing down.

Critical-Thinking Questions

1. Why does Procter and Gamble draw so many job applicants?

2. How did Procter and Gamble influence the creation of their industry as it pertains to safety?

Resources:

Burla, A. (2017). What is the corporate culture like at Procter & Gamble? How is the culture different than other companies? *Quora.* Retrieved from https://www.quora.com/What-is-the-corporate-culture-like-at-Procter-Gamble-How-is-the-culture-different-than-other-companies

Fisman, R. (2013). Culture clash: Even a merger made in heaven can get off to a rocky start. *Slate.* Retrieved from http://www.slate.com/articles/business/the_enlightened_manager/2013/12/corporate_culture_clashes_what_managers_can_learn_from_the_rocky_first_days.html

Horowitz, A. (2011). How Procter & Gamble became the maker of EVERYTHING you buy for your house. *Business Insider.* Retrieved from http://www.businessinsider.com/protor-gamble-makes-everything-2011-2

Marketplace. (n.d.). *Procter & Gamble corporate history.* Retrieved from https://www.marketplace.org/2008/05/20/procter-gamble-corporate-history

P&G. (n.d.). *Policies & practices.* Retrieved from http://us.pg.com/who-we-are/our-approach/purpose-values-principles

P&G. (n.d.). *Who we are.* Retrieved from http://us.pg.com/who-we-are/heritage/history-of-innovation

Smithson, N. (2017). Procter & Gamble's organizational culture of mission fulfillment. *Panmore Institute.* Retrieved from http://panmore.com/procter-gamble-organizational-culture-mission-fulfillment

What Is Leadership?

>> LO 12.1   Explain the basic concept of leadership

Our Proctor & Gamble (P&G) case shows the different ways in which organizations can lead. P&G is a leading brand because of its commitment to innovation, branding, safety, and excellent leadership training programs. Organizations this successful need good leaders. But what does it mean to be a good leader? The search for what makes a good leader has been going on for centuries and, in spite of myriad studies, there are no conclusive answers. Although many definitions exist, for our purposes, **leadership** is a process of providing general direction from a position of influence to individuals or groups toward the successful attainment of goals.[1]

The Internet has revolutionized society by giving millions of people a voice and the ability to communicate across cultural and geographical barriers. With enough online resources to access most corners of the world, almost anybody can be a leader, with or without formal authority, given the right skills and a strong initiative. In our global world, effective leaders need to connect and collaborate with people from different types of social groups through global networks in order to be heard.

What makes a great leader? Would you single out presidents and prime ministers, sports coaches, or CEOs as examples of iconic leaders? On what basis do you identify them as leaders? Popularity? Achievement? The way they communicate? The way they engage with you through social media? For example, do you like leaders who tweet? Perhaps it's something intangible, like a leader's charisma. President Donald Trump has been described as a charismatic leader who uses emotion to engage a crowd.[2] Societal norms and media influence have much to do with our perceptions about what makes an effective leader, and sometimes they create a false impression of **leader emergence**, which occurs when someone naturally becomes the leader of a leaderless group.[3] As a result, we can fall prey to stereotypes. Dianne Bevelander, professor of management education at Erasmus University's Rotterdam School of Management, has challenged business schools to drop the tendency to stereotype leaders when teaching business courses. Bevelander says, "New leadership no longer looks like a white man rescuing companies." "It is far more diverse and includes women, people of color, and people with different sexual orientations," she said.[4]

SAGE edge™

Master the content
**edge.sagepub.com/
neckob2e**

Leadership: The process of providing general direction, from a position of influence, to individuals or groups toward the successful attainment of goals

Leader emergence: The natural occurrence of someone becoming the leader of a leaderless group

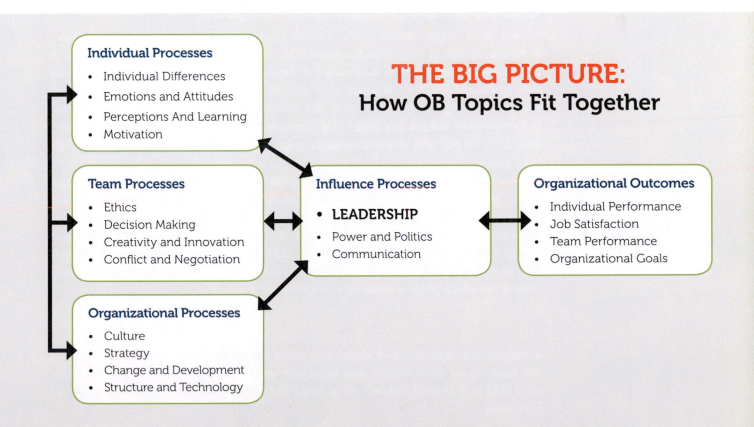

THE BIG PICTURE:
How OB Topics Fit Together

Individual Processes
- Individual Differences
- Emotions and Attitudes
- Perceptions And Learning
- Motivation

Team Processes
- Ethics
- Decision Making
- Creativity and Innovation
- Conflict and Negotiation

Organizational Processes
- Culture
- Strategy
- Change and Development
- Structure and Technology

Influence Processes
- **LEADERSHIP**
- Power and Politics
- Communication

Organizational Outcomes
- Individual Performance
- Job Satisfaction
- Team Performance
- Organizational Goals

Despite numerous debates regarding the nature of leadership, there is a general view that today's leaders are most likely to be critical thinkers who lead from a position of influence rather than power, and who use their decision-making, motivational, and communication skills to inspire others with their vision in order to generate results. Researchers have discovered that effective leadership can produce astonishing results in terms of increasing a company's profits, maintaining a successful corporate culture, motivating employees through good times and bad, increasing production levels, connecting with the community, and leading the charge on sustainability.

As an example of effective leadership, refer to the OB in the Real World feature to read about Scott Whitfield, project manager at IBM.

THINKING CRITICALLY

1.   Provide two examples of people (alive or dead) whom you consider to be great leaders. What characteristics defined their leadership abilities?

2.   Do you agree that adopting a "masculine" style could help make a woman a more effective leader? Why or why not?

3.   Have you ever had a manager or boss whose leadership disappointed you? If so, explain what made him or her a less than effective leader. If not, describe the most effective manager or boss with whom you have ever worked. What made this person an effective leader?

Formal and Informal Leadership

>> LO 12.2   Distinguish between formal and informal leadership and between leadership and management

Within most organizations there are two types of leaders: formal and informal.[5] A formal leader is officially designated by the organization, like a CEO who is appointed by the board of directors. For example, although Marillyn Hewson was only appointed CEO of Lockheed Martin in 2013, she has been named as one of the best-performing CEOs in the world.[6] An informal leader does not receive a title but is perceived by others as a leader. For example, in the teaching profession, teachers hold both formal and informal roles in order to provide leadership by example for their peers.[7]

Formal leaders must act in the best interests of the organization and have certain rights and privileges that allow them to reward or discipline employees. Informal leaders do not have official appointments and therefore do not have the same rights as formal leaders, but team members may rely on them to motivate and help them realize their goals. When both formal and informal leaders exist in an organization, it is important for them to share the same vision and ensure the teams are working toward the same goals in order to avoid conflict.

Management versus Leadership

Although management and leadership share some similarities, they do not mean the same thing. Both leaders and managers work with people, set goals, and influence others in order to achieve those goals, but several distinctions separate the two functions.

OB IN THE REAL WORLD

Scott Whitfield, Project Executive, IBM

Scott Whitfield is a twenty-year veteran and project executive at IBM. A Naval Academy graduate with a math background, he always saw himself going into a field driven by data where he could put his technical nature to good use. While at the Naval Academy, Scott was given some of the best leadership training in the world and uses some of that training in IBM, especially with regard to how people react to change and to pressure. Scott firmly believes that each person has the ability to add value. That's why his goal is to develop the best in everyone that he comes into contact with, which he also believes should be the goal of all business leaders.

While he acknowledges that a bad team member can drag everyone down, he also points out that it is quite rare to find someone who doesn't contribute anything.

Scott says, "Some of the best teams that I have ever been on have started with a weak link, but with a little cultivating that same team member often becomes a leader in his or her own way." He believes that a leader who complains about a team member that "doesn't fit" is a way of admitting defeat, and ignoring the possibility that the member could possibly offer something to the team that nobody else could.

Scott says, "I love having the person on my team that can take this outsider (a team member that may not fit at first) and bring them into the group to allow them to contribute. There is only so close to a situation like this that a manager can get to the employee team, but having an employee that understands the perks of getting everyone to contribute is a valuable thing."

Scott admits that sometimes team members don't lead like this, and then the responsibility falls on the team leader's shoulders. When this is the case, Scott says that he always learns something about himself and about the dynamics of a team and finds those times valuable. He also acknowledges that if he hadn't had someone to help him develop when he needed it, he would not be the leader he is today.

Critical-Thinking Questions

1. What does Scott see as the goal of all business leaders regarding their employees?

2. What does Scott think about the idea of a "weak link"? ●

Source: Interview with Scott Whitfield conducted on June 30th, 2017

First, leadership has been around far longer than management. History records the strategies employed by military leaders such as Alexander the Great (336–323 BC) and Attila the Hun (406–453 BC). Managers, in contrast, are mainly a product of industrialization in the 20th century, an era when large-scale production and manufacturing demanded the organizational skills necessary to plan, organize, staff, and control the operation. These skills are still highly relevant in the 21st-century workplace.

Second, leadership consists of creating a vision, introducing change and movement, and influencing others to achieve goals, while managers maintain the status quo, promote stability, and ensure the smooth running of operations.[8] There is an overlap between managers and leaders, however. For example, if you are a manager running a project and setting goals for your team, then you are leading your team. Similarly, if you are a leader and you are engaged in the daily organization

FIGURE 12.1

Comparison of a Leader and a Manager

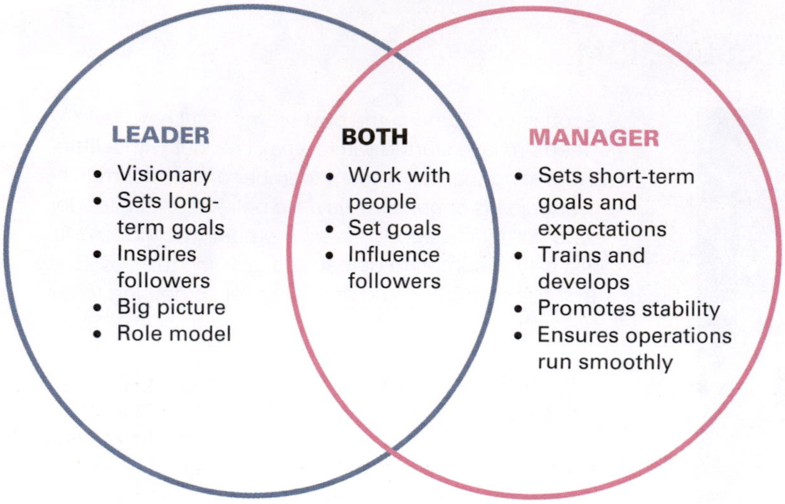

LEADER
- Visionary
- Sets long-term goals
- Inspires followers
- Big picture
- Role model

BOTH
- Work with people
- Set goals
- Influence followers

MANAGER
- Sets short-term goals and expectations
- Trains and develops
- Promotes stability
- Ensures operations run smoothly

of operations, then you are fulfilling management functions. In each case, both managers and leaders are leading from a position of influence. For example, Scott Whitfield at IBM is a project manager who also leads from a position of influence to bring the best out of his team. Therefore, it could be argued that organizations need strong leaders *and* strong managers to be successful.

However, realistically, not all managers are leaders, nor for that matter all leaders managers. For example, managers who put their own interests above those of their employees or who fail to motivate, guide, or positively influence their teams would not be classified as good leaders. Effective managers need to possess some leadership traits in order to optimize the performance of others (see Figure 12.1).

However, although it is useful for leaders to have managerial skills, it is not essential; certainly, it is advantageous for leaders to understand the discipline of management and have a background in the management functions, but it doesn't mean they need to be managers as well as leaders. Their primary strength lies in the ability to influence the behaviors and work of others in order to realize their vision and achieve set goals.

THINKING CRITICALLY

1. Do informal leaders have the potential to be as powerful as or more powerful than a formal leader in an organization? Why or why not?

2. Do leaders or managers require more training to be successful? Explain your answer.

Basic Leadership Types

» LO 12.3 Contrast the four basic types of leadership

Four distinct types of leadership behavior, originally proposed by Charles C. Manz and Henry P. Sims Jr., and since refined by other leadership theorists, are directive leadership, transactional leadership, visionary leadership, and empowering leadership (also known as "superleadership").[9] (See Table 12.1.)

Directive leadership behavior consists of implementing guidelines, providing information about what is expected, setting performance standards, and ensuring that individuals follow rules. Directive leaders are sometimes known as **production-oriented leaders** because they tend to focus more on the technical or task aspects of the job. Directive leaders also tend to rule with an **autocratic style**, making decisions without asking for suggestions from others. They also rely on the power to use their authority to command, reprimand, or intimidate in order to get the desired results from their subordinates.

Directive leadership: A leadership style characterized by implementing guidelines, managing expectations, setting definite performance standards, and ensuring that individuals follow rules

Production-oriented leader: A leader who tends to focus more on the technical or task aspects of the job

Autocratic style: A leadership style based on making decisions without asking for suggestions from others

TABLE 12.1

Four Basic Types of Leaders

Directive Leaders	Transactional Leaders
• Implement guidelines • Provide expectations • Set performance standards • Ensure rules are followed	• Set goals for followers • Motivate with rewards
Visionary Leaders	**Empowering Leaders**
• Create vision to motivate followers • Utilize charisma to gain support • Expect commitment from followers	• Develop followers' skills • Encourage followers to take ownership of their work • Lead others to lead themselves

Transactional leadership assumes employees are motivated by goals and equitable rewards. The transactional leader offers clear and objective goals for followers in order to gain **compliance**, which occurs when the targets of influence readily agree to carry out the leader's requests.

Visionary leadership, often contrasted with transactional leadership, creates visions to motivate, inspire, and stimulate employees. A visionary leader uses charisma to encourage followers to share in the mission and expects them to commit to him or her and work toward the desired goal. Finally, **empowering leadership**, or "superleadership," shifts the focus from the leader to the follower through the idea of self-leadership.[10] Empowering leaders help to develop the individual skills and abilities of their followers, allowing them to utilize these skills, take ownership of their work, and contribute to organizational performance. The idea of "superleadership" has been defined as the "process of leading others to lead themselves."[11]

Transactional leadership: A behavioral type of leadership that proposes that employees are motivated by goals and equitable rewards

Compliance: The behavior of targets of influence who agree to readily carry out the requests of the leader

Visionary leadership: A behavioral type of leadership that creates visions to motivate, inspire, and stimulate employees

Empowering leadership: A behavioral type of leadership that empowers leaders to help develop the individual skills and abilities of their followers. Also known as "superleadership"

THINKING CRITICALLY

1. A parent who rewards a child with stickers each time the child performs a desired behavior is enacting which type of leadership (directive, transactional, visionary, empowering)? Explain your answer.

2. The expression "Give a man a fish and he'll eat for a day; teach a man to fish and he'll eat for the rest of his life" is tacitly encouraging which type of leadership? Explain your answer.

Early Leadership Perspectives

>> **LO 12.4** Describe the trait, behavioral, and contingency leadership perspectives

As we have learned, there is no set definition or combination of characteristics that describes a good leader. However, in order to support our current understanding of leadership, it is useful to explore the early theories of leadership, each of which focuses on different ways in which a great leader is created. These include trait, behavioral, and contingency theories.

Trait Leadership Perspective

The **trait leadership perspective** is a theory that explores the relationship between leaders' personal qualities and characteristics and the way their traits differentiate

Trait leadership perspective: A theory that explores the relationship between leaders and personal qualities and characteristics and how they differentiate leaders from nonleaders

Early trait theorists studied famous leaders like Winston Churchill and Joan of Arc to determine whether certain characteristics were indicative of strong leadership qualities.

them from nonleaders. In other words, the theory assumes effective leaders are born, not made. Famous leaders such as Gandhi, Churchill, Lincoln, Joan of Arc, and Alexander the Great were studied by early trait theorists, who explored characteristics such as physical appearance, personality, and ability and sought to link them to individuals' leadership qualities. However, trait theory has since been widely criticized for its limiting methodology and inaccurate conclusions.[12] Researchers believed that traits in isolation could not predict leadership success.

Despite skepticism about early trait theory, the study of leadership traits has made a bit of a comeback in recent years since researchers have discovered patterns of traits.[13] Modern theorists now believe that leadership characteristics can be nurtured and developed over time, and that leaders must use a combination of these traits effectively to become successful leaders. The following is a list of leadership core traits identified in more recent research studies:[14]

- **Drive.** Leaders are ambitious and motivated and have a natural desire to succeed.
- **Desire to lead.** Leaders are motivated by a keen desire to lead and influence others, and to gain power.
- **Integrity.** Successful leaders are honest, trustworthy, and ethical and maintain behavior consistent with these values.
- **Self-confidence.** Leaders have a high degree of self-confidence in their leadership abilities.
- **Cognitive ability.** Leaders who have a wide range of cognitive skills have the ability to gather, integrate, and process complex information.
- **Knowledge of domain.** Leaders who possess a keen knowledge of their field are better at making decisions, predicting potential problems, and understanding the impact of their actions.
- **Openness to new experiences.** Leaders must be flexible, open to new experiences, and willing to adopt the ideas of others.
- **Extraversion.** Leaders who enjoy engaging with others tend to form relationships that support them in problem solving and in seeking new opportunities.

THE OHIO STATE STUDIES	THE UNIVERSITY OF MICHIGAN STUDIES
1. Initiating structure	1. Job-Centered Leadership Style
2. Consideration	2. Employee-Centered Leadership Style

TABLE 12.2

Behavioral Leadership Perspective Studies

Sources: Based on Hemphill, J. K., and A. E. Coons, *Leader Behavior: Its Description and Measurement*. Research Monograph No. 88 (Columbus: Ohio State University, Bureau of Business Research, 1957); Likert, Rensis. *New Patterns of Management* (New York: McGraw-Hill, 1961).

Although modern trait theory proposes that leadership traits can be nurtured over time, the behavioral leadership perspective focuses on a set of specific behaviors displayed by leaders in any given situation.

Behavioral Leadership Perspective

The **behavioral leadership perspective** proposes that specific behaviors distinguish leaders from nonleaders. During the 1950s, independent researchers at both Ohio State University and University of Michigan conducted studies of leadership behavior (see Table 12.2).

Ohio State University Studies

In the 1940s, researchers at Ohio State University administered a questionnaire to hundreds of people working in the military, business, and educational fields in order to assess leadership styles. The aim was to ascertain how employees perceived the types of leadership behavior exhibited by their superiors. From the results, researchers proposed a two-dimensional view of leadership behavior based on leadership styles they called initiating structure, and consideration.[15] **Initiating structure** is a behavior demonstrated by leaders who define the roles of the employees, set clear guidelines and procedures, and establish distinct patterns of organization and communication. **Consideration** is a behavior demonstrated by leaders who develop mutual trust and respect and actively build interpersonal relationships with their followers.

These two dimensions are similar to the theories proposed by the Michigan studies a few years later.

University of Michigan Studies

In an effort to identify the patterns of leadership behavior, University of Michigan researchers under the general direction of Rensis Likert in the 1950s interviewed leaders from both private and public companies and asked them to complete a questionnaire. The results helped the researchers establish two styles of leadership behavior: *job-centered leadership style*, a behavioral leadership style that emphasizes employee tasks and the methods used to accomplish them, and *employee-centered leadership style*, a behavioral leadership style that emphasizes the personal needs of employees and the development of interpersonal relationships.[16]

Researchers investigated the impact each leadership style had on rates of productivity, staff turnover, job satisfaction, and absenteeism and concluded that because employee-centered leaders had better results in these areas, they were more effective than job-centered leaders. However, there were some inconsistencies within the

Behavioral leadership perspective: The belief that specific behaviors distinguish leaders from nonleaders

Initiating structure: A behavioral leadership style demonstrated by leaders who define the roles of the employees, set clear guidelines and procedures, and establish distinct patterns of organization and communication

Consideration: A behavioral leadership style demonstrated by leaders who develop mutual trust and respect and actively build interpersonal relationships with their followers

FIGURE 12.2

The Blake Mouton Leadership Grid

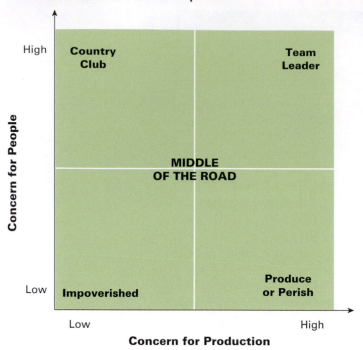

Source: Adapted from Blake, R. R., and J. S. Mouton, *The Managerial Grid* (Houston, TX: Gulf Publishing, 1964).

Leadership grid: An approach that plots concern for production on the horizontal axis and concern for people on the vertical axis where 1 is the least concern and 9 is the greatest concern

studies, mainly due to the fact that researchers were skeptical that leaders could possess characteristics from both styles rather than just one, which other theorists thought cast doubt on the results.

The two dimensions of initiating structure and consideration suggested in the Ohio studies are similar to the theories proposed by the Michigan studies. For example, initiating structure is similar to job-centered leadership because both behaviors place an emphasis on assigning tasks and getting the job done, and consideration is comparable to employee-centered leadership, with its focus on employee welfare and development. Although there are similarities between the Michigan and Ohio State studies, the Ohio State studies offer a more rounded view of leadership behavior by demonstrating that leaders could exhibit characteristics from both dimensions rather than just one.

The Leadership Grid

As an extension of the results published from the Ohio State studies, management researchers Robert R. Blake and Jane S. Mouton designed the **leadership grid**, an approach that plots concern for production on the horizontal axis and concern for people on the vertical axis (Figure 12.2). Each axis is a scale, with 1 representing the least concern and 9 the most. The five leadership styles are country club, produce or perish, impoverished, middle of the road, and team leader.[17]

Leaders who get a low score for production and a high score for people are known as "country club" leaders. This style of leader is more concerned about the well-being of his employees than about production and feels confident that a happy, relaxed workforce is the most productive. However, because of the lack of control and direction, this type of leadership can inhibit productivity.

"Produce or perish" leaders emphasize production over people and lead with an authoritarian rule, using punishment as a motivator. "Impoverished" leaders have very little concern for production *or* for people, which means they are ineffective for the most part. Leaders who are "middle-of-the-road" appear to have achieved the right balance between concern for people and concern for production, but this requires compromise; the problem with compromise is that the needs of both factions are not fully met, resulting in an average performance. Finally, the "team leader" rates production needs and people needs equally highly. According to the Blake-Mouton model, the team leader is the ideal leader, because he or she creates an environment in which teams are motivated and committed to furthering the success of the organization, leading to high production and satisfied employees.

The leadership grid reaffirmed the findings of the Ohio State studies that consideration of employees leads to a higher-performing workforce; however, it also introduced the idea that both people and production should be treated with the highest concern in order for the organization to achieve optimal results.

FIGURE 12.3

Least-Preferred Coworker Scale

Unfriendly	1 2 3 4 5 6 7 8	Friendly
Unpleasant	1 2 3 4 5 6 7 8	Pleasant
Rejecting	1 2 3 4 5 6 7 8	Accepting
Tense	1 2 3 4 5 6 7 8	Relaxed
Cold	1 2 3 4 5 6 7 8	Warm
Boring	1 2 3 4 5 6 7 8	Interesting
Backbiting	1 2 3 4 5 6 7 8	Loyal
Uncooperative	1 2 3 4 5 6 7 8	Cooperative
Hostile	1 2 3 4 5 6 7 8	Supportive
Guarded	1 2 3 4 5 6 7 8	Open
Insincere	1 2 3 4 5 6 7 8	Sincere
Unkind	1 2 3 4 5 6 7 8	Kind
Inconsiderate	1 2 3 4 5 6 7 8	Considerate
Untrustworthy	1 2 3 4 5 6 7 8	Trustworthy
Gloomy	1 2 3 4 5 6 7 8	Cheerful
Quarrelsome	1 2 3 4 5 6 7 8	Harmonious

Source: Adapted from Fiedler, F. E., and M. M. Chemers. *Improving Leadership Effectiveness: The Leaders Match Concept* (2nd ed.) (New York: Wiley, 1984).

Contingency Leadership Perspective

The **contingency leadership perspective**, pioneered by Fred E. Fiedler, claimed that the effectiveness of the leader depended on there being an appropriate match between the leader's traits or behaviors and the demands and characteristics of the contingency or situation.[18] Fiedler sought to identify the different types of leadership styles in certain situations and devised a scale called **least-preferred coworker (LPC)**, an instrument that evaluates whether a person is task oriented or relationship oriented.

To use the LPC scale, leaders were asked to think of a work situation in which they encountered a person they least enjoyed working with and rate that person's standing based on adjectives such as "friendly" or "unfriendly"; "considerate" or "inconsiderate," and so on (Figure 12.3).

Leaders who gave high scores on the LPC scale were thought to be relationship-motivated, because they tended to describe their least preferred coworker in a positive light. Those who had a more negative view of their coworkers received a low LPC score and were believed to be more task motivated.

In the next stage of this theory, Fiedler set out to prove that leadership style was dependent on the following situational variables:

- **Leader-member relations** describe the degree of confidence, trust, and respect that exist between subordinates and their leaders. Leaders who are well regarded can better influence events and outcomes.

Contingency leadership perspective: The view that the effectiveness of the leader relates to the interaction of the leader's traits or behaviors with situational factors

Least-preferred coworker (LPC) questionnaire: An instrument that purports to measure whether a person is task oriented or relationship oriented

Leader-member relations: Relationships that reflect the degree of confidence, trust, and respect that exists between subordinates and their leaders

FIGURE 12.4

Fiedler's Contingency Model

Leader-Member Relations	GOOD				POOR			
Task Structure	High		Low		High		Low	
Position Power	Strong	Weak	Strong	Weak	Strong	Weak	Strong	Weak
	1	2	3	4	5	6	7	8
Preferred Leadership Style	Low LPCs Middle LPCs				High LPCs			Low LPCs

Source: Adapted from F. E. Fiedler, *A Theory of Leadership Effectiveness* (New York: McGraw-Hill, 1967).

Task structure: The degree to which job assignments are defined

Leader's position power: The level of power a leader possesses to reward or punish, or promote and demote

- **Task structure** is the degree to which job assignments are defined. Leaders who provide clear, structured tasks are viewed more favorably.

- **Leader's position power** is the level of power a leader possesses to reward or punish, or promote and demote.

Fiedler's contingency model (Figure 12.4) is designed to predict the effectiveness of leadership styles in certain situations, on a scale from 1 to 8. For example, in instances of high situational control where leader-member relations are good, task structure is low, and the leader has strong position power, the model gives a score of 3, suggesting a low LPC leadership or task-driven style is most effective. Conversely, in instances of low situational control when leader-member relations are poor, task structure is high, and the leader has weak position power, the model assigns a rating of 6, suggesting a high LPC leadership or relationship-driven style is best. Fiedler found that the most favorable situations occurred when leader-member relations, task structure, and position power are all high because then leaders have the most control over the situation.

Although Fiedler's model is useful for matching optimal leadership styles to certain situations, it has been criticized for its lack of flexibility, primarily its assumption that leadership styles cannot be changed. For example, according to the theory, leaders with low LPC ratings (more task driven) in situations where a high LPC approach (relationship driven) would be more suitable should be replaced by leaders with a natural flair for building relationships, even though it might be equally effective to encourage the low LPC leaders to adopt a different style or to develop their skills through training or other measures.

Hersey and Blanchard's Situational Leadership Model

Situational leadership model: A leadership model that proposes leaders should adapt their leadership style based on the types of people they are leading and the requirements of the task

Telling: A leadership behavior characterized by giving clear instructions and guidance to followers, informing them exactly how and when to complete the task

Developed in 1969 by Paul Hersey and Ken Blanchard, the **situational leadership model** proposes that leaders should adapt their leadership style based on the types of people they are leading and the requirements of the task.[19] Drawing from the findings of the Ohio State studies, Hersey and Blanchard applied concepts similar to "initiating structure" and "consideration" to the following four main leadership styles:

- **Telling** (S1). Telling is a directive approach in which leaders give clear instructions and guidance to followers, informing them exactly how and when to complete the task. This leadership style works best within environments that have high initiating structure and low consideration, where the completion of the task takes precedence over the relationship with employees. For example, in an emergency people would rather be told what to do in order to deal with the situation as quickly and safely as possible.

- **Selling** (S2). Leaders who adopt the selling style provide support to followers through communicating and "selling" the goals of the task in order to gain commitment. This style is appropriate for issues with high initiating structure and high consideration. For example, a leader of a sales team has to meet regular sales targets but also needs to foster a good relationship with the sales reps in order to motivate them to meet their goals.

- **Participating** (S3). Leaders and followers work together and share in the decision-making responsibilities of the task in the participating style. It works best in situations where there is low initiating structure and high consideration. For example, an employee may have picked up some skills on the job but needs more guidance to complete a task. In this case, the leader will include the follower in decisions and help develop his or her knowledge base.

- **Delegating** (S4). Leaders give most of the responsibility to followers in the delegating style yet still monitor progress. Delegating occurs in instances of low initiating structure and low consideration. For example, when employees are fully functional and skilled to complete a task, there is little need for leadership involvement.

Telling and selling are more task-oriented leadership styles, whereas participating and delegating are more focused on the development of team members' ability to work independently to complete the task.

But which leadership style is most appropriate? And how do leaders know which one to use? According to Hersey and Blanchard, the choice of leadership style depends on the willingness and ability of followers, in other words, their level of readiness to get the job done.

The Hersey-Blanchard model expands on previous theories by emphasizing the importance of the readiness or maturity of followers when completing a task. It also allows for greater flexibility in leadership behaviors when it comes to dealing with different types of people in the workforce.

House's Path–Goal Theory

Originally developed by Robert House in 1971, **path–goal leadership theory** suggests that leadership effectiveness is the degree to which the leader enhances the performance of followers by guiding them on a defined track toward achieving their goals.[20] Leaders can help followers by clarifying the routes they need to take to achieve their goals, removing obstacles, and providing incentives at certain milestones. The level of support and assistance provided to followers depends on the situation, the complexity of the task, and the motivational capabilities of the followers.

House describes how leadership effectiveness is influenced by the interaction among the four main leadership styles:

- **Directive leadership.** Leadership behavior characterized by implementing guidelines, managing expectations, setting definite performance standards, and ensuring that individuals follow rules. This type of leadership is appropriate in the military, where commands are expected to be followed immediately and without question.

Selling: Leadership behavior characterized by support provided to followers through communication and "selling" them the aims of the task in order to gain commitment

Participating: Leadership behavior in which both leaders and followers work together and share in the decision-making responsibilities of the task

Delegating: The act of giving most of the responsibility to followers while still monitoring progress

Path–goal leadership theory: A theory that proposes that leadership effectiveness depends on the degree to which the leader enhances the performance of followers by guiding them on a defined track toward achieving their goals

FIGURE 12.5

Path–Goal Theory Model

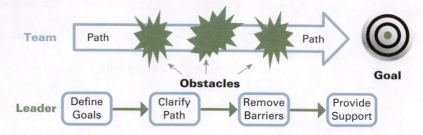

Sources: House, R. "Path-Goal Theory of Leadership: Lessons, Legacy, and a Reformulated Theory." *Leadership Quarterly* 7, no. 3 (1996): 323–352; model adapted from Northouse, P. *Leadership: Theory and Practice* (4th ed.) (Thousand Oaks, CA: Sage, 2007): 128.

Supportive leadership:
A leadership behavior characterized by friendliness and concern for the welfare of others

Participative leadership: A leadership style that favors consulting with followers and considering their input in decision making

Achievement-oriented leadership: Leadership behavior characterized by setting challenging goals, improving performance, and assisting training

- **Supportive leadership.** A type of leadership behavior characterized by friendliness and concern for the welfare of others. For example, a leader might work with followers struggling with a task until they feel empowered enough to carry out the task themselves.

- **Participative leadership**. Leadership behavior that consists of consulting with followers and considering their input in decision making. For example, a marketing leader might gather his or her followers to collect input about the possibility of launching a new product or taking a product off the market.

- **Achievement-oriented leadership.** Leadership behavior characterized by setting challenging goals, improving performance, and assisting in employee training. This style of leadership is often used by football quarterbacks, who are expected to direct the team to perform certain plays at the right time in order to win the game.

According to House, certain styles of leadership may be more suitable in some situations than others in order to influence follower satisfaction, motivation for the task, and acceptance of the leader. There are two main situational contingencies:

Subordinate characteristics: Situational contingencies such as anxiety, inflexibility, perceived ability, locus of control, and close-mindedness

Task characteristics: Situational contingencies outside the follower's control, such as team dynamics, authority systems, and task structure

- **Subordinate characteristics** such as anxiety, inflexibility, perceived ability, locus of control, and close-mindedness.

- **Task characteristics** outside the follower's control such as team dynamics, authority systems, and task structure.

The theory suggests that leaders can adjust their leadership styles to compensate for employee limitations. For example, a leader may take a supportive approach with a disgruntled employee in an effort to get to the root of the problem and find a resolution.

In contrast to the Fiedler contingency model, the path–goal model states that the four leadership styles are flexible, and that effective leaders can possess and adopt more than one style to help, motivate, and support their employees by removing obstacles on the path to achieving goals (Figure 12.5). Unlike earlier theories, the path–goal model also offers specific suggestions for how leaders can help employees by taking into account relevant contingency factors such as employee characteristics and environmental factors.

Substitutes for Leadership Model

Although path–goal theory focuses on the centrality of the leadership role to employee satisfaction and work performance, the **substitutes for leadership model**[21] proposes that certain characteristics of individuals, the job, and/or the organization can act as substitutes for leadership or neutralize leadership impact altogether. In this context, **neutralizing** means replacing leadership attributes that do not affect followers' outcomes.

A team that is well run, experienced, and organized might substitute for or neutralize the need for a task-oriented leader because the team already knows how to carry out the requirements of their roles. For example, organizations like W. L. Gore, tomato processor Morning Star, and steelmaker Worthington Industries cultivate environments in which teams are largely left to manage themselves.[22]

> **Substitutes for leadership model:** A model that suggests certain characteristics of the situation can constrain the influence of the leader.
>
> **Neutralizing:** The substitution of leadership attributes that do not affect follower outcomes

THINKING CRITICALLY

1. Consider the eight traits identified by the Trait Leadership Perspective: drive, desire to lead, integrity, self-confidence, cognitive ability, knowledge of domain, openness to new experiences, and extraversion. Imagine you are a teacher trying to cultivate leadership qualities in your students. Describe the steps you could take to foster one of the traits in the list. Identify the traits that would be easier to develop. Which traits would be more difficult to develop? Explain your reasoning.

2. Which type of leader identified by Blake Mouton's Leadership Grid—country club, produce or perish, impoverished, middle of the road, or team leader—would command the most respect from employees? Explain your answer.

3. Use the Least-Preferred Coworker Scale to rank your least preferred coworker or fellow student. Based on the results, do you think you are more relationship-motivated or task-motivated as a leader? Why?

4. Compare the pros and cons of adopting a participating leadership style versus a delegating leadership style. Are there situations where one style would be more advantageous over the other style? Why or why not?

5. Consider the leadership approaches discussed thus far in this chapter. Which of these leadership approaches best fit your leadership style? Explain why the leadership approach in your answer best fits you and why some of the other approaches do not?

Contemporary Leadership Perspectives

>> **LO 12.5** Compare the inspirational, relational, and follower-centered leadership perspectives

Although early leadership perspectives enhanced our understanding of leadership and follower behavior, more recent inspirational and relational leadership perspectives have built on these theories to explain how leaders motivate and build relationships with followers to achieve performance beyond expectations. Popular contemporary perspectives include leader-member exchange (LMX), transformational leadership, and charismatic leadership (Table 12.3).

Leader-Member Exchange (LMX) Theory

The **leader-member exchange (LMX) theory**[23] builds on the idea that leaders develop different relationships with different followers. The quality of the relationship determines whether the leader (often subconsciously) places the follower in the "in-group exchange" or the "out-group exchange" (Figure 12.6).

Source: Gupta, Ashum. "Leader Member Exchange." *Practical Management.* June 6, 2009. http://practical-management.com/pdf/Leadership-Development/Leader-Member-Exchange.pdf?format=phocapdf. Copyright © practical-management.com.

Leader-exchange theory: A theory of leadership that focuses on the relationships between leaders and their group members.

In-group exchange: Interaction that occurs when leaders and followers develop good working relationships based on mutual trust, respect, and a sense of sharing common fates

Out-group exchange: Interaction that occurs when leaders and followers fail to create a sense of mutual trust, respect, or common fate

Idealized influence: Behavior that gains the admiration, trust, and respect of followers, who in turn follow the leader's example with their own actions

Inspirational motivation: Leadership behaviors that promote commitment to a shared vision of the future

Intellectual stimulation: Stimuli that encourage people to think and promote intelligence, logic, and problem solving

Individualized consideration: Leader behavior associated with creating mutual respect or trust and a genuine concern for the needs and desires of others

- **In-group exchange.** Typically, team members who are loyal, trustworthy, and skilled have high-quality relationships with leaders. The leader devotes more attention to this in-group, assigns challenging tasks, and often spends more one-to-one time with members. People in this group are given more opportunities for growth and advancement and often mirror the leader's work ethic and characteristics.

- **Out-group exchange.** People who are perceived to be incompetent, unmotivated, untrustworthy team members have low-quality relationships with their leaders. Leaders tend to assign simple, limited tasks to this group, communicate with them only when necessary, and often withhold opportunities for growth or advancement.

LMX theory demonstrates the dangers of overclassifying individuals. Once an individual is in the out-group and the leader's perception of that person has been sealed, it is almost impossible to change that perception, and often the individual has no recourse but to leave the team or organization. Leaders need to nurture all relationships with their followers to draw out everyone's best efforts and achieve organizational success.

Transformational Leadership

Transformational leaders inspire their followers to transcend their self-interests for the good of the organization and commit to a shared vision, while also serving as a role model. Transformational leadership is becoming an increasingly popular model for today's leaders. Amazon CEO Jeff Bezos and Emmanuel Faber, CEO of world food company Danone, are good examples of transformational leaders who have transformed their companies by inspiring their teams to achieve goals.[24] In addition, Heather Clark, founder of apparel company Pomchies featured in OB in the Real World, uses transformational leadership to motivate her employees. The four dimensions of transformational leadership are[25]

- **Idealized influence** (also referred to as *charisma*) is behavior that gains the admiration, trust, and respect of followers.

- **Inspirational motivation** promotes commitment to a shared vision of the future.

- **Intellectual stimulation** encourages people to view problems from a different perspective and to think about innovative and alternative ways to address them.

- **Individualized consideration** creates mutual respect or trust and a genuine concern for the needs and desires of others.

TABLE 12.3

Differences between Transactional, Transformational, and Charismatic Leaders

TRANSACTIONAL LEADERS	TRANSFORMATIONAL LEADERS	CHARISMATIC LEADERS
Set goals for followers.	Involve followers in collaborative goal-setting.	Use charm and personality to motivate employees to achieve goals.
Motivate through rewards and punishments.	Motivate by inspiring followers to work as a team.	Stimulate followers by sharing their vision and ideology.
Maintain status quo.	Encourage followers to be creative and innovative in problem-solving.	Inspire confidence in followers through empathy and support.
Monitor and control.	Empower teams which ultimately leads to employee engagement.	Establishes high performance expectations.
Work within an existing organizational culture.	Works toward changing an organizational culture by implementing new initiatives.	

In direct opposition to transformational leadership is **laissez-faire leadership**, in which a leader fully delegates responsibility to others.[26] This type of leader has little involvement with followers, almost no control over the task, and little interest in making decisions unless forced into it. Investor Warren Buffett is an example of a laissez-faire leader, who prefers to give his management teams a lot of freedom to make decisions rather than monitoring them to any great degree. Yet although Buffett is famously hands-off in monitoring his businesses, he is still actively involved in pricing. Given his extensive experience, Buffett is more willing to take risks than some of the CEOs running his companies.[27]

Laissez-faire leadership: Leadership behavior that fully delegates responsibility to others

Charismatic Leadership

Transformational leadership theory was inspired by Max Weber's concept of **charismatic leadership**, which is the ability of a leader to use his or her personality or charm to inspire, motivate, and acquire loyalty and commitment from employees.[28]

Charismatic leaders are similar to transformational leaders in that they both use inspirational techniques to energize and motivate their followers. They can certainly use their exceptional leadership skills for good. However, though transformational leaders are focused on the best interests of the individuals and the organization, charismatic leaders may place more emphasis on their own needs and interests[29] and become caught up in their own hype. Leaders who follow their own agendas become inflexible, believe they can do no wrong, and tend to dismiss advice from others if it diverges from their own convictions. Adolf Hitler is an example of a charismatic leader who inspired devotion in others to carry out his own extreme political agenda—to horrifying and tragic results.

In addition, serious repercussions can occur when charismatic leaders become convinced of their own infallibility—their followers may also buy into this belief and perceive such leaders as invincible. The danger is that followers will relate their own personal job satisfaction and the success of the organization directly to the presence of the leader. In this situation, the departure of a charismatic leader can have a devastating effect on followers. Therefore, the charismatic leader needs to be an appropriate role model for followers.

Charismatic leadership: The ability of a leader to use his or her personality or charm to inspire, motivate, and acquire loyalty and commitment from employees

OB IN THE REAL WORLD

Heather Clark, Founder and Owner, Pomchies

Not everyone travels out of their home country; fewer still actually live in multiple different countries. Fewer even still have the strategic intelligence to live in four different countries, move for family matters multiple times, and start multiple successful businesses all at once. Heather Clark is no average entrepreneur, and she is the founder and owner of her latest success: Pomchies. Pomchies, a certified women-owned business entity, manufactures and sells creative and practical apparel made only from unique swimsuit fabric.

Heather manages her lean team in the United States, but Pomchies owns their supply chain all the way up to the factory in Vietnam. They sell to over 6,000 stores all around the world, and they engage in eCommerce. Heather didn't find her success by accident: she has had organizational strategies her whole business career, and she has engaged in operational planning through her travels. In many ways, her strategic management has been most effective in managing her own time and her organization's core competencies. One of her greatest assets has been her ability to lead her employees and her company to success.

Heather began in Switzerland, and then moved to Hong Kong and worked in the hospitality business. Heather then moved to the Philippines to support her then husband—and she began enacting her operational plans to become an entrepreneur. It started with bringing small consumer products between Hong Kong and the Philippines with her and selling them to fascinated friends. Next came a swimsuit manufacturing company, where she produced swimsuits, to be sold in the United States, out of sun protective fabrics. While this venture was a success, she created a plan to grow from the scraps of her swimsuit business, literally. Using fabric scraps, she created Pomchies. Now the product is a worldwide hit, and she insists on manufacturing it with the same materials.

Currently the biggest Pomchies sellers are Pom ID's, which are creative luggage tags for the strategic airport-goer. But leading Pomchies is not simply about inventing new products and showcasing them; Heather has involved many important leadership techniques in growing her business. When asked how she manages her team, Heather says, "You have to be very in touch and hands on with your employees. I make sure my employees are happy and learning at all times." To Heather, "mentoring is a very important part of leadership," and she strives to mentor her employees both professionally and personally. In this way, Heather can impact her organization with more than just her formal leadership role as owner.

Of course, Heather cannot lead a successful business entirely on her own—Heather is always on the lookout for the next emerging leader. She says, "You can tell when an employee is totally committed to you, when they love their work, love their job, and love working for you." She has a "right hand man," an employee with the leadership potential to fill Heather's shoes. On top of seeking out leaders within her organization, Heather actively engages her team by involving them in important conversations and processes. The text speaks on the concept of shared leadership, and Heather uses the technique often. Pomchies strives to stay ahead of the market with their latest designs and styles, a process which, Heather says, heavily involves her whole team and her husband, whom she calls "foundational" in the process. According to Heather, "We test new items all the time, and someone might make a suggestion I hadn't thought of."

In leading their employees, all managers should devote time and resources to articulating their plans for their organization in the way that Heather has. For example, recently a member of her team told the group that she has a liking and knack for photography. Shortly after, Heather and the rest of the management team seized the opportunity to facilitate learning and growth by using company funds to pay for photography classes and equipment. This form of transformational leadership puts the goals of the organization as the highest good, and rewards employees who wish to put in an extraordinary effort. Ever since then, Pomchies media platforms have been enriched by more dynamic photography than ever, produced by a preexisting employee.

Heather says they invest in employees with a strong drive to improve the organization because "We're small, but we have to keep up." And, as successful corporate managers usually do, Heather has shown throughout her life an inexhaustible drive to succeed. When asked how she has maintained the dedication to make it through the long nights and hard work, Heather says simply "I love what I am doing. If you don't like what you're doing, your mind will always wander while you work."

Critical-Thinking Questions

1. Name the leadership tactics from this chapter that Heather uses.

2. Why has Heather's successful leadership played such an important role in the success of Pomchies? ●

Source: Interviews with Heather Clark conducted June 23, 2017, and February 28, 2018

Follower-Centered Leadership Perspective

Recently, researchers have begun to explore a more follower-centered approach that focuses less on different types of leaders and their behaviors. **Followership** is the capacity of individuals to cooperate with leaders.[30] The theory that studies it stems from cognitive categorization theory, which explores the idea that people tend to label others on the basis of a first impression.[31]

The follower-centered leadership perspective focuses on how followers view leaders and how they view themselves. There are two types of theories in this approach: implicit leadership theories, and implicit followership theories.

According to **implicit leadership theories**, we have a natural tendency to apply traits and attributes to others to determine whether they are leaders.[32] Relevant traits and attributes include charismatic, attractive, intelligent, dedicated, tyrannical, and strong. These traits are called **leadership prototypes** and are behaviors we associate with leadership.[33]

Implicit followership theories are preconceived notions about the types of behaviors that leaders believe characterize followers and nonfollowers.[34] Common prototypes ascribed to good followers included enthusiasm, industriousness, and being a good citizen. Ineffective or nonfollowers are characterized as easily influenced, lacking humility, lacking experience, working slowly, and behaving unprofessionally. Like LMX theory, followership theories show that opinions based on first impressions or very quick judgments can prejudice our views of others and create negativity within groups.

Although transformational and empowering leadership approaches may dominate today's views on leadership, a number of cutting-edge perspectives are quickly gaining ground. Recent theorists have criticized directive leaders for using fear as a motivator, questioned the "carrot-and-stick" methodology of transactional leadership, and argued that transformational leaders may impede independent thinking in followers.

It may be impossible to wrap the constituents of leadership into a neat package. Perhaps, however, we can conclude from the evolution of leadership theories that different situations require different kinds of leaders. Next we focus on emerging leadership perspectives, and how they enhance the skills and improve the effectiveness of 21st-century leaders.

Followership: Individuals' capacity to cooperate with leaders

Implicit leadership theories: Hypotheses that explore the extent to which we distinguish leaders and nonleaders based on underlying assumptions, stereotypes, and beliefs

Leadership prototypes: Behaviors that people associate with leadership

Implicit followership theories: Preconceived notions about the types of behaviors that characterize followers and nonfollowers

THINKING CRITICALLY

1. Who do you think is responsible for employees being placed in the "in-group" or the "out-group"—the leaders or the employees themselves? Explain your answer.

2. Which do you think requires leaders to have more confidence in their followers, transformational leadership or laissez-faire leadership? Defend your answer.

3. Consider the potential benefits and potential drawbacks of charismatic leadership. In what situations might charismatic leadership be useful to an organization? In what situations could a charismatic leader create problems within an organization? In general, do you believe that charismatic leaders are an asset or a liability? Why?

4. The text suggests that different situations require different kinds of leaders. Do you agree with this idea? Why or why not?

Power-Distributing Leadership Perspectives

>> **LO 12.6**   Discuss the power-distributing leadership perspectives of empowering, shared, and self-leadership

The concept of "distributed leadership" has grown in popularity over the past few years and serves as an alternative to those theories that have focused on leadership traits, characteristics, and behaviors. Instead, distributed leadership calls for sharing the power and influence within organizations. Let's return to our narrative to further explore the three main facets of power-distributing leadership: empowering, shared, and self-leadership.

Bill Gates demonstrated empowering leadership by encouraging employees to share their ideas, innovate, and build on their strengths.

Empowering Leadership

Empowering leadership is the practice of delegating power that motivates employees and inspires them to achieve goals.[35] Facebook COO Sheryl Sandberg is a good example of an empowering leader because she has introduced the support group for women, Leanin.Org, and launched the campaign "Together Women Can" to encourage women to empower other women in the workplace.[36]

Empowering leadership is similar to participative leadership, in which leaders allow their employees to partake in decision-making processes and provide them with the resources and support to carry out their roles. Empowering leaders encourage their employees to act independently and make decisions without the presence of a formal leader. Here are some of the behaviors they use:

- **Leading by example.** Empowering leaders inspire their employees by demonstrating a strong commitment to their work. A CEO who attends the company's diversity training workshop leads by example by demonstrating his commitment to his employees in relation to diversity.[37]

- **Coaching.** Empowering leaders take active steps to educate and train their employees so they can become more independent. A study carried

FIGURE 12.7

Traditional Leadership versus Shared Leadership

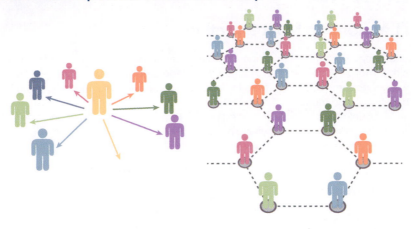

Traditional Leadership Model   **Shared Leadership Model**

out by leadership development company Zenger Folkman showed that good coaching improves productivity, increases staff retention, and boosts employee engagement.[38]

- **Participative decision making.** Empowering leaders encourage employees to make suggestions and express their ideas. For example, UK-based hardware company Screwfix engages their employees by giving them the opportunity to give their honest feedback and ideas to their managers, every two weeks.[39]

- **Informing.** Empowering leaders keep their employees up to date with company information and goals. For example, GE (General Electric) has fostered a culture of transparency and makes sure its employees are kept well-informed about big organizational changes.[40]

- **Showing concern.** Empowering leaders take an interest in the well-being of their employees and treat them with respect. Renowned entrepreneur Richard Branson believes in the value of treating his employees well. He says, "Your employees are your company's real competitive advantage. They're the ones making the magic happen—so long as their needs are being met."[41]

Shared Leadership

Shared leadership distributes influence among groups and individuals to achieve organizational or team goals.[42] Rather than being solely responsible for decision making, the leader shares responsibility with the group as members strive to achieve common goals (Figure 12.7).

Shared leadership is becoming more frequent in patient care and top management teams. For shared leadership to be effective, employees must share the same vision and goals, be provided with the right resources to carry out their tasks, maintain similar levels of knowledge and skills, work in a collaborative environment that fosters trust and cooperation, and be flexible enough to adapt to changing conditions. Recent research shows that shared leadership in change management and virtual or startup teams can lead to improved organizational performance.[43]

Shared leadership: A style of leadership that distributes influence among groups and individuals to achieve organizational or team goals

EXAMINING THE EVIDENCE

When Is Empowering Leadership Most Effective?

Empowering leadership involves sharing power and decision-making authority in ways that motivate employees to achieve goals and work autonomously. But when is empowering leadership likely to be most effective? A recent study by Natalia M. Lorinkova and Sara Jansen Perry published in the *Journal of Management** examined this question. Their results suggest that empowering leader behaviors reduce employee cynicism both directly and indirectly through employee feelings of psychological empowerment. Cynicism, in turn, was significantly related to time theft, which occurs when employees "steal" time at work by focusing on personal matters during working hours. However, the relationship between empowering leadership and psychological empowerment was only significant when the empowering leader had a high-quality relationship with his or her own boss. These findings suggest that simply exhibiting empowering leadership behaviors may not be enough. In addition, would-be empowering leaders should strive to develop good working relationships with their own supervisors if they want their followers to feel increased psychological empowerment and decreased cynicism.

Critical-Thinking Questions

1. How can empowering leaders most effectively improve or sustain the quality of their relationships with their own leaders?

2. How can organizations help to reduce employee cynicism and time theft? ●

*Lorinkova, Natalia M., and Sara Jansen Perry. 2017. "When Is Empowerment Effective? The Role of Leader-Leader Exchange in Empowering Leadership, Cynicism, and Time Theft." *Journal of Management* 43, no. 5: 1631–1654.

Self-Leadership

Self-leadership: A process whereby people intentionally influence their thinking and behavior to achieve their objectives

Both empowering and shared leadership facilitate and encourage self-leadership. **Self-leadership** is a process through which people intentionally influence their thinking and behavior to achieve their objectives.[44] In other words, people can deliberately guide themselves toward attaining favorable outcomes. Author and management expert Ken Blanchard uses self-leadership techniques to remove constraints, identify points of power, and collaborate with others.[45] There are three main categories of self-leadership strategies.[46]

Behavior-focused strategies are targeted toward increasing our self-awareness and managing our own conduct. They include self-observation, self-goal setting, self-reward, self-correcting feedback, and self-cueing.[47] Self-observation entails analyzing our own behaviors for the purposes of identifying those that need to be adjusted, enhanced, or eliminated altogether. For example, setting goals that challenge us motivates us to achieve them. Self-reward helps us motivate ourselves and improve performance by mentally praising our own achievements and giving ourselves positive feedback and corrections. Self-cueing strategies, such as writing to-do lists or keeping an efficient record of information, helps to focus our attention on assigned tasks.

Natural reward strategies help us to find pleasure in certain aspects of our roles, leading to an enhanced sense of competence, self-discipline, and application.[48] For example, if you are given a particularly tedious assignment, you could decide to complete the most onerous part of the task first before turning your attention to the more rewarding part. Even external reward strategies can make a difference in the way we work. For example, adding personal touches to your desk can have a calming effect when work becomes frustrating.

Constructive thought pattern strategies focus on the modification of certain key mental processes.[49] That is, the more positive and optimistic our thinking patterns, the better our work performance. Mental imagery is one strategy we can use to shape our thought processes by visualizing the successful attainment of the goal before we begin. This is a common technique among top athletes; for example, 18-gold-medal Olympic swimmer Michael Phelps used mental imagery to help him succeed. Phelps's coach Bob Bowman describes how Phelps uses visualization to his advantage: "For months before a race Michael gets into a relaxed state. He mentally rehearses for two hours a day in the pool. He sees himself winning. He smells the air, tastes the water, hears the sounds, sees the clock."[50]

THINKING CRITICALLY

1. Contrast the effectiveness of an empowering leadership style versus a charismatic leadership style in furthering one's own career and motivating a team.

2. What challenges might an organization with a shared-leadership structure encounter? Discuss at least three potential problems that could arise.

3. To what extent do you engage in self-leadership? What techniques have you employed, and how have these techniques helped you succeed at your tasks?

Values-Based Leadership Perspectives

>> **LO 12.7** Describe the values-based leadership perspectives of authentic, spiritual, servant, and ethical leadership

Following the economic turbulence over the last few years, there has been a shift from power-based leadership to values-based leadership. Values-based leaders act in concert with a set of principles in order to equip others with the right tools to unleash their potential so that they can act for the greater good.[51] There are four types of values-based leadership: authentic, spiritual, servant, and ethical.

Authentic Leadership

Authentic leadership is a pattern of leadership behavior based on honesty, practicality, and ethicality.[52] Support for this type of leadership has been gaining ground as a reaction to the number of corporate scandals and blunders made by high-profile leaders. Cargill CEO David MacLennan believes in the importance of authenticity:

"A critical part of transparency and a real test of leadership authenticity is having people come up to you and say, 'Hey this is what I think is wrong. Were you aware of this?' as opposed to, 'Look out. There's the CEO. I better not speak up.' Your real 'authenticity audit' is the degree to which people are open to you, because you have been open, vulnerable and honest with them."[53] When authentic leaders find their "true north" or moral compass, they are more focused on empowering their employees, forming meaningful relationships, and fostering an ethical environment.[54] Authentic leadership has been associated with improved job performance, increased job satisfaction, greater trust in the leader/follower relationship, and organizational commitment.[55]

Authentic leadership: A pattern of leadership behavior based on honesty, practicality, and ethicality

Spiritual Leadership

Spiritual leadership is a values-based style of leadership that motivates employees through faith, hope, and vision and encourages positive social emotions such as forgiveness and gratitude.[56] The concept of spirituality is not necessarily connected

Spiritual leadership: A values-based style of leadership that motivates employees through faith, hope, and vision and encourages positive social emotions such as forgiveness and gratitude

Richard Murphy's legacy of servant leadership lives on in successful programs like the Harlem Children's Zone in New York, providing services for children and families in need.

with religion; rather it is communicated in the workplace through shared values, attitudes, and behaviors. Spiritual leaders use their charisma to unite followers and to encourage them to view their roles as an opportunity for growth and meaningful contribution. Spiritual leadership may be linked to higher organizational commitment and productivity.[57]

Servant Leadership

Servant leadership is a pattern of leadership that places an emphasis on employees and the community rather than on the leader.[58] Servant leaders share their power and tend to "lead from behind," ensuring the team (not the leader) receives recognition for hard work. They are usually empathic, good listeners, perceptive, and committed to growth in the organization and the community. Servant leadership has been connected with high morale, loyalty, and ethics.

Sameer Dholakia, CEO of Denver-based email delivery platform SendGrid, is a good example of a servant leader. Dholakia spends around half his working day meeting with or checking in with his employees. He encourages honest feedback and offers his help and support at the end of each meeting. Because of this approach, employees feel comfortable enough to share their concerns and to ask for help when they need it.[59]

Servant leadership: A pattern of leadership that places an emphasis on employees and the community rather than on the leader

Ethical Leadership

Ethical leadership is a means of influencing others through personal values, morals, and beliefs.[60] By following their own values as well as the organization's values, ethical leaders are role models for ethical conduct. They communicate honestly and openly about the importance of ethical behavior and hold their followers accountable for failing to uphold organizational values, often rewarding those who consistently demonstrate ethical behavior. Typically, they are fair, honest, principled people who excel at making fair, balanced decisions and who practice what they preach. Sally Osberg, CEO of social entrepreneurship organization Skoll Foundation, is an ethical leader who works hard to foster social change by uniting innovators and entrepreneurs to devise creative solutions to the world's toughest problems.[61]

Ethical leadership: A means of influencing others through personal values, morals, and beliefs

THINKING CRITICALLY

1. Consider each of the four types of values-based leaders (authentic, spiritual, servant, and ethical). Is each style equally applicable to all organizations or do certain types lend themselves to particular types of organizations, like nonprofits or religious entities? Defend your answer.

2. Which type of values-based leader would you prefer to follow? Why?

3. Can you think of a drawback or negative of leading via value based leadership? Yes or no? Please explain your answer.

Cross-Cultural Leadership

>> **LO 12.8** **Discuss leadership across cultures**

Cross-cultural leadership is the process of leading across different cultures. Many companies and organizations of all sizes employ people from different cultural backgrounds, have branches in other countries, outsource parts of their business abroad, or use foreign suppliers. Shellye Archambeau, CEO of Silicon Valley-based governance, risk, and compliance firm MetricStream, is the first African American woman to obtain this leadership role. Archambeau fully believes in the importance of hiring people from different cultural backgrounds and genders and works hard to achieve a high level of diversity in her organization.[62]

For 21st-century leaders to lead effectively, they need to be proficient at managing people from different cultural backgrounds.

Project GLOBE (Global Leadership and Organizational Behavior Effectiveness) is the largest research study to date on cross-cultural leadership.[63] Conducted over the course of eleven years, the project surveyed 17,300 managers from 951 organizations, in 62 societal cultures, and relied on about 140 country coinvestigators. It concluded that individuals from different cultures or "societal clusters" associate certain sets of beliefs or preconceived notions with leaders. This is in line with *implicit leadership theory* or ILT, which explains our tendency as individuals to assign personality characteristics, skills, and behaviors to certain leaders. Our personal belief systems (also referred to as prototypes, mental models, and stereotypes) are thus thought to influence the extent to which we accept leaders. The GLOBE project researchers wanted to discover whether societal and organizational culture has a bearing on how people perceive leadership. In short, they tested the same concept as ILT but on a universal level.

The key findings of the GLOBE project centered around six global leadership attributes perceived by businesspeople worldwide to either contribute to or inhibit leadership; these are known as *culturally endorsed leadership theory* or CLT.[64]

The six dimensions of the CLT leadership profiles are [65]

- **Charismatic/value-based**. This dimension captures the leader's capacity to inspire, motivate, and expect high performance outcomes from others. All cultures believed this CLT profile to be a key contributor to outstanding leadership.

- **Team oriented**. Team orientation highlights effective team building and the implementation of a common purpose or goal among team members. Again, all cultures surveyed found this dimension to be a major contributor to outstanding leadership.

- **Participative**. This CLT describes the extent to which managers engage others in making and implementing decisions.

- **Humane oriented**. The leadership dimension that signifies supportive, considerate, compassionate, and generous leadership was thought to be only a moderate contributor to outstanding leadership across all the cultures.

- **Autonomous**. This CLT describes independent and individualistic leadership. Unlike the other dimensions, autonomous leadership is thought to impede or only slightly facilitate outstanding leadership.

- **Self-protective.** This leadership dimension describes the self-interests of the leader in terms of face saving, safety, and security and is generally reported to inhibit outstanding leadership.

Cross-cultural leadership: The process of leading across cultures

TABLE 12.4

Summary of Comparisons for CLT Leadership Dimensions

SOCIETAL CLUSTER	CLT LEADERSHIP DIMENSIONS					
	CHARISMATIC/ VALUE-BASED	TEAM-ORIENTED	PARTICIPATIVE	HUMANE ORIENTED	AUTONOMOUS	SELF-PROTECTIVE
Eastern Europe	M	M	L	M	H/H	H
Latin America	H	H	M	M	L	M/H
Latin Europe	M/H	M	M	L	L	M
Confucian Asia	M	M/H	L	M/H	M	H
Nordic Europe	H	M	H	L	M	L
Anglo	H	M	H	H	M	L
Sub-Sahara Africa	M	M	M	H	L	M
Southern Asia	H	M/H	L	H	M	H/H
Germanic Europe	H	M/L	H	M	H/H	L
Middle East	L	L	L	M	M	H/H

Source: Republished with permission of Academy of Management, from Javidan, Mansour, Peter W. Dorfman, Mary Sully De Luque, and Robert J. House. "In the Eye of the Beholder: Cross Cultural Lessons in Leadership from Project GLOBE." *Academy of Management Perspectives* 20, no. 1 (February 2006): 67–90; permission conveyed through Copyright Clearance Center, Inc.
Note: For letters separated by a /, the first letter indicates rank with respect to the absolute score, second letter with respect to a response bias corrected score.
H = high rank; M = medium rank; L = low rank.
H or L (bold) indicates highest or lowest cluster score for a specific CLT dimension.

The findings of GLOBE's empirical study (illustrated in Table 12.4) have improved our knowledge of what professionals across sixty-two societies perceive to be the key contributors to outstanding leadership. This evidence is essential to today's leaders who will be expected to exhibit cross-cultural skills in most aspects of their roles.

Leadership and Gender

>> **LO 12.9** **Identify gender issues in the context of leadership**

Gender inequality remains a source of much discussion and debate. Although more women are achieving leadership positions, there is no doubt that in the United States and other countries they are still underrepresented in the higher levels of organizations. Overall, there are fifteen female leaders worldwide—a figure that has doubled since 2000.[66] History shows that there has never been a female leader as president. In the business world, women make up just over 50 percent of the US population, with only thirty-two women CEOs in the Fortune 500.[67]

Studies suggest that gender inequality in organizations is due to several likely causes.[68]

Leadership style and expectations. Some studies suggest that men and women differ in their overall leadership styles. Men tend to be autocratic while women employ a more transformational style.[69] Given widespread expectations of leaders employing more traditionally masculine styles of leadership, women may be perceived as less suited for leadership positions. In cases where women do embrace more autocratic styles, however, they may be perceived more negatively than a man

FIGURE 12.8

Maternity Leave Policies around the World

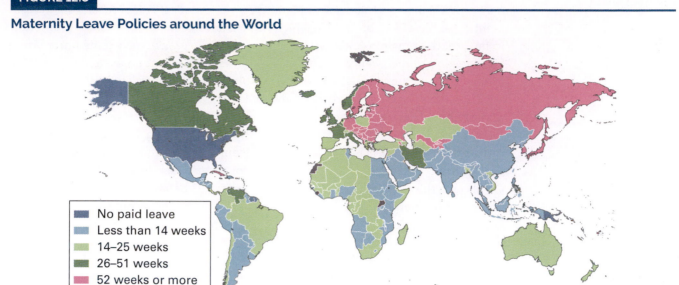

- No paid leave
- Less than 14 weeks
- 14–25 weeks
- 26–51 weeks
- 52 weeks or more

Source: © 2015 WORLD Policy Analysis Center. Retrieved from http://worldpolicycenter.org/policies/is-paid-leave-available-to-mothers-and-fathers-of-infants.

displaying similar characteristics. More of today's leaders, regardless of gender, are adopting a participative approach to leadership because it is considered to be more effective. This trend may help to accelerate the promotion of more women to leadership positions.

Family and career demands. The burden of balancing domestic and child and elder care responsibilities with work falls heavily on women.[70] In fact, the United States is the only developed country in the world that doesn't guarantee paid maternal leave. As Figure 12.8 shows, it shares this policy only with Papua New Guinea, Suriname, and five small Pacific Island nations.[71] However, the Trump administration has included a plan in its 2018 budget proposal to provide six weeks of paid parental leave. If the proposal becomes policy, it will be a major development in the issue of paid leave.[72]

Studies also find that employers may elect not to assign more challenging tasks to women because of assumed domestic responsibilities.[73] Less challenging work assignments generally result in fewer promotions and contribute to the glass ceiling effect discussed in Chapter 2.

Professional networks. Another line of research suggests that women who juggle familial and work duties have less time for socializing with colleagues and building professional networks.[74] When career advancement depends largely on who you know, inability to network can be a drag on advancement. However, even when women devote time to building relationships outside work, they may still face an uphill struggle—many of the most powerful and instrumental organizational networks are composed of men who typically engage in male-bonding activities. Walmart, for example, was sued for gender discrimination because it promoted male-oriented activities such as quail hunting and visiting strip clubs and Hooters restaurants.[75] Tech companies Yahoo, Twitter, Facebook, and Microsoft have also been sued for gender discrimination.[76]

Discrimination and stereotypes. Discrimination and stereotypical views of women may provide barriers to advancement.[77] Over the decades, numerous sexual harassment cases have been brought in which women have been passed over for promotion in favor of their male counterparts, and many more instances have gone unreported. Uber recently fired twenty employees in the wake of sexual harassment claims by former Uber engineer Susan Fowler. In a blog post, Fowler alleged that her manager made inappropriate sexual comments to her, while a director made disparaging remarks about the capability of women engineers.[78]

Many people still possess traditional views equating leadership with men rather than women. These views place women in a difficult position: Should they exhibit "male" behaviors (like being tough and task oriented) to get ahead? Or should they embrace the perceived "feminine" behaviors in supporting and encouraging their followers? There is no easy answer to carry out a role effectively. Ultimately, it is attitudes and perceptual distortions that need to be altered, not leadership styles.

Organizations can play a big part in challenging these patterns. For example, they can:

Eliminate prejudice. Organizations can raise awareness of the stereotypes and prejudices toward women leaders through diversity training and workshops. However, managers throughout the organization must also reinforce these lessons. Cultural change begins at the top.

Adjust evaluation process. Many organizations assess employee performance by measuring the number of hours people work rather than by the quality of the work they produce. This tends to skew results, because the employee who works late into the night might not be as productive as the employee who leaves at 5:00 p.m. to pick up the kids from child care. In fact, some employees put in extra-long hours to impress the boss with their commitment or to catch up on work they have neglected to do during the day. Organizations need to assess performance more objectively.

Adopt open-recruitment methods. Organizations need to be transparent in their recruitment by hiring through external agencies and advertising. Internal recruitment should also be as visible as possible to reduce informal processes that can favor male employees over female employees.

Redress the balance. Organizations can make active efforts to recruit and promote women to leadership positions. A higher proportion of women in senior roles will result in less focus on their gender and more on their individual abilities.

Encourage networking. Socializing and network building are key to career advancement. Organizations can provide more opportunities for informal socializing and encourage all employees to participate. They can also establish mentoring programs to help women take advantage of networking opportunities and create new ones.

Provide management opportunities. If organizations do not provide an opportunity for employees to develop the skills and knowledge required for promotion, employees will find it difficult to advance to the next level. They may instead be forced to change companies to find more challenging roles with broader responsibility and better compensation.

Establish family-friendly practices. The high cost of full-time child care can work out to more than an average working salary, leading many working parents to question the point of having one parent work at all. More women are leaving traditional organizations to pursue entrepreneurial ventures or to work for more flexible companies that allow employees to create their own hours. For example, woman-led Geller Law Group believes its employees can still have plenty of family time with their children without giving up their legal careers.[79] However, organizations can encourage both parents to stay in the traditional workforce by providing flextime, job sharing, telecommuting, child care benefits, and on-site child care. Allowing both parents to work more flexible hours helps them balance the vigorous demands of children with a working life.

Encourage men to use family-friendly benefits. Although parental leave and part-time work provide valuable support to mothers, taking advantage of them can also delay career progression. To even the playing field, organizations should encourage men to choose these options if desired, giving more women the opportunity to access managerial roles.

Allow time to achieve. Some organizations expect employees to ascend the career ladder at a rapid pace and ask those who do not keep up—often those with parental responsibilities—to leave. This is not to say employees with children are not capable of performing as well as those without children; they are simply unable to put in the same hours. Firms should capitalize on their initial investment in employees by giving the parents of young children—especially young mothers, who typically bear greater childcare responsibilities—more time to prove themselves and achieve promotion.

Keep the door open. Organizations should stay in touch with high-performing women who leave their roles because of changing personal circumstances. Keeping the lines of communication with former employees open conveys a message that it is still possible to return to work if and when the situation allows.

Although more progress is needed, organizations clearly have a variety of options for fostering a more gender diverse workforce. Achieving more representative numbers of women in leadership positions will encourage nuanced assessments of individual leadership styles.

LGBT Employees in the Workplace

In the United States, it is legal in twenty-eight states for companies to fire employees if they are gay or transgender.[80] Yet these laws do not reflect public opinion. According to a recent PRRI poll, 70 percent of Americans support laws to protect LGBT people from discrimination in the workplace, and outside. But despite this support, 40 percent of gays and bisexuals still experience discrimination and harassment at work, with 97 percent of transgender employees reporting similar ill-treatment.[81]

Regardless of their sexual orientation, all employees should feel respected, comfortable, and accepted in the workplace. Here are three ways managers can ensure LGBT people are protected from discrimination at work:[82]

1.   Foster LGBT networks

It is essential that companies encourage an internal LGBT network across the organization to nurture friendships and build a sense of community between LGBT members.

2. Create a culture of inclusiveness

Organizations need to cultivate an inclusive culture by actively demonstrating its commitment in this area. This involves extensive employee training, revised employee policies to reflect any new changes, and clear communications to reinforce the message that negativity or harassment will not be tolerated.

3. Support LGBT issues outside the organization

Employers who really want to demonstrate their commitment to inclusiveness could start by supporting local LGBT events and supporting LGBT issues. This might involve encouraging employees to march in the local Gay Pride Parade, or take a stance against a law that might have a negative impact on LGBT employees.

While there may be a large and varied set of theories surrounding leadership, we still do not have a set definition. However, these theories help us to separate good leaders from bad, and further our understanding of what effective leadership really means. While leadership styles tend to vary according to the context or the situation, we would argue that someone who uses critical thinking, leads from a position of influence, cultivates a culture of inclusiveness, and uses decision-making and motivational skills to inspire others, is likely to be an effective leader.

THINKING CRITICALLY

1. Do you agree with the section's argument that the underrepresentation of women in organizational leadership positions is a problem? Why or why not?

2. Rank the causes of workplace gender discrimination in order of highest impact to lowest impact. Defend your ranking. Do you believe that any causes of gender discrimination are missing from the discussion?

3. Rank the proposed solutions to workplace gender discrimination from highest impact to lowest impact. Defend your ranking.

4. Assume you are the CEO of a large company and you want to encourage your company to support LGBT issues. How would you approach this with employees who want to participate without offending those who don't? ●

Visit **edge.sagepub.com/neckob2e** to help you accomplish your coursework goals in an easy-to-use learning environment.

- Mobile-friendly eFlashcards and practice quizzes
- Video and multimedia content
- Chapter summaries with learning objectives
- EXCLUSIVE! Access to full-text SAGE journal articles

12.1 Explain the basic concept of leadership

Leadership is a process of providing general direction, from a position of influence, to individuals or groups toward the successful attainment of goals. Effective leaders today are most likely to be critical thinkers who lead from a position of influence rather than power, and who use their decision-making, motivational, and communication skills to inspire others with their vision in order to generate results.

12.2 Distinguish between formal and informal leadership and between leadership and management

A formal leader such as a CEO is designated by the organization, whereas an informal leader does not have a formal designation but may still be perceived by others as a leader. Leaders create visions, introduce change, and influence others to achieve goals, while managers maintain the status quo, promote stability, and ensure the smooth running of operations.

12.3 Contrast the four basic types of leadership

Directive leadership is characterized by implementing guidelines, providing information on what is expected, setting definite performance standards, and ensuring that individuals follow rules. **Transactional leadership** is a behavioral type of leadership that proposes that employees are motivated by goals and equitable rewards. **Visionary leadership** uses charisma to encourage followers to share in the mission and commit to and work toward the desired goal. **Empowering leadership** shifts the focus from the leader to the follower through the idea of self-leadership.

12.4 Describe the trait, behavioral, and contingency leadership perspectives

The **trait leadership perspective** explores the relationship between leaders and personal qualities and characteristics, and how we differentiate leaders from nonleaders. It assumes effective leaders are born, not made. The **behavioral leadership perspective** proposes that specific behaviors distinguish leaders from nonleaders. Subsequently, the **contingency leadership perspective** suggests the effectiveness of the leader relates to the interaction of the leader's traits or behaviors and situational factors.

12.5 Compare the inspirational, relational, and follower-centered leadership perspectives

Although early leadership perspectives enhanced our understanding of leadership and follower behavior, inspirational and relational leadership perspectives built on these theories to examine how leaders motivate and build relationships with followers to achieve performance beyond expectations. More recently, there has been a shift from a leadership-centric to a follower-centered approach.

12.6 Discuss the power-distributing leadership perspectives of empowering, shared, and self-leadership

Empowering leadership gives or delegates power to employees that motivates and inspires them to achieve goals. **Shared leadership** distributes influence among groups and individuals to achieve organizational or team goals, or both. **Self-leadership** is a process through which people intentionally influence their thinking and behavior to achieve their objectives, using behavior-focused strategies, natural reward strategies, and constructive thought pattern strategies.

12.7 Describe the values-based leadership perspectives of authentic, spiritual, servant, and ethical leadership

Authentic leadership is a pattern of leadership behavior based on honesty, practicality, and ethicality. **Spiritual leadership** is a values-based style of leadership that motivates employees through faith, hope, and vision and encourages positive social emotions such as forgiveness and gratitude. The concept of spirituality is not necessarily connected with religion; rather it is communicated in the workplace through shared values, attitudes, and behaviors. **Servant leadership** emphasizes employees and the community rather than the leader. Servant leaders share their power and are empathic, good listeners, perceptive, and committed to growth in the organization and the community. **Ethical leadership** is the influence of others through personal values, morals, and beliefs.

12.8 Discuss leadership across cultures

Cross-cultural leadership is the process of leading across different cultures. The key findings of the GLOBE project centered around six global leadership attributes: (1) charismatic/value-based, (2) team-oriented, (3) participative, (4) humane oriented, (5) autonomous, and (6) self-protective.

12.9 Identify gender issues in the context of leadership

Although more women are achieving leadership positions, they are still underrepresented in higher levels of organizations around the world. Factors that contribute to gender inequality are leadership style, the unequal burden of family and career demands, unequal access to professional networks, discrimination, and stereotypes.

KEY TERMS

Achievement-oriented leadership   348
Authentic leadership   357
Autocratic style   340
Behavioral leadership perspective   343
Charismatic leadership   351
Compliance   341
Consideration   343
Contingency leadership perspective   345
Cross-cultural leadership   359
Delegating   347
Directive leadership   340
Empowering leadership   341
Ethical leadership   358
Followership   353
Idealized influence   350
Implicit followership theories   353
Implicit leadership theories   353
In-group exchange   350
Individualized consideration   350
Initiating structure   343
Inspirational motivation   350
Intellectual stimulation   350
Laissez-faire leadership   351
Leader emergence   337
Leader-exchange theory   350
Leader-member relations   345
Leader's position power   346

Leadership   337
Leadership grid   344
Leadership prototypes   353
Least-preferred coworker (LPC)
   questionnaire   345
Neutralizing   349
Out-group exchange   350
Participating   347
Participative leadership   348
Path–goal leadership theory   347
Production-oriented leader   340
Self-leadership   356
Selling   347
Servant leadership   358
Shared leadership   355
Situational leadership model   346
Spiritual leadership   357
Subordinate characteristics   348
Substitutes for leadership model   349
Supportive leadership   348
Task characteristics   348
Task structure   346
Telling   346
Trait leadership perspective   341
Transactional leadership   341
Visionary leadership   341

UP FOR DEBATE: Hierarchy of Leadership

The best and most effective form of leadership is one where the leader and his decisions are made distanced from the general population of employees. This requires the responsibilities and control to be centralized toward the top of the hierarchy, leaving little leadership needs toward the bottom. Each member toward the bottom of the decision-making ladder is only responsible for what they are told to do and nothing else, providing structure. Agree or disagree? Explain your answer.

EXERCISE 12.1: Identifying Types of Leadership

Objective

The purpose of this exercise is to be able to identify the four basic types of leaders.

Instructions

Your text identifies four types of leaders:

- **Directive leadership**—leadership style characterized by implementing guidelines, managing expectations, setting definite performance standards, and ensuring that individuals follow rules
- **Transactional leadership**—a behavioral type of leadership that proposes that employees are motivated by goals and equitable rewards
- **Visionary leadership**—a behavioral type of leadership that creates visions to motivate, inspire, and stimulate employees
- **Empowering leadership**—a behavioral type of leadership that empowers leaders to help develop the individual skills and abilities of their followers

The instructor will ask for eight to twelve volunteers from the class for a series of role-plays (two to three participants for each type of leader). Each group of participants will be given one of the four leadership types above. Then, each group will take five to ten minutes to devise a scenario or skit that demonstrates that particular type of leader. For example, one group will create a role-play demonstrating directive leadership, another, transactional leadership, and so on.

The student volunteers will then take turns performing their role-play in front of the class.

The remaining students will attempt to guess which type of leadership is being shown based upon the words and interactions of the students at the front of the room. Students should write down their opinion as to which type of leadership is shown and the correct identification is not given until all four groups of students have completed their skit.

Reflection Questions

1. For each group of students, how could you tell which type of leader was being demonstrated? What cues or clues were given that showcased that particular type of leader?
2. Which of the four types of leaders is your current or most recent supervisor? Explain.
3. What type of leader do you think of yourself as? Why?
4. What type of leader would you like to be in the future? Why?

Exercise contributed by Steven Stovall, Southeast Missouri State University.

EXERCISE 12.2: Leadership Jolt

Objectives

This exercise will help you to better explain basic leadership concepts.

Instructions

While standing in line and talking about your organizational behavior class with some friends at a local coffee house, the person in front of you overhears and asks you a question about leadership. She is the head of a moderate sized, but extremely well connected office supply company and wants to improve the leadership of her managers. She asks you what the most important leadership concept is for making improvements in workplace outcomes, and also says that many other CEOs she knows would be interested in having a presentation on the same subject. She turns around to pay for and pick up her order, so you have a few minutes to collect your thoughts. But you also know that she will not have too long to listen to your idea, and this is your chance to make some very good contacts for your future career.

Step 1. Choose the leadership concept you feel is the most useful for improving workplace outcomes. Write an overview of this concept, what outcomes can be improved by adopting the leadership behavior, and why it is practical to try and model the leadership behavior. (5 minutes)

Step 2. Be prepared to present your description to the class. (1 to 3 minutes)

Reflection Questions

1. How did framing a description of a leadership concept in terms of a persuasive presentation change your view of the concept?

2. What new insights did you gain from having to make such a succinct overview of the concept?

3. What new ways of applying the concept did you discover through this process?

4. What surprised you most about your classmates' presentations?

Exercise contributed by Milton R. Mayfield, Professor of Business, Texas A&M International University, and Jacqueline R. Mayfield, Professor of Business, Texas A&M International University.

EXERCISE 12.3: The Challenge of Leadership

Objectives

Successful completion of this exercise will help you to better explain basic leadership concepts and distinguish between formal and informal leadership.

Instructions

Step 1. Select a person that you feel is (or was) a leader in an organization, but did not have a formal leadership position. (This person should be someone that you have had personal interactions with.) Develop an argument about why that person was a leader using chapter concepts and terms. In your description, make sure that you describe the circumstances and environment relevant to this person's informal leadership role. (5 minutes)

Step 2. Find two other people and select one person to act as a judge. (If no one wants to volunteer, select the person who has had the most recent birthday.) Have each of the contestants present her or his argument for the selected person being an informal leader. If someone selects a person who actually holds a formal leadership role, that person is automatically disqualified. Otherwise, judge the arguments based on how well the argument is supported with chapter concepts.

The judge should award each person 1 point for every argument that is supported by a relevant chapter concept. If no concept is used for support, or if a concept is used incorrectly, then the person has one point deducted from her or his score. After each person has had a chance to present her or his argument, then the judge should tally the scores. Whoever has the highest score wins. In case of a tie, the winner is the person who has the highest proportion of supported arguments to total arguments. (10 to 15 minutes)

Step 3. The judge should be prepared to present the winning person's argument to the class. (5 minutes)

Reflection Questions

1. What new insights did you learn about informal leadership?

2. Did you notice any recurring circumstances that lead to someone becoming an informal leader?

3. What were the aspects of informal leadership that surprised you?

Exercise contributed by Milton R. Mayfield, Professor of Business, Texas A&M International University, and Jacqueline R. Mayfield, Professor of Business, Texas A&M International University.

ONLINE EXERCISE 12.1: Assessing Leadership of a CEO

Objective

The purpose of this exercise is to gain an appreciation for current business leaders.

Instructions

Conduct an online search of a current CEO or president of a large for-profit company. Once you have identified this individual, learn as much as you can about him or her through further online research. Based upon what you discover, write a two- to three-page paper for your instructor where you assess the following:

- How long has this person been with this company? Did he or she become president by working up to that position from lower ranks within the company or arrive at the position from outside the firm?

- Discuss the person's ability to manage versus ability to lead.

- Which of the four basic types of leadership is this president (directive, transactional, visionary, or empowering)?

- Would this person be considered a charismatic leader? Why or why not?

Reflection Questions

1. How did you choose a CEO for this assignment? What criteria did you use in your selection?

2. Without personally knowing this individual, describe the difficulty of this assignment.

3. If you were to conduct this same analysis of your current or previous manager, what would your analysis state about this person?

4. What if you were to conduct this same analysis of yourself? What would be your response for each question?

Exercise contributed by Steven Stovall, Southeast Missouri State University.

CASE STUDY 12.1: Leadership Perspective at Chobani

Chobani's story is that of a fairy tale. What started as an immigrant's risky venture has become a market-consuming conglomerate worth billions of dollars. Hamdi Ulukaya, a Turkish immigrant of Kurdish ethnicity, opened his own wholesale feta cheese plant in 2002 after tasting the inferior local American cheese. Over the years, this small local plant expanded its operations and its vision as it took risks to deliver a product that was simply better. The company has also made headlines for its investment in its people. Its management philosophy has proven successful, as the company now owns over 50 percent of the market share in the yogurt space. This would not be possible without the man leading the operation. The chapter seeks to define what makes a great leader. It defines leadership as the process of providing general direction from a position of influence to individuals or groups toward the successful attainment of goals. It asks the question, however, what part of the process separates an average leader from a great leader. Communication? Popularity? Achievement? Looking closely at Chobani's leadership, it's clear that a great leader cannot be defined by a set of specific attributes; rather, great leaders are defined by what makes them different from everyone else.

Taking Risks and Defining Moments of Leadership

Starting a business of your own is a daunting task. To say that it takes hard work and commitment is an understatement. It takes blood, sweat, tears, and sometimes a little bit of luck to be a successful entrepreneur. In fact, 70 percent of businesses started in the United States fail after the first ten years of operation. These are massive odds to go against for anyone. Now imagine that you're an immigrant in a foreign country. Hamdi Ulukaya permanently immigrated to the United States in 1994 with the intention of studying English and taking business courses at a small college in upstate New York. He found work as a hand on a farm nearby. In 2002, Ulukaya's father visited him in the States and was disgusted with the quality of cheese he was served. He suggested that Ulukaya import cheese from Turkey to sell around town. Upon doing so, the cheese became popular and Ulukaya decided that he was going to produce it himself. After two years of barely breaking even, an interesting opportunity presented itself to Ulukaya on a piece of junk mail advertising the sale of an old Kroger cheese manufacturing plant that had just been shut down. He toured the plant the following day, took out a loan from the US government, and bought it within five months. This was arguably the most risky move of his career, but it was necessary to expand the operations and improve efficiencies of his cheese business.

Ulukaya needed employees to run his new cheese manufacturing plant so he hired up all the recently fired Kroger employees. He understood that they would have their doubts about working for him, an immigrant entrepreneur with no experience in the cheese business. While his position of authority made him a formal leader, a leader who is officially designated by the organization, he knew that he needed to be more in order for his new workforce to buy into the operation. According to the book, formal leaders must act in the best interests of the organization and have certain rights and privileges that allow them to reward or discipline employees. Informal leaders, on the other hand, are relied on by team members for motivation and to help them realize their goals. Knowing that his position of authority was not enough at this stage of his operation, Ulukaya leveraged one of his greatest attributes: the fact that he genuinely cares about his people. Hence, he paid his new employees significantly more than they were receiving while they worked at Kroger. According to Ulukaya, "Finding and training new members of our team is ultimately a tax on our productivity. And replacing an employee can cost up to double his or her salary in lost knowledge, not to mention hiring and training time. With many of our original employees still working with us at our plants, we're proof that the long-term benefit to our company and our community far outweighs the short-term cost. . . . Because Chobani is a private and independent company, we have the freedom of following our own conscience when it comes to our business practices." Ulukaya complemented his formal leadership with qualities that naturally made him an excellent informal leader.

Manager versus Leader

Hamdi Ulukaya's business philosophy is evident when you look at all aspects of the Chobani brand. The product itself is made out of all natural, healthy ingredients. There are no preservatives, gelatine, or dairy used from cows injected with growth hormones. He is an extremely generous employer, giving every employee an ownership stake in the company. The company also sponsors numerous worldwide initiatives. As an immigrant fleeing what he described as an unjust political atmosphere, Ulukaya has made Chobani a leader in hiring refugees who come to look for asylum and a fresh start. He has consistently maintained on multiple different occasions that companies should focus on their impact on humanity as a whole and not just their profit margins, and strongly believes that "business is still the strongest, most effective way to change the world."

The common theme surrounding all of Ulukaya's ventures is that he is always doing things differently. He has positioned himself as much more than a manager. This chapter examines the similarities and differences between managers and leaders. Managers set short-term goals, train and develop employees, promote stability, and ensure operations run smoothly. Leaders are visionaries, they set long-term goals, they inspire followers, they maintain a big-picture mind-set, and they are role models. Ulukaya is so successful because he has been able to be both a leader and a manager. In doing so, he has been a huge influence on the industry in which he works and in the communities in which his business has a presence.

Critical-Thinking Questions

1. How has Ulukaya's different approach to running a business been his most valuable attribute?

2. Could there be any potential weaknesses associated with Chobani's corporate philosophy?

3. Why might a leader not necessarily be a good manager? And vice versa?

Resources

Financial Times. (n.d.). *Make informed decisions with the FT.* Retrieved from https://www.ft.com/content/fe252dc2-a07b-11e2a6e1-00144feabdc0#axzz2kiqtoyLa

Henry, P. (2017, February 18). Why some startups succeed (and why most Fail). *Entrepreneur.* Retrieved from https://www.entrepreneur.com/article/288769

Ulukaya, H. (2016, March 31). Chobani founder: Higher wages important to our success. *CNN Money.* Retrieved from http://money.cnn.com/2016/03/31/news/economy/chobani-minimum-wage/index.html

Leadership Type Preference

For each statement, check the circle that best describes your actions when leading others based on the following scale:

	NOT AT ALL ACCURATE	SOMEWHAT ACCURATE	A LITTLE ACCURATE	MOSTLY ACCURATE	COMPLETELY ACCURATE
1. I give followers instructions about how to do their jobs.	☐	☐	☐	☐	☐
2. When followers perform well, I recommend that they be rewarded.	☐	☐	☐	☐	☐
3. I provide my followers with a clear vision of where we are going.	☐	☐	☐	☐	☐
4. I advise followers to solve problems without always seeking my approval.	☐	☐	☐	☐	☐
5. I establish performance goals for my followers.	☐	☐	☐	☐	☐
6. I provide special recognition for follower performance that is especially good.	☐	☐	☐	☐	☐
7. I inspire followers to strive for achievements they normally would not pursue.	☐	☐	☐	☐	☐
8. I provide followers the opportunity to take initiative on their own.	☐	☐	☐	☐	☐
9. I am often critical of my followers' work.	☐	☐	☐	☐	☐
10. I work with my followers to establish performance goals and associated rewards.	☐	☐	☐	☐	☐
11. I am driven by higher purposes or ideals.	☐	☐	☐	☐	☐
12. I encourage my followers to find their own favorite ways to get their work done.	☐	☐	☐	☐	☐

Scoring

Directive leadership (add items 1, 5, 9 and write your score in the blank) _____

Characterized by implementing guidelines, providing information on what is expected, setting definite performance standards, and ensuring that individuals follow rules

Transactional leadership (add items 2, 6, 10 and write your score in the blank) _____

Proposes that employees are motivated by goals and equitable rewards, offers clear and objective goals for the followers in order to gain compliance

Visionary leadership (add items 3, 7, 11 and write your score in the blank) _____

Creates visions to motivate, inspire, and stimulate employees using charisma to encourage followers to share a mission resulting in commitment toward a desired goal

Empowering leadership (add items 4, 8, 12 and write your score in the blank) _____

Helps to develop the individual skills and abilities of followers so that they may utilize these skills to take ownership of their work in order to contribute to organizational performance

What was your strongest leadership type? What are the advantages and disadvantages of this type of leadership?

What was your weakest leadership type? What are the advantages and disadvantages of this type of leadership?

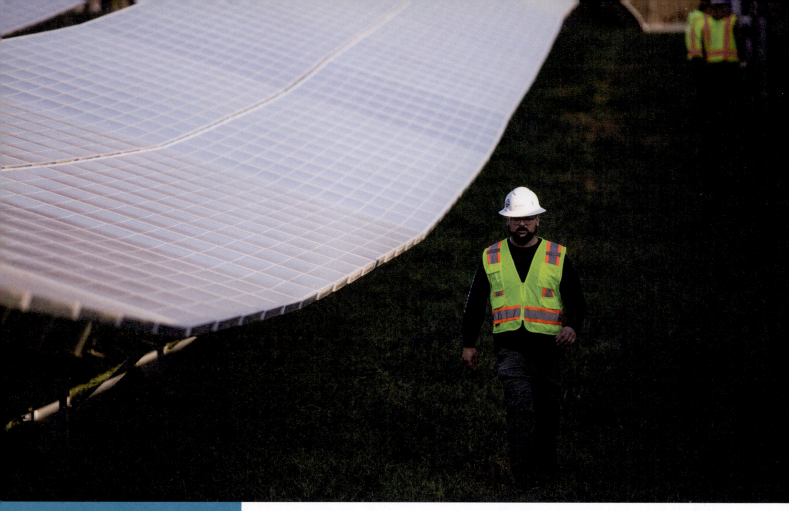

13

Influence, Power, and Politics

The most common way people give up their power is by thinking they don't have any.

—*Alice Walker, American author and activist*

Learning Objectives

By the end of this chapter, you will be able to:

13.1   Discuss the concept of power and its relationship to leadership

13.2   Identify the various sources of power

13.3   Describe tactics for influencing others

13.4   Outline the results of the various influence tactics

13.5   Identify the causes and possible consequences of organizational politics

13.6   Discuss the four different types of organizational politics

CASE STUDY: MANAGERIAL POWER AT NEXTERA ENERGY, INC.

All large companies which are traded publicly on stock exchanges must constantly engage in the process of organizing effective organizational influence, power, and politics. A single mistake or lie among management can devastate an entire company's standing in the public market. One company pairs that duty with its own huge renewable energy production arm which must heavily engage with both federal and state governments: NextEra Energy, Inc. (NYSE: NEE). A $65 billion market cap company, NextEra Energy, based in South Florida, is a member of the Forbes 200 business list; it has a subsidiary which provides publicly regulated electricity to nearly half of Florida, it produces more megawatts of renewable electricity than any company in the world and NextEra Energy, Inc., and its subsidiary companies have over 14,300 employees.

Power Structures in a Large Cap Incorporation

The first challenge for managers at NextEra is simply adequately leading a company with so many employees and interests. They confront this by employing many layers of legitimate power, and, in fact, operating separate subsidiary businesses. First, NextEra Energy, Inc. operates Florida Power and Light, the largest electricity utility in Florida. NextEra also created NextEra Energy Resources, which is the group in charge of national and international energy production, which engages in many renewable energy ventures. In addition to those, NextEra Energy Capital Holdings provides capital management support. In spite of the vast array of engineers, project managers, financial experts, accountants, and more, NextEra Energy, Inc. has a chain of command. The CEO is James "Jim" Robo; he and the rest of the management at NextEra say that their vision is "Be North America's Leader in the Generation and Delivery of Clean Energy." In operating, their stated corporate values are as follows: "We Are Committed to Excellence. We Do the Right Thing. We Treat People with Respect."

A corporate structure with legitimate power, paired with these vision and values statements, is a key component in managing the organizational behavior at NextEra Energy. Managers in businesses of all sizes must enforce legitimate power, but they often should do so through stated goals and values. In this way, NextEra cares for its employees, and their hard work is a willful return for the respect of their leaders. In order to adequately manage all of its arms, there are separate CEOs from NextEra Energy, Inc. for both NextEra Energy Resources and Florida Power and Light. Beyond that, there are multiple executive vice presidents, each with an entire section of the company to look after. Businesses of all sizes can engage in this type of structure: whether or not a business is large enough to justify splitting into separate entities, a single leader always has to delegate to other managers or to his or her employees.

Corporate Referent Power

NextEra Energy says to future employees: "We will reward your time, talent, and commitment with pay, benefits, career development opportunities, a supportive work environment, and many more advantages." And they mean it. Employees at many of their locations enjoy free or highly discounted access to wellness centers, doctor's checkups, gymnasiums, and relaxing corporate environments. This is a form of referent power—in a sense, NextEra is a corporation to which the employees are referent. NextEra dedicates millions of corporate dollars to Human Resources departments and comprehensive employee benefits, and in return employees show loyalty to the company and its executives. This attitude trickles down among managers, leading to a widespread coherence among managers and employees.

In large-scale business operations, it is paramount that employees enjoy their work. It is easier to fall into anonymity in large corporations, so any managing directors in such places must constantly remember to show their team the care and hard work that reap referent power. In all industries and scales of operations there are employee-manager relationships that must go beyond simple legitimate power structures. Whether a manager employs benefits to create reward power or to simply engage with his or her employees, a manager is in charge of finding ways to add value to work beyond a paycheck.

A clear description of the importance of influencing the behavior of employees can be seen in the consequences listed in this chapter. There are entire organizational effects that differ when employees behave out of either resistance, compliance, or commitment. Resistance to proper management is purely a negative progress; successful companies and employees spend time organizing projects and making deals, not arguing among themselves to a harmful extent about how to do it. Even compliance alone fails to fuel a successful team. Without committed employees and managers, a company will always struggle to succeed, so NextEra Energy and other companies devote countless resources to cultivating a committed group of employees—all 14,300 of them. And the final piece to achieving the same results NextEra achieves, which cannot be forgotten, is that an employer provides benefits and rewards out of sincerity as opposed to contrived manipulation. From the CEO to the lowest level of employee on the organizational chart, members of all businesses recognize respect and good treatment just as easily as they recognize when they're being used.

Risk Factors

Organizational politics become more important as the intensity of the larger external global political climate escalates, and this is true at NextEra as much as in any organization. Oftentimes members of organizations like NextEra Energy, which produces huge amounts of renewable energy, or any organization in a heavily regulated industry, make the news for giving in to corrupt organizational politics. There are important lines between acceptable benefits for employees, whether they are gifted by governments or private parties such as investment banks. NextEra Energy has consolidated revenues over $16 billion a year—this means they constantly spend money and borrow money in order to operate a massive conglomerate of ever-growing projects. This presents one of the biggest organizational political risks: with this much money moving around, outside sources are always trying to gain access to the corporation. This industry often involves forms of bribery, and NextEra wholeheartedly attempts to remain a neutral, fair business partner. On a smaller scale, employees and managers can monitor their own risk of inappropriate organizational politics by treating all members of their organizations and other organizations with equal respect and care, but not with inappropriate gifts. Lastly, employees and managers can mitigate the risk of bribery by setting clear, articulated guidelines on the types of rewards that may be given and accepted, a practice in which NextEra Energy engages.

NextEra Energy and its subsidiaries provide a useful template for all managers in maintaining a professional corporate environment that rewards employees. Accordingly, the management is effective, and NextEra continues to post better results while producing happy, hardworking employees. This template is only useful to an extent: all forms of management require a unique mixture of power forms, and one of the best ways to discover them is by finding ways to make employees feel appreciated.

Critical-Thinking Questions

1. Why should managers employ more than legitimate power to influence workers?

2. What is the purpose of monitoring organizational politics?

3. Describe how NextEra Energy maintains professional organizational politics.

Resources:

Bloomberg. (2018). *Independent power and renewable electricity producers: Company overview of NextEra Energy capital holdings, Inc.* Retrieved from https://www.bloomberg.com/research/stocks/private/snapshot.asp?privcapId=3152359

Forbes. (n.d.). *#182 NextEra Energy.* Retrieved from https://www.forbes.com/companies/nextera-energy/

McKenzie, B. (n.d.). Bribery and corruption - FSA tells investment banks to improve procedures. *Lexology.* Retrieved from http://www.lexology.com/library/detail.aspx?g=ce18fc3a-e86a-4101-869b-b1d76043f136

NextEra Energy. (2017). *Investing in America's energy infrastructure sustainably and responsibly.* Retrieved from http://www.nexteraenergy.com/pdf/profile.pdf

NextEra Energy. (n.d.). *Leading the nation in energy storage.* Retrieved from http://www.nexteraenergy.com/

NextEra Energy. (n.d.). *NextEra Energy corporate governance: Political engagement policy.* Retrieved from http://www.investor.nexteraenergy.com/phoenix.zhtml?c=88486&p=irol-politicalcontributions

NextEra Energy. (n.d.). *Our leadership.* Retrieved from http://www.nexteraenergy.com/company/bios.shtml

NextEra Energy. (n.d.). *Benefits.* Retrieved from http://www.nexteraenergy.com/careers/benefits.shtml

NextEra Energy Inc. (n.d.). *News.* Retrieved from http://quotes.wsj.com/NEE

United States Environmental Protection Agency. (2018). *Green power partnership national top 100.* Retrieved from https://www.epa.gov/greenpower/green-power-partnership-national-top-100

Power: Definition and Overview

>> **LO 13.1** Discuss the concept of power and its relationship to leadership

NextEra Energy is a good example of an organization that uses its power for good. Not only is the organization determined to be the leader of clean energy, but its CEO Jim Robo is also committed to treating his employees with fairness and respect. In return, workers at NextEra Energy work hard together toward the fulfillment of

$SAGE edge™

Master the content
**edge.sagepub.com/
neckob2e**

Power: The capacity to influence the actions of others

the company's vision and goals. The concept of **power**, the capacity to influence the actions of others, is inextricably linked with leadership.[1] Leaders have power for different reasons. In organizations, some leaders may be perceived as powerful by their followers because of their ability to give raises or bonuses, assign important tasks, or hire and fire. The power of other types of leaders may lie in their professional or technical expertise, or they may have personal qualities that inspire admiration in their followers. Being aware of why you are influenced by someone else helps you recognize your own power, decide whether you want to accept the way the power is being used, and build on your own leadership skills to learn how to be a positive influence in your organization.

However, there are different ways in which leaders can use their influence. For example, in Chapter 11, we learned about the power that authoritarian leaders wield over their followers to force compliance. But we also learned about transactional, transformational, and charismatic leaders, who are just as influential but instead obtain results by initiating shared goals, building meaningful relationships, and gaining the respect and esteem of others.

Indeed, recent psychological research has suggested that coercive power is a less effective method for gaining power, and that *social intelligence,* or our ability to negotiate, resolve conflicts, and understand the goals of others as well as group norms is the key to moving up in hierarchies.[2] Drawing from this theory, "leaders that treat their subordinates with respect, share power, and generate a sense of camaraderie and trust are considered more just and fair."[3] We might conclude that depending on their psychological make-up, different types of leaders may exert their power to influence in different ways, which can lead to positive or negative outcomes.

THINKING CRITICALLY

1. Discuss the relationship of power to leadership. What types of power can formal leaders exert? What types of power can informal leaders exert?

2. Consider the idea that social intelligence is more likely to lead to power than coercive power. Why might that be the case? Under what circumstances and in what areas might coercive power still prove more effective?

Basic Sources of Power

>> LO 13.2 Identify the various sources of power

To truly understand the concept of power, we need to explore the underlying sources of power. There are two: organizational power and personal power.[4]

Organizational Power

Organizations are political structures that operate in a system for distributing power and authority among individuals and teams. Depending on how it is used, power can lead to either positive or negative outcomes in an organization.

There are three main aspects of power within organizations:

Legitimate power: The degree to which a person has the right to ask others to do things that are considered within the scope of their authority

- **Legitimate power** is the leader's officially sanctioned authority to ask others to do things. For example, an organization such as the military that operates within a hierarchical structure places managers in a position of legitimate power. This means that by virtue of their organizational position managers have the formal authority or power to give orders and approve or deny employee requests. James "Jim" Robo, CEO of NextEra Energy, is an example of a leader with legitimate power because of the senior position he holds.

- **Reward power** is the use of incentives to influence the actions of others. For example, a manager may inspire employees by promising salary raises, bonuses, promotions, and so on. For example, at the end of 2016, Gary Bertch, CEO of Iowa-based Bertch Cabinets, rewarded his 800 employees for their hard work by taking them on a five-day all-expenses-paid Caribbean cruise. The staff had been informed of the trip at the beginning of the year as an incentive to work hard. Bertch says, "We just tried to get all of our people pumped up a little more to achieve the various goals, both customer-oriented goals and financial goals."[5]

    When used appropriately, reward power can motivate, but if rewards are used unethically or distributed based on favoritism, they can lead to demoralization and apathy.

- **Coercive power** is the means by which a person controls the behavior of others through punishments, threats, or sanctions. For example, a manager might have the power to fire or punish employees if they are perceived as violating the organization's policies and norms. In today's organizations, coercive power is perceived by many leaders as a negative power and is usually used as a last resort.

FIGURE 13.1

Sources of Power

Organizational Power	Personal Power
Legitimate Power	Expert Power
Reward Power	Referent Power
Coercive Power	

Reward power: The extent to which someone uses incentives to influence the actions of others

Coercive power: A strategy by which a person controls the behavior of others through punishments, threats, or sanctions

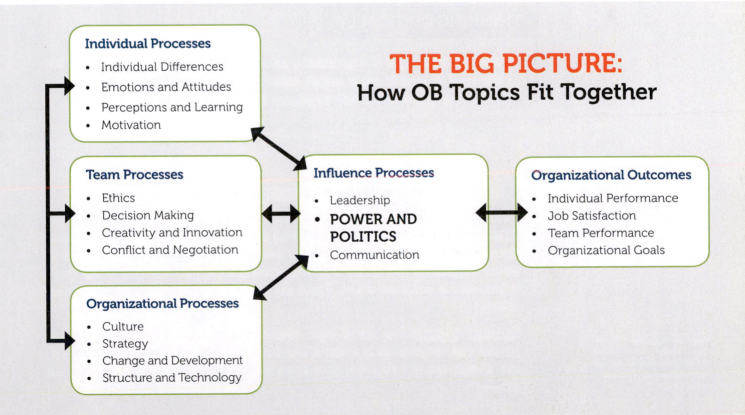

THE BIG PICTURE:
How OB Topics Fit Together

Individual Processes
- Individual Differences
- Emotions and Attitudes
- Perceptions and Learning
- Motivation

Team Processes
- Ethics
- Decision Making
- Creativity and Innovation
- Conflict and Negotiation

Organizational Processes
- Culture
- Strategy
- Change and Development
- Structure and Technology

Influence Processes
- Leadership
- **POWER AND POLITICS**
- Communication

Organizational Outcomes
- Individual Performance
- Job Satisfaction
- Team Performance
- Organizational Goals

Toshiba's former CEO Hisao Tanaka, Volkswagen's former CEO Martin Winterkorn, and Third Avenue Management's former CEO David Barse were known to use coercive power to intimidate employees.[6]

Personal Power

Personal power comes from within the individual and is independent of the position he or she holds in an organization. Personality and specialist knowledge in a certain area can be useful tools of personal power and influence. There are two main types of personal power:

Expert power: The ability to influence the behavior of others through the amount of knowledge or expertise possessed by an individual on which others depend

- **Expert power** is the ability to influence the behavior of others through the possession of knowledge or expertise on which others depend. For example, a team working on a project will look to their leader for guidance if he or she is the one with the knowledge and experience necessary for the task to be done. Expert power is easily gained by using the wealth of information resources around us. For a start, if you're working in an organization, you can develop expert power by reading the company's annual report or paying attention to important memos and emails.[7] Once you have developed your own expert base, you get the opportunity to share your own knowledge and contribute to important topics.

Referent power: The degree to which a leader can influence others through their desire to identify and be associated with them

- **Referent power** is the influence a leader gains over others when they desire to identify and be associated with him or her. For example, people will naturally gravitate toward a leader who comes across as fair, approachable, and adept at handling certain situations. Pam Nicholson, CEO of Enterprise Holdings, features as one of the most popular CEOs in America, according to a survey conducted by *Forbes*.[8] Nicholson is respected for her focus on the importance of ethics and rewarding those who do the right thing.

THINKING CRITICALLY

1. Rank the three types of organizational power (legitimate, reward, coercive) and the two types of personal power (expert, referent) in order of most to least likely to yield effective long-term results from employees. Defend your ranking.

Using Power: Tactics for Influencing Others

>> LO 13.3 Describe tactics for influencing others

The way we use power is important when it comes to influencing others. In organizations, people often use different forms of power tactics to get what they want. Recognizing these tactics at play in the workplace is important as it allows us to better understand how to deal with coworkers or managers who tend to use these maneuvers to influence others. There are eleven primary tactics for influencing others:[9]

Rational appeals: The use of logic, reason, and evidence to convince another person that cooperation in a task is worthwhile

Rational appeals: The use of logic, reason, and evidence to convince another person that cooperation in a task is worthwhile. Billionaire investor Warren Buffett is regarded as a naturally persuasive person as he uses logic to explain his actions.[10]

FIGURE 13.2

Characteristics of Inspirational Leadership

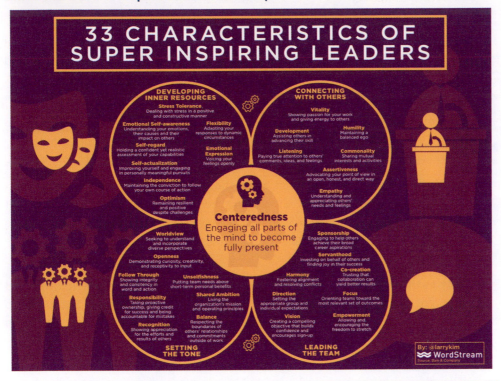

Source: Republished with permission of Mansuento Ventures LLC, from Kim, Larry. (2016). "33 Traits of the Most Inspiring Leaders." *Inc;* permission conveyed through Copyright Clearance Center, Inc.

Inspirational appeals: The use of emotions to rouse enthusiasm for the task by appealing to the values and ideals of others. Recent research carried out by global management consulting firm Bain & Company shows that there are thirty-three characteristics of inspirational leadership, made up into four groups: the skills associated with leading a team; how leaders connect with others; how leaders handle themselves; and how leaders work in groups (see Figure 13.2).[11] The study also found that people are inspired by leaders who deal positively with stress, have the courage of their convictions when others disagree with them, and have the ability to remain centered by being fully present at all times.

Upward appeals: The argument that the task has been requested by higher management, or a request to higher management to assist in gaining cooperation. For example, when trying to persuade a colleague to complete a task, you might use the argument that the request has come from the top, and that's why it needs to be done.

Personal appeals: A request to cooperate on the basis of friendship or as a personal favor. However, asking for or accepting favors requires a degree of caution. For example, Maurice S. Herbert of Tufts Healthcare Plan, featured in OB in the Real World, sets strict rules regarding the types of gifts the employees receive from vendors. Accepting gifts may give the impression that employees will be more open to doing special favors for their clients in the future.

Consultation: The offer of participation or consultation in the decision-making process. For example, Jim Whitehurst, CEO of software company Red Hat,

Inspirational appeals: The use of emotions to raise enthusiasm for the task by appealing to the values and ideals of others

Upward appeals: The argument that the task has been requested by higher management, or a request to higher management to assist in gaining cooperation

Personal appeals: Requests to cooperate on the basis of friendship or as a personal favor

Consultation: The offer of participation or consultation in the decision-making process

headquartered in North Carolina, involves employees in major decision making which he believes results in creative solutions. Whitehurst calls this tactic, "inclusive decision making."[12]

Exchange: The promise of rewards to persuade another person to cooperate

Exchange: The promise of rewards to persuade another person to cooperate. NextEra Energy, featured in our case study, rewards its employees for their hard work with generous salaries, benefits, career development opportunities, and additional perks such as free or highly discounted access to wellness centers, doctor's checkups, gymnasiums, and relaxing corporate environments.

Coalition building: Gathering the support of others as a reason for another person to agree to a request

Coalition building: Reference to the support of others as a reason for someone to agree to a request. For example, unions often build coalitions to make collective demands on an organization, and may threaten to strike if demands are not met.

Ingratiation: A strategy of winning favor and putting oneself in the good graces of others before making a request

Ingratiation: An effort to win favor and the good graces of others before making a request. Yet ingratiation should only be taken so far. For instance, recent research shows that managers who use ingratiation as a tactic with their CEOs may start to feel resentment against their bosses, especially when they believe the CEO is benefiting at their expense.[13]

Silent authority: An influencing tactic that relies on unspoken but acknowledged power

Silent authority: A passive tactic that relies on unspoken but acknowledged power. For example, when leaders use silence as a tactic, they are better able to hear what is being said and what remains unsaid, which allows them to reach the truth much more easily.

Information control: A hard influencing tactic in which key information is withheld in order to manipulate outcomes

Information control: Withholding key information to influence outcomes. Recent studies show that employees who withhold information may do so through a fear of speaking their minds. However, researchers found that in organizations where employees are allowed to speak freely, there is a higher rate of retention and performance.[14]

Assertiveness: The use of demands or threats to persuade someone to carry out a task. Elon Musk, technology innovator and founder of Tesla and SpaceX, has a reputation for making extreme demands and putting excessive pressure on his employees.[15]

Influencing employees by explaining how their efforts contribute to a greater good is an example of an inspirational appeal.

Assertiveness: The use of demands or threats to persuade someone to carry out a task

Choosing a particular tactic depends on the situation. Effective leaders know when to choose "hard" tactics such as assertiveness and information control, and when they should tread more carefully and adopt "soft" tactics such as personal appeals, inspirational appeals, or exchange. The key to influencing others is to identify which situation calls for a particular type of tactic.

THINKING CRITICALLY

1. Which influence tactics are more likely to be used by people wielding each type of organizational power (legitimate, reward, coercive)? Which are more likely to be used by people wielding each type of personal power (expert, referent)? Explain your reasoning.

2. To what extent should the type of power you have in an organization affect the influencing tactics you use? Defend your answer.

3. Think of a time that you may have used the assertiveness tactic to try to get your way in a situation at work or outside of work. Did the tactic work? Why or why not?

Consequences of Influence Tactics

>> LO 13.4   Outline the results of the various influence tactics

When employed successfully, influence tactics can motivate employees, help managers obtain support and resources, and instigate effort, commitment, and cooperation. One of the best ways of choosing the right influence tactic is to understand how people react to different forms of influence. We can explore the effectiveness of an influence tactic by looking at three different possible outcomes: commitment, compliance, and resistance (Figure 13.3).[16]

Commitment occurs when people are enthusiastic and fully in agreement with an action or decision and are motivated to put in the extra effort to successfully reach a goal. This is the best reaction to an influence tactic.

Compliance occurs when people are indifferent to a task and make only the minimal effort necessary to complete a goal. Although this reaction is not ideal for tasks that require more commitment, compliance has its place, especially when it comes to simple requests. For example, a manager telling an employee to do a routine, monotonous task like scanning a stack of documents may not receive an enthusiastic response, but the task will ultimately get done. In this scenario, compliance may be considered a successful outcome.

Resistance takes place when people oppose the influencer's request by refusing to do it or arguing against carrying out the task. This is the worst reaction to an influence tactic, and it also causes bad feeling and distrust.

In general, people tend to react better to "soft" rather than "hard" tactics. Soft tactics are more likely to result in commitment and are a frequent choice of leaders with personal sources of power such as expert and referent power. In contrast, hard tactics are more likely to generate compliance or resistance, and they are used by leaders with position power such as legitimate, reward, and coercive power.

It's helpful to know which soft influence tactics are the most effective in a given situation and why. For example, people with more knowledge and expertise tend to achieve better results through rational appeals because they have the necessary factual and logical evidence to support their requests. The success of ingratiation, inspirational appeals, or personal appeals largely depends on the sincerity of the person making the request. False behavior displayed by leaders tends to cause their staff to lose respect. Similarly, exchange and consultation as soft influence tactics must be meant sincerely to achieve the desired reaction.

What about hard tactics? People with strong legitimate power usually have more success using silent

Compliance is the lowest level of commitment an employee can make as a result of influence tactics. However, compliance is just the right level of commitment an employee needs to make for simple tasks, like making photocopies.

©iStockphoto.com/AleksandarNakic

FIGURE 13.3

Consequences of Influence Tactics

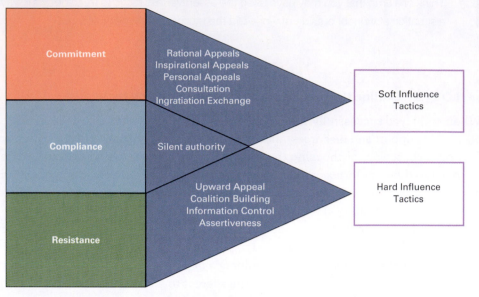

Source: Based on Falbe, Cecilia M., and Gary Yukl. "Consequences for Managers of Using Single Influence Tactics and Combinations of Tactics." *Academy of Management Journal* 35, no. 3 (August 1992): 638–652.

authority to have their requests fulfilled. For example, a CEO of an organization might expect subordinates to immediately carry out his requests even if they might not necessarily agree.

The choice of the most suitable influence tactic depends on personal, organizational, and cultural values. For example, people with an inclination toward power may prefer to use assertiveness to get their demands met, whereas those who prefer to toe the line may seek support from others higher up in the organization through upward appeals. At an organizational level, people in companies with a competitive culture are more likely to build coalitions to protest or debate an issue, or they may deliberately control information to manipulate; both these tactics can generate resistance, and ultimately damage future relationships.

Influence tactics also vary across different cultures. Though extensive studies have been carried out to identify which cultures use certain influence tactics more commonly than others, the results are mixed at best. Some studies suggest information control is more common in Hong Kong than in the United States,[17] while others propose that coalition building is more effective in the United States and Switzerland than in China.[18] Despite these studies, knowledge gaps still exist, and further research is necessary to explain the cultural variations and effectiveness of influence tactics.

THINKING CRITICALLY

1. List at least five sorts of business tasks where commitment would be far better than compliance. List at least five sorts of business tasks where compliance is acceptable and would not damage organizational goals or working relationships.

2. To what extent does an effective leader need to be able to employ both soft and hard influence tactics? Under what circumstances are soft tactics more likely to be effective? Under what circumstances are hard tactics more likely to be effective?

EXAMINING THE EVIDENCE

Political Behavior: A Viable Coping Strategy for Organizational Politics?

Research suggests that political behavior often results in negative outcomes for individuals and organizations. But in certain situations it may have positive outcomes. Researchers Shuhua Sun of Tulane University and Huaizhong Chen of West Virginia University found that when employees choose to "play the political game" and engage in political behavior, it can serve as a coping mechanism that reduces the negative effects of perceived organizational politics on employee psychological empowerment and ultimately on employee task performance. However, it appears that these positive benefits may come with an associated cost. Their findings also suggest that political behavior also *increases* the negative effects of perceived organizational politics on employee emotional exhaustion, thereby reducing task performance. These researchers suggest that employees should be aware of both the positive and negative effects of political behavior as a coping strategy, while managers should attempt to minimize employee perceptions of organizational politics. As long as employees perceive organizational politics, they are likely to suffer one way or the other. If they actively "play the political game," they may gain a sense of greater control, but at the cost of more emotional exhaustion. On the other hand, if they choose not to politick, they will likely experience lower levels of psychological empowerment.

Critical-Thinking Questions

1. How can managers most effectively leverage the positive effects of organizational politics?

2. In what ways can managers minimize employee perceptions of organizational politics? ●

Source: Sun, S., & Chen, H. (2017, May 22). Is Political Behavior a Viable Coping Strategy to Perceived Organizational Politics? Unveiling the Underlying Resource Dynamics. *Journal of Applied Psychology.* Advance online publication. http://dx.doi.org/10.1037/apl0000239.

Organizational Politics

>> **LO 13.5** **Identify the causes and possible consequences of organizational politics**

The word *politics* often elicits more negative than positive connotations. Popular culture generally portrays politicians as underhanded, power hungry, and ruthless in their ambition to make it to the top. Yet all people are capable of engaging in self-serving behavior. Politics exist wherever there is conflict and competition between employees in the scramble up the career ladder. We define **organizational politics** as behavior that is not formally sanctioned by the organization and that is focused on maximizing our self-interest, often at the expense of the organization or other employees.[19] Whether you choose to engage in it or avoid it, organizational politics is a reality in every workplace.

Organizational politics: Behavior that is not formally sanctioned by the organization and that is focused on maximizing our self-interest, often at the expense of the organization or other employees

How do people behave when they are engaging in political behaviors? Political behaviors include ingratiation, self-promotion, strong influence tactics, coalition building, the forging of connections with powerful allies, taking credit for positive events and the success of others, and the circumvention of legitimate channels to secure resources that would otherwise be unattainable.[20] You may notice that some of these terms appeared in section 13.3; political behaviors are indeed closely aligned with tactical influence. People who "play the game" seek to influence others to get ahead, whether it's for their own interests or for the best interests of the organization.

Why is organizational politics an inevitable part of working life? There are two main factors at play: organizational factors and individual factors.[21]

©iStockphoto.com/wellesenterprises

When Cisco started laying off large numbers of employees in 2012, their remaining workforce started competing for the positions and opportunities that remained. This is an example of how organizational factors can influence political behavior.

Organizational Factors

People are more likely to engage in political behavior in organizations where resources such as monetary rewards or promotions are limited. In today's uncertain economy, many companies have implemented austerity measures and cut back on overhead, often by conducting layoffs. For example, National Oilwell Varco, Walmart, and oil company Schlumberger are among the biggest companies who have announced the most layoffs in 2016.[22]

These cost-cutting steps can fuel political behavior as employees compete for dwindling resources and rewards. "Zero-sum rewards," programs that compensate only one or a few team members at the expense of the others, can have negative consequences for those who do not receive anything, creating bad feeling and driving unhealthy competition. Similarly, organizations going through periods of organizational change tend to have more politically centered workforces. For example, rumors of layoffs may encourage some employees to use political tactics to ensure that their jobs are secure.

An organization's environment or culture is a good indicator of the extent of politics that exists in it. For example, in organizations that fail to implement formal rules, that tolerate a lack of trust between employees and management, or that put employees under serious pressure to perform, competition and politics prevail.

Individual Factors

Even if your organization is highly political, the extent to which you engage in political behavior depends on your personality. For example, you may be someone who has a strong desire for power and operates with a high internal locus of control (the belief that you can control outcomes). Or you could be a high self-monitor, someone who is more sensitive to social cues, can relate well to others, and inspires trust and confidence. Finally, you might have a Machiavellian personality and be willing to manipulate others and use power to advance your own self-interests.

Possible Outcomes of Political Behavior

The vast majority of research evidence suggests that organizational politics has negative effects, including increased strain and stress, higher organizational turnover, decreased job satisfaction and performance, lower morale, and reduced organizational commitment.[23] However, politics can be used for positive means when people possess **political skill,** the ability to understand and influence others for the good of the organization.[24] In other words, when people hold the interests of the organization above their own interests, provide high levels of feedback to colleagues and direct reports, and maintain good working relationships to achieve results, then organizational politics can have positive results. Regardless of how you feel about it, there is no doubt that politics will be prevalent in most organizations you join. Organizational politics refers to a variety of activities associated with the use of influence tactics to improve personal or organizational interests. Studies show that individuals with political skills tend to do better in gaining more personal power as well as managing stress and job demands, than their politically naive counterparts.[25] They also have a greater impact on organizational outcomes. Yet

Political skill: The ability to understand and influence others for the good of the organization

OB IN THE REAL WORLD

Maurice S. Hebert, Senior Vice President, Tufts Health Plan

Tufts Health Plan is a growing nonprofit health provider which is based out of Massachusetts and operates in Rhode Island and New Hampshire. They now employ over 2,400 people and provide great care for over one million. Compared to some health care providers, Tufts Health Plan is relatively small—which is partly why their senior vice president of finance left his place at a larger company to work for Tufts.

Maurice Hebert, a graduate from Louisiana State University, has been with Tufts since the start of 2016. His department consists of seventy-five employees, and he came to Tufts in order to hold a position from which he could truly influence an organization and improve the lives of customers. He says that he "took the opportunity to make a larger and more substantive impact on a company." In order to do so, he employs many of the tactics mentioned in this chapter in order to influence his employees, his company, and himself. His department is organized so that he directly supervises five people, but Maurice has weekly meetings with his vice presidents and one-on-one meetings with his directors to make sure that his department is running smoothly. He also holds a quarterly all-hands meeting in order to connect with his seventy-five finance employees.

Maurice says this about his experience with legitimate power, which he says plays a daily role in operating, "In

the real world, your position and rank certainly affords you power." But he says that this structural power is greatly enhanced by reward power; to be successful, he must use a few forms of influence. Specifically, Maurice constantly assures his employees with recognition for their work, and he challenges them. "If I can get my employees to feel as if they are owners in the company, then they will act with a vested interest in the success of the company. So I challenge them to give insight and ideas for devising processes and plans to fulfill goals," Maurice says. Maurice places a high level of importance on hearing the perspective of as many of his employees as he can. He says it benefits the company and the employee when ideas are fielded: "If employee input is solicited and acted upon, it motivates them. There is a reward in itself: my idea was heard, and somebody seriously considered it, and in some cases adopted it."

Maurice emphasizes that last aspect of collecting ideas: implementing them. He has found throughout his career in health care that the best finance department is the one that serves as a business partner to the operations and caregiving sides of the company. He and his team have a responsibility to provide useful and immediate data on the financial impact of each decision the company makes and each change in the political world in order to assist each branch of the company in making better and better decisions.

The process of informing other departments requires different types of influence. Maurice's expert power, derived from his knowledge of his field, is instrumental, as he puts it, "Especially in Finance, which is a very technical field, expert power plays a huge role." This alone is not effective enough, though. He has found that, regarding expert power, "It's only as valuable as it can be if you are teaching and imparting your expert knowledge on other people. You must empower your department to develop the same knowledge; this builds strength and capable players." Maurice has discovered that expert power goes hand in hand with referent power. When he structures his department in order to impart knowledge to employees, they develop a respect and admiration for him. Likewise, among his peers in the company, his expert knowledge serves as a tool for gaining respect. The respect other senior VPs have for Maurice and his department allows him to give serious propositions and feedback to all sections of Tufts, which is the best way to see the ideas of his department implemented in the overall business.

Influencing his peers and employees is not all Maurice must worry about as a manager. In regards to

(Continued)

(Continued)

organizational politics, Maurice and Tufts have set clear restrictions on the types of gifts they can receive from vendors. Maurice says that having clearly defined rules makes it much easier to uphold organizational ethics in decision making. He says that governmental politics play a huge role in health care, so his department is constantly updated on the changing political world. If government subsidies for patients are altered, it affects the way the finance department must price plans.

Maurice must also use his influence to ensure that his department's mission is effective, and that it lines up with the overall mission of Tufts, which is "to improve the health and wellness of the diverse communities we serve." Sometimes when sitting in front of financial data and spreadsheets, Maurice and his team can lose track of their overall mission to improve the health of customers. To fix this, Maurice makes sure to remind his team that an effective finance department directly

assists customers, in two ways. If they recommend improved options to the operations and caregiving side of Tufts, then the finance department can assist in delivering higher quality care. Secondly, cost-saving activities that they can engage in are passed on directly to customers. For these reasons, Maurice and his team can feel engaged in the Tufts Health Plan Mission, and they can effectively improve the operations of the company.

Critical-Thinking Questions

1. Name and describe the types of power that Maurice uses as chief financial officer.

2. What is one effective method of keeping organizational politics ethical? ●

Source: Interview with Maurice Hebert conducted on April 28th, 2017

---

as the Examining the Evidence feature shows, playing the political game can also come at a price. Take a look at how Maurice S. Herbert, senior vice president of Tufts Health Plan featured in OB in the Real World, manages organizational politics in his company.

If you are aiming for a promotion, you will need to network with the right people and take on high-profile projects in order to increase your **visibility,** which is others' awareness of your presence in an organization.[26] Ultimately, your rewards, bonuses, and promotional prospects depend on the relationships you have with others. You don't need to behave in an underhanded way to stand out, but with so much competition in the workplace there is nothing wrong with ensuring that your hard work is acknowledged and fairly rewarded. Of course, you can choose to stay out of politics altogether, but this may mean getting passed over for promotions simply because the people responsible for promotional decisions and rewards are unaware of your skills, talents, and contributions. The next section provides a greater understanding of the political landscape that exists in most organizations.

Visibility: The awareness of others regarding your presence in an organization

THINKING CRITICALLY

1. Do you agree with the statement that organizational politics is a reality in every workplace? Why or why not?

2. To what extent are small, innovative start-ups more or less likely to be characterized by organizational politics and political behavior than large, well-established multinationals? How does the size of a company affect the extent of organizational politics?

Four Different Types of Organizational Politics

>> **LO 13.6**   Discuss the four different types of organizational politics

In organizations, political behavior can either be destructive or a force for good. Regardless of the situation, it is important to understand the four main types of organizational politics to navigate the political landscape. These are the weeds, the rocks, the high ground, and the woods.[27] Two dimensions operate across these four types. The first dimension involves just one person who engages in political activity, which expands to group-level politics as others get involved, before evolving into organizational politics. The second dimension is the degree to which the power is used; it can either be "soft" power, where people make informal use of their own influence or relationships; or "hard" power where people use their own authority and expertise to engage in political activity. Being aware of these two dimensions can help us to understand the types of politics around us.

The Weeds

The weeds describes a place where people engage in politics using personal influence and informal networks. For example, a not-for-profit organization relies on donors to keep the business afloat. The secretary general starts behaving unethically and underperforming. There is a concern among the staff that his behavior will put off current and future donors. A group of employees gets together to discuss the problem informally. Over time, the problem gets worse, but the group's influence grows stronger, and within a year the secretary general is removed from his role in order to protect the company's reputation. This shows that informal groups have the political power to be a force for good.

However, informal groups can be destructive if they are set up to hamper legitimate change or disrupt the long-term interests of the organization. To counteract the negative aspect of groups operating in "the weeds," managers need to understand the nature of the politics, identify the key players, and communicate with them to find the source of their discontent.

The Rocks

When in "the rocks," people in authority use hard power to enforce decisions. Often these people operate in high-status groups such as finance committees or senior management teams. While using hard power can be a stabilizing force particularly during turbulent times when tough decisions need to be made, there are also downsides to using this type of political behavior. For example, a mid-size advertising agency is implementing a growth strategy, but the CEO is using her formal power to block the changes. She questions decisions, changes her mind, and takes people off projects without telling them. Her use of this type of political behavior is destructive and self-serving.

In this situation, it is better to try and find a way to persuade the CEO that these changes are positive in the long-term. For instance, growth is in the interests of the company and she will be leaving behind an impressive legacy if she steers the company in the right way.

The High Ground

The high ground describes a type of organizational politics where the rules, structures, and policy guidelines are set formally in place. While rules and regulations are necessary for a well-functioning organization, too much formal authority can lead to overly bureaucratic structures which impede innovation and change. One way of tackling this level of rigidity is to set up task forces, or separate groups outside the formal structure of the organization to analyze the problem and make a case for change. For example, one public agency was failing to collect millions of tax revenues because of its cumbersome internal structures and policies. A dedicated task force was created outside of the formal organizational structure to discuss a solution. The group's suggestions were implemented over time, leading to a change in processes and a much higher recovery rate. Car manufacturer Nissan and British supermarket retailer Asda are just two examples of companies that have used task forces to remove the barriers of bureaucracy to implement change and innovation.

The Woods

Besides their rules and regulations, organizations have certain norms (see Chapter 7 for further information on norms), which can sometimes prove to be a political minefield. Organizations can get lost in "the woods" by focusing on the issues rather than the hidden, unseen, underlying norms that could well be the key source of the problem. One way of identifying these unspoken habits is to ask people outside the organization such as clients, temporary contractors, or recent hires to share their thoughts on how the company operates. Their feedback will determine whether the cultural norms are hindering or helping the organization.

For example, a newly merged telecoms company engaged in a simple exercise where people from both companies were asked to describe their respective cultural norms and those of the other parties. Discussing these norms openly bridged the gap between the two parties, who began to work as a team to roll out a key project.

Each type of organizational politics has a positive and negative aspect. It is essential that managers understand the drivers of these behaviors in order to avoid getting drawn into the dark side of politics.

So far, we have explored the role of power and politics and how it influences relationships in organizations. In the next chapter, we will illustrate the importance of positive culture and its impact on organizational behavior.

THINKING CRITICALLY

1. Do you agree with the statement that organizational politics is a reality in every workplace? Why or why not?

2. To what extent are small, innovative start-ups more or less likely to be characterized by organizational politics and political behavior than large, well-established multinationals? How does the size of a company affect the extent of organizational politics?

3. Discuss the four types of organizational politics presented in this chapter. What are the positives and negatives of each type? How as a manager could you offset or reduce the negative outcomes associated with each type? ●

Visit **edge.sagepub.com/neckob2e** to help you accomplish your coursework goals in an easy-to-use learning environment.

- Mobile-friendly eFlashcards and practice quizzes
- Video and multimedia content
- Chapter summaries with learning objectives
- EXCLUSIVE! Access to full-text SAGE journal articles

IN REVIEW

13.1 **Discuss the concept of power and its relationship to leadership**

The concept of **power,** which is the capacity to influence the actions of others, is inextricably linked with leadership. Recent psychological research has suggested that coercive power is a myth, and that true power lies in social intelligence or our ability to negotiate, resolve conflicts, and understand the goals of others. Depending on their psychological make-up, different types of leaders may exert their power to influence in different ways, which can lead to positive or negative outcomes.

13.2 Identify the various sources of power

Organizational power can be broken into three main aspects: legitimate power, reward power, and coercive power. Legitimate power is the right to ask others to do things within the scope of the leader's authority. Reward power is the use of incentives to influence the actions of others. Coercive power controls the behavior of others through punishments, threats, or sanctions.

Personal power can be broken into two main types: expert power and referent power. Expert power is the ability to influence the behavior of others through the possession of knowledge or expertise on which they depend. Referent power is influence over others based on their desire to identify and be associated with the leader.

13.3 Describe tactics for influencing others

There are several different types of tactics we can use to influence others:

- **Rational appeals**: The use of logic, reason, and evidence to convince another person that cooperation in a task is worthwhile
- **Inspirational appeals**: The use of emotions to rouse enthusiasm for the task by appealing to the values and ideals of others
- **Upward appeals**: The argument that the task has been requested by higher management, or a request to higher management to assist in gaining cooperation
- **Personal appeals**: Requests to cooperate on the basis of friendship or as a personal favor
- **Consultation:** The offer of participation or consultation in the decision-making process
- **Exchange:** The promise of rewards to persuade another person to cooperate
- **Coalition building:** Reference to the support of others as a reason for someone to agree to a request
- **Ingratiation:** An effort to win favor and the good graces of others before making a request
- **Silent authority:** A passive tactic that relies on unspoken but acknowledged power.
- **Information control**: Withholding key information to influence outcomes.
- **Assertiveness:** The use of demands or threats to persuade someone to carry out a task

13.4 Outline the results of the various influence tactics

The three basic outcomes of influence tactics are commitment, compliance, and resistance. *Commitment* occurs when people are enthusiastic and fully in agreement with an action or decision and are motivated to put in the extra effort to successfully reach a goal. *Compliance* occurs when people are indifferent to a task and make only the minimal effort necessary to complete a goal. *Resistance* takes place when people oppose the influencer's request by refusing to carry out a task or arguing against carrying out a task.

13.5 Identify the causes and possible consequences of organizational politics

Organizational politics is behavior that is not formally sanctioned by the organization and that is focused on maximizing our self-interest, often at the expense of the organization or other employees. They include ingratiation, self-promotion, strong influence tactics, coalition building, connections with powerful allies, the taking of credit for positive events and the success of others, and the circumvention of legitimate channels to secure resources that would be otherwise unattainable.

People are more likely to engage in political behavior in organizations in which resources such as monetary rewards or promotions are limited. Similarly, organizations going through periods of organizational change tend to have a more politically centered workforce.

The vast majority of research evidence suggests negative effects of organizational politics, including increased strain and stress, higher organizational turnover, decreased job satisfaction and performance, lower morale, and reduced organizational commitment. However, politics can be used for positive means when people possess **political skill,** the ability to understand and influence others for the good of the organization, and hold the interests of the organization above their own interests, provide high levels of feedback to employees, and maintain good working relationships to achieve results.

13.6 **Discuss the four different types of organizational politics**

It is important to understand the four main types of organizational politics to navigate the political landscape. These are the weeds, the rocks, the high ground, and the woods. The weeds describes a place where people engage in politics using personal influence and informal networks. When in the rocks, people in authority use hard power to enforce decisions. The high ground describes a type of organizational politics where the rules, structures, and policy guidelines are set formally in place. Finally, organizations can get lost in the woods by focusing on the issues rather than the hidden, unseen, underlying norms that could well be the key source of the problem.

KEY TERMS

Assertiveness 380	Organizational politics 383
Coalition building 380	Personal appeals 379
Coercive power 377	Political skill 384
Consultation 379	Power 376
Exchange 380	Rational appeals 378
Expert power 378	Referent power 378
Information control 380	Reward power 377
Ingratiation 380	Silent authority 380
Inspirational appeals 379	Upward appeals 379
Legitimate power 376	Visibility 386

UP FOR DEBATE: Managerial Benefits

A boss has the right to use his position of leadership and esteem to enjoy benefits offered by clients, such as gifts and tickets to events. A boss has done the necessary work to make it to a high-level position, so there should be no problem with enjoying the benefits that come with it. Agree or disagree? Explain your answer.

EXERCISE 13.1: Tactics for Influencing Others

Objective

The purpose of this exercise is to gain a greater appreciation of the eleven primary tactics for influencing others.

Instructions

The text discusses eleven primary tactics for influencing others (rational appeals, inspirational appeals, etc.). In groups of three to five students, select any two of the tactics. Then, brainstorm a TV show or online series that has a character who utilizes your selected tactics. You may have two different shows/characters for the two tactics.

Once you have identified the two tactics and characters, what examples can you cite or behaviors these characters exhibit that demonstrate their use of these influencing tactics? How do other characters react to these tactics? In other words, are the tactics effective?

Reflection Questions

1. What tactics does your current or previous supervisor use to influence employees? How effective are these tactics?

2. Which tactics do you rely on to influence others? Why?

3. Which of the eleven tactics do you not respond to well? Which is a tactic that works on you most of the time? Explain.

Exercise contributed by Steven Stovall, Southeast Missouri State University.

Objectives

This exercise will help you to be able to better *discuss* the concept of power and *identify* various sources of power.

Instructions

Step 1. Think of an organization of which you are a member. For each power type (legitimate, reward, coercive, expert, and referent), describe why you do or do not have that particular power. Since power is an exchange process and differs in various relationships, you may also need to specify with who (or what group of people) you have that power. (5 minutes)

Step 2. Find a partner (ideally someone who you do not work with on a regular basis), and prepare a list of similarities and differences in your influence relationships. (10 minutes)

Step 3. Choose a spokesperson for your pair and be prepared to discuss your comparison with the class. (1 to 3 minutes)

Reflection Questions

1. How would you expect your power bases to change in a different organization?

2. How do you expect your power bases to change after you graduate from your program?

3. What power bases do you prefer to use? How could you improve those power bases?

4. What power bases would you expect to transfer between organizations and positions?

Exercise contributed by Milton R. Mayfield, Professor of Business, Texas A&M International University, and Jacqueline R. Mayfield, Professor of Business, Texas A&M International University.

EXERCISE 13.3: Grappling with Organizational Politics

Objective

The purpose of this exercise is to grasp the concept of the four different types of organizational politics.

Instructions

Your text identifies four types of organizational politics:

- **The weeds**—a place where people engage in politics using personal influence and informal networks

- **The rocks**—a place where people in authority use hard power to enforce decisions

- **The high ground**—situation where the rules, structures, and policy guidelines are set formally in place

- **The woods**—a situation where members of the organization focus on issues rather than the hidden, unseen, underlying norms that could well be the source of the problem

The instructor will ask for eight to twelve volunteers from the class for a series of role-plays (two to three participants for each type of organizational politics). Each group of participants will be given one of the four types above. Then, each group will take five to ten minutes to devise a scenario or skit that demonstrates that particular type of organizational politics. For example, one group will create a role-play demonstrating the weeds, another, the rocks, and so on.

The student volunteers will then take turns performing their role-play in front of the class.

The remaining students will attempt to guess which type of organizational politics is being shown based upon the words and interactions of the students at the front of the room. Students should write down their opinion as to which type of politics is shown and the correct identification is not given until all four groups of students have completed their skit.

Reflection Questions

1. For each group of students, how could you tell which type of organizational politics was being demonstrated? What cues or clues were given that showcased that particular type?

2. Which of the four types of organizational politics are you currently experiencing in your job or at a previous job? Explain.

3. What type of organizational politics would you most thrive in? Why?

4. What type of organizational politics would you least like? Why?

Exercise contributed by Steven Stovall, Southeast Missouri State University.

ONLINE EXERCISE 13.1: Understanding the Consequences of Influence Tactics

Objective

The purpose of this exercise is to gain an appreciation for the possible outcomes of influence tactics.

Description of Exercise

This exercise utilizes a discussion board to explore the three possible outcomes a person may have to influence tactics. Those three outcomes are:

- **Commitment**—occurs when people are enthusiastic and fully in agreement with an action or decision and are motivated to put in the extra effort to successfully reach a goal

- **Compliance**—occurs when people are indifferent to a task and make only the minimal effort necessary to complete a goal

- **Resistance**—occurs when people oppose the influencer's request by refusing to do it or arguing against carrying out the task

On the discussion board, post an example from your experience where commitment was the outcome to an influence tactic of a supervisor. Allow others to also post their experiences as well. Once everyone has posted, discuss the similarities of tactics and responses people had. Explore how there may also be differences. Then, repeat this discussion with compliance and resistance.

Discussion Questions

1. What did you learn about others' responses to various influence tactics that will help you in the future as you encounter these?

2. Do you think the type of outcome to influence tactics is a result of the manager's behavior and words or the entire culture of the organization? Explain.

3. How can organizations move away from a resistance outcome to one that is more commitment focused?

4. If you were hired as a new manager and you discover that the previous supervisor used harsh tactics in attempting to influence the employees which have resulted in a climate of compliance and resistance, what steps would you take to change the situation?

CASE STUDY 13.1: Monsanto Company

Depending on whom you talk to, Monsanto Company, the chemical and agricultural biotechnology multinational based in Creve Coeur, Missouri, is either the "devil incarnate" or the answer to some of humanity's most vexing problems. Do a quick Google search and you'll find a wide array of opinion in articles with titles ranging from "Monsanto Named 2013's Most Evil Corporation in New Poll" and "Monsanto Connected to at Least 200,000 Suicides in India throughout Past Decade" to "One of *CR* Magazine's 100 Best Corporate Citizens for 2014"

(CR stands for corporate responsibility). One thing is for sure: Monsanto is a powerful force on the world stage, with more than 22,000 employees, $14.87 billion in annual sales, and heavy political clout in the United States and beyond.

And it's everywhere. "Like Intel's dominance in the chip market, almost every soybean in America has Monsanto inside," wrote Scott Tong on *Marketplace.org*. Soybeans are the second-largest US crop after corn—they cover nearly a quarter of the country's farmland—and Monsanto is responsible for planting and harvesting about 90 percent of the nation's crop. The animals that produce our milk, eggs, meat, leather, gelatin, and wool feed on soybean meal. About 60 percent of the vegetable fats found in processed *human* food are soy based, too.

Monsanto's agricultural dominance can be traced in part to 1983, when it became a pioneer by genetically modifying a plant cell to become hardier. This was part of a wider GMO movement that for some "constitutes a massive experiment on the planet, with potentially devastating effects on human health and the global environment," as columnist Adam Kapp wrote in 2002. But that innovation, among others, has helped Monsanto produce soybeans cheaply and reliably to feed a growing global population.

Monsanto is also an innovator in pesticides, among other chemicals and technologies. Founded in 1901, over the years the company has led breakthrough research on catalytic asymmetric hydrogenation and light-emitting diodes (LEDs) and produced the insecticide DDT, PCBs, Agent Orange, and bovine growth hormone. Borrowing from biotechnology's and the pharmaceutical industry's playbooks (its founder was a pharmacist), Monsanto spends millions on R&D and biological patents, making much of its money back (and then some) on its patents' reuse. Today, the company is both revered and reviled for its influence in the soybean trade and for the production of Roundup, a powerful pesticide the company insists is safe. Its introduction of the herbicide Roundup-ready Soybeans—meaning farmers can spray their fields to keep away the pests while theoretically keeping their Monsanto soybeans safe—unleashed even louder protests from environmentalists and the organic- and small-farmer movements in 2000 that continues today.

Why all the fuss? The world's population is growing at an unprecedented rate, and determining how to feed everyone is essential to our survival—which Monsanto claims is one of its core goals. But detractors say that GMO crops are nutritionally inferior and hazardous to humans and the environment. Scientists mostly agree that genetic engineering is also leading to the growth of "super" weeds and pests that withstand not only Roundup but any pesticide.

Author Bret Frazer, on *The Northern Light.org*, explains why Monsanto is not just "bad" but *"evil"*: "Monsanto . . . epitomizes the undermining of democracy. Monsanto is an example of revolving door politics." He points out that Supreme Court Justice Clarence Thomas worked as a Monsanto attorney in the 1970s. In 2001, Thomas wrote the majority opinion for *J.E.M. Ag Supply, Inc. v. Pioneer Hi-Bred International, Inc.,* which found that "newly developed plant breeds are patentable," allowing GMO producers like Monsanto to make billions from generations of seeds and sue those farmers who did not abide by strict patent-protecting policies. Linda Fisher, Monsanto vice president from 1995 to 2000, was made deputy administrator of the EPA (Environmental Protection Agency) in 2001. Michael Taylor was once employed by a law firm that lobbied for FDA approval of Monsanto's artificial growth hormone. President Barack Obama reappointed him deputy commissioner of the FDA (Food and Drug Administration) in 2009. In "Why Is Monsanto Evil, but DuPont Isn't?," Stephen D. Simpson of *The Motley Fool* reports that when corporate lobbying "Monsanto does indeed spend millions . . . around $5 million or $6 million a year by most reports." But it is certainly not the first major corporation whose executives have made the transition to the federal payroll.

But perhaps the most ire has been raised by Monsanto's use of litigation to protect its patented crops and its perceived unfair influence within the very government that regulates its industry.

Monsanto has sued farmers, claiming they used its patented seeds without permission (sometimes the seeds in question were several generations removed from the original patented seeds). In 2013, a case taken all the way to the Supreme Court was resolved in favor of Monsanto when Indiana farmer Vernon Hugh Bowman was ordered to pay the company $84,000 for patent infringement.

But thanks in part to grassroots, social media-fueled movements, the legislative tide may turn against Monsanto. In 2014, Vermont passed a bill that mandates the labeling of GMO foods—so consumers can choose to eliminate GMO foods from their grocery carts—and other states may soon follow suit. It doesn't take effect until July 2016, and lawsuits from the agriculture industry are expected to follow.

Simpson sees Monsanto's business practices as par for the course. "Every crop science company works to protect its intellectual property, every crop science company looks to get a good price for its technology, and every crop science company opens its wallet to attempt to sway public and governmental opinion to their side—just as companies in technology, healthcare, banking and virtually every other industry do, and have done for decades."

Whatever argument about Monsanto's behavior sways you, it's clear the company won't be leaving the headlines—or our dinner tables—any time soon. As activists protest more loudly and Vermont and others heed their call, perhaps consumers will have greater purchasing power than ever before.

Case Questions

1. Describe how Monsanto became so powerful in the chemical and agricultural biotechnology industry.

2. Describe how Monsanto uses organizational power.

3. What sort of power do environmentalists and other activists hold in their fight against Monsanto's policies? Where does it come from? How can they best use or increase their power?

4. Describe Monsanto as an example of revolving door politics and the way it gives the company additional organizational power.

Sources

Adams, Mike. "Monsanto Voted Most Evil Corporation of the Year by NaturalNews Readers." *NaturalNews.com*. January 10, 2011. www.naturalnews.com/030967_Monsanto_evil.html## ixzz31WiamJFP.

Bunge, Jacob. "For Weed Control, Farmers Widen Their Arsenal of Herbicides." *Wall Street Journal*. April 25, 2014. http://online.wsj.com/news/articles/SB1000142405270230384780457 9481641717350038.

Chatsko, Maxx. "Is Monsanto Company Wrong about Pest Resistance?" *Motley Fool*. April 18, 2014. www.fool.com/investing/general/2014/04/18/is-monsanto-company-wrong-about-pest-resistance.aspx.

Huff, Ethan A. "Monsanto Connected to at Least 200,000 Suicides in India throughout Past Decade." *Naturalnews.com*. January 4, 2011. www.naturalnews.com/030913_Monsanto_suicides.html#.

Kresser, Chris. "Are GMOs Safe?" *Chriskresser.com*. n.d. chriskresser.com/are-gmos-safe.

Liptak, Adam. "Supreme Court Supports Monsanto in Seed-Replication Case." *New York Times*. May 13, 2013. http://www.nytimes.com/2013/05/14/business/monsanto-victorious-in-genetic-seed-case.html?_r=0.

"Monsanto Named as a Top Company for Diversity." *Monsanto.com*. April 24, 2014. news. monsanto.com/press-release/recognition/monsanto%C2%A0named%C2%A0as%C2%A0a%C 2%A0top-company%C2%A0-diversity.

Philpott, Tom. "Chicken Nuggets, with a Side of Respiratory Distress." *Motherjones.com*. April 30, 2014. www.motherjones.com/tom-philpott/2014/04/superweeds-arent-only-trouble-gmo-s.

Sheets, Connor Adams. "Monsanto Named 2013's 'Most Evil Corporation' in New Poll." *International Business Times*. June 10, 2013. www.ibtimes.com/monsanto-named-2013s-most-evil-corporation-new-poll-1300217.

Simpson, Stephen D. "Why Is Monsanto Evil, but DuPont Isn't?" *Investopedia.com*. June 19, 2013. www.investopedia.com/articles/investing/061913/why-monsanto-evil-dupont-isnt.asp.

Smith, Jeffrey. "Monsanto Voted World's Most Evil Corp Year after Year for Good Reasons." *RT.com*. October 11, 2013. rt.com/op-edge/monsanto-technique-ruins-evolution-016.

Tong, Scott. "Monsanto: The Behemoth That Controls 90 Percent of Soybean Production." *Marketplace.org* May 13, 2013. www.marketplace.org/topics/sustainability/monsanto-behemoth-controls-90-percent-soybean-production.

"USDA Creates New Government Certification for GMO-Free." *New York Times*. May 14, 2015. www.nytimes.com/aponline/2015/05/14/us/politics/ap-us-genetically-modified-foods-labeling.html?_r=0.

How Political Is My Organization?

Consider an organization in which you are a member. This could be an organization for which you work, a fraternity or sorority or other campus organization, a social or community organization, or the like.

For each statement, circle the number that best describes your organization on the following scale:

	NOT AT ALL ACCURATE	SOMEWHAT ACCURATE	A LITTLE ACCURATE	MOSTLY ACCURATE	COMPLETELY ACCURATE
1. The most successful people in my organization are fairly adept at the art of ingratiation.	1	2	3	4	5
2. The people who get ahead in my organization are very good at self-promotion.	1	2	3	4	5
3. Strong influence tactics must be used in order to accomplish objectives in my organization.	1	2	3	4	5
4. Building coalitions tends to be very important for success in my organization.	1	2	3	4	5
5. The people who are most successful in my organization tend to have connections with powerful allies.	1	2	3	4	5
6. Successful members of my organization do not hesitate in taking credit for positive events and/or the success of others.	1	2	3	4	5
7. Circumventing legitimate channels to secure resources that would be otherwise unattainable is a fairly common practice for success in my organization.	1	2	3	4	5
8. People seem to enjoy the political process in my organization.	1	2	3	4	5

Scoring

Add the numbers circled and write your score in the blank _____.

Interpretation

32 and above = Your organization is highly political. It will take a significant amount of political skill and political behavior to be successful in this organization.

24–31 = Your organization is moderately political. High levels of political skill and savvy may be helpful in certain situations.

23 and below = Your organization is not very political. High levels of political skill and behaviors are not needed to be successful and may even be detrimental to success in certain situations.

PART V

Organizational Context

14

Organizations and Culture

Employees who believe that management is concerned about them as a whole person—not just an employee—are more productive, more satisfied, more fulfilled. Satisfied employees mean satisfied customers, which leads to profitability.

—Anne M. Mulcahy, CEO of Xerox

Learning Objectives

By the end of this chapter, you will be able to:

14.1 Describe the basic characteristics of organizational culture

14.2 Discuss the various artifacts of organizational culture

14.3 Identify the functions of organizational culture

14.4 Compare various types of organizational cultures

14.5 Identify key ways in which organizations adapt their practices across cultures

14.6 Describe how international assignments can be used for employee development

14.7 Contrast differing approaches for shaping organizational culture

CASE STUDY: RECREATIONAL EQUIPMENT INCORPORATED'S (REI) ORGANIZATIONAL CULTURE

REI started as a Seattle-based equipment shop for experienced climbers back in 1938. Founded by Lloyd and Mary Anderson, REI was a cooperative to help outdoor enthusiasts acquire good quality climbing gear at reasonable prices. From the beginning, they both knew that in order for customers to buy their products they would need all employees to be experienced with whatever they were selling. In any business, especially one like REI, disengaged employees drag down others and impact customer service, sales, and quality. REI created a culture of engaged employees and continues to lead the way in doing so even today.

In order to take on the most experienced staff, they have always prioritized the well-being of their employees, hoping that the employees would then care for the well-being of each and every customer. With this in mind, it is no surprise then that their first full-time employee was also the first American to summit Mount Everest, and would also become their CEO during the 1960s. What was a small gear rental co-op had diversified into the family camping market focused more on consumer goods by the '80s. With a new less-experienced market of customers required a shift in employee type that made each store member an even more vital piece of the operation. Now that their clientele was made up of fewer mountaineers and more family campers, they needed a staff whose advice families could depend on, making REI a prime example of employee-focused organizational culture.

Today, REI is one of the largest stores of their kind with revenues of $38 billion and over 10,000 employees. While no longer a small company, REI maintains its small-store feel where employees are required to have an intimate knowledge of each product they are selling for the sake of the customer. REI has experienced restructuring over their long history such as their above change in the 1980s from a "co-op" style retailer to a more standard format that offered a wide range of sporting products. Then again, in 2014, REI made another shift back toward that of a cooperative-style store, even rebranding to reflect the new change of business model. All of these changes reflect what the consumer wants at the time and show REI's intimate connection with the needs and wants of their customers.

Innovation is required in order to manage organizational culture long term, and while many companies try to create new fun ideas to handle this, many fail in doing so. REI has something called "company campfire" where associates and executives have the ability to share their thoughts and participate in debates on social media. More than 4,500 of its 11,000 employees have logged on and contributed since its creation. Ideas like this are at the essence of organizational culture. For employees, it offers a voice on things that matter in the most direct way, and for managers, it gives a direct line to the conversations, worries, and complaints of all employees. This is corporate innovation at its finest but without an organizational culture that fits with this method, employees could feel afraid of speaking their minds on important topics, but not at REI.

REI is continually changing and improving, yet the aspect about the retailer that has never changed is how REI treats its customers and employees. While they have an excellent culture and method for managing employees, they understand the need for incentives. Employees in any business are greatly affected by incentives; however, the types of incentives and the way they influence employees varies from industry to industry. REI is consistently a top-ranked company to work for and has been ranked in the top 100 Companies to Work for in the United States since the list's creation in 1998. Of course, there is a reason that REI is in the *Fortune Magazine* Employer Hall of Fame: in fact, there are many. Of its 11,000 employees, all of them have access to healthcare benefits. While many employers give employees discounts on products, REI gives discounts on merchandise, outdoor classes, and also "Yay Day" passes which entitle employees to spend six hours outdoors for pay. When more and more retailers were opening their doors on Thanksgiving to accommodate for Black Friday shopping, REI chose to close their stores for Black Friday altogether. They halted all business both online and in-store and gave employees a paid day off. These are just some of the things that REI does to make sure that its employees are taken care of and happy with their jobs.

These initiatives by REI are what make them a leader in retail, thanks to their satisfied and motivated staff of outdoor enthusiasts. REI understands that the best way to sell outdoors gear is to build itself a staff that is experienced in the outdoors so that they know what they would buy. They create the best employees by hiring the most loyal customers. They aren't just hiring a workforce, they are hiring a walking opinion on all things outdoors. By doing everything they can to incentivize employees to frequent the outdoors, REI shows that it is committed to providing a helpful staff with enough experience to comfortably recommend products on a customer-by-customer basis. These perks along with benefits for all employees and a handful of other incentives leaves REI a large enough pool of potential employees to always have a quality staff on-hand.

With programs like "company campfire" in the place of water-cooler conversations and "#optoutside" in the place of Black Friday frenzies, REI shows that they have always been committed to putting their organizational culture above all else. It shows that REI is committed to their future by protecting their two most vital resources: a place to use their products and employees to sell them. With these two resources intact, REI's business should be a lasting one and should continually grow and change. They continually innovate new ideas to do this more efficiently and to effectively manage their image and it has paid off immensely.

Critical-Thinking Questions

1. Why does REI need employees who are experienced with their equipment just to sell products?

2. Why doesn't REI take part in Black Friday even though it is many stores' most successful day?

Resources:

Boué, K. (2015, September 29). Yay for corporate culture. *Outdoor Industry Association.* Retrieved from https://outdoorindustry.org/article/yay-for-corporate-culture/

Purposeful Connections. (2016, July 14). *REI'S #Optoutside – 10 critical insights for authentic and powerful purpose creation.* Retrieved from http://www.purposecollaborative.com/reis-optoutside-10-critical-insights-for-authentic-and-powerful-purpose-creation/

Silicon Bayou News. (2016, September 7). *How REI, Southwest and Whole Foods built company cultures that drive their success, and so can you.* Retrieved from http://siliconbayounews.com/2016/09/07/rei-southwest-whole-foods-built-company-cultures-drive-success-can/

Vorhauser-Smith, S. (2013, August 14). How the best places to work are nailing employee engagement. *Forbes.* Retrieved from https://www.forbes.com/forbes/welcome/?toURL=https://www.forbes.com/sites/sylviavorhausersmith/2013/08/14/how-the-best-places-to-work-are-nailing-employee-engagement/&refURL=https://www.google.com/&referrer=https://www.google.com/

What Is Organizational Culture?

>> LO 14.1   **Describe the basic characteristics of organizational culture**

The culture of an organization often influences its degree of success or failure. REI profiled in our case study measures its success by the level of knowledge exhibited by its employees when selling equipment to outdoor enthusiasts. We define **organizational culture** as a pattern of shared norms, rules, values, and beliefs that guides the attitudes and behaviors of its employees.[1] People are the most important asset to an organization, and the behavioral side of a culture is as important as, if not more important than, the financial side. REI shows appreciation for its employees by giving them discounts on merchandise, paid days off, and "Yay Day" passes. As we will see, a company that neglects its internal culture is likely to suffer economically.

> **Organizational culture:**
> A pattern of shared norms, rules, values, and beliefs that guides the attitudes and behaviors of its employees

On a more personal level, the type of organizational culture also affects an employee's chance of fitting in and doing well. So how do you know which kind of culture is best for you? Some corporate cultures encourage long hours with few breaks, while others are more relaxed and informal. This is why doing your research on different organizations before you join one is essential. Finding out how employees rate their companies can be a good way of determining whether an organization is the right one for you. Take the 2017 Employees' Choice Awards conducted by online jobs and career community Glassdoor, for instance. Consulting firm Bain topped the list, followed by Facebook and World Wide Technology (WWT), ranking second and third, respectively, on the list of top 50 best companies to work for in the United States. While Bain and Facebook employees credited smart coworkers to be one of the main reasons they enjoyed work, both sets commented that the long hours were definitely a negative. Perhaps one of the most

Facebook employees enjoy a strengths-based organizational culture where they believe in what they are doing and value their relationship with others.

surprising results involved online hospitality service Airbnb which fell from the number 1 spot in 2015 to 35th place in 2017. This big slip in the rankings highlights the cultural tension between Airbnb management and their employees. According to the report, poor communication, fewer opportunities for career growth, and decreased work/life balance were just a few of the complaints made by Airbnb employees.[2]

Take a look at how Julius Veloria, senior account executive at Datavard, views the importance of organizational culture in the OB in the Real World feature.

Components of Culture

Organizational culture can be subtle, with some of its components hidden beneath the surface. As illustrated in Figure 14.1, there are two main components of culture: observable and unobservable.

Observable culture refers to the components of culture that we can see in an organization. For example, personal appearances and dress codes, processes and structures, behaviors and attitudes, and *artifacts* of the culture like awards, myths, and stories[3] (described in more detail following) are all observable parts of organizational culture.

Unobservable culture consists of the components that lie beneath the surface of an organization, such as company values and assumptions.[4] For instance, Dallas-based leading mechanical construction company TDIndustries integrates trust, empowerment, commitment, and humility within its corporate culture. Because of its values-based culture, TD has been ranked in *Fortune* magazine's 100 Best Companies list for the last twenty years.[5]

The components of unobservable culture are often demonstrated in employee behaviors and attitudes. In some cases, the assumptions and values that make up unobservable culture can become so ingrained in employees' mind-sets that their perspectives and behaviors become difficult to change.

Observable culture: The components of culture that can be seen in an organization

Unobservable culture: The components that lie beneath the surface of an organization, such as company values and assumptions

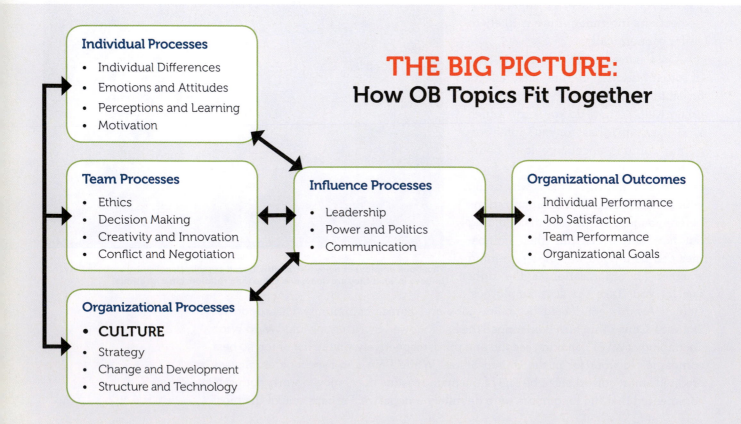

THE BIG PICTURE:
How OB Topics Fit Together

Individual Processes
- Individual Differences
- Emotions and Attitudes
- Perceptions and Learning
- Motivation

Team Processes
- Ethics
- Decision Making
- Creativity and Innovation
- Conflict and Negotiation

Organizational Processes
- **CULTURE**
- Strategy
- Change and Development
- Structure and Technology

Influence Processes
- Leadership
- Power and Politics
- Communication

Organizational Outcomes
- Individual Performance
- Job Satisfaction
- Team Performance
- Organizational Goals

OB IN THE REAL WORLD

Julius Veloria, Senior Account Executive, Datavard

Julius Veloria, the senior account executive at Datavard for North America, has built an acumen in the fields of marketing, technology, and business development. As he looks back at his career, he feels an even sharper sense for the importance of organizational culture. Julius started out of college as a consultant for Accenture and since then has worked at companies from Microsoft to HP and even recently for Taser. Each culture was different regarding the relationship between employees and their respective bosses. Having worn a variety of hats in fields like consulting and data processing, he has seen plenty of examples of when organizational culture goes right and when it goes wrong. Organizational culture, he believes, is often the decider of success or failure even at the start-up level. For this reason, the way that managers approach leadership and the softer sides of an organization contribute greatly to the bottom line. Julius says that the one thing that he has seen differentiate good organizational cultures from bad ones is communication between managers and employees.

The first step toward excellent organizational culture begins with hiring the right people with the right motivations. Julius believes that while it is not the single largest factor, without a motivated group of employees, most initiatives become harder. Julius says, "The best way to be sure that your organization is up to a task is to know that you have a capable team to tackle it." Having worked in a number of organizations with very different cultures, Julius feels confident in saying that organizational culture fit is vital for employee happiness. If an organization does not have the most competent employees, neither they nor the employee has anything to gain. With this in mind, the hiring and human resources are a vital aspect to organizational success.

The next advice that Julius gave for achieving a strong organizational culture was to have a diversity of opinions to make the best decisions. He prefaces this advice by first saying, "While a large amount of diversity in an organization is healthiest, too much of it can cause friction and if managed well, this friction can bring about the best results. If not managed well this friction could become poisonous to success."

Having a diverse formal educational background himself, Julius went to Tufts for mechanical engineering before attending Northwestern's Kellogg School of Management. He says that having degrees in both engineering and business has allowed him to think outside the box in the boardroom and has given him keen insights into how businesses function.

As a manager for many years in a handful of different businesses, Julius has seen that a breakdown in communication between managers and employees happens on both ends. Having a deficiency in the above areas comes from and leads to a breakdown in communication between employees and managers. He finds that poor organizational behavior begets poor organizational culture. Julius says, "When I was consultant, as an outsider, it was so clear when we went into an organization to see if managers and employees were communicating well. Within the first day of being on a project we could tell if everyone was seeing eye to eye and often they were not. What was often the case from my experience was that this lack of communication that we immediately saw was the cause of many of the problems that we were hired to fix." Employees that feel they don't have a voice tend to not speak up and managers that feel they aren't listened to tend to do things that employees disagree with. This bad behavior begetting bad culture is poisonous for an organization and leaves employees unhappy and particularly unsatisfied with their work.

Critical-Thinking Questions

1. What are the two things that a company needs to have in a work force in order to create healthy channels of communication?

2. What are the effects of diversity of opinions amongst employees? ●

Source: Interview with Julius conducted on May 24th, 2017; https://www.linkedin.com/in/veloria/

The Competing Values Framework

Competing values framework:
A procedure that provides a way
to identify, measure, and change
organizational culture

One popular way of approaching the study of organization culture is the **competing values framework (CVF),** which provides a means to identify, measure, and change culture.[6] It is a useful tool to help managers develop the behavioral skills required to deal with the issues arising from an increasingly complex workplace.

FIGURE 14.1

The Cultural Iceberg: Components of Organizational Culture

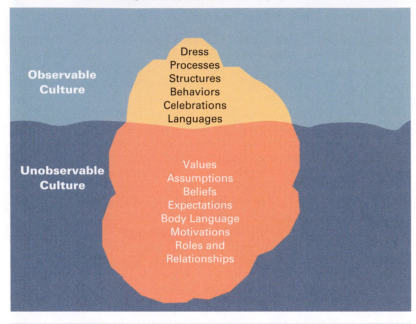

Source: Based on Hall, Edward T. *Beyond Culture* (Oxford: Anchor, 1976).

Gregory Rec/Portland Press Herald via Getty Images

Tom Chappell, founder of Tom's of Maine, fosters a company culture that feels more like a family. This is an example of clan culture.

This model highlights two main value dimensions: the first dimension differentiates *flexibility* and *discretion* from *stability* and *control*. This means that some organizations benefit from a more adaptable, flexible culture whereas others might thrive on a more stable and mechanical culture. The second dimension differentiates *internal focus* and *integration* from an *external focus* in the workplace. In other words, some organizations are effective if they focus on the internal culture, for example ensuring that employees share the same values, integrate well, and work harmoniously, while other organizations focus on building successful relationships outside the organization such as with suppliers, clients, and customers to make themselves more competitive. Amazon, Apple, Costco, and Salesforce are examples of organizations that have focused on enhancing the customer experience to build excellent customer relationships.[7] These two dimensions combined result in four different types of culture: clan, hierarchy, adhocracy, and market (see Figure 14.2).

The *clan* culture falls under the flexibility and internal focus dimension. Typically, clan cultures are welcoming places where employees openly share and form strong personal relationships. Leaders tend to be perceived as mentors and coaches who focus on bringing out the best in each of their employees. The clan culture also furnishes a collaborative environment in which loyalty and commitment are high. Organizations with a clan culture primarily gauge their success against the performance and satisfaction of their employees. Tom's of Maine is a good example of the clan culture. Tom Chappell founded his company, which produces all-natural toothpastes, soaps, and related hygiene products, on the basis of developing strong relationships with a number of stakeholders

FIGURE 14.2

Competing Values Framework

CULTURE TYPE	ASSUMPTIONS	BELIEFS	VALUES	BEHAVIORS	RESULTS
Clan	Human relationships	People are more likely to be loyal and committed when they have trust in an organization.	Collaboration, trust, loyalty, and support	Teamwork, engagement, open communication	Loyalty, commitment, and job satisfaction
Hierarchy	Stability	People behave appropriately in formal organizations governed by rules and procedures.	Communication, consistency, and formalization	Obedience and probability	Efficiency, productivity, and timeliness
Market	Accomplishment	People are more motivated to reach goals when they are rewarded for their achievements.	Communication, capability, and achievement	Goal-setting, competitiveness, planning, researching the competition	Increasing market share and profit, productivity
Adhocracy	Change	People create and innovate when they understand the need for the change.	Growth, inspiration, attention to detail	Creativity, flexibility, adaptability	Innovation

Source: Adapted from Robert E. Quinn and John R. Kimberly, "Paradox, Planning, and Perseverance: Guidelines for Managerial Practice," in *New Futures: The Challenge of Managing Corporate Transitions* (pp. 295–313), edited by J. R. Kimberly and R. E. Quinn, 1984, Homewood, IL: Dow Jones–Irwin.

including employees, customers, suppliers, the community, and the environment. Like many clan cultures, Tom's of Maine, is essentially an "extended family" with Tom serving as the mentor or parental figure.[8] In 2017, Tom's of Maine strengthened ties with the local and greater communities by partnering with New Jersey–based recycling company TerraCycle to collect, donate, and recycle unwanted toys from households across the United States during Earth Month.[9]

The *hierarchy* culture exhibits a combination of stability and an internal focus. Unlike organizations adopting the clan culture, hierarchical organizations like the military can be formal and structured places where employees are

Oracle uses a market culture to justify demanding work schedules, keeping their eye on the competition.

©iStockphoto.com/drserg

primarily guided by processes, rules, and procedures. Hierarchical cultures are run via a formal chain of command populated by leaders who use their positions to manage their employees and to emphasize the importance of efficiency, productivity, and organization in the day-to-day running of operations. McDonald's, the military, or the Department of Motor Vehicles are good examples of organizations operating hierarchical cultures.[10] Organizations that are too rigid and bureaucratic, however, tend not to react well to change.

The Relationship among Dominant Culture, Subculture, and Counterculture

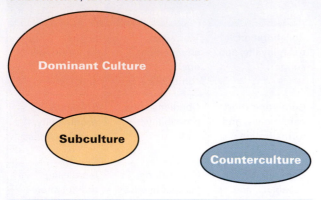

Like the hierarchy culture, the *market* culture is also positioned under the control and stability dimension but places more emphasis on interactions conducted outside the organization with a view to increasing company competitiveness. Leaders tend to be driven and goal oriented and to gauge success on the basis of market performance. General Electric and software giant Oracle are two examples of organizations that drive employees hard in order to beat the competition.[11] Because this is a results-driven culture, there can sometimes be unhealthy competition between employees.

The *adhocracy* culture focuses on flexibility and discretion with an external emphasis. These organizations are fast moving and the quickest to adapt to changing markets. Leaders tend to be entrepreneurs and risk takers who encourage their employees to experiment and generate innovative ideas. Success is measured by company growth and the production of unique, cutting-edge, and innovative products and services. Facebook demonstrates its adhocracy culture by encouraging rapid innovation, based on CEO Mark Zuckerberg's demand to "Move fast and break things—unless you are breaking stuff, you are not moving fast enough."[12]

Although most organizations have elements of all four of these cultural types, some emphasize one type over another. For example, a small family-run business might exhibit characteristics of a clan culture; an investment bank with a strong emphasis on the bottom line may operate as a hierarchy; a results-driven company such as a call center that makes hundreds of sales every day is characterized by elements of a market culture; and start-ups and high-tech firms often have an adhocracy culture.

Though most organizations require different elements from each of the four cultures to operate effectively, none of the elements should be taken to extremes. For example, an organization that is too bureaucratic tends to stifle creativity and can be slow to react to change. Similarly, organizations that are rigidly results driven can damage relationships between competing employees. In the current business environment we find a focus on clan and adhocracy cultures, with an emphasis on strong relationships based on mutual respect built inside and outside the workplace, and in the most successful organizations an environment that nurtures creativity and innovation.[13]

Dominant Culture, Subculture, Counterculture

Dominant culture: Set of core values shared by the majority of organizational employees

Every cultural group has its distinctions. The **dominant culture** is the set of core values shared by the bulk of organizational employees.[14] So, for instance, the executive management team at software company Cadence based in San Jose teaches its employees the importance of giving back by encouraging them to take an extra week off to volunteer for work to help their community.[15]

Subcultures: Groups in an organization who share different values to those held by the majority

In addition to this dominant culture, **subcultures** may spring up, which are groups in an organization that share different values from those held by the majority (Figure 14.3).[16] For example, the Department of Defense consists of different branches such as the Army, Marines, and the Navy. Overall, the dominant culture pervades, but each individual branch has its own subculture made up of unique characteristics. However, it is more common for subcultures to arise in companies where there is no dominant culture, or in the merger of two companies, each of which has a different culture.

An extreme type of subculture whose values strongly differ from those of the larger organization is a **counterculture**.[17] Such groups openly reject the company's values, embrace change, and challenge the status quo. It might seem that these "rebel" groups would be bad for an organization, but a counterculture can also produce positive results. It can instigate a revolution that brings about much-needed change, and contribute valuable perspectives and creative ideas. For example, John DeLorean, division head at General Motors in the 1970s, took steps to create a counterculture that was in direct opposition to GM's corporate culture. The GM culture at that time was based on hierarchy, bureaucracy, and con-

John DeLorean's forward-thinking style ran counter to GM's bureaucratic corporate culture. He eventually left GM to start his own company and created one of the most iconic cars of all time.

formity; employees were expected to defer to seniority and be conservative in their choice of work clothes and office decoration. DeLorean sought to change all this by rallying a group of followers to reject the bureaucratic decision making and conformity, dressing in modern styles and redecorating their offices in bright colors. Although GM tolerated DeLorean's counterculture for a while, when he left to start the DeLorean Motor Company (producer of the famous DeLorean DMC-12, featured in Hollywood's blockbuster *Back to the Future* series), the counterculture he left behind fell apart.

Counterculture: Values that differ strongly from those of the larger organization

Strong and Weak Cultures

When the majority of employees are aligned with the values of an organization, the organization has a strong culture; there is less need for detailed policies and procedures because the rules are accepted and understood.[18] Often cultural values are embedded in value statements; for example, Google communicates 10 "truths" to its employees, one of which focuses on the importance of the user; LinkedIn describes itself as a "human service" business; and wealth management firm RW Baird calls its culture "unique."[19]

In contrast, an organization with a weak culture is one whose core values are not embraced or shared by its employees. This occurs mainly because the core values are not defined or communicated well, which can lead to inconsistent behavior among employees, which in turn can lead to bad service. For example, banking giant Wells Fargo came under fire for opening up to 1.4 million fake bank and credit card accounts. The bank has blamed poor sales practices where employees were placed under immense pressure to reach unrealistic sales goals. Wells Fargo has committed to changing its unhealthy work culture by hiring new management, doing away with its sales goals, and paying millions in refunds to affected customers.[20]

Although strong organizational cultures are valuable for nurturing a sense of unity and providing direction, they usually take a long time to develop and can be difficult to adapt in a rapidly changing environment. In addition, employees can become conditioned to think the same way as their peers and become reluctant to share

©iStockphoto.com/Thomas Faull

After a number of White House lawn security breaches in 2015, an independent investigation into the culture of the Secret Service showed that the organization needed new cultural leadership.

different views—a phenomenon known as **groupthink**.[21] Too much groupthink in an organization can lead to stifled creativity, lack of innovation, and cultural clashes. For example, in 2017, Google employee James Damore was fired for publishing a 10-page document criticizing Google's diversity efforts and ideology. Some employees believe Damore was unfairly dismissed and believe his arguments should have paved the way for further discussion about gender in the workplace. Some believe the Google ideology is so entrenched that groupthink is responsible for pressuring employees to fit into a culture that they don't necessarily agree with.[22]

Groupthink: A phenomenon whereby employees can become conditioned to think the same way as their peers and become reluctant to share different views

THINKING CRITICALLY

1. Why is it important for company leaders to seek employee feedback about their successes and challenges, and what should leaders do with the feedback they obtain?

2. What factors might contribute to the success of a clan culture? Why do these factors affect the company's ability to thrive?

3. Why might a hierarchy culture be comparatively ineffective in dealing with change?

4. Under what circumstances might a counterculture be most likely to arise within a company, and why?

Artifacts of Organizational Culture

>> LO 14.2   Discuss the various artifacts of organizational culture

The artifacts or identifiable elements of an organization provide members and outsiders with a better understanding of its culture.[23]

Stories: Narratives based on real organizational experiences that have become embellished over time and illustrate core cultural values

Newcomers to the company are often told **stories**, narratives based on real organizational experiences that have become embellished over time and illustrate core cultural values. For example, in an effort to attract new talent, technology company Cisco encouraged its employees to provide photos and stories about why they liked working for Cisco. This storytelling approach boosted Cisco's Twitter following four-fold in six months, and increased the amount of traffic to its online career site.[24]

Symbols: Objects that provide meaning about a culture

Organizations may also have a number of **symbols**, which are objects that express meaning about a culture. For example, casually dressed staff gives the impression to any outsider that the organization is a relaxed place to work. The owner of computer service company New York Computer Help believes casual dress is the key to employee satisfaction and higher productivity. He says, "Comfort is definitely king in our workplace. I saw our staff [become] ten times happier and more productive after making the change [to casual wear] a few years back."[25] Few top management staff, and very little hierarchy in the organization is a symbol of its empowering culture.

Rituals: Formalized actions and planned routines

The culture is also supported by **rituals**, formalized actions, and planned routines. A small organization where staff gather Monday at 9:00 a.m. for a question-and-answer and feedback session with the CEO is an example of a company ritual. Another example is senior managers offering an open-door policy that gives employees the opportunity for one-to-one conversations with management at any time.

Another cultural artifact includes **ceremonies**, events that reinforce the relationship between employees and the organization. For example, employee engagement platform TinyPulse hold an annual holiday party to announce the recipients of several awards, honoring employees who go the extra mile, show the most spirit, and demonstrate the most promise ("rookie of the year").[26]

Some companies have a particular **organizational language** which involves the staff using certain words or metaphors and expressions regularly in conversation with each other. For example, in the Google culture, Google employees are called "Googlers," new employees are called "Newglers," and employees who bike together are called "Bikeglers."[27]

Organizations with the most positive cultural artifacts are ones which cultivate independent and innovative thinking, provide meaningful feedback, and emphasize personal responsibility.

Ceremonies: Events that reinforce the relationship between employees and the organization

Organizational language: Words or metaphors and expressions specific to an organization

THINKING CRITICALLY

1. What is the value of an organization's practice of telling stories to new employees? Who do you think would make the most effective storytellers—company leaders or employees of a similar stature?

2. What are three examples of symbols a company could use to demonstrate it cultivates a culture of employee satisfaction?

3. Based on your own experiences, what types of ceremonies might work best to motivate employees, and why?

Functions of Organizational Culture

>> LO 14.3 Identify the functions of organizational culture

Two major functions of organizational culture imperative to an organization's survival are external adaptation and internal integration.[28] **External adaptation** is the way an organization reacts to outside influences. To achieve external adaptation to its environment, the organization must arrive at some basic shared assumptions about its mission and strategy, about the goals, tasks, and methods the organization needs to achieve, and about ways of managing both success and failure.[29] For example, Facebook has responded to competition from image messaging and multimedia mobile application Snapchat by adding similar tools to Snapchat, such as visuals and stories to all of its major Facebook social media apps.[30]

Internal integration, in contrast, is the process of creating a shared identity among employees by adopting a common language, group boundaries, an accepted distribution of power and status, and norms of trust, rewards, and punishment.[31] Every company, regardless of size, needs a degree of internal integration to succeed. Internal integration allows teams to communicate effectively, develop friendships and norms, and define acceptable and unacceptable behaviors. American entertainment company Netflix promotes internal integration by evaluating employees according to their abilities and achievements rather than the number of hours worked. While Netflix sets high expectations, providing its employees with a high degree of autonomy motivates and inspires them to reach their goals.[32]

External adaptation: A pattern of basic assumptions shared between employees of the goals, tasks, and methods that need to be achieved, together with ways of managing success and failure

Internal integration: A shared identity with agreed-upon methods of working together

Potential Dysfunctions of Culture

What happens when cultures become a liability rather than an asset? There are at least three situations in which organizational culture can become dysfunctional and create hindrances: during organizational change, under organizational diversity, and during mergers and acquisitions.

Change hindrances: Obstacles that impede progress and make it difficult for the organization to adapt to different situations

Change hindrances are cultural obstacles that impede progress and make it difficult for the organization to adapt to different situations.[33] Examples of change hindrances are ineffective communication with employees, unclear processes and procedures, disorganized leadership, failure to involve employees, and inadequate resources. For managers to effectively implement change, such as introducing a new system or restructuring a team, they need to minimize resistance by communicating clear objectives, engaging their employees in decision making, equipping them with the necessary resources to support the change, and keeping them fully informed about how and why the change is taking place.

Diversity hindrances: Obstacles that limit the range of employees in organizations

Diversity hindrances are cultural obstacles that limit the range of employee demographics in organizations.[34] As we explored in Chapter 2, diversity can span a wide range of areas, including age/generation, race/ethnicity, gender, and ability. Many of today's organizations cultivate a diverse workforce because of the benefits diversity can bring.

However, despite the trend toward creating more diverse workplaces, managers at many organizations must still overcome cultural and other obstacles to achieve this ideal. Organizations with strong cultures tend to select the same types of employees because they are perceived to best fit the culture. Technology companies in particular score low on workplace diversity, including Facebook, Apple, Twitter, Google, Amazon, Netflix, and Uber.

Organizations that continue to hire the same types of people limit the level of diversity in their organization, which often leads to inequality. For example, the pay inequity between men and women in the workplace has been well documented, as has the lack of minorities in senior positions. Organizations that work hard to overcome diversity hindrances and recognize the value of differences are more likely to have a rich, varied, and productive workforce.

Mergers and acquisition hindrances: Obstacles that make it difficult for two organizations to join together

Mergers and acquisitions hindrances are cultural obstacles that make it difficult for two organizations to join together.[35] Mismatched cultures can lead to a "culture clash" that can have a devastating impact on the success of the merger.[36] For example, since the Amazon and Whole Foods merger in 2017, there has been much speculation about the potential effects of cultural differences between the two organizations. While Amazon has a reputation for being a "hothouse" where employees are expected to work at a relentless pace, Whole Foods fosters a nurturing environment which primarily focuses on the well-being and happiness of its employees. Only time will tell whether these two industry giants can harmonize their very different cultures to create a successful organization.[37]

An organization that encourages innovation through informal interaction may not blend well with one that follows more formal processes and procedures. To break down these cultural barriers, managers in both organizations need to adopt cultural initiatives, which include promoting open communication with and among employees, providing a forum for questions and concerns, and engaging employees in major decisions.

THINKING CRITICALLY

1. Can you think of a company that does well with internal integration and external adaption? Explain how this company does both.

2. Why is it necessary or desirable for employees to understand how and why a company change is taking place? To what extent do you think this best practice is actually followed in the real world?

3. How would a company with a strong culture, and an accompanying tendency to hire the same type of employees, best go about overcoming its diversity hindrances?

FIGURE 14.4

Organizational Cultures

CULTURE	ATTRIBUTES
Positive Organizational Culture	• Employees' strengths supported • High morale • Good work is rewarded
Communal Culture	• Employees think alike • Employees share knowledge • Have clear focus on goals • Goals achieved as a team
Fragmented Culture	• Little socializing • Work as individuals
Mercenary Culture	• Employees measured by level of performance and productivity • High commitment expected • Financial goals are top priority • Little socializing
Networked Culture	• High degree of trust • Employees communicate openly and share information • Mostly work independently, but come together to share ideas • Highly creative
Ethical Culture	• Managers act as ethical role models • Ethical standards communicated clearly • Employees trained to behave ethically
Spiritual Culture	• Focus on tasks that contribute to the good of society • Prioritizes caring, compassion, and support over profit

Types of Organizational Cultures

>> LO 14.4 Compare various types of organizational cultures

Earlier in this chapter, we explored the different types of organizational cultures, namely the adhocracy, clan, hierarchy, and market cultures, through the competing values framework. As we see next, however, many more types of culture exist in the workplace (see Figure 14.4).

Positive Organizational Culture

Organizations with positive organizational cultures focus on supporting employees' strengths, increasing morale, and providing rewards for good work.[38] In this type of culture, employees are active in decision making and kept informed of the organization's vision and direction. They tend to be productive, engaged, and committed to the company. Prescription eyewear brand Warby Parker is a good example of an organization with a positive culture. Its employees are fully committed to the organization's vision, values, and mind-set. Warby Parker fosters an environment which encourages teamwork and fun—sometimes combining the two. For instance, random employees are often sent off to have lunch together in order to boost collaboration.[39]

Communal Culture

Organizations that nurture a communal culture environment are home to employees who tend to think alike, are happy to share knowledge, and have a clear focus on the direction of the task.[40] They are sociable and responsive and work well together to achieve goals. Southwest Airlines has created a communal culture that encourages staff to work together by pitching in and helping out where necessary.[41] The airline has been able to sustain this type of culture because of its very deliberate hiring process—Southwest only hires people who are a good fit.[42]

Fragmented Culture

Fragmented culture is found in companies where employees tend to keep to themselves, avoid socializing, and work as individuals rather than as part of a team.[43] For example, computer programmers often spend long periods of time working alone, which may cause distance and disconnection from the rest of the group.

Mercenary Culture

As the name suggests, mercenary cultures exist in organizations where making money is the top priority.[44] Employees are measured by their levels of performance and productivity and are expected to have a high commitment to achieving organizational goals. Because the culture is task driven, they do not tend to socialize, which can sometimes result in an unfriendly working environment. Uber came under the spotlight in 2017 for its hugely competitive and mercenary culture, where values included "toe-stepping" and "Always Be Hustlin'."[45]

Networked Cultures

Networked cultures are characterized by a high degree of trust between employees and a willingness to communicate and share information.[46] Employees may work independently of each other, but they come together on an informal basis to swap and exchange ideas. Highly creative organizations such as Google, Apple, and Pixar, in which people are encouraged to think differently, tend to have networked cultures.

Ethical Culture

Because of well-documented ethical scandals during the past few years, many organizations are focused on creating more ethical cultures.[47] This means managers need to be role models themselves, communicate ethical standards, and train employees to behave in an ethical manner. To reinforce this type of culture, employees should be rewarded for ethical behavior and punished for unethical behavior. An example of an organization with a strong ethical culture is leading beauty company L'Oréal, which has been recognized by the Ethisphere Institute as the most ethical company in the world because of its strong commitment to responsible innovation, environmental awareness, and social responsibility.[48]

Spiritual Culture

Spiritual culture focuses on opportunities for employees to grow in the workplace by carrying out meaningful tasks that contribute to the good of society as a whole.[49] Organizations with a spiritual culture prioritize caring, compassion, and support for others over profit. There has been some debate over the effectiveness of spiritual organizations, with supporters believing that workplace spirituality enhances the value of the organization, and critics questioning the legitimacy of this type of culture as well as its effectiveness in terms of profit and financial success.[50]

EXAMINING THE EVIDENCE

Organizational Culture and Firm Performance

Organizational culture emerged in the 1970s and 1980s as a concept popularized by practitioner-focused books such as Tom Peters's and Robert Waterman's *In Search of Excellence* and Edgar Schein's *Organizational Culture and Leadership*. Two basic premises developed from these and other similar writings. The first is that organizational culture is derived primarily from the personalities, values, and behaviors of the founders and top executives of organizations. The second premise is that organizational culture is a key determinant of an organization's performance.

More than forty years later, these fundamental assumptions about organizational culture remain largely in place, yet as researchers Charles A. O'Reilly III of Stanford University, David F. Caldwell of Santa Clara University, and Jennifer A. Chatman and Bernadette Doerr of University of California, Berkeley, point out, empirical evidence supporting them is fragmented and inconclusive. These researchers conducted a comprehensive study of sixty firms in the United States and forty-four firms in Ireland to examine these basic assumptions of organizational culture. Their findings provide support for the hypotheses that CEO personality is related to certain types of organizational cultures and that culture is related to firm performance. More specifically, CEOs who are high in openness to experience are more likely to be associated with cultures that emphasize adaptability, CEOs who are high in conscientiousness tend to have more detail-oriented cultures, and CEOs who are low in agreeableness are more likely to have cultures that are results oriented. Their results further show that more adaptable and detail-oriented cultures tend to have higher financial performance outcomes.

Critical-Thinking Questions

1. Why do you think CEO personality and organizational culture affect firm performance? What are the implications for organizations?

2. Based on this evidence, what specific actions can organizational decision makers take to enhance firm performance? ●

Source: O'Reilly, Charles A., David F. Caldwell, Jennifer A. Chatman, and Bernadette Doerr. "The Promise and Problems of Organizational Culture: CEO Personality, Culture, and Firm Performance." *Group and Organization Management* 39, no. 6 (December 2014): 595–625.

Many organizations strive to build an organizational culture that promotes respect and trust for others, loyalty and commitment to the company, and positivity and creativity. Yet achieving a desired organizational culture does not happen overnight; indeed, building culture is a slowly evolving process shaped over time.

THINKING CRITICALLY

1. Of the types of organizational cultures discussed in this section, which would you most like to work within? Which would you least like to work within? Explain your answer.

2. Do you think that promoting a communal culture is compatible with promoting company diversity? Why or why not?

3. If employees don't mind or actually enjoy working in a fragmented culture, should company leaders encourage the continuation of this type of culture? Why or why not?

4. What would be an effective way to reward employees for ethical behavior and to punish them for unethical behavior?

5. Why do critics call into question the legitimacy of spiritual culture? In what types of organizations and industries might spiritual culture be more productive and effective than more common culture types?

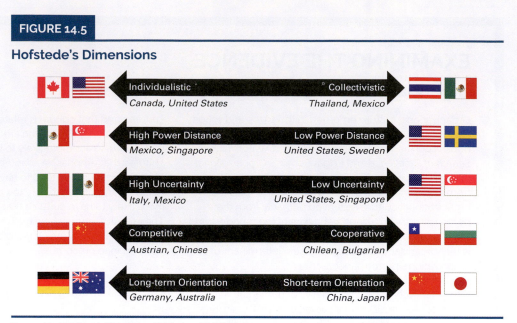

FIGURE 14.5

Hofstede's Dimensions

Source: Neck, C. (2013). *Management* (Hoboken, NJ: Wiley): 122.

Adapting Organizational Practices across Cultures

>> LO 14.5   Identify key ways in which organizations adapt their practices across cultures

One of the main criteria for a successful global expansion is an understanding of different organizational cultures.

One of the most valuable studies in measuring culture was conducted by Dutch sociologist Geert Hofstede. Hofstede identified five ways of measuring culture based on research analyzing the interactions between people from different cultures all over the world. Known as Hofstede's dimensions, these five measures, each of which is shown as a continuum in Figure 14.5, have been used by organizations to improve understanding and cooperation between cultures.[51]

Hofstede's Dimensions

The **individualist–collectivist** dimension focuses on the degree to which citizens in a given culture believe they have the right to live their lives as they see fit, choose their own values, and act on their own judgment. This dimension is usually high in individualist cultures like the United States. In collectivist cultures such as Thailand, people are more likely to value the welfare of the group over that of any particular individual and suspend personal values and judgment for the sake of the "greater good." **Power distance** expresses the extent to which people in different societies accept the way power is distributed. People in countries with *high power distance* such as Mexico and Singapore are more likely to accept the idea of hierarchy and depend on those with power to make the decisions. At the organizational level, high power distance is most common in hierarchical structures where there is very little interaction between lower- and higher-level employees. In *low power distance* countries such as the United States and Sweden, in contrast, people tend to prefer consultation with others and strive to ensure the distribution of power is equalized as fairly as possible.

Uncertainty avoidance measures the degree to which people are able to deal with the unexpected and how they cope with uncertainty in unstructured environments. As Figure 14.5 shows, Italy and Mexico have cultures that emphasize more predictable

Individualist–collectivist: The degree to which employees believe they have the right to live their lives as they see fit, choose their own values, and act on their own judgment

Power distance: The extent to which people in different societies accept the way power is distributed.

Uncertainty avoidance: The degree to which people are able to deal with the unexpected and how they cope with uncertainty in unstructured environments

structures, while the United States and Singapore emphasize variable environments. In countries with a competitive culture, such as Austria and China, employees generally tend to display more assertive, striving, merit-oriented personality traits. In contrast, countries with cooperative cultures such as Chile and Bulgaria tend to take a more compassionate, tolerant, and caring approach. Hofstede used the terms "masculine" and "feminine" to denote the competitive versus cooperative continuum in his work, but the authors consider this nomenclature outdated. Cultures that lean toward **long-term orientation** measure values such as perseverance, respect for tradition, and thrift against **short-term orientation** values such as meeting social obligations and avoiding embarrassment or shame.

Singaporeans are more suited to dealing with a variable environment. This cultural characteristic is reflected in their unique and modern skyline.

Long-term orientation: The measurement of values such as perseverance, respect for tradition, and thrift

Short-term orientation: The measurement of values such as meeting social obligations and avoiding embarrassment or shame

Hofstede has been criticized for using surveys to measure cultural differences, and overgeneralizing national populations on the basis of the limited size of the model, in that there weren't enough respondents to the questionnaires to draw the conclusions that Hofstede had made. Hofstede has responded to these criticisms by defending his use of surveys, noting that the results closely correlated with other data that represented whole national populations.[52]

Although Hofstede's cultural dimensions provide a useful guideline for organizations considering branching out into new territories, every organization is different and will need to take its own particular traits into consideration. At the same time, an understanding of Hofstede's cultural dimensions may help management in one culture determine how best to launch a business in another culture and support new employees.

Global Integration versus Local Responsiveness

International companies face challenges in two major areas when they operate in foreign countries: global integration and local responsiveness.[53] This means they often have to strike a balance between following their own global strategies—determining how their products are made and marketed and how employees are treated—and meeting the legal, financial, employment, and other requirements of their host government. Firms may have to change or tailor their operations to remain in compliance with those requirements. As a result, they have to consider how much they should either standardize or localize their practices.

Standardization is the degree to which employees are expected to follow the same rules and policies everywhere.[54] For example, in a manufacturing plant, teams might follow best practices that are applied globally, such as adhering to certain protocols for safety reasons and ensuring operations go smoothly. When introducing a new product under a global standardized process, teams may perform *upstream functions* such as identifying the market need, devising strategies, and brainstorming ways to bring the product to market. These functions take place behind the scenes and are invisible to the customer.

Standardization: The degree to which employees are expected to follow the same rules and policies everywhere

Localization, in contrast, is the process of adapting certain functions to accommodate the language, culture, or governing laws of a different country.[55] In the case of a new product, teams working in a foreign country might step in to manage the *downstream functions* that focus on sales and marketing of the product after the launch. These functions are centered on improving the flow of the product to the customer.

Localization: The process of adapting certain functions to accommodate the language, culture, or governing laws of a country

1. Do different cultures experience high power or low power distance in business as a reflection of their mode of political governance? Explain your answer.

2. What are two types of industries that would particularly benefit from standardization? What are two types of industries that would particularly benefit from localization? Why?

International Assignments and Career Development

>> LO 14.6   **Describe how international assignments can be used for employee development**

Expatriate: An employee who lives and works in a foreign country on a temporary basis

HIPOs: High-potential employees who are flexible, committed, and motivated

Culture shock: Feelings of nervousness, doubt, and confusion arising from being in a foreign environment

Sometimes employees are sent abroad on international assignments in order to further their personal and career development. An **expatriate** is an employee who lives and works in a foreign country on a temporary basis.[56] High-potential employees or **HIPOs** are employees who are flexible, committed, and motivated.[57] Such employees are often chosen to work on international assignments as part of their career development.

Although international assignments sound like exciting prospects, they can have downsides. Many people underestimate the difficulty of moving to a different country as an expatriate and experiencing **culture shock,** a feeling of nervousness, doubt, and confusion arising from being in a foreign and unfamiliar environment.[58]

If you ever have the opportunity to work on a long-term foreign assignment, avoid culture shock by doing your homework. Research the culture and the language, talk to people who have been in that country to get their advice and feedback, and make sure the job you will be doing is clear from the very beginning. Many employees have accepted assignments overseas only to find the role or the culture (or both) to be nothing like they envisioned. Ideally, organizations should offer support and provide cultural knowledge and language training if necessary to prepare their employees for an overseas experience.[59]

Stages of Cultural Adaptation

Typically, there are five stages of cultural adaptation.[60] (See Figure 14.6.) The first is the *honeymoon* stage that takes place soon after arrival in the new country. Everything is exciting and novel and there is an immediate impulse to explore and soak up the new culture. However, after a few weeks, the *disintegration* stage sets in, the gloss starts to wear off, and feelings of nervousness and insecurity may appear. It might be difficult to communicate with the residents, the food might seem strange, business and social etiquette might be a struggle, and the local laws may seem confusing. For example, in Singapore you can incur a heavy fine for drinking any kind of liquid on public transportation, including water; in Germany putting your hands in your pockets while you are talking to someone is considered rude; and in India saying the word "no" during a business meeting is frowned upon (people say "possibly" or "we'll see" instead).

The third stage is *reintegration,* which typically occurs after a few months in the foreign location. At this stage, you probably have reached an understanding about how the business and social cultures operate and have accepted the factors that seemed strange in the beginning. You may still have mixed feelings about living and working in the society, but you are starting to adjust. During the *autonomy* stage you are more confident about knowing how to function in your new environment, you know how to interact with people and where to socialize, and you have a clearer understanding of business practices. In short, you are beginning to settle in.

This leads to the *independence* stage, in which you understand how the culture operates, feel confident that you can handle most situations, and value the culture for its differences from as well as its similarities to your own.

Expatriate Failure

Global firms hope that most employees who are sent on foreign assignments, particularly expatriates who might be expected to last for a couple of years or more, will reach the independence stage. However, expatriates sometimes return home early for a variety of reasons. There are several reasons why expatriates fail to complete the duration of their stay in a different country.[61] The most common is family stress.[62] Although the employee is experiencing a novel and exciting environment and making new friends at work, the spouse, who may have left a job or career behind at home, may be lonely and struggling to adjust to the new culture, which can put an enormous amount of pressure on a relationship.

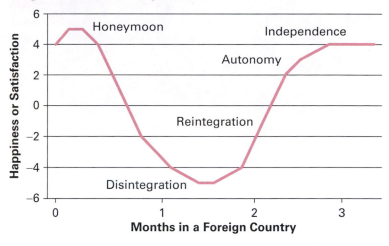

FIGURE 14.6

Stages of Cultural Adaptation

Source: Adapted from Winkelman, Michael. "Cultural Shock and Adaptation." *Journal of Counseling and Development* 73, no. 2 (November 1994): 121–126.

Another factor is that foreign assignments often come with a higher degree of responsibility, which some people find overwhelming. Managing people from different cultures can be frustrating and perplexing, especially if the expatriate is not familiar with local customs. If an expatriate is unable to fulfill the requirements of his or her role or does not possess the emotional maturity to handle additional responsibility, then the organization itself may choose to terminate the assignment.

Finally, another reason for expatriate failure is inability to adjust to cultural or language differences, which often occurs because of poor advance preparation. This can lead to severe homesickness and an early return home.

Benefits and Costs of International Assignments

Are expatriate assignments worth the cost and extra effort to the employee, the family, and the firm? In some companies, a person's career development depends on his or her taking international assignments. For example, an employee working in a US investment bank in New York with branches located globally can gain great experience and make valuable new contacts in one of the firm's international offices. However, "out of sight, out of mind" can also operate. In other words, sometimes expatriates can return home to find they have been overlooked for career opportunities or promotions while away. To combat this issue, employees working abroad must manage their careers by staying in touch with their mentors and remaining in close contact with their biggest work champions back at headquarters, either through modern technology such as Skype, face-to-face when returning to the main office on scheduled trips, or both.[63]

THINKING CRITICALLY

1. What factors should a CEO of an organization take most into account when deciding which U.S. employee to relocate to another country?

Jeff Weiner's values and behaviors are embraced by LinkedIn employees, who are encouraged to follow their passions and take action.

David Paul Morris/Bloomberg via Getty Images

Shaping Organizational Culture

>> **LO 14.7**   **Contrast differing approaches for shaping organizational culture**

Organizational culture can be difficult to change. Unlike many other management functions, shaping organizational culture requires changing mind-sets. In short, it is an emotional process rather than a rational or analytical one, and as we have learned, dealing with emotions in the workplace can be tricky.

Consultancy firm Booz & Co. has outlined a concept called "the critical few" that presents managers with ways to implement effective change within the organizational culture.[64] First, organizations need to define a few *critical behaviors* that managers would like their employees to embody—for example, hire only people who energize others, or make sure employees provide excellent customer service. Once these critical behaviors have been identified, they can be strengthened and nurtured through training until they become a natural part of the company ethos.

Second, focus on a few *cultural traits* that have an emotional effect on employees. What makes employees take pride in their work? What kinds of traits motivate them—loyalty, commitment, trust? Once these traits have been identified, managers can promote them with the goal of encouraging every employee to embrace them.

Finally, managers need to identify the *informal leaders* in the organization. These leaders can exist at every level. They are well liked, trusted, and respected and have a natural way of influencing the behavior of others. Managers need to get these informal leaders motivated to help champion changes and get buy-in from others.

However, change starts at the top, and one of the most important catalysts for change is the behavior of top management.

Influence of Founders and Top Management

Successful organizations tend to be led by top managers who embody certain beliefs, values, and assumptions, thereby influencing employees to do the same.[65] LinkedIn CEO Jeff Weiner is a good example of a leader whose behaviors and values have been embraced by the LinkedIn staff and have become the core of the company's mission. Employees are expected to adhere to five main values: transformation, integrity, collaboration, humor, results. LinkedIn employees are given the freedom to work on projects they are most interested in and are encouraged to take action and contribute ideas.[66]

Selection Practices

Person-organization fit: The degree of compatibility between job candidates and organizations

Managers working in organizations with a certain culture tend to select candidates whose personalities, behaviors, values, and attitudes best match that culture and values.[67] This match is called **person-organization fit.** Research has shown that hiring for organizational fit can be beneficial for both the organization and the employee. Employees who feel that they "fit in" tend to have low levels of absenteeism, are likely to feel stressed about their day-to-day tasks, and experience higher levels of job satisfaction, performance, and productivity. Netflix, LinkedIn, and grooming products organization Walker & Company are just three examples of companies that hire on the basis of person-organization fit.[68] Julius Veloria, featured in OB in the Real World, believes that cultural fit is essential to employee happiness.

Socialization Methods

New hires are integrated into the company's corporate culture through **socialization**, the process through which an organization communicates its values to new employees.[69] For example, when you were hired for your current or most recent job, training probably happened as part of your socialization process. There are three main forms of socialization: context, content, and social dynamics.[70]

Context

Socialization depends on the *context* in which the information is imparted. For example, organizations can choose to socialize new hires through an informal or formal process, and on an individual or collective basis.

New Red Hat employees receive special group training and are each given a red fedora to show that they are now part of the team.

Socialization: The process through which an organization communicates its values to new employees

During an informal process, new hires are put to work immediately so they can learn the company's values through on-the-job training. For example, new hires at house-cleaner matching service Homejoy, regardless of job title, are instructed to go on a "test clean" (scrubbing sinks and toilets) to get a true insight into the company's values and culture.[71]

However, most organizations advocate a more formal approach, including a ceremonial induction or orientation program that introduces new hires to the specifics of the culture and helps build a sense of cohesiveness and identity.

Content

Organizations often provide new hires with *content,* which is information regarding the activities and tasks they may be expected to carry out, and the time each activity should take to complete. This gives new hires a sense of career direction and provides them with an understanding about what they are expected to do and why they are doing it.

Social Dynamics

Socialization also depends on the nature of *social dynamics* that take place once an employee has been hired. Some organizations assign new hires to specific employees who act as role models or mentors. In an effort to promote inclusion in the workplace, PayPal's Unity Mentorship program pairs women with people from the same or different departments and from mixed genders. The goal of the program is to help women thrive through an emphasis on "human connection."[72]

However, in many cases, new hires do not receive formal social support from team members. Left to their own devices, they are forced to figure out the dynamics by themselves, which can result in uncertainty and confusion.

Organizations with successful socialization strategies are more likely to have a positive organizational culture and perform better as a result.

Feldman's Model of Organizational Socialization

Researcher Daniel Feldman identified three phases of organizational socialization experienced by an employee before and after entering an organization.[73] These three phases are anticipatory socialization, encounter phase, and change and acquisition phase. (See Figure 14.7.)

Anticipatory Socialization

Anticipatory socialization takes place before the individual joins the organization. This can happen in several ways. For example, the individual may have talked to current employees to get their opinions about what they like and dislike about the

FIGURE 14.7

Feldman's Three Stages of Organizational Socialization

Source: Based on Feldman, Daniel Charles. "A Contingency Theory of Socialization." *Administrative Science Quarterly* 21, no. 3 (September 1976): 433–452.

organization, or he or she may have researched the company online to get a better sense of the working environment.

Encounter Phase

The encounter phase begins when the individual signs an employment contract and learns more about what the organization is really like. During this phase, the organization may use a number of socializing techniques to help the new employee become better acquainted with the working environment, such as introductions to key members of the organization, classroom or online training, or written guidelines about the company.

Change and Acquisition Phase

When socialization is successful, the employee will have a clear understanding of his or her role and will have learned how to confidently carry out new tasks and skills. This is also the period when new employees adjust to group values and norms and come to understand where they fit into the team dynamic.

Successful organizations work hard to shape the culture by building trust and leading by example. They foster an environment where employees are treated like accountable adults who want to take responsibility for their work processes and do good work. Organizations that take the right steps to nurture a positive culture will go a long way toward maintaining employee engagement, morale, and overall happiness.

THINKING CRITICALLY

1. If change starts at the top, why is it important to identify the informal leaders of a company and motivate them to support company change?

2. How might the beliefs and values of the CEO of an organization with a positive culture compare to the CEO of an organization with a mercenary culture? How would socialization methods for new employees at an organization with a mercenary culture differ from those from a positive culture?

3. How would you rank the three main forms of employee socialization (context, content, and social dynamics) in order of importance to a new employee, and why?

4. What do you consider the most effective way for a new employee to benefit from anticipatory socialization? Explain your answer. ●

Visit **edge.sagepub.com/neckob2e** to help you accomplish your coursework goals in an easy-to-use learning environment.

- Mobile-friendly eFlashcards and practice quizzes
- Video and multimedia content
- Chapter summaries with learning objectives
- EXCLUSIVE! Access to full-text SAGE journal articles

IN REVIEW

14.1 Describe the basic characteristics of organizational culture

Organizational culture is a pattern of shared norms, rules, values, and beliefs that guide the attitudes and behaviors of its employees. Observable culture refers to the components that can be seen in an organization such as dress, structures, behaviors, and artifacts. **Unobservable culture** consists of the components that lie beneath the surface, such as company values and assumptions.

14.2 Discuss the various artifacts of organizational culture

Symbols are objects that provide meaning about a culture. **Rituals** are formalized actions and planned routines. **Ceremonies** are events that reinforce the relationship between employees and the organization. **Organizational language** consists of certain words or metaphors, and expressions the staff use regularly.

14.3 Identify the functions of organizational culture

External adaptation is a shared understanding of the goals, tasks, and methods that need to be achieved, together with ways of managing success and failure. Every company, regardless of how big or small, needs a degree of **internal integration**, which creates a shared identity with agreed-upon methods of working together.

14.4 Compare various types of organizational cultures

Organizations with a *positive organizational culture* focus on building on employee strengths, increasing morale, and providing rewards for good work. Employees in a *communal culture* tend to think alike, are happy to share knowledge, and have a clear focus on the direction of the task. Organizations with a *fragmented culture* have employees who tend to keep to themselves, avoid socializing, and work as individuals rather than part of a team. As the name suggests, *mercenary cultures* exist in organizations where making money is the top priority. Employees are measured by their levels of performance and productivity and expected to have a high commitment toward achieving organizational goals. In *networked cultures* there is a high degree of trust between employees and a willingness to communicate and share information. In an *ethical culture* managers need to be role models themselves, communicate ethical standards, and train employees to behave in an ethical manner. Organizations with a *spiritual culture* focus on the opportunities for employees to grow in the workplace by carrying out meaningful tasks that contribute to the good of society as a whole.

14.5 Identify key ways in which organizations adapt their practices across cultures

Standardization is the degree to which all employees are expected to follow the same rules and policies. **Localization** is the process of adapting certain functions to accommodate the language, culture, or governing laws of a country.

14.6 Describe how international assignments can be used for employee development

The first stage of cultural adaptation is the *honeymoon* stage in which everything seems exciting and new and there is an immediate impulse to explore and soak up the new culture. After a few weeks, the *disintegration* stage sets in, the gloss starts to wear off, and feelings of nervousness and insecurity set in. In *reintegration* the expatriate reaches an understanding about how the business and social cultures operate and accepts the factors that may have seemed strange in the beginning. During the *autonomy* stage he or she knows how to function in the new environment and has a clearer understanding of business practices. This leads on to the *independence* stage of complete understanding about how the culture operates, enough confidence to handle most situations, and appreciation of the culture for its differences as well as its similarities.

14.7 **Contrast differing approaches for shaping organizational culture**

Managers working in organizations with a certain culture tend to select candidates whose personalities and attitudes best match that culture and values. This match is called **person-organization fit**. New hires are integrated into the company's corporate culture through a process of **socialization**, which is a way an organization communicates its values to employees.

KEY TERMS

Ceremonies 409

Change hindrances 410

Competing values framework 404

Counterculture 407

Culture shock 416

Diversity hindrances 410

Dominant culture 406

Expatriate 416

External adaptation 409

Groupthink 408

HIPOs 416

Individualist-collectivist 414

Internal integration 409

Localization 415

Long-term orientation 415

Mergers and acquisition hindrances 410

Observable culture 402

Organizational culture 401

Organizational language 409

Person-organization fit 418

Power distance 414

Rituals 408

Short-term orientation 415

Socialization 419

Standardization 415

Stories 408

Subcultures 406

Symbols 408

Uncertainty avoidance 414

Unobservable culture 402

UP FOR DEBATE: The Importance of Organizational Culture

Organizational culture is what separates a good company from a great company because it is the fastest way toward excellence in all company business activities. A good organizational culture will retain the best employees in a way that cash incentives never will. Agree or disagree? Explain your answer.

EXERCISE 14.1: That's the Way We Do Things around Here!

Consider an organization with which you are very familiar. Ideally, it is one for which you have worked, volunteered, or otherwise served as a member.

Observable Aspects of Culture

If an outsider were to come into your organization, what would he or she see? What would appear striking and characteristic of your organization?

1. List some specific structures and processes, behaviors, and dress and personal appearance factors an outsider might find striking.

    _____

    _____

    _____

    _____

2. What cultural artifacts (stories, rituals, symbols, language) are especially representative of your organization's underlying culture?

_____

_____

_____

_____

Unobservable Aspects of Culture

What aspects of the culture would be less visible to an outside observer? What values, norms, and assumptions are hidden beneath the surface?

1. List the core values, the primary or dominant values that are accepted throughout your organization.

_____

_____

_____

_____

2. What are the basic underlying assumptions of your organization, the taken-for-granted beliefs and philosophies that are so ingrained that members act on them in a given situation without questioning the validity of their own actions?

_____

_____

_____

_____

Categorizing Your Culture

1. Which type of culture does your organization most resemble according to the competing values framework (clan, adhocracy, hierarchy, market)?

_____

_____

_____

_____

2. Perhaps your organization's culture more closely resembles one of the other types of cultures discussed in the chapter (positive, communal, fragmented, mercenary, networked, ethical, spiritual).

_____

_____

_____

_____

3.   Or possibly you would categorize your organization's culture in terms different from any of the following categories described:

_____

_____

_____

_____

Thinking Critically about Your Culture

1.   What aspects of your organization's culture have enabled it to be successful?

_____

_____

_____

_____

2.   What aspects of your organization's culture have constrained or inhibited it from succeeding?

_____

_____

_____

_____

EXERCISE 14.2: What Are the Artifacts of Your University?

Objective

The purpose of this exercise is to grasp the concept of cultural artifacts of organizations.

Instructions

For members of an organizational culture to fully understand their culture, artifacts help articulate the culture in ways that the members can readily appreciate and, in some cases, explain to outsiders.

The text discusses five typical artifacts of organizational culture. They are explained in more detail in the text, but here are short definitions of each:

- **Stories**—narratives based on real organizational experiences that have become embellished over time and illustrate core cultural values
- **Symbols**—objects that provide meaning about a culture
- **Rituals**—formalized actions and planned routines
- **Ceremonies**—events that reinforce the relationship between employees and the organization
- **Organizational language**—words or metaphors and expressions specific to an organization

In this exercise, a student will lead a discussion with the class to determine how each of the artifacts is demonstrated at your university. Once a volunteer student is selected, that student will come to the front of the room and proceed through each of the five artifacts mentioned above as they relate to your university. In other words, what stories are told about the university that truly represent the culture? What symbols exist on campus that express the university's culture? And so on.

Reflection Questions

1. How does your, and even the class's, view about the university's culture differ from that of an employee of the university? Would a student and a university employee completely agree on the culture of the university? Why or why not?

2. Choose an organization you have either worked with in the past or which you are currently employed. What stories, symbols, rituals, ceremonies, and organizational language can you identify in that organization?

3. Who is more likely to *accurately* identify the cultural artifacts of an organization: employees within that organization or outsiders? Explain.

Exercise contributed by Steven Stovall, Southeast Missouri State University.

EXERCISE 14.3: You Got Lucky

Objectives

1. Describe the basic characteristics of organizational culture.
2. Contrast differing approaches for shaping organizational culture.

Background

Upon completing your university degree, you have been hired as a store manager for Clover Supermarkets, and can expect to be promoted to a district manager for McQueen Foods (the corporate owner of Clover Supermarkets) in six to eighteen months if you can show success at Clover. McQueen Foods is a large grocery store chain that has been buying out smaller grocery store chains such as Clover Supermarkets over the past few years. During college, you had worked at a McQueen store and worked your way up to shift manager. You know that McQueen prides itself on caring for its employees and providing excellent customer service while still selling groceries at competitive prices.

You have been managing one of the last free standing Clover Supermarkets for about a month, and you have noticed a big difference between the cultures of McQueen and Clover stores. While all of the Clover employees are polite, none of them seem to have any special drive to provide the extra customer service that McQueen is known for. When customers call, they can be left on hold for long periods of time, and it is very difficult for customers to find help with locating items when they are in the store. Many customers have to bag their own groceries, and it is rare that there is someone who can help customers carry their groceries out to the car. In addition, when workers are asked questions about products, they will rarely be able to answer such questions. And while the store does have a system in place to add new items based on customer requests, such items rarely appear on store shelves.

You are convinced that this lack of customer service has hurt Clover's performance, and that it needs to be changed. Such a change will also help bring the Clover culture in line with the McQueen culture. You are aware of the difficulty in changing any culture, and that if you want to align the Clover culture with the McQueen culture, then you cannot change the service aspect by hurting the respect for company employees or by making prices noncompetitive.

However, you also see this change as a career opportunity for you. If you can successfully change the Clover culture, and provide a blueprint for similar changes at the other stores that McQueen has recently acquired, this accomplishment will greatly help your career progression at McQueen Foods.

To help generate ideas for this change, you have invited other new McQueen store managers that you met in your training program to discuss possibilities.

Instructions

Step 1. Form into groups of five to seven members and develop an outline for the cultural change. The plan must include a clear description of the current culture, a vision for the desired future culture, and methods for changing the current culture to match the future culture. Because of the difficulty in changing cultures, you will want to list multiple methods for changing the key cultural aspects. Also, sequence the cultural change steps as necessary, and list where expected resistance to change can come from. Describe what approaches you might take to overcome these roadblocks. (15 to 30 minutes)

Step 2. Be prepared to present your change plan to the class. (5 to 10 minutes)

Reflection Questions

1. What insights did you gain from thinking of organizational cultures from a change perspective?

2. What disagreements arose about cultural diagnosis in your team?

3. What cultural change ideas were the most difficult for your team to develop?

4. How did the constraints of maintaining worker support and competitive prices make the cultural change more challenging?

Exercise contributed by Milton R. Mayfield, Professor of Business, Texas A&M International University, and Jacqueline R. Mayfield, Professor of Business, Texas A&M International University.

ONLINE EXERCISE 14.1: Examples of Poor Communication

Objective

The purpose of this exercise is to gain an appreciation for organizational culture.

Instructions

In addition to social media, there are many websites available that give a window into the culture of a particular organization. Sites such as glassdoor.com, indeed.com, and careerbliss.com have reviews written about thousands of companies and what it is like to work in those firms.

Choose a large company you are familiar with. Next, go to that company's website—especially the part of the website that describes career opportunities and what the culture is like at that organization. Also, read posts the company has placed on various social media platforms describing what it is like to work at that firm.

Then, read about the company on the career websites just mentioned. Write a two- to three-page report to your instructor that demonstrates what the organization says the organizational culture is like and then compare/contrast what is on the company's website with the anonymous reviews posted on websites such as glassdoor.com.

Reflection Questions

1. Did the company you chose describe an organizational culture that is congruent with what you found on the career websites? How were they similar? Different?

2. How does the firm you currently work for (or your most recent employer) describe its organizational culture? How does that differ from what you have experienced at the organization?

3. Why is there sometimes a difference between what a company promotes on its website and in social media to potential employees about its positive culture and what current and former employees state about the culture?

4. What is the best way to know what an organization's culture is like? Explain.

Exercise contributed by Steven Stovall, Southeast Missouri State University.

CASE STUDY 14.1: Zappos' Organizational Culture

A mind-boggling array of shoes and merchandise, free return policy, and extraordinary customer service helped Zappos reach $1 billion in sales in its eighth year of operation—making it one of the most successful Internet retailers in history and culminating in its purchase by Amazon for nearly $1 billion in 2009. But it's the quirky HR policies and emphasis on happiness and human connection that have earned Zappos thousands of loyal customers and a regular presence on lists of the "Best Places to Work."

Zappos got its start in 1999 when founder Nick Swinmurn pitched the idea of selling shoes online to venture capitalists Tony Hsieh and Alfred Lin. While Hsieh admits he had his doubts, shortly after the launch he jumped on the opportunity to become co-CEO and began developing his "dream corporate culture" and people-centered management style not long after.

Hsieh had sold his start-up, LinkExchange, to Microsoft for $265 million in 1999. But the reason he agreed to sell wasn't price; it was culture. With a hiring strategy based on skills and expertise only, LinkExchange's culture went from exuberant to downtrodden. Hsieh pledged that he'd never run a company that way again and became intrigued with the idea of creating a corporate culture that was everything his earlier start-up was not. He hit the mark with Zappos, which considers itself a customer service company that happens to sell online merchandise.

Something of a philosopher, Hsieh has used Zappos to test his theories on happiness, which is what he claims the company strives to provide. But Zappos doesn't go about ensuring happiness in the typical way. Its salaries aren't great—they are often below market, in fact, and except for 100 percent paid health care benefits, there are few perks. There are, however, lots of great intangibles: nights out with bosses and coworkers that Hsieh often attends; a nap room; a requirement that managers spend 10 percent to 20 percent of their time "goofing off" with their employees; and an emphasis on fun and "weirdness" that affords the opportunity to express yourself at work and feel empowered while doing it.

There are no limits on the time a call center operator can spend on the phone with a customer, for example (the company made headlines in December 2012 with a record-breaking call that lasted 10½ hours), and no scripts to recite. Employees are empowered to make decisions without consulting higher-ups—like offering refunds, or in one case following up a refund with flowers sent to a customer whose husband died unexpectedly after she had ordered him a pair of shoes. Employees are encouraged to be individuals and treat their customers as such—not just as sales figures. All this contributes to what Hsieh calls the "wow" factor in customer service, which keeps his turnover low and his customers coming back while singing the company's praises to others.

"Our philosophy has been that most of the money we might ordinarily have spent on advertising should be invested in customer service, so that our customers will do the marketing for us through word of mouth," said Hsieh. In the beginning, this was a necessity for the cash-strapped company. Now, it's one of its greatest keys to success.

Of course, extending this much freedom to employees implies risk—and this is why Zappos goes to great lengths to make sure it hires the right employees, those who will fit within and contribute to its carefully crafted culture. Its intensive training comes with a unique twist—at its conclusion, prospective employees are offered $2,000 plus compensation for training hours to quit. It's Hsieh's way of weeding out those who are in it for just the paycheck or the goodies—not the type he wants working for him. "We want people who are passionate about what Zappos is about—service. I don't care if they're passionate about shoes."

In late 2013, Hsieh announced he would eliminate hierarchy and job titles in favor of the "holacracy" model in which all work is done in circles. There are "leads" but no managers; circle members make important decisions while leads simply facilitate. The idea is to eliminate politics and bottlenecks and increase innovation. Time will tell whether Hsieh's radical makeover of Zappos' internal workings will produce the intended results. In the meantime, the business world is watching.

Case Questions

1. What was Tony Hsieh's goal regarding organization culture when he became co-CEO of Zappos?

2. Evaluate how the functions of organizational culture are implemented at Zappos.

3. What type of organizational culture does Zappos have? Explain your answer.

Sources

Bloxham, Eleanor. "Zappos and the Search for a Better Way to Run a Business." *CNNMoney.com.* January 29, 2014. http://management.fortune.cnn.com/2014/01/29/zappos-holacracy/.

Bryant, Adam. "On a Scale of 1 to 10, How Weird Are You?" *New York Times.* January 9, 2010. www.nytimes.com/2010/01/10/business/10corner.html?pagewanted=all&_r=0.

Chafkin, Max. "The Zappos Way of Managing." *Inc.* May 1, 2009; http://inc.com/magazine/20090501/the-zappos-way-of-managing.html?nav=next.

Gelles, David. "At Zappos, Pushing Shoes and a Vision." *New York Times.* July 17, 2015. www.nytimes.com/2015/07/19/business/at-zappos-selling-shoes-and-a-vision.html.

Hsieh, Tony. "How I Did It: Zappos's CEO on Going to Extremes for Customers." *Harvard Business Review.* July 2010. http://hbr.org/2010/07/how-i-did-it-zapposs-ceo-on-going-to-extremes-for-customers/ar/1.

"Meet Our Monkies." http://about.zappos.com/meet-our-monkeys/tony-hsieh-ceo.

O'Connor, Clare. "Zappos Mogul Tony Hsieh's Latest Bet: High Tech Fashion." *Forbes.com.* January 1, 2014. www.forbes.com/sites/clareoconnor/2014/01/30/zappos-mogul-tony-hsiehs-latest-bet-high-tech-fashion/.

Rich, Motoko. "Why Is This Man Smiling?" *New York Times.* April 8, 2011. www.nytimes.com/2011/04/10/fashion/10HSEIH.html?pagewanted=all&_r=0.

SELF-ASSESSMENT 14.1

What Is My Cultural Preference?

When considering job opportunities, people generally consider factors such as salary and benefits, but seldom consider their fit with the culture of the organization. This assessment will help you to determine your organizational cultural preference using the competing values framework.

For each item, circle the number that best describes how well the words appeal to you using the following scale:

		NOT AT ALL APPEALING	SOMEWHAT APPEALING	A LITTLE APPEALING	VERY APPEALING	EXTREMELY APPEALING
1.	Strict chain of command	1	2	3	4	5
2.	Outward looking	1	2	3	4	5
3.	Flexibility	1	2	3	4	5
4.	Independence	1	2	3	4	5
5.	Respect for position and power	1	2	3	4	5
6.	Bargaining and decision making	1	2	3	4	5
7.	Vision and shared goals	1	2	3	4	5
8.	Speed and adaptability	1	2	3	4	5
9.	Well-defined policies, processes, and procedures	1	2	3	4	5
10.	Results oriented	1	2	3	4	5
11.	Autonomy	1	2	3	4	5
12.	Experimentation	1	2	3	4	5

	NOT AT ALL APPEALING	SOMEWHAT APPEALING	A LITTLE APPEALING	VERY APPEALING	EXTREMELY APPEALING
13. Coordination and organization	1	2	3	4	5
14. Hard-driving competition	1	2	3	4	5
15. Facilitative and supportive	1	2	3	4	5
16. Innovation	1	2	3	4	5

Scoring

Preference for Hierarchy

Total for items 1, 5, 9, and 13 _____

Preference for Market

Total for items 2, 6, 10 and 14 _____

Preference for Clan

Total for items 3, 7, 11, and 15 _____

Preference for Adhocracy

Total for items 4, 8, 12 and 16 _____

What was your strongest organizational culture preference?

What are some examples of observable aspects of culture (structures and processes, behaviors, dress and personal appearance, stories, rituals, symbols) that might help you recognize this type of culture in an organization you may be considering joining?

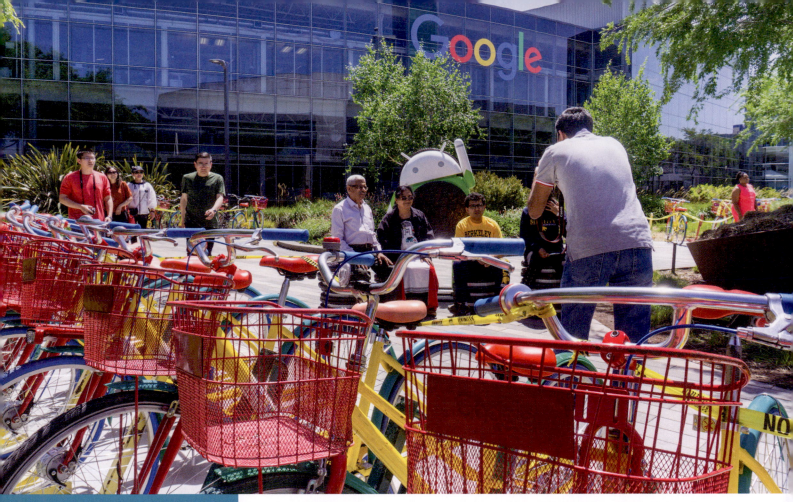

15

Organizational Change and Structure

Imagine a world where most organizations were the best place to work. Imagine what we could be getting done on the planet if it were true.

–Karen May, VP of People Development, Google

Learning Objectives

By the end of this chapter, you will be able to:

15.1 Compare and contrast various conceptualizations of the change process

15.2 Identify the forces for change in organizations

15.3 Describe where resistance to change comes from and how to reduce it

15.4 Discuss how organizational structure helps shape behavior in organizations

15.5 Describe the concept of organizational development in organizations and identify different types of OD change interventions

CASE STUDY: GOOGLE'S ORGANIZATIONAL DEVELOPMENT AND CHANGE

There have been very few companies in the world's history that have had as profound an impact on human life in such a short period of time as Google. In the past eighteen years, Google has grown from a two-man start-up based in a garage to a worldwide tech conglomerate with over 57,000 employees in forty different countries, and around $90 billion in revenues. This kind of growth seems unsustainable. However, Google has shown the world that all it really takes is tireless dedication to corporate adaptability and complete commitment to smooth organizational change and development. Over the course of its life, Google has displayed these attributes excellently through its structural interventions, in terms of altering its rewards systems, changing its culture, and reorganizing the structure itself through job design and division of labor. The tech industry is, by far, the most competitive industry on the planet right now. Tens of thousands of highly qualified candidates from around the world are constantly vying for an opportunity to work at Google. Google not only has greater prestige and growth opportunities than other tech companies but it also has some of the best, if not the best, compensation packages in the world with entry-level employees earning six-figure salaries right off the bat.

In one instance, a Google software engineer was offered a $500,000 salary to leave Google and work for a tech start-up in Silicon Valley but he turned it down because at Google he was being paid a salary worth $3 million! Additionally, around the world Google is known for providing some of the best accommodation allowances in the industry. Thousands of employees have moved from country to country working for the Google brand across the globe and the company has vowed to make this a stress-free activity by essentially paying for all of it. This is one of Google's best offerings to prospective employees in almost every corner of the planet. However, this remuneration philosophy has proven to be, surprisingly, ineffective in the southernmost regions of the Middle East, particularly the United Arab Emirates. According to Marc Schoenen, who himself has moved from the headquarters in California to the United Kingdom and travels frequently, "We try to have a globally consistent model, but it wasn't working in Dubai, so we changed it. Situations like this highlight ongoing discussions about global uniformity and local customization." In order to gain a competitive advantage in the recruiting space in Dubai, Google needed to change how they compensated their employees completely.

After much deliberation, Google decided that the right strategy moving forward was to pay their employees "unfairly," as some have called it, when in reality employees' compensation is entirely based on the impact they have in the organization. This means that, potentially, lower-level employees could earn more than senior employees. "There have been situations where one person received a stock award of $10,000 and another working in the same area received $1,000,000. This isn't the norm, but the range of rewards at almost any level can easily vary by 300 percent to 500 percent, and even then, there is plenty of room for outliers," says Lazlo Bock, Google's Senior Vice President of People Operations.

In the highly competitive tech industry, paying star employees above the average is the only way to ward off competitors such as Uber, Facebook, LinkedIn, and Twitter. Similarly, in the film and sports industries, it simply makes sense to pay top performers top dollar. Schoenen argues, "We believe you can apply the same sports structure to engineering, coding and legal expertise. If you have the right metrics, you can identify star performers in every function. It might only be three people out of one thousand, but these are the people driving your organization and you need to appreciate them." The strategy Google implemented in Dubai is a fantastic example of how important it is to adapt the ways that employees are rewarded to the times. Google identified that, in its competitive industry, allowing competition to continue to thrive within the workplace is what drives maximum output in Dubai. The structure of the employee rewards was altered and now Google is reaping the benefits of its own adaptability.

One of Google's more well-known initiatives is that of its workplace culture. Walking into Google's headquarters to see the swings dangling from the ceilings and beanbags on the floors might make one question if they are actually looking at a Fortune 100 company, but they would be mistaken if they came to any other conclusion. Google identified a very interesting opportunity to be different from every single one of their competitors simply by changing their culture. Years ago, Google set out on a mission to have its various offices and campuses around the globe "reflect the company's overarching philosophy, which is nothing less than 'to create the happiest, most productive workplace in the world', according to a Google spokesman, Jordan Newman." Google's mission was and still is inherently in the favor of every single one of its employees so when this change was implemented there was almost no resistance to it. Often times, widespread organizational change comes with a significant amount of resistance from employees who are accustomed to the status quo. This status quo can lead to what is called structural inertia which makes the process of changing a huge pain for companies. Google was able to steer clear of this barricade by implementing new changes every day, effectively forcing the employees to adapt. That may seem like a very aggressive strategy, however, when you are pushing to make your culture more playful and relaxing by bringing puppies into work and buying thousands of bean bags for your employees, there isn't much pushback from the start. More recently, Google has undergone even more change following a decision to restructure its many components into a series of companies under a new umbrella corporation called Alphabet.

Organizational development, change, and structure is often a very grueling process for even the most successful companies. Yet, Google has mastered the art of OD by integrating a philosophy of adaptability that has become second nature to its workforce as it has swept through all of the silos in the company. Especially in the competitive tech industry, companies like Google must continue to be both agile and adaptive to deal with the pressure of continual change and development.

Critical-Thinking Questions

1. Why might Google's tactics for employee compensation need to vary in different places in the world?

2. Why do companies often run into resistance when trying to implement new organizational development and changes?

Resources:

Crowley, M. C. (2013). Not a happy accident: How Google deliberately designs workplace satisfaction. *Fast Company.* Retrieved from https://www.fastcompany.com/3007268/not-happy-accident-how-google-deliberately-designs-workplace-satisfaction

Google. (n.d.). Retrieved from https://en.wikipedia.org/wiki/Google

Walker, T. (2013, September 20). Perks for employees and how Google changed the way we work (while waiting in line). *Independent.* Retrieved from http://www.independent.co.uk/news/world/americas/perks-for-employees-and-how-google-changedthe-way-we-work-while-waiting-in-line-8830243.html

Yarow, J. (2015, August). Google just announced a massive overhaul of its business structure. *Business Insider.* Retrieved from http://www.businessinsider.com/google-new-operating-structure-2015-8

Master the content
**edge.sagepub.com/
neckob2e**

The Change Process

>> LO 15.1   Compare and contrast various conceptualizations of the change process

Google is a great example of an organization which implements changes in order to stay current. Its advocacy for change has been at the forefront of its success in becoming a global technology giant. Like Google, organizations must be both agile and adaptive to deal with the pressure of continual change. It's not easy to implement change inside an organization, however, and successful change requires careful planning, hard work, cooperation, and excellent communication. Change management has been around for more than fifty years, yet studies show that 60 to 70 percent of organizational change projects fail, despite huge investments in training and education to support them. What are the reasons for these failures? One theory proposes that too many organizations hire outside consultants or experts to design the change projects rather than assigning the responsibility to the managers inside the organization. This means that managers do not get the opportunity to fully embrace the changes, and it weakens their ability to implement the changes effectively.[1]

What happens when a whole industry needs to change? In 2017, sexual harassment claims were made against movie director mogul Harvey Weinstein. Over thirty women came forward to tell their stories about the abuse they had suffered from the now-disgraced Hollywood legend, including major movie stars Angelina Jolie, Gwyneth Paltrow, and Ashley Judd. Since the news broke, dozens of other women have come forward with claims of sexual harassment made by other studio executives. Questions have been raised about how this ongoing abuse has managed to span so many decades without being addressed. Gail Berman, co-owner and founder of production studio the Jackal Group, believes the lack of diversity in Hollywood studios plays a large part—when men outnumber women, they have the power to sustain a culture of abuse, rather than prevent it. "The more women there are in powerful positions, that makes this less likely to happen," says Berman. "As we all know, it's a power issue."[2]

Director Kirby Dick also agrees that more women in the entertainment industry is an effective way to implement change. "Studies show that when women in an institution hold 30 percent or more of the positions of authority, the institution

Chicago Bears quarterback Jay Cutler, along with head coach Marc Trestman, spoke out against hazing new team members and instead promoted a culture of respect in the locker room.

begins to make significant changes," said Dick. "Hollywood is nowhere near that figure."[3]

Although no change in Hollywood studio culture will happen overnight, these shocking allegations will hopefully change attitudes and provoke much-needed discussions about the way women are treated, not only in the entertainment industry, but in workplaces all over the world.

However, in many cases, change does work if it is approached in the right manner. Take the huge changes at petroleum refineries company Hess Corporation, for example. In an effort to strengthen engagement, CEO John Hess challenged the leadership to provide solutions to improve decision making, minimize costs, and become more agile. In addition, Hess created a champions team responsible for ensuring changes were implemented throughout the organization. This all-hands-on-deck approach to change management ensured everyone's involvement in the initiative which made the changes easier to enforce.

THE BIG PICTURE:
How OB Topics Fit Together

Individual Processes
- Individual Differences
- Emotions and Attitudes
- Perceptions and Learning
- Motivation

Team Processes
- Ethics
- Decision Making
- Creativity and Innovation
- Conflict and Negotiation

Organizational Processes
- Culture
- STRATEGY
- **CHANGE AND DEVELOPMENT**
- STRUCTURE AND TECHNOLOGY

Influence Processes
- Leadership
- Power and Politics
- Communication

Organizational Outcomes
- Individual Performance
- Job Satisfaction
- Team Performance
- Organizational Goals

OB IN THE REAL WORLD

Cristina Weekes, *Senior VP, Central Garden and Pet*

Organizational change and development play a daily role in nearly all industries, and they are especially present among growing, successful companies. Perfectly suited to speak on the topic, Cristina Weekes is a Senior VP at Central Garden and Pet (NASDAQ: CENT); she has been with the company for seven years. The $1.55 billion market cap company, based in California, has grown significantly over the last five years, and Cristina primarily manages the dog and cat pet supplies departments. The company supplies many retailers from brick and mortar to e-commerce and owns multiple pet product brands from equine to dog and cat to bird, as well as multiple garden product brands from weed control to grass seed. Cristina has been involved with multiple acquisitions and has become acutely aware of the driving forces behind organizational change, especially during times of complete reorganization.

In 2015, Central Garden and Pet bought a $100 million, thirty-year-old private company. Cristina's close involvement with the merging of the two companies provided her with the chance to direct organizational change on a large scale. The first step to organizational change, as described in the chapter, is unfreezing, and she had firsthand managerial experience with it. The new company had an established culture; it was accustomed to being a privately owned company and the employees had little to no experience with an Enterprise Resource Planning (ERP) system the size of the one used by Central Garden and Pet. Describing the organizational change and unfreezing process, she says, "I had to start

with microcosms of changes and move into larger ones. We started by forming small functional teams from both the old and new companies. The first small project was a demand planning software implementation. This way everyone rolled up their sleeves, worked hard and felt the effects of some success." In this case, Cristina used effective tools in order to unfreeze the traditional operations of the acquisitioned company: start with small steps, and document the changes.

After success with this step-by-step program, Cristina says the company could "rip off the Band-Aid and lean into the system-wide changes." This process, called transformation, involves consistent training, revision, proper timing, and supervision. It took her eight months to complete the merging tasks properly so that the new Central Garden and Pet employees would use the ERP systems efficiently and mix in with the preexisting employees. Cristina says she had to constantly collect feedback from her teams and make informed decisions on the development process. They had to decide when to aggressively require change and adaptation, as well as when to take a step back and let employees move at their own pace. She says she now knows that finding the right employees for the right tasks is one of the most important aspects of the transformation process. Once the new and existing employees were working together, and as soon as they like each other, "the ideas just start flowing," according to Cristina. From that point on, her organization's changes produced a pipeline of collaboration and innovation.

The last step in the process of organizational change, large or small, is to refreeze the new implementations. Cristina gives a simple description of this final step: "Once everyone is looking through the same lens, the last phase is knowing your metrics, and that is when you know you really have a combined culture." Include metrics with a consistent benchmarking effort, and an organization can maintain its new culture, processes, and changes. Her experience is that once new employees begin working toward goals with the same resources alongside existing employees, the company-wide change becomes refrozen as part of the organization. Recording this progress serves to help solidify it.

The three phases of organizational change have played significant roles in Cristina's time with Central Garden and Pet, but she holds a wealth of knowledge about other elements of an organization's change management. She says her own department, as well as the others in the company, actively promote intrapreneurship—in more ways than one. First, employees have open access to

(Continued)

(Continued)

an internal portal called Idea Central, through which they can send their thoughts to other members of the organization. Furthermore, there are regular ideation sessions, in which Cristina brings in experts from across the company; she says this is an effective way to "cross-pollinate between sectors of the company." Then they constantly prototype new concepts. An effective method of managing organizational change is to take steps like these to get out ahead of the competition. The risk of a company not promoting intrapreneurship is that the industry will evolve and leave a company behind.

Like all managers, Cristina experiences resistance to change from her employees. She says that part of her position requires understanding the direction of the company and communicating the company's goals to her many employees. This includes making sure that employees accept the company's goals. Her experience with resistance is that, oftentimes, it solves many problems to allow employees to voice their concerns and to peel back a layer of their frustration in order to investigate the root cause. She says that convincing an employee of the importance of a change is impossible if he or she carries on harboring unspoken complaints.

At times, it requires a negotiation process to manage resistant employees. This process requires that managers show true interest in the concerns and well-being of their teams. In her company, Cristina has discovered that "when people have the opportunity to go to a seminar or take a course, employees know that the company has invested in them, and they are excited to take the course." Something like a seminar is useful, but it is not the only method of convincing employees. Cristina says that it is necessary to promote and accept some form of resistance, and she does every day, because it ensures that a company's direction is well vetted. Through her open communication channels, employee courses, and genuine concern for employee requests, Cristina is able to be an effective change maker. The final piece of the negotiation process for her, and perhaps the most important, is clarity and honesty. "The more honest you are up front, the easier it is to negotiate changes downstream. When employees are clear on the *why*, they can accept the *what* much easier," she says. Managing processes and employees in this way serves to secure long-term, consistent success like Cristina's.

Critical-Thinking Questions

1. List and explain the three primary aspects of an organizational change.

2. Do you think Cristina is an effective change manager? Why or why not? ●

Source: Interview with Cristina Weekes conducted on July 8th, 2017

Overworked and undervalued nurses may suffer from burnout. The position is one of high turnover in certain cultures due to poor working conditions.

©iStockphoto.com/Dean Mitchell

DADA syndrome: Four stages—denial, anger, depression, and acceptance—experienced by individuals when they are faced with unwanted change

Take a look at how, Cristina Weekes, Senior VP at California-based Central Garden and Pet, implemented change arising from a merger in the OB in the Real World feature.

The DADA Process

Managers must tread carefully when addressing concerns; otherwise, they run the risk of inciting the **DADA syndrome**, experienced by individuals faced with unwanted change. The syndrome consists of four stages: denial, anger, depression, and finally acceptance.[4] During the denial stage, people deliberately ignore the change; in the anger stage, they begin to express rage about the change; in the depression stage, they often experience low emotional states and lack of motivation; and finally, in the acceptance stage, they begin to come around to the idea of the change and try and make the best of it. In worst-case scenarios, people will leave an organization if they are unable to accept the changes being implemented.

Lewin's Basic Change Model

Lewin's basic change model to help facilitate the change process. Kurt Lewin was a German American psychologist who developed a three-stage model of planned change that explained how to initiate, manage, and stabilize the change process. The three stages are known as *unfreezing*, *transforming*, and *refreezing*.[5]

Unfreezing

Unfreezing requires explaining the rationale for change, breaking down the status quo, challenging existing beliefs, and understanding how starting on a new path is essential for the company's survival. This is the most difficult and stressful part of the change process, because challenging deeply held beliefs about the way things are done can provoke strong reactions from people.

Following a merger, Cristina Weekes managed the unfreezing process at Central Garden and Pet by forming teams composed of preexisting and new employees to work together on a new project. This was an effective way for employees to get to know each other and bond over a current goal.

Transforming

After the unfreezing stage comes the **transforming** stage, in which people begin to make peace with their doubts and uncertainties and embrace the new direction of the company. However, transformation does not happen overnight. Managers need to give employees time to adjust to change and ensure they are communicating with them consistently and effectively. They need to reinforce their vision for change by providing evidence such as research, documentation, and success stories of other companies that have implemented similar changes. Employees who are still struggling with the changes must be offered more support through training and additional resources when necessary.

Transforming: The process that occurs when people begin to make peace with their doubts and uncertainties and begin to embrace the new direction of the company

Refreezing

When employees appear to have embraced the change, managers use refreezing to reinforce the new approach and help people internalize the changes. This is done by creating reward systems, tracking behaviors, and setting up continuous training to further enhance skills. During this stage, it is very important for managers to promote a sense of stability and consistency in order for the changes to be fully incorporated into daily working life.

Lewin's Force Field Analysis

Before implementing any changes, organizations need to assess the validity of the change. Force field analysis (see Figure 15.1) is a useful decision-making technique that helps to assess the reasons for and against making certain changes.[6] The drivers for change must be stronger than the restraining forces in order for the change to work.

FIGURE 15.1

Lewin's Force Field Analysis Model

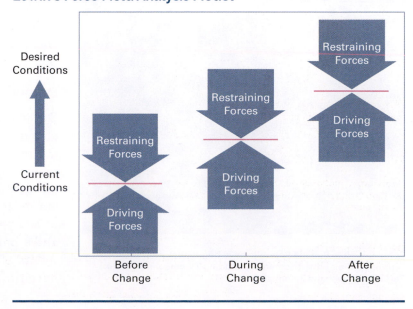

THINKING CRITICALLY

1. Discuss the pros and cons of hiring outside consultants to design change projects. The section mentions that failing to assign this responsibility to managers inside an organization prevents managers from fully embracing changes and weakens their ability to implement them, but what other obstacles to change acceptance and implementation might outside consultants create in an organization?

2. Describe an approach you could take to encourage people to become "unfrozen." Why do you think this approach might work?

3. List possible reasons why an employee would be skeptical of a collaborative organizational culture. As a manager, how could you help an employee overcome such skepticism?

Forces for Change

External forces: Outside influences for change

Internal forces: Inside influences for change

>> **LO 15.2**   **Identify the forces for change in organizations**

Every day, employees are affected by a range of internal and external forces as they try to perform their roles in organizations. Managers who promote an awareness of these forces and make an effort to counteract them have a better chance of creating a more productive and loyal workforce. This means organizations need to adapt to **external forces**, which are outside influences such as competitors' actions and customers' changing preferences, and to **internal forces**, which are inside influences such as company culture and employee diversity.[7]

External Forces for Change

Organizations cannot function in a vacuum—they need to be aware of and respond to events and trends in the outside world. Some examples of these external forces are customers' demographic characteristics, technological advancements, customer and market changes, social and political pressures, and generational changes. Let's consider each.

Demographic Characteristics

Organizations need to adapt to demographic changes such as aging and increasingly diversified customer populations. To deal with these changes, many organizations have tailored their marketing strategies to appeal to a variety of different consumers and to ensure fair treatment for people regardless of age, religion, sexual orientation, gender, or race and ethnicity. For example, brands from the United Colors of Benetton to Banana Republic to Expedia have run ad campaigns featuring interracial or gay

Paul Archuleta/FilmMagic

Companies like Banana Republic have begun featuring same-sex couples in their advertisements, including TV personality Nate Berkus and husband Jeremiah Brent.

couples, while other brands including Amazon.com, CoverGirl, and Microsoft have featured Muslims in their ad campaigns in a quest to involve those who may feel isolated because of their religion.[8]

Technological Advancements

The rapid rise of and continuous innovation in computer and wireless technology means that organizations must move equally fast to compete. Many organizations now use social networks to market their products, build awareness of their brands, and connect more fully with their consumers. For instance, Belgian beer company Maes Beer used social media to spread product awareness by offering a free barrel of beer to anyone who had the last name "Maes" on the condition that they had to share it with twenty of their friends. As a result, over seven thousand people changed their last names to Maes on Facebook, and over the course of six weeks, the beer company received over seventy-five thousand "likes" and half a million visits to their Facebook page.[9]

Customer and Market Changes

Social media has given customers a platform for sharing their opinions in ways that companies have never had to deal with before. Negative feedback from customers that has the potential to reach countless others online can immediately influence sales, and it can also enhance or damage the organization's reputation in the long term. For example, customer comments on review sites like Tripadvisor, Angie's List, and Yelp can help or hurt hotels, local businesses, tourist attractions, and restaurants. Another force for change is changing customer demands, which put pressure on organizations to stay ahead of the competition. Organizations that listen to their customers and keep up with the evolving market landscape are more likely to succeed than those who don't.

Social and Political Pressures

Social values are changing. Consumers are interested in buying environmentally safe products that have been manufactured in an ethical manner, and many organizations have adapted their practices to cater to these values. For example, PACT apparel ensures that every step of the supply chain process is carried out in an ethical manner, including the growing and harvesting of organic nongenetically modified (non-GMO) cotton, before the final high-quality products reach their customers.[10]

Organizations can also be subject to political pressures, and organizations must often comply with new regulations or adapt to existing ones. For example, Facebook, Google, and Twitter could face new regulations on political advertising following the Russian involvement in the 2016 presidential election. Under the new regulations, these social media companies would have to provide greater transparency in political advertising.[11] Facebook and Twitter already have launched new transparency tools that provide users detailed information about the ads running on their social networks.[12]

Generational Changes

Organizations need to be prepared for generational changes which are already impact the workforce. Baby boomers are already retiring and millions more will start exiting their companies over the next few years. When they go, they take with them years of talent, skills, and experience, leaving companies to find ways to bridge the enormous talent gap. Some organizations have already begun to put strategies in place to prepare for this situation, such as promoting millennials to higher management, and creating partnerships where boomers take on roles as mentors and transfer their extensive knowledge to the younger generation.[13]

Internal Forces for Change

Although it is essential that organizations respond to external forces, it is just as important to look inside the organization at the internal forces at play. Issues such as low job satisfaction can influence productivity and cause conflict or strikes. Organizations must address internal problems as soon as they arise and strive to build a positive working environment based on mutual respect, teamwork, and collaboration.[14] Management changes, organizational restructuring, and intrapreneurship are some examples of the internal forces that affect organizations.

Management Change

New CEOs or executive management can have a significant impact on an organization's culture and strategy. For example, when Satya Nadella joined Microsoft as CEO in 2014, he changed the bureaucratic company culture to focus on two main areas: building new technology and making sure teams worked together rather than tearing each other apart. Since Nadella took over as CEO, Microsoft has increased its market share and his leadership style has been widely praised by Microsoft veterans.[15]

Organizational Restructuring

There may be instances when organizations need to change their organizational structure in order to adapt to new strategies, new product lines, or global expansion. For example, WalMart has announced that it is restructuring its divisional and regional groups in order to enhance communication and improve decision making, to keep up with rapid change in the retail sector.[16]

Changing structures means disruption for employees. Communication and training are essential during a reorganization to ensure that employees understand the reasons for the change and the implications it will have for their daily duties.

Intrapreneurship

Intrapreneurship: when employees within a company take risks and come up with new ideas in an effort to solve a given problem.

Many organizations foster a spirit of **intrapreneurship** in their employees by encouraging them to come up with new ideas and new ways of doing things. When an employee suggests something innovative, the organization must consider the best way of implementing the idea, which may mean allocating more resources, putting more people to work on the initiative, or coming up with different branding in the case of a new product. Google is well known for encouraging intrapreneurship: Gmail, Google News, Google Maps, AdWords, AdSense, Driverless Cars, Google Glasses are just a few examples of innovations devised by Google employees from inside the organization.[17]

Although organizations must be aware of both external and internal forces for change, they must also be able to manage resistance to change and understand how to reduce it. We look at this challenge next.

1. Consider the recent move on the part of food manufacturers to remove trans fats from processed foods such as margarine and vegetable shortening. What external force or forces for change (demographic characteristics, technological advancements, customer and market changes, social and political pressures) do you think caused this to occur? Explain and defend your answer.

2. Of the various forces for internal change (management change, organizational restructuring, and intrapreneurship), which do you think has the greatest potential for employee empowerment? Explain and defend your answer.

Resistance to Change

>> **LO 15.3** **Describe where resistance to change comes from and how to reduce it**

One of the main obstacles to implementing organizational changes is **resistance to change**, people's unwillingness to accept or support modifications in the work-place.[18] When people resist change it can affect their productivity, performance, and relationships (see Figure 15.2).

Resistance to change: The unwillingness to accept or support modifications in the workplace

Individual Sources of Resistance to Change

There are ten main reasons for employees resisting change.[19]

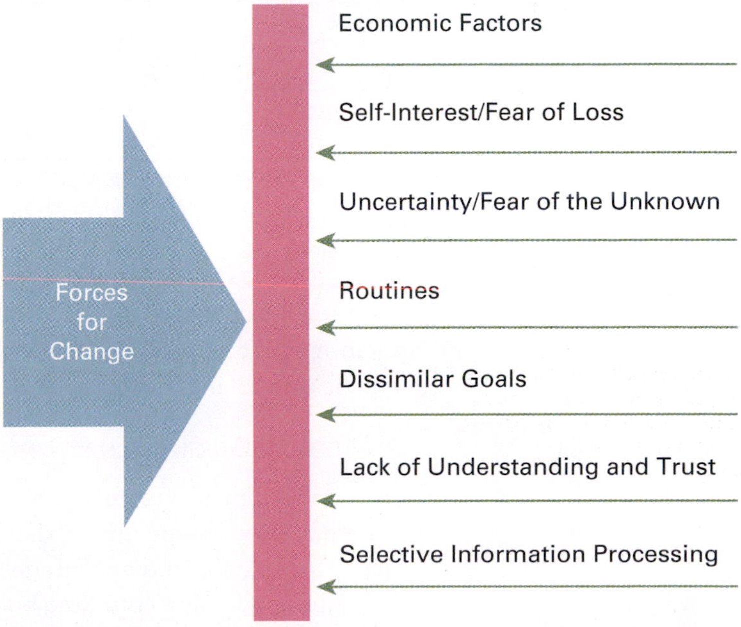

1. **Lack of clarity:** When the argument for change is not communicated clearly, there can be cause for misunderstandings and resistance—especially from long-standing employees, used to the current model who do not see why things have to change at all.

2. **Fear of the unknown:** Concerns about what may lie ahead are a common reason why people resist change. This barrier will only be removed when people are reassured that moving forward is better than standing still.

3. **Lack of skills:** Some people worry that they won't have the right skills to cope with the change. The right communication and appropriate training help to assuage these concerns.

4. **Overcommitment to the current model:** Some people are so invested in the "old way" of doing things, that they perceive any suggested changes as a threat.

5. **Lack of trust:** If employees don't have any trust in their organization, then it is less likely for them to get on board with the changes.

FIGURE 15.2

Sources of Resistance to Change

- Economic Factors
- Self-Interest/Fear of Loss
- Uncertainty/Fear of the Unknown
- Routines
- Dissimilar Goals
- Lack of Understanding and Trust
- Selective Information Processing

Forces for Change

6. **Being left out:** People are more likely to support change if they are well-informed and made aware of the reasons that have led to the changes. This is especially important if their jobs are going to be affected.

7. **Change to routine:** It can be difficult to coax people out of their comfort zones in order to embrace new changes, especially if they have been with the company over a long period of time.

8. **Resignation:** Some people go along with change because they are too jaded to resist it. However, compliance does not lead to job satisfaction. For the changes to really work, people have to be motivated enough to support them properly.

9. **Perceptions of change:** People may resist change if they believe the change is more beneficial to another department or area or if they feel that they will be worse off once the change has been implemented.

10. **Inadequate benefits and rewards:** Many employees will oppose change if they feel unfairly compensated for making the change.

FIGURE 15.3

Psychological Reactions to Change

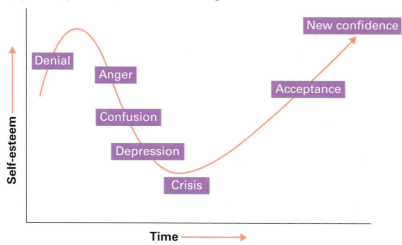

Source: Rick, Torben. 2011. "Top 12 Reasons Why People Resist Change." *Meliorate.* https://www.torbenrick.eu/blog/change-management/12-reasons-why-people-resist-change/

As Figure 15.3 illustrates, poorly communicated policies for change can raise a number of strong emotions such as denial, anger, confusion, and depression. A successful change management model will help to lead employees toward acceptance and provide them with the confidence to cope with the changes.

Kotter's 8-Step Change Model

Research conducted by Harvard business school professor and change expert John Kotter shows that only 30 percent of organizations successfully implement organizational change. As a result of his findings, Kotter created an 8-Step Change Model for leading change in organizations (see Figure 15.4).[20]

1. Create a Sense of Urgency

During the first step, employees must be made aware of how important the change is to them and the organization. This requires honest and open dialogue, outlining the threats and risks of not making the change, and the importance of taking action at this time.

2. Create a Guiding Coalition

It is important to create a project team, preferably composed of employees from different roles and positions, that focuses on the changes required by the organization. This team would encourage the rest of the employees to get on board with the changes and act as a sounding board for those who have any questions or concerns.

3. Create a Vision for Change

For change to work, people need a clear vision of what the organization is trying to achieve. Employees will need to be a part of that vision in order for them to accept the changes ahead.

FIGURE 15.4

Kotter's 8-Step Change Model

Source: Kotter, John P. and Cohen, Dan S., *The Heart of Change*. Boston: Harvard Business School Press.

4. Communicate the Vision

Once the vision has been formulated, it is essential that it is communicated effectively to all employees across the entire organization. Talking to employees and keeping them informed increases the chances of acceptance, especially when their opinions and concerns are taken into account.

5. Remove Obstacles

Change will not be successful unless all obstacles are removed beforehand. In this context, the obstacles are usually employees who are resisting the change. Talking to these employees is the best way of understanding the reasons why they don't want the changes to go ahead. Incorporating their ideas into the change process is also a powerful way to get them onboard.

6. Create Short-Term Wins

Change can be a long process, and employees need to be motivated in order to go the distance. This is why it is important to create short-term goals, where employees are given rewards and acknowledgment when they have successfully achieved their targets. Not only will this encourage employees to continue to pursue long-term goals, but it sends a message to the rest of the organization that the change is definitely going ahead.

7. Consolidate Improvements

Kotter believed that many change processes tend to fail because victory is declared too soon. Change is an ongoing process which needs to be incorporated into the overall organizational culture. Therefore, organizations must promote the idea of continuous change and constantly look for ways to improve processes.

8. Anchor the Changes

For change to stick, it needs to be at the core of an organization. It must match the company's vision and values as well as the behavior of its employees. As time goes on, the changes must still be supported by employees. Building in this new climate of change involves telling success stories, ensuring new hires are made aware of the change ideals and values, and publicly acknowledging the employees most instrumental in the change process.

By following these 8 steps, organizations have a better chance of gaining support from employees, implementing and consolidating the change, and overall creating the right environment for change to take place in the future.

Organizational Sources of Resistance to Change

In addition to individual sources of resistance to change, organizational factors may prove to be barriers. For example, many organizations are based on stability—people are recruited because they fit in with the organizational culture and are then socialized to behave in certain ways through training, rules, processes, and procedures. However, this uniformity can lead to *structural inertia,* which makes an organization slow to change after having followed the same rules and procedures for many years.

Organizations can also fall prey to *limited focus of change,* which arises when only a small number of departments apply the change rather than the whole organization. Confusion often results because the change is not being fully enforced. Another organizational source of resistance to change is *group inertia*. This means that even if individuals agree with the change, they may be constrained by group norms—a situation that often occurs in unions.[21] Groups may also feel that organizational changes are a *threat to expertise*. For example, a data analysis department may feel threatened when a computer program is brought in to perform many of the data functions. The group may resist learning the program for fear it will render their roles obsolete. Furthermore, the group may not want to entertain *decisions that disrupt cultural traditions or group relationships*, which means they will cling to the familiar way of doing things.

Finally, an organization can experience *threat to established power relationships,* particularly when it is undergoing a reorganization. Companies moving from an autocratic structure to a participative or self-managed one are likely to experience opposition from middle managers who may feel their source of power is being threatened.

Reducing Resistance to Change

Typically organizations use different types of methods to deal with resistance to change.[22]

Education and Communication

One of the most common approaches to addressing resistance to change is education and communication. It is best to teach people about the change before it takes place and ensure the message is communicated clearly and effectively. For instance, when Google CEO Larry Page made the significant decision to restructure Google into a series of companies under a new umbrella corporation called Alphabet, he made sure everyone at Google understood the reasons for such a radical change. Page clearly explained why the changes made sense: under the new model, employees would be free to focus on their own goals without being concerned with Google's overall mission, as well as benefiting from more purposeful innovation. While Page acknowledged that change wasn't easy, he felt it was fundamentally necessary to restructure such a diverse organization, "in the technology industry, where revolutionary ideas drive the next big growth areas, you need to be a bit uncomfortable to stay relevant."[23]

Participation

When employees are involved in the change, they are more likely to support it rather than resist it. For example, Jim Whitehurst, CEO of Red Hat, an IT products and solutions organization, believes in including his staff in decisions before they are made. That way, everybody has a voice and an opportunity to share their solutions thereby becoming part of the change process. Whitehurst says, "The best way that I can describe how that feels is that we move most of the 'change management' activities into the decision-making process itself."[24]

Involving employees in organizational changes will make them more invested and more likely to support them.

Negotiation

The negotiation method is generally useful when the employees resisting the change feel they have something to lose. Through negotiation, managers can offer them an improved compensation package or other incentives in exchange for agreeing to implement the changes. However, this approach can be expensive and might encourage others to seek the same treatment.

Manipulation

In certain circumstances, corporate management may use manipulation to encourage their employees to accept changes. For example, an influential figure of seniority might be drafted into the change process, not necessarily to play an active role, but to give endorsement to the change and convince the rest of the staff that the change is a good idea. However, if employees suspect they are being manipulated, it can lead to even more disruption.

Coercion

Coercion is most commonly used in a crisis when leaders need everyone on board with the changes and right away. However, although threatening job losses or providing poor performance evaluations might work in the short term, it usually leaves employees bitter and ultimately less committed to the changes. Research has shown that companies that threaten to fire their employees as a means of motivation can result in insecurity, poor health, burnout, and reduced levels of job satisfaction and performance.[25]

THINKING CRITICALLY

1. Assume you are a senior manager and you want to teach your junior managers skills that may help them adjust their attitude, behavior, and management approach toward colleagues. What are two concrete examples of skills you might teach them, and how would these help?

2. Of the various methods of addressing resistance to change (education and communication, participation, negotiation, manipulation, and coercion), are there any that you feel should never be used by effective managers? Explain your answer.

Organizational Structure

>> LO 15.4 **Describe how organizational structure helps shape behavior in organizations**

So far, we have focused on organizational change. Although change is fundamental to many of today's organizations, it would not be possible without the support of an underlying structure. For instance, implementing change requires installing and empowering people at the right levels of authority, and reacting to change is possible only when the organization's structure reflects its business goals and objectives. We define **organizational structure** as the framework of work roles and functions that helps shape and support employee behavior.[26] There are many different ways to organize work. For instance, Starbucks' global corporate structure is organized around three geographical regions: China and Asia-Pacific; the Americas; and Europe, Middle East, Russia, and Africa.[27]

In contrast, General Mills' US retail operations are structured into divisions based on five product areas: baking, cereal, meals, snacks, and yogurt.[28] On a smaller scale, think of a superstore like a Walmart or Target organized into departments like pharmacy, grocery, housewares, outdoor, and clothing.

Lines of reporting that define who reports to whom are also examples of organizational structure. Workers can report to a shift supervisor who reports to a manager, as at McDonald's; they can function as a team that manages itself, as at W. L. Gore;[29] or they can simultaneously report to multiple managers in different areas of the firm, as at cosmetics manufacturer Procter and Gamble.[30] We take a closer look at all these structures later in the chapter.

For now, note that the structure of an organization has a significant influence on the behavior of its employees. It groups and separates people geographically, hierarchically, or both; it builds and limits relationships by setting up lines of reporting and teams; and it defines employees' responsibilities by outlining their areas of influence and accountability. Many types of organizational structures are possible, and the most successful choices of structure are made with knowledge of the way each structure shapes behavior, including work performance and, to a degree, working relationships. Organizations can undertake rapid reorganizations to make themselves more competitive and adaptable to change. Examples include the division of HP into two separate companies[31] and the splitting of payments system PayPal from eBay.[32] In 2016, South Korean manufacturer Samsung announced that it may split the company in two—one would be a holding company and the other would manage operations—in order to appease shareholders, many of whom believe Samsung's current organizational structure to be too complex.[33]

An organization's structure affects how successfully it can coordinate and accomplish its work activities. (Think about why elementary and high schools organize their students by age rather than by height, for instance.) Several different organizing concepts, such as how specialized a given job is and how many people report to an individual manager, describe the kinds of choices an organization's top managers must make in choosing the most appropriate structure. Let's look at these.

Specialization and Division of Labor

Work specialization, also known as **division of labor,** is the degree to which jobs are divided into specific tasks.[34] When work is specialized, employees who work in a certain department carry out only the tasks that relate to their roles. For example, at a restaurant there might be someone greeting the customers, another person showing them to their table, someone taking their orders, and another person bussing the tables, but all the employees would not perform all these tasks to accomplish the job of feeding customers. The advantages of specialization may include increased efficiency and more accurate production as workers become more skilled in a particular task.

Organizational structure: A framework of work roles that helps shape and support employee behavior

Division of labor: The degree to which certain jobs are divided into specific tasks

However, many organizations are moving away from specialization because too much of it—as when employees repeatedly perform the same few tasks—can lead to bored employees with narrow skill sets. Instead, many companies are widening the scope of their employees' roles and creating environments in which employees can rotate among tasks to broaden their skill base.

Departmentalization

Departmentalization is a process of grouping people with related job duties, skills, and experiences into the same area within the overall organizational structure.[35] Many midsized and larger companies structure their organizations in this way. For example, a manufacturing plant may be divided into production, sales and marketing, accounting, and human resources with very little crossover between the departments (see Figure 15.5).

Chain of Command

Some organizations devise a **chain of command,** a flow of authority and power from the highest to the lowest levels of the organization (see Figure 15.6).[36] As we have explored during the course of this book, many organizations such as Campbell Soup and Microsoft are advocating a more inclusive and participative

A hostess at a restaurant performs different skills from a server or a chef. These specializations allow each employee to be more skilled and efficient at their designated jobs.

©iStockphoto.com/andresr

FIGURE 15.5

Example of Departmentalization Structure

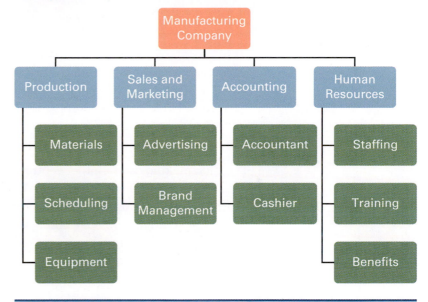

Departmentalization: A process of grouping people with related job duties, skills, and experiences into different areas within the overall organizational structure

Chain of command: The flow of authority and power from the highest to the lowest levels of the organization

FIGURE 15.6

Example of Chain of Command

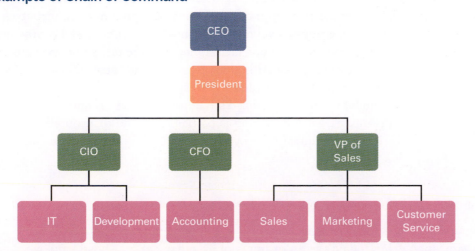

©iStockphoto.com/albertobrian

McDonald's operates with a centralized organizational structure, with decisions and standards being handed down to individual stores from the corporate office.

approach, rather than a strict chain of command such as in the military, as a way to meet organizational goals and objectives.

Span of Control

When organizations expand by hiring more people, the number of direct reports to a given manager usually increases, giving that manager a wider span of control.[37] Some of the advantages for both employees and managers of a wide span of control are better communication and collaboration as more employees are included in the decision-making process, and higher morale as employees are given more responsibility and less supervision. Some of the disadvantages are that managers may lose control over what employees are doing, and they can become overloaded with work.

Companies like Google, Apple, and Facebook prefer a wider span because it encourages the sharing of ideas and communication,[38] although in an organization like U.S. Steel we historically find a narrower span of control, applied in an effort to exert more control over workers.[39]

Centralization and Decentralization

Decision making can be either centralized or decentralized.[40] In a centralized organizational structure, such as McDonald's or Burger King, senior management makes all the major decisions, whereas in a decentralized organization, like New York–based HR solutions provider Lifion, employees are empowered to make decisions without seeking approval from senior management.[41] Again, many organizations are seeking to move toward a decentralized approach because the evidence suggests that empowered employees are a key factor of organizational success.[42]

Mechanistic and Organic Models

Mechanistic model: A formalized structure based on centralization and departmentalization

The **mechanistic model** is a formalized structure based on centralization and departmentalization.[43] There is a definite chain of command, employees tend to work separately rather than collaborating, and there is very little communication between lower-level employees and upper-level management. This sort of model is predominant in manufacturing, where everyone is assigned specific tasks and expected to follow certain rules and procedures. Although the mechanistic structure is relatively easy to implement, it can be difficult to adapt it to rapid change.

Organic model: A less formalized structure based on decentralization and cross-functional teams

The **organic model** is a less formalized structure based on decentralization and cross-functional teams.[44] Decision making is participative and distributed throughout the organization. Communication is open and frequent, and employees are more likely to accept and adapt to change.

Formalization and Bureaucracy

Formalization: The degree to which rules and procedures are standardized in an organization

Formalization is the degree to which rules and procedures are standardized in an organization.[45] McDonald's is an example of an organization whose employees are

EXAMINING THE EVIDENCE

Centralization versus Decentralization: Does Organizational Structure Matter?

Given the trend toward employee empowerment and flexible organizations that can adjust rapidly to changes in the competitive environment, in recent years many organizations have moved in the direction of decentralized organizational structures. But, depending on the situation, can centralized structures be more effective for accomplishing work tasks? That's the question investigated by researchers John D. McCluskey of Rochester Institute of Technology, Jeffrey M. Cancino of Texas State University-San Marcos, and Marie Skubak Tillyer and Rob Tillyer of the University of Texas-San Antonio in a recent study of the organizational structure of detectives in the San Antonio Police Department. On one hand, a community-policing model suggests that decentralized detective units that patrol the streets could develop closer ties with the communities they serve and see better processes and outcomes. On the other hand, the centralization of resources, staff, and decision making could help coordinate information processing when following up leads and provide more rationality and objectivity. The percentage of robberies cleared (solved) by an arrest increased after a reorganization from a decentralized to centralized organizational structure in the San Antonio robbery detectives' department. Interviews with detectives suggested that changes in the collection and use of information, cooperation among detectives, and police-prosecutor interface all improved as a result of the reorganization. These findings suggest that centralized organizational structures remain beneficial in certain situations.

Critical-Thinking Questions

1. What other types of organizations may benefit from centralized structures? Would their employees differ from those in the San Antonio Police Department? How?

2. What are the dangers of generalizing or applying the results of this study to other organizations? ●

Source: McCluskey, John D., Jeffrey M. Cancino, Marie Skubak Tillyer, and Rob Tillyer. "Does Organizational Structure Matter? Investigation Centralization, Case Clearances, and Robberies." *Police Quarterly* 17, no. 3 (September 2014): 250–275.

---

expected to follow strict guidelines. Although there are some benefits to having strict rules, such as less confusion about how and why things are done, employees may become frustrated at the lack of opportunity to exercise their own judgment. Today's organizations tend to follow a less formalized structure to manage employee behavior.

Bureaucracy is characterized by formalized rules and regulation, specialized routine tasks, division of labor, and centralized authority.[46] Bureaucratic structures, such as the IRS or the Motor Vehicle Bureau, tend to follow a chain of command with decision making and power firmly at the top.

There are four main types of organizational structures: simple structures, functional structures, divisional structures, and matrix structures.[47]

Simple structures (see Figure 15.7) are more common in small organizations where there is one central authority figure, usually a business owner, who tends to make the decisions. For example, the owner of a small clothing store might have to manage a cashier and salespeople. Because there are no layers of management, decisions can be made and implemented quickly. However, this structure has its drawbacks. The business owner may become overloaded with work or may be reluctant to delegate when necessary, which could slow down the progress of the organization.

Functional structures group employees according to the tasks they perform for the organization, such as marketing, finance, and human resources. Here employees are

FIGURE 15.7

Simple Structure

Bureaucracy: An organizational style characterized by formalized rules and regulation, specialized routine tasks, division of labor, and centralized authority

Simple structures: Organizational structures, common in small organizations, where is there is one central authority figure, usually a business owner, who tends to make decisions

Functional structures: Organizational structures that group employees according to the tasks they perform for the organization

Divisional structure: (sometimes called *multidivisional structure*) An organizational structure that groups employees by products and services, geographic regions, or customers

managed by means of clear levels of authority. In general, this structure works well for smaller organizations, but there is a risk of lack of communication between the departments because of their tendency to work separately from each other (Figure 15.8).

The **divisional structure**—sometimes called *multidivisional structure*—groups employees by products and services, by geographic regions, or by customers (Figure 15.9).

FIGURE 15.8

Current Pioneering Health Frankfurt Organizational Structure

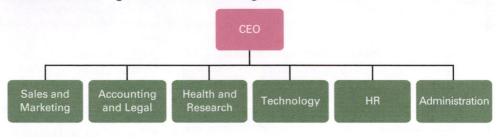

FIGURE 15.9

Pioneering Health and Domestic and Global Divisions

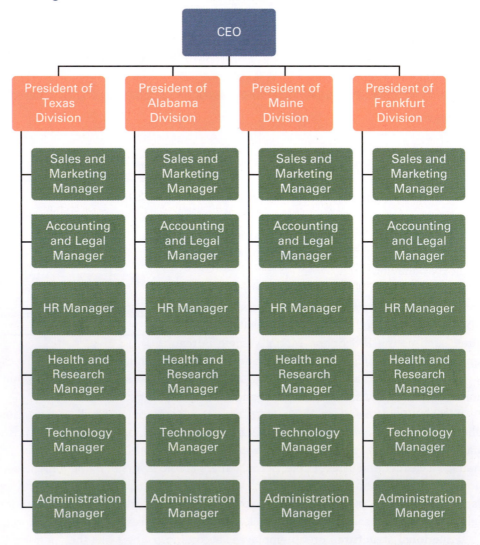

FIGURE 15.10

Matrix Structure

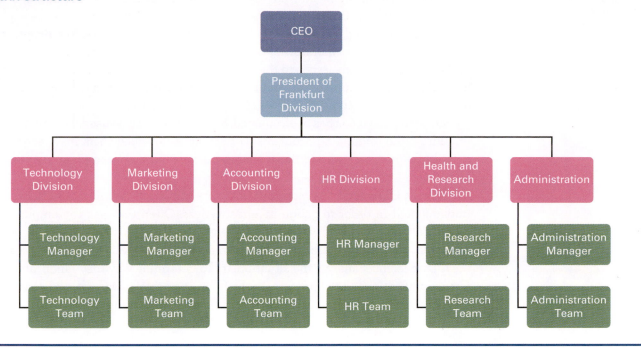

Although divisional structures are ideally placed to meet external demands, divisions that are performing similar tasks—in different locations, for example—may be at risk of duplicating their work. They may also compete for shared resources.

The **matrix structure** is an organizational structure that combines both functional and divisional departmentalization, with dual lines of authority (see Figure 15.10).

Matrix structure: An organizational structure that combines both functional and divisional departmentalization together with dual lines of authority

Organizational development (OD): A deliberately planned system that uses behavioral science knowledge to increase the efficiency and effectiveness of an organization

THINKING CRITICALLY

In what ways will a matrix structure encourage collaboration and communication within an organization more than a functional structure or a divisional structure? Explain your reasoning.

Organizational Development

>> **LO 15.5** Describe the concept of organizational development in organizations and identify different types of OD change interventions

To further reinforce organizational learning, many organizations use **organizational development (OD)**, a planned system that uses behavioral science knowledge to increase an organization's efficiency and effectiveness[48] to cope with internal and external changes. OD researchers and practitioners observe the culture, strategy, and climate of an organization and try to answer

FIGURE 15.11

Organizational Development Techniques

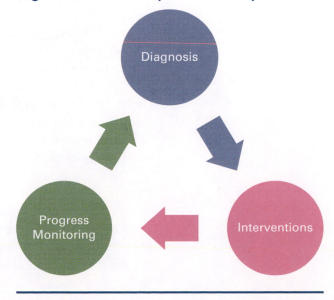

questions such as how do employees communicate? What are their cultural norms, attitudes, and beliefs? How are problems resolved? What is the mood or personality of an organization? Once they have identified these factors, they can begin to work out how to influence the employees' behavior.

Researchers tend to follow three basic steps in an OD model: diagnosis, interventions, and progress monitoring (see Figure 15.11).[49] First they seek to *diagnose* the problem and bring any issues to the surface so they can be resolved. The most common diagnostic techniques are employee surveys (such as job satisfaction surveys), questionnaires, and interviews.

Once this feedback has been collated, *interventions* can be used that are designed to address the underlying problems. For example, OD specialists may recommend team-building exercises, additional training, or role restructuring for employees who appear to be experiencing job dissatisfaction.

Finally, OD specialists *monitor* the effects of the intervention after it has been implemented in order to gauge its effectiveness. Often they ask the employees to complete the same survey post-implementation. This helps identify the change objectives that have and have not been met. When goals have not been reached, the OD specialists analyze the situation, try to determine why they failed, and introduce modifications to the process. In the following section, we take a more in-depth view of the types of OD interventions adopted in organizations.

Types of OD Change Interventions

OD interventions are plans consisting of specific steps to address problems and create solutions in order to implement change in some facet of an organization, with the overall goal of improving the entire organization. Five different types of change interventions are commonly used in organizations: structural interventions, task-technology interventions, sociotechnical systems design, quality of worklife interventions, and people-focused interventions.[50] Let's explore how these interventions work.

Structural Interventions

Structural interventions focus on job design, tasks, and division of labor. Typically, structural intervention is carried out in three different ways: changing rewards systems, changing the culture, and reorganizing the structure itself.[51]

The millennial generation has forced more and more companies to adjust the way employees are rewarded. Research reported by Sodexo Benefits and Rewards Services shows that 84 percent of millennials would prefer to receive experiential rewards over cash rewards, with 17 percent disclosing they would like to share these rewards with their teams. These rewards may include spa trips, days out, or free cinema or theme park tickets.[52]

Chris Baldwin, director of Consumer Programmes at Sodexo, said, "This research shows how important it is to revise benefits and rewards programmes in line with changing employee demands. Rewarding millennial employees with something they can share with others has a number of clear benefits for the business, including team bonding, incentive to continue delivering quality work and greater loyalty."[53]

Clearly, this new approach to employee rewards seems to be working, with over 60 percent of the high performing organizations surveyed showing a clear preference for this type of reward system.

Another type of intervention employed in organizations is *changing the culture*. For example, human resources software company Workday has initiated a small but effective cultural change by moving away from a "performance management" approach, which penalizes low performers, to one which boosts employee efforts through a "performance enhancement" approach. Greg Pryor, vice president of leadership and organizational effectiveness says, "That's only a one-word difference, but it's an important shift."[54]

This subtle cultural change has been supported by a revised employee feedback system, which surveys staff on a weekly basis, to help management understand how they feel about their goals and performance. Pryor believes the system appeals to millennials in particular, who often need regular feedback and dialogue to feel motivated by their roles.

A new generation in the workforce responds more positively to praise as motivation, encouraging many companies to integrate praise into their day-to-day operations.

Finally, organizations may choose to *change the structure* of the organization in order to improve communication, problem-solving, and goal-setting techniques. For example, companies like Zappos and adventure travel company G Adventures advocate flat, more open organizational structures as a means of engaging employees, reaching goals, and staying competitive.

Task-Technology Interventions

Task-technology intervention focuses on changing the tasks people perform or the technological processes they use to carry out their roles in order to enhance productivity and increase job satisfaction.[55] For example, communication platform Slack allows employees to easily exchange messages and files with their managers and coworkers. Yelp, Airbnb, Salesforce, Stripe, and Spotify are among the top companies that use Slack to manage their day-to-day office communications.[56]

Sociotechnical Systems Redesign

In organizational development, **sociotechnical systems** consist of the interaction between human behavior and technical systems.[57] The concept of the sociotechnical system was established to improve the relationship between people and machines to increase organizational effectiveness and efficiency. For example, car manufacturer Volvo was one of the first pioneers of sociotechnical systems redesign. It ended its mechanistic approach—in which people worked separately on a production line, specializing in one task—by creating a sociotechnical system in which a group of highly skilled employees worked together to assemble the cars using a collection of parts. As a result, people no longer felt like they were "machines" and became more motivated, productive, and effective.

Sociotechnical systems:
The interaction between human behavior and technical systems

Thus, if a company is introducing a new technical system, its managers need to consider the people who will be learning and using it. Unlike technology, people are not mechanistic and cannot be "programmed" in the same way. However, many organizations treat the technical system and the users as two separate entities. This is why the organizational change team and the technical team need to communicate regularly throughout the process of redesigning their sociotechnical system to ensure that the new system meets both organizational and human needs. Studies have shown that organizations like Volvo that focus on improving both technical and human systems have a better chance of adapting and responding to change.

Quality of Worklife Interventions

Quality of worklife (QWL): The relationship between the employees and the workplace

Another type of OD intervention is **quality of worklife (QWL)**, which alters the relationship between the employees and the workplace.[58] QWL efforts focus on improving employee satisfaction with pay, compensation, job security, responsibilities, performance, work/life balance, health, and career opportunities. For example, food retailer Trader Joe's nurtures a QWL intervention by providing flexible work hours for their employees, stating on its website, "We don't believe you have to compromise important priorities in your life to be in ours."

People-Focused Interventions

Sensitivity training: A type of program designed to raise awareness of group dynamics and any existing prejudices toward others

Finally, organizations can use different types of people-focused interventions during times of change. **Sensitivity training** is a type of program designed to raise awareness of group dynamics and any existing prejudices toward others.[59] Typically, the members of an organization are encouraged to participate in group discussions, exercises, and role-plays. They are also invited to share their perspectives and to raise any issues that concern them about dealing with different groups. Then they are shown productive ways to alleviate tensions without causing conflict. For instance, soldiers in the US Army and civilians who work with soldiers have begun mandatory transgender sensitivity training to "assist soldiers in understanding Army policy for the military service of transgender soldiers so that they can implement the policy while maintaining morale, readiness, and good order and discipline."[60]

Process consultation: An intervention that involves increasing group awareness and/or understanding

We've seen that organizations sometimes use *survey feedback* to assess the level of job satisfaction in the workplace and take steps to reduce any problems that may hinder success. **Process consultation** is another form of intervention, which attempts to increase groups' awareness or understanding of their behaviors in the workplace.[61] Usually, an outside observer such as a trainer will study the way groups interact with each other and then provide feedback to members in the hope of making them more aware of their attitudes and behaviors and to develop practical solutions to identified problems.

Intergroup development: The process of finding ways to change the attitudes, perceptions, and stereotypes that employees may have of each other

Most organizations use *team-building* exercises to help improve the relationship between groups of employees.[62] These exercises might include physical challenges such as obstacle courses or rowing, or weekend retreats designed to bond employees and teams by giving them a place away from the office to spend time together in informal activities. Team building is also a fundamental part of **intergroup development**, which is finding ways to change the attitudes, perceptions, and stereotypes that employees may have of each other.[63] Part of this approach is to gather different groups together, listen to their perspectives on others, and seek to resolve these views through exercises and discussion.

Over the course of this textbook we have explored many different facets of organizational behavior supported by the latest theory and research, media, and firsthand accounts. As you have learned, organizational behavior isn't just about "common sense"—it is a way of understanding the people you may work with: people who you will likely spend more time with than anybody else—and navigating all their different learning styles, personality traits, and other complexities. Learning the language of OB is an essential skill to master in managing your own behavior as well as the behavior of others.

THINKING CRITICALLY

1. Within the context of an OD model, what research instruments or actions can help managers diagnose problems occurring among their employees?

2. What are some of the types of interventions managers can use to deal with employee-related challenges? Do you see any of these interventions being more effective than the others listed? Why or why not? ●

Visit **edge.sagepub.com/neckob2e** to help you accomplish your coursework goals in an easy-to-use learning environment.

- Mobile-friendly eFlashcards and practice quizzes
- Video and multimedia content
- Chapter summaries with learning objectives
- EXCLUSIVE! Access to full-text SAGE journal articles

IN REVIEW

15.1 Compare and contrast various conceptualizations of the change process

The **DADA syndrome** experienced by individuals faced with unwanted change consists of four stages: denial, anger, depression, and acceptance. Lewin's basic change model is a three-stage model of planned change that explains how to initiate, manage, and stabilize the change process by *unfreezing*, *transforming*, and *refreezing*. Lewin's force field analysis model is a decision-making technique that helps assess the reasons for and against making certain changes.

15.2 Identify the forces for change in organizations

For organizations to succeed they need to adapt to **external forces,** or outside influences such as customers' demographic characteristics, technological advancements, customer and market changes, and social and political pressures, and **internal forces,** or inside influences such as management changes, organizational restructuring, and intrapreneurship.

15.3 Describe where resistance to change comes from and how to reduce it

Some individual sources of **resistance to change** are fear of the unknown, insecurity, and habit. Organizational sources include structural inertia, limited focus of change, group inertia, threat to expertise, and threat to established power relationships.

One of the most common ways to address resistance to change is education and communication before the change takes place. Other methods include participation, negotiation, manipulation, and coercion.

15.4 Describe how organizational structure helps shape behavior in organizations

Organizational structure is a framework of work roles that helps shape and support employee behavior. The structure of an organization has significant influence over the behavior of its employees. It groups and separates people geographically, hierarchically, or both; it builds and limits relationships by setting up lines of reporting and teams; and it defines employees' responsibilities by outlining their area of influence and accountability.

15.5 Describe the concept of organizational development in organizations and identify types of OD change interventions

Organizational development (OD) is a planned system that uses behavioral science knowledge to increase the efficiency and effectiveness of an organization. OD researchers tend to follow three basic steps in an OD model: diagnosis, interventions, and progress monitoring. **Structural intervention** is carried out in three different ways: changing rewards systems, changing the culture, and reorganizing the structure itself. **Task-technology interventions** restructure tasks, redesign roles, or reconfigure sociotechnical systems. **Sociotechnical systems** redesign improves the interaction between human behavior and technical systems. The concept of the sociotechnical system was established to improve the relationship between people and machines to increase organizational effectiveness and efficiency.

Quality of worklife (QWL) interventions focus on employee satisfaction with pay, compensation, job security, responsibilities, performance, work/life balance, health, and career opportunities. Finally, organizations can use different types of **people-focused interventions** during times of change.

KEY TERMS

Bureaucracy   449
Chain of command   447
DADA syndrome   436
Departmentalization   447
Division of labor   446
Divisional structure   450
External forces   438
Formalization   448
Functional structures   449
Intergroup development   454
Internal forces   438
Intrapreneurship   440

Matrix structure   451
Mechanistic model   448
Organic model   448
Organizational development   451
Organizational structure   446
Process consultation   454
Quality of worklife   454
Resistance to change   441
Sensitivity training   454
Simple structures   449
Sociotechnical systems   453
Transforming   437

UP FOR DEBATE: Management's Role in Organizational Change

In the United States, when companies want to execute a major change in the company (e.g., changing a major product or implementing a new system for employee bonuses), upper-level management is under zero obligation to consult employees at all organizational levels to have a voice in the change. What do you think? Agree or disagree? Explain your answer

EXERCISE 15.1: Overcoming Resistance to Change

Objective

The purpose of this exercise is to understand resistance to change.

Instructions

This exercise is a class discussion based upon employees' resistance to change. The text discusses ten individual sources of resistance to change. The ten reasons are provided below and are explained in detail within the text:

- Lack of clarity
- Fear of the unknown
- Lack of skills
- Overcommitment to the current model
- Lack of trust
- Being left out
- Change to routine
- Resignation
- Perceptions of change
- Inadequate benefits and rewards

Your instructor will write each on the board or provide a slide with the ten reasons delineated. As a class, discuss each one from a manager's perspective. As you proceed through the reasons, offer suggestions for steps a manager could take to lessen or remove that particular resistance to change. Be as specific as possible with detailed actions or words the manager could employ in combating each resistance to change.

Reflection Questions

1. Which of the ten reasons for resistance to change is the most challenging for a manager to address? Why?

2. Which of the ten reasons for resistance to change do you engage in most often at work? Explain.

3. What successful strategies have you personally experienced that a manager utilized to combat two or more of the reasons listed above? Why were they so effective?

Exercise contributed by Steven Stovall, Southeast Missouri State University.

EXERCISE 15.2: The Structure versus Strategy Debate

Objective

The purpose of this exercise is to grasp the synergies of structure and strategy.

Instructions

Among organizational behavior researchers, there is often a debate as to which comes first: organizational structure or organizational strategy. On one hand, those who believe that structure is set first suggest that in order to effectively determine the strategy of an organization, organizational structure must be established. In other words, the only way strategy could be crafted is if a structure is in place first. But, on the other hand, those who posit that strategy is implemented first believe that the structure of the organization is created based upon the strategy that the top managers of the organization want to execute. This position of the debate requires that first strategy must be determined before any structure could be created.

This exercise utilizes a debate format to consider the importance of structure and strategy. The instructor will ask the group who believes structure is first priority and who feels that strategy is the first priority. Once everyone has raised their hand for either side of this issue, move to the section of the room that believes the same as you about structure and strategy.

Once you are with those who feel similarly as you, elect two spokespeople to represent your side. The group will offer suggestions, making the case that either structure comes first, or that strategy does. After ten minutes of preparation, the four representatives—two from each side—come to the front of the classroom and begin the debate.

The format of the debate is as follows:

A coin is tossed to determine which side goes first.

The first side has three minutes to make an opening statement. Then, the other side has three minutes to make their opening statement.

After the opening statements, the representatives who made the first opening statement have two minutes to respond. Then, the other side has two minutes for rebuttal.

This continues—two minutes per side—for thirty minutes (or an appropriate amount of time, given any time constraints associated with the class).

Finally, three-minute closing statements are made. The side that gave the first opening statement goes first and then the side that gave the second opening statement has the final word.

During opening and closing statements as well as responses and rebuttals, there can be no interruptions or distractions from the other side or the audience.

Those who remain in the audience can still participate. If they readily see an opportunity for the perfect response, they should write their idea down and hand it to one of their representatives.

Reflection Questions

1. Based upon what you saw and heard during the debate, where do you stand on this issue? Do you think structure determines strategy or that strategy determines structure? Explain.

2. Is your stance on this debate the same if the organization is new (such as an entrepreneurial start-up) or if it is a well-established company (over one hundred years old) that suddenly hires a president from outside the company who wants to establish new strategies and restructure the organization? Explain.

3. In your current or most recent place of employment, has structure taken precedence or has strategy? Explain.

Exercise contributed by Steven Stovall, Southeast Missouri State University.

EXERCISE 15.3: Road to Change and Development

Objectives

This exercise gives you practice in *identifying* organizational change forces, and *describing* change resistance and methods for reducing this change resistance.

Instructions

Background—It is five years in the future and you are working for your state's department of transportation. You have been placed on a task force to provide a smooth transition to automating highway and road maintenance tasks. This change is expected to take two years to implement, and is expected to enable the department to increase efficiency and reduce costs for many maintenance tasks. It is projected that through a combination of retraining and normal workforce attrition, the department can keep 80 percent of the existing workforce and see a 20 percent reduction in its operational budget. As an alternative, 100 percent of the workforce can be retained, but operational savings will be only 10 percent. All cost reductions will be beneficial, but there are political forces that are pushing for the maximum savings possible. In addition, there is a high level of cohesion and solidarity among the road maintenance workers, and they see these potential changes as threats to their and their colleagues' jobs.

For the initial meeting of your task force, you will need to identify the forces that are promoting change, and the forces that will resist the change. In identifying these elements, be sure to discuss both the technical and nontechnical issues related to change, and discuss methods for reducing change resistance. You should concentrate your discussion on concepts from this chapter, but you will also need to bring in relevant concepts from other chapters when developing your plan. You should include both change methods (80 percent and 100 percent worker retention) in your discussion.

You will also find it useful to start with identifying and specifying the desirable future state of your organization.

To develop this plan, you should form into teams of five to seven people. Once you have formed a team, take twenty to thirty minutes to develop the plan and be prepared to have a team spokesperson present your plan in a five- to ten-minute presentation.

Reflection Questions

1. How did the change plans differ under the two scenarios?

2. What elements remained consistent between the two scenarios?

3. What disputes about the change plans arose in your team?

4. What were the easiest change elements to identify and decide upon?

5. How would you expect the change resistance elements to differ if the change time period was substantially longer or shorter?

Exercise contributed by Milton R. Mayfield, Professor of Business, Texas A&M International University, and Jacqueline R. Mayfield, Professor of Business, Texas A&M International University.

ONLINE EXERCISE 15.1: Analyzing Organizational Structure

Objective

The purpose of this exercise is to gain an appreciation for aspects of organizational structure.

Instructions

Conduct an online search of a large company you are familiar with. Try and locate an organizational chart that illustrates the structure of the firm. Once you have found a recent organizational chart, write an analysis for your instructor that describes the organizational structure.

Specifically, your analysis should address the following:

- Discuss the division of labor—does the company seem to employ primarily specialists or generalists?

- Describe the departmentalization—how is the firm departmentalized?

- Assess the chain of command—is chain of command from the front-line associates to the president clearly defined?

- Discuss the span of control—are managers supervising an appropriate number of employees?

- Determine the degree of centralization—based upon the organizational chart, is this company centralized or decentralized?

- Describe the structural model—does the company exhibit a mechanistic or organic model?

Reflection Questions

1. What was the most challenging aspect of organizational structure for you to assess in this assignment? Why?

2. For the organization you currently work for, or a recent employer, assess the organizational structure you have experienced.

3. What kind of organizational structure would you most like to work in? Least? Explain.

4. Why do companies have varying organizational structures? Why are they not all the same?

Exercise contributed by Steven Stovall, Southeast Missouri State University.

CASE STUDY 15.1: Organizational Change and Structure at General Electric (GE)

General Electric (NYSE: GE), headquartered in Boston, is one of the most storied and successful corporations in American history. They have roots all the way back to Thomas Edison and his invention of the incandescent light bulb, when they purchased his company, Edison General, in 1892. General Electric can be found all across homes, consumer products markets, and business-to-business transactions around the world; they are involved in providing everything from refrigerators to wind turbines to financial services and banking. As impressive as their history is, GE must constantly adapt and change their business to stay alive.

The Change Process

Jeff Immelt, the Chief Executive Officer of GE from 2000 until 2017, saw huge success and huge failure, and he found ways to help General Electric adapt to the world around it. The text speaks about internal and external forces, which are forces from inside and outside a company, respectively, that demand action. GE, with Immelt in the corner office, saw much of both. For example, the 2008 financial crisis did not leave GE unscathed: their stock price in 2007 was $40, and by 2009 it was below $10. It makes it difficult for a large conglomeration of companies like General Electric to function effectively when their share price is so low and equity markets are ineffective for raising capital to continue growth and operations, but this external force led to positive organizational change. According to Jeff Immelt, "The changes that took place in the world from 2001, when I assumed the company's leadership, to 2017 are too numerous to mention. The task of the CEO has never been as difficult as it is today." And he is right: when the internet came around, and with it a technology boom, General Electric could have easily been left in the dust as an old industrial corporation. To adapt, GE has become an innovator in technology, began investing in many new businesses, and redesigned old ones.

Immelt, when looking back on his time as CEO and discussing the change-making process, remarks, "It's the leader's job to connect the dots for everyone in the organization." This is a tough task, but an important one. The text mentions resistance to change: a very common phenomenon where employees or managers refuse to embrace change; sometimes they do not want to learn a new method, or they simply do not believe there is a need for a change. Part of connecting the dots, as Immelt puts it, is "to get people in your organization to see the need for change as existential." All future managers should be aware of that fact—that without their full dedication and leadership, they will never get their team to get on board with serious organizational change.

GE Transformations

There is no way for a company to survive a hundred years, or even ten, without undergoing some changes in their identity or services. There are three elements of Lewin's Basic Change model, and General Electric has become familiar with the one in the middle: transformation. This occurs when managers accept the need for change, and begin the difficult process of implementation; this involves important things, like making sure employees are aligned with the transformation. For example, GE started a branch named GE Capital as far back as 1932, and it has grown into a very large financial services operator and financier. The management found, though, that their company had gone astray with too many subsidiaries involved in their essential business offerings, so they defined their core business as industrial businesses and technology. After defining the change, they spent years reframing GE Capital and many other business units to put an emphasis on supporting the core industrial activities.

GE has done a few more things to promote a transformation in the 2000s. They doubled investment in research and development (R&D) in order to ensure they are at the front of the pack in the technology they manufacture; a longstanding company can be disrupted by a start-up on any day unless they transform and innovate constantly. Changes like that require convincing: management has to agree to spend the money, the funds have to be found somewhere, and new teams of employees must be created and work well together. GE also transformed into a global company, and they have operations in over 180 countries. This, too, is part of their core mission to add value in the digital age and stay ahead of disruptors and external forces.

General Electric: Still an Open Case

Charles Dow created the still-famous Dow Jones Industrial index out of twelve companies in 1896, and GE was the only original member still standing up until 2018. Their removal after such a long stay on the list of companies used to measure the health of the American market is only one of General Electric's new problems and largely occurred in response to their recent poor performance in some areas. They have the biggest pension deficit of any company on Standard and Poor's 500 index, meaning that they have outstanding debt to their employees of over $28 billion. They have had to make cuts to their dividends, the money they pay shareholders quarterly, and they will have to raise capital and sell off business units until they can manage both problems, and return to their historic profitability.

GE has seen times worse than these, and they have learned to adapt all throughout the 21st century. The open case now is whether they will change, transform, and fix their problems like they have in the past.

Case Questions

1. Name two transformations that GE has undergone since the turn of the century.

2. What is an external force? Describe one which GE had to react to.

3. Why is GE an open case?

Resources

The Editors of Encyclopaedia Britannica (2018). General Electric: American Corporation. In *Encyclopaedia Britannica*. Retrieved from https://www.britannica.com/topic/General-Electric Immelt, Jeffrey R. "How I Remade GE." Harvard Business Review. September–October 2017 Issue. https://hbr.org/2017/09/inside-ges-transformation

"The 10 Oldest Dow Components." Forbes. May 26, 2011. https://www.forbes.com/2011/05/26/dow-at-115-longest-tenured-stocks_slide/#234d73084e14

Clough, Rick and Kochkodin, Brandon. "GE Cuts $2.4 Billion From Biggest Pension Deficit on S&P 500." Bloomberg. February 23, 2018. https://www.bloomberg.com/news/articles/2018-02-23/general-electric-cuts-2-4-billion-off-s-p-worst-pension-deficit

SELF-ASSESSMENT 15.1

How Resistant Am I to Change?

For each statement, circle the number that best describes you based on the following scale:

	NOT AT ALL ACCURATE	SOMEWHAT ACCURATE	A LITTLE ACCURATE	MOSTLY ACCURATE	COMPLETELY ACCURATE
1. I tend to consider change to be a bad thing.	1	2	3	4	5
2. I prefer daily routine over new and unexpected events.	1	2	3	4	5
3. I would rather be bored than surprised.	1	2	3	4	5
4. When plans change, I tend to get stressed.	1	2	3	4	5
5. If I were told that there would be a major change in how things are done at school or at work, I would probably feel tense about it.	1	2	3	4	5
6. I really dislike changing my plans.	1	2	3	4	5
7. If one of my professors changed the grading criteria in a class, I would feel uncomfortable even if I thought I would do just as well with no additional effort.	1	2	3	4	5
8. I tend to avoid changes despite knowing that they will probably be for the best.	1	2	3	4	5
9. When others pressure me to make changes, I tend to resist even if I think the changes will benefit me.	1	2	3	4	5
10. I tend to avoid changes, even if I know they will be beneficial for me.	1	2	3	4	5
11. I seldom change my mind.	1	2	3	4	5
12. I tend to maintain the same opinions and viewpoints over time.	1	2	3	4	5

Scoring

Add the numbers circled: _____

Interpretation

48 and above = You are highly resistant to change. You prefer set routines and predictability. Even changes that may benefit you may appear threatening.

25–47 = You have moderate level of resistance to change. Although you are comfortable with established routines, you are occasionally open new approaches and changes of plans.

24 and below = You have a low level of change resistance. You are open to new ways of doing things and actively seek ways to break established routines.

Source: Adapted from Oreg, Shaul. "Resistance to Change: Developing an Individual Differences Measure." *Journal of Applied Psychology* 88, no. 4 (August 2003): 680–693.

GLOSSARY

A

Ability diversity. The representation of people with different levels of mental and physical abilities within an organization

Achievement-oriented leadership. Leadership behavior characterized by setting challenging goals, improving performance, and assisting training

Acquired needs theory. Theory that suggests three main categories of needs: need for achievement, need for affiliation, and need for power

Active listening. The act of concentrating on the true meaning of what others are saying

Adjourning. The stage when individuals either leave the team or have no reason to be in further contact with their teammates

Affects. The range of feelings in form of emotions and moods that people experience

Age diversity. People of all different ages included within the workplace

Anchoring and adjustment heuristic. A process whereby people base their decisions on the first piece of information they are given without taking other probabilities into account

Antecedents of conflict. Factors that set the scene for potential dispute

Anthropology. The study of people and their activities in relation to societal, environmental, and cultural influences

Arbitrator. A neutral third party officially assigned to settle a dispute

Assertiveness. The use of demands or threats to persuade someone to carry out a task

Attitude. A learned tendency to consistently respond positively or negatively to people or events

Attribution theory. A theory that holds that people look for two causes to explain the behavior of others: internal attributions, which are personal characteristics of others, and external attributions, which are situational factors

Authentic leadership. A pattern of leadership behavior based on honesty, practicality, and ethicality

Autocratic style. A leadership style based on making decisions without asking for suggestions from others

Availability heuristic. A rule of thumb for making judgments on examples and events that immediately spring to mind

Awareness of others. The way we are aware (or unaware) of the feelings, behaviors, personalities, likes, and dislikes in other people

B

BATNA. The best possible alternative to a negotiable agreement

Behavioral goals (proximal goals). Short-term goals

Behavioral leadership perspective. The belief that specific behaviors distinguish leaders from nonleaders

Big Five model. Five basic dimensions of personality to include neuroticism and frequently used to evaluate and assess people in the workplace

Bonus pay. A pay plan that rewards employees for recent performance rather than historical performance

Bounded rationality. The idea that we are restricted by a variety of constraints when making decisions

Brainstorming. The process of generating creative, spontaneous ideas from all members of a group without any criticism or judgment

Bureaucracy. An organizational style characterized by formalized rules and regulation, specialized routine tasks, division of labor, and centralized authority

C

Ceremonies. Events that reinforce the relationship between employees and the organization

Chain of command. The flow of authority and power from the highest to the lowest levels of the organization

Change hindrances. Obstacles that impede progress and make it difficult for the organization to adapt to different situations

Channel richness. The capacity to communicate and understand information between people and organizations

Charismatic leadership. The ability of a leader to use his or her personality or charm to inspire, motivate, and acquire loyalty and commitment from employees

Classical conditioning. A conditioning concept developed by Russian physiologist Ivan Pavlov that suggests that learning can be accomplished through the use of stimuli

Cluster chain. A type of communication that occurs when a group of people broadcast information within a larger group

Coalition building. Gathering the support of others as a reason for another person to agree to a request

Coercive power. A strategy by which a person controls the behavior of others through punishments, threats, or sanctions

Cognitive dissonance. The inconsistency between a person's beliefs, attitudes, or behaviors

Cohesion. The degree to which team members connect with each other

Common-information bias. The inclination to overemphasize information held by the majority of group members while failing to consider other perspectives held by the minority

Communication. The act of transmitting thoughts, processes, and ideas through a variety of channels

Competence. The ability to perform work tasks successfully

Competing values framework. A procedure that provides a way to identify, measure, and change organizational culture

Competitive advantage. The edge that gives organizations a more beneficial position than their competitors and allows them to generate more profits and retain more customers

Complete rationality. The assumption that we take in to account every single criterion or possible alternative to make a decision

Compliance. The behavior of targets of influence who agree to readily carry out the requests of the leader

Compressed workweeks. A work arrangement that gives employees the benefit of an extra day off by allowing them to work their usual number of hours in fewer days per pay period

Conceptual skill. The capacity to see the organization as a whole and understand how each part relates to each other and how it fits into its overall environment

Conciliator. A neutral third party who is informally assigned to persuade opponents to communicate

Confirmation bias. The tendency to seek out information that fuels our preexisting views and to discount information that conflicts with our worldview

Conflict. A clash between individuals or groups in relation to different opinions, thought processes, and perceptions

Consideration. A behavioral leadership style demonstrated by leaders who develop mutual trust and respect and actively build interpersonal relationships with their followers

Consultation. The offer of participation or consultation in the decision-making process

Content theories. Theories that explain why people have different needs at different times and how these needs motivate behavior, such as Maslow's hierarchy of needs, Alderfer's ERG theory, McClelland's need theory, and Herzberg's two-factor theory

Contingency leadership perspective. The view that the effectiveness of the leader relates to the interaction of the leader's traits or behaviors with situational factors

Contingency thinking. The approach that describes actions as dependent on the nature of the situation; one size does not fit all

Continuous reinforcement. A reinforcement schedule in which a reward occurs after each instance of a behavior or set of behaviors

Contrast effect. An effect that takes place when people rank something higher or lower than they should as a result of exposure to recent events or situations

Conventional morality. The second stage (adolescence and early adulthood) of moral development where moral decisions are based on standards set by adult role models and societal norms

Coping. The effort to manage, reduce, or minimize stressors

Corporate social responsibility (CSR). A business approach that delivers economic, social, and environmental benefits to stakeholders in order to contribute to sustainable development

Correlation. A reciprocal relationship between two or more factors

Counterculture. Values that differ strongly from those of the larger organization

Counterproductive work behaviors. Voluntary behaviors that purposefully disrupt or harm the organization

Creative potential. The skills and capacity to generate ideas

Creativity. The generation of meaningful ideas by individuals or teams

Critical thinking. The ability to use intelligence, knowledge, and skills to question and carefully explore situations and arrive at thoughtful conclusions based on evidence and reason

Cross-cultural leadership. The process of leading across cultures

Cross-functional team. A group of workers from different units with various areas of expertise, assembled to address certain issues

Culture shock. Feelings of nervousness, doubt, and confusion arising from being in a foreign environment

D

DADA syndrome. Four stages—denial, anger, depression, and acceptance—experienced by individuals when they are faced with unwanted change

Decentralization. The distribution of power across all levels of the organization

Decision making. The action or process of identifying a strategy to resolve problems

Deep acting. Efforts to change your actual emotions to better match the required emotions of the situation

Deep-level diversity. Differences in verbal and nonverbal behaviors that are not as easily perceived because they lie below the surface, such as differences in attitudes, values, beliefs, and personality

Delegating. The act of giving most of the responsibility to followers while still monitoring progress

Delphi technique. A method of decision making in which information is gathered from a group of respondents within their area of expertise

Departmentalization. A process of grouping people with related job duties, skills, and experiences into different areas within the overall organizational structure

Dependent variable. Factor affected by independent variables

Differing perceptions. The way in which our interpretations of situations clashes with the perceptions of others

Directive leadership. A leadership style characterized by implementing guidelines, managing expectations, setting definite performance standards, and ensuring that individuals follow rules

Discretionary responsibility. Involves going beyond the call of duty to benefit society

Display rules. Basic norms that govern which emotions should be displayed and which should be suppressed

Distress. High levels of stressors that have destructive and negative effects on effort and performance

Distributive bargaining. A strategy that involves two parties trying to claim a "fixed pie" of resources

Distributive justice. The degree to which people think outcomes are fair

Diversity hindrances. Obstacles that limit the range of employees in organizations

Division of labor. The degree to which certain jobs are divided into specific tasks

Divisional structure (*sometimes called multidivisional structure*). An organizational structure that groups employees by products and services, geographic regions, or customers

Dominant culture. Set of core values shared by the majority of organizational employees

Downward communication. Messages sent from the upper levels of the organizational hierarchy to the lower levels

Dysfunctional conflict. A dispute or disagreement that has negative effects on individuals or teams

E

Ease-of-recall bias. The propensity to over-rely on information recollected from memory when making a decision

Economic responsibility. Organizations must be economically and financially sound to enable them to become socially responsible in the first place

Electronic communication. The ability to transmit messages through e-mail, Skype, videoconferencing, blogs, fax, instant messaging, texting, and social networking

Emotional contagion. A phenomenon in which emotions which are experienced by few people of a work group are spread to the others

Emotional dissonance. A discrepancy between the emotions a person displays and the emotions he or she actually feels

Emotional intelligence. The ability to understand emotions in oneself and others in order to effectively manage one's own behaviors and relationships with others

Emotional labor. The process of managing one's feelings to present positive emotions even when they are contrary to one's actual feelings

Emotional regulation. A set of processes through which people influence their own emotions and the ways in which they experience and express them

Emotional stability. The extent to which we can remain calm and composed

Emotion-focused coping. An effort to try to change a person's emotional reaction to a stressor by using positive language and distracting techniques

Emotions. Intense feelings directed at a specific object or person

Employee engagement. A connection with the organization and passion for one's job

Employee stock ownership plans (ESOPs). Plans in which employees purchase stock, often at below market price as a part of their benefits

Empowering leadership. A behavioral type of leadership that empowers leaders to help develop the individual skills and abilities of their followers. Also known as "SuperLeadership"

Equity theory. Theory that holds that motivation is based on our perception of fairness in comparison with others

ERG theory. Theory that suggests that people are motivated by three categories of needs arranged in the form of a hierarchy

Escalation of commitment. The increased commitment to a decision despite negative information

Ethical dilemma. A conflict between two or more morally unpleasant alternatives

Ethical leadership. A means of influencing others through personal values, morals, and beliefs

Ethics. Moral principles of duty and virtue that prescribe how we should behave

Ethical responsibility. Being morally aware to enough to do the right thing in relation to the environment, fair wages, or who the company does business with

Ethnicity. Sociological factors such as nationality, culture, language, and ancestry

Ethnocentrism. The tendency to believe that your culture or ethnicity is superior to everyone else's

Eustress. Moderate levels of stressors that have constructive and positive effects on effort and performance

Evidence-based management. The practice of using research-based facts to make decisions

Exchange. The promise of rewards to persuade another person to cooperate

Expatriate. An employee who lives and works in a foreign country on a temporary basis

Expectancy. The probability that the amount of work effort invested by an individual will result in a high level of performance

Expectancy theory. Theory that holds that people will choose certain behaviors over others with the expectation of a certain outcome

Expert power. The ability to influence the behavior of others through the amount of knowledge or expertise possessed by an individual on which others depend

Exploitative innovation. The enhancement and reuse of existing products and processes

Exploratory innovation. Risk taking, radical thinking, and experimentation

External adaptation. A pattern of basic assumptions shared between employees of the goals, tasks, and methods that need to be achieved, together with ways of managing success and failure

External forces. Outside influences for change

External locus of control. The extent to which people believe their performance is the product of circumstances which are beyond their immediate control

Extinction. A reinforcement contingency in which a behavior is followed by the absence of any consequence, thereby reducing the likelihood that the behavior will be repeated in the same or similar situations

Extrinsic rewards. External awards to employees such as salary, bonuses, and paid vacations

F

Filtering. The process of screening and then manipulating a message from a sender before passing it on to the intended receiver

Flextime. Flexible working hours in which employees customize their own work hours within limits established by management

Followership. Individuals' capacity to cooperate with leaders

Formal networks. The transmission of messages established and approved by the organizational hierarchy

Formalization. The degree to which rules and procedures are standardized in an organization

Forming. A process whereby team members meet for the first time, get to know each other, and try to understand where they fit in to the team structure

Framing error. The tendency to highlight certain aspects of a situation depending on whether they are positive or negative to solve a problem while ignoring other aspects

Free agents. Independent workers that supply organizations with short-term talent for projects or time-bound objectives

Functional conflict. A constructive and healthy dispute between individuals or groups

Functional structures. Organizational structures that group employees according to the tasks they perform for the organization

Fundamental attribution error. The tendency to underestimate the influence of external factors and overestimate the impact of internal factors when making judgments about the behavior of others

G

Gain sharing. A system whereby managers agree to share the benefits of cost savings with staff in return for their contribution to the company's performance

Gender diversity. The way different genders are treated in the workplace

Glass ceiling. An invisible barrier that limits one's ability to progress to more senior positions

Globalization. The integration of economy, trade, and finance on an international scale

Goal-setting theory. Theory that suggests that human performance is directed by conscious goals and intentions

Gossip chains. A type of communication that occurs when one individual creates and spreads untrue or inaccurate information through the organization

Grapevine. An unofficial line of communication between individuals or groups

Group. Three or more people who work independently to attain organizational goals

Groupthink. A psychological phenomenon in which people in a cohesive group go along with the group consensus rather than offering their own opinions

H

Halo effect. A perception problem through which we form a positive or negative bias of an individual based on our overall impressions of that person

Heuristics. Shortcuts or "rules of thumb" that allow us to make judgments and decisions quickly and efficiently

Hierarchy of needs theory. Maslow's theory that suggests people are motivated by their desire to satisfy specific needs, and that needs are arranged in a hierarchy with physiological needs at the bottom and self-actualization needs at the top

High-context cultures. Cultures in which meaning is conveyed through body language, nonverbal cues, and the circumstances in which the communication is taking place

High-involvement management. The way managers empower employees to make decisions, provide them with extensive training and the opportunities to increase their knowledge base, share important information, and provide incentive compensation

Hindsight bias. The tendency to overestimate the ability to predict an outcome of an event

Human capital. People's skills, knowledge, experience, and general attributes

Human capital inimitability. The degree to which the skills and talents of employees can be emulated by other organizations

Human capital rareness. The skills and talents of an organization's people that are unique in the industry

Human capital value. The way employees work toward the strategic goals of an organization to achieve competitive advantage

Human skills. The ability to relate to other people

Hygiene factors. Sources of job satisfaction such as salary, status, and security

Hypothesis. A statement that specifies the relationships between the two variables

I

Idealized influence. Behavior that gains the admiration, trust, and respect of followers, who in turn follow the leader's example with their own actions

Impact. The feeling of making a difference

Implicit followership theories. Preconceived notions about the types of behaviors that characterize followers and nonfollowers

Implicit leadership theories. Hypotheses that explore the extent to which we distinguish leaders and nonleaders based on underlying assumptions, stereotypes, and beliefs

Impression management. The process by which we attempt to influence the perceptions others may have of us

Independent variables. Factors that remain unchanged

Individual differences. The degree to which people exhibit behavioral similarities and differences

Individualized consideration. Leader behavior associated with creating mutual respect or trust and a genuine concern for the needs and desires of others

Informal networks. A casual form of sharing information between employees across company divisions

Information control. a hard influencing tactic in which key information is withheld in order to manipulate outcomes

Information overload. Exposure to an overwhelming amount of information

Information technology (IT). A set of tools, processes, systems, and data communications based on microelectronic technology, designed to disseminate information to provide support to individuals in an organization

Ingratiation. A strategy of winning favor and putting oneself in the good graces of others before making a request

In-group exchange. Interaction that occurs when leaders and followers develop good working relationships based on mutual trust, respect, and a sense of sharing common fates

Initiating structure. A behavioral leadership style demonstrated by leaders who define the roles of the employees, set clear guidelines and procedures, and establish distinct patterns of organization and communication

Innovation. The creation and development of a new product or service

Inspirational appeals. The use of emotions to raise enthusiasm for the task by appealing to the values and ideals of others

Inspirational motivation. Leadership behaviors that promote commitment to a shared vision of the future

Instrumentality. The probability that good performance will lead to various work outcomes

Integrative bargaining. A strategy that involves both parties negotiating a win-win solution

Intellectual stimulation. Stimuli that encourage people to think and promote intelligence, logic, and problem solving

Interdependence. The extent to which team members rely on each other to complete their work tasks

Intergroup development. The process of finding ways to change the attitudes, perceptions, and stereotypes that employees may have of each other

Intermittent reinforcement. Reinforcement schedule in which a reward does not occur after each instance of a behavior or set of behaviors

Internal forces. Inside influences for change

Internal integration. A shared identity with agreed-upon methods of working together

Internal locus of control. The degree to which people believe they control the events and consequences which affect their lives

Intrinsic motivation. The performance of tasks for our own innate satisfaction

Intuition. An unconscious process of making decisions based on imagination and possibilities

J

Job characteristics model. Five core dimensions of jobs: skill variety, task identity, task significance, autonomy, and feedback

Job content–based pay. A salary paid based on the evaluation of a job's worth

Job design. A method of setting duties and responsibilities of a job with the intention of improving productivity and performance

Job enlargement. An increase in the range of tasks and duties associated with a job

Job enrichment. An increase in the scope of a job to make it more complex, interesting, stimulating, and satisfying for employees

Job rotation. A process of periodically moving staff employees from one job to another

Job satisfaction. The degree to which an individual feels positive or negative about a job

Job sharing. An employment option in which one full-time job is divided among two or more people according to predetermined hours

Justice approach. A classical decision-making approach that advocates basing decisions on fairness

L

Lack of participation error. The inclination to exclude certain people from the decision-making process

Laissez-faire leadership. Leadership behavior that fully delegates responsibility to others

Lateral communication. Messages sent between and among the same hierarchical levels across organizations

Leader emergence. The natural occurrence of someone becoming the leader of a leaderless group

Leader-exchange theory. A theory of leadership that focuses on the relationships between leaders and their group members

Leader-member relations. Relationships that reflect the degree of confidence, trust, and respect that exists between subordinates and their leaders

Leader's position power. The level of power a leader possesses to reward or punish, or promote and demote

Leadership. The process of providing general direction, from a position of influence, to individuals or groups toward the successful attainment of goals

Leadership grid. An approach that plots concern for production on the horizontal axis and concern for people on the vertical axis where 1 is the least concern and 9 is the greatest concern

Leadership prototypes. Behaviors that people associate with leadership

Learning. An ongoing process through which individuals adjust their behavior based on experience

Least-preferred coworker (LPC) questionnaire. An instrument that purports to measure whether a person is task oriented or relationship oriented

Legal responsibility. Organizations must make every effort is made to comply with legal requirements

Legitimate power. The degree to which a person has the right to ask others to do things that are considered within the scope of their authority

Locus of control. The extent to which people feel they have influence over events

Low-context cultures. Cultures that depend on explicit messages conveyed through the spoken or written word

M

Machiavellianism. A philosophy that describes people who manipulate others and use unethical practices for personal gain

Manifest conflict stage. The stage at which people engage in behaviors that provoke a response

Matrix structure. An organizational structure that combines both functional and divisional departmentalization together with dual lines of authority

Meaningfulness. The value of work tasks in line with a person's own self-concepts and ideals

Mechanistic model. A formalized structure based on centralization and departmentalization

Mediator. A neutral third party who attempts to assist parties in a negotiation to find a resolution or come to an agreement using rational arguments and persuasion

Mergers and acquisition hindrances. Obstacles that make it difficult for two organizations to join together

Merit pay. A pay plan consisting of a pay rise which is linked directly to performance

Model. A simplified snapshot of reality

Moods. Generalized positive or negative feelings of mind

Motivation. Forces from within individuals that stimulate and drive them to achieve goals

Motivators. Sources of job satisfaction such as achievement, recognition, and responsibility

N

Need for achievement. Need to perform well against a standard of excellence

Need for affiliation. Need to be liked and to stay on good terms with most other people

Need for competence. The motivation derived from stretching and exercising our capabilities

Need for power. Desire to influence people and events

Need for self-determination. The state of motivation and control gained through making efforts that are not reliant on any external influences

Negative affect. A mood dimension that consists of emotions such as boredom, lethargy, and depression

Negative reinforcement. A reinforcement contingency through which behaviors are followed by the removal of previously experienced negative consequences, resulting in the likelihood that the behavior will occur again in the same or similar situations

Negotiation. The process of reaching an agreement that both parties find acceptable

Neuroticism. A personality trait that involves being tense, moody, irritable, and temperamental

Neutralizing. The substitution of leadership attributes that do not affect follower outcomes

Nominal group technique. A structured way for team members to generate ideas and identify solutions in which each member is asked the same question in relation to a work issue and requested to write as many answers as possible. Answers are read aloud and voted upon

Nonprogrammed decisions. New or nonroutine problems for which there are no proven answers

Nonverbal communication. The transmission of wordless cues between people

Norming. The process by which team members resolve the conflict and begin to work well together and become more cohesive

Norms. The informal rules of a team's behavior that govern the team

O

Observable culture. The components of culture that can be seen in an organization

Open systems theory. The assumption that organizations are systems that interact with their environments to obtain resources or inputs and transform them into outputs returned to the environment for consumption

Operant conditioning. The process of forming associations between learning and behavior by controlling its consequences

Operations technology. The combination of processes, knowledge, and techniques that creates product or service value for an organization

Oral communication. The ability to give and exchange information, ideas, and processes verbally, either one on one or as a group

Organic model. A less formalized structure based on decentralization and cross-functional teams

Organization. A structured arrangement of people working together to accomplish specific goals

Organization structural innovation. The introduction or modification of work assignments, authority relationships, and communication and reward systems within an organization

Organizational behavior. A field of study focused on understanding, explaining, and improving attitudes of individuals and groups in organizations

Organizational behavior modification. The use of behavioral techniques to reinforce positive work behavior and discourage unhelpful work behavior

Organizational citizenship behavior. Discretionary and voluntary behavior that is not a part of the employee's specific role requirements and is not formally rewarded

Organizational cultural lag. The deficit in organizations that fail to keep up with new emerging innovations

Organizational culture. A pattern of shared norms, rules, values, and beliefs that guides the attitudes and behaviors of its employees

Organizational design. The process of creating or changing a structure of an organization to integrate people, information, and technology

Organizational development (OD). A deliberately planned system that uses behavioral science knowledge to increase the efficiency and effectiveness of an organization

Organizational justice. The perception of fairness in workplace practices

Organizational language. Words or metaphors and expressions specific to an organization

Organizational politics. Behavior that is not formally sanctioned by the organization and that is focused on maximizing our self-interest, often at the expense of the organization or other employees

Organizational structure. A framework of work roles that helps shape and support employee behavior

Outcomes of conflict stage. The stage that describes the consequences of the dispute

Out-group exchange. Interaction that occurs when leaders and followers fail to create a sense of mutual trust, respect, or common fate

P

Participating. Leadership behavior in which both leaders and followers work together and share in the decision-making responsibilities of the task

Participative leadership. A leadership style that favors consulting with followers and considering their input in decision making

Part-time workers. (similar to *free agents*). Independent workers who supply organizations with part-time talent for projects or time-bound objectives

Path–goal leadership theory. A theory that proposes that leadership effectiveness depends on the degree to which the leader enhances the performance of followers by guiding them on a defined track towards achieving their goals

People innovation. Changes in the beliefs and behaviors of individuals working in an organization

Perceived inequity. The sense of feeling under-rewarded or over-rewarded in comparison with others

Perceived/felt conflict stage. The stage at which emotional differences are sensed and felt

Perception. The process by which we receive and interpret information from our environment

Performance goals (distal). Long-term goals set into the future

Performance-based pay. A financial incentive awarded to employees for meeting certain goals or objectives

Performing. The way in which a team is invested towards achieving its goals and operates as a unit

Personal appeals. Requests to cooperate on the basis of friendship or as a personal favor

Personal conception. The degree to which individuals relate to and think about their social and physical environment and their personal beliefs regarding a range of issues

Personality. A stable and unique pattern of traits, characteristics, and resulting behaviors that gives an individual his or her identity

Personality traits. Characteristics that describe our thoughts, feelings, and behaviors

Person-organization fit. The degree of compatibility between job candidates and organizations

Piece rate. A pay plan in which workers are paid a fixed sum for each unit of production completed

Political science. The study of the behavior of individuals and groups within a political environment

Political skill. The ability to understand and influence others for the good of the organization

Pooled interdependence. An organizational model in which each team member produces a piece of work independently of the other members

Positive affect. A mood dimension that consists of emotions such as excitement, self-assurance, and cheerfulness at the high end and boredom, sluggishness, and tiredness at the low end

Positive organizational behavior. The strengths, virtues, vitality, and resilience of individuals and organizations

Positive reinforcement. A reinforcement contingency through which behaviors followed by positive consequences, are more likely to occur again in the same or similar situations

Postconventional morality. The final stage of moral development (mature adults), where individual judgment is based on a chosen belief system, which shapes moral views

Power. The capacity to influence the actions of others

Practiced creativity. The ability to seize opportunities to apply creative skills in the workplace

Preconventional morality. A stage that applies to very young children whose morality tends to be based on obedience, self-protection, and self-interest

Primacy effect. A perception problem through which an individual assesses a person quickly on the basis of the first information encountered

Proactive personality. The tendency for individuals to take the initiative to change their circumstances

Problem-focused coping. A type of coping that aims at reducing or eliminating stressors by attempting to understand the problem and seeking practical ways in which to resolve it

Problem-solving team. A group of workers coming together for a set amount of time to discuss specific issues

Procedural justice. The degree to which people perceive the implementation of company policies and procedures to be fair

Process conflict. The clash in viewpoints in relation to how to carry out work

Process consultation. An intervention that involves increasing group awareness and/or understanding

Process gains. Factors that contribute to team effectiveness

Process innovation. The introduction of new or improved operational and work methods

Process losses. Factors that detract from team effectiveness

Process theories. Theories that describe the cognitive processes through which needs are translated into behavior, such as equity theory, expectancy theory, and goal-setting theory

Processing. The act of understanding and remembering what is being said as well as making an effort to empathize with the speaker's feelings and thoughts and the situation at hand

Product innovation. The development of new or improved goods or services that are sold to meet customer needs

Production-oriented leader. A leader who tends to focus more on the technical or task aspects of the job

Productive forgetting. The ability to abandon a solution that isn't working in favor of a new one

Profit sharing. Sharing profits with employees of an organization by the owners

Programmed decisions. Automatic responses to routine and recurring situations

Projecting. A process through which people ascribe their own personal attributes onto others

Projection bias. The inclination to believe other people think, feel, and act the same way we do

Psychological empowerment. The extent to which employees feel a sense of personal fulfillment and intent when carrying out tasks, together with a belief that their work contributes to some larger purpose

Psychology. The scientific study of the human mind that seeks to measure and explain behavioral characteristics

Punishment. A reinforcement contingency that discourages undesirable behavior by administering unpleasant consequences

Q

Quality of worklife (QWL). The relationship between the employees and the workplace

R

Race. Identifying biological factors such as skin, hair, or eye color

Randomness error. The tendency for people to believe they can predict the outcome of chance events based on false information or superstition

Rational appeals. The use of logic, reason, and evidence to convince another person that cooperation in a task is worthwhile

Recency effect. A perception problem through which we use the most recent information available to assess a person

Reciprocal interdependence. An organizational model in which team members work closely together on a piece of work, consulting with each other, providing each other with advice, and exchanging information

Referent power. The degree to which a leader can influence others through their desire to identify and be associated with them

Reinforcement. The application of consequences to establish patterns of behavior

Reinforcement theory. A theory that states that behavior is a function of its consequences and is determined exclusively by environmental factors such as external stimuli and other reinforcers

Relationship conflict. The clash in personalities between two or more individuals

Representativeness heuristic. A shortcut that bases a decision on our existing mental prototype and similar stereotypes

Resistance to change. The unwillingness to accept or support modifications in the workplace

Responding. The way active listeners provide feedback to the speaker

Reward power. The extent to which someone uses incentives to influence the actions of others

Rights approach. A classical decision-making approach that fosters decisions made on moral principles that infringe as little as possible on the entitlements of others

Risk-taking propensity. The tendency to engage in behaviors that might have positive or negative outcomes

Rituals. Formalized actions and planned routines

S

Satisficing decisions. Solutions that aim for acceptable results rather than for the best or optimal ones

Scientific management. Early 20th-century theory introduced by Frederick Taylor and his colleagues that analyzes workflow through systematic observation or reasoning

Selective attention. The tendency to selectively focus on aspects of situations that are most aligned with our own interests, values, and attitudes

Self-awareness. Being aware of our own feelings, behaviors, personalities, likes, and dislikes

Self-concept. The beliefs we have about who we are and how we feel about ourselves

Self-determination. The understanding of skills, knowledge, and strengths that enable a person to make choices and initiate work tasks

Self-efficacy. The belief we have in our ability to succeed in a specific task or situation

Self-esteem. The beliefs we have about our own worth following the self-evaluation process

Self-fulfilling prophecy. The way a person behaves based on preexisting expectations about another person or situation so as to create an outcome that is aligned with those expectations

Self-leadership. A process whereby people intentionally influence their thinking and behavior to achieve their objectives

Self-managing team. A group of workers who manage their daily duties under little to no supervision

Self-monitoring. Adjusting our behavior to accommodate different situations

Self-regulation. A process whereby people set goals, creating a discrepancy between the desired state and the current state

Self-serving bias. The tendency for individuals to attribute their own successes to internal factors and put the blame for failures on external factors

Selling. Leadership behavior characterized by support provided to followers through communication and "selling" them the aims of the task in order to gain commitment

Seniority-based pay. Guaranteed wages and salary increases based on the amount of time the employee has spent with the organization

Sensing. The way listeners pay attention to the signals sent from the speaker

Sensitivity training. A type of program designed to raise awareness of group dynamics and any existing prejudices toward others

Sequential interdependence. An organizational model in which one team member completes a piece of work and passes it on to the next member for their input, similar to an assembly line

Servant leadership. A pattern of leadership that places an emphasis on employees and the community rather than on the leader

Sexual orientation. A person's sexual identity and the gender(s) to which she or he is attracted

Shared leadership. A style of leadership that distributes influence among groups and individuals to achieve organizational or team goals

Silent authority. an influencing tactic that relies on unspoken but acknowledged power

Simple structures. Organizational structures, common in small organizations where is there is one central authority figure, usually a business owner, who tends to make decisions

Situational leadership model. A leadership model that proposes leaders should adapt their leadership style based on the types of people they are leading and the requirements of the task

Skill-based pay. A system of pay that rewards employees for the acquisition and the development of new skills that lead to enhanced work performance

Social cognitive theory. A theory that proposes that learning takes place through the observation, imitation, and the modeling of others within a social context

Social facilitation. The tendency for individuals to perform tasks better when they are in the presence of others

Social loafing. A phenomenon wherein people put forth less effort when they work in teams than when they work alone

Social psychology. The social science that blends concepts from sociology and psychology and focuses on how people influence each other in a social setting

Socialization. The process through which an organization communicates its values to new employees

Sociology. The study of the behavior of groups and how they relate to each other in a social setting

Sociotechnical systems. The interaction between human behavior and technical systems

Span of control. The number of direct reports to a given manager following an expansion

Spiritual leadership. A values-based style of leadership that motivates employees through faith, hope, and vision and encourages positive social emotions such has forgiveness and gratitude

Stereotypes. An individual's fixed beliefs about the characteristics of a particular group

Stories. Narratives based on real organizational experiences that have become embellished over time and illustrate core cultural values

Storming. A phase during which, after a period of time, tension may arise between members and different personalities might clash, leading to tension and conflict in the team

Strategic OB approach. The idea that people are the key to productivity, competitive edge, and financial success

Stressors. Environmental stimuli that place demands on individuals

Subcultures. Groups in an organization who share different values to those held by the majority

Subordinate characteristics. Situational contingencies such as anxiety, inflexibility, perceived ability, locus of control, and close-mindedness

Substitutes for leadership model. A model that suggests certain characteristics of the situation can constrain the influence of the leader

Sunk cost bias. The decision to continue an investment based on past investments of time, effort, and/or money

Supportive leadership. A leadership behavior characterized by friendliness and concern for the welfare of others

Surface acting. A person suppresses their true feelings while displaying the organizationally desirable ones

Surface-level diversity. Easily perceived differences between people, such as age/generation, race/ethnicity, gender, and ability

Symbols. Objects that provide meaning about a culture

Synergy. The concept that the total amount of work produced by a team is greater than the amount of work produced by individual members working independently

T

Task characteristics. Situational contingencies outside the follower's control, such as team dynamics, authority systems, and task structure

Task conflict. The clash between individuals in relation to the direction, content, or goal of a certain assignment

Task structure. The degree to which job assignments are defined

Team. A group of people brought together to use their individual skills on a common project or goal

Technical skill. The aptitude to perform and apply specialized tasks

Technology. The development of scientific knowledge as applied to machinery and devices

Telecommuting. Working from home or from a remote location on a computer or other advanced telecommunications that are linked to the office

Telling. A leadership behavior characterized by giving clear instructions and guidance to followers, informing them exactly how and when to complete the task

Theory. A set of principles intended to explain behavioral phenomena in organizations

Three-component model of creativity. A model proposing that individual creativity relies on domain-relevant skills and expertise, creativity-relevant processes, and intrinsic task motivation

Trait leadership perspective. A theory that explores the relationship between leaders and personal qualities and characteristics and how they differentiate leaders from nonleaders

Transactional leadership. A behavioral type of leadership that proposes that employees are motivated by goals and equitable rewards

Transforming. The process that occurs when people begin to make peace with their doubts and uncertainties and begin to embrace the new direction of the company

Triadic reciprocal model of behavior. A model that shows human functioning shaped by three factors that are reciprocally related: reinforcement, cognitive processes, and behavior

Trust. The dependence on the integrity, ability, honesty, and reliability of someone or something else

Two-factor theory (*motivation-hygiene theory or dual theory***).** The impact of motivational influences on job satisfaction

Type A orientation. The way people are characterized as competitive, impatient, aggressive, and achievement oriented

Type B orientation. The way people are characterized as relaxed, easygoing, patient, and noncompetitive

U

Unobservable culture. The components that lie beneath the surface of an organization, such as company values and assumptions

Upward appeals. The argument that the task has been requested by higher management, or a request to higher management to assist in gaining cooperation

Upward communication. Messages sent from the lower levels of the organizational hierarchy to the higher levels

Utilitarian approach. A classical decision-making approach that focuses on taking action that results in the greater good for the majority of people

V

Valence. The value individuals place on work outcomes

Value chain. The sequence of activities carried out by organizations to create valued goods and services to consumers

Virtual teams. Groups of individuals from different locations work together through e-mail, video conferencing, instant messaging, and other electronic media

Visibility. The awareness of others regarding your presence in an organization

Visionary leadership. A behavioral type of leadership that creates visions to motivate, inspire, and stimulate employees

W

Wellness program. A personal or organizational effort to promote health and wellbeing through providing access to services like medical screenings, weight management, health advice, and exercise programs

Workplace diversity. The degree to which an organization represents different cultures

Written communication. Messages communicated through the written word, such as e-mails, reports, memos, letters, and other channels

Z

ZOPA. The zone of possible agreement, the area where two sides in a negotiation may find common ground

NOTES

Chapter 1

1. For an overview of the field of organizational behavior see: Thompson, Leigh, and Jo-Ellen Pozner. "Organizational Behavior." In *Social Psychology: Handbook of Basic Principles* (2nd ed.), 913–939 (New York: Guilford, 2007); Greenberg, Jerald. *Organizational Behavior: The State of the Science* (2nd ed.) (Mahwah, NJ: Erlbaum, 2003).

2. Kiisel, Ty. "65% of Americans Choose a Better Boss Over a Raise — Here's Why." *Forbes,* October 16, 2012. https://www.forbes.com/sites/tykiisel/2012/10/16/65-of-americans-choose-a-better-boss-over-a-raise-heres-why/#d129a7a76d29.

3. Kalish, Alyse. "Free Food's Great, But People Would Give It Up in Exchange for a Better Boss." *The Muse,* October 4, 2016. https://www.themuse.com/advice/free-foods-great-but-people-would-give-it-up-in-exchange-for-a-better-boss.

4. Lipman, Victor. "People Leave Managers, Not Companies." *Forbes,* August 4, 2015. https://www.forbes.com/sites/victorlipman/2015/08/04/people-leave-managers-not-companies/#2eadc8d747a9.

5. Fayol, Henri. *Industrial and General Administration* (Paris: Dunod, 1916).

6. Katz, Robert L. "Skills of an Effective Administrator." *Harvard Business Review* 34, no. 2 (March 1956): 127; Cai, Houqing. "Management Development: A Principles Framework and Critical Skills Approach." *Human Systems Management* 33, no. 4 (September 2014): 207–212.

7. Ibid.

8. Ibid.

9. Salovey, Peter, and John D. Mayer. "Emotional Intelligence." *Imagination, Cognition and Personality* 9, no. 3 (1989): 185–211; Miao, Chao, Ronald H. Humphrey, and Shanshan Qian. "A meta-analysis of emotional intelligence and work attitudes." *Journal of Occupational and Organizational Psychology* 90, no. 2 (June 2017): 177–202.

10. Katz, "Skills of an Effective Administrator; Cai, "Management Development."

11. Crook, T. Russell, Samuel Y. Todd, James G. Combs, David J. Woehr, and David J. Ketchen Jr. "Does Human Capital Matter? A Meta-analysis of the Relationship between Human Capital and Firm Performance." *Journal of Applied Psychology* 96, no. 3 (May 2011): 443–456; Wright, Patrick M., Russell Coff, and Thomas P. Moliterno. "Strategic Human Capital: Crossing the Great Divide." *Journal of Management* 40, no. 2 (February 2014): 353–370.

12. Hatch, Nile W., and Jeffrey H. Dyer. "Human Capital and Learning as a Source of Sustainable Competitive Advantage." *Strategic Management* 25, no. 12 (December 2004): 1155–1178; Lawler, Edward E. III. "Make Human Capital a Source of Competitive Advantage." *Organizational Dynamics* 38, no. 1 (January 2009): 1–7; Campbell, Benjamin A., Russell Coff, and David Kryscynski. "Rethinking Sustained Competitive Advantage from Human Capital." *Academy of Management Review* 37, no. 3 (July 2012): 376–395.

13. Ibid.

14. See for example, Dwyer, Christopher P. *Critical thinking: Conceptual perspectives and practical guidelines.* New York, NY: Cambridge University Press, 2017; Lack, Caleb W., and Jacques Rousseau. *Critical Thinking, Science, and Pseudoscience: Why We Can't Trust Our Brains.* (New York: Springer Publishing Co, 2016).

15. See for example, Lennon, Chauncy. "Lack of Skilled Workers Threatens Economic Growth." *U.S. News & World Report,* October 30, 2014. www.usnews.com/news/stem-solutions/articles/2014/10/30/lack-of-skilled-workers-threatens-economic-growth-in-stem-fields; Schramm, Jen. "Survey: Qualified Workers Are Harder to Find." *HR Today,* June 1, 2016. https://www.shrm.org/hr-today/news/hr-magazine/0616/pages/0616-hr-recruiting-difficulties-rise.aspx.

16. Casserly, Meghan. "The 10 Skills That Will Get You Hired in 2013." Forbes.com. December 10, 2012. www.forbes.com/sites/meghancasserly/2012/12/10/the-10-skills-that-will-get-you-a-job-in-2013/.

17. Conference Board, Are They Really Ready to Work? Employers' Perspectives on the Basic Knowledge and Applied Skills of New Entrants to the 21st-Century U.S. Workforce. Study conducted by The Conference Board, Partnership for 21st-Century Skills, Corporate Voices for Working Families, and the Society for Human Resource Management, 2006.

18. B. Hagemann and J. M. Chartrand. 2009 Trends in Executive Development: A Benchmark Report. Technical report (Oklahoma City: Executive Development Associates, 2009).

19. Deniz S. Ones, and Stephan Dilchert. "How Special Are Executives? How Special Should Executive Selection Be? Observations and Recommendations." *Industrial and Organizational Psychology* 2, no. 2 (June 2009): 163–170.

20. Casserly, "10 Skills."

21. "Why Critical Thinking and Teamwork Matter the Most." *www.ThinkingHabits.com,* July 30, 2016. http://www.thinkinghabitats.com/blog/why-critical-thinking-and-teamwork-matter-the-most.

22. Wolfe, Alexandra. "Weekend Confidential: Daniel Ek." *Wall Street Journal,* June 21, 2013. http://online.wsj.com/news/articles/SB10001424127887323566804578553691334279504.

23. Russell, Jon. "Spotify Reaches 50 Million Paying Users." *Tech Crunch,* March 2, 2017. https://techcrunch.com/2017/03/02/spotify-50-million/.

24. For an overview of the scientific method and theory testing in the behavioral sciences see: Marczyk, Geoffrey, David DeMatteo, and David Festinger. *Essentials of Research Design and Methodology* (Hoboken, NJ: Wiley, 2005).

25. Rousseau, Denise M. (Ed.). *The Oxford Handbook of Evidence-Based Management* (New York: Oxford University Press, 2012).

26. Emery, Merrelyn. "Refutation of Kira and van Eijnatten's Critique of the Emery's Open Systems Theory." *Systems Research and Behavioral Science* 27, no. 6 (November 2010): 697–712; Rosen, Ned A. "Open Systems Theory in an Organizational Sub-System: A Field Experiment." *Organizational Behavior and Human Performance* 5, no. 3 (1970): 245–265.

27. Acquier, Aurélien, Bertrand Valiorgue, and Thibault Daudigeos. "Sharing the Shared Value: A Transaction Cost Perspective on Strategic CSR Policies in Global Value Chains." *Journal of Business Ethics* 144, no. 1 (August 2017): 139–152; Gertner, Moryosseff Iris. "The Value Chain and Value Creation." *Advances in Management* 6, no. 10 (October 2013): 1–4; Champion, David. "Mastering the Value Chain." *Harvard Business Review* 79, no. 6 (June 2001): 108–115.

28. Choi, Jin Nam, Sun Young Sung, and Zhengtang Zhang. "Workforce Diversity in Manufacturing Companies and Organizational Performance: The Role of Status-Relatedness and Internal Processes." *The International Journal of Human Resource Management* 28, no. 19 (October 2017): 2738–2761;

Kundu, Subhash C., and Archana Mor. "Workforce Diversity and Organizational Performance: A Study of IT Industry in India." *Employee Relations* 39, no. 2 (2017): 160–183.

29. See for example, Thompson and Pozner, *Organizational Behavior.*

30. Van Wyden, Genevieve, "Examples of Great Teamwork." *Houston Chronicle.* http://smallbusiness.chron.com/examples-great-teamwork-12607.html.

31. Frenz, Roslyn, "Google's Organizational Structure." http://www.ehow.co.uk/about_6692920_google_s-organizational-structure.htm.

32. Campbell Quick, James, Cary L. Cooper, Philip C. Gibbs, Laura M. Little, and Debra L. Nelson. "Positive Organizational Behavior at Work." In *International Review of Industrial and Organizational Psychology* 2010 (Vol. 25), 253–291 (n.p.: Wiley-Blackwell, 2010); Luthans, Fred, and Bruce J. Avolio. "The 'Point' of Positive Organizational Behavior." *Journal of Organizational Behavior* 30, no. 2 (February 2009): 291–307; Warren, Meg A., Stewart I. Donaldson, and Fred Luthans. "Taking Positive Psychology to the Workplace: Positive Organizational Psychology, Positive Organizational Behavior, and Positive Organizational Scholarship." In *Scientific Advances in Positive Psychology*, 195–227. (Santa Barbara, CA, US: Praeger/ABC-CLIO, 2017).

33. Ying, Zhou, and Zou Min. "The Effect of High Involvement Management on Employee Well-Being in Britain." *Academy Of Management Annual Meeting Proceedings* 2016, no. 1 (January 2016): 1. Wood, Stephen, Marc Van Veldhoven, Marcel Croon, and Lilian M. de Menezes. "Enriched Job Design, High Involvement Management and Organizational Performance: The Mediating Roles of Job Satisfaction and Well-Being." *Human Relations* 65, no. 4 (April 2012): 419–445.

34. Steiner Sports. "Healthy Discrimination." June 3, 2013. http://brandonsteiner.com/blog/healthy-discrimination/.

35. Ibid.

36. Ibid.

Chapter 2

1. https://www.nytimes.com/2017/04/05/business/kendall-jenner-pepsi-ad.html.

2. For a recent review of diversity research see: Plaut, Victoria C., Sapna Cheryan, and Flannery G. Stevens, "New Frontiers in Diversity Research: Conceptions of Diversity and Their Theoretical and Practical Implications." In *APA Handbook of Personality and Social Psychology, Volume 1: Attitudes and Social Cognition*, 593–619 (Washington, DC: American Psychological Association, 2015).

3. Shepherd, Jack. "Oscars 2016: Everyone who Boycotted the Academy Awards and Why, from Jada Pinkett Smith to Spike Lee." *Independent*, February 28, 2016. https://www.independent.co.uk/arts-entertainment/films/news/oscars-2016-everyone-boycotting-the-academy-awards-and-why-from-jada-pinkett-smith-to-spike-lee-a6902121.html.

4. Lu, Chia-Mei, Shyh-Jer Chen, Pei-Chi Huang, and Jui-Ching Chien, "Effect of Diversity on Human Resource Management and Organizational Performance." *Journal of Business Research* 68, no. 4 (April 2015): 857–861; Peretz, Hilla, Ariel Levi, and Yitzhak Fried, "Organizational Diversity Programs across Cultures: Effects on Absenteeism, Turnover, Performance and Innovation." *International Journal of Human Resource Management* 26, no. 6 (March 2015). 875–903; *Global Diversity and Inclusion: Fostering Innovation through a Diverse Workforce* (New York: Forbes/Insights).

5. https://www.diversityinc.com/st/DI_Top_50.

6. Broughton, Ashley. "Minorities Expected to Be Majority in 2050." *CNN*. August 13, 2008. http://edition.cnn.com/2008/US/08/13/census.minorities/.

7. Harrison, David A., Kenneth H. Price, Joanne H. Gavin, and Anna T. Florey. "Time, Teams, and Task Performance: Changing Effects of Surface- and Deep-Level Diversity on Group Functioning." *Academy of Management Journal* 45, no. 5 (October 2002): 1029–1045.

8. Bieling, Gisela I., and Florian Dorozalla. "Making the Most of Age Diversity: How Age Diversity Climate Contributes to Employee Performance." *Academy of Management Annual Meeting Proceedings* (January 2014): 1308–1314; Seong, Jee Young, and Doo-Seung Hong. "Age Diversity, Group Organisational Citizenship Behaviour, and Group Performance: Exploring the Moderating Role of Charismatic Leadership and Participation in Decision-Making." *Human Resource Management Journal* (May 25, 2018); Stone, Dianna L., and Lois E. Tetrick. "Understanding and Facilitating Age Diversity in Organizations." *Journal of Managerial Psychology* 28, no. 7–8 (2013): 725–728.

9. Kane, Libby. "Meet Generation Z, the 'Millennials on Steroids' Who Could Lead the Charge for Change in the US." *Business Insider*, December 4, 2017. http://www.businessinsider.com/generation-z-profile-2017-9/?r=UK&IR=T/#technology-has-shaped-their-daily-lives-and-their-worldview-1.

10. Byars-Winston, Angela, Nadya Fouad, and Yao Wen. "Race/Ethnicity and Sex in U.S. Occupations, 1970–2010: Implications for Research, Practice, and Policy." *Journal of Vocational Behavior* 87, (April 2015): 54–70; Humes, Karen, and Howard Hogan. "Do Current Race and Ethnicity Concepts Reflect a Changing America?" In *Race and Social Problems: Restructuring Inequality*, 15–38 (New York: Springer Science + Business Media, 2015).

11. See for example: Roh, Hyuntak, and Eugene Kim. "The Business Case for Gender Diversity: Examining the Role of Human Resource Management Investments." *Human Resource Management* (June 22, 2015): 000–000: *PsycINFO*, EBSCOhost; Muzio, Daniel, and Jennifer Tomlinson. "Editorial: Researching Gender, Inclusion and Diversity in Contemporary Professions and Professional Organizations." *Gender, Work and Organization* 19, no. 5 (September 2012): 455–466.

12. See for example: Ng, Eddy S., and Greg J. Sears. "The Glass Ceiling in Context: The Influence of CEO Gender, Recruitment Practices and Firm Internationalisation on the Representation of Women in Management." *Human Resource Management Journal* 27, no. 1 (January 2017): 133–151.

13. Sheth, Sonam, Shayanne Gal, and Skye Gould. "6 Charts Show How Much More Men Make Than Women." *Business Insider*, April 10, 2018. http://www.businessinsider.com/gender-wage-pay-gap-charts-2017-3?r=UK&IR=T.

14. Bellis, Rich. "Here's Everywhere In America You Can Still Get Fired for Being Gay or Trans." *Fast Company*, March 3, 2016. https://www.fastcompany.com/3057357/heres-everywhere-in-america-you-can-still-get-fired-for-being-lgbt.

15. www.census.gov/newsroom/releases/archives/miscellaneous/cb12-134.html.

16. Dobbin, Frank, Alexandra Kalev, and Erin Kelly. "Diversity Management in Corporate America." *Contexts* 6, no. 4 (2007): 21–27.

17. Dobbin, Frank, and Alexandra Kalev. "Why Diversity Programs Fail." *Harvard Business Review*, July-August 2016. https://hbr.org/2016/07/why-diversity-programs-fail.

18. http://cdn.culturewizard.com/PDF/Trends_in_VT_Report_4-17-2016.pdf.

19. This section is based in part on "Understanding Workplace Cultures Globally." www.SHRM.org, November 30, 2015. https://www.shrm.org/resourcesandtools/tools-and-samples/toolkits/pages/understandingworkplaceculturesglobally.aspx.

20. For an overview of individual differences research, see Mikulincer, Mario, Phillip R. Shaver, M. Lynne Cooper, and Randy J. Larsen. *APA Handbook of Personality and Social Psychology,*

Volume 4: Personality Processes and Individual Differences. (Washington, DC: American Psychological Association, 2015).

21. Carver, Charles S. "Self-Awareness." In *Handbook of Self and Identity* (2nd ed.), 50–68 (New York: Guilford, 2012); Proust, Joëlle. *The Philosophy of Metacognition: Mental Agency and Self-Awareness.* (New York: Oxford University Press, 2015).

22. Figurski, Thomas J. "Self-Awareness and Other-Awareness: The Use of Perspective in Everyday Life." In *Self and Identity: Psychosocial Perspectives*, 197–210 (Oxford: Wiley, 1987); Reddy, Vasudevi. "Experiencing Others: A Second-Person Approach to Other-Awareness." In *Social Life and Social Knowledge: Toward a Process Account of Development*, 123–144 (New York: Taylor & Francis / Erlbaum, 2008).

23. Amey, Rachel, and Chad E. Forbes. "The Role of Top-Down and Bottom-Up Mechanisms in the Maintenance of the Self-Concept: A Behavioral and Neuroscience Review." In *Handbook of Categorization in Cognitive Science*, 55–74. (San Diego: Elsevier Academic Press, 2017); Har, Sunil S., and Michael Kyrios. "The Self-Concept: Theory and Research." In *The Self in Understanding and Treating Psychological Disorders*, 8–18. (New York: Cambridge University Press, 2016).

24. MacKinnon, Neil J. *Self-Esteem and Beyond.* (New York: Palgrave Macmillan, 2015); Ferris, D. Lance, Huiwen Lian, Douglas J. Brown, and Rachel Morrison. "Ostracism, Self-Esteem, and Job Performance: When Do We Self-Verify and When Do We Self-Enhance?." *Academy Of Management Journal* 58, no. 1 (February 2015): 279–297.

25. Bandura, Albert. *Self-Efficacy: The Exercise of Control.* (New York: W H Freeman/Times Books/Henry Holt, 1997); Bandura, Albert. "On the Functional Properties of Perceived Self-Efficacy Revisited." *Journal of Management* 38, no. 1 (January 2012): 9–44; Beck, James W., and Aaron M. Schmidt. "Negative Relationships Between Self-Efficacy and Performance Can Be Adaptive: The Mediating Role of Resource Allocation." *Journal Of Management* 44, no. 2 (February 2018): 555–558.

26. For an overview or personality theory and research, see Cervone, Daniel, and Lawrence A. Pervin, *Personality: Theory and Research* (14th ed.) (New York: Wiley, 2018).

27. Bornstein, Robert F. "Personality Traits and Dynamics." In *APA Handbook of Clinical Psychology: Applications and Methods*, 81–101. (Washington, DC: American Psychological Association, 2016); Paunonen, Sampo V., and Ryan Y. Hong. "On the Properties of Personality Traits." In *APA Handbook of Personality and Social Psychology, Volume 4: Personality Processes and Individual Differences*, 233–259. (Washington, DC: American Psychological Association, 2015).

28. See for example, Quenk, Naomi L. *Essentials of Myers-Briggs Type Indicator® Assessment* (2nd ed.) (Hoboken, NJ: Wiley, 2009).

29. McCaulley, Mary H. "The Myers-Briggs Type Indicator: A Measure for Individuals and Groups." *Measurement and Evaluation in Counseling and Development* 22, no. 4 (January 1990): 181–195.

30. Bower, Kay M. "Coaching with the Myers Briggs Type Indicator: A Valuable Tool for Client Self-Awareness." *Journal of Practical Consulting* 5, no. 2 (Winter 2015): 10–18; Mi-Ran, Kim, and Han Su-Jeong. "Relationships between the Myers-Briggs Type Indicator Personality Profiling, Academic Performance and Student Satisfaction in Nursing Students." *International Journal of Bio-Science & Bio-Technology* 6, no. 6 (December 2014): 1–11; McCaulley, "The Myers-Briggs Type Indicator."

31. For additional details see www.myersbriggs.org/my-mbti-personality-type/my-mbti-results/how-frequent-is-my-type.htm.

32. Barrick, Murray R., and Michael K. Mount. "The Big Five Personality Dimensions and Job Performance: A Meta-Analysis." *Personnel Psychology* 44, no. 1 (Spring 1991): 1–26; John, Oliver P., and Sanjay Srivastava. "The Big Five Trait Taxonomy: History, Measurement, and Theoretical Perspectives." In *Handbook of Personality: Theory and Research* (2nd ed.), 102–138 (New York: Guilford, 1999).

33. See for example, Gurven, Michael, Christopher von Rueden, Maxim Massenkoff, Hillard Kaplan, and Marino Lero Vie. "How Universal is the Big Five? Testing the Five-Factor Model of Personality Variation among Forager–Farmers in the Bolivian Amazon." *Journal of Personality and Social Psychology* 104, no. 2 (February 2013): 354–370.

34. See for example, Saucier, Gerard, and Sanjay Srivastava. "What Makes a Good Structural Model of Personality? Evaluating the Big Five and Alternatives." In *APA Handbook of Personality and Social Psychology, Volume 4: Personality Processes and Individual Differences*, 283–305. (Washington, DC: American Psychological Association, 2015).

35. Chang, Chu-Hsiang (Daisy), D. Lance Ferris, Russell E. Johnson, Christopher C. Rosen, and James A. Tan. "Core Self-Evaluations: A Review and Evaluation of the Literature." *Journal of Management* 38, no. 1 (January 2012): 81–128; Mäkikangas, Anne, Ulla Kinnunen, Saija Mauno, and Eva Selenko. "Factor Structure and Longitudinal Factorial Validity of the Core Self-Evaluation Scale: Exploratory Structural Equation Modeling." *European Journal of Psychological Assessment* (October 7, 2016).

36. McDonald, Roy, Vincent J. Tempone, and William L. Simmons, "Locus of Control as a Personality and Situational Variable." *Perceptual and Motor Skills* 27, no. 1 (1968): 135–141; Rotter, Julian B., and Ray C. Mulry, "Internal versus External Control of Reinforcement and Decision Time." *Journal of Personality and Social Psychology* 2, no. 4 (October 1965): 598–604.

37. Deloitte. *CFO Insights: The Power of Business Chemistry.* www.deloitte.com/view/en_US/us/Services/additional-services/chief-financial-officer/cfo-insights/ae6743f2b7886310VgnVCM2000001b56f00aRCRD.htm.

38. Jones, Daniel N. "The Nature of Machiavellianism: Distinct Patterns of Misbehavior." In *The Dark Side of Personality: Science and Practice in Social, Personality, and Clinical Psychology*, 87–107. (Washington, DC: American Psychological Association, 2016); Bagozzi, Richard P., Willem J. M. I. Verbeke, Roeland C. Dietvorst, Frank D. Belschak, Wouter E. van den Berg, and Wim J. R. Rietdijk. "Theory of Mind and Empathic Explanations of Machiavellianism: A Neuroscience Perspective." *Journal of Management* 39, no. 7 (November 2013): 1760–1798.

39. Rachman, Gideon. "The Kremlin's Machiavelli Has Led Russia to Disaster." *Financial Times*, July 21, 2014. https://www.ft.com/content/cc3ca75c-10c5-11e4-812b-00144feabdc0.

40. Fuglestad, Paul T., and Mark Snyder. "Self-Monitoring." In *Handbook of Individual Differences in Social Behavior*, 574–591 (New York: Guilford, 2009); Oh, In-Sue, Steven D. Charlier, Michael K. Mount, and Christopher M. Berry. "The Two Faces of High Self-Monitors: Chameleonic Moderating Effects of Self-Monitoring on the Relationships between Personality Traits and Counterproductive Work Behaviors." *Journal of Organizational Behavior* 35, no. 1 (January 2014): 92–111; Pillow, David R., Willie J. Jr. Hale, Meghan A. Crabtree, and Trisha L. Hinojosa. "Exploring the relations between self-monitoring, authenticity, and well-being." *Personality and Individual Differences* 116, (October 1, 2017): 393–398.

41. Lebowitz, Shana. "The Fact That No One Knows Much About Google's New CEO May Be One Reason For His Success." *Business Insider*, April 11, 2016. http://www.businessinsider.com/sundar-pichai-self-monitoring-2016-4?r=UK&IR=T

42. Li, Wen-Dong, Doris Fay, Michael Frese, Peter D. Harms, and Xiang Yu Gao. "Reciprocal Relationship between Proactive Personality and Work Characteristics: A Latent Change Score Approach." *Journal of Applied Psychology* (March 17, 2014); Park, Joon Hyung, and Richard S. DeFrank. "The Role of Proactive Personality in the Stressor–Strain Model." *International Journal of Stress Management* 25, no. 1 (February 2018): 44–59.

43. Van Rooy, David. "The Little-Known Personality Trait That Predicts Entrepreneurial Success." *Inc.*, August 28, 2014. https://www.inc.com/david-van-rooy/the-little-known-personality-trait-that-predicts-entrepreneurial-success.html.

44. Ganster, Daniel C., John Schaubroeck, Wesley E. Sime, and Bronston T. Mayes. "The Nomological Validity of the Type A Personality among Employed Adults." *Journal of Applied Psychology* 76, no. 1 (February 1991): 143–168; Billing, Tejinder K., and Pamela Steverson. "Moderating Role of Type-A Personality on Stress-Outcome Relationships." *Management Decision* 51, no. 9 (November 2013): 1893–1904; Naseer, Saima, Usman Raja, and Magda Bezerra Leite Donia. "Effect of Perceived Politics and Perceived Support on Bullying and Emotional Exhaustion: The Moderating Role of Type A Personality." *The Journal of Psychology: Interdisciplinary and Applied* 150, no. 5 (July 2016): 606–624.

45. Josef, Anika K., David Richter, Gregory R. Samanez-Larkin, Gert G. Wagner, Ralph Hertwig, and Rui Mata. "Stability and Change in Risk-Taking Propensity across the Adult Life Span." *Journal of Personality and Social Psychology* 111, no. 3 (September 2016): 430–450; Gardiner, Elliroma, and Chris J. Jackson. "Workplace Mavericks: How Personality and Risk-Taking Propensity Predicts Maverickism." *British Journal of Psychology* 103, no. 4 (November 2012): 497–519.

46. Casselman, Ben. "Risk-Averse Culture Infects U.S. Workers, Entrepreneurs." *Wall Street Journal*, June 2, 2013. http://online.wsj.com/article/SB10001424127887324031404578481162903760052.html.

47. Schwartz, Barry. *The Paradox of Choice: Why More Is Less* (New York: HarperCollins, 2004).

Chapter 3

1. Weingartern, Gene. "Pearls before Breakfast." *Washington Post,* April 8, 2007. www.washingtonpost.com/wp-dyn/content/article/2007/04/04/AR2007040401721.html.

2. See for example, Coren, Stanley. "Sensation and Perception." In *Handbook of Psychology, Vol. 1: History of Psychology* (2nd ed.), 100–128 (Hoboken, NJ: Wiley, 2013); Kass, Sarah, and Brent Dean Robbins. "Sensation and Perception." In *Humanistic Contributions for Psychology 101: Growth, Choice, and Responsibility*, 25–41: University Professors Press, 2016.

3. Ritchie, Hannah. "Read All about It: The Biggest Fake News Stories of 2016." *www.CNBC.com*, December 30, 2016. https://www.cnbc.com/2016/12/30/read-all-about-it-the-biggest-fake-news-stories-of-2016.html.

4. Silverman, Craig. "This Analysis Shows How Viral Fake Election News Stories Outperformed Real News on Facebook." www.BuzzFeed.com, November 16, 2016. https://www.buzzfeed.com/craigsilverman/viral-fake-election-news-outperformed-real-news-on-facebook?utm_term=.vpBZY5DLJQ#.sfgBgK64dr.

5. Barthel, Michael, Amy Mitchell, and Jesse Holcomb. "Many Americans Believe Fake News Is Sowing Confusion." *Pew Research Center,* December 15, 2016. http://www.journalism.org/2016/12/15/many-americans-believe-fake-news-is-sowing-confusion/.

6. Haden, Jeff. "Why What Kind of Car You Drive Matters." *Inc.* August 10, 2012. www.inc.com/jeff-haden/small-business-owners-does-it-matter-what-you-drive.html.

7. Lewin, Kurt, Fritz Heider, and Grace M. Heider. *Principles of Topological Psychology* (New York: McGraw-Hill, 1936).

8. Silcox, Beth. "Perception Is Everything." *Success.* n.d. www.success.com/article/perception-is-everything.

9. Devos, Thierry. "Stereotypes and Intergroup Attitudes." In *APA Handbook of Multicultural Psychology, Vol. 1: Theory and Research*, 341–360 (Washington, DC: American Psychological Association, 2014).

10. Swayne, Matt. "Real Stereotypes Continue to Exist in Virtual Worlds." *Penn State News,* May 4, 2105. https://news.psu.edu/story/355909/2015/05/04/research/real-stereotypes-continue-exist-virtual-worlds.

11. Lamy, Dominique, Andrew B. Leber, and Howard E. Egeth. "Selective Attention." In *Handbook of Psychology, Vol. 4: Experimental Psychology* (2nd ed.), 267–294 (Hoboken, NJ: Wiley, 2013).

12. http://www.theinvisiblegorilla.com/gorilla_experiment.html.

13. https://www.youtube.com/watch?v=FWSxSQsspiQ.

14. Lammers, William J., Sarah Davis, Olivia Davidson, and Kellie Hogue. "Impact of Positive, Negative, and No Personality Descriptors on the Attractiveness Halo Effect." *Psi Chi Journal of Psychological Research* 21, no. 1 (Spr 2016): 29–34.

15. Cherry, Kendra. "The Halo Effect." www.verywellmind.com, May 1, 2018. https://www.verywellmind.com/what-is-the-halo-effect-2795906.

16. Raffel, G. "Two Determinants of the Effect of Primacy." *American Journal of Psychology* 48 (1936): 654–657; Nahari, Galit, and Gershon Ben-Shakhar. "Primacy Effect in Credibility Judgements: The Vulnerability of Verbal Cues to Biased Interpretations." *Applied Cognitive Psychology* 27, no. 2 (March 2013): 247–255.

17. Swider, Brian, Brad Harris, and Murray Barrick. "Should You Chat Informally Before an Interview?" *Harvard Business Review,* September 14, 2016. https://hbr.org/2016/09/should-you-chat-informally-before-an-interview.

18. Postman, Leo, and Jerome S. Bruner. "Hypothesis and the Principle of Closure: The Effect of Frequency and Recency." *Journal of Psychology: Interdisciplinary and Applied* 33 (1952): 113–125; Plonsky, Ori, and Ido Erev. "Learning in Settings with Partial Feedback and the Wavy Recency Effect of Rare Events." *Cognitive Psychology* 93, (March 2017): 18–43.

19. Preston, M. G. "Contrast Effects and the Psychometric Function." *American Journal of Psychology* 48, (1936): 625–631; Kopelman, M. D. "The Contrast Effect in the Selection Interview." *British Journal of Educational Psychology* 45, no. 3 (November 1975): 333–336; Boillaud, Eric, and Guylaine Molina. "Are Judgments a Form of Data Clustering? Reexamining Contrast Effects with the k-Means Algorithm." *Journal of Experimental Psychology: Human Perception and Performance* 41, no. 2 (April 2015): 415–430.

20. Pratt, Siofra. "How Badly Is Your Unconscious Bias Affecting Your Recruiting Skills?" www.socialtalent.com, June 23, 2015. https://www.socialtalent.com/blog/recruitment/how-badly-is-your-unconscious-bias-affecting-your-recruiting-skills.

21. Thomsen, A. "Psychological Projection and the Election: A Simple Class Experiment." *Journal of Psychology: Interdisciplinary and Applied* 11 (1941): 115–117; Chang, Valerie T., Nickola C. Overall, Helen Madden, and Rachel S. T. Low. "Expressive Suppression Tendencies, Projection Bias in Memory of Negative Emotions, and Well-Being." *Emotion* (February 1, 2018).

22. "Psychological Projection: Dealing with Undesirable Emotions." www.everydayhealth.com, November 15, 2017. https://www.everydayhealth.com/emotional-health/psychological-projection-dealing-with-undesirable-emotions/.

23. Clark, Jenna L., and Melanie C. Green. "Self-Fulfilling Prophecies: Perceived Reality of Online Interaction Drives Expected Outcomes of Online Communication." *Personality and Individual Differences* (August 30, 2017); Jussim, Lee. "Accuracy, Bias, Self-Fulfilling Prophecies, and Scientific Self-Correction." *Behavioral and Brain Sciences* 40, (March 22, 2017).

24. Crossman, Ashley. "Definition of Self-Fulfilling Prophecy." *www.ThoughtCo.com,* March 6, 2017. https://www.thoughtco.com/self-fulfilling-prophecy-3026577.

25. Bourdage, Joshua S., Jocelyn Wiltshire, and Kibeom Lee. "Personality and Workplace Impression Management: Correlates and Implications." *Journal of Applied Psychology*

100, no. 2 (March 2015): 537–546; Kacmar, K. Michele, John E. Delery, and Gerald R. Ferris. "Differential Effectiveness of Applicant Impression Management Tactics on Employment Interview Decisions." *Journal of Applied Social Psychology* 22, no. 16 (August 1992): 1250–1272; Kacmar, K. Michele, and Dawn S. Carlson. "Effectiveness of Impression Management Tactics across Human Resource Situations." *Journal of Applied Social Psychology* 29, no. 6 (June 1999): 1293–1315.

26.   Roulin, Nicolas, and Julia Levashina. "Impression Management and Social Media Profiles." In *Social Media in Employee Selection and Recruitment: Theory, Practice, and Current Challenges*, 223–248. (Cham, Switzerland: Springer International Publishing, 2016).

27.   Keeves, Gareth, James Westphal, and Michael McDonald. "Research: Executives Who Flatter Their CEOs Are More Likely to Criticize Them to the Press." *Harvard Business Review*, April 5, 2017. https://hbr.org/2017/04/research-executives-who-flatter-their-ceos-are-more-likely-to-criticize-them-to-the-press.

28.   Dweck, Carol S. "Reflections on the Legacy of Attribution Theory." *Motivation Science* 4, no. 1 (March 2018): 17–18; Martinko, Mark J., Scott C. Douglas, and Paul Harvey. "Attribution Theory in Industrial and Organizational Psychology: A Review." In *International Review of Industrial and Organizational Psychology 2006* (Vol. 21), 127–187 (Hoboken, NJ: Wiley, 2006).

29.   Harvey, Paul, Kristen Madison, Mark Martinko, T. Russell Crook, and Tamara A. Crook. "Attribution Theory in the Organizational Sciences: The Road Traveled and the Path Ahead." *Academy of Management Perspectives* 28, no. 2 (May 2014): 128–146; Mehlman, Rick C., and C. R. Snyder. "Excuse Theory: A Test of the Self-Protective Role of Attributions." *Journal of Personality and Social Psychology* 49, no. 4 (October 1985): 994–1001.

30.   Heath, Dan. "The Fundamental Attribution Error: It's the Situation, Not the Person." *Fast Company*, June 9, 2010. https://www.fastcompany.com/1657515/fundamental-attribution-error-its-situation-not-person.

31.   Harvey, John H., and Richard P. McGlynn. "Matching Words to Phenomena: The Case of the Fundamental Attribution Error." *Journal of Personality and Social Psychology* 43, no. 2 (August 1982): 345–346; Ross, Lee D., Teresa M. Amabile, and Julia L. Steinmetz. "Social Roles, Social Control, and Biases in Social-Perception Processes." *Journal of Personality and Social Psychology* 35, no. 7 (July 1977): 485–494; Jouffre, Stéphane, and Jean-Claude Croizet. "Empowering and Legitimizing the Fundamental Attribution Error: Power and Legitimization Exacerbate the Translation of Role-Constrained Behaviors into Ability Differences." *European Journal of Social Psychology* 46, no. 5 (August 2016): 621–631.

32.   Seppala, Emma. "When Giving Critical Feedback, Focus on Your Nonverbal Cues." *Harvard Business Review*, January 20, 2017. https://hbr.org/2017/01/when-giving-critical-feedback-focus-on-your-nonverbal-cues.

33.   Larson Jr., James R. "Evidence for a Self-Serving Bias in the Attribution of Causality." *Journal of Personality* 45, no. 3 (September 1977): 430–441; Arkin, Robert M., et al. "Self-Presentation, Self-Monitoring, and the Self-Serving Bias in Causal Attribution." *Personality and Social Psychology Bulletin* 5, no. 1 (January 1979): 73–76; ee-Bates, Benjamin, Daniel C. Billing, Peter Caputi, Greg L. Carstairs, Denise Linnane, and Kane Middleton. "The Application of Subjective Job Task Analysis Techniques in Physically Demanding Occupations: Evidence for the Presence of Self-Serving Bias." *Ergonomics* 60, no. 9 (September 2017): 1240–1249.

34.   Cherry, Kendra. "How the Self-Serving Bias Protects Self-Esteem." www.verywellmind.com, February 12, 2018. https://www.verywellmind.com/what-is-the-self-serving-bias-2795032.

35.   See for example, Allport, Floyd H. "Perception and Theories of Learning: The Behavior Theory Approach." In *Theories of Perception and the Concept of Structure: A Review and Critical Analysis with an Introduction to a Dynamic-Structural Theory of Behavior*, 437–466 (Hoboken, NJ: Wiley, 1955).

36.   Robson, David. "Old Schooled: You Never Stop Learning Like a Child." *Neuroscience*. May 26, 2013. http://neurosciencestuff.tumblr.com/post/51428289471/old-schooled-you-never-stop-learning-like-a-child?utm_source=Dan+Pink%27s+Newsletter&utm_campaign=f2973b957c-august_newsletter&utm_medium=email&utm_term=0_4d8277f97a-f2973b957c-306048817.

37.   Clark, Robert E. "The Classical Origins of Pavlov's Conditioning." *Integrative Physiological and Behavioral Science* 39, no. 4 (October 2004): 279–294.

38.   Davey, Graham, and Chris Cullen. *Human Operant Conditioning and Behavior Modification* (Oxford: Wiley, 1988).

39.   Thorndike, E. L. "The Law of Effect." *American Journal of Psychology* 39, (1927): 212–222.

40.   Skinner, B. F. "The Effect on the Amount of Conditioning of an Interval of Time before Reinforcement." *Journal of General Psychology* 14, (1936): 279–295; Scriven, Michael, James J. Gallagher, Allen D. Calvin, Charles Hanley, James V. McConnell, and F. J. McGuigan. "An Overview of Stimulus-Response Reinforcement Theory." In *Psychology*, 321–329 (Needham Heights, MA: Allyn & Bacon, 1961).

41.   Luthans, Fred, and Mark J. Martinko. "Organizational Behavior Modification: A Way to Bridge the Gap between Academic Research and Real World Application." *Journal of Organizational Behavior Management* 3, no. 3 (1981): 33–50; Stajkovic, Alexander D., and Fred Luthans. "A Meta-Analysis of the Effects of Organizational Behavior Modification on Task Performance, 1975–95." *Academy of Management Journal* 40, no. 5 (October 1997): 1122–1149.

42.   Caprino, Kathy. "Six Essential Ways to Build a Positive Organization." *Forbes.com*. December 13, 2013. www.forbes.com/sites/kathycaprino/2013/12/13/6-essential-ways-to-build-a-positive-organization/.

43.   Wexley, Kenneth N., and Wayne F. Nemeroff. "Effectiveness of Positive Reinforcement and Goal Setting as Methods of Management Development." *Journal of Applied Psychology* 60, no. 4 (August 1975): 446–450; Briefer Freymond, Sabrina, Elodie F. Briefer, Anja Zollinger, Yveline Gindrat-von Allmen, Christa Wyss, and Iris Bachmann. "Behaviour of Horses in a Judgment Bias Test Associated with Positive or Negative Reinforcement." *Applied Animal Behaviour Science* 158 (September 2014): 34–45.

44.   Jones, Bruce. "How Positive Reinforcement Keeps Employees Engaged." *Harvard Business Review*, February 28, 2017. https://hbr.org/sponsored/2017/02/how-positive-reinforcement-keeps-employees-engaged.

45.   Alessandri, Jérôme, Carlos R. X. Cançado, and Josele Abreu-Rodrigues. "Effects of Reinforcement Value on Instruction Following under Schedules of Negative Reinforcement." *Behavioural Processes* 145, (December 2017): 27–30.

46.   Burger, Richard. "The Marvelous Benefits of Positive and Negative Reinforcement." *Selah Independent*. March 11, 2009.

47.   McConnell, James V. "Negative Reinforcement and Positive Punishment." *Teaching of Psychology* 17, no. 4 (December 1990): 247–249; Harbeck, Emma L., A. Ian Glendon, and Trevor J. Hine. "Reward versus Punishment: Reinforcement Sensitivity Theory, Young Novice Drivers' Perceived Risk, and Risky Driving." *Transportation Research Part F: Traffic Psychology and Behaviour* 47, (May 2017): 13–22.

48.   Ibid.

49.   Chan, C. K. J., and Justin A. Harris. "Extinction of Pavlovian Conditioning: The Influence of Trial Number and Reinforcement History." *Behavioural Processes* 141, no. Part 1 (August 2017): 19–25; Kunnavatana, S. Shanun, Sarah E. Bloom, Andrew L. Samaha, Timothy A. Slocum, and Casey J. Clay. "Manipulating Parameters of Reinforcement to Reduce Problem Behavior

without Extinction." *Journal of Applied Behavior Analysis* 51, no. 2 (Spr 2018): 283–302.

50. Lundin, Robert W. "Schedules of Reinforcement." In *Personality: An Experimental Approach*, 76–101 (New York: MacMillan, 1961).

51. Ibid.

52. Crossman, Edward K. "Schedules of Reinforcement." In *Human Behavior in Today's World*, 133–138 (New York, Praeger, 1991); Okouchi, Hiroto. "An Exploration of Remote History Effects in Humans: II. The Effects under Fixed-Interval, Variable-Interval, and Fixed-Ratio Schedules." *Psychological Record* 60, no. 1 (Winter 2010): 27–42.

53. Ibid.

54. Ibid.

55. Ibid.

56. Bandura, Albert. *Social Learning Theory* (Oxford: Prentice-Hall, 1977); Bandura, Albert. "Social Cognitive Theory of Self-Regulation." *Organizational Behavior and Human Decision Processes* 50, no. 2 (December 1991): 248–287; Bandura, Albert. "Social Cognitive Theory." In *Handbook of Theories of Social Psychology* (Vol. 1), 349–373. (Thousand Oaks, CA: Sage, 2012).

57. Bandura, Albert. *Self-Efficacy: The Exercise of Control* (New York: W H Freeman/Times Books/Henry Holt & Co, 1997); Bandura, Albert. "The Role of Self-Efficacy in Goal-Based Motivation." In *New Developments in Goal Setting and Task Performance*, 147–157 (New York: Routledge/Taylor & Francis Group, 2013).

58. Ibid.

59. Rousmaniere, Dana. "Help Your Employees Learn from Each Other." *Harvard Business Review*, January 28, 2016. https://hbr.org/tip/2016/01/help-your-employees-learn-from-each-other.

60. "Is Your Company Encouraging Employees to Share What They Know?" *Business Mirror*, November 16, 2015. http://businessmirror.com.ph/is-your-company-encouraging-employees-to-share-what-they-know/.

61. Bandura. "Social Cognitive Theory of Personality"; Hoover, J. Duane, Robert C. Giambatista, and Liuba Y. Belkin. "Eyes On, Hands On: Vicarious Observational Learning as an Enhancement of Direct Experience." *Academy Of Management Learning and Education* 11, no. 4 (December 2012): 591–608.

62. Bandura. "Social Cognitive Theory of Personality"; Bandura. "Social Cognitive Theory of Self-Regulation.

63. Bandura, Albert. "Human Agency in Social Cognitive Theory." *American Psychologist* 44, no. 9 (September 1989): 1175–1184; Wood, Robert, and Albert Bandura. "Social Cognitive Theory of Organizational Management." *Academy of Management Review* 14, no. 3 (July 1989): 361–384.

Chapter 4

1. Augustine, Adam A., and Randy J. Larsen. "Personality, Affect, and Affect Regulation." In *APA Handbook of Personality and Social Psychology, Volume 4: Personality Processes and Individual Differences*, 147–165 (Washington, DC: American Psychological Association, 2015); George, Jennifer M. "Trait and State Affect." In *Individual Differences and Behavior in Organizations,* edited by Kevin R. Murphy, 145 (San Francisco: Jossey-Bass, 1996).

2. Charles, Susan T., and Jennifer W. Robinette. "Emotion and Emotion Regulation." In *APA Handbook of Clinical Geropsychology, Vol. 1: History and Status of the Field and Perspectives on Aging*, 235–258 (Washington, DC: American Psychological Association, 2015); Frijda, Nico H. "Moods, Emotion Episodes, and Emotions." In *Handbook of Emotions*, 381–403 (New York: Guilford, 1993).

3. Ong, Anthony D., and Alex J. Zautra. "Intraindividual Variability in Mood and Mood Regulation in Adulthood." In *Handbook of Intraindividual Variability across the Life Span*, 198–215 (New York: Routledge/Taylor & Francis Group, 2015); Guterman, Yossi, Inbal Kleifeld, and Rachel Vegmister. "Just Think! Mood Regulation Effects of Cognitive Activity." In *Emotional Intelligence: Current Evidence from Psychophysiological, Educational and Organizational Perspectives*, 57–70 (Hauppauge, NY: Nova Science Publishers, 2015).

4. Lang, Annie, and David R. Ewoldsen. "The Measurement of Positive and Negative Affect in Media Research." In *The Routledge Handbook of Emotions and Mass Media*, 79–98. (New York: Routledge/Taylor & Francis Group, 2015); Rice, Frances, Shiri Davidovich, and Sandra Dunsmuir. "Emotion Regulation and Depression: Maintaining Equilibrium between Positive and Negative Affect." In *Emotion Regulation and Psychopathology in Children and Adolescents*, 171–195. (New York: Oxford University Press, 2017).

5. Wilding, Melody. "5 Signs You're About To Make a Bad Career Decision." *Forbes,* November 14, 2016. https://www.forbes.com/sites/melodywilding/2016/11/14/5-signs-youre-about-to-make-a-bad-career-decision/#3ee28df4207c.

6. Wong, Julia Carrie. "Uber CEO Travis Kalanick Caught on Video Arguing with Driver about Fares." *The Guardian,* March 1, 2017. https://www.theguardian.com/technology/2017/feb/28/uber-ceo-travis-kalanick-driver-argument-video-fare-prices.

7. Goudreau, Jenna. "From Crying to Temper Tantrums: How to Manage Emotions at Work." *Forbes.com.* January 9, 2013. www.forbes.com/sites/jennagoudreau/2013/01/09/from-crying-to-temper-tantrums-how-to-manage-emotions-at-work/.

8. Tee, Eugene Y. J. "The Emotional Link: Leadership and the Role of Implict and Explicit Emotional Contagion Processes across Multiple Organizational Levels." *Leadership Quarterly* (June 23, 2015): *PsycINFO*, EBSCO*host*; Hatfield, Elaine, John T. Cacioppo, and Richard L. Rapson. *Emotional contagion* (New York, NY: Cambridge University Press, 1994).

9. Niiler, Eric. "The Psychology behind Violence at Trump Rallies." *Wired,* March 18, 2016. https://www.wired.com/2016/03/psychology-behind-violence-trump-rallies/.

10. Gabriel, Allison S., Michael A. Daniels, James M. Diefendorff, and Gary J. Greguras. "Emotional Labor Actors: A Latent Profile Analysis of Emotional Labor Strategies." *Journal of Applied Psychology* 100, no. 3 (May 2015): 863–879; Ashforth, Blake E., and Ronald H. Humphrey. "Emotional Labor in Service Roles: The Influence of Identity." *Academy of Management Review* 18, no. 1 (January 1993): 88–115; Hochschild, Arlie R. *The Managed Heart: Commercialization of Human Feeling* (Berkeley: University of California Press, 1983).

11. Christoforou, Paraskevi S., and Blake E. Ashforth. "Revisiting the Debate on the Relationship between Display Rules and Performance: Considering the Explicitness of Display Rules." *Journal of Applied Psychology* 100, no. 1 (January 2015): 249–261; Ashforth, Blake E., and Ronald H. Humphrey. "Emotional Labor in Service Roles: The Influence of Identity." *Academy of Management Review* 18, no. 1 (January 1993): 88–115; Rafaeli, Anat, and Robert I. Sutton. "The Expression of Emotion in Organizational Life." *Research in Organizational Behavior* 11 (January 1989): 1–42.

12. Côté, Stéphane. "A Social Interaction Model of the Effects of Emotion Regulation on Work Strain." *Academy of Management Review* 30, no. 3 (July 2005): 509–530; Kenworthy, Jared, Cara Fay, Mark Frame, and Robyn Petree. "A Meta-analytic Review of the Relationship between Emotional Dissonance and Emotional Exhaustion." *Journal of Applied Social Psychology* 44, no. 2 (February 2014): 94–105.

13. Côté. "A Social Interaction Model"; Grandey, Alicia A. "When 'The Show Must Go On': Surface Acting and Deep Acting as Determinants of Emotional Exhaustion and Peer-Rated Service Delivery." *Academy of Management Journal* 46, no. 1 (February 2003): 86–96; Xanthopoulou, Despoina, Arnold B. Bakker, Wido G.M. Oerlemans, and Maria Koszucka. "Need for

Recovery after Emotional Labor: Differential Effects of Daily Deep and Surface Acting." *Journal of Organizational Behavior* (November 27, 2017).

14. Braunstein, Laura Martin, James J. Gross, and Kevin N. Ochsner. "Explicit and Implicit Emotion Regulation: A Multi-Level Framework." *Social Cognitive and Affective Neuroscience* 12, no. 10 (October 2017): 1545–1557; Gross, James J., and Ross A. Thompson. "Emotion Regulation: Conceptual Foundations." In *Handbook of Emotion Regulation*, 3–24 (New York: Guilford, 2007).

15. Appleton, Allison A., Eric B. Loucks, Stephen L. Buka, and Laura D. Kubzansky. "Divergent Associations of Antecedent- and Response-Focused Emotion Regulation Strategies with Midlife Cardiovascular Disease Risk." *Annals of Behavioral Medicine* 48, no. 2 (October 2014): 246–255; Gross, James J. "Antecedent- and Response-Focused Emotion Regulation: Divergent Consequences for Experience, Expression, and Physiology." *Journal of Personality and Social Psychology* 74, no. 1 (January 1998): 224–237.

16. Appleton et al. "Divergent Associations of Antecedent- and Response-Focused Emotion Regulation Strategies; Gross. "Antecedent- and Response-Focused Emotion Regulation."

17. Salovey, Peter, and John D. Mayer. "Emotional Intelligence." *Imagination, Cognition and Personality* 9, no. 3 (1989): 185–211; Joseph, Dana L., Jing Jin, Daniel A. Newman, and Ernest H. O'Boyle. "Why Does Self-Reported Emotional Intelligence Predict Job Performance? A Meta-Analytic Investigation of Mixed EI." *Journal of Applied Psychology* 100, no. 2 (March 2015): 298–342.

18. Goleman, Daniel. *Emotional Intelligence* (New York: Bantam Books, 1995); Goleman, Daniel, Richard Boyatzis, and Annie McKee. *Primal Leadership: Realizing the Power of Emotional Intelligence* (Boston: Harvard Business School Press, 2002).

19. Deutschendorf, Harvey. "7 Reasons Why Emotional Intelligence Is One of the Fastest-Growing Job Skills." *Fast Company,* May 4, 2016. https://www.fastcompany.com/3059481/7-reasons-why-emotional-intelligence-is-one-of-the-fastest-growing-job-skills.

20. Thygesen, Kes. "Why Emotional Intelligence Is More Important to Hiring Than You Think." *Fast Company.* April 21, 2014. www.fastcompany.com/3029306/why-you-should-make-emotional-intelligence-the-cornerstone-of-your-hiring-strategy.

21. Molinsky, Andy. "Emotional Intelligence Doesn't Translate across Borders." *Harvard Business Review.* April 20, 2015. https://hbr.org/2015/04/emotional-intelligence-doesnt-translate-across-borders.

22. Nishi, Dennis. "'Soft Skills' Can Help You Get Ahead." *Wall Street Journal.* May 18, 2013. http://online.wsj.com/article/SB10001424127887324715704578481290888822474.html.

23. Goleman. *Emotional Intelligence*; Goleman, Boyatzis, and McKee. *Primal Leadership*.

24. See for example, Harms, P. D., and Marcus Credé. "Remaining Issues in Emotional Intelligence Research: Construct Overlap, Method Artifacts, and Lack of Incremental Validity." *Industrial and Organizational Psychology: Perspectives on Science and Practice* 3, no. 2 (June 2010): 154–158; Murphy, Kevin R. *A Critique of Emotional Intelligence: What Are the Problems and How Can They Be Fixed?* (Mahwah, NJ: Erlbaum, 2006).

25. Murphy, Mark. "Why New Hires Fail (Emotional Intelligence vs. Skills)." *www.LeadershipIQ.com,* June 22, 2015. https://www.leadershipiq.com/blogs/leadershipiq/35354241-why-new-hires-fail-emotional-intelligence-vs-skills#.

26. Allport, G. W. "Attitudes." In *A Handbook of Social Psychology*, 798–844 (Worcester, MA: Clark University Press, 1935); Bem, Daryl J. *Beliefs, Attitudes, and Human Affairs* (Oxford: Brooks/Cole, 1970); McVittie, Chris, and Andy McKinlay. "Attitudes and Attributions." In *The Palgrave Handbook of Critical Social Psychology*, 269–289. (New York: Palgrave Macmillan, 2017).

27. Ajzen, Icek, and Martin Fishbein. "The Influence of Attitudes on Behavior." In *The Handbook of Attitudes*, 173–221 (Mahwah, NJ: Erlbaum, 2005); Ajzen, Icek, and Martin Fishbein. "Attitudes and Normative Beliefs as Factors Influencing Behavioral Intentions." *Journal of Personality and Social Psychology* 21, no. 1 (January 1972): 1–9; Ajzen, Icek. "The Theory of Planned Behavior." *Organizational Behavior and Human Decision Processes* 50, no. 2 (December 1991): 179–211.

28. Festinger, Leon. *A Theory of Cognitive Dissonance* (Stanford, CA: Stanford University Press, 1957); Morvan, Camille, and Alexander O'Connor. *An Analysis of Leon Festinger's A Theory of Cognitive Dissonance.* (New York: Routledge/Taylor & Francis Group, 2017).

29. Eggerth, Donald E. "Job Satisfaction, Job Performance, and Success." In *APA Handbook of Career Intervention, Volume 2: Applications*, 453–463. (Washington, DC: American Psychological Association, 2015).

30. Loudenback, Tanza, Emmie Martin, and Alexa Pipia. "13 of the Happiest Companies in America." *Business Insider,* April 29, 2016. http://www.businessinsider.com/payscale-best-companies-with-happiest-employees-in-america-2016-4?r=UK&IR=T.

31. Byrne, Zinta S. *Understanding Employee Engagement: Theory, Research, and Practice.* (New York: Routledge/Taylor & Francis Group, 2015); Mone, Edward M., and Manuel London. *Employee Engagement through Effective Performance Management: A Practical Guide for Managers., 2nd ed.* (New York: Routledge/Taylor & Francis Group, 2018).

32. Maier, Steffen. "5 Companies Getting Employee Engagement Right." *Entrepreneur,* December 28, 2016. https://www.entrepreneur.com/article/285052.

33. Ibid.

34. Organ, Dennis W. *Organizational Citizenship Behavior: The Good Soldier Syndrome* (Lexington, MA: Lexington Books/D. C. Heath, 1988); Smith, C. Ann, Dennis W. Organ, and Janet P. Near. "Organizational Citizenship Behavior: Its Nature and Antecedents." In *Work and Organisational Psychology: Research Methodology; Assessment and Selection; Organisational Change and Development; Human Resource and Performance Management; Emerging Trends: Innovation/Globalisation/Technology*, 129–144. (Thousand Oaks, CA: Sage, 2016).

35. Wilson, Tamara. "Teacher Goes Above and Beyond for Students in Need." *CNN,* December 22, 2015. https://edition.cnn.com/2015/12/22/us/gif-sonya-romero/index.html.

36. Ones, Deniz S., and Stephan Dilchert. "Counterproductive Work Behaviors: Concepts, Measurement, and Nomological Network." In *APA Handbook of Testing and Assessment in Psychology, Vol. 1: Test Theory and Testing and Assessment in Industrial and Organizational Psychology*, 643–659 (Washington, DC: American Psychological Association, 2013).

37. Steel, Emily and Michael S. Schmidt. "Bill O'Reilly Is Forced Out at Fox News." *New York Times,* April 19, 2017. https://www.nytimes.com/2017/04/19/business/media/bill-oreilly-fox-news-allegations.html

38. Boas, Ana Alice Vilas, and Estelle M. Morin. "Work-Related Stress, Psychological Well-Being, and Work Engagement: Effects and Relation to Quality of Working Life." In *Stress and Quality of Working Life: Interpersonal and Occupation-Based Stress*, 109–129. (Charlotte, NC: IAP Information Age Publishing, 2016); Yang, Julia. "Understanding Work Stress." In *Stress in the Modern World: Understanding Science and Society*, 175–185. (Santa Barbara, CA): Greenwood Press/ABC-CLIO, 2017).

39. For details see https://www.stress.org/americas-1-health-problem/.

40. For details see www.stress.org/stress-is-killing-you/.

41. Fulton, April. "Work Can Be Stressful, Dangerous And Sometimes Great." *NPR,* August 14, 2017. https://www.npr.org/sections/health-shots/2017/08/14/542907572/work-can-be-stressful-dangerous-and-sometimes-great.

42.   Abbas, Muhammad, and Usman Raja. "Challenge-Hindrance Stressors and Job Outcomes: The Moderating Role of Conscientiousness." *Journal of Business and Psychology* (April 2, 2018); Lepine, Jeffery A., Nathan P. Podsakoff, and Marcie A. Lepine. "A Meta-Analytic Test of the Challenge Stressor—Hindrance Stressor Framework: An Explanation for Inconsistent Relationships among Stressors and Performance." *Academy of Management Journal* 48, no. 5 (October 2005): 764–775.

43.   https://www.ncbi.nlm.nih.gov/pmc/articles/PMC5244684/.

44.   http://www.hrrevolution.me/challenge-stressors-versus-hindrance-stressors-and-resources-to-overcome-stressors/.

45.   Cao, X, Masood, A, Luqman, A, & Ali, A. "Excessive Use of Mobile Social Networking Sites and Poor Academic Performance: Antecedents and Consequences from Stressor-Strain-Outcome Perspective." *Computers in Human Behavior* 85, (August 2018): 163–174; Cheung, Francis, and Catherine Tang. 2010. "The Influence of Emotional Dissonance on Subjective Health and Job Satisfaction: Testing the Stress–Strain–Outcome Model." *Journal of Applied Social Psychology* 40, no. 12: 3192–3217.

46.   Sonnentag, Sabine, and Charlotte Fritz. 2015. "Recovery from Job Stress: The Stressor-Detachment Model as an Integrative Framework." *Journal of Organizational Behavior* 36, no. Suppl 1: S72–S103.

47.   Nelson, Debra L., and Bret L. Simmons. "Savoring Eustress While Coping with Distress: The Holistic Model of Stress." In *Handbook of Occupational Health Psychology* (2nd ed.), 55–74 (Washington, DC: American Psychological Association, 2011).

48.   Ibid.

49.   Perrewé, Pamela L., Christopher C. Rosen, and Christina Maslach. "Organizational Politics and Stress: The Development of a Process Model." In *Politics in Organizations: Theory and Research Considerations*, 213–255 (New York: Routledge/Taylor & Francis Group, 2012).

50.   Banerjee, Ab. "It's Time to End the Cult of the CEO." *Management Today.* https://www.managementtoday.co.uk/its-time-end-cult-ceo/leadership-lessons/article/1431285.

51.   George, Bill. "The Massive Difference between Negative and Positive Leadership." *Fortune,* March 21, 2016. http://fortune.com/2016/03/21/negative-positive-leadership-politics-ford-alan-mulally/.

52.   Gouthro, Dan. "The Employee Burnout Crisis: Study Reveals Big Workplace Challenge in 2017." www.kronos.com, January 9, 2017. https://www.kronos.com/about-us/newsroom/employee-burnout-crisis-study-reveals-big-workplace-challenge-2017.

53.   Penwell-Waines, Lauren M., Kevin T. Larkin, and Jeffrey L. Goodie. "Coping." In *Biopsychosocial Assessment in Clinical Health Psychology*, 154–170 (New York: Guilford, 2015); Steptoe, Andrew. "Psychological Coping, Individual Differences and Physiological Stress Responses." In *Personality and Stress: Individual Differences in the Stress Process*, 205–233 (Oxford: Wiley, 1991).

54.   Penwell-Waines et al. "Coping"; Steptoe. "Psychological Coping."

55.   Bradberry, Travis. "How Successful People Handle Toxic People." *Forbes,* October 21, 2014. https://www.forbes.com/sites/travisbradberry/2014/10/21/how-successful-people-handle-toxic-people/#609b6ae32a92.

56.   Moninger, Jeannette. "10 Relaxation Techniques That Zap Stress Fast." WebMD, https://www.webmd.com/balance/guide/blissing-out-10-relaxation-techniques-reduce-stress-spot#1.

57.   Sung Doo, Kim, Elaine C. Hollensbe, Catherine E. Schwoerer, and Jonathon R. B. Halbesleben. "Dynamics of a Wellness Program: A Conservation of Resources Perspective." *Journal of Occupational Health Psychology* 20, no. 1 (January 2015): 62–71.

58.   Farr, Christina. "How Fitbit Became the Next Big Thing In Corporate Wellness." *Fast Company,* April 18, 2016. https://www.fastcompany.com/3058462/how-fitbit-became-the-next-big-thing-in-corporate-wellness.

59.   Rothfeld, Lindsay. "7 Companies with Amazingly Unique Wellness Programs." *www.Mashable.com,* May 15, 2015. https://mashable.com/2015/05/15/unique-corporate-wellness-programs/#MLDBcedeyEqm.

60.   "Six Easy-to-Implement Workplace Wellness Programs." *Medium.com,* January 17, 2017. https://medium.com/@ManagedbyQ/six-easy-to-implement-workplace-wellness-programs-9ebc00b11302.

61.   Purcell, Jim. "Meet the Wellness Programs That Save Companies Money." *Harvard Business Review,* April 20, 2016. https://hbr.org/2016/04/meet-the-wellness-programs-that-save-companies-money.

62.   Kohll, Alan. "The Top Corporate Wellness Trends to Watch For in 2017." *Forbes,* January 18, 2017. https://www.forbes.com/sites/alankohll/2017/01/18/the-top-corporate-wellness-trends-to-watch-for-in-2017/2/#1c6732164a80.

63.   https://safetymanagement.eku.edu/resources/infographics/work-related-stress-on-employees-health/.

Chapter 5

1.   Refer to the following for an overview of work motivation theory: Grant, Adam M., and Jihae Shin. "Work Motivation: Directing, Energizing, and Maintaining Effort (and Research)." In Richard M. Ryan (Ed.), *Oxford Handbook of Motivation,* 505–519 (New York: Oxford University Press, 2012); Kanfer, Ruth. "Work Motivation: Theory, Practice, and Future Directions." In *The Oxford Handbook of Organizational Psychology, Vol. 1,* 455–495. (New York: Oxford University Press, 2012); Kanfer, Ruth, Michael Frese, and Russell E. Johnson. "Motivation Related to Work: A Century of Progress." *Journal of Applied Psychology* 102, no. 3 (March 2017): 338–355.

2.   Kanfer, Ruth. "Motivation Theory and Industrial and Organizational Psychology." In Marvin D. Dunnette (Ed.), *Handbook of Industrial and Organizational Psychology,* 2nd ed., Vol. 1, 75–130 (Palo Alto, CA: Consulting Psychologists Press).

3.   Kanfer, Ruth, Michael Frese, and Russell E. Johnson. "Motivation Related to Work: A Century of Progress." *Journal of Applied Psychology* 102, no. 3 (March 2017): 338–355.

4.   Maslow, A. H. "A Theory of Human Motivation," *Psychological Review* 50, no. 4 (July 1943): 370–396.

5.   Wahba, Mahmoud A., and Lawrence G. Bridwell. "Maslow Reconsidered: A Review of Research on the Need. Hierarchy Theory." *Organizational Behavior and Human Performance* 15, no. 2 (April 1976): 212–240; Harrigan, William Joseph, and Michael Lamport Commons. "Replacing Maslow's Needs Hierarchy with an Account Based on Stage and Value." *Behavioral Development Bulletin* 20, no. 1 (April 2015): 24–31.

6.   Ibid.

7.   Alderfer, Clayton P. "An Empirical Test of a New Theory of Human Needs," *Organizational Behavior and Human Performance* 4, no. 2 (1969): 142–175; Cao, Juan, Qin An, and Hao Chen. "A qualitative research of the psychological need of the elderly in ERG theory perspective." *Chinese Journal of Clinical Psychology* 23, no. 2 (April 2015): 343–345; Schneider, Benjamin, and Clayton P. Alderfer. "Three Studies of Measures of Need Satisfaction in Organizations." *Administrative Science Quarterly* 18, no. 4 (December 1973): 489–505.

8.   Herzberg, F., B. Mausner, and B. Snyderman. *The Motivation to Work,* 2nd ed. (Oxford: Wiley, 1959); Herzberg, Frederick. "One More Time: How Do You Motivate Employees?" *Harvard Business Review* 81, no. 1 (January 2003): 87–96; Holmberg, Christopher, Jino Caro, and Iwona Sobis. "Job Satisfaction among Swedish Mental Health Nursing Personnel: Revisiting the Two-Factor Theory." *International Journal of Mental Health Nursing* (April 10, 2017).

9. Ibid.

10. http://www.leadership-central.com/two-factor-theory.html#axzz3YDaoZUtX.

11. King, Nathan. "Clarification and Evaluation of the Two-Factor Theory of Job Satisfaction." *Psychological Bulletin* 74, no. 1 (July 1970): 18–31; Wall, Toby D., and Geoffrey M. Stephenson. "Herzberg's Two-Factor Theory of Job Attitudes: A Critical Evaluation and Some Fresh Evidence." *Industrial Relations Journal* 1, no. 3 (September 1970); Furnham, Adrian, Andreas Eracleous, and Tomas Chamorro-Premuzic. "Personality, Motivation and Job Satisfaction: Hertzberg Meets the Big Five." *Journal of Managerial Psychology* 24, no. 8 (2009): 765–779; Sledge, Sally, Angela K. Miles, and Samuel Coppage. "What Role Does Culture Play? A Look at Motivation and Job Satisfaction among Hotel Workers in Brazil." *International Journal of Human Resource Management* 19, no. 9 (September 2008): 1667–1682.

12. McClelland, David C. *The Achieving Society* (New York: Van Nostrand, 1961); McClelland, David C. *Power: The Inner Experience* (New York: Irvington, 1975); Harrell, Adrian M., and Michael J. Stahl. "A Behavioral Decision Theory Approach for Measuring McClelland's Trichotomy of Needs." *Journal of Applied Psychology* 66, no. 2 (April 1981): 242–247; Liu, Yu-Shan, and Susan Wohlsdorf Arendt. "Development and Validation of a Work Motive Measurement Scale." *International Journal of Contemporary Hospitality Management* 28, no. 4 (June 2016): 700–716.

13. https://www.biography.com/people/sara-blakely-031416.

14. Sailor, Craig. "No Regrets for Dan Price: CEO Who Put $70k Minimum Wage in Place Is Here to Stay." *The News Tribune,* February 11, 2017. http://www.thenewstribune.com/news/business/article131986394.html.

15. Greenblatt, Drew. "A Simple Spreadsheet for Motivation and Versatility," *Inc.*, January 8, 2013, www.inc.com/drew-greenblatt/simple-spreadsheet-for-motivation-and-versatility.html.

16. Broughton, Anne Claire. "How Marlin Steel Got Lean by Paying for Skills." *Forbes,* March 14, 2016. https://www.forbes.com/sites/thehitachifoundation/2016/03/14/how-marlin-steel-got-lean-by-paying-for-skills/#4573f9c22b0e.

17. "Free Food! Free Travel! 10 Corporate Perks We Love." The Muse. https://www.themuse.com/advice/free-food-free-travel-10-corporate-perks-we-love.

18. Latham, Gary P., and Edwin A. Locke. "Goal Setting—A Motivational Technique That Works." *Organizational Dynamics* 8, no. 2 (September 1979): 68–80; Locke, Edwin A., and Gary P. Latham, "Building a Practically Useful Theory of Goal Setting and Task Motivation: A 35-Year Odyssey." *American Psychologist* 57, no. 9 (September 2002): 705–717; Locke, Edwin A., and Gary P. Latham. *A Theory of Goal Setting and Task Performance* (Englewood Cliffs, NJ: Prentice Hall, 1990); Epton, Tracy, Sinead Currie, and Christopher J. Armitage. "Unique Effects of Setting Goals on Behavior Change: Systematic Review and Meta-Analysis." *Journal of Consulting and Clinical Psychology* 85, no. 12 (December 2017): 1182–1198.

19. Gregory, Jane Brodie, and Paul E. Levy. "How Feedback and Goals Drive Behavior: Control Theory." In *Using Feedback in Organizational Consulting*, 21–30 (Washington, DC: American Psychological Association, 2015); Clayton, Michael, and Samantha Nesnidol. "Reducing Electricity Use on Campus: The Use of Prompts, Feedback, and Goal Setting to Decrease Excessive Classroom Lighting." *Journal of Organizational Behavior Management* 37, no. 2 (April 2017): 196–206; Neubert, Mitchell J. "The Value of Feedback and Goal Setting over Goal Setting Alone and Potential Moderators of This Effect: A Meta-analysis." *Human Performance* 11, no. 4 (1998): 321–335.

20. Locke and Latham, 1990; Latham, Gary P., and J. James Baldes, "The 'Practical Significance' of Locke's Theory of Goal Setting." *Journal of Applied Psychology* 60, no. 1 (February 1975):

21. Ibid.

22. Dishman, Lydia. "10 Ways to Be a Better Employee in 2017." *Fast Company,* January 1, 2017. https://www.fastcompany.com/3066691/how-to-be-a-better-employee-in-2017.

23. Locke, Edwin A., Gary P. Latham, and Miriam Erez. "The Determinants of Goal Commitment." *Academy of Management Review* 13, no. 1 (January 1988): 23–39; Swaim, James, and Amy Henley. "The Use of Influence Tactics and Outcome Valence on Goal Commitment for Assigned Student Team Projects." *Journal of Management Education* 41, no. 1 (February 2017): 118–145.

24. "Human Capital 30: Companies That Put Employees Front and Center." *Fortune,* March 8, 2016. http://fortune.com/2016/03/08/human-capital-30/.

25. Clear, James. "The Goldilocks Rule: How to Stay Motivated in Life and Business." *https://jamesclear.com/goldilocks-rule.*

26. Erez, Miriam. "Feedback: A Necessary Condition for the Goal Setting–Performance Relationship." *Journal of Applied Psychology* 62, no. 5 (October 1977): 624–627; Kim, Jay S., and W. C. Hamner. "Effect of Performance Feedback and Goal Setting on Productivity and Satisfaction in an Organizational Setting." *Journal of Applied Psychology* 61, no. 1 (February 1976): 48–57; Wack, Stephanie R., Kimberly A. Crosland, and Raymond G. Miltenberger. "Using Goal Setting and Feedback to Increase Weekly Running Distance." *Journal of Applied Behavior Analysis* 47, no. 1 (Spring 2014): 181–185.

27. http://delvv.io/blog/read/9-famous-quotes-about-feedback-along-with-images.

28. Latham, Gary P., and Gerard H. Seijts. "The Effects of Proximal and Distal Goals on Performance on a Moderately Complex Task." *Journal of Organizational Behavior* 20, no. 4 (July 1999): 421–429; Latham, Gary P., and Edwin A. Locke. "New Developments In and Directions for Goal-Setting Research." *European Psychologist* 12, no. 4 (2007): 290–300; Ford, Robert C. "Combining Performance, Learning, and Behavioral Goals to Match Job with Person: Three Steps to Enhance Employee Performance with Goal Setting." *Business Horizons* 60, no. 3 (May 2017): 345–352.

29. Adams, J. Stacy. "Towards an Understanding of Inequity." *Journal of Abnormal and Social Psychology* 67, no. 5 (November 1963): 422–436; Polk, Denise M, "Evaluating Fairness: Critical Assessment of Equity Theory." In *Theories in Social Psychology* (Chichester, West Sussex, UK: Wiley-Blackwell, 2011), 163–190; Ryan, James Christopher. "Old Knowledge for New Impacts: Equity Theory and Workforce Nationalization." *Journal of Business Research* 69, no. 5 (May 2016): 1587–1592.

30. Greenberg, Jerald. "Cognitive Reevaluation of Outcomes in Response to Underpayment Inequity." *Academy of Management Journal* 32, no. 1 (March 1989): 174–184.

31. Thibaut, John. "An Experimental Study of the Cohesiveness of Underprivileged Groups." *Human Relations* 3, (1950): 251–278.

32. Colquitt, Jason A., Donald E. Conlon, Michael J. Wesson, Christopher O. L. H. Porter, and K. Yee Ng, "Justice at the Millennium: A Meta-analytic Review of 25 Years of Organizational Justice Research." *Journal of Applied Psychology* 86, no. 3 (June 2001): 425–445; Greenberg, Jerald, and Jason A. Colquitt. *Handbook of Organizational Justice* (Mahwah, NJ: Erlbaum, 2005); Wang, Hai-jiang, Chang-qin Lu, and Oi-ling Siu. "Job Insecurity and Job Performance: The Moderating Role of Organizational Justice and the Mediating Role of Work Engagement." *Journal of Applied Psychology* 100, no. 4 (July 2015): 1249–1258.

33. Covey, Stephen M. R., and Douglas R. Conant. "The Connection between Employee Trust and Financial Performance." *Harvard Business Review,* July 18, 2016. https://hbr.org/2016/07/the-connection-between-employee-trust-and-financial-performance.

122–124; Kleingeld et al. "The Effect of Goal Setting on Group Performance."

34. Graf, Nikki, Anna Brown, and Eileen Patten. "The Narrowing, but Persistent, Gender Gap in Pay." *Pew Research Center,* April 9, 2018. http://www.pewresearch.org/fact-tank/2018/04/09/gender-pay-gap-facts/.

35. Adamczyk, Alicia. "6 Excuses for the Gender Pay Gap You Can Stop Using." *Money,* April 12, 2016. http://time.com/money/4285843/gender-pay-gap-excuses-wrong/.

36. Fleischman, Edward. "The Dangers of Playing Favorites at Work." *Fortune,* August 4, 2015. http://fortune.com/2015/08/04/favoritism-careers-leadership/.

37. Greenberg, Jerald. "Employee Theft as a Reaction to Underpayment Inequity: The Hidden Cost of pay Cuts." *Journal of Applied Psychology* 75, no. 5 (October 1990): 561–568.

38. Vroom, Victor H. *Work and Motivation* (New York: Wiley, 1964); Matsui, Tamao, and Toshitake Terai. "A Cross-Cultural Study of the Validity of the Expectancy Theory of Work Motivation." *Journal of Applied Psychology* 60, no. 2 (April 1975): 263–265; Barba-Sánchez, Virginia, and Carlos Atienza-Sahuquillo. "Entrepreneurial Motivation and Self-Employment: Evidence from Expectancy Theory." *International Entrepreneurship And Management Journal* 13, no. 4 (December 2017): 1097–1115.

39. Ellingson, Jill E., and Lynn A. McFarland. "Understanding Faking Behavior through the Lens of Motivation: An Application of VIE Theory." *Human Performance* 24, no. 4 (September 2011): 322–337.

40. Adapted from Lunenburg, Fred C. "Expectancy Theory of Motivation: Motivating by Altering Expectations." *International Journal of Management, Business, and Administration* 15, no. 1 (2011): 1–6.

Chapter 6

1. Deci, Edward L. *Intrinsic Motivation* (New York: Plenum, 1975); Hagger, Martin S., Severine Koch, and Nikos L. D. Chatzisarantis. "The Effect of Causality Orientations and Positive Competence-Enhancing Feedback on Intrinsic Motivation: A Test of Additive and Interactive Effects." *Personality and Individual Differences* 72 (January 2015): 107–111.

2. Deci, *Intrinsic Motivation*; Deci, Edward L. "The Effects of Contingent and Noncontingent Rewards and Controls on Intrinsic Motivation." *Organizational Behavior and Human Performance* 8, no. 2 (October 1972): 217–229; Deci, Edward L., and Richard Koestner. "The Undermining Effect Is a Reality After All." *Psychological Bulletin* 125, no. 6 (November 1999): 692; Pritchard, Robert D., Kathleen M. Campbell, and Donald J. Campbell. "Effects of Extrinsic Financial Rewards on Intrinsic Motivation." *Journal of Applied Psychology* 62, no. 1 (February 1977): 9–15; Olafsen, Anja H., Hallgeir Halvari, Jacques Forest, and Edward L. Deci. "Show Them the Money? The Role of Pay, Managerial Need Support, and Justice in a Self-Determination Theory Model of Intrinsic Work Motivation." *Scandinavian Journal of Psychology* (March 24, 2015): PsycINFO, EBSCOhost.

3. De Meulenaere, Kim, Christophe Boone, and Tine Buyl. "What Is the Impact of Seniority-Based Pay on Labor Productivity?" *Academy of Management Annual Meeting Proceedings* 2015, no. 1 (January 2015): 1.

4. Oi, Mariko. "Japan Seeks Alternatives to Its Pay System." *BBC News,* March 22, 2016. https://www.bbc.com/news/35868599.

5. Pierson, David A., Karen S. Koziara, and Russel E. Johannesson. "Equal Pay for Jobs of Comparable Worth: A Quantified Job Content Approach." *Public Personnel Management* 12, no. 4 (Winter 1983): 445; Singh, Manjari, Jatin Pandey, Shrihari S. Sohani, Jatinder Jha, and Biju Varkkey. "Job Points Model: An Open Source Tool to Determine the Comparable Worth of Jobs." *Indian Journal of Industrial Relations* 53, no. 4 (April 2018): 711–716; Patten, Thomas H. Jr. *Fair Pay: The Managerial Challenge of Comparable Job Worth and Job Evaluation* (San Francisco:

Jossey-Bass, 1988); Gittleman, Maury, and Brooks Pierce. "Inter-Industry Wage Differentials, Job Content and Unobserved Ability." *Industrial and Labor Relations Review* 64, no. 2 (January 2011): 356–374.

6. Gupta, Shalene. "The 10 Top-Paying Companies." *Fortune,* March 5, 2015. http://fortune.com/2015/03/05/top-paying-best-companies/.

7. Mitra, Atul, Nina Gupta, and Jason D. Shaw. "A Comparative Examination of Traditional and Skill-Based Pay Plans." *Journal of Managerial Psychology* 26, no. 4 (2011): 278–296; Murray, Brian, and Barry Gerhart. "Skill-Based Pay and Skill Seeking." *Human Resource Management Review* 10, no. 3 (2000): 271–287; Léné, Alexandre. "Skill-Based Pay in Practice: An Interactional Justice Perspective." *European Journal of Training & Development* 38, no. 7 (September 2014): 628–641.

8. Boinott, John. "Being Too Good at Your Job Could Actually Hurt Your Career." *Business Insider,* July 17, 2015. http://www.businessinsider.com/being-too-good-at-your-job-could-actually-hurt-your-career-2015-7?IR=T.

9. Boachie-Mensah, Francis, and Ophelia Delali Dogbe. "Performance–Based Pay as a Motivational Tool for Achieving Organisational Performance: An Exploratory Case Study." *International Journal of Business and Management* 6, no. 12 (December 2011): 270–285; Wang, Taiyuan, Stewart Thornhill, and Bin Zhao. "Pay-for-Performance, Employee Participation, and SME Performance." *Journal of Small Business Management* 56, no. 3 (July 2018): 412–434.

10. Fisher, Anne. "Why Performance Bonuses and Merit Raises Don't Work." *Fortune,* February 24, 2016. http://fortune.com/2016/02/24/salary-bonuses-merit-raises-effectiveness/.

11. https://www.payscale.com/about/press-releases/payscale-research-reveals-successful-companies-embrace-modern-compensation-practices-to-retain-their-best-employees.

12. Ogbonnaya, Chidiebere, Kevin Daniels, and Karina Nielsen. "Does Contingent Pay Encourage Positive Employee Attitudes and Intensify Work?" *Human Resource Management Journal* 27, no. 1 (January 2017): 94–112.

13. Brooks, Chad. "Performance-Based Pay Won't Motivate Employees as Much as You Think." *Business News Daily,* January 25, 2017. https://www.businessnewsdaily.com/9712-performance-based-pay.html.

14. Arthur, Jeffrey B., and Dong-One Kim. "Gainsharing and Knowledge Sharing: The Effects of Labour–Management Co-operation." *International Journal of Human Resource Management* 16, no. 9 (September 2005): 1564–1582; Benson, George S., and Edward E. III Lawler. "Employee Involvement: Research Foundations." In *The Psychologically Healthy Workplace: Building a Win-Win Environment for Organizations and Employees*, 13–33. (Washington, DC: American Psychological Association, 2016).

15. "Five-year Pact Includes Increases in Benefits, Pension and Wages, as Well as Language to Support Seniority and Safety." *www.saultstar.com,* May 31, 2017. http://www.saultstar.com/2017/05/31/five-year-pact-includes-increases-in-benefits-pension-and-wages-as-well-as-language-to-support-seniority-and-safety.

16. Florkowski, Gary W. "The Organizational Impact of Profit Sharing." *Academy of Management Review* 12, no. 4 (October 1987): 622–636; Magnan, Michel, and Sylvie St-Onge. "The Impact of Profit Sharing on the Performance of Financial Services Firms." *Journal of Management Studies* 42, no. 4 (June 2005): 761–791; Lee, Joung Hun, Yuki Kubo, Takahiro Fujiwara, Ratih Madya Septiana, Slamet Riyanto, and Yoh Iwasa. "Profit Sharing as a Management Strategy for a State-Owned Teak Plantation at High Risk for Illegal Logging." *Ecological Economics* 149, (July 2018): 140–148.

17. Roberts, John Jeff. "How Delta Landed on the 100 Best Companies to Work For List." *Fortune,* March 10, 2017. http://fortune.com/2017/03/10/delta-air-lines-best-companies-list/.

18. Ettling, Jennifer. "Winning and Losing with ESOPs: The Design of Effective Employee Stock Ownership Plans." *Academy of Management Best Papers Proceedings* (August 1990): 269–273; Parrish, Steve, and Geoffrey PeConga. "Incentive Strategies for Employee Stock Ownership Plan-Owned Companies." *Journal of Financial Service Professionals* 69, no. 2 (March 2015): 31–33. ; Bergstein, Warren M., and Wanda Williams. "The Benefits of Employee Stock Ownership Plans." *CPA Journal* 83, no. 4 (April 2013): 54–57.

19. Erb, George. "At Northwest Firms with ESOPs, Employees Act like They Own the Place." *The Seattle Times,* January 21, 2017. https://www.seattletimes.com/business/at-northwest-firms-with-esops-employees-act-like-they-own-the-place/.

20. Mangla, Ismat Sarah. "Researchers Have Identified the Types of Intelligence That Make Aging Workers Valuable." *Quartz,* December 9, 2016. https://qz.com/857430/researchers-have-identified-the-types-of-intelligence-that-make-aging-workers-valuable/.

21. Ibid.

22. Twenge, Jean M., Stacy M. Campbell, Brian J. Hoffman, and Charles E. Lance. "Generational Differences in Work Values: Leisure and Extrinsic Values Increasing, Social and Intrinsic Values Decreasing." *Journal of Management* 36, no. 5 (September 2010): 1117–1142.

23. Johns, Gary, Xie Jia Lin, and Fang Yongqing. "Mediating and Moderating Effects in Job Design." *Journal of Management* 18, no. 4 (December 1992): 657; Kempner, T., and Ray Wild. "Job Design and Productivity." *Journal of Management Studies* 10, no. 1 (February 1973): 62–81; Daniels, Kevin, Cigdem Gedikli, David Watson, Antonina Semkina, and Oluwafunmilayo Vaughn. "Job Design, Employment Practices and Well-Being: A Systematic Review of Intervention Studies." *Ergonomics* 60, no. 9 (September 2017): 1177–1196; Cullinane, Sarah-Jane, Janine Bosak, Patrick C. Flood, and Evangelia Demerouti. "Job Design under Lean Manufacturing and the Quality of Working Life: A Job Demands and Resources Perspective." *International Journal of Human Resource Management* 25, no. 21 (November 2014): 2996–3015.

24. Chung, Kae H., and Monica F. Ross. "Differences in Motivational Properties between Job Enlargement and Job Enrichment." *Academy of Management Review* 2, no. 1 (January 1977): 113–122; Bishop, Ronald C., and James W. Hill. "Effects of Job Enlargement and Job Change on Contiguous but Nonmanipulated Jobs as a Function of Workers' Status." *Journal of Applied Psychology* 55, no. 3 (June 1971): 175–181; Berdicchia, Domenico, Francesco Nicolli, and Giovanni Masino. "Job Enlargement, Job Crafting and the Moderating Role of Self-Competence." *Journal of Managerial Psychology* 31, no. 2 (2016): 318–330.

25. Campion, Michael A., Lisa Cheraskin, and Michael J. Stevens. "Career–Related Antecedents and Outcomes of Job Rotation." *Academy of Management Journal* 37, no. 6 (December 1994): 1518–1542; Jeon, In Sik, Byung Yong Jeong, and Ji Hyun Jeong. "Preferred 11 Different Job Rotation Types in Automotive Company and Their Effects on Productivity, Quality and Musculoskeletal Disorders: Comparison between Subjective and Actual Scores by Workers' Age." *Ergonomics* 59, no. 10 (October 2016): 1318–1326.

26. Zimmerman, Kaytie. "Are Rotational Programs the Key to Retaining Millennial Employees?" *Forbes,* August 8, 2016. https://www.forbes.com/sites/kaytiezimmerman/2016/08/08/can-a-millennial-quarter-life-crisis-be-cured-by-their-employer/#4968b5a446f6.

27. Ibid.

28. Chung, Kae H., and Monica F. Ross. "Differences in Motivational Properties between Job Enlargement and Job Enrichment." *Academy of Management Review* 2, no. 1 (January 1977): 113–122; Duffield, Christine, Richard Baldwin, Michael Roche, and Sarah Wise. 2014. "Job Enrichment: Creating Meaningful Career Development Opportunities for Nurses." *Journal of Nursing Management* 22, no. 6: 697–706.

29. Choudhary, Supriya. "Job Enrichment: A Tool for Employee Motivation." *International Journal of Applied Research* 2, no. 5 (2016): 1020–1024.

30. Hackman, J. Richard, and Greg R. Oldham. *Work Redesign* (Reading, MA: Addison–Wesley, 1980); Hackman, J. Richard, and Greg R. Oldham. "Motivation through the Design of Work: Test of a Theory." *Organizational Behavior and Human Performance* 16, no. 2 (August 1976): 250–279; Blanz, Mathias. "Employees' Job Satisfaction: A Test of the Job Characteristics Model among Social Work Practitioners." *Journal of Evidence-Informed Social Work* 14, no. 1 (January 2017): 35–50.

31. Bullock, Robert. "Motivating Employees Has Everything to Do with Giving Them Feelings of Ownership." *Forbes,* September 25, 2014. https://www.forbes.com/sites/datafreaks/2014/09/25/motivating-employees-has-almost-nothing-to-do-with-their-attitude-and-almost-everything-to-do-with-feelings-of-ownership/#735b51fb1140.

32. Straz, Matt. "This Is What Happens When Employees Find Meaning at Work." *Entrepreneur,* June 13, 2016. https://www.entrepreneur.com/article/277199.

33. Mankins, Michael, and Eric Garton. "How Spotify Balances Employee Autonomy and Accountability." *Harvard Business Review,* February 9, 2017. https://hbr.org/2017/02/how-spotify-balances-employee-autonomy-and-accountability.

34. Ward, Marguerite. "Ex-Google Exec Reveals the Leadership Strategy She Learned from Larry Page." *CNBC,* April 27, 2017. https://www.cnbc.com/2017/04/27/ex-google-exec-on-the-leadership-strategy-she-learned-from-larry-page.html.

35. Spreitzer, Gretchen M. "Psychological, Empowerment in the Workplace: Dimensions, Measurement and Validation." *Academy of Management Journal* 38, no. 5 (October 1995): 1442–1465; Spreitzer, Gretchen M., Mark A. Kizilos, and Stephen W. Nason. "A Dimensional Analysis of the Relationship between Psychological Empowerment and Effectiveness, Satisfaction, and Strain." *Journal of Management* 23, no. 5 (December 15, 1997): 679; Dust, Scott B., Christian J. Resick, Jaclyn A. Margolis, Mary B. Mawritz, and Rebecca L. Greenbaum. "Ethical Leadership and Employee Success: Examining the Roles of Psychological Empowerment and Emotional Exhaustion." *The Leadership Quarterly* (February 12, 2018).

36. Ibid.

37. Koval, Christy Zhou, Michelle R. vanDellen, Gráinne M. Fitzsimons, and Krista W. Ranby. "The Burden of Responsibility: Interpersonal Costs of High Self-Control." *Journal of Personality and Social Psychology* 108, no. 5 (May 2015): 750–766.

38. Spreitzer, Gretchen M. "Psychological, Empowerment in the Workplace: Dimensions, Measurement and Validation." *Academy of Management Journal* 38, no. 5 (October 1995): 1442–1465; Spreitzer, Gretchen M., Mark A. Kizilos, and Stephen W. Nason. "A Dimensional Analysis of the Relationship between Psychological Empowerment and Effectiveness, Satisfaction, and Strain." *Journal of Management* 23, no. 5 (December 15, 1997): 679; Dust, Scott B., Christian J. Resick, Jaclyn A. Margolis, Mary B. Mawritz, and Rebecca L. Greenbaum. "Ethical Leadership and Employee Success: Examining the Roles of Psychological Empowerment and Emotional Exhaustion." *The Leadership Quarterly* (February 12, 2018).

39. Ibid.

40. Ibid.

41. Schwantes, Marcel. "The World's 10 Top CEOs (They Lead in a Totally Unique Way)." *Inc.*, March 29, 2017. https://www.inc.com/marcel-schwantes/heres-a-top-10-list-of-the-worlds-best-ceos-but-they-lead-in-a-totally-unique-wa.html.

42. Spreitzer, Gretchen M. "Psychological, Empowerment in the Workplace: Dimensions, Measurement and Validation." *Academy of Management Journal* 38, no. 5 (October 1995): 1442–1465; Spreitzer, Gretchen M., Mark A. Kizilos, and Stephen W. Nason. "A Dimensional Analysis of the Relationship between Psychological Empowerment and Effectiveness, Satisfaction, and Strain." *Journal of Management* 23, no. 5 (December 15, 1997): 679; Dust, Scott B., Christian J. Resick, Jaclyn A. Margolis, Mary B. Mawritz, and Rebecca L. Greenbaum. "Ethical Leadership and Employee Success: Examining the Roles of Psychological Empowerment and Emotional Exhaustion." *The Leadership Quarterly* (February 12, 2018).

43. Bailey, Catherine, and Adrian Madden. "What Makes Work Meaningful—or Meaningless." *MIT Sloan Management Review,* June 1, 2016. https://sloanreview.mit.edu/article/what-makes-work-meaningful-or-meaningless/.

44. Ibid.

45. Pink, Daniel H. *Free Agent Nation: The Future of Working for Yourself* (New York: Warner Business Books, 2001); Pfeffer, Jeffrey, "Why Free Agents Don't Feel Free," *Business 2.0* 7, no. 9 (October 2006): 78.

46. Reynolds, Brie. "FlexJobs Survey: Millennials More Interested in Travel, Work Flexibility than Gen X, Baby Boomers." *www.flexjobs.com,* September 30, 2016. https://www.flexjobs.com/employer-blog/flexjobs-survey-millennials-interested-travel-work-flexibility/.

47. Fry, Richard. "Millennials Aren't Job-Hopping any Faster than Generation X Did." *Pew Research Center,* April 19, 2017. http://www.pewresearch.org/fact-tank/2017/04/19/millennials-arent-job-hopping-any-faster-than-generation-x-did/.

48. Goudreau, Jenna. "Back to the Stone Age? New Yahoo CEO Marissa Mayer Bans Working from Home," *Forbes.* February 25, 2013; www.forbes.com/sites/jennagoudreau/2013/02/25/back-to-the-stone-age-new-yahoo-ceo-marissa-mayer-bans-working-from-home/.

49. Lindsay, Greg. "Yahoo Says That Killing Working From Home Is Turning Out Perfectly." *Forbes,* October 30, 2013. https://www.fastcompany.com/3020930/yahoo-says-that-killing-working-from-home-is-turning-out-perfectly.

50. Weller, Chris. "IBM Was a Pioneer in the Work-from-Home Revolution—Now It's Cracking Down." *Business Insider,* March 27, 2017. http://www.businessinsider.com/ibm-slashes-work-from-home-policy-2017-3?r=UK&IR=T.

51. Hicks, William D., and Richard J. Klimoski. "The Impact of Flextime on Employee Attitudes." *Academy of Management Journal* 24, no. 2 (June 1981): 333–341; Spieler, Ines, Susanne Scheibe, Christian Stamov-Roßnagel, and Arvid Kappas. "Help or Hindrance? Day-Level Relationships between Flextime Use, Work–Nonwork Boundaries, and Affective Well-Being." *Journal of Applied Psychology* 102, no. 1 (January 2017): 67–87.

52. Arbon, Chyleen A., Rex L. Facer II, and Lori L. Wadsworth. "Compressed Workweeks—Strategies for Successful Implementation." *Public Personnel Management* 41, no. 3 (Fall 2012): 389–405; Baltes, Boris B., Thomas E. Briggs, Joseph W. Huff, Julie A. Wright, and George A. Neuman. "Flexible and Compressed Workweek Schedules: A Meta–Analysis of Their Effects on Work-Related Criteria." *Journal of Applied Psychology* 84, no. 4 (August 1999): 496–513; Hyatt, Edward, and Erica Coslor. "Compressed Lives: How "Flexible" Are Employer-Imposed Compressed Work Schedules?." *Personnel Review* 47, no. 2 (March 2018): 278–293.

53. Christensen, Stephanie Taylor. "Job Sharing: The Devil Is in the Details." *Managing People at Work* no. 363 (June 2012): 3; Daniels, Lucy. "The Person's Relating to Others at Work Questionnaire (PROWQ): A Modified Version of the PROQ Applied to Job Sharing at Senior Levels in the Workplace." In *Relating Theory— Clinical and Forensic Applications,* 123–135. (New York: Palgrave Macmillan, 2016).

54. Diab, Ann. "5 Flexible Work Strategies and the Companies That Use Them." *Fast Company,* March 30, 2016. https://www.fastcompany.com/3058344/5-flexible-work-strategies-and-the-companies-who-use-them.

55. Golden, Timothy D. "Unraveling Telecommuting and Satisfaction: Towards a Relational View." *Academy of Management Proceedings* (August 2004): F1–F6; Allen, Tammy D., Timothy D. Golden, and Kristen M. Shockley. "How Effective is Telecommuting? Assessing the Status of Our Scientific Findings." *Psychological Science in the Public Interest* 16, no. 2 (October 2015): 40–68.

56. Frost, Aja. "10 Crazy Flexible Companies That Understand You Need Freedom." https://www.themuse.com/advice/10-crazy-flexible-companies-that-understand-you-need-freedom.

Chapter 7

1. For an overview of teams in organizations, see Kozlowski, Steve W. J., and Bradford S. Bell. "Work Groups and Teams in Organizations." In *Handbook of Psychology,* Vol. 12: *Industrial and Organizational Psychology* (2nd ed.), 412–469 (Hoboken, NJ: Wiley, 2013).

2. Kesling, Ben, and James R. Hagerty. "'Soft Skills' Can Help You Get Ahead." *Wall Street Journal.* April 2, 2013. http://online.wsj.com/news/articles/SB10001424127887323466204578383022434680196?mg=reno64-wsj&url=http%3A%2F%2Fonline.wsj.com%2Farticle%2FSB100014241278873234662045783830224 34680196.html.

3. Zábojník, Ján. "Centralized and Decentralized Decision Making in Organizations." *Journal of Labor Economics* 20, no. 1 (January 2002): 1–22.

4. Venkatraman, Rohini. "3 Ways to Collaborate with Your Team That Will Actually Boost Creativity." *Inc.,* February 7, 2017. https://www.inc.com/rohini-venkatraman/is-collaboration-killing-your-teams-creativity-psychology-has-answers-for-bringi.html.

5. Katzenbach, Jon R., and Douglas K. Smith. "The Discipline of Teams." *Harvard Business Review* 83, no. 7/8 (July 2005): 162–171; Stewart, Greg L., Charles C. Manz, and Henry P. Sims, *Team Work and Group Dynamics* (New York: Wiley, 1999).

6. Ibid.

7. Thomson, Stephanie. "Google's Surprising Discovery about Effective Teams." *World Economic Forum,* December 9, 2015. https://www.weforum.org/agenda/2015/12/googles-surprising-discovery-about-effective-teams/.

8. Newman, Alexander, Ross Donohue, and Nathan Eva. "Psychological Safety: A Systematic Review of the Literature." *Human Resource Management Review* 27, no. 3 (September 2017): 521–535.

9. Clark, Nancy F. "How to Build the Amazing Team of Your Dreams." *Forbes,* January 19, 2018. https://www.forbes.com/sites/womensmedia/2018/01/19/how-to-build-the-amazing-team-of-your-dreams/2/#2d5de1593a5e.

10. Bonebright, Denise A. "Forty Years of Storming: A Historical Review of Tuckman's Model of Small Group Development." *Human Resource Development International* 13, no. 1 (February 2010): 111–120; Tuckman, Bruce W. "Developmental Sequence in Small Groups." *Psychological Bulletin* 63, no. 6 (June 1965): 384–399; Tuckman, Bruce W., and Mary Ann C. Jensen. "Stages of Small-Group Development Revisited." *Group and Organization Studies* 2, no. 4 (December 1977): 419–427.

11. Gersick, Connie J.G. 1988. "Time and Transition in Work Teams: Toward a New Model of Group Development." *Academy of Management Journal* 31, no. 1: 9–41; Gersick, Connie J. G. "Revolutionary Change Theories: A Multilevel Exploration of the Punctuated Equilibrium Paradigm." *Academy of Management Review* 16, no. 1 (January 1991): 10–36.

12. Celani, Anthony, and Kevin Tasa. "We're All in This Together: Examining Associations between Collectivistic Group Norms, Collective Efficacy, and Team Performance." *Academy of Management Annual Meeting Proceedings* (August 2010): 1–6; Chatman, Jennifer A., and Francis J. Flynn. "The Influence of Demographic Heterogeneity on the Emergence and Consequences of Cooperative Norms in Work Teams." *Academy of Management Journal* 44, no. 5 (October 2001): 956–974; De Jong, Bart A., and Katinka M. Bijlsma-Frankema. "When and How Does Norm-Based Peer Control Affect the Performance of Self-Managing Teams?" *Academy of Management Annual Meeting Proceedings* (August 2009): 1–6; Gavac, Sarah, Sohad Murrar, and Markus Brauer. "Group Perception and Social Norms." In *Social psychology: How Other People Influence Our Thoughts and Actions*, 333–359; (Santa Barbara, CA: Greenwood Press/ABC-CLIO, 2017); Taggar, Simon, and Robert Ellis. "The Role of Leaders in Shaping Formal Team Norms." *Leadership Quarterly* 18, no. 2 (April 2007): 105–120.

13. Karten, Naomi. "How Team Norms Can Boost Team Effectiveness." www.techwell.com, October 17, 2012. https://www.techwell.com/techwell-insights/2012/10/how-team-norms-can-boost-team-effectiveness.

14. "Google Finds That Successful Teams Are about Norms Not Just Smarts." *www.hunterwalk.com*, September 3, 2016. https://hunterwalk.com/2016/09/03/google-finds-that-successful-teams-are-about-norms-not-just-smarts/.

15. Beal, Daniel J., Robin R. Cohen, Michael J. Burke, and Christy L. McLendon. "Cohesion and Performance in Groups: A Meta-Analytic Clarification of Construct Relations." *Journal of Applied Psychology* 88, no. 6 (December 2003): 989–1004; Carron, Albert V., Mark A. Eys, and Shauna M. Burke. "Team Cohesion: Nature, Correlates, and Development." In *Social Psychology in Sport*, 91–101 (Champaign, IL: Human Kinetics, 2007); Cruwys, Tegan, Amber M. Gaffney, and Yvonne Skipper. "Uncertainty in Transition: The Influence of Group Cohesion on Learning." In *Self and Social Identity in Educational Contexts*, 193–208. (New York: Routledge/Taylor & Francis Group, 2017).

16. "Your Project Needs a Charter. Here's What That Means." *Harvard Business Review*, November 3, 2016. https://hbr.org/2016/11/your-project-needs-a-charter-heres-what-that-means.

17. Stagl, Kevin C., C. Shawn Burke, Eduardo Salas, and Linda Pierce. "Team Adaptation: Realizing Team Synergy." In *Understanding Adaptability: A Prerequisite for Effective Performance within Complex Environments*, 117–141 (Amsterdam, Netherlands: Elsevier, 2006); Gal, Amit. "Synergy Work and Synergistic Membership: Towards a Theory of Beneficial Social Interactions in Teams." *Academy of Management Annual Meeting Proceedings* 2015, no. 1 (January 2015): 1.

18. Felps, Will, Terence R. Mitchell, and Eliza Byington. "How, When, and Why Bad Apples Spoil the Barrel: Negative Group Members and Dysfunctional Groups." *Research in Organizational Behavior* 27, (January 2006): 175–222.

19. Barrick, Murray R., Greg L. Stewart, Mitchell J. Neubert, and Michael K. Mount. "Relating Member Ability and Personality to Work-Team Processes and Team Effectiveness." *Journal of Applied Psychology* 83, no. 3 (June 1998): 377–391.

20. Miner, Frederick C. "Group versus Individual Decision Making: An Investigation of Performance Measures, Decision Strategies, and Process Losses/Gains." *Organizational Behavior and Human Performance* 33, no. 1 (February 1984): 112–124; Steiner, Ivan D. "Models for Inferring Relationships between Group Size and Potential Group Productivity." *Behavioral Science* 11, no. 4 (1966): 273–283; Mejias, Roberto J. "The Interaction of Process Losses, Process Gains, and Meeting Satisfaction within Technology-Supported Environments." *Small Group Research* 38, no. 1 (February 2007): 156–194.

21. Ibid.

22. Chamorro-Premuzic, Tomas. "Why Group Brainstorming Is a Waste of Time." *Harvard Business Review*, March 25, 2015. https://hbr.org/2015/03/why-group-brainstorming-is-a-waste-of-time.

23. Mercado, Brittany K., Casey Giordano, and Stephan Dilchert. "A Meta-Analytic Investigation of Cyberloafing." *The Career Development International* 22, no. 5 (2017): 546–564.

24. Zakrzewski, Cat. "The Key to Getting Workers to Stop Wasting Time Online." *The Wall Street Journal*, March 13, 2016. https://www.wsj.com/articles/the-key-to-getting-workers-to-stop-wasting-time-online-1457921545.

25. Ibid.

26. Glassman, J, Prosch, M, & Shao, B, "To Monitor or Not to Monitor: Effectiveness of a Cyberloafing Countermeasure." *Information & Management* 52, no. 2 (2015): 170–182.

27. Zakrzewski, Cat. "The Key to Getting Workers to Stop Wasting Time Online." *The Wall Street Journal*, March 13, 2016. https://www.wsj.com/articles/the-key-to-getting-workers-to-stop-wasting-time-online-1457921545.

28. Steinmetz, Janina, and Stefan Pfattheicher. "Beyond Social Facilitation: A Review of the Far-Reaching Effects of Social Attention." *Social Cognition* 35, no. 5 (October 2017): 585–599; Williamson, E. G. "Allport's Experiments in 'Social Facilitation.'" *Psychological Monographs* 35, no. 2 (1926): 138–143.

29. Kirkman, Bradley L., Benson Rosen, Paul E. Tesluk, and Cristina B. Gibson. "The Impact of Team Empowerment on Virtual Team Performance: The Moderating Role of Face-to-Face Interaction." *Academy of Management Journal* 47, no. 2 (April 2004): 175–192; Malhotra, Arvind, Ann Majchrzak, and Benson Rosen. "Leading Virtual Teams." *Academy of Management Perspectives* 21, no. 1 (February 2007): 60–70; Montoya-Weiss, Mitzi M., Anne P. Massey, and Michael Song. "Getting It Together: Temporal Coordination and Conflict Management in Global Virtual Teams." *Academy of Management Journal* 44, no. 6 (December 2001): 1251–1262; Klitmøller, Anders, Susan Carol Schneider, and Karsten Jonsen. "Speaking of Global Virtual Teams: Language Differences, Social Categorization and Media Choice." *Personnel Review* 44, no. 2 (2015): 270–285.

30. http://globalworkplaceanalytics.com/telecommuting-statistics.

31. https://risepeople.com/blog/6-virtual-companies/

32. Schell, Adam. "Trends in Global Virtual Teams." *Culture Wizard*, April 26, 2016. https://www.rw-3.com/blog/trends-in-global-virtual-teams.

33. Magpili, Nina Cristina, and Pilar Pazos. "Self-Managing Team Performance: A Systematic Review of Multilevel Input Factors." *Small Group Research* 49, no. 1 (February 2018): 3–33; Neck, Christopher P., Mary L. Connerley, and Charles C. Manz. "Toward a Continuum of Self-Managing Team Development." In *Advances in Interdisciplinary Studies of Work Teams*, Vol. 4, 193–216 (Stamford, CT: Elsevier Science/JAI Press, 1997).

34. Blakeman, Chuck. "Why Self-Managed Teams Are the Future of Business." *Inc.*, November 25, 2014. https://www.inc.com/chuck-blakeman/why-self-managed-teams-are-the-future-of-business.html.

35. Blakeman, Chuck. "Companies without Managers Do Better by Every Metric." *Inc.*, July 22, 2014. https://www.inc.com/chuck-blakeman/companies-without-managers-do-better-by-every-metric.html.

36. deLeon, Linda. "Accountability for Individuating Behaviors in Self-Managing Teams." *Organization Development Journal* 19,

no. 4 (Win 2001): 7–19; Langfred, Claus W. "The Downside of Self-Management: A Longitudinal Study of the Effects of Conflict on Trust, Autonomy, and Task Interdependence in Self-Managing Teams." *Academy of Management Journal* 50, no. 4 (August 2007): 885–900.

37. Rosenfield, Sylvia, Markeda Newell, Scott Jr. Zwolski, and Lauren E. Benishek. "Evaluating Problem-Solving Teams in K–12 Schools: Do They Work?." *American Psychologist* 73, no. 4 (May 2018): 407–419; Scott, Jonathan T. "Chapter 10: Managing Teams and Work Groups." In *Concise Handbook of Management: A Practitioner's Approach*, 79–84 (n.p.: 2005).

38. Reynolds, Alison, and David Lewis. "Teams Solve Problems Faster When They're More Cognitively Diverse." *Harvard Business Review*, March 30, 2017. https://hbr.org/2017/03/teams-solve-problems-faster-when-theyre-more-cognitively-diverse.

39. Aime, Federico, Stephen Humphrey, D. Scott Derue, and Jeffrey B. Paul. "The Riddle of Heterarchy: Power Transitions in Cross-Functional Teams." *Academy of Management Journal* 57, no. 2 (April 2014): 327–352; Boroş, Smaranda, et al. "Breaking Silos: A Field Experiment on Relational Conflict Management in Cross-Functional Teams." *Group Decision and Negotiation* 26, no. 2 (March 2017): 327–356.

40. Bruzzese, Anita. "How to Improve Cross-Functional Collaborations." *Quick Base*, May 2, 2016. https://www.quickbase.com/blog/how-to-improve-cross-functional-collaborations.

41. Ibid.

42. See for example, Hackman, J. R. "The Design of Work Teams." In *Handbook of Organizational Behavior*, edited by J. W. Lorsch, 315–342 (Englewood Cliffs, NJ: Prentice-Hall, 1987); Ilgen, Daniel R., John R. Hollenbeck, Michael Johnson, and Dustin Jundt. "Teams In Organizations: From Input-Process-Output Models to IMOI Models." *Annual Review of Psychology* 56, no. 1 (February 2005): 517–543; McGrath, J. E. *Social Psychology: A Brief Introduction* (New York: Rinehart and Winston, 1964); Stock, Ruth Maria. "How Should Customers Be Integrated for Effective Interorganizational NPD Teams? An Input-Process-Output Perspective." *Journal of Product Innovation Management* 31, no. 3 (May 2014): 535–551.

43. Stewart et al. *Team Work and Group Dynamics*; Thompson, James D. *Organizations in Action: Social Science Bases of Administrative Theory* (New York: McGraw-Hill, 1967).

44. Daft, Richard L. *Organization Theory and Design* (Boston: Cengage, 2015).

45. Chakravarty, Amiya K. *Supply Chain Transformation: Evolving with Emerging Business Paradigms* (Heidelberg, Germany: Springer, 2014).

46. Daft, *Organization Theory and Design*.

47. Larson, Erik. "3 Best Practices for High Performance Decision-Making Teams." *Forbes*, March 23, 2017. https://www.forbes.com/sites/eriklarson/2017/03/23/3-best-practices-for-high-performance-decision-making-teams/#6ff322ebf971.

48. Barry, Bruce, and Greg L. Stewart. "Composition, Process, and Performance in Self-Managed Groups: The Role of Personality." *Journal of Applied Psychology* 82, no. 1 (February 1997): 62–78.

49. Peeters, Miranda A. G., Harrie F. J. M. Van Tuijl, Christel G. Rutte, and Isabelle M. M. J. Reymen. "Personality and Team Performance: A Meta-analysis." *European Journal of Personality* 20, no. 5 (August 2006): 377–396.

50. Schneider, Benjamin. "The People Make the Place." *Personnel Psychology* 40, no. 3 (September 1987): 437–453; Schneider, Benjamin, Harold W. Goldstein, and D. Brent Smith. "The ASA Framework: An Update." *Personnel Psychology* 48, no. 4 (Winter 1995): 747–773.

51. Bretz, Robert D. Jr., Ronald A. Ash, and George F. Dreher. "Do People Make the Place? An Examination of the Attraction-Selection-Attrition Hypothesis." *Personnel Psychology* 42, no. 3 (September 1989): 561–581; Butler, Brian S., Patrick J. Bateman, Peter H. Gray, and E. Ilana Diamant. "An Attraction–Selection–Attrition Theory of Online Community Size and Resilience." *MIS Quarterly* 38, no. 3 (September 2014): 699–728; Ployhart, Robert E., Jeff A. Weekley, and Kathryn Baughman. "The Structure and Function of Human Capital Emergence: A Multilevel Examination of the Attraction-Selection-Attrition Model." *Academy of Management Journal* 49, no. 4 (August 2006): 661–677; Schneider, Benjamin, D. Brent Smith, and Michelle C. Paul. "P–E Fit and the Attraction-Selection-Attrition Model of Organizational Functioning: Introduction and Overview." In *Work Motivation in the Context of a Globalizing Economy*, 231–246 (Mahwah, NJ: Erlbaum, 2001).

52. Gregersen, Hal. "Better Brainstorming." *Harvard Business Review* 96, no. 2 (March 2018): 64–71; Litchfield, Robert C. "Brainstorming Reconsidered: A Goal-Based View." *Academy of Management Review* 33, no. 3 (July 2008): 649–668; Taylor, Donald W., Paul C. Berry, and Clifford H. Block. "Does Group Participation When Using Brainstorming Facilitate or Inhibit Creative Thinking?" *Administrative Science Quarterly* 3, no. 1 (June 1958): 23–47.

53. Markman, Art. "Your Team Is Brainstorming All Wrong." *Harvard Business Review*, May 18, 2017. https://hbr.org/2017/05/your-team-is-brainstorming-all-wrong.

54. Ibid.

55. Lafargue, Veronique. "How to Brainstorm Like a Googler." *Fast Company*, June 20, 2016. https://www.fastcompany.com/3061059/how-to-brainstorm-like-a-googler.

56. Delbecq, Andre L., and Van de Ven Andrew. H. "A Group Process Model for Problem Identification and Program Planning." *Journal of Applied Behavioral Science* no. 7 (July/August, 1971), 466–91; Foth, Thomas, Nikolaos Efstathiou, Brandi Vanderspank-Wright, Lee-Anne Ufholz, Nadin Dütthorn, Manuel Zimansky, and Susan Humphrey-Murto. "The Use of Delphi and Nominal Group Technique in Nursing Education: A Review." *International Journal of Nursing Studies* 60, (August 2016): 112–120; Van de Ven, Andrew H., and Andre L. Delbecq. "The Effectiveness of Nominal, Delphi, and Interacting Group Decision Making Processes." *Academy of Management Journal* 17, no. 4 (December 1974): 605–621.

57. Ibid.

58. Larson, Erik. "3 Best Practices for High Performance Decision-Making Teams." *Forbes*, March 23, 2017. https://www.forbes.com/sites/eriklarson/2017/03/23/3-best-practices-for-high-performance-decision-making-teams/#b7a1caef971b.

59. For detailed discussions of groupthink, see Janis, Irving L. "Groupthink." *Psychology Today* 5, no. 6 (November 1971): 43–46, 74–76; Janis, Irving L. *Victims of Groupthink: A Psychological Study of Foreign-Policy Decisions and Fiascoes* (Boston: Houghton Mifflin, 1972); Janis, Irving L. *Groupthink: Psychological Studies of Policy Decisions and Fiascoes* (Boston: Houghton Mifflin, 1982); Russell, Jeffrey, John Hawthorne, and Lara Buchak. "Groupthink." *Philosophical Studies* 172, no. 5 (May 2015): 1287–1309.

60. Mitchell, Amy, Jeffrey Gottfried, Jocelyn Kiley, and Katerina Eva Matsa. "Political Polarization & Media Habits." *Pew Research Center*, October 21, 2014. http://www.journalism.org/2014/10/21/political-polarization-media-habits/.

61. Leetaru, Kalev. "Why 2017 Was the Year of the Filter Bubble?" *Forbes*, December 18, 2017. https://www.forbes.com/sites/kalevleetaru/2017/12/18/why-was-2017-the-year-of-the-filter-bubble/#2bf17d3f746b.

62. Schkade, David, Cass R. Sunstein, and Reid Hastie. "What Happened on Deliberation Day?" *California Law Review* 95, no. 3 (June 2007): 915–940.

Chapter 8

1. For overviews see Koopman, Paul L., Jan Willem Broekhuijsen, and André F. M. Wierdsma. "Complex Decision-Making in Organizations." In *Handbook of Work and Organizational Psychology: Organizational Psychology*, 357–386. (Hove, England: Psychology Press/Erlbaum (UK) Taylor & Francis, 1998); Miller, Susan J., David J. Hickson, and David C. Wilson. "Decision-Making in Organizations." In *Handbook of Organization Studies*, 293–312 (Thousand Oaks, CA: Sage, 1996).

2. Simon, Herbert A. *The New Science of Management Decision* (New York: Harper & Brothers, 1960); Osmani, Juliana. "Group Decision-Making: Factors That Affect Group Effectiveness." *Academic Journal of Business, Administration, Law & Social Sciences* 2, no. 1 (March 2016): 23–38.

3. Haroun, Chris. "Why the Best Companies Always Have the Best Customer Service." *Inc.*, April 25, 2016. https://www.inc.com/chris-haroun/why-companies-like-apple-and-amazon-always-have-the-best-customer-service.html.

4. Post, Jennifer. "The 10 Biggest Challenges for CEOs in 2017." *Business News Daily,* January 26, 2017. https://www.businessnewsdaily.com/3625-new-year-challenges.html.

5. Foss, Nicolai J., and Libby Weber. "Moving Opportunism to the Back Seat: Bounded Rationality, Costly Conflict, and Hierarchical Forms." *Academy of Management Review* 41, no. 1 (January 2016): 61–79; Lorkowski, Joe, and Vladik Kreinovich. *Bounded Rationality in Decision Making under Uncertainty: Towards Optimal Granularity.* (Cham, Switzerland: Springer International Publishing, 2018).

6. Ibid.

7. Baumol, William J. "On Rational Satisficing." In *Models of a Man: Essays in Memory of Herbert A. Simon*, 57–66 (Cambridge, MA: MIT Press, 2004); Janis, Irving L., and Leon Mann. "Satisficing." In *The Effective Manager: Perspectives and Illustrations*, 157–159 (Thousand Oaks, CA: Sage, 1996); Luan, Mo, Lisha Fu, and Hong Li. "Do Maximizers Maximize for Others? Self-Other Decision-Making Differences in Maximizing and Satisficing." *Personality and Individual Differences* 121, (January 15, 2018): 52–56.

8. Hermann, Helena, Manuel Trachsel, and Nikola Biller-Andorno. "Accounting for Intuition in Decision-Making Capacity: Rethinking the Reasoning Standard?" *Philosophy, Psychiatry, & Psychology* 24, no. 4 (December 2017): 313–324; Strack, Fritz, and Roland Deutsch. "Intuition." In *Social Cognition: The Basis of Human Interaction*, 179–197 (New York: Psychology Press, 2009); Plessner, Henning, and Sabine Czenna. "The Benefits of Intuition." In *Intuition in Judgment and Decision Making*, 251–265 (Mahwah, NJ: Erlbaum, 2008).

9. Dearborn, George Van N. "Intuition." *Psychological Review* 23, no. 6 (November 1916): 465–483; Isenman, Lois. "Understanding Unconscious Intelligence and Intuition: 'Blink' and Beyond." *Perspectives in Biology and Medicine* 56, no. 1 (Winter 2013): 148–166.

10. Ferenstein, Gregory. "Netflix CEO Explains Why 'Gut' Decisions Still Rule in the Era of Big Data." *Forbes,* January 22, 2016. https://www.forbes.com/sites/gregoryferenstein/2016/01/22/netflix-ceo-explains-why-gut-decisions-still-rule-in-the-era-of-big-data/#2ef203d41e09.

11. Gigerenzer, Gerd, Ralph Hertwig, and Thorsten Pachur. *Heuristics: The Foundations of Adaptive Behavior* (New York: Oxford University Press, 2011).

12. Chen, Chieh-Shuo, Jia-Chi Cheng, Fang-Chi Lin, and Chihwei Peng. "The Role of House Money Effect and Availability Heuristic in Investor Behavior." *Management Decision* 55, no. 8 (2017): 1598–1612; Schwarz, Norbert, and Leigh Ann Vaughn. "The Availability Heuristic Revisited: Ease of Recall and Content of Recall as Distinct Sources of Information." In *Heuristics and Biases: The Psychology of Intuitive Judgment*, 103–119 (New York: Cambridge University Press, 2002).

13. Mass, Harold. "The Odds Are 11 Million to 1 That You'll Die in a Plane Crash." *The Week.* July 8, 2013. http://theweek.com/article/index/246552/the-odds-are-11-million-to-1-that-youll-die-in-a-plane-crash.

14. Kahneman, Daniel. *Thinking, Fast and Slow.* (New York: Farrar, Straus and Giroux, 2011).

15. Epley, Nicholas, and Thomas Gilovich. "The Anchoring-and-Adjustment Heuristic: Why the Adjustments Are Insufficient." *Psychological Science* 17, no. 4 (April 2006): 311–318.

16. Dumm, Randy, David Eckles, Charles Nyce, and Jacqueline Volkman-Wise. "Demand for Windstorm Insurance Coverage and the Representative Heuristic." *Geneva Risk & Insurance Review* 42, no. 2 (September 2017): 117–139; Nilsson, Håkan, Peter Juslin, and Henrik Olsson. "Exemplars in the Mist: The Cognitive Substrate of the Representativeness Heuristic." *Scandinavian Journal of Psychology* 49, no. 3 (June 2008): 201–212.

17. Stasser, Garold, and William Titus. "Effects of Information Load and Percentage of Shared Information on the Dissemination of Unshared Information during Group Discussion." *Journal of Personality and Social Psychology* 53, no. 1 (July 1987): 81–93; Zhang, Haisu, Timothy M. Basadur, and Jeffrey B. Schmidt. "Information Distribution, Utilization, and Decisions by New Product Development Teams." *Journal of Product Innovation Management* 31, (December 2, 2014): 189–204.

18. Green, David W. "Confirmation Bias, Problem-Solving and Cognitive Models." In *Cognitive Biases*, 553–562 (Oxford: North-Holland, 1990); Winking, Jeffrey. "Exploring the Great Schism in the Social Sciences: Confirmation Bias and the Interpretation of Results Relating to Biological Influences on Human Behavior and Psychology." *Evolutionary Psychology* 16, no. 1 (January 17, 2018).

19. Buontempo, Gina, and Joel Brockner. "Emotional Intelligence and the Ease of Recall Judgment Bias: The Mediating Effect of Private Self-Focused Attention." *Journal of Applied Social Psychology* 38, no. 1 (January 2008): 159–172; Weingarten, Evan, and J. Wesley Hutchinson. "Does Ease Mediate the Ease-of-Retrieval Effect? A Meta-Analysis." *Psychological Bulletin* 144, no. 3 (March 2018): 227–283.

20. Bhattacharya, Chandrima, and John D. Jasper. "Degree of Handedness: A Unique Individual Differences Factor for Predicting and Understanding Hindsight Bias." *Personality and Individual Differences* 125 (April 15, 2018): 97–101; Hoffrage, Ulrich, Ralph Hertwig, and Gerd Gigerenzer. "Hindsight Bias: A By-Product of Knowledge Updating?" In *Heuristics: The Foundations of Adaptive Behavior*, 223–241 (New York: Oxford University Press, 2011); Hoffrage, Ulrich, and Ralph Hertwig. "Hindsight Bias: A Price Worth Paying for Fast and Frugal Memory." In *Simple Heuristics That Make Us Smart*, 191–208 (New York: Oxford University Press, 1999).

21. Chang, Valerie T., Nickola C. Overall, Helen Madden, and Rachel S. T. Low. "Expressive Suppression Tendencies, Projection Bias in Memory of Negative Emotions, and Well-Being." *Emotion* (February 1, 2018); Krueger, Joachim I., and Melissa Acevedo. "Social Projection and the Psychology of Choice." In *The Self in Social Judgment*, 17–41 (New York: Psychology Press, 2005).

22. Kalmanovich-Cohen, Hanna, Matthew J. Pearsall, and Jessica Siegel Christian. "The Effects of Leadership Change on Team Escalation of Commitment." *The Leadership Quarterly* (April 5, 2018); Staw, Barry M. "The Escalation of Commitment: An Update and Appraisal." In *Organizational Decision Making*, 191–215 (New York: Cambridge University Press, 1997).

23. Emich, Kyle J., and Jin Seok Pyone. "Let It Go: Positive Affect Attenuates Sunk Cost Bias by Enhancing Cognitive Flexibility." *Journal of Consumer Psychology* (February 2, 2018); Hsuchi, Ting, and Thomas S. Wallsten. "A Query Theory Account of the Effect of Memory Retrieval on the Sunk Cost Bias." *Psychonomic Bulletin and Review* 18, no. 4 (August 2011): 767–773.

24. Steele-Johnson, Debra, and Zachary T. Kalinoski. "Error Framing Effects on Performance: Cognitive, Motivational, and Affective Pathways." *Journal of Psychology: Interdisciplinary and Applied* 148, no. 1 (January 2014): 93–111.

25. For overviews of creativity in organizations see: Anderson, Neil, Kristina Potočnik, and Jing Zhou. "Innovation and Creativity in Organizations: A State-of-the-Science Review, Prospective Commentary, and Guiding Framework." *Journal of Management* 40, no. 5 (July 2014): 1297–1333; van Knippenberg, Daan, and Giles Hirst. "A Cross-Level Perspective on Creativity at Work: Person-in-Situation Interactions." In *The Oxford Handbook of Creativity, Innovation, and Entrepreneurship*, 225–244. (New York: Oxford University Press, 2015); Zhou, Jing, and Inga J. Hoever. "Research on Workplace Creativity: A Review and Redirection." *Annual Review of Organizational Psychology and Organizational Behavior* 1, (2014): 333–359.

26. For overviews of innovation in organizations see: Ahlstrom, David. "Innovation and Growth: How Business Contributes to Society." *Academy of Management Perspectives* 24, no. 3 (August 2010): 11-24; Anthony, Scott D. "The Little Black Book of Innovation: How It Works, How to Do It." *Harvard Business School Press Books* (January 2012): 1; Neiva, Elaine Rabelo, Helenides Mendonça, Maria Cristina Ferreira, and Leela Lacerda Francischeto. "Innovation in Organizations: Main Research Results and Their Practical Implications." In *Organizational Psychology and Evidence-Based Management: What Science Says about Practice*, 157–185. (Cham, Switzerland: Springer International Publishing, 2017).

27. Maycock, Dan. "5 Creative Tools Used Every Day by Google, IDEO, and Other Top Innovation Firms." *Inc.*, January 5, 2017. https://www.inc.com/dan-maycock/5-creative-tools-used-every-day-by-google-ideo-and-other-top-innovation-firms.html.

28. Rogers, Bruce. "Innovation In Action: My Interview with EY's Global Chief Innovation Officer Jeff Wong." *Forbes*, August 17, 2017. https://www.forbes.com/sites/brucerogers/2017/08/17/innovation-in-action-my-interview-with-eys-global-chief-innovation-officer-jeff-wong/3/#3d88ebbd609f.

29. https://www.fastcompany.com/person/rupal-patel.

30. Amabile, Teresa M. "The Social Psychology of Creativity: A Componential Conceptualization." *Journal of Personality and Social Psychology* 45, no. 2 (August 1983): 357–376; Amabile, Teresa M. "How to Kill Creativity." *Harvard Business Review* 76, no. 5 (September 1998): 76–87.

31. Ibid.

32. Ibid.

33. Ibid.

34. Ibid.

35. DiLiello, Trudy C., and Jeffery D. Houghton. "Creative Potential and Practised Creativity: Identifying Untapped Creativity in Organizations." *Creativity and Innovation Management* 17, no. 1 (March 2008): 37–46.

36. Naiman, Linda. "How Artists, Scientists and Entrepreneurs Get Their Creative Juices Flowing." *Inc.*, June 17, 2017. https://www.inc.com/linda-naiman/5-ways-to-get-your-creative-juices-flowing-this-weekend-and-all-week-long.html.

37. Amabile, Teresa M., Regina Conti, Heather Coon, Jeffrey Lazenby, and Michael Herron. "Assessing the Work Environment for Creativity." *Academy of Management Journal* 39, no. 5 (October 1996): 1154–1184; DiLiello, Trudy C., Jeffery D. Houghton, and David Dawley. "Narrowing the Creativity Gap: The Moderating Effects of Perceived Support for Creativity." *Journal of Psychology: Interdisciplinary and Applied* 145, no. 3 (March 2011): 151–172; Zhang, Li, Qiong Bu, and Sooyeon Wee. "Effect of Perceived Organizational Support on Employee Creativity: Moderating Role of Job Stressors." *International Journal of Stress Management* 23, no. 4 (November 2016): 400–417.

38. Lai-DuMone, Van. "Creativity Is Good for Business." *Thrive Global*, February 4, 2017. https://medium.com/thrive-global/creativity-is-good-for-business-c2512761c829.

39. DiLiello et al., "Narrowing the Creativity Gap."

40. Ibid.

41. Amabile et al., "Assessing the Work Environment for Creativity"; DiLiello et al. "Narrowing the Creativity Gap."

42. Ibid.

43. Ibid.

44. Dupere, Katie. "21 Incredible Innovations That Improved the World in 2016." *Mashable*, December 18, 2016. https://mashable.com/2016/12/18/social-good-innovations-2016/#Vz7cBiUixmqS.

45. Gale, Adam. "Meet the French Entrepreneur Bringing Romance Back to Online Dating." *Management Today*. https://www.managementtoday.co.uk/meet-french-entrepreneur-bringing-romance-back-online-dating/entrepreneurs/article/1434824.

46. Dupere, "21 Incredible Innovations that Improved the World in 2016."

47. Knight, Kenneth E. "A Descriptive Model of the Intra-firm Innovation Process." *Journal of Business* 40, no. 4 (October 1967): 478–496.

48. Baer, Salem. "The 3 Types of Innovation: Product, Process, & Business Model." *www.differential.com*, January 16, 2017. https://differential.com/insights/the3typesofinnovation/.

49. Knight "A Descriptive Model of the Intra-firm Innovation Process."

50. "Here's How Nike Is Innovating to Scale Up Its Manufacturing." *Forbes*, May 18, 2016. https://www.forbes.com/sites/greatspeculations/2016/05/18/heres-how-nike-is-innovating-to-scale-up-its-manufacturing/#4a0670fe1497.

51. Knight "A Descriptive Model of the Intra-firm Innovation Process."

52. Guzman, Zack. "Zappos CEO Tony Hsieh on Getting Rid of Managers: What I Wish I'd Done Differently." *CNBC*, September 13, 2016. https://www.cnbc.com/2016/09/13/zappos-ceo-tony-hsieh-the-thing-i-regret-about-getting-rid-of-managers.html.

53. Knight "A Descriptive Model of the Intra-firm Innovation Process."

54. Mooney, Chris. "Virgin Atlantic Just Used Behavioral Science to 'Nudge' Its Pilots into Using Less Fuel. It Worked." *The Washington Post*, June 22, 2016. https://www.washingtonpost.com/news/energy-environment/wp/2016/06/22/virgin-atlantic-just-used-behavioral-science-to-nudge-its-pilots-into-saving-lots-of-fuel/?noredirect=on&utm_term=.ffdbe6335da4.

55. Hong, Jin, Bojun Hou, Kejia Zhu, and Dora Marinova. "Exploratory Innovation, Exploitative Innovation and Employee Creativity." *Chinese Management Studies* 12, no. 2 (April 2018): 268–286.

56. Ibid.

57. Ogburn, William F. "Cultural Lag as Theory." *Sociology and Social Research* 41, (1957): 167–174; Langan, Debra, Nicole Schott, Timothy Wykes, Justin Szeto, Samantha Kolpin, Carla Lopez, and Nathan Smith. "Students' Use of Personal Technologies in the University Classroom: Analysing the Perceptions of the Digital Generation." *Technology, Pedagogy and Education* 25, no. 1 (January 2016): 101–117.

58. Smith and Tushman, "Managing Strategic Contradictions."

Chapter 9

1. For a detailed overviews of ethics in business organizations see: Collins, Denis. *Business Ethics, 2e.* (Thousand Oaks, CA: Sage, 2018); Johnson, Craig E. *Organizational Ethics: A Practical Approach 3e.* (Thousand Oaks, CA: Sage, 2016).

2. Di Miceli da Silveira, Alexandre. "The Enron Scandal a Decade Later: Lessons Learned?" *Homo Oeconomicus* 30, no. 3 (July 2013): 315–347; Petrick, Joseph A., and Robert F. Scherer. "The Enron Scandal and the Neglect of Management Integrity Capacity." *Mid-American Journal of Business* 18, no. 1 (Spr 2003): 37–49.

3. Matthews, Chris, and Matthew Heimer. "The 5 Biggest Corporate Scandals of 2016." *Fortune,* December 28, 2016. http://fortune.com/2016/12/28/biggest-corporate-scandals-2016/.

4. Duprey, Rich. "How Skechers U.S.A. Lost Ground to Adidas." *Fox Business,* November 17, 2016. https://www.foxbusiness.com/markets/how-skechers-u-s-a-lost-ground-to-adidas.

5. Clifford, Catherine. "Hundreds of A.I. Experts Echo Elon Musk, Stephen Hawking in Call for a Ban on Killer Robots." *CNBC,* November 8, 2017. https://www.cnbc.com/2017/11/08/ai-experts-join-elon-musk-stephen-hawking-call-for-killer-robot-ban.html.

6. Mutnick, Ally. "New Business School Aims to Build Moral Corporate Leaders." *USA Today,* June 5, 2013. www.usatoday.com/story/news/nation/2013/06/04/catholic-university-business-school/2389499/.

7. Isaza, Marcela, and Leanne Italie. "60 Million Pairs of Shoes and 10 Years Later: TOMS Shoes Founder Reflects." *The Seattle Times,* May 13, 2016. https://www.seattletimes.com/life/fashion/60-million-pairs-of-shoes-and-10-years-later-toms-shoes-founder-reflects/.

8. See, for example, Linehan, Carol, and Elaine O'Brien. "From Tell-Tale Signs to Irreconcilable Struggles: The Value of Emotion in Exploring the Ethical Dilemmas of Human Resource Professionals." *Journal of Business Ethics* 141, no. 4 (April 8, 2017): 763–777.

9. Giang, Vivian. "7 Business Leaders Share How They Solved the Biggest Moral Dilemmas of Their Careers." *Fast Company,* June 2, 2015. https://www.fastcompany.com/3046630/7-business-leaders-share-how-they-solved-the-biggest-moral-dilemmas-of-their.

10. Gustafson, Andrew. "In Defense of a Utilitarian Business Ethic." *Business and Society Review* 118, no. 3 (Fall 2013): 325–360; Schumann, Paul L. "A Moral Principles Framework for Human Resource Management Ethics." *Human Resource Management Review* 11, nos. 1/2 (Summer 2001): 93.

11. Ibid.

12. Ibid.

13. Johnson, Craig E. *Organizational Ethics: A Practical Approach 3e.* (Thousand Oaks, CA: Sage, 2016).

14. Khan, Roomy. "Equifax, SEC And Deloitte Cyber Breaches: Is It Time to Remove Executive Immunity from Prosecutions?" *Forbes,* October 3, 2017. https://www.forbes.com/sites/roomykhan/2017/10/03/equifax-sec-and-deloitte-cyber-breaches-is-it-time-to-remove-executive-immunity-from-prosecutions/#2e064c09727f.

15. Johnson, *Organizational Ethics: A Practical Approach 3e.*

16. Kohlberg, Lawrence, and Richard H. Hersh. "Moral Development: A Review of the Theory." *Theory into Practice* 16, no. 2 (April 1977): 53–59.

17. Kohlberg, Lawrence. "The Development of Children's Orientations toward a Moral Order: I. Sequence in the Development of Moral Thought." *Vita Humana* 6, no. 1–2 (1963): 11–33.

18. Heyman, Gail D., and Kang Lee. "Moral Development: Revisiting Kohlberg's Stages." In *Developmental Psychology: Revisiting the Classic Xtudies,* 164–175. (Thousand Oaks, CA: Sage, 2012).

19. http://josephsoninstitute.org/about/.

20. Josephson, Michael. "Six Pillars of Character." *Personal Excellence* (October 2007): 4.

21. https://charactercounts.org/.

22. Ibid.

23. Ibid.

24. Josephson. "Six Pillars of Character."

25. Josephson, Michael S., and Wes Hanson. *Making Ethical Decisions.* (Los Angeles, CA: Josephson Institute of Ethics, 1992).

26. Golshan, Tara. "Study Finds 75 Percent of Workplace Harassment Victims Experienced Retaliation When They Spoke Up." *Vox,* October 15, 2017. https://www.vox.com/identities/2017/10/15/16438750/weinstein-sexual-harassment-facts.

27. Keltner, Dacher. "Sex, Power, and the Systems That Enable Men like Harvey Weinstein." *Harvard Business Review,* October 13, 2017. https://hbr.org/2017/10/sex-power-and-the-systems-that-enable-men-like-harvey-weinstein.

28. Nicks, Denver. "Mark Zuckerberg Bought Four Houses Just to Tear Them Down." *Money,* May 24, 2016. http://time.com/money/4346766/mark-zuckerberg-houses/.

29. Donnelly, Grace. "Top CEOs Make More in Two Days Than an Average Employee Does in One Year." *Fortune,* June 20, 2017. http://fortune.com/2017/07/20/ceo-pay-ratio-2016/.

30. Rodionova, Zlata. "Chobani Yoghurt CEO Gives 10% of His Shares to Workers, Potentially Making Them Millionaires." *Independent,* April 27, 2016. https://www.independent.co.uk/news/business/news/chobani-yoghurt-ceo-gives-10-of-his-shares-to-workers-potentially-making-them-millionaires-a7003511.html.

31. Karlsson, Per-Ola, DeAnne Aguirre, and Kristin Rivera. "Are CEOs Less Ethical Than in the Past?" *Strategy+Business,* May 15, 2017. https://www.strategy-business.com/feature/Are-CEOs-Less-Ethical-Than-in-the-Past?gko=50774.

32. Brian, Matt. "Toshiba CEO Quits after Company Lied about $1.2 Billion Profits." *www.engadget.com,* July 21, 2015. https://www.engadget.com/2015/07/21/toshiba-ceo-quits-profit-scandal/.

33. Knight, Rebecca. "How Managers Can Avoid Playing Favorites." *Harvard Business Review,* March 15, 2017. https://hbr.org/2017/03/how-managers-can-avoid-playing-favorites.

34. Ibid.

35. "Volkswagen Chief Apologises to Shareholders over Emissions Scandal." *ABC,* June 22, 2016. http://www.abc.net.au/news/2016-06-22/vw-chief-tells-shareholders-sorry-for-emissions-scandal/7534844.

36. Dickey, Megan Rose. "Former Startup CEO Indicted for Allegedly Defrauding Employees." *www.techcrunch.com,* June 8, 2017. https://techcrunch.com/2017/06/08/wrkriot-ceo-indicted/.

37. Haroun, Chris. "Why the Best Companies Always Have the Best Customer Service." *Inc.,* April 25, 2016. https://www.inc.com/chris-haroun/why-companies-like-apple-and-amazon-always-have-the-best-customer-service.html.

38. Kasai, Toshinobu. "Companies Are Demanding More Productivity. But Overworked Employees Are Not the Answer." *World Economic Forum,* November 8, 2016. https://www.weforum.org/agenda/2016/11/companies-are-demanding-more-productivity-but-overworked-employees-are-not-the-answer/.

39. Goldhill, Olivia. "Neuroscientists Have Found a Basis for the 'I Was Just Following Orders' Excuse." *Quartz,* February 21, 2016. https://qz.com/621274/neuroscientists-have-found-a-basis-for-the-i-was-just-following-orders-excuse/.

40. "Employees with Supportive Managers May Be Less Cynical of Workplace, but May Not Feel More Loyal to Company." *www.physorg.com*, April 16, 2016. https://phys.org/news/2016-04-employees-cynical-workplace-loyal-company.html.

41. Scott, Kristyn A., and David Zweig. "Understanding and Mitigating Cynicism in the Workplace." *Journal of Managerial Psychology* 31, no. 2 (2016): 552–569.

42. "Employees with Supportive Managers May Be Less Cynical of Workplace, but May Not Feel More Loyal to Company."

43. Garner, Johny T. "How to Communicate Dissent at Work." *Harvard Business Review,* February 4, 2013. https://hbr.org/2013/02/how-to-communicate-dissent-at.

44. Kolvek, Robin. "Three Leadership Lessons from the Wells Fargo Scandal." *Credit Union Journal,* November 4, 2016. https://www.cujournal.com/opinion/three-leadership-lessons-from-the-wells-fargo-scandal.

45. Van Edwards, Vanessa. "The Scientifically Proven Ways to Deliver Bad News." *Entrepreneur,* November 9, 2017. https://www.entrepreneur.com/article/302091.

46. For an overview of corporate social responsibility see: Ciani, Adriano, Francesco Diotallevi, Lucia Rocchi, Anna Maria Grigore, Cinzia Coduti, and Elisa Belgrado. "Corporate Social Responsibility (CSR): Theory, Regulations, and New Paradigms in the Framework of Sustainable Development Strategy." In *Empowering Organizations through Corporate Social Responsibility,* 166–190. (Hershey, PA: Business Science Reference/IGI Global, 2015).

47. http://www.nielsen.com/us/en/insights/reports/2015/the-sustainability-imperative.html?afflt=ntrt15340001&afflt_uid=GMhUXXsH-8M.4uFP4cNEorg8kUE0PIHeB7YsM-iP8TTn&afflt_uid_2=AFFLT_ID_2.

48. Thomson, Mason Dubbink, Wim, and Luc Liedekerke. "A Neo-Kantian Foundation of Corporate Social Responsibility." *Ethical Theory & Moral Practice* 12, no. 2 (March 2009): 117–136.

49. "Companies Pay Out More Than £1.5m for Breaking Environment Laws." *The Guardian,* January 30, 2017. https://www.theguardian.com/environment/2017/jan/30/companies-pay-out-more-than-15m-for-breaking-environment-laws.

50. Baldelomar, Raquel. "Where Is the Line between Ethical and Legal?" *Forbes,* July 21, 2016. https://www.forbes.com/sites/raquelbaldelomar/2016/07/21/where-is-the-line-between-what-is-ethical-and-legal/#8e2ac0250bb7.

51. Venkatraman, Rohini. "3 Companies That Broke the Rules and Got Ahead–Without Hurting Anyone Along the Way." *Inc.,* September 20, 2017. https://www.inc.com/rohini-venkatraman/these-3-founders-broke-the-rules-ethically-and-saw.html.

52. Preston, Caroline. "The 20 Most Generous Companies of the Fortune 500." *Fortune,* June 22, 2016. http://fortune.com/2016/06/22/fortune-500-most-charitable-companies/.

53. Loudenback, Tanzen. "12 Entrepreneurs Who Are Changing the World." *Business Insider,* April 2, 2016. http://www.businessinsider.com/entrepreneurs-who-are-changing-the-world-2016-3?r=UK&IR=T.

54. https://lynnsocialentrepreneur.wordpress.com/2017/07/06/jacks-soap-a-social-enterprise-that-helps-children-in-need/.

55. Economy, Peter. "The 7 Remarkably Powerful Core Values of a Chef." *Inc.,* April 15, 2016. https://www.inc.com/peter-economy/the-7-remarkably-powerful-core-values-of-a-chef.html.

56. Whittemore, Christine. "What Great Brands Do with Mission Statements: 27 Examples." *www.simplemarketingnow.com,* October 10, 2017. https://www.simplemarketingnow.com/blog/flooring-the-consumer/bid/168520/what-great-brands-do-with-mission-statements-8-examples.

57. "Your Organization Needs a Code of Conduct—Here's Why." www.knowledgecity.com, August 2, 2017. https://www.knowledgecity.com/blog/organization-needs-code-conduct-here.

58. Swisher, Kara. "Google Fires Employee Who Penned Controversial Memo on Women and Tech." *CNBC,* August 7, 2017. https://www.cnbc.com/2017/08/07/firing-expected-after-google-ceo-says-employee-who-penned-controversial-memo-on-women-has-violated-its-code-of-conduct.html.

59. McLaverty, Christopher, and Annie McKee. "What You Can Do to Improve Ethics at Your Company." *Harvard Business Review,* December 29, 2016. https://hbr.org/2016/12/what-you-can-do-to-improve-ethics-at-your-company.

60. Pontefract, Dan. "Wells Fargo Proves Corporate Culture Can Also Be a Competitive Disadvantage." *Forbes,* September 15, 2016. https://www.forbes.com/sites/danpontefract/2016/09/15/wells-fargo-proves-corporate-culture-can-also-be-a-competitive-disadvantage/#5fe717252d10.

61. Sherman, Len. "Why Boards Must Step Up to Deter Corporate Scandals." *Forbes,* March 13, 2017. https://www.forbes.com/sites/lensherman/2017/03/13/why-boards-must-step-up-to-deter-corporate-scandals/#3648248a1b79.

62. Lally, Rosemarie. "Study Shows Rise in Ethics and Compliance Reporting Rates." *www.shrm.org*, April 14, 2017. https://www.shrm.org/resourcesandtools/hr-topics/behavioral-competencies/ethical-practice/pages/benchmark-reporting-ethics.aspx.

63. https://www.loreal.com/media/press-releases/2016/jan/loreals-chief-ethics-officer-recognized-for-leadership-in-corporate-ethics.

64. Wells, Deborah, and Marshall Schminke. "Ethical Development and Human Resources Training: An Integrative Framework." *Human Resource Management Review* 11, no. 1–2 (Spr-Sum 2001): 135–158.

Chapter 10

1. For an overview, see May, Steve, and Dennis K. Mumby, *Engaging Organizational Communication Theory and Research: Multiple Perspective* (Thousand Oaks, CA: Sage, 2005); Mumby, Dennis K., and Timothy R. Kuhn. *Organizational Communication: A Critical Introduction 2e.* (Thousand Oaks, CA: Sage, 2018).

2. Berlo, D. K. *The Process of Communication* (New York: Holt, Rinehart, & Winston, 1960); Shannon, C. E., & W. Weaver. *The Mathematical Theory of Communication* (Urbana: University of Illinois Press, 1949).

3. Collins, Keith. "Victims of the WannaCry Ransomware Attacks Have Stopped Paying Up." *Quartz,* May 17, 2017. https://qz.com/986094/wannacry-ransomware-attacks-victims-have-stopped-paying-the-ransom/.

4. Gifford, Robert. "The Role of Nonverbal Communication in Interpersonal Relations," In *Handbook of Interpersonal Psychology: Theory, Research, Assessment, and Therapeutic Interventions,* 171–190 (Hoboken, NJ: Wiley, 2011); Matsumoto, David, Hyisung C. Hwang, and Mark G. Frank. *APA Handbook of Nonverbal Communication.* (Washington, DC, US: American Psychological Association, 2016).

5. Gausepohl, Shannon. "What Is Your Body Language Telling Colleagues about You?" *Business News Daily,* October 7, 2016. https://www.businessnewsdaily.com/9469-body-language-workplace-communication.html.

6. Smith, Jacqueline. "15 Email-Etiquette Rules Every Professional Should Know." *Business Insider,* February 1, 2016. http://www.businessinsider.com/email-etiquette-rules-every-professional-needs-to-know-2016-1/?r=UK&IR=T/#1-include-a-clear-direct-subject-line-1.

7. Petter, Olivia. "'Smiley' Emojis in the Workplace Imply Incompetence, Finds Study." *Independent,* August 14, 2017. https://www.independent.co.uk/life-style/smiley-emojiis-workplace-incompetence-study-emoticons-messaging-emails-a7891876.html.

8. Williams, Ellie. "The Etiquette of Texting in the Workplace." *www.thenest.com.* https://woman.thenest.com/etiquette-texting-workplace-3927.html.

9. Gopalakrishnan, Manasi. "Should Businesses Follow Deutsche Bank and Ban Texting?" *www.dw.com,* January 14, 2017. http://www.dw.com/en/should-businesses-follow-deutsche-bank-and-ban-texting/a-37135029.

10. Button, Kenneth, and Fabio Rossera. "Barriers to Communication." *Annals of Regional Science* 24, no. 4 (December 1990): 337; Chen, Ming-Huei, and Somya Agrawal. "Do Communication Barriers in Student Teams Impede Creative Behavior in the Long Run?—A Time-Lagged Perspective." *Thinking Skills and Creativity* 26, (December 2017): 154–167.

11. Yarrow, Kit. "The Science of How Marketers (and Politicians) Manipulate Us." *Money,* September 29, 2016. http://time.com/money/4511709/marketing-politicians-manipulation-psychology/.

12. Haughton, Jermain. "When Leaders Lose Their Rag." *www.managers.org.uk,* May 5, 2017. https://www.managers.org.uk/insights/news/2017/may/when-leaders-lose-their-rag.

13. Guillot, Craig. "How CEOs Can Reduce Their Information Overload." *Chief Executive,* August 31, 2016. https://chiefexecutive.net/ceos-can-reduce-information-overload/.

14. O'Malley, Brian. "Millennials and 'Their Destruction of Civilization.'" *Forbes,* April 25, 2016. https://www.forbes.com/sites/valleyvoices/2016/04/25/millennials-and-their-destruction-of-civilization/#175fce502830.

15. See http://innolectinc.com/services-overview/the-cost-of-poor-listening/.

16. See, for example, Weger, Harry Jr, Gina Castle Bell, and Melissa C. Robinson. "The Relative Effectiveness of Active Listening in Initial Interactions." *International Journal of Listening* 28, no. 1 (January 2014): 13–31.

17. Keyser, John. "Listening Is a Leader's Most Important Skill." *www.td.com,* July 15, 2014. https://www.td.org/insights/listening-is-a-leaders-most-important-skill.

18. Tiseo, Vincent. "Active Listening in the Age of Social Media." *www.gsam.com,* February 14, 2017. https://www.gsam.com/content/gsam/us/en/advisors/market-insights/gsam-connect/2017/active-listening-in-the-age-of-social-media.html.

19. Drollinger, Tanya, Lucette B. Comer, and Patricia T. Warrington. "Development and Validation of the Active Empathetic Listening Scale." *Psychology and Marketing* 23, no. 2 (February 2006): 161–180; Shrivastava, Archana. "Active Empathic Listening as a Tool for Better Communication." *International Journal of Marketing & Business Communication* 3, no. 3/4 (July 2014): 13–18.

20. Brodsky, Andrew, and Sigal Barsade. "Advancing Research on Interpersonal Communication: Communicating in All Directions." *Academy of Management Annual Meeting Proceedings* 2016, no. 1 (January 2016): 1; Lunenburg, Fred C. "Formal Communication Channels: Upward, Downward, Horizontal, and External." *Focus on Colleges, Universities, and Schools* 4, no. 1 (2010): 1–7; Roberts, Karlene H., and Charles A. O'Reilly. "Measuring Organizational Communication." *Journal of Applied Psychology* 59, no. 3 (June 1974): 321–326.

21. Shurenberg, Eric. "Richard Branson: Why Customers Come Second at Virgin." *Inc.* https://www.inc.com/eric-schurenberg/sir-richard-branson-put-your-staff-first-customers-second-and-shareholders-third.html.

22. Kelley, Tom, and Jonathan Littman. *The Art of Innovation: Lessons in Creativity from IDEO, America's Leading Design Firm* (New York: Doubleday, 2001).

23. Hopkins, Cassidy. "Those Ringing Bells at Trader Joe's Are Actually Part of a Secret Morse Code for Employees." *Insider,* June 1, 2017. http://www.thisisinsider.com/what-the-ringing-bells-at-trader-joes-mean-2017-3.

24. Lewis, Len. "Fostering a Loyal Workforce at Trader Joe's." *Workforce.* June 2, 2005. www.workforce.com/articles/fostering-a-loyal-workforce-at-trader-joe-s.

25. Song, Xiao, Wen Shi, Yaofei Ma, and Chen Yang. "Impact of Informal Networks on Opinion Dynamics in Hierarchically Formal Organization." *Physica A* 436, (October 15, 2015): 916–924; Langan-Fox, Janice. "Communication in Organizations: Speed, Diversity, Networks, and Influence on Organizational Effectiveness, Human Health, and Relationships." In *Handbook of Industrial, Work and Organizational Psychology.* Vol. 2: *Organizational Psychology,* 188–205 (Thousand Oaks, CA: Sage, 2002).

26. Davis, Keith. "Management Communication and the Grapevine." *Harvard Business Review* 31, no. 5 (September 1953): 43–49; Baerjee, Pratyush, and Sweta Singh. "Managers' Perspectives on the Effects of Online Grapevine Communication: A Qualitative Inquiry." *Qualitative Report* 20, no. 6 (June 2015): 765–779; Nicoll, David Cathmoir. "Acknowledge and Use Your Grapevine." *Management Decision* 32, no. 6 (August 1994): 25; Smith, Bob. "Care and Feeding of the Office Grapevine." *Management Review* 85, no. 2 (February 1996): 6.

27. Broderick, Ryan, and Emanuella Grinberg, "10 People Who Learned Social Media Can Get You Fired." *CNN,* June 1, 2013. http://edition.cnn.com/2013/06/06/living/buzzfeed-social-media-fired/index.html.

28. Davis, Keith, "Management Communication and the Grapevine." *Harvard Business Review* 31, no. 5 (September 1953): 43–49; Drapkin, Jennifer. "The Dirty Little Secret about Gossip." *Psychology Today* 38, no. 6 (November 2005): 54–60; Foster, Eric K., and Ralph L. Rosnow. "Gossip and Network Relationships." In *Relating Difficulty: The Processes of Constructing and Managing Difficult Interaction*, 161–180 (Mahwah, NJ: Erlbaum, 2006).

29. Ibid.

30. Mishra, "Managing the Grapevine."

31. Keith, Kenneth D. "Ethnocentrism: Our Window on the World." In *Culture across the Curriculum: A Psychology Teacher's Handbook*, 391–406. (New York: Cambridge University Press, 2018).

32. "I have said School of the South; because in reality, our north is the South. There must not be north, for us, except in opposition to our South. Therefore we now turn the map upside down, and then we have a true idea of our position, and not as the rest of the world wishes. The point of America, from now on, forever, insistently points to the South, our north." (Joaquin Torres Garcia, *Constructive Universalism*, BS AS, *Poseidon*, 1941).

33. Hall, Edward T. *Beyond Culture* (Oxford: Anchor, 1976); Jeong, Ji Youn, and John L. Crompton. "Do Subjects from High and Low Context Cultures Attribute Different Meanings to Tourism Services with 9-Ending Prices?." *Tourism Management* 64, (February 2018): 110–118; Kittler, Markus G., David Rygl, and Alex Mackinnon. "Beyond Culture or Beyond Control? Reviewing the Use of Hall's High-/Low-Context Concept." *International Journal of Cross Cultural Management* 11, no. 1 (April 2011): 63–82.

34. Bennett, Brian. "Aides Warned Trump Not to Attack North Korea's Leader Personally before His Fiery U.N. Address." *Los Angeles Times,* September 22, 2017. http://www.latimes.com/politics/la-fg-trump-northkorea-20170922-story.html.

35. Ferraro, Gary P., and Elizabeth K. Briody. *The Cultural Dimensions of Global Business* (7th ed.) (Upper Saddle River, NJ: Pearson, 2012).

36. Ibid.

37. Ibid.

38. Melas, Cloe. "Will Ferrell Breaks into Song during USC Commencement Speech." *CNN,* May 12. 2017. https://edition.cnn.com/2017/05/12/celebrities/will-ferrell-usc-commencement-speech/index.html.

39. Toegel, Ginka, and Jean-Louis Barsoux. "3 Situations Where Cross-Cultural Communication Breaks Down." *Harvard Business Review,* June 8, 2016. https://hbr.org/2016/06/3-situations-where-cross-cultural-communication-breaks-down.

Chapter 11

1. For detailed overviews of organizational trust definitions and research, see De Jong, Bart A., David P. Kroon, and Oliver Schilke. "The Future of Organizational Trust Research: A Content-Analytic Synthesis of Scholarly Recommendations and Review of Recent Developments." In *Trust in Social Dilemmas,* 173–194. (New York: Oxford University Press, 2017); García, Ana Belén, Erica Pender, and Patricia Elgoibar. "The State of Art: Trust and Conflict Management in Organizational Industrial Relations." In *Building Trust and Constructive Conflict Management in Organizations,* 29–51. (Cham, Switzerland: Springer International Publishing, 2016).

2. Smith, Courtenay. "Reader's Digest Trust Poll: The 100 Most Trusted People in America." *Reader's Digest.* https://www.rd.com/culture/readers-digest-trust-poll-the-100-most-trusted-people-in-america/1/.

3. "Maria Sharapova Claims She 'Fought for Truth' as Tennis Doping Ban Return Nears." *The Guardian.* March 29, 2017. https://www.theguardian.com/sport/2017/mar/29/maria-sharapova-tennis-fought-for-truth-doping-ban.

4. Choi, Byoung Kwon, Hyoung Koo Moon, and Eun Young Nae. "Cognition- and Affect-Based Trust and Feedback-Seeking Behavior: The Roles of Value, Cost, and Goal Orientations." *Journal of Psychology* 148, no. 5 (September 2014): 603–620; Mayer, Roger C., James H. Davis, and F. David Schoorman. "An Integrative Model of Organizational Trust." *Academy of Management Review* 20, no. 3 (July 1995): 709–734; McAllister, Daniel J. "Affect- and Cognition-Based Trust as Foundations for Interpersonal Cooperation in Organizations." *Academy of Management Journal* 38, no. 1 (February 1995): 24–59.

5. Colquitt, Jason A., Brent A. Scott, and Jeffery A. LePine. "Trust, Trustworthiness, and Trust Propensity: A Meta-analytic Test of Their Unique Relationships with Risk Taking and Job Performance." *Journal of Applied Psychology* 92, no. 4 (July 2007): 909–927; Mayer, Roger C., and Mark B. Gavin. "Trust in Management and Performance: Who Minds the Shop While the Employees Watch the Boss?" *Academy of Management Journal* 48, no. 5 (October 2005): 874–888.

6. Ibid.

7. Guest, David E. "Trust and the Role of the Psychological Contract in Contemporary Employment Relations." In *Building Trust and Constructive Conflict Management in Organizations,* 137–149. (Cham, Switzerland: Springer International Publishing, 2016); Rousseau, Denise M. "The Individual–Organization Relationship: The Psychological Contract." In *APA Handbook of Industrial and Organizational Psychology, Vol 3: Maintaining, Expanding, and Contracting the Organization,* 191–220. (Washington, DC: American Psychological Association, 2011).

8. Delgado-Márquez, Blanca L., Maksim Belitski, and Luisa Delgado-Márquez. "The Role of Individuals' Social Networks Density on Their Transfers of Trust Behaviors and Expectations: A Social Capital Approach." In *Psychology of Trust: New Research,* 305–324. (Hauppauge, NY, US: Nova Science Publishers, 2013).

9. Das, T. K., and Bing-Sheng Teng. "The Risk-Based View of Trust: A Conceptual Framework." *Journal of Business and Psychology* 19, no. 1 (Fal 2004): 85–116.

10. Kauflin, Jeff. "The Worst CEO Screw-Ups of 2016." *Forbes,* December 20, 2016. https://www.forbes.com/sites/jeffkauflin/2016/12/20/the-worst-ceo-screw-ups-of-2016/#78f337125e36.

11. For an overview see Elgoibar, Patricia, Martin Euwema, and Lourdes Munduate. *Building Trust and Constructive Conflict Management in Organizations.* (Cham, Switzerland: Springer International Publishing, 2016); Roche, William K., Paul Teague, and Alexander J. S. Colvin. *The Oxford Handbook of Conflict Management in Organizations.* (New York: Oxford University Press, 2016).

12. Turkewitz, Julie. "Prayer Dispute between Somalis and Plant Reshapes a Colorado Town, Again." *The New York Times,* March 7, 2016. https://www.nytimes.com/2016/03/08/us/prayer-dispute-between-somalis-and-plant-reshapes-a-colorado-town-again.html?mcubz=0.

13. Venkatesh, Sudhir. "How to Use Conflict to Unlock Creativity." *Fast Company,* June 15, 2015. https://www.fastcompany.com/1682575/how-to-use-conflict-to-unlock-creativity.

14. Berger, Laura. "Five Conflict Management Strategies." *Forbes,* June 7, 2017. https://www.forbes.com/sites/forbescoachescouncil/2017/06/07/five-conflict-management-strategies/#56e6de71521d.

15. Amason, Allen C. "Distinguishing the Effects of Functional and Dysfunctional Conflict on Strategic Decision Making: Resolving a Paradox for Top Management Teams." *Academy of Management Journal* 39, no. 1 (February 1996): 123–148; Bobot, Lionel. "Functional and Dysfunctional Conflicts in Retailer-Supplier Relationships." *International Journal of Retail & Distribution Management* 39, no. 1 (January 2011): 25–50.

16. Ibid.

17. Jehn, Karen A. "A Qualitative Analysis of Conflict Types and Dimensions in Organizational Groups." *Administrative Science Quarterly* 42, no. 3 (September 1997): 530–557; Marineau, Joshua E., Anthony C. Hood, and Giuseppe 'Joe' Labianca. "Multiplex Conflict: Examining the Effects of Overlapping Task and Relationship Conflict on Advice Seeking in Organizations." *Journal of Business and Psychology* (August 22, 2017).

18. Pondy, Louis R. "Organizational Conflict: Concepts and Models." *Administrative Science Quarterly* 12, no. 2 (September 1967): 296–320.

19. https://www.osha.gov/SLTC/workplaceviolence/.

20. Chang, Wen-Long, and Chun-Yi Lee. "Virtual Team E-Leadership: The Effects of Leadership Style and Conflict Management Mode on the Online Learning Performance of Students in a Business-Planning Course." *British Journal of Educational Technology* 44, no. 6 (November 2013): 986–999; Kilmann, Ralph H., and Kenneth W. Thomas. "Interpersonal Conflict-Handling Behavior as Reflections of Jungian Personality Dimensions." *Psychological Reports* 37, no. 3, Pt 1 (December 1975): 971–980.

21. For overviews, see Dreu, Carsten K. W. de, Hillie Aaldering, and Özüm Saygi. "Conflict and Negotiation within and between Groups." In *APA Handbook of Personality and Social Psychology, Volume 2: Group Processes,* 151–176. (Washington, DC: American Psychological Association, 2015); Thompson, Leigh L., Jiunwen Wang, and Brian C. Gunia. "Negotiation." In *Group Processes,* 55–84 (New York: Psychology Press, 2013).

22. The negotiation process explained here is based on information contained in Lewicki, Roy J., Stephen E. Weiss, and David Lewin. "Models of Conflict, Negotiation and Third Party Intervention: A Review and Synthesis." *Journal of Organizational Behavior* 13, no. 3 (May 1992): 209–252.

23. "Seven Keys To Effective Negotiation." www.mitsloan.mit.edu, February 17, 2016. http://mitsloan.mit.edu/newsroom/articles/seven-keys-to-effective-negotiation/.

24. "Emotional Triggers: How Emotions Affect Your Negotiating Ability." www.pon.harvard.edu, April 26, 2018. https://www.pon.harvard.edu/daily/negotiation-skills-daily/how-emotions-affect-your-talks/.

25. Quast, Lisa. "10 Tips to Help You Win Every Negotiation." *Forbes,* August 8, 2016. https://www.forbes.com/sites/

lisaquast/2016/08/08/10-tips-to-help-you-win-every-negotiation/#35c9bc4436d0.

26. Angoff, Samuel E. "Impartial Opinion and Constructive Criticism of Mediators, Mediation Agencies and Conciliators." *Labor Law Journal* 12, no. 1 (January 1961): 67; Lewicki et al., "Models of Conflict, Negotiation and Third Party Intervention."; Ross, William H., and Donald E. Conlon. "Hybrid Forms of Third-Party Dispute Resolution: Theoretical Implications of Combining Mediation and Arbitration." *Academy of Management Review* 25, no. 2 (April 2000): 416–427.

27. Gorman, Thomas. "The Arbitration Process." *Baseball Prospectus.* January 18, 2012. www.baseballprospectus.com/article.php?articleid=15864.

28. Lewicki et al., "Models of Conflict, Negotiation and Third Party Intervention."

29. Ibid.; Fisher, Roger. "Getting to Yes." *Management Review* 71, no. 2 (February 1982): 16–21.

30. Ibid.

31. Hedges, Kristi. "How to Negotiate a Higher Salary." *Forbes Woman.* April 24, 2013. www.forbes.com/sites/work-in-progress/2013/04/24/how-to-negotiate-a-higher-salary/.

32. Fisher, Roger, and William Ury. "What If They Are More Powerful? (Develop Your BATNA—Best Alternative to a Negotiated Agreement)." In *Getting to Yes*, 101–111 (n.p.: 1983).

33. Sebenius, James K. "Negotiation Analysis: A Characterization and Review." In *Negotiation, Decision Making and Conflict Management*, Vols. 1–3, 18–41 (Northampton, MA: Edward Elgar, 2005).

Chapter 12

1. For an overview of leadership research see one or more of the following: Bass, Bernard M. *The Bass Handbook of Leadership: Theory, Research, and Managerial Applications* (4th ed.) (New York: Free Press, 2008); Day, David V. *The Oxford Handbook of Leadership and Organizations.* (New York: Oxford University Press, 2014); House, Robert J., and Ram N. Aditya. "The Social Scientific Study of Leadership: Quo Vadis?" *Journal of Management* 23, no. 3 (1997 Special Issue 1997): 409; Jago, Arthur G. "Leadership: Perspectives in Theory and Research." *Management Science* 28, no. 3 (March 1982): 315–336.

2. Khazan, Olga. "Why People Fall for Charismatic Leaders." *The Atlantic,* October 13, 2016. https://www.theatlantic.com/science/archive/2016/10/why-people-fall-for-charismatic-leaders/503906/.

3. See for example Foti, Roseanne J., and Neil M. A. Hauenstein. "Pattern and Variable Approaches in Leadership Emergence and Effectiveness." *Journal of Applied Psychology* 92, no. 2 (March 2007): 347–355; Kwok, Navio, Samuel Hanig, Douglas J. Brown, and Winny Shen. "How Leader Role Identity Influences the Process of Leader Emergence: A Social Network Analysis." *The Leadership Quarterly* (April 28, 2018).

4. Elmes, John. "Business Schools 'Must Challenge Leader Stereotypes.'" *Times Higher Education,* February 4, 2016. https://www.timeshighereducation.com/news/business-schools-must-challenge-leader-stereotypes.

5. See, for instance, Neubert, Mitchell J., and Simon Taggar. "Pathways to Informal Leadership: The Moderating Role of Gender on the Relationship of Individual Differences and Team Member Network Centrality to Informal Leadership Emergence." *Leadership Quarterly* 15, no. 2 (April 2004): 175–194; Pan, Jingzhou, Songbo Liu, Bin Ma, and Zhiyao Qu. "How Does Proactive Personality Promote Creativity? A Multilevel Examination of the Interplay between Formal and Informal Leadership." *Journal of Occupational and Organizational Psychology* (May 10, 2018).

6. "The Best-Performing CEOs in the World." *Harvard Business Review,* November 2016. https://hbr.org/2016/11/the-best-performing-ceos-in-the-world.

7. Kearney, Patrick J. "5 Tips for Teacher Leaders." *Huffington Post,* August 23, 2017. https://www.huffingtonpost.com/entry/five-tips-for-teacher-leaders_us_599dd57ae4b0b87d38cbe701.

8. Chiu, Chia-Yen (Chad), Prasad Balkundi, and Frankie Jason Weinberg. "When Managers Become Leaders: The Role of Manager Network Centralities, Social Power, and Followers' Perception of Leadership." *The Leadership Quarterly* 28, no. 2 (April 2017): 334–348; Clemens, John K. "Leaders versus Managers: The Case of Captain Vere." *Journal of Leadership Studies* 1, no. 3 (June 1994): 117–128; Watkins, Michael D. "How Managers Become Leaders." *Harvard Business Review* 90, no. 6 (June 2012): 64–72; Zaleznik, Abraham. "Managers and Leaders: Are They Different?" *Harvard Business Review* 55, no. 3 (May 1977): 67–78.

9. Manz, Charles C., and Henry P. Sims Jr. "SuperLeadership: Beyond the Myth of Heroic Leadership." *Organizational Dynamics* 19, no. 4 (1991): 18–35; Pearce, Craig L., Henry P. Jr. Sims, Jonathan F. Cox, Gail Ball, Eugene Schnell, Ken A. Smith, and Linda Trevino. "Transactors, Transformers and Beyond: A Multi-Method Development of a Theoretical Typology of Leadership." *Journal of Management Development* 22, no. 4 (2003): 273–307.

10. Manz and Sims, "SuperLeadership"; Manz, Charles C., and Henry P. Sims Jr. *The New SuperLeadership: Leading Others to Lead Themselves* (San Francisco: Berrett-Koehler, 2001); Pearce, Craig L., and Henry P. Jr. Sims. "Vertical versus Shared Leadership as Predictors of the Effectiveness of Change Management Teams: An Examination of Aversive, Directive, Transactional, Transformational, and Empowering Leader Behaviors." *Group Dynamics: Theory, Research, and Practice* 6, no. 2 (June 2002): 172–197.

11. Ibid.

12. See, for example, Jenkins, William O. "A Review of Leadership Studies with Particular Reference to Military Problems." *Psychological Bulletin* 44, no. 1 (January 1947): 54–79; Stogdill, Ralph M. "Personal Factors Associated with Leadership: A Survey of the Literature." *Journal of Psychology: Interdisciplinary and Applied* 25 (1948): 35–71; Wyatt, Madeleine, and Jo Silvester. "Do Voters Get It Right? A Test of the Ascription-Actuality Trait Theory of Leadership with Political Elites." *The Leadership Quarterly* (February 14, 2018).

13. Colbert, Amy E., Timothy A. Judge, Daejeong Choi, and Gang Wang. "Assessing the Trait Theory of Leadership Using Self and Observer Ratings of Personality: The Mediating Role of Contributions to Group Success." *Leadership Quarterly* 23, no. 4 (August 2012): 670–685; Derue, D. Scott, Jennifer D. Nahrgang, Ned Wellman, and Stephen E. Humphrey. "Trait and Behavioral Theories of Leadership: An Integration and Meta-analytic Test of Their Relative Validity." *Personnel Psychology* 64, no. 1 (2011): 7–52; Penney, Samantha A., E. Kevin Kelloway, and Damian O'Keefe. "Trait Theories of Leadership." In *Leadership in Sport*, 19–33. (New York: Routledge/Taylor & Francis Group, 2015).

14. Kirkpatrick, Shelley A., and Edwin A. Locke. "Leadership: Do Traits Matter?" *Academy of Management Executive* 5, no. 2 (May 1991): 48–60; Zaccaro, Stephen J. "Trait-Based Perspectives of Leadership." *American Psychologist* 62, no. 1 (January 2007): 6–16.

15. Hemphill, J. K., and A. E. Coons. *Leader Behavior: Its Description and Measurement* (Research Monograph No. 88) (Columbus: Ohio State University, Bureau of Business Research, 1957); Tremblay, Michel, Marie-Claude Gaudet, and Xavier Parent-Rocheleau. "Good Things Are Not Eternal: How Consideration Leadership and Initiating Structure Influence the Dynamic Nature of Organizational Justice and Extra-Role Behaviors at the Collective Level." *Journal of Leadership & Organizational Studies* 25, no. 2 (2018): 211–232.

16. Cartwright, D. and A. Zander. *Group Dynamics Research and Theory* (Evanston, IL: Row, Peterson, 1960); Katz, D. and R. L. Kahn. "Human Organization and Worker Motivation." *Industrial Productivity* (Madison, WI: Industrial Relations Research Association, 1951); Likert, Rensis. *New Patterns of Management* (New York: McGraw-Hill, 1961).

17. Blake, R. R., and J. S. Mouton, *The Managerial Grid* (Houston, TX: Gulf, 1964).

18. See, for example, Barbour, JoAnn Danelo. "Contingency Management and Situational Leadership Theories." In *The Handbook of Educational Theories*, 917–921. (Charlotte, NC: IAP Information Age Publishing, 2013); Hughes, Richard L., Robert C. Ginnett, and Gordon J. Curphy. "Contingency Theories of Leadership." In *Leading Organizations: Perspectives for a New Era*, 141–157 (Thousand Oaks, CA: Sage, 1998); Fiedler, F. E. "A Contingency Model of Leadership Effectiveness." In *Advances in Experimental Social Psychology,* Vol. 1, edited by L. Berkowitz, 149–190 (New York: Academic Press, 1964); Fiedler, F. E. *A Theory of Leadership Effectiveness* (New York: McGraw-Hill, 1967).

19. Hersey, Paul, and Kenneth H. Blanchard *Management of Organizational Behavior: Utilizing Human Resources* (Englewood Cliffs, NJ: Prentice Hall, 1969); Blanchard, Kenneth H., Drea Zigarmi, and Robert B. Nelson. "Situational Leadership® After 25 Years: A Retrospective." *Journal of Leadership Studies* 1, no. 1 (November 1993): 21–36; Luo, Haibin, and Shanshi Liu. "Effect of Situational Leadership and Employee Readiness Match on Organizational Citizenship Behavior in China." *Social Behavior and Personality* 42, no. 10 (2014): 1725–1732; Tortorella, Guilherme, and Flávio Fogliatto. "Implementation of Lean Manufacturing and Situational Leadership Styles: An Empirical Study." *Leadership & Organization Development Journal* 38, no. 7 (2017): 946–968.

20. House, Robert J. "A Path Goal Theory of Leader Effectiveness." *Administrative Science Quarterly* 16, no. 3 (September 1971): 321–339; House, Robert J. "Path-Goal Theory of Leadership: Lessons, Legacy, and a Reformulated Theory." *Leadership Quarterly* (Fall 1996): 323; House, Robert J., and Terence R. Mitchell. "Path-Goal Theory of Leadership." In *Leadership: Understanding the Dynamics of Power and Influence in Organizations* (2nd ed.), 241–254; Bickle, Jason T. "Developing Remote Training Consultants as Leaders-Dialogic/Network Application of Path-Goal Leadership Theory in Leadership Development." *Performance Improvement* 56, no. 9 (October 2017): 32–39.

21. Kerr, Steven, and John M. Jermier. "Substitutes for Leadership: Their Meaning and Measurement." *Organizational Behavior and Human Performance* 22, no. 3 (December 1978): 375–403; Nübold, Annika, Peter M. Muck, and Günter W. Maier. "A New Substitute for Leadership? Followers' State Core Self-Evaluations." *Leadership Quarterly* 24, no. 1 (February 2013): 29–44; Velez, M. J., and P. Neves. "The Relationship between Abusive Supervision, Distributive Justice and Job Satisfaction: A Substitutes for Leadership Approach." *European Review of Applied Psychology / Revue Européenne De Psychologie Appliquée* 67, no. 4 (July 2017): 187–198.

22. Colvin, Geoff. "The Art of the Self-Managing Team." *Fortune,* December 5, 2012. http://fortune.com/2012/12/05/the-art-of-the-self-managing-team/.

23. Dansereau, Fred, George Graen, and William J. Haga. "A Vertical Dyad Linkage Approach to Leadership within Formal Organizations: A Longitudinal Investigation of the Role Making Process." *Organizational Behavior and Human Performance* 13, no. 1 (February 1975): 46–78; Gerstner, Charlotte R., and David V. Day. "Meta-Analytic Review of Leader-Member Exchange Theory: Correlates and Construct Issues." *Journal of Applied Psychology* 82, no. 6 (December 1997): 827–844; Seo, Jungmin (Jamie), Jennifer D. Nahrgang, Min Z. Carter, and Peter W. Hom. "Not All Differentiation is the Same: Examining the Moderating Effects of Leader-Member Exchange (LMX) Configurations." *Journal of Applied Psychology* 103, no. 5 (May 2018): 478–495.

24. Anthony, Scott, and Evan I. Schwartz. "What the Best Transformational Leaders Do." *Harvard Business Review,* May 8, 2017. https://hbr.org/2017/05/what-the-best-transformational-leaders-do.

25. Bass, Bernard M. *Leadership and Performance beyond Expectations* (New York: Free Press, 1985); Avolio, Bruce J., and Bernard M. Bass. "Transformational Leadership, Charisma, and Beyond." In *Emerging Leadership Vistas* (Lexington, MA: Lexington Books, 1988): 29–49.

26. Bass, *Leadership and Performance beyond Expectations;* Hinkin, Timothy R., and Chester A. Schriesheim. "An Examination of 'Nonleadership': From Laissez-Faire Leadership to Leader Reward Omission and Punishment Omission." *Journal of Applied Psychology* 93, no. 6 (November 2008): 1234–1248; Buch, Robert, Øyvind L. Martinsen, and Bård Kuvaas. "The Destructiveness of Laissez-Faire Leadership Behavior: The Mediating Role of Economic Leader–Member Exchange Relationships." *Journal of Leadership & Organizational Studies* 22, no. 1 (February 2015): 115–124.

27. Colvin, Geoff. "Warren Buffett's Very Ordinary Management." *Fortune,* December 14, 2016. http://fortune.com/2016/12/14/warren-buffetts-very-ordinary-management/.

28. Conger, Jay A., and Rabindra N. Kanungo. "Toward a Behavioral Theory of Charismatic Leadership in Organizational Settings." *Academy of Management Review* 12, no. 4 (1987): 637–647; Conger, Jay A. "Charismatic and Transformational Leadership in Organizations: An Insider's Perspective on These Developing Streams of Research." *Leadership Quarterly* 10, no. 2 (Summer 99 1999): 145; Sy, Thomas, Calen Horton, and Ronald Riggio. "Charismatic Leadership: Eliciting and Channeling Follower Emotions." *The Leadership Quarterly* (January 3, 2018).

29. Conger, Jay A. "The Dark Side of Leadership." *Organizational Dynamics* 19, no. 2 (September 1990): 44–55; Howell, Jane M. "Two Faces of Charisma: Socialized and Personalized Leadership in Organizations." In *Charismatic Leadership: The Elusive Factor in Organizational Effectiveness* (San Francisco: Jossey-Bass, 1988): 213–236.

30. Andersson, Thomas. "Followership: An Important Social Resource for Organizational Resilience." In *The Resilience Framework: Organizing for Sustained Viability*, 147–162. (New York: Springer Science + Business Media, 2018); Carsten, Melissa K., Mary Uhl-Bien, Bradley J. West, Jaime L. Patera, and Rob McGregor. "Exploring Social Constructions of Followership: A Qualitative Study." *Leadership Quarterly* 21, no. 3 (June 2010): 543–562.

31. See, for example, Hogg, Michael A. "Social Categorization, Depersonalization, and Group Behavior." In *Self and Social Identity*, 203–231 (Malden, MA: Blackwell, 2004).

32. Foti, Roseanne J., Tiffany Keller Hansbrough, Olga Epitropaki, and Patrick T. Coyle. "Dynamic Viewpoints on Implicit Leadership and Followership Theories: Approaches, Findings, and Future Directions." *The Leadership Quarterly* 28, no. 2 (April 2017): 261–267; Junker, Nina Mareen, and Rolf van Dick. "Implicit Theories in Organizational Settings: A Systematic Review and Research Agenda of Implicit Leadership and Followership Theories." *The Leadership Quarterly* 25, no. 6 (December 2014): 1154–1173.

33. Foti, Roseanne J., Scott L. Fraser, and Robert G. Lord. "Effect of Leadership Labels and Prototypes on Perceptions of Political Leaders." *Journal of Applied Psychology* 67, no. 3 (June 1982): 326–333; Harkiolakis, Nicholas, Daphne Halkias, and Marcos Komodromos. "A Historical View of Leadership Prototypes: Looking Backward to Move Forward." *International Leadership Journal* 9, no. 2 (June 2017): 3–16.

34. Junker, Nina M., Sebastian Stegmann, Stephan Braun, and Rolf Van Dick. "The Ideal and the Counter-Ideal Follower—Advancing Implicit Followership Theories." *Leadership & Organization Development Journal* 37, no. 8 (2016): 1205–1222; Shondrick, Sara J., and Robert G. Lord. "Implicit Leadership and Followership

Theories: Dynamic Structures for Leadership Perceptions, Memory, and Leader–Follower Processes." In *International Review of Industrial and Organizational Psychology 2010*, Vol. 25, 1–33 (n.p.: Wiley-Blackwell, 2010): Sy, Thomas. "What Do You Think of Followers? Examining the Content, Structure, and Consequences of Implicit Followership Theories." *Organizational Behavior and Human Decision Processes* 113, no. 2 (November 2019): 73–84.

35. Arnold, Josh A., Sharon Arad, Jonathan A. Rhoades, and Fritz Drasgow. "The Empowering Leadership Questionnaire: The Construction and Validation of a New Scale for . . . " *Journal of Organizational Behavior* 21, no. 3 (May 2000): 249–269; Vecchio, Robert P., Joseph E. Justin, and Craig L. Pearce. "Empowering Leadership: An Examination of Mediating Mechanisms within a Hierarchical Structure." *Leadership Quarterly* 21, no. 3 (June 2010): 530–542; Zhang, Xiaomeng, and Kathryn M. Bartol. "Linking Empowering Leadership and Employee Creativity: The Influence of Psychological Empowerment, Intrinsic Motivation, and Creative Process Engagement." *Academy of Management Journal* 53, no. 1 (February 2010): 107–128; Zhang, Shuxia, Xudong Ke, Xiao-Hua Frank Wang, and Jun Liu. "Empowering Leadership and Employee Creativity: A Dual-Mechanism Perspective." *Journal of Occupational and Organizational Psychology* (April 18, 2018).

36. Wolfson, Rachel. "Why Women Are Key for Empowering Other Women." *Huffington Post*, July 1, 2016. https://www.huffingtonpost.com/rachel-wolfson/4-women-offer-advice-on-s_b_10718812.html.

37. Schrage, Michael. "Like It or Not, You Are Always Leading by Example." *Harvard Business Review*, October 5, 2016. https://hbr.org/2016/10/like-it-or-not-you-are-always-leading-by-example.

38. Folkman, Joseph. "5 Business Payoffs for Being an Effective Coach." *Forbes*, February 19, 2015. https://www.forbes.com/sites/joefolkman/2015/02/19/5-business-payoffs-for-being-an-effective-coach/#4b8eca8a2afb.

39. Maier, Steffen. "5 Companies Getting Employee Engagement Right." *Entrepreneur*, December 28, 2016. https://www.entrepreneur.com/article/285052.

40. Guisbond, Amanda. "Four Corporate Communications Best Practices to Learn from GE." *Forbes*, May 1, 2017. https://www.forbes.com/sites/forbescommunicationscouncil/2017/05/01/four-corporate-communications-best-practices-to-learn-from-ge/#37b298243b87.

41. Patterson, Sarah. "Why You Should Treat Your Employees Like Your Most Loyal Customers." *Fast Company*, June 18, 2015. https://www.fastcompany.com/3047366/why-you-should-treat-your-employees-like-your-most-loyal-customers.

42. Drescher, Marcus A., M. Audrey Korsgaard, Isabell M. Welpe, Arnold Picot, and Rolf T. Wigand. "The Dynamics of Shared Leadership: Building Trust and Enhancing Performance." *Journal of Applied Psychology* (April 14, 2014); Pearce, Craig L., and Charles C. Manz. "The New Silver Bullets of Leadership: The Importance of Self- and Shared Leadership in Knowledge Work." *Organizational Dynamics* 34, no. 2 (May 2005): 130–140; Pearce, Craig L. "The Future of Leadership: Combining Vertical and Shared Leadership to Transform Knowledge Work." *Academy of Management Executive* 18, no. 1 (February 2004): 47–57; Zhu, Jinlong, Zhenyu Liao, Kai Chi Yam, and Russell E. Johnson. "Shared Leadership: A State-of-the-Art Review and Future Research Agenda." *Journal of Organizational Behavior* (June 8, 2018).

43. Fitzsimons, Declan. "How Shared Leadership Changes Our Relationships at Work." *Harvard Business Review*, May 12, 2016. https://hbr.org/2016/05/how-shared-leadership-changes-our-relationships-at-work.

44. Manz, Charles C. "Self-Leadership: Toward an Expanded Theory of Self-Influence Processes in Organizations." *Academy of*

Management Review 11, no. 3 (July 1986): 585–600; Stewart, Greg L., Stephen H. Courtright, and Charles C. Manz. "Self-Leadership: A Multilevel Review." *Journal of Management* 37, no. 1 (January 2011): 185–222; Neck, Christopher P., and Jeffery D. Houghton. "Two Decades of Self-Leadership Theory and Research." *Journal of Managerial Psychology* 21, no. 4 (June 2006): 270–295; Stewart, G.L., Courtright, S.H., & Manz, C.C. (2019). Self-Leadership: A Paradoxical Core of Organizational Behavior. *Annual Review of Organizational Psychology and Organizational Behavior*, vol. 6.

45. Blanchard, Ken. "Three Ways To Be An Effective Self-Leader: You Can't Lead Others If You Can't Lead Yourself, And You Can't Lead Yourself without The Right Tools." *Fast Company*. February 6, 2014. www.fastcompany.com/3026046/leadership-now/3-ways-to-be-an-effective-self-leader.

46. Neck and Houghton, "Two Decades of Self-Leadership Theory and Research."

47. Ibid.

48. Ibid.

49. Ibid.; Neck, Chris P., and Charles C. Manz. "Thought Self-Leadership: The Influence of Self-Talk and Mental Imagery on Performance." *Journal of Organizational Behavior* 13, no. 7 (December 1992): 681–699.

50. Gallo, Carmine. "3 Daily Habits of Peak Performers, According To Michael Phelps' Coach." *Forbes*, May 24, 2016. https://www.forbes.com/sites/carminegallo/2016/05/24/3-daily-habits-of-peak-performers-according-to-michael-phelps-coach/#2264c0dd102c.

51. McGuire, Jeanne. *The Case for Values Based Leadership: Maximizing People and Profitability* (White paper). Corporate Education Group. www.corpedgroup.com/resources/ml/ValuesBasedLeadership.asp.

52. Gardner, William L., Claudia C. Cogliser, Kelly M. Davis, and Matthew P. Dickens. "Authentic Leadership: A Review of the Literature and Research Agenda." *Leadership Quarterly* 22, no. 6 (December 2011): 1120–1145; Walumbwa, Fred O., Bruce J. Avolio, William L. Gardner, Tara S. Wernsing, and Suzanne J. Peterson. "Authentic Leadership: Development and Validation of a Theory-Based Measure." *Journal of Management* 34, no. 1 (February 2008): 89–126; Sidani, Yusuf M., and W. Glenn Rowe. "A Reconceptualization of Authentic Leadership: Leader Legitimation Via Follower-Centered Assessment of the Moral Dimension." *The Leadership Quarterly* (May 2, 2018).

53. Cashman, Kevin. "Ten Authentic Leadership Practices." *Forbes*, April 24, 2017. https://www.forbes.com/sites/kevincashman/2017/04/24/ten-authentic-leadership-practices/#1ea64adb4e0a.

54. Cashman, Kevin, *Awakening the Leader Within: A Story of Transformation* (Hoboken, NJ: Wiley, 2003); George, Bill. *True North: Discover Your Authentic Leadership* (San Francisco: Jossey-Bass, 2007).

55. Peus, Claudia, Jenny Sarah Wesche, Bernhard Streicher, Susanne Braun, and Dieter Frey. "Authentic Leadership: An Empirical Test of Its Antecedents, Consequences, and Mediating Mechanisms." *Journal of Business Ethics* 107, no. 3 (May 2012): 331–348; Walumbwa et al. "Authentic leadership"; Clapp-Smith, Rachel, Gretchen R. Vogelgesang, and James B. Avey. "Authentic Leadership and Positive Psychological Capital: The Mediating Role of Trust at the Group Level of Analysis." *Journal of Leadership and Organizational Studies* 15, no. 3 (February 2009): 227–240.

56. Fry, Louis W. "Toward a Theory of Spiritual Leadership." *Leadership Quarterly* 14, no. 6 (December 2003): 693–727; Fry, Louis W. "Spiritual Leadership and Faith and Spirituality in the Workplace." In *Handbook of Faith and Spirituality in the Workplace: Emerging Research and Practice*, 697–704 (New York: Springer Science + Business Media, 2013); Yang, Fu, Jun

Liu, Zhen Wang, and Yucheng Zhang. "Feeling Energized: A Multilevel Model of Spiritual Leadership, Leader Integrity, Relational Energy, and Job Performance." *Journal of Business Ethics* (October 13, 2017).

57.   Fry, Louis W., Sean T. Hannah, Michael Noel, and Fred O. Walumbwa. "Impact of Spiritual Leadership on Unit Performance." *Leadership Quarterly* 22, no. 2 (April 2011): 259–270; Fry, Louis W., Sean T. Hannah, Michael Noel, and Fred O. Walumbwa. "Corrigendum to 'Impact of Spiritual Leadership on Unit Performance.' [The Leadership Quarterly. 22 (2011) 259–270]." *Leadership Quarterly* 23, no. 3 (June 2012): 641.

58.   Greenleaf, R. K. *The Servant as Leader* (Newton Centre, MA: Robert Greenleaf Center, 1970); Lu, Junting, Zhe Zhang, and Ming Jia. "Does Servant Leadership Affect Employees' Emotional Labor? A Social Information-Processing Perspective." *Journal of Business Ethics* (February 19, 2018); Neubert, Mitchell J., K. Michele Kacmar, Dawn S. Carlson, Lawrence B. Chonko, and James A. Roberts. "Regulatory Focus as a Mediator of the Influence of Initiating Structure and Servant Leadership on Employee Behavior." *Journal of Applied Psychology* 93, no. 6 (November 2008): 1220–1233.

59.   Kauflin, Jeff. "The Unusual Management Style of One of the Most Highly Rated CEOs in Tech." *Forbes,* August 10, 2017. https://www.forbes.com/sites/jeffkauflin/2017/08/10/the-unusual-management-style-of-one-of-the-most-highly-rated-ceos-in-tech/#43d7504e715b.

60.   Brown, Michael E., and Linda K. Treviño. "Ethical Leadership: A Review and Future Directions." *Leadership Quarterly* 17, no. 6 (December 2006): 595–616; Brown, Michael E., Linda K. Treviño, and David A. Harrison. "Ethical Leadership: A Social Learning Perspective for Construct Development and Testing." *Organizational Behavior and Human Decision Processes* 97, no. 2 (July 2005): 117–134; Mostafa, Ahmed Mohammed Sayed. "Ethical Leadership and Organizational Citizenship Behaviours: The Moderating Role of Organizational Identification." *European Journal of Work and Organizational Psychology* (May 10, 2018).

61.   Williams, Nate. "10 Most Ethical CEOs of 2016." *Retire at the Top, http://blog.retireatthetop.com/10-most-ethical-ceos-of-2016/.*

62.   Tulshyan, Ruchika. "Racially Diverse Companies Outperform Industry Norms by 35%." *Forbes,* January 30, 2015. https://www.forbes.com/sites/ruchikatulshyan/2015/01/30/racially-diverse-companies-outperform-industry-norms-by-30/#36ccad391132.

63.   Chhokar, Jagdeep S., Felix C. Brodbeck, and Robert J. House. *Culture and Leadership across the World: The GLOBE Book of In-Depth Studies of 25 Societies* (Mahwah, NJ: Erlbaum, 2008); Gabrenya, William K. Jr., and Peter B. Smith. "Project GLOBE for Scientists and Practitioners: Drawing Clarity from Controversy." In *Leading Global Teams: Translating Multidisciplinary Science to Practice*, 33–65. (New York: Springer Science + Business Media, 2015); Javidan, Masour, Peter W. Dorfman, Mary Sully De Luque, and Robert J. House. "In the Eye of the Beholder: Cross Cultural Lessons in Leadership from Project GLOBE." *Academy of Management Perspectives* 20, no. 1 (February 2006): 67–90.

64.   Ibid.

65.   Ibid.

66.   Geiger, Abigail, and Lauren Kent. "Number of Women Leaders around the World Has Grown, but They're Still a Small Group." *Pew Research Center,* March 8, 2017. http://www.pewresearch.org/fact-tank/2017/03/08/women-leaders-around-the-world/.

67.   McGregor, Jena. "The Number of Women CEOs in the Fortune 500 Is at an All-Time High — of 32." *The Washington Post,* June 7, 2017. https://www.washingtonpost.com/news/on-leadership/wp/2017/06/07/the-number-of-women-ceos-in-the-fortune-500-is-at-an-all-time-high-of-32/?utm_term=.25ee52f2264b.

68.   Fairchild, Caroline. "Women CEOs in the Fortune 1000: By the Numbers." *Fortune.* July 8, 2014. http://fortune.com/2014/07/08/women-ceos-fortune-500-1000/.

69.   For an overview see Eagly, Alice H., and Linda L. Carli. "Women and Men as Leaders." In *The Nature of Leadership*, 279–301 (Thousand Oaks, CA: Sage, 2004).

70.   Eagly, Alice H., Mary C. Johannesen-Schmidt, and Marloes L. van Engen. "Transformational, Transactional, and Laissez-Faire Leadership Styles: A Meta-Analysis Comparing Women and Men." *Psychological Bulletin* 129, no. 4 (July 2003): 569–591; Eagly, A. H., and B. T. Johnson. "Gender and Leadership Style: A Meta-Analysis." *Psychological Bulletin* 108, no. 2 (September 1990): 233.

71.   Eagly, Alice H., and Linda L. Carli. "Women and the Labyrinth of Leadership." *Harvard Business Review* 85, no. 9 (September 2007): 63–71.

72.   Turner, Matt. "Here's How Much Paid Leave New Mothers and Fathers Get in 11 Different Countries." *Business Insider,* September 7, 2017. http://www.businessinsider.com/maternity-leave-worldwide-2017-8/?r=UK&IR=T#australia-there-is-a-legal-requirement-to-provide-12-months-maternity-leave-1.

73.   "Is Paid Leave Available to Mothers and Fathers of Infants?" (2018). Retrieved June 27, 2018, from http://worldpolicycenter.org/policies/is-paid-leave-available-to-mothers-and-fathers-of-infants.

74.   Hoobler, Jenny M., Sandy J. Wayne, and Grace Lemmon. "Bosses' Perceptions of Family-Work Conflict and Women's Promotability: Glass Ceiling Effects." *Academy of Management Journal* 52, no. 5 (October 2009): 939–957.

75.   Eagly and Carli. "Women and the Labyrinth of Leadership."

76.   Wong, Julia Carrie. "Former Yahoo Employee Accuses Company of Gender Bias—against Men." *The Guardian,* February 2, 2016. https://www.theguardian.com/technology/2016/feb/02/gender-discrimination-lawsuit-male-former-employee-yahoo-marissa-mayer.

77.   Eagly and Carli. "Women and the Labyrinth of Leadership."

78.   Solon, Olivia. "Uber Fires More Than 20 Employees after Sexual Harassment Investigation." *The Guardian,* June 6, 2017. https://www.theguardian.com/technology/2017/jun/06/uber-fires-employees-sexual-harassment-investigation.

79.   Eagly and Carli. "Women and the Labyrinth of Leadership."

80.   Bellis, Rich. "Here's Everywhere in the U.S. You Can Still Get Fired for Being Gay or Trans." *Fast Company,* August 28, 2017. https://www.fastcompany.com/40456937/heres-everywhere-in-the-u-s-you-can-still-get-fired-for-being-gay-or-trans.

81.   Baksh, Karina. "Workplace Discrimination: The LGBT Workforce." *Huffington Post,* December 6, 2017. https://www.huffingtonpost.com/kurina-baksh/workplace-discrimination-_b_10606030.html.

82.   Miller-Merrell, Jessica. "4 Ways to Create an LGBT Friendly Workplace." *Rework,* February 6, 2017. https://www.cornerstoneondemand.com/rework/4-ways-create-lgbt-friendly-workplace.

Chapter 13

1.   Brass, Daniel J., and David M. Krackhardt. "Power, Politics, and Social Networks in Organizations." In *Politics in Organizations: Theory and Research Considerations*, 355–375. (New York: Routledge/Taylor & Francis Group, 2012).

2.   Keltner, Dacher. "The Power Paradox." *Greater Good.* December 1, 2007. http://greatergood.berkeley.edu/article/item/power_paradox.

3.   Ibid.

4. French, John R., and Bertram Raven. D. Cartwright, ed. *The Bases of Social Power* (Ann Arbor, MI: Institute for Social Research, 1959); Wood, Jay K. "Fight the Power: Comparing and Evaluating Two Measures of French and Raven's (1959) Bases of Social Power." *Current Research in Social Psychology* 21 (2013): PsycINFO, EBSCOhost.

5. Malloy, Mark. "World's Best Boss? CEO Rewards 800 Staff with Caribbean Cruise." *The Telegraph,* December 26, 2016. https://www.telegraph.co.uk/news/2016/12/28/worlds-best-boss-ceo-rewards-800-staff-caribbean-cruise/.

6. Kelly, Ric. "3 Ways Coercive Leaders Can Change Their Ways." *Entrepreneur,* September 22, 2016. https://www.entrepreneur.com/article/281914.

7. Murphy, Mark. "How to Get More Power at Work." *Forbes,* March 11, 2016. https://www.forbes.com/sites/markmurphy/2016/03/11/how-to-get-more-power-at-work/#44867e34f4f3.

8. Cain, Aine. "The 26 Most Popular CEOs in America, According to Glassdoor." *Business Insider,* June 21, 2017. http://www.businessinsider.com/most-loved-ceos-in-america-2017-6/?r=UK&IR=T/#2-jim-kavanaugh-world-wide-technology-2.

9. Yukl, Gary, and Cecilia M. Falbe. "Influence Tactics and Objectives in Upward, Downward, and Lateral Influence Attempts." *Journal of Applied Psychology* 75, no. 2 (April 1990): 132–140; Kipnis, David, Stuart M. Schmidt, and Ian Wilkinson. "Intraorganizational Influence Tactics: Explorations in Getting One's Way." *Journal of Applied Psychology* 65, no. 4 (August 1980): 440–452.

10. Clifford, Catherine. "Warren Buffett Uses This Simple Psychological Trick to Be Persuasive and So Can You, Says Influence Expert." *CNBC,* July 12, 2017. https://www.cnbc.com/2017/07/12/use-warren-buffetts-simple-psychological-trick-to-be-persuasive.html.

11. Kim, Larry. "33 Traits of the Most Inspiring Leaders." *Inc.,* November 18, 2016. https://www.inc.com/larry-kim/33-characteristics-of-super-inspiring-leaders.html.

12. Whitehurst, Jim. "Decisions Are More Effective When More People Are Involved from the Start." *Harvard Business Review,* March 15, 2016. https://hbr.org/2016/03/decisions-are-more-effective-when-more-people-are-involved-from-the-start.

13. Keeves, Gareth, James Westphal, and Michael McDonald. "Office Politics: When Managers Flatter the CEO, but Undermine Him with Journalists." *LSE Business Review,* January 20, 2017. http://blogs.lse.ac.uk/businessreview/2017/01/20/office-politics-when-managers-flatter-the-ceo-but-undermine-him-with-journalists/.

14. Detert, James R., and Ethan R. Burris. "Can Your Employees Really Speak Freely?" *Harvard Business Review,* January–February 2016. https://hbr.org/2016/01/can-your-employees-really-speak-freely.

15. Wadhwa, Vivek. "The Best Companies in the World Are Run by Enlightened Dictators." *Quartz,* June 8, 2016. https://qz.com/701895/the-best-companies-in-the-world-are-run-by-enlightened-dictators/.

16. Falbe, Cecilia M, and Gary Yukl. "Consequences for Managers of Using Single Influence Tactics and Combinations of Tactics." *Academy of Management Journal* 35, no. 3 (August 1992): 638–652; Rhodes, Julius E., and Linda G. Rhodes. "Managing Up: Using Influence & Collaboration." *Professional Safety* 62, no. 5 (May 2017): 30–31.

17. Ralston, David A., David J. Gustafson, Fanny M. Cheung, and Robert H. Terpstra. "Differences in Managerial Values: A Study of U.S., Hong Kong and PRC Managers." *Journal of International Business Studies* 24, no. 2 (June 1993): 249–275.

18. Yukl, G., P. P. Fu, and R. McDonald. "Cross-Cultural Differences in Perceived Effectiveness of Influence Tactics for Initiating or Resisting Change." *Applied Psychology: An International Review* 52, no. 1 (January 2003): 68–82.

19. Ferris, Gerald R., and Wayne A. Hochwarter. "Organizational Politics." In *APA Handbook of Industrial and Organizational Psychology,* Vol. 3: *Maintaining, Expanding, and Contracting the Organization,* 435–459 (Washington, DC: American Psychological Association, 2011); Landells, Erin M., and Simon L. Albrecht. "The Positives and Negatives of Organizational Politics: A Qualitative Study." *Journal of Business And Psychology* 32, no. 1 (February 2017): 41–58.

20. Ferris, Gerald R., Gail S. Russ, and Patricia M. Fandt. "Politics in Organizations." In *Impression Management in the Organization,* 143–170 (Hillsdale, NJ: Erlbaum, 1989); Munyon, Timothy P., James K. Summers, Katina M. Thompson, and Gerald R. Ferris. "Political Skill and Work Outcomes: A Theoretical Extension, Meta-Analytic Investigation, and Agenda for the Future." *Personnel Psychology* 68, no. 1 (Spring 2015): 143–184.

21. Parker, Christopher P., Robert L. Dipboye, and Stacy L. Jackson. "Perceptions of Organizational Politics: An Investigation of Antecedents and Consequences." *Journal of Management* 21, no. 5 (December 1995): 891–912; Sultan, Sarwat, Frasat Kanwal, and Shahzad Gul. "Factors of Perceived Organizational Politics: An Analysis of What Contributes the Most?." *Pakistan Journal of Commerce & Social Sciences* 9, no. 3 (September 2015): 999–1011.

22. Long, Heather. "America's Top 10 Job-Killing Companies." *CNN,* May 17, 2016. http://money.cnn.com/2016/05/15/news/economy/america-job-killing-companies/index.html.

23. Chang, Chu-Hsiang, Christopher C. Rosen, and Paul E. Levy. "The Relationship between Perceptions of Organizational Politics and Employee Attitudes, Strain, and Behavior: A Meta-Analytic Examination." *Academy of Management Journal* 52, no. 4 (August 2009): 779–801; Ejaz, Aqsa, and Delphine Lacaze. "Organizational Politics and Work Outcomes: A Moderated Mediation Model." *Academy Of Management Annual Meeting Proceedings* 2016, no. 1 (January 2016): 1; Ferris, Gerald R., Dwight D. Frink, Maria Carmen Galang, Jing Zhou, and Jack L. Howard. "Perceptions of Organizational Politics: Prediction, Stress-Related Implications, and Outcomes." *Human Relations* 49, no. 2 (February 1996): 233–266.

24. Ferris, Gerald R., Darren C. Treadway, Robyn L. Brouer, and Timothy P. Munyon. "Political Skill in the Organizational Sciences." In *Politics in Organizations: Theory and Research Considerations,* 487–528 (New York: Routledge/Taylor & Francis Group, 2012); Rosen, Christopher C., and Pamela L. Perrewé. *Power, Politics, and Political Skill in Job Stress.* (Bingley, United Kingdom: Emerald Group Publishing, 2017).

25. Jarrett, Michael. "The 4 Types of Organizational Politics." *Harvard Business Review,* April 24, 2017. https://hbr.org/2017/04/the-4-types-of-organizational-politics.

26. Warren, Donald I. "Power, Visibility, and Conformity in Formal Organizations." *American Sociological Review* 33, no. 6 (1968): 951–970; Lewis, Patricia, and Ruth Simpson. "Kanter Revisited: Gender, Power and (In)visibility." *International Journal of Management Reviews* 14, no. 2 (June 2012): 141–158.

27. Jarrett. "The 4 Types of Organizational Politics."

Chapter 14

1. For overviews of organizational culture see: Ehrhart, Mark G., Benjamin Schneider, and William H. Macey. *Organizational Climate and Culture: An Introduction to Theory, Research, and Practice* (New York: Routledge/Taylor & Francis Group, 2014); Fleming, Mark, and Frank Guldenmund. "Organizational Culture." In *APA Handbook of Human Systems Integration,* 589–604. (Washington, DC: American Psychological Association, 2015); Ostroff, Cheri, Angelo J. Kinicki, and Rabiah S. Muhammad. "Organizational Culture and Climate." In *Handbook of Psychology,* Vol. 12: *Industrial and Organizational Psychology* (2nd ed.), 643–676 (Hoboken, NJ: Wiley, 2013).

2. Kauflin, Jeff. "The Best Places to Work in 2017." *Forbes,* December 7, 2016. https://www.forbes.com/sites/jeffkauflin/2016/12/07/the-best-places-to-work-in-2017/#7be169378b16.

3. Schein, Edgar H. "Organizational Culture." *American Psychologist* 45, no. 2 (February 1990): 109–119.

4. Ibid.

5. Schwantes, Marcel. "The World's 10 Top CEOs (They Lead in a Totally Unique Way)." *Inc.,* March 29, 2017. https://www.inc.com/marcel-schwantes/heres-a-top-10-list-of-the-worlds-best-ceos-but-they-lead-in-a-totally-unique-wa.html.

6. Hartnell, Chad A., Amy Yi Ou, and Angelo Kinicki. "Organizational Culture and Organizational Effectiveness: A Meta-Analytic Investigation of the Competing Values Framework's Theoretical Suppositions." *Journal of Applied Psychology* 96, no. 4 (July 2011): 677–694; Tong, Yew Kwan, and Richard D Arvey. "Managing Complexity via the Competing Values Framework." *Journal of Management Development* 34, no. 6 (2015): 653–673.

7. Haroun, Chris. "Why the Best Companies Always Have the Best Customer Service." *Inc.,* April 25, 2016. https://www.inc.com/chris-haroun/why-companies-like-apple-and-amazon-always-have-the-best-customer-service.html.

8. Tharp, Bruce M. "Four Organizational Culture Types." *Haworth.* Organizational Culture White Paper (2009). http://faculty.mu.edu.sa/public/uploads/1360757023.3588organizational%20cult98.pdf.

9. Szczepanski, Mallory. "TerraCycle Partners with Tom's of Maine to Donate, Recycle Toys." *Waste360,* March 20, 2017. http://www.waste360.com/waste-reduction/terracycle-partners-tom-s-maine-donate-recycle-toys.

10. https://popinnow.com/four-types-organizational-culture/.

11. Ibid.

12. Ibid.

13. Hartnell, Chad A., Amy Yi Ou, and Angelo Kinicki. "Organizational Culture and Organizational Effectiveness: A Meta-Analytic Investigation of the Competing Values Framework's Theoretical Suppositions." *Journal of Applied Psychology* 96, no. 4 (July 2011): 677–694; Quinn, Robert E., and John Rohrbaugh. "A Spatial Model of Effectiveness Criteria: Towards a Competing Values Approach to Organizational Analysis." *Management Science* 29, no. 3 (March 1983): 363–377.

14. Hofstede, Geert. "Identifying Organizational Subcultures: An Empirical Approach." *Journal of Management Studies* 35, no. 1 (January 1998): 1–12; Martin, Joanne, and Caren Siehl. "Organizational Culture and Counterculture: An Uneasy Symbiosis." *Organizational Dynamics* 12, no. 2 (September 1983): 52–64.

15. "The 50 Best Workplaces for Giving Back." *Fortune,* February 9, 2017. http://fortune.com/2017/02/09/best-workplaces-giving-back/.

16. Hofstede. "Identifying Organizational Subcultures"; Martin and Siehl. "Organizational Culture and Counterculture."

17. Ibid.

18. Denison, Daniel R. "Bringing Corporate Culture to the Bottom Line." *Organizational Dynamics* 13, no. 2 (September 1984): 5–22; Saffold III, Guy S. "Culture Traits, Strength, and Organizational Performance: Moving Beyond "Strong" Culture." *Academy of Management Review* 13, no. 4 (October 1988): 546–558; Kotter, John P. *Corporate Culture and Performance* (New York: Simon and Schuster, 2008); Pandu, A., and S. Kamaraj. "Correlates of Organizational Culture and Social Responsibility: An Empirical Study of College Teachers." *Journal of Organisation & Human Behaviour* 5, no. 2 (April 2016): 14–22.

19. Bersin, Josh. "Culture: Why It's The Hottest Topic In Business Today." *Forbes,* March 13, 2015. https://www.forbes.com/sites/joshbersin/2015/03/13/culture-why-its-the-hottest-topic-in-business-today/#589d63d627f6.

20. Egan, Matt. "Wells Fargo Uncovers up to 1.4 Million More Fake Accounts." *CNN,* August 31, 2017. http://money.cnn.com/2017/08/31/investing/wells-fargo-fake-accounts/index.html.

21. Janis, Irving L. "Groupthink and Group Dynamics: A Social Psychological Analysis of Defective Policy Decisions." *Policy Studies Journal* 2, no. 1 (September 1973): 19–25; Sunstein, Cass, and Reid Hastie. "Wiser: Getting Beyond Groupthink to Make Groups Smarter." *Harvard Business School Press Books* (January 2015).

22. Salon, Olivia. "'There Was a Witch-Hunt': Silicon Valley Conservatives Decry Google Groupthink." *The Guardian,* August 9, 2017. https://www.theguardian.com/technology/2017/aug/09/google-diversity-memo-conservatives-react.

23. Schein, Edgar H. "Organizational Culture." *American Psychologist* 45, no. 2 (February 1990): 109–119; Schneider, Benjamin, Mark G. Ehrhart, and William H. Macey. "Perspectives on Organizational Climate and Culture." In *APA Handbook of Industrial and Organizational Psychology, Vol 1: Building and Developing the Organization,* 373–414. (Washington, DC: American Psychological Association, 2011).

24. Sanders, Ian. "The Untold Story: The Power of Corporate Storytelling." *Financial Times / IE Corporate Learning Alliance,* March 28, 2017. http://www.ftiecla.com/2017/03/28/the-untold-story-the-power-of-corporate-storytelling/.

25. Salemi, Vicki. "If You Want Productive Employees, Let Them Wear Sweatpants." *New York Post,* April 4, 2016. https://nypost.com/2016/04/04/if-you-want-productive-employees-let-them-wear-sweatpants/.

26. https://bonus.ly/employee-recognition-guide/employee-recognition-examples.

27. Karch, Marziah. "Odd Google Jargon Terms." *Lifewire,* May 19, 2018. https://www.lifewire.com/google-jargon-terms-1616202.

28. Schein. "Organizational Culture."

29. Ibid.

30. Constine, Josh. "Zuck Says Copying Snapchat Was Just Step 1 of Facebook's AR Platform." *Tech Crunch,* April 18, 2017. https://techcrunch.com/2017/04/18/will-snap-copy-the-fb-platform/.

31. Schein. "Organizational Culture."

32. Arruda, William. "5 Great Companies That Get Corporate Culture Right." *Forbes,* August 17, 2017. https://www.forbes.com/sites/williamarruda/2017/08/17/5-great-companies-that-get-corporate-culture-right/#948397315828.

33. Schein. "Organizational Culture."

34. Arnold, Pamela, and Terri Kruzan. "Organizational Culture Roadblocks and Shortcuts for Leveraging Diversity: Part 1." *Profiles in Diversity* 14, no. 3 (May 2012): 71.

35. Schein, "Organizational Culture"; Schraeder, Mike, and Dennis R. Self. "Enhancing the Success of Mergers and Acquisitions: An Organizational Culture Perspective." *Management Decision* 41, no. 5 (2003): 511–522; Dewan, Astha. "Organizational Culture & Human Resource Management: A Scenario in The Case of Mergers & Acquisitions." *Amity Global HRM Review* 6, (September 2016): 62–65.

36. Bligh, Michelle C. "Surviving Post-Merger 'Culture Clash': Can Cultural Leadership Lessen the Casualties?" *Leadership* 2, no. 4 (November 2006): 395–426; Van den Steen, Eric. "Culture Clash: The Costs and Benefits of Homogeneity." *Management Science* 56, no. 10 (October 2010): 1718–1738; Milligan, Susan. "Culture Clash!" *HR Magazine* 59, no. 8 (August 2014): 18–24.

37. Wartzman, Rick. "Amazon and Whole Foods Are Headed for a Culture Clash." *Fortune,* June 26, 2017. http://fortune

.com/2017/06/26/amazon-whole-foods-corporate-culture-clash-jeff-bezos-john-mackey/.

38. Laschinger, Heather K. Spence, Carol A. Wong, Greta G. Cummings, and Ashley L. Grau. "Resonant Leadership and Workplace Empowerment: The Value of Positive Organizational Cultures in Reducing Workplace Incivility." *Nursing Economics* 32, no. 1 (January 2014): 5–44; Rinke, Wolf J. "How to Build a Positive Organizational Culture." *Food Management* 33, no. 11 (November 1998): 17.

39. Arruda. "5 Great Companies That Get Corporate Culture Right."

40. Goffee, Rob, and Gareth Jones. *The Character of a Corporation* (New York: Harper Collins, 1998).

41. Makovsky, Ken. "Behind the Southwest Airlines Culture." *Forbes.* November 21, 2013. www.forbes.com/sites/kenmakovsky/2013/11/21/behind-the-southwest-airlines-culture/.

42. Schawbel, Dan. "Patrick Lencioni: 3 Indispensable Virtues That Make Teams Successful." *Forbes,* April 26, 2016. https://www.forbes.com/sites/danschawbel/2016/04/26/patrick-lencioni-3-indispensable-virtues-that-make-teams-successful/#c5d43677fdc8.

43. Goffee and Jones, *The Character of a Corporation.*

44. Ibid.

45. Titcomb, James. "Uber Boss Travis Kalanick to Take Leave of Absence after Series of Scandals." *The Telegraph,* June 13, 2017. https://www.telegraph.co.uk/technology/2017/06/13/uber-boss-travis-kalanick-take-leave-absence-series-scandals/.

46. Goffee and Jones, *The Character of a Corporation.*

47. Ruiz-Palomino, Pablo, Ricardo Martínez-Cañas, and Joan Fontrodona. "Ethical Culture and Employee Outcomes: The Mediating Role of Person-Organization Fit." *Journal of Business Ethics* 116, no. 1 (August 2013): 173–188; Meinert, Dori. "Creating an Ethical Culture." *HR* 59, no. 4 (April 2014): 22–27.

48. http://www.loreal.com/media/press-releases/2017/mar/loreal-named-as-a-2017-worlds-most-ethical-company-.

49. Dolan, Simon L. "Values, Spirituality and Organizational Culture." *Developing Leaders* no. 21 (October 2015): 22–27; Fawcett, Stanley E., James C. Brau, Gary K. Rhoads, David Whitlark, and Amydee M. Fawcett. "Spirituality and Organizational Culture: Cultivating the ABCs of an Inspiring Workplace." *International Journal of Public Administration* 31, no. 4 (March 2008): 420–438.

50. See, for example, Case, Peter, and Jonathan Gosling. "The Spiritual Organization: Critical Reflections on the Instrumentality of Workplace Spirituality." *Journal of Management, Spirituality and Religion* 7, no. 4 (December 2010): 257–282.

51. Maylie, Devon. "Mining Debate Rattles South Africa." *Wall Street Journal,* May 15, 2013. www.wsj.com/articles/SB10001424127887323309604578430833278491840.

52. Hofstede, Geert. "Culture and Organizations." *International Studies of Management and Organization* 10, no. 4 (1980): 15–41; Hofstede, Geert. "National Cultures in Four Dimensions." *International Studies of Management and Organization* 13, no. 1/2 (Summer 1983): 46–74; Taras, Vas, Bradley L. Kirkman, and Piers Steel. "Examining the Impact of Culture's Consequences: A Three-Decade, Multilevel, Meta-analytic Review of Hofstede's Cultural Value Dimensions." *Journal of Applied Psychology* 95, no. 3 (May 2010): 405–439.

53. McSweeney, Brendan. "Hofstede's Model of National Cultural Differences and Their Consequences: A Triumph of Faith—a Failure of Analysis." *Human Relations* 55, no. 1 (2002): 89–118; Hofstede, Geert. "Dimensions Do Not Exist: A Reply to Brendan McSweeney." *Human Relations* 55, no. 11 (2002): 1355–1361.

54. Bartlett, Christopher A., and Sumantra Ghoshal. *Managing across Borders: The Transnational Solution* (2nd edition) (Boston: Harvard Business School Press, 2002).

55. Evans, Paul, Vladimir Pucik, Jean-Louis Barsoux. *The Global Challenge: Frameworks for International Human Resource Management* (Boston: McGraw-Hill, 2002).

56. Guzzo, Richard A. "The Expatriate Employee." In *Trends in Organizational Behavior,* Vol. 3: 123–137 (Hoboken, NJ: Wiley, 1996); Lee, Yosup, and Laurie Larwood. "The Socialization of Expatriate Managers in Multinational Firms." *Academy of Management Journal* 26, no. 4 (December 1983): 657–665; Tung, Rosalie L. *The New Expatriates: Managing Human Resources Abroad.* (New York: Ballinger/Harper & Row, 1988).

57. Derr, C. Brooklyn, Candace Jones, and Edmund L. Toomey. "Managing High-Potential Employees: Current Practices in Thirty-Three U.S. Corporations." *Human Resource Management* 27, no. 3 (Fall 1988): 273–290; Gelens, Jolyn, Joeri Hofmans, Nicky Dries, and Roland Pepermans. "Talent Management and Organisational Justice: Employee Reactions to High Potential Identification." *Human Resource Management Journal* 24, no. 2 (April 2014): 159–175.

58. Feldman, Daniel C., and Holly B. Tompson. "Entry Shock, Culture Shock: Socializing the New Breed of Global Managers." *Human Resource Management* 31, no. 4 (Winter 1992): 345–362; Ward, Colleen, Stephen Bochner, and Adrian Furnham. *The Psychology of Culture Shock* (2nd ed.). (New York: Routledge, 2001).

59. Winkelman, Michael. "Cultural Shock and Adaptation." *Journal of Counseling and Development* 73, no. 2 (November 1994): 121–126.

60. Shaules, Joseph. "Are You Struggling with Expat Culture Shock?" *Telegraph,* May 4, 2015. www.telegraph.co.uk/expat/before-you-go/11553062/Are-you-struggling-with-expat-culture-shock.html.

61. Hays, Richard D. "Ascribed Behavioral Determinants of Success-Failure Among U.S. Expatriate Managers." *Journal of International Business Studies* 2, no. 2 (Fall 1971): 40–46; Tung, Rosalie L. "Expatriate Assignments: Enhancing Success and Minimizing Failure." *Academy of Management Executive* 1, no. 2 (May 1987): 117–125; Kataria, Neeraj, and Shweta Sethi. "Making Successful Expatriates in Multinational Corporations." *Asian Journal of Business and Economics* 3, no. 3 (2013): 1–12.

62. Tung, Rosalie L. "Expatriate Assignments: Enhancing Success and Minimizing Failure." *Academy of Management Executive* 1, no. 2 (May 1987): 117–125; Gupta, Ritu, Pratyush Banerjee, and Jighyasu Gaur. "Exploring the Role of the Spouse in Expatriate Failure: A Grounded Theory-Based Investigation of Expatriate' Spouse Adjustment Issues from India." *International Journal of Human Resource Management* 23, no. 17 (October 2012): 3559–3577.

63. Driscoll, Ian. "Expat's Dilemma: Out of Sight—and Mind?" *BBC.* October 21, 2014. www.bbc.com/capital/story/20141020-expat-woes-out-of-sight-and-mind.

64. Schachter, Harvey. "Key Steps to Change Corporate Culture." *Globe and Mail.* March 23, 2014. www.theglobeandmail.com/report-on-business/careers/management/key-steps-to-change-corporate-culture/article17557724/.

65. Schein, E. "The Role of the Founder in Creating Organizational Culture." *Organizational Dynamics* 12, no. 1 (Summer 1983): 13–28; Hambrick, Donald C, and Phyllis A. Mason. "Upper Echelons: The Organization as a Reflection of Its Top Managers." *Academy of Management Review* 9, no. 2 (April 1984): 193–206.

66. Lowe, Ruby. "3 Reasons LinkedIn Is an Awesome Place to Work." *Undercover Recruiter.* https://theundercoverrecruiter.com/linkedin-culture/.

67. O'Reilly III, Charles A., Jennifer Chatman, and David F. Caldwell. "People and Organizational Culture: A Profile Comparison Approach to Assessing Person-Organization Fit." *Academy of Management Journal* 34, no. 3 (September 1991): 487–516; Swider, Brian W., Ryan D. Zimmerman, and Murray R. Barrick. "Searching for the Right Fit: Development of Applicant Person-Organization Fit Perceptions during the Recruitment Process." *Journal of Applied Psychology* 100, no. 3 (2015): 880–893.

68. Eyring, Alison. "Why You Need to Only Hire People Who Fit Your Culture (No Matter How Qualified They Are)." *Inc.*, August 24, 2017. https://www.inc.com/alison-eyring/why-linkedin-and-netflix-only-hire-people-who-fit-.html.

69. Cranmer, Gregory A., Zachary W. Goldman, and Melanie Booth-Butterfield. "The Mediated Relationship between Received Support and Job Satisfaction: An Initial Application of Socialization Resources Theory." *Western Journal of Communication* 81, no. 1 (January 2017): 64–86; Kammeyer-Mueller, John, Connie Wanberg, Alex Rubenstein, and Song Zhaoli. "Support, Undermining, and Newcomer Socialization: Fitting In during The First 90 Days." *Academy of Management Journal* 56, no. 4 (August 2013): 1104–1124; Chao, Georgia T., Anne M. O'Leary-Kelly, Samantha Wolf, Howard J. Klein, and Philip D. Gardner. "Organizational Socialization: Its Content and Consequences." *Journal of Applied Psychology* 79, no. 5 (October 1994): 730–743.

70. Ashforth, Blake E., Alan M. Saks, and Raymond T. Lee. "Socialization and Newcomer Adjustment: The Role of Organizational Context." *Human Relations* 51, no. 7 (July 1998): 897–926; Ashforth, Blake E., David M. Sluss, and Spencer H. Harrison. "Socialization in Organizational Contexts." In *International Review of Industrial and Organizational Psychology 2007* (Vol. 22): 1–70 (New York: Wiley, 2007).

71. Truong, Alice. "Homejoy, the Startup That Makes All New Hires Scrub Toilets." *Fast Company*, February 13, 2014. https://www.fastcompany.com/3026170/homejoy-the-startup-that-makes-all-new-hires-scrub-toilets.

72. Ward, Katie. "These Companies Run Mentorship Programs That Actually Work." *Fast Company*, October 5, 2016. https://www.fastcompany.com/3064292/these-companies-run-mentorship-programs-that-actually-work.

73. Feldman, Daniel Charles. "A Contingency Theory of Socialization." *Administrative Science Quarterly* 21, no. 3 (September 1976): 433–452; Feldman, Daniel C. "A Practical Program for Employee Socialization." *Organizational Dynamics* 5, no. 2 (September 1976): 64–80; Feldman, Daniel C., and Olivia Amanda O'Neill. "The Role of Socialization, Orientation, and Training Programs in Transmitting Culture and Climate and Enhancing Performance." In *The Oxford Handbook of Oorganizational Climate and Culture*, 44–64. (New York: Oxford University Press, 2014).

Chapter 15

1. Ashkenas, Ron. "Change Management Needs to Change: Interaction." *Harvard Business Review*. April 16, 2013. https://hbr.org/2013/04/change-management-needs-to-change/.

2. Lang, Brent, and Elizabeth Wagmeister. "Judgment Day: Harvey Weinstein Scandal Could Finally Change Hollywood's Culture of Secrecy." *Variety*, October 18, 2017. https://variety.com/2017/film/news/harvey-weinstein-game-over-judgment-day-scandal-culture-secrecy-1202591437/.

3. Ibid.

4. The DADA syndrome is an adaptation of the Kübler-Ross death and dying model to the context of organizational change as outlined in the following sources: Morano, Richard A. "How to Manage Change to Reduce Stress." *Management Review* 66, no. 11 (November 1977): 21; Rashford, Nicholas S., and David Coghan. "Phases and Levels of Organisational Change." In *The Effective Manager: Perspectives and Illustrations*, 119–130 (Thousand Oaks, CA; Maidenhead, BRK, England: Sage, 1996); Zell, Deone. "Organizational Changes as a Process of Death, Dying and Rebirth." *Journal of Applied Behavioral Science* 39, no. 1 (March 2003): 73–96.

5. Lewin, Kurt. "Frontiers in Group Dynamics: Concept, Method and Reality in Social Science: Social Equilibria and Social Change." *Human Relations* 1, (1947): 5–41; Burnes, Bernard. "Kurt Lewin

and the Planned Approach to Change: A Re-appraisal." *Journal of Management Studies* 41, no. 6 (September 2004): 977–1002; Bakari, Haroon, Ahmed Imran Hunjra, and Ghulam Shabbir Khan Niazi. "How Does Authentic Leadership Influence Planned Organizational Change? The Role of Employees' Perceptions: Integration of Theory of Planned Behavior and Lewin's Three Step Model." *Journal of Change Management* 17, no. 2 (April 2017): 155–187.

6. Lewin, Kurt. *Field Theory in Social Science: Selected Theoretical Papers.* Edited by Dorwin Cartwright (Oxford: Harpers, 1951); Burnes, "Kurt Lewin and the Planned Approach to Change"; Ennis, Gerry. "What Does It Take to Change This?" *Supervision* 78, no. 10 (October 2017): 15–18.

7. Maxwell, Paul D. "Resistance to Change and Change Management." In *Organizational Behavior in Health Care*, 379–411. (Boston: Jones and Bartlett, 2005); Nelson-Brantley, Heather V., and Debra J. Ford. "Leading Change: A Concept Analysis." *Journal of Advanced Nursing* 73, no. 4 (April 2017): 834–846.

8. Maheshwari, Sapna. "In Year of Anti-Muslim Vitriol, Brands Promote Inclusion," *The New York Times*, January 1, 2017. https://www.nytimes.com/2017/01/01/business/media/anti-muslim-vitriol-brands-promote-inclusion.html.

9. Cloutier, Chris. "30 Businesses That Are Rocking Social Media." *Small Business Trends*, November 1, 2017. https://smallbiztrends.com/2014/07/best-social-media-marketing-examples.html.

10. http://www.thegoodtrade.com/features/fair-trade-clothing.

11. Shaban, Hamza, and Karoun Demirjian. "Facebook and Google Might Be One Step Closer to New Regulations on Ad Transparency." *The Washington Post*, October 19, 2017. https://www.washingtonpost.com/news/the-switch/wp/2017/10/19/facebook-and-google-might-be-one-step-closer-to-new-regulations-on-ad-transparency/?noredirect=on&utm_term=.b6ea75787f7a.

12. Newcomb, Alyssa. "Facebook and Twitter Launch Ad Transparency Tools Ahead of Midterms." *NBC News*, June 28, 2018. https://www.nbcnews.com/tech/tech-news/facebook-twitter-launch-ad-transparency-tools-ahead-midterms-n887496.

13. Boitnott, John. "How the Baby Boomers' Exit Will Affect the Way You Do Business." *Inc.*, February 9, 2016. https://www.inc.com/john-boitnott/how-to-bridge-the-talent-gap-as-baby-boomers-leave-your-company.html.

14. Daniel, Teresa A. "Tools for Building a Positive Employee Relations Environment." *Employment Relations Today* 30, no. 2 (Summer 2003): 51–64; "Positive Employee Relations Key to Defeating Corporate Campaigns." *Management Report for Nonunion Organizations* 33, no. 3 (March 2010): 7–8.

15. Weinberger, Matt. "Microsoft CEO Satya Nadella Explains the 'Not Universally Loved' Changes He Made to a Luxury Executive Retreat." *Business Insider UK*, September 26, 2017. http://uk.businessinsider.com/microsoft-satya-nadella-company-culture-2017-9?r=US&IR=T.

16. Garcia, Tonya. "Wal-Mart Shifting Organizational Structure to Keep Up with Rapid Changes in Retail." *Market Watch*, September 12, 2017. https://www.marketwatch.com/story/wal-mart-shifting-organizational-structure-to-keep-up-with-rapid-changes-in-retail-2017-09-12.

17. Deeb, George. "Big Companies Must Embrace Intrapreneurship To Survive." *Fortune*, February 18, 2016. https://www.forbes.com/sites/georgedeeb/2016/02/18/big-companies-must-embrace-intrapreneurship-to-survive/#73caeaa348ab.

18. Alas, Ruth. "Resistance to Institutional and Organizational Change: An Individual Perspective." In *Change Management and the Human Factor: Advances, Challenges and Contradictions in Organizational Development*, 153–165 (Cham, Switzerland: Springer International, 2015); Kotter, John P., and Leonard A.

19. Rick, Torbin. "Top 12 Reasons Why People Resist Change." *www.torbenrick.eu*, May 23, 2011. https://www.torbenrick.eu/blog/change-management/12-reasons-why-people-resist-change/.

20. Kotter, John P. "Leading Change, With a New Preface by the Author." *Harvard Business School Press Books* (October 2012).

21. Youngblood, Stuart A., Angelo S. DeNisi, Julie L. Molleston, and William H. Mobley. "The Impact of Work Environment, Instrumentality Beliefs, Perceived Labor Union Image, and Subjective Norms on Union Voting Intentions." *Academy of Management Journal* 27, no. 3 (September 1984): 576–590; Mulder, Catherine P. "Unions' Resistance to Capital and the Potential for Class Transformation." *Rethinking Marxism* 25, no. 1 (January 2013): 114–120.

22. Alas, "Resistance to Institutional and Organizational Change"; Kotter and Schlesinger, "Choosing Strategies for Change."

23. Troyani, Laura. "3 Examples of Organizational Change Done Right." *Tiny Pulse,* May 25, 2107. https://www.tinypulse.com/blog/3-examples-of-organizational-change-and-why-they-got-it-right.

24. Whitehurst, Jim. "Decisions Are More Effective When More People Are Involved from the Start." *Harvard Business Review,* March 15, 2016. https://hbr.org/2016/03/decisions-are-more-effective-when-more-people-are-involved-from-the-start.

25. Nisen, Max. "Threatening to Fire Workers Doesn't Make Them More Productive." *Quartz,* May 19, 2014. https://qz.com/210884/threatening-to-fire-workers-doesnt-make-them-more-productive/.

26. Gibson, Linda K., Bruce Finnie, and Jeffrey L Stuart. "A Mathematical Model for Exploring the Evolution of Organizational Structure." *International Journal of Organizational Analysis* 23, no. 1 (2015): 21–24; Peiró, José M. "Organizational Structure." In *Advances in Organizational Psychology: An International Review*, 191–206 (Thousand Oaks, CA: Sage, 1987); Bourgeois, L. J. III, Daniel W. McAllister, and Terence R. Mitchell. "The Effects of Different Organizational Environments upon Decisions about Organizational Structure." *Academy of Management Journal* 21, no. 3 (September 1978): 508–514.

27. Meyer, Pauline. "Starbucks Coffee Company's Organizational Structure." *Panmore Institute,* January 31, 2017. http://panmore.com/starbucks-coffee-company-organizational-structure.

28. http://www.generalmills.com/en/Company/Businesses/US-retail.

29. Blakeman, Chuck. "Why Self-Managed Teams Are the Future of Business." *Inc.com.* November 25, 2014. www.inc.com/chuck-blakeman/why-self-managed-teams-are-the-future-of-business.html.

30. Bradt, George. "12 Ways To Make Matrix Organizations More Effective." *Forbes,* January 10, 2017. https://www.forbes.com/sites/georgebradt/2017/01/10/%EF%BB%BF12-ways-to-make-matrix-organizations-more-effective/#1debb7684066.

31. "Hewlett-Packard to Split into Two Companies." *BBC News.* October 6, 2014. www.bbc.com/news/business-29501235.

32. "eBay to Split Off PayPal Online Payment Business." *BBC News.* September 30, 2014. www.bbc.com/news/business-29423251.

33. Grothaus, Michael. "Samsung Says It Will Consider Splitting into Two Separate Companies." *Fast Company,* November 29, 2016. https://www.fastcompany.com/4025945/samsung-says-it-will-consider-splitting-into-two-separate-companies.

34. Shepard, Jon M. "Functional Specialization and Work Attitudes." *Industrial Relations* 8, no. 2 (February 1969): 185–194; Jagoda, Agnieszka. "Deskilling as the Dark Side of the Work Specialization." *International Journal of Academic Research* 5, no. 3 (May 2013): 331–334.

35. Nieberding, Amy Owen. "Employee Engagement and Other Bonding Forces in Organizations." *Consulting Psychology Journal: Practice and Research* 66, no. 4 (December 2014): 320–323; Price, James L. "The Impact of Departmentalization on Interoccupational Cooperation." *Human Organization* 27, no. 4 (Winter 1968): 362; Yeh, Dowming, and Jeng Jing-Hwa. "An Empirical Study of the Influence of Departmentalization and Organizational Position on Software Maintenance." *Journal of Software Maintenance and Evolution: Research and Practice* 14, no. 1 (January 2002): 65–82.

36. Davis, Stanley M. "Two Models of Organization: Unity of Command versus Balance of Power." *Sloan Management Review* 16, no. 1 (Fall 1974): 29–40; Fayol, Henri. *General and Industrial Management.* Trans. C. Storrs (London: Sir Isaac Pitman & Sons, 1949); Wren, Daniel A., Arthur G. Bedeian, and John D. Breeze. "The Foundations of Henri Fayol's Administrative Theory," *Management Decision* 40, no. 9 (October 2002): 906; Krause, Ryan, Michael C. Withers, and Matthew Semadeni. "Compromise on the Board: Investigating the Antecedents and Consequences of Lead Independent Director Appointment." *Academy of Management Journal* 60, no. 6 (December 2017): 2239–2265.

37. Wong, Carol A., Pat Elliott-Miller, Heather Laschinger, Michael Cuddihy, Raquel M. Meyer, Margaret Keatings, Camille Burnett, and Natalie Szudy. "Examining the Relationships between Span of Control and Manager Job and Unit Performance Outcomes." *Journal of Nursing Management* 23, no. 2 (March 2015): 156–168; Entwisle, Doris R., and John Walton. "Observations on the Span of Control." *Administrative Science Quarterly* 5, no. 4 (March 1961): 522–533; Ouchi, William G., and John B. Dowling. "Defining the Span of Control." *Administrative Science Quarterly* 19, no. 3 (September 1974): 357–365; Udell, Jon G. "An Empirical Test of Hypotheses Relating to Span of Control." *Administrative Science Quarterly* 12, no. 3 (December 1967): 420–439; Urwick, Lyndall F. "The Manager's Span of Control." *Harvard Business Review* 34, no. 3 (May 1956): 39–47; Urwick, L. F. "V. A. Graicunas and the Span of Control." *Academy of Management Journal* 17, no. 2 (June 1974): 349–354.

38. See, for example, Lebowitz, Shana. "Apple CEO Tim Cook Now Has 17 Direct Reports—and That's Probably Too Many." *Business Insider.* July 8, 2015. www.businessinsider.com/apple-ceo-tim-cook-has-too-many-direct-reports-2015-7?r=UK&IR=T.

39. Stone, Katherine. "The Origins of Job Structures in the Steel Industry." *Review of Radical Political Economics* 6 (Summer 1974): 61–97.

40. Bayramzadeh, Sara, and Mariam F. Alkazemi. "Centralized vs. Decentralized Nursing Stations: An Evaluation of the Implications of Communication Technologies in Healthcare." *Health Environments Research and Design Journal (HERD) (Vendome Group LLC)* 7, no. 4 (Summer 2014): 62–80; Fayol, *General and Industrial Management*; Wren et al., "The Foundations of Henri Fayol's Administrative Theory"; Zábojník, Ján. "Centralized and Decentralized Decision Making in Organizations." *Journal of Labor Economics* 20, no. 1 (January 2002): 1.

41. Maimon, Amit. "4 Ways to Guide Your Employees Toward Empowered Decisions." *Entrepreneur,* December 23, 2016. https://www.entrepreneur.com/article/286971.

42. See, for example, Fong, Kai Hung, and Ed Snape. "Empowering Leadership, Psychological Empowerment and Employee Outcomes: Testing a Multi-level Mediating Model." *British Journal of Management* 26, no. 1 (January 2015): 126–138; Frazier, M. Lance, and Stav Fainshmidt. "Voice Climate, Work Outcomes, and the Mediating Role of Psychological Empowerment: A Multilevel Examination." *Group and Organization Management* 37, no. 6 (December 2012): 691–715.

43. Courtright, John A., Gail T. Fairhurst, and L. Edna Rogers. "Interaction Patterns in Organic and Mechanistic System." *Academy of Management Journal* 32, no. 4 (December 1989):

773–802; Gillen, Dennis J., and Stephen J. Carroll. "Relationship of Managerial Ability to Unit Effectiveness in More Organic Versus More Mechanistic Departments." *Journal of Management Studies* 22, no. 6 (November 1985): 668–676; Zanzi, Alberto. "How Organic Is Your Organization? Determinants of Organic/Mechanistic Tendencies in a Public Accounting Firm." *Journal of Management Studies* 24, no. 2 (March 1987): 125–142; Dust, Scott B., Christian J. Resick, and Mary Bardes Mawritz. "Transformational Leadership, Psychological Empowerment, and the Moderating Role of Mechanistic–Organic Contexts." *Journal of Organizational Behavior* 35, no. 3 (April 2014): 413–433.

44. Ibid.

45. Podsakoff, Philip M., Larry J. Williams, and William D. Todor. "Effects of Organizational Formalization on Alienation among Professionals and Nonprofessionals." *Academy of Management Journal* 29, no. 4 (December 1986): 820–831; Peters, Gangolf. "Organisation as Social Relationship, Formalisation, and Standardisation: A Weberian Approach to Concept Formation." *International Sociology* 3, no. 3 (September 1988): 267–282; Mattes, Jannika. "Formalisation and Flexibilisation in Organisations—Dynamic and Selective Approaches in Corporate Innovation Processes." *European Management Journal* 32, no. 3 (June 2014): 475–486.

46. Toren, Nina. "Bureaucracy and Professionalism: A Reconsideration of Weber's Thesis." *Academy of Management Review* 1, no. 3 (July 1976): 36–46; Spicer, Michael W. "Public Administration in a Disenchanted World: Reflections on Max Weber's Value Pluralism and His Views on Politics and Bureaucracy." *Administration & Society* 47, no. 1 (January 2015): 24–43; Walton, Eric J. "The Persistence of Bureaucracy: A Meta-analysis of Weber's Model of Bureaucratic Control." *Organization Studies* 26, no. 4 (April 2005): 569–600; Weiss, Richard M. "Weber on Bureaucracy: Management Consultant or Political Theorist?" *Academy of Management Review* 8, no. 2 (April 1983): 242–248.

47. Concepts presented in the following discussion are taken in part from these sources: Anand, N., and Richard L. Daft "What Is the Right Organization Design?" *Organizational Dynamics* 36, no. 4 (November 2007): 329–344; Duncan, Robert. "What Is the Right Organization Structure? Decision Tree Analysis Provides the Answer" *Organizational Dynamics* 7, no. 3 (Winter 1979): 59–80; Galbraith, Jay R. *Designing Complex Organizations* (Reading, MA: Addison–Wesley, 1973); Galbraith, Jay R. *Organization Design* (Reading, MA: Addison-Wesley, 1977); Galbraith, Jay R. "Matrix Organization Designs." *Business Horizons* 14, no. 1 (February 1971): 29.

48. Bartunek, Jean M., and Richard W. Woodman. "Organizational Development." In *The Oxford Handbook of Positive Organizational Scholarship*, 727–736 (New York: Oxford University Press, 2012); Dievernich, Frank E. P., Kim Oliver Tokarski, and Jie Gong. *Change Management and the Human Factor: Advances, Challenges and Contradictions in Organizational Development*. (Cham, Switzerland: Springer International Publishing, 2015).

49. For an overview of OD process models see McLean, Gary L. *Organization Development: Principles, Processes, Practices* (San Francisco: Berrett-Koehler, 2006).

50. For reviews of differing types of OD interventions see Friedlander, Frank, and L. Dave Brown. "Organization Development." *Annual Review of Psychology* 25, no. 1 (February 1974): 313; Neuman, George A., Jack E. Edwards, and Nambury S. Raju. "Organizational Development Interventions: A Meta-analysis of Their Effects on Satisfaction and Other Attitudes." *Personnel Psychology* 42, no. 3 (September 1989): 461–489; Coghlan, David, and A. B. (Rami) Shani. "Organizational-Development Research Interventions: Perspectives from Action Research and Collaborative Management Research." In *The Wiley-Blackwell Handbook of the Psychology of Leadership, Change, and Organizational Development*, 443–460 (Wiley-Blackwell, 2013).

51. Margulies, Newton, Penny L. Wright, and Richard W. Scholl. "Organization Development Techniques: Their Impact on Change." *Group and Organization Studies* 2, no. 4 (December 1977): 428–448; Kiel, Joan M. "Using Organizational Development for Electronic Medical Record Transformation." *The Health Care Manager* 35, no. 4 (October 2016): 305–311.

52. "Millennials Prefer Experiential Rewards." *Reward,* February 23, 2017. https://www.reward-guide.co.uk/millennials-prefer-experiential-rewards/1167.article.

53. Ibid.

54. Kell, John. "Meet the Culture Warriors: 3 Companies Changing the Game." *Fortune*, March 14, 2017. http://fortune.com/2017/03/14/best-companies-to-work-for-culture/.

55. Margulies et al., "Organization Development Techniques."

56. Locke, Charlie. "Finally, Slack Is Living Up To Its Name." *Wired,* June 9, 2016. https://www.wired.com/2016/06/slack-social-network/.

57. Emery, Fred. "Characteristics of Socio-Technical Systems." In *The Social Engagement of Social Science: A Tavistock Anthology*, Vol. 2: *The Socio-technical Perspective*, 157–186 (Philadelphia: University of Pennsylvania Press, 1993); Eijnatten, Frans M. van. "Developments in Socio-Technical Systems Design (STSD)." In *Handbook of Work and Organizational Psychology*. Vol. 4: *Organizational Psychology* (2nd ed.), 61–88 (Hove, England: Psychology Press/Erlbaum (UK)/Taylor & Francis, 1998); Hughes, Helen P. N., Chris W. Clegg, Lucy E. Bolton, and Lauren C. Machon. "Systems Scenarios: A Tool for Facilitating the Socio-Technical Design of Work Systems." *Ergonomics* 60, no. 10 (October 2017): 1319–1335.

58. Hammer, Leslie B., and Kristi L. Zimmerman. "Quality of Work Life." In *APA Handbook of Industrial and Organizational Psychology*. Vol 3: *Maintaining, Expanding, and Contracting the Organization*, 399–431 (Washington, DC: American Psychological Association, 2011); Kocman, Andreas, and Germain Weber. "Job Satisfaction, Quality of Work Life and Work Motivation in Employees with Intellectual Disability: A Systematic Review." *Journal of Applied Research in Intellectual Disabilities* 31, no. 1 (January 2018): 1–22.

59. Lomranz, Jacob, Martin Lakin, and Harold Schiffman. "A Three-Valued Typology for Sensitivity Training and Encounter Groups." *Human Relations* 26, no. 3 (June 1973): 339; Nikels, Holly J., Grace Ann Mims, and Matthew J. Mims. "Allies against Hate: A School-Based Diversity Sensitivity Training Experience." *Journal for Specialists in Group Work* 32, no. 2 (June 2007): 126–138; Thomason, Angela R., Patricia B. Naro, Paula A. Thompson, and Maryam Iranikhah. "Education of Pharmacy Students with Geriatric Sensitivity Training Exercise." *Pharmacy Education: An International Journal Of Pharmaceutical Education* 16, (2016): 6–10.

60. Vanden Brook, Tom. "Army Orders Soldiers to Undergo Training to Accept Transgender Troops." *USA Today,* June 13, 2017. https://www.usatoday.com/story/news/politics/2017/06/13/transgender-troops-defense-secretary-jim-mattis-army-marine-corps/102822598/.

61. Jason, Leonard A., Louise Ferone, and Thomas Anderegg. "Evaluating Ecological, Behavioral, and Process Consultation Interventions." *Journal of School Psychology* 17, no. 2 (Summer 1979): 103–115; Lipshitz, Raanan, and John J. Sherwood. "The Effectiveness of Third-Party Processes Consultation as a Function of the Consultant's Prestige and Style of Intervention." *Journal of Applied Behavioral Science* 14, no. 4 (October 1978): 493–509; Lalonde, Carole, and Chloé Adler. "Information Asymmetry in Process Consultation: An Empirical Research on Leader-Client/Consultant Relationship in Healthcare

Organizations." *Leadership & Organization Development Journal* 36, no. 2 (2015): 177–211.

62. Beauchamp, Mark R., Desmond McEwan, and Katrina J. Waldhauser. "Team Building: Conceptual, Methodological, and Applied Considerations." *Current Opinion in Psychology* 16, (August 2017): 114–117; Dyer, William G., W. Gibb Dyer Jr., and Jeffrey H. Dyer. *Team Building: Proven Strategies for Improving Team Performance, 4e* (San Francisco: Jossey-Bass, 2007); Murrell, Kenneth L., and E. H. Valsan. "A Team-Building Workshop as an OD Intervention in Egypt."

Leadership and Organization Development Journal 6, no. 2 (1985): 11–16.

63. Randolph, W. Alan, and Barry Z. Posner. "The Effects of an Intergroup Development OD Intervention as Conditioned by the Life Cycle State of Organizations: A Laboratory Experiment." *Group and Organization Studies* 7, no. 3 (September 1982): 335–352; Killen, Melanie, Aline Hitti, and Kelly Lynn Mulvey. "Social Development and Intergroup Relations." In *APA Handbook of Personality and Social Psychology.* Vol. 2: *Group Processes*, 177–201 (Washington, DC: American Psychological Association, 2015).

Abboy, R., 309
Adams, J. S.
Adams, M., 394
Adams, N. E., 85
Ajzen, I., 105
Alber, L., 41
Alderfer, C., 132
Alexander the Great, 339, 342
Allison, L. K., 198
Amabile, T. M., 226
Andersen, L., 399
Andersen, M., 399
Angelou, M., 36, 305
Anton, J., 184
Asch, S., 193
Ashkanasy, N. M., 113
Ashton, M. C., 55
Attila the Hun, 339
Aubrey, W. A., 65
Aung San, S. K., 302

Backman, M., 127
Baer, D., 176
Bailey, J., 270
Baldwin, C., 452
Bandura, A., 85, 93
Barrick, M. R., 54
Barse, D., 378
Bauer, T., 7
Beck, J., 224
Becker, W. J., 285
Beersma, B., 331
Bell, J., 71, 73
Bennett, M., 47
Berkus, N., 438
Berman, G., 433
Bevelander, D., 337
Bezos, J., 223, 350
Bhatia, H., 334
Blake, R. R., 344
Blakely, S., 133
Blanchard, K., 346–347
Bloxham, E., 428
Boch, L., 432
Boone, E. H., 31
Boswell, W. R., 285
Bourdage, J. S., 55
Bowman, B., 357
Bradt, G., 275
Branson, R., 286, 355
Brent, J., 438
Briggs, K. C., 51
Bryant, A., 428
Buckley, G. W., 298
Buffer, 195
Buffett, W., 378
Bunge, J., 394
Butterfield, J., 209
Butts, M. M., 285

Caldwell, D. F., 413
Cancino, J. M., 449
Carlson, N., 71
Carpenter, M., 7
Chafkin, M., 428

Chappell, T., 404–405
Chatman, J. A., 413
Chatsko, M., 394
Chemers, M. M., 345
Chen, H., 383
Choi, I., 257
Churchill, W., 342
Cissone, S., 184
Clark, H., 352–353
Clark, M. A., 198
Clifton, J., 2
Clinton, H. R., 72, 277
Clough, R., 32
Cohen, D. S., 443
Collins, A., 106
Collins, C., 100, 106
Comer, L. B., 284
Cook, D., 277–278
Cook, M., 45
Coons, A. E., 343
Côté, S., 101
Crow, M., 213, 214, 228
Curhan, J., 318
Curry, S., 96
Cutler, J., 434

Daft, D. L., 282
Damore, J., 408
Davis, J. H., 306
DeBonal, E., 68
DeDreu, C. K. W., 331
DeLorean, J., 407
DeLuque, M. S., 360
Deupree, R., 336
de Vries, R. E., 55
de Witt, F.R.C., 314
Dholakia, S., 358
Dick, K., 433–434
Dickson, M. W., 198
DiLiello, T. C., 240
Dillon, K., 256
Disney, R. E., 74
Disney, W., 153, 154
Doerr, B., 413
Doolen, T. L., 198
Dorfman, P. W., 360
Dorsey, J., 70
Doughtery, J., 64
Drollinger, T., 284

Egan, J., 150
Eisenhower, D. D., 124
Ek, D., 15
Endres, M., 40
Engelbert, C., 45
Epictetus, 283
Erdogan, B., 7
Evers, A., 331

Faber, E., 350
Falbe, C. M., 382
Farfan, B., 150
Fay, B., 284
Feldman, D. C., 419, 420
Fenzi, F., 176

SUBJECT INDEX